TRAINING DISTANCE RUNNERS

David E. Martin, PhD
Department of Cardiopulmonary Care Science
Georgia State University

Peter N. Coe
Coach of Sebastian Coe and Wendy Sly

Leisure Press
Champaign, Illinois

Library of Congress Cataloging-in-Publication Data

Martin, David E., 1939-
    Training distance runners / by David E. Martin and Peter N. Coe.
      p. cm.

    ISBN 0-88011-404-5
    1. Marathon running--Training. 2. Running races. I. Coe, Peter
GV1065.17.T73M37 1991   90-33486
796.42'5--dc20   CIP

ISBN: 0-87322-727-1 (paper)
ISBN: 0-88011-404-5 (cloth)

Acquisitions Editor: Brian Holding; **Developmental Editor:** Peggy Rupert; **Managing Editor:** Robert King; **Assistant Editor:** Kari Nelson; **Copyeditor:** Barbara Walsh; **Proofreader:** Karin Leszcynski; **Indexer:** Barbara Cohen; **Production Director:** Ernie Noa; **Typesetters:** Sandra Meier, Yvonne Winsor, Kathy Boudreau-Fuoss; **Text Design:** Keith Blomberg; **Text Layout:** Tara Welsch, Denise Lowry; **Cover Design:** Jack Davis; **Cover Photo:** Agence/Shot (Seb Coe leading GDR's Jens-Peter Herold at World Cup 1,500m race, Barcelona); **Illustrations:** Mark Fetkewicz, Jerry Thompson, David Gregory; **Printer:** BookCrafters

Figure 1.10 (p. 16) courtesy of Mark Shearman.
Figures 3.8, 4.9, 4.15, and 4.19c (pp. 160, 195, 198, and 200) courtesy of Hugh Hastings.
Figures 4.31 through 4.39 (pp. 214-215) courtesy of Georgia State University Department of Public Information.

Leisure Press books are available at special discounts for bulk purchase for sales promotions, premiums, fundraising, or educational use. Special editions or book excerpts can also be created to specification. For details, contact the Special Sales Manager at Leisure Press.

Printed in the United States of America   10 9 8 7 6 5 4 3 2

Leisure Press
A Division of Human Kinetics
P.O. Box 5076, Champaign, IL 61825-5076
1-800-747-4457

Canada: Human Kinetics, Box 24040, Windsor, ON N8Y 4Y9
1-800-465-7301 (in Canada only)

Europe: Human Kinetics, P.O. Box IW14, Leeds LS16 6TR, England
(44) 532 781708

Australia: Human Kinetics, 2 Ingrid Street, Clapham 5062, South Australia
(08) 371 3755

New Zealand: Human Kinetics, P.O. Box 105-231, Auckland 1
(09) 309 2259

Contents

Foreword

W.C. Fields was supposed to have been asked if poker was a game of chance. "Not the way I play it," he drawled.

Trying to minimize the element of chance by leaving no stone unturned in his quest for coaching excellence is the cornerstone of Peter Coe's thinking. This philosophy kept me at the forefront of world athletics for more than a decade. David Martin is of the same creed; an established physiologist, his dedication to research and its practical application is total.

Together they have combined their expertise to produce a book that has been long overdue. Watching them work together has been like experiencing firsthand the work of composer and librettist. The result is a book of complementary disciplines and harmony.

Although sports scientists have made theoretical contributions to training knowledge, they have been less ready to practically apply this work to coaching. Similarly, many coaches are still slow in realizing that by working within a theoretical framework and with the application of scientific evaluation, they can make much greater progress. Science is a discipline; coaching should be one also. Both have much to contribute to each other, but this is effective only in dialogue. In practice, their paths have often been only parallel; they have not touched frequently enough.

I am privileged to have been helped by Peter and David along the way from club athlete to Olympic golds in 1980 and 1984—a voyage of discovery during which obstacles and hazards became navigable challenges.

Successful coaching is both an art and a science. *Training Distance Runners* is a synthesis of the two. This book is the pooling of two people's special talents, and, more than that, it is a very significant contribution to the literature on the sport of athletics. I believe it to be the best yet in linking together the science and the art of developing distance runners.

Sebastian Coe

Preface

If two people share a common goal long enough, there is a fair chance that they will meet. Looking back, it seems that, although we didn't know each other, living on separate continents and pursuing different professions, for nearly a decade during the 1970s we were already on the road to collaboration. Specifically, we both had the goal of linking together the craftiness of coaching artistry with the rapidly evolving body of knowledge in sports science and sports medicine so that the athletes with whom we were working could have the best opportunity for competitive success. The people most likely to achieve such a goal are those who not only have experience in scientific methodology but who also are working in the trenches at the front lines of battle preparing runners for top-level racing proficiency. When they combine their skills of data acquisition and analysis (both scientifically in the laboratory and practically in the field) with close personal working relationships with their athletes, they are in the best position to discover what works, what does not, and the best explanations for both. Delightfully, the two of us have enjoyed this most priceless privilege for what now between us totals nearly 40 years of our lives.

One of us (Peter Coe), a professional engineer, assumed the task of training a single athlete from the beginning as a young lad through a career that lasted more than 20 years. Sebastian Coe is arguably the greatest middle-distance runner in athletics history. Perhaps the most detailed and continuous daily record in existence for any elite-level runner's development and performance has produced a very powerful game plan with many elements that can be used sensibly and practically by others. The systematic approach developed for Seb's training did not change conceptually throughout this entire period, attesting to its basic worth.

Eventual expansion of activities led to a working relationship with more runners as well. Restricting attention to a very small group of individual athletes at any one time instead of becoming a coaching administrator for an entire club program has always ensured a focus on the most important task at hand, namely the constant monitoring and subtle modifying of assigned work loads that best help athletes achieve their planned development. Initially it was not easy to persuade runners who already had tasted some measure of success with one type of training regimen to alter quite significantly their training to fit Coe's system, a system albeit tried and tested with singular success on one male athlete. Their willingness to work, along with Coe's careful nurturing, brought successful results.

At the moment, half of Coe's athlete charges are female. Women distance runners are mentally and physically just as durable and delightful to work with as men. They are competitive and desirous of success, even to the point of needing a restraining hand to save them from the problems caused by the excesses of overenthusiasm. At the 1988 British Olympic Trials one of his female runners earned a bronze medal at 800m, and the other (Wendy Sly) won a bronze at 3,000m and a silver at 10,000m on consecutive days. As a result, Wendy was selected to a 3,000m spot on the British team for her second Olympic Games. Although she lost considerable time in the years following the Los Angeles Olympics due to overtraining and overuse problems that resolved slowly, her progressive improvement when exposed to the system of multi-tier and multi-pace training that is described in this book provided her with the developmental sparkle she needed to regain her performance excellence at the highest level.

The other author (David Martin), a physiologist by profession, established a human performance evaluation laboratory in 1975. One of its goals was the identification and implementation of methodology to quantify aerobic and anaerobic fitness changes occurring during an athlete's training season. Another was to interpret these changes from the perspective of the specific kinds of training utilized by that athlete. By evaluating elite-level distance runners three to four times each year, sufficient knowledge was acquired that could permit practical suggestions, specific to each runner, to guide the athletes in fine-tuning their training for steady forward progress. Enhancing these studies was a comprehensive health evaluation program including blood chemistry profiling, musculoskeletal evaluation, and nutritional assessment, a primary goal being the early identification of overuse injury or overtraining. Initially, participation was limited to those elite-level athletes passing through Atlanta to or from competitions, as travel funds specifically for health and fitness profiling were difficult to acquire from either research grant sources or sporting goods companies with which athletes had promotional contracts. The success of the project through word-of-mouth reports from participants soon created a waiting list of athletes desiring involvement. Several athletes have continued to return for periods now approaching 10 years, and they are still reaping the benefits.

Since 1981, funding from the United States Olympic Committee (USOC) to The Athletics Congress of the United States (TAC/USA) has provided a continuity for these studies and has also increased the number of athletes that can be accommodated. The athletes who have received benefits from this USOC/TAC Elite Athlete Special Project form a contemporary who's who of American distance running. Some of those with whom we have been privileged to develop close working relationships spanning several years include, in alphabetical order, Dick Beardsley, Bruce Bickford, Keith Brantly, Tom Byers, Jim Cooper, Ed Eyestone, John and Chris Gregorek, Janis Klecker, Mike Pinocci, Pat Porter, Anthony Sandoval, Linda Sheskey, Steve Spence, Jim Spivey, Jon Sinclair, John Tuttle, and Craig Virgin. With a few of these athletes, a personal coaching relationship has developed. With others, a tripartite exchange between athlete, coach, and scientist has been equally productive. For still others, who are self-coached, the technical input has also been valuable.

The catalyst in the fusion of our special interests was Sebastian Coe, in whom we both recognized and appreciated a very special talent. Although one of us, of course, has been both father and coach, the other first met Seb at the European Championships (Prague) in 1978 purely by accident, in helping to resolve a translation problem as some of the East German media, familiar with Seb's then arch-rival Olaf Beyer, sought details of Seb's training. An abiding friendship was born.

Our own conversations together date back to the early 1980s, when we would meet, usually unexpectedly, at various European cross-country and track gatherings. Our track- or turf-side postmortem observations as we watched our athletes compete, together with our late-night discussions in local pubs, made us realize that much of what we perceived as gaps in knowledge or inaccuracies in application of scientific information to the practical realities of working with athletes was common to both sides of the Atlantic. From these discussions developed a joint yearning to do our best to resolve a few of these gaps and inaccuracies, thus permitting our own runners, to whom we were so dedicated, ultimately to benefit.

By this time Seb was an outstanding athlete with an already long career, and it was for the improvement and extension of that career that we joined forces in a practical way, encouraged by Seb himself. There is a great need for planning and management skills in coaching, and these were brought to bear in this most productive environment. Being a British-based coach did not prevent Coe from recognizing and, most importantly, using powerful (and friendly!) resources in the United States. (Chauvinism and parochialism are formidable obstacles to progress, and we have both steadfastly fought to be free of their entanglement!) The opportunity for Seb and Wendy Sly to combine wintering in Florida with access to a physiology laboratory in Atlanta as well as a scientist-coach in whom they could confide and discuss developmental strategies was too good to pass up. Then again, as Martin realized that athletics seemed far better researched in Europe than in the U.S., particularly with regard to long-term and individualized athlete care, his being an American-based physiologist did not prevent him from frequenting the European scene—studying it and learning from it.

Seb became an important force in permitting these interactions to continue. The fruits of our labor bear witness to the value of that collaboration—Seb's unique second gold medal in Los Angeles for his Olympic-record 1,500m performance, and his first major victory 2 years later in the 800m at the 1986 European Championships. Although he happily commenced training in preparation for a third Olympic

Games in Seoul, Seb's participation in those Games was not to be, snuffed out by a decision of his nation's athletic body that he not participate.

Each of us has thus been motivated by the desire to bring together the two languages of coaching and sports science as they pertain to distance running. Each discipline can learn so much from the other, yet they seem so far apart when viewed alone. The two knowledge bases should be woven into a unified whole. We owe this to our athletes, who urge constantly that we be of practical benefit to them, because the bottom line in our practical collaboration is their best preparation for an excellent race.

We have enjoyed taking the teacher's approach of putting our ideas and experiences into writing under cover of a book. It should be emphasized most clearly that this is not intended as a treatise on exercise physiology, nor is it an encyclopedia of coaching. It is, however, a summary of some of the major information areas that we have found important not only for our own understanding but also in teaching our athletes, so that they might know more about themselves as they seek excellence in their event specialties. Our goal has been to achieve a balance between describing basic principles and exploring controversial ideas, thereby providing an appreciation for both problems solved and the many problems we still face.

We hope we have provided clarity without oversimplification. At the same time, some topics are difficult to understand without considerable thought and some background knowledge. Other topics are fraught with misunderstanding and controversy, caused mainly by disagreements in the definition of terms or problems with precise conceptual descrip-

tions. If coaches and athletes become a little distressed as the pace of reading slows considerably while they grapple with the lactate/ventilatory threshold, the Krebs cycle, and muscle fiber types, they can take comfort in realizing that their scientific friends will have equal challenge a few chapters later in comprehending the nuances of reps and sets in training plan design or planning strategy in 800m versus 5,000m racing! All of these topics are simply different facets on the diamond that represents athletic performance competence.

We hope that this book will serve as a legacy for the athletes from whom we have learned so much, and as a basis from which our continuing interest can help us (and others) learn more. We fully anticipate that some (in some respects nontraditional) elements of our total approach to working with distance runners may stimulate vigorous debate and reaction. Indeed, by the time this is read, the present explosion of knowledge may very well have already answered some of the questions we pose and proved incorrect some suggestions offered from more recent literature. Such change can serve only as an exciting stimulus for advancing a more reasoned view. As with all aspects of education, we are climbing mountains to see more mountains to climb. If better performances in distance running result from the thought and application resulting from such analysis of our ideas, we will have achieved our purpose.

David E. Martin, Atlanta
Peter Coe, London

Special Acknowledgments

We cannot name all those who have influenced us during our time devoted to athletics; there simply are too many. But each of us must mention those few who, from our individual perspective, have had a special place in making it all possible. It is appropriate that we name them separately.

From Peter Coe:

In coaching, there is my old friend Frank Horwill, who founded the British Milers Club. His devotion to miling has been obscured by his prickly and contentious ways, but nevertheless he has put a lot of thought into the sport. In 1970 he made what for me was a very seminal observation: In Britain the fastest milers were the 5,000m athletes who had come down in distance, and the best half-milers were 400m runners who had stepped up an event. This gave me a new direction in coaching and in structuring training around the correct paces.

In journalism, writers should not overglamorize, nor should they pen needlessly cruel copy; it must be analytical and fair. For me there are two particular writers who temper their analytical eyes with a passionate love of the game and are sensitive to the individual behind the medals and the records. Both are respected friends from prestigious journals. The first is Robert Parienté, editor of the great French newspaper *L'Equipe*, and the other is Kenny Moore of *Sports Illustrated*, a fine Olympian and marathoner as well. Kenny's search for the inside story borders on the extreme, and the results of his rambles are

chronicled with class. He was brave enough on one occasion to join a painfully difficult training session with Seb Coe on an even harsher English winter day, a session that I, protected from the icy wind and rain, directed from a following car.

And finally, I thank meet promoter Andreas Brugger of Zurich, whose longtime assistance and friendship has helped me to cope with the many hazards and vicissitudes of the international circuit.

From David E. Martin:

Financial resources and top-quality "people-power" are at the heart of most successful endeavors, and the present situation is no exception. The close working relationships I established early on with coaches, athletes, and sports scientists at the forefront of both the European track and cross-country circuits and the Asian marathon circuit have been the sources of much knowledge I've needed to confront the technical and practical challenge of athlete preparation for top-level competitions.

The Center for Exercise Physiology and Pulmonary Function in the Department of Cardiopulmonary Care Sciences at Georgia State University has been the site of our scientific studies with distance runners. The dedication and expertise over many years by a small but devoted and talented cadre of professional colleagues—notably Donald F. May, Susan P. Pilbeam, Meryl Sheard, and Richard Eib—have ensured an unusually high standard of test-retest reliability so indispensable for the success of periodic physiological data acquisition when the study subjects are serving as their own controls. Their talents have been essential in helping to mesh the nuances of changing equipment and technology with the challenging demands of monitoring the performance capabilities of some of the most gifted athletes the sport of distance running has ever seen. Collaboration with David H. Vroon, MD, Director of the Clinical Laboratory of Grady Memorial Hospital, has been instrumental in providing the kind of long-term comprehensive blood chemistry profiling program required to document from many viewpoints the various metabolic changes occurring in distance runners as they proceed through a training season.

Since 1981, substantial funding to defray travel and laboratory testing costs for elite-level athletes has been acquired through the highly competitive research and support services grant programs of the USOC, administered through the Elite Athlete Special Project and TAC's Men's Development Committee. The travel assistance has been especially valuable in allowing athletes to reap the practical benefits of long-term profiling, as their visits can be scheduled at important points during their development rather than coincidental with other travel through Atlanta. Additional funding sources have included the Urban Life Foundation of Georgia State University and the Atlanta Track Club.

Lastly, I shall always cherish the friendships developed with the athletes who have visited our laboratory. Their confidence that we could be of substantial benefit to their developing athletic careers has motivated us to work with a devotion matched perhaps only by their own, so that we might be of service to them. It has been a rare privilege to study with them the details of their training plans, to help them identify their performance strengths and liabilities, and to help design strategies for continuing their quest for athletic success. We have always challenged them to learn as much from us as we do from them. They have indeed accepted and met that challenge!

Both of us as authors also owe a great debt of gratitude to Rainer Martens of Human Kinetics Publishers, who agreed with our view that this book could be of benefit to the athletics community. Developmental editor Peggy Rupert has shown enormous patience and understanding as we have attempted to fit the preparation of this manuscript into our busy days. Her expertise with format and the myriad other details of this undertaking are impressive and helped immeasurably to make this project a success.

Introduction

It is quite simple to lump into a single word the task for any distance runner aspiring to further excellence: *train*. However, that word embraces a multiplicity of assignments. Ideally, we see the following as requirements for a distance runner to have the best chance for achieving success:

1. Find a competent coach or advisor with whom to work, and try to learn as much as possible about the dynamics of training—how organ systems are affected, why rest is so crucial, and how to best plan work loads that improve fitness.
2. Define and create a development plan based upon achievable goals.
3. Do the physical and mental training necessary to improve performance.
4. Develop a support system for maintaining good health, preventing overtraining, and monitoring fitness/performance assets and liabilities, using qualified people who can interact effectively with athlete and coach.
5. Evaluate the results of development by a combination of carefully planned periodic time trials, laboratory physiological evaluation, and races.
6. Enter each major competitive period with confidence, and deliver good performances.

The purpose of this book is to help athletes with their aspirations of success in distance running and to help the coaches and scientists working with them. The first two chapters provide a scientific foundation. Chapter 1 discusses some of the essentials of physiology, biomechanics, and fuel metabolism that relate to movement in general and running in particular. Chapter 2 outlines the means by which the cardiopulmonary system and blood ensure the distribution of fuels and other substances essential to high-level work to the various organs of greatest need. The next two chapters relate specifically to the design of training plans. Chapter 3 deals with the concept of periodization, or layout, of a training plan and emphasizes the running-related activities for that plan. Chapter 4 discusses all the other aspects of total body fitness that make the difference between simply a trained runner and a complete athlete.

Chapter 5 is an event-by-event analysis of racing strategies for several Olympic distance events and provides a few hints and suggestions to serve as a catalyst for coping with the vast knowledge that athletes will soon acquire as they experience the world of competitive sport. Finally, chapter 6 examines the problem of managing the enormous physiological and psychological stress load facing athletes whose goal is top-level training and competition. Their willingness to train so arduously that the resulting injury and exhaustion from overuse and overtraining can ruin their careers must instead be channeled into a more reasoned approach to identify what is necessary and master it well. Important in this process is the interaction with an effective coach/advisor who can help design a useful plan and a good sports scientist who can help monitor progress using the constancy and technology of laboratory profiling. Some perspective on both these roles of assisting personnel are appropriate.

Defining the Role of a Coach

Finding a good description for the complex relationship between athletes and the people who work closely with them isn't easy. And current English language usage certainly doesn't help very much (Flexner & Hauck, 1987). The word *coach* when used as a verb means "to give instruction or advice to." The word *train*, however, when used as a verb, can refer both to what the athlete does (i.e., "to get oneself into condition for an athletic performance through exercise, diet, practice, etc."), or to what a coach does (i.e., "to give the discipline and instruction, drill, practice, etc. designed to impart proficiency or efficiency"). We might conclude from this that both athletes and coaches are trainers; that is, people who train (themselves or others). And indeed, the word *trainer*, used as a noun, can either refer to "a person who trains" or "a person who trains athletes." (Not all coaches are athletes, however, although some athletes make good coaches.) But a trainer can also be "a staff member of an athletic team who gives first aid and therapy to injured players," and as well "a person who trains racehorses or other animals for contests, shows, or performances." The French word *entraineur* means "trainer (of horses) or coach (of a team)," the latter referring to humans (Mansion, 1968). Indeed, most coaches for whom English is not their primary language use the term trainer rather than coach in reference to working with athlete development. Interestingly, the official entry list for the 1984 Los Angeles Olympic Games, with French and English as the two official languages, used "coach/entraineur" as one heading for team staff, and "trainer/soigneur" as another. The French verb *soigner* means "to attend to, to look after, to take care of."

In striving to improve and in striving to win, athletes require excellent coaching, management, and competition. Frank Dick (1983) very nicely defines a coach as "the director of an athlete's athletic ambition" (p. 6). If we substitute the word career for ambition, the concept becomes clearer still. If a coach and athlete have agreed to a collaboration leading in the direction of the athlete achieving all-around excellence in competitive sport, then the coach must undertake to provide input into and manage all aspects of the plan. The thinking should be done first, before training begins. Goals should be identified at that time—both long- and short-term—that set the stage for meaningful subsequent decisions. Training plans then become relatively simple to create. A good coach thus must also be well-rounded and provide a good example to make value judgments with conviction and credibility.

It may be that the simplest one-word definition we are seeking that sums up the concept of being a coach is simply *manager*. A good manager blends all the ingredients of a successful undertaking into a functional whole. A successful coach knows what to blend, how much of each ingredient to mix and when, and has an appreciation of how the end result may reflect more than simply the sum of all the ingredients. A competent coach is an expert at creating a master development plan and is able and willing to utilize the expertise of qualified and trusted people to assist with the execution of this plan. All along the way, a steady grip is kept on the path of forward progress for optimum athlete development. It is hoped that this can provide the direction an athlete needs to help inherent skills develop optimally into continuing success in later years.

Coaching a talented athlete thus would appear to be almost a full-time job, or at the very least not a job that can be done with a large group of athletes. A one-on-one athlete-coach relationship is probably most productive in the long run (pun perhaps intended), but it is practically difficult to achieve. A coach in a club situation may be required to work actively with a dozen or more athletes, all with differing talents and levels of fitness. College and university coaches may, in addition to managing the administrative details of an entire program, be hostage to the "payment by results" system, threatened by dismissal every year if their team doesn't win. For a coach to create useful training plans, individualized to athlete needs, a sizable time commitment is required. The greater the totality of ancillary demands upon one aspiring to coach a few talented athletes, the less is the probability that those athletes will obtain the individualized care that they need and deserve.

Using an academic analogy, a coach is someone who prepares students (athletes) to perform well in their examinations. Make no mistake: An important championship race is indeed a searching test of mastery. Good coaches are also good students, learning what others have done and documenting carefully what they are doing with their own athletes. Discovering blind alleys in advance of entry into them can save time and keep one on the path of progress. This path is really the plan (and thus we return to the implicit need for goals—they give direction to the plan).

In preparing athletes, however, a coach cannot know it all. Today there are more and more information subspecialties, all of which can add to multifaceted athlete development. Coaches need to establish a working awareness of all these sources of assistance and interweave their potential benefits effectively into the master development plan. Podiatric care, biomechanical film analysis, blood chemistry profiling, strength and circuit training, psychological preparation, treadmill runs to measure cardiopulmonary conditioning, and more all have their value—when implemented judiciously as part of the overall process of improving athletes' running skills and fitness. And added to these are all the varied aspects of these athletes' interaction with the world around them that need effective management—not only short-term (such as the details of upcoming competitions and training plan design) but also long-term (such as completing college education, managing financial affairs, possible public engagements or promotional opportunities, etc.). Sport is indeed a microcosm of life itself; the greater an athlete's success, the more complex this world becomes.

The Successful Athlete-Coach Relationship

The necessity for an athlete to be self-motivated is of great importance. A coach may, and should, broaden an athlete's horizon and suggest higher standards or goals to seek, so long as they are within the boundaries of reason and good sense. But a coach cannot be the inner drive that a winner must possess—that would be rather like the morbid analogy of a doctor being the donor in a slow but continuing blood transfusion wherein doctor and patient both die.

The best athletes are coach-oriented but not coach-dependent. The best relationship is a partnership. When an athlete chooses a coach, there comes also the obligation to submit willingly to that coach's discipline. A primary example includes doing no greater quantity or intensity of training than that assigned. If the coach is unaware of such additional training, erroneous judgment occurs in interpreting the effect of the assigned (plus unassigned) work load. The coach then has difficulty in devising subsequent meaningful training plans. But the coach must also be sensitive to athletes' unique needs and must work with those needs in devising the master plan. If an athlete-coach relationship is to be a journey of mutual discovery, both minds must be working together, not separately.

As the athlete progresses in excellence, it may become entirely appropriate for certain aspects of athletic life to be handled independently of the coach. Highly media-visible athletes can acquire sizable financial rewards, for example, making the addition of a good financial manager to the team advantageous. This decision should be a joint one by coach and athlete, usually initiated by the athlete.

Success depends so much on mutual trust. Even in the closest of partnerships, athletes will be away from their coaches for variable periods, and may not even live in the same city. A coach with the slightest doubt about an athlete's dedication or whether the athlete is doing the work assigned is a frustrated coach for whom dispassionate judgment is difficult. The coach must have the confidence (instilled by the athlete—and here's where the mutual trust appears) that, within reason, agreed-upon assignments will be completed. The real champions are self-disciplined and willing to make considerable personal sacrifice. Communication between athlete and coach must be effective, for both utilize the knowledge provided by each other's perspective on the training process and its effects. Indeed, knowledge is power, and the synergism of two experts (coach and athlete) bound by desire to create a superlative performance is powerful indeed.

No theory can be proved correct. The best we can hope for is that no test can be devised that proves our theory incorrect (Katch, 1986). It is the repeated testing for failure and falseness that affords a measure of confidence in the knowledge that coaches bring to the training process. Athletes are essentially unique ''experiments of one'' in how they are put together, and the more elite the athlete, the more unique the experiment. Individuals they may all be, yet their similarities far outweigh their differences. It is only because the human body functions physiologically in known laboratory-tested ways that training methods have gotten anywhere beyond guesswork. This is why it is very useful for a good coach to be well versed in the scientific essentials explaining human performance and its enhancement by adaptation to specific work loads. A college degree in the subject may not be necessary, but the knowledge is. It may not be possible to have close proximity to a human performance testing center, although the data obtained by such a facility, when interpreted properly, can be invaluable. Careful observation and recording of training responses and results of time trials can be adequate by themselves to permit meaningful analysis of progress and preparation. The coach and athlete must work closely to ensure the kind of communication that permits such analysis.

Of course, an obvious truth is that no one is completely knowable. Therefore, the best coach-athlete relationships are those in which each can tune in to each other with the greatest success. In part it stems from classic intuition—seeing the truth without reason or knowledge. But in part it comes from years of working together. It is the coach's responsibility to assign the work of training, raising or lowering its intensity to balance its tolerability. Thus, the coach constantly must have all antennae tuned in to pick up clues that will identify small changes that, when made, assure steady progress or identify areas needing improvement. The more intense the training, or the closer a major competition, the more sensitive this fine-tuning should be. Good coaches can arrive at a sense of what needs to be done, sometimes without being able to articulate fully the reasoning or the actions identifying that decision. This is a far different kind of assessment than simple gut reactions of would-be quasi-coaches acting on impulse. Very often, a coach well-tuned in to an athlete will be able to discuss overall progress in such a way that both together delineate a sensible plan of action.

Successful Athletes Are High Achievers

Competitively successful athletes, just like those people competent in other walks of life, have behavioral characteristics consistent with their achievement. Knowledge of these characteristics permits the athletes to better understand themselves and also permits coaches to interact more effectively with them. For example, successful athletes have a high degree of persistence at practicing the tasks required to improve. Thus, it is important that they know which tasks are important for improvement, and for this, good coaching is beneficial. It is often said that our best coaches ought to work with our youngest athletes, and the reason for this is clear. Wasting time and energy at tasks that will not necessarily improve the ability to perform in the sport event merely contaminate an athlete's developmental plan. This is a critical issue particularly with a sport such as distance running, which has injury risks from overuse and chronic fatigue.

High achievers also have a high completion rate at the tasks they do that are related to their intended goal of performance improvement. Their focus is more task-centered than person-centered. They are self-directed. Once given instructions, they proceed competently on their own, with no problem in taking control or command over their task-oriented focus. They assume responsibility willingly and enjoy involvement in decision making with regard to the design of tasks that will improve performance. As they continue to work, they strive for a high completion rate in their assigned tasks. It is thus crucial that the work load approximate closely the athlete's ability. If the work load is too easy, frustration occurs because of insufficient challenge. If the assignment is too difficult, injury may occur because the athlete will persist relentlessly toward what is perceived as an achievable goal. The final result in a properly directed program of development for a highly motivated athlete is improved performance quality. Good planning is very important in this regard.

Scientific Evaluation of Health and Fitness

There is no doubt that hard work over a long period of time is the primary route toward achieving athletic performance potential. To that end, training, competing, and sharing experiences and feelings with other athletes form the primary basis for essential development. Successful training and racing, however, can occur only in the context of excellent general health. And it would be nice to ensure that a continual improvement in fitness is resulting from the assigned training. This centers around prevention of habituation to training and identification of optimum training. Habituation is really bad adaptation. If one habituates to a training load, one is no longer responding to the training environment by improvement; there is no further adaptation. We desire continued, steady adaptation to the work load assigned. This is an important reason for the recent considerable interest among coaches and athletes for teaming up with knowledgeable scientists: to monitor ongoing health changes, to quantify training effectiveness, and to identify more specifically what should be done during training to further enhance performance. Long-term periodic fitness and health evaluation, using athletes as their own controls, provides the best opportunity for combining the art of coaching and the science of sport into a unified whole.

Changes in tolerance to training loads over time can be sensed subjectively by athlete and coach and interpreted along with objective evidence in managing time trials or small competitions. Coupled with this, however, careful laboratory monitoring of performance capabilities—with minimum contamination by such factors as temperature, wind, humidity, terrain, and tactics—can provide an additional objective assessment of changes in fitness over time. The longer this collaboration of knowledge acquisition occurs, the more confident we can be about the conclusions obtained. Careful review of training logs in light of this combined wisdom can suggest the best plan for further training, tapering, or racing. Final advice for the best racing strategies will optimize performance strengths and rely least on capabilities less well developed. The latter will be reserved for subsequent training, thereby continuing the fine-tuning process.

Unfortunately, athletes and coaches have not always found the world of sports science very useful in helping them refine their training strategies. Too often in the past, athletes have very willingly agreed to be evaluated in scientific laboratories but were provided with little or no direct feedback of useful information for their training. There have been at least two reasons for this. Although scientists have been fascinated with the amazing performance capabilities of elite athletes and the extent to which these abilities exceed the norm, a large proportion of studies have been simply descriptive, with practical relevance not immediately obvious. Scientists who are not coaches or athletes also may not have as well-developed an appreciation for the need to search for such practical application of the laboratory results to training methodology.

A second reason is that quite often the discovery of information about how physiological processes function simply reinforces what athletes already have experienced. A champion marathoner who finds training sessions of fast running difficult to accomplish and who has never excelled at shorter distance races will learn little from a biopsy evaluation of his skeletal muscle fibers that shows a biochemical specialization for endurance- rather than quickness-oriented performance. This new information by itself does little to improve training effectiveness. It is our view that, for elite-level athletes whose careers are determined solely by the quality of their competitive results, emphasis of studies done with them should be directed toward acquisition of specific practical knowledge that, when incorporated properly into their training lifestyles, can preserve excellent health and/or improve their fitness. Progress in this area is improving significantly.

Three kinds of information have been identified as useful for assisting athletes and coaches with performance enhancement. The first includes information related to basic health. Monitoring blood chemistry markers to evaluate health and the risk of overtraining is one general example. Detecting a trend toward anemia by observing steadily decreasing hemoglobin levels obtained via blood chemistry profiling is one specific example. Nutritional suggestions for enhancing fuel absorption and replenishment in working skeletal muscles is another. The second includes information indicating risks for disease or musculoskeletal injury. Evaluation of pulmonary function in athletes with exercise-induced asthma, with a view toward identifying the effectiveness of appropriate approved medications to cope with and minimize its debilitating effects, is an example. The third includes measurement of specific performance-related variables that can be affected by training. An example might be cardiopulmonary system evaluation using treadmill runs to identify optimum training paces for delaying the onset of accumulating metabolic acids, or increasing the maximum amount of oxygen uptake during fast running.

Changes in specific variables by themselves are not likely to be identifiable as cause-and-effect predictors of individual competitive performances. The sum total of the interactive effects of all the training variables over time, plus others unmeasured, contribute to performance. And, of course, on the day of competition there is the inner mental drive to perform well that may never be exactly quantifiable. But a healthy athlete whose training plan has brought development to a peak at the appropriate moment has the ideal opportunity to combine the will to win with superlative fitness into a personal best performance. This book is about optimum development of distance runners through health maintenance and adaptation to training.

REFERENCES

Dick, F. (1983). Value judgements and the coach. *Track & Field Quarterly Review*, **83**(3):6-9.

Flexner, S.B., & Hauck, L.C. (1987). *The Random House dictionary of the English Language* (2nd ed.). New York: Random House.

Katch, V. (1986). The burden of disproof* . . . *Medicine and Science in Sports and Exercise*, **18**, 593-595.

Mansion, J.E. (1968). *Heath's standard French and English dictionary*. Boston: D.C. Heath.

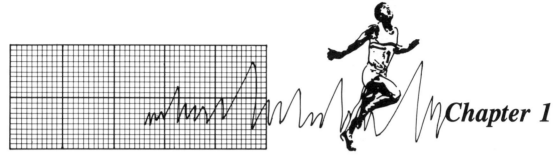

The Coupling of Movement and Metabolism

Where there is life, there is movement. Walking and running are intricate motor skills that develop over time, with repeated practice, and are our most familiar forms of movement. Running is often considered mankind's oldest form of sport—a simple test of one's ability to move quickly from one point to another. The Olympic motto *Citius, Altius, Fortius* literally means "faster, higher, braver," although "swifter, higher, stronger" seems more commonly accepted. From ancient Greece to modern times, running fast and long has been popular.

The desire to know how to run faster or farther is essentially as old as our willingness to try harder. Talented athletes very often are highly motivated, even to the extent that their enthusiasm may need tempering rather than enhancement. Running is a neuromuscular skill, performed in accordance with the principles of biomechanics and dependent on metabolic energy. Practice, so often it is told, makes perfect. When inefficient movement patterns are refined out of a runner's natural style through months of such practice, which we call training, movement economy improves, permitting potentially greater speed or endurance. But it isn't just practice that brings perfection. Knowing *how* to practice is essential; we must have an effective plan derived from the best information available as to the kinds of work that will bring improvement. Knowing the results of that practice then can provide essential feedback for more refined activity. Excessive motivation to train and improve can overchallenge the body's ability to provide the required energy and increase the likelihood of fatigue as well as soreness and injuries. Thus motivation, movement, and metabolism are closely coupled.

As soon as runners begin to improve their abilities over time through training, they become desirous of any and all information that might enhance this development. Coaches as well continually search for answers to questions that might provide them with additional knowledge to help their athletes acquire the winning edge over their competitors. How is running acquired as a skill? How do the nervous and musculoskeletal systems interact to permit running to occur? Can an individual's running style be improved, and would this likely improve competitive performance abilities? How can running injuries be prevented? What occurs during the training process that makes muscles more fatigue-resistant? Are these changes related solely to the neuromuscular system, or does the cardiovascular system interact in this regard? Because energy is required for movement, how are the various available fuels converted into energy? How is this energy stored and made available for use by working muscles? How can this knowledge be applied practically by athletes and coaches to provide the best possible physiological environment for adaptation to the various training loads that will be assigned over a season of training and competing?

It's a tall order to answer all of these questions, but we'll try. Let us begin by first summarizing some of the basic concepts relating to movement and development of the skill aspect of running. This is an important part of the discipline of kinesiology. Then we can proceed to review some of the mechanical principles governing how we run. This falls under the purview of the rapidly evolving discipline of sport biomechanics. From there we will be in a better position to consider our working skeletal muscles in greater detail, not only from the perspective of their role in movement but also in terms of how they produce energy in a manner that permits competitiveness over the broad range of distances that are of interest to the middle- and long-distance athlete.

INTRODUCTION TO KINESIOLOGY: THE STUDY OF MOVEMENT

Kinesiology is the science of human motion. It utilizes relevant principles from such disciplines as anatomy, physiology, and physics and applies them appropriately to the understanding of bodily movement. Our particular interest is to better understand the movement patterns that permit running. Each structure contributing to such body movement acts in obedience to biomechanical and physiological principles. Understanding these principles puts us in a better position to identify the best plan for helping runners become more skilled in their sport. Because running is such a fundamental aspect of human movement, it is a skill learned quite early in life. Improved skill combined with the benefits of training contributes to performance enhancement. Thus, once runners are in their high school, college, and postcollegiate years, increases in performance ability are achieved primarily through greater fitness.

Terminology and Concepts

We define **movement** as a position change by any segment of the body. A more complex **movement pattern** is thus a sequence of movements in a particular time-space relationship. Running is a specifically structured movement pattern. Sometimes the phrases ''motor activity'' or ''motor pattern'' are substituted-for movement pattern. A **motor skill** is defined as a group of simple, natural movements combined toward achieving a predetermined goal. Three primary demands on muscular performance are imposed in acquiring any motor skill: strength, endurance, and speed. Coordination links these three together to permit smoothly executed movement patterns (Henatsch & Langer, 1985).

Fundamental motor skills set the stage for the development of more advanced and specialized motor activities. **Fundamental motor patterns** thus are the general sequence of movements required to perform a fundamental skill. A small child just beginning to run a few steps has acquired fundamental motor patterns for running. Over time, and with practice, marked improvement will be noted. This refinement has various features that comprise the developmental motor pattern. Although this developing runner is by no means as accomplished as he or she will be gradually over time, there is still a vast increase in competence beyond the fundamental running motor pattern. Thus, motor skills are learned. Inborn natural (unconditioned) responses are eventually modified to permit their triggering by other-than-natural (conditioned) stimuli, in new combinations and sequences. This occurs because the plasticity of the nervous system permits reinterpretation (and, it is hoped, a refinement) of nervous input, over time and with repetition.

When asked to run laps around a 400-meter (m) track at a specific pace, novice runners typically demonstrate considerable variation in lap times. If the runner is asked to maintain a 75-second (sec) pace, for example, for six laps, with half a minute (min) rest between laps, variation of as much as 2 to 3 sec and more for each lap can be common. Not so with an experienced distance runner, who after years of good coaching can achieve a constancy, despite weather or progressive fatigue, that over distances from 200 m to 800 m may not vary by more than a few 10ths of 1 sec.

A **sport skill** is a fundamental skill that has been refined and specialized to permit participation in a particular sport. Thus, whereas the simple act of running may be a fundamental skill, the art of running competitively is a sport skill. The concept of *form* or *style* refers to the visual effect produced by motor patterns. If the visual effect is smooth and efficient, then good form (style) ought to equate at least to some extent with increased skill. Finally, performance describes an assigned motor activity. A **sport performance** is thus a specialized sport skill that is assigned, typically with the intent of producing the best possible display of motor patterns.

Ability Versus Capacity

In all activities—athletic, artistic, literary—individuals who have subjected themselves to intensive training typically demonstrate a wide range of abilities. The inference is that they must have started with unequal capacities to learn. There is thus a distinction between ability and capacity. *Capacity* is synonymous with readiness for use, whereas *ability* presupposes training. It is quite possible that each individual is endowed with a general motor capacity comparable to his or her general intellectual capacity. Whereas capacity is a condition, ability can be observed and measured.

An ability is invariably the result of training, and the degree of ability is related to the quantity of such training. The common phrase "inherent ability" really refers to capacity.

The capacity of the brain to engender new motor patterns seems almost unlimited. Incorporation of incoming new sensory information leads to further perceptive and cognitive integration, which in turn permits progressively more effective motor responses. Not only can we create movements in the images of our thinking, but we also can improve their execution. This mental assimilation comes from training. There is no substitute for proper training if movement patterns are to develop optimally. The extent of performance improvement is greatest among those athletes whose development programs have been not only very intense but also most specific to the sport skills being developed. Training, coaching, and specificity are the keys.

Evidently, the acquisition of human skill presupposes not only physical abilities but also the realization of distinct aims and objectives. The latter in turn are conceived in the image of historical, social, cultural, and scientific precedents. Thus, developing athletes become aware of the excellence of past athletes (such as Olympian Jesse Owens), identify with a particular event (such as the short sprints), and develop a yearning for excellence (such as a desire someday also to compete in the Olympic Games). This provides a base for their motivation and goal setting toward achieving excellence (through collaboration with coaches who have demonstrated competence).

Development of Skill in Movement

Both training and technique are essential in improving sport skill levels. The human body is a self-optimizing machine in that it gradually adapts to a given movement challenge by improving the efficiency with which the movement is performed. Ostensibly, this permits the imposition of an even greater challenge, with eventual adaptation to that as well. Peak physical performance occurs when limits to further adaptation are reached. It is essentially the result of a balance between natural abilities (both physical and mental) and proper training. The training aspect is seen in the biochemical and physiological adaptations occurring within cells. The skill aspect is seen in improved movement pattern efficiency; visually we see an improved running style.

At least five characteristics are observable as a skilled performer optimizes energy expenditure to permit the highest quality of performance:

1. There is improved balance and coordination, thereby reducing postural work.

2. Unnecessary and exuberant movements are eliminated.

3. Necessary movements are refined to ensure that these occur in the proper direction, with optimum quickness to minimize loss of kinetic energy.

4. The most important muscles for movement (the **prime movers**) are used more effectively. This includes the most efficient coordination of **agonists** (those muscles active for generating movement), **antagonists** (those muscles which have opposing motion and are either relaxed or stabilizing the involved joints when the agonists are active), and **synergists** (those muscles assisting the prime movers). The end result is minimum energy devoted to initiating the movement, minimum opposing resistance, and minimum force required to terminate or reverse the direction of movement.

5. Continually controlled movements are gradually replaced by ballistic strokes. This final characteristic needs further elaboration.

For practical purposes, the limiting factor in the rapidity of a movement—be it tapping a finger or running down a street—is set by the natural movement frequency of the involved body part; this is its resonance. A reciprocal movement such as running is essentially a series of ballistic strokes. A **ballistic stroke** can be conceptualized here as a single oscillation of a moving pendulum formed by the arm or leg. Movement is initiated by sudden generation of tension in shortening muscles until acceleration has been completed, at which time the limb continues to move under its own momentum. As movement patterns are being learned, the stroke velocity is slow due to uncertainty, and tension application may occur throughout much of the range of motion. As skill is acquired, movement velocity increases. With it, there is a gradual shift from prolonged muscle activity through the range of motion to short ballistic bursts that initiate limb acceleration in the precise direction and extent required to complete the movement.

In a fashion similar to acceleration, a decelerating action due to tension generation in the antagonistic muscles continues for sufficient time to reverse the movement and initiate a ballistic stroke in the opposite direction. If the optimum resonant frequency of a limb is exceeded, movement becomes less efficient because more energy is required. Resonance thus limits the rate of running through limitation of stride frequency. Once the optimum frequency is attained, greater velocity occurs by lengthening the stride. This is achieved by strengthening, which comes with proper training over time.

These concepts can help us understand the developmental process as runners progress from novice to elite levels. For example, a well-trained runner brings the thigh of the lead leg forward at closer to the maximum velocity permitted by resonance and may take a stride that is several centimeters (cm) longer than a novice runner with a similar relationship between leg length and body height. The increased velocity requires more intense tension generation in the agonist muscles, and the longer stride mandates a greater relaxation of the antagonists to accommodate the increased range of motion. If the quadriceps muscles, for example, are the agonist muscles providing forward thrust in running, then the hamstrings are the antagonists. Inflexible hamstrings can thus limit efficient stride maintenance at higher running intensities or can be prone to injury if the much stronger quadriceps group stretches them inappropriately. Thus, optimum relationships among muscle strength, muscle length, and joint range of motion are important for promoting injury-free improvement in performance. As an accompaniment to a training plan that includes various patterns of running to provide specific development (see chapter 3), we also recommend a plan to develop these other more general aspects of fitness (commonly called total body conditioning; see chapter 4).

Brain Initiation and Execution of Movement

Many regions of the brain and spinal cord interact as a team to set the stage for and permit initiation of functionally useful and efficient movement. The cerebral cortex, as the seat of our volitional thoughts, is only one of the regions in the brain involved in directing movement. Many other brain and spinal cord regions are also involved with movement, and they interact with the cerebral cortex. Gaining a complete understanding could be the challenge of college courses in neuroanatomy and neurophysiology. Here we can only briefly discuss some of the more important concepts that will provide a basis for better understanding of running as a form of movement and how this movement is organized.

It is useful to view movement as a phenomenon in direct conflict with posture. Movement causes variable changes in the position of the body parts over time. Posture is exactly the reverse: The body position is fixed. To resolve this conflict, the renowned neurologist Denny-Brown suggested that we think of movement as simply a series of postures. In Figure 1.1, from left to right, three contemporary male 800m runners (Seb Coe [Great Britain], Steve Cram [Great Britain], and Ryszard Ostrowski [Poland]) demonstrate what we shall later describe as, respectively, the midsupport, follow-through, and foot descent

periods of a running cycle. Of interest to us at the moment, however, is understanding which structures of the central nervous system interact to initiate and permit these very rapid sequential postural changes that we call running.

Figure 1.1   Three of many postures assumed during a running sequence. Shown here, from left to right, and identifiable by their side numbers, are Sebastian Coe (GBR—#1), Steve Cram (GBR—#3), and Ryszard Ostrowski (POL—#2). Coe's right leg is in the midsupport period, Cram's left leg is in the follow-through period, and Ostrowski's left leg is in the foot descent period of the running cycle.

The reticular formation in the brain stem (Figure 1.2) plays one of the most fundamental roles. This is the oldest part of the brain, and it assumes responsibility for the three primary requirements of postural maintenance:

1. Support against gravity
2. Orientation in space
3. Balance

Cues from several sensory systems are utilized to satisfy this responsibility. The visual system is probably the most familiar, providing visual orientation in space. The vestibular system in the inner ear provides cues about position of the center of mass as well as changes in acceleration or deceleration. *Neuromuscular spindles* distributed among all the skeletal muscle fibers detect static as well as dynamic muscle length. *Golgi tendon organs* are specialized for

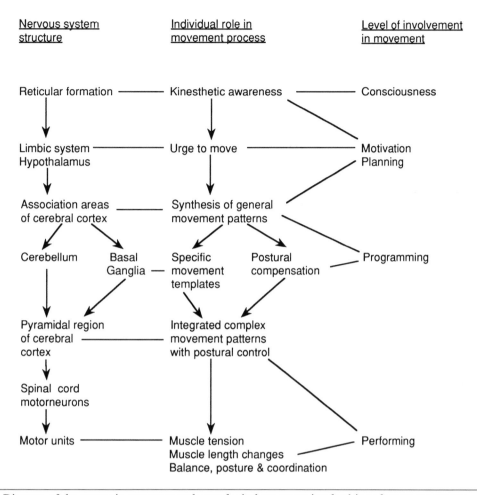

Nervous system structure

Reticular formation

Limbic system
Hypothalamus

Association areas
of cerebral cortex

Cerebellum   Basal
                  Ganglia

Pyramidal region
of cerebral
cortex

Spinal cord
motorneurons

Motor units

Individual role in movement process

Kinesthetic awareness

Urge to move

Synthesis of general
movement patterns

Specific   Postural
movement   compensation
templates

Integrated complex
movement patterns
with postural control

Muscle tension
Muscle length changes
Balance, posture & coordination

Level of involvement in movement

Consciousness

Motivation
Planning

Programming

Performing

Figure 1.2   Diagram of the anatomic structures and neurological processes involved in voluntary movement.

measuring changes in tension or force in skeletal muscles. These various receptors are often grouped together as *proprioceptors*. The Latin prefix *proprio* refers to "one's own," and thus proprioceptors identify the position of one's body in space. Information from all of these systems is sent to the reticular formation, via either brain nerve pathways or spinal cord pathways.

The cerebellum is another quite primitive brain region, acting as a kind of computer to process incoming information from a variety of levels of sophistication—volitional, automatic, and reflex. It interacts with both the reticular formation and the cerebral cortex to ensure that volitional commands for movement sequences produce the most efficient and coordinated result possible while still permitting appropriate postural maintenance.

The signals to initiate movement originate in regions just below the cerebral cortex, notably the limbic system and hypothalamus. Here is where motivation and the urge to move (the drive to act) are developed. Stimuli from these areas then signal regions of the

cerebral cortex known as association areas, and at this time the synthesis of movement patterns is created. Signals from the association areas are then sent to two regions. Those going to the cerebellum result in movement patterns involving ballistic strokes and great precision. Signals sent to the basal ganglia just below the cerebral cortex create movement templates directed toward postural compensation when the movement begins. Both the basal ganglia and cerebellum send their integrated movement pattern signals back to the cerebral cortex, specifically to its motor or pyramidal region (so-called because many of its large cell bodies resemble small pyramids).

Then, initiating signals are sent from the cerebral cortex down through the spinal cord to the various muscles involved not only in permitting the movement but also in postural maintenance. As movement begins and posture is altered, this will, of course, be monitored in exquisite detail via action of the proprioceptors. Such incoming information will be used to help the brain determine how much volitional output is required to permit efficient and effective movement for the particular movement pattern attempted. Figure 1.2 summarizes these various levels of organization and processes that permit voluntary movements.

The Need for Training in Skill Acquisition

Achievement in sport is essentially the product of testing capabilities (how well one performs, in either a competition, a time trial, or a practice session) multiplied by skill level. Motivation is required for both, but it is particularly influential in providing the persistence required for the training and practice necessary to improve skill levels. For achievement at anything, one needs

- reasonable capabilities for that activity,
- the capacity (motivation plus environment) to train diligently, and
- effective use of learned skills in a test situation.

Observing and thinking do not suffice by themselves for the acquisition of skills. In sports as well as the arts, a long period of conditioning and practice precedes mastery of a task. The personal history of every champion athlete reveals the determining role played by intensive and dedicated training. Sustained practice of precisely designed movement sequences establishes advanced levels of control, differentiation, and precision of motor patterns that are beyond the integrative control of the untrained individual. Along with basic neuromotor skill, the cognitive qualities of awareness and judgment are also required for performance excellence.

The eventual goal of motor learning is to develop the ability to perform with minimum conscious concern for exactly how the performance is being achieved. Frequent practice of a complex skill helps make it automatic rather than voluntary, and the increasing smoothness thereby reduces error frequency. The execution of all rapid movements depends greatly on timing—generating and relaxing tension in individual muscles in a closely planned sequence. People vary in their abilities to store such movement sequences within the brain. Considerable time is spent practicing to develop one's potentialities within the complex neurological framework that permits movement patterns in the context of postural balance. Once movement patterns have been learned, then attention need only be shifted from the elements of the task to the initiating signal for skill competence. Thus, bowlers are taught to take their stance and then focus on the pins rather than on the ball or their body position behind the foul line. Tennis players are taught not to look at their rackets or arms but rather at the oncoming ball being returned or served. We mentioned earlier that running involves much more fitness than technique because it is not a complex technique-oriented skill.

Runners in a race automatically select a stride length, stride frequency, and breathing rate that fit their level of exertion and running velocity. This permits other aspects to be dealt with more from a cognitive viewpoint, such as assessing their own level of perceived exertion and how it seems to compare to the level of the runners around them (listening to their breathing patterns, viewing their expressions, etc.), and determining the appropriateness of using tactics for improving race position. Is this automatically selected combination of stride length and stride frequency in fact always the most energy efficient? To answer this question, we need to better understand some of the basic concepts involving the application of biomechanics to running.

BIOMECHANICS OF RUNNING

Successful distance runners improve steadily with training and experience minimum setbacks with structural injury in any parts of the connecting limbs (bones, tendons, muscles, joints). More training can bring better fitness, and thus better performance capabilities, but only within limits. The challenge is to identify those limits before they are reached. The large volumes of training required to improve fitness result in an enormous net impact stress on the feet and legs.

An example can give an idea of the magnitude of the problem. Let us define a running **cycle** as consisting of two strides; that is, beginning and ending with one particular foot striking the ground (Mann, 1982). (Some investigators substitute *stride* for *cycle* and *step* for *stride* [Cavanagh & Kram, 1990].) Assuming a stride length of 60 inches (in.), or 5 feet (ft), at a pace of 6:30/mile (mi), with each landing foot bearing the impact of twice the body weight, a 10-mi run for a 130-pound (lb) male runner would involve 5,280 landings per foot, with a total impact force per foot of 686 U.S. tons, as shown by the following calculations:

$$(1 \text{ stride}/5 \text{ ft} \times 5{,}280 \text{ ft/mi} \times 10 \text{ mi})/2 = 5{,}280 \text{ landings/foot}$$

$$(130 \text{ lb} \times 2 \text{ body weight})/\text{stride} \times 5{,}280 \text{ strides} \times 1 \text{ U.S. ton}/2{,}000 \text{ lb} = 686 \text{ U.S. tons} \qquad (1.1)$$

If running velocity increases, the stride length will increase, reducing the number of landings per unit distance. But the impact will increase to as much as five or six times body weight.

For those readers more familiar with the metric system, we can recalculate the preceding example using metric equivalents. A 59-kilogram (kg) runner with a stride length of 1.52 m completing a 16.1-km run would have 5,296 landings per foot and a total impact force per foot of 624,928 kg! A similar calculation for a female distance runner could be made by substituting 110 lb (50 kg) and a 55-in. (1.40m) stride length at 6:30/mi and is left as an exercise for interested readers.

Runners aspiring to excellence are in an almost no-win situation. Running is required as training to improve running skills. As records become more difficult to break, more training (quantity, quality, or both) is required to achieve the performance level necessary for such a feat. This is true for individual records as much as for world, Olympic, or school records. The greater the volume or intensity of distance run, the greater the stress and thus the risk of injury. As shown previously, even one run provides enormous stresses to the lower limbs. Not to train very extensively makes one ill prepared to compete successfully with those who have done so but haven't (yet) become injured. At the top level, it is not unusual for an elite 10,000m runner or marathoner to have several-week blocks of endurance-oriented training that can exceed 100 mi (161 km) each week (Kaggestad, 1987). Using the arithmetic format illustrated in Equation 1.1, a calculation of the number of footstrikes or amount of landing force (in lb or kg) for such a week gives results that are almost unimaginable. Try it!

Thus, the conflict between the need for training for improvement and the limit imposed by load-related stress that results in injury has stimulated considerable interest in understanding what occurs during a running cycle, how biomechanics can be improved, and how the weakest links can be identified that might predispose a runner to injury as repetitive stress accumulates. If improved running mechanics in fact decrease the energy costs associated with the muscular forces of running, the resulting improved efficiency should decrease the oxygen (O_2) cost of running at any given submaximum pace. Presumably, this ought to increase the maximum maintainable pace, thereby improving performance. Athletes and coaches ought to understand these basic concepts, including the proper terminology related to running biomechanics. They then can communicate more effectively with the various experts—biomechanists, podiatrists, orthopedists, and other coaches—who have the skills to assist them in identifying optimum training conditions for performance enhancement with injury freedom.

Application of Biomechanical Principles to Running

At least four important principles of biomechanics explain what occurs during a running cycle. Understanding these principles permits greater appreciation for the limb and postural adjustments that occur.

Principle 1:
Force Must be Applied to Change the Velocity of an Object in Motion

In humans, muscular tension generation serves as the producer of force. This force can start, accelerate, decelerate, stop, or change direction of movement. As an example, a runner experiences a slight loss of velocity during the airborne phase of each stride. Thus, to maintain continuity of motion, appropriate force must be applied by the support leg at takeoff.

Principle 2:
Linear and Angular Motion Need Integration to Permit Optimum Performance of Movement Patterns

The lower limbs function by flexion and extension through the range of motion of their joints. The pelvis transmits the body weight to the alternating surface-striking limbs through the hip joints and the lumbothoracic spine. As the lower limbs alternate from support phase through swing phase, thigh extension and flexion are accompanied by rotatory movements (to increase stride length) as well as abduction and adduction at the hips, and lateral flexion and rotation of the spine. All these movements about various planes need to be complementary and not contradictory.

Principle 3:
The Longer the Length of a Lever, the Greater the Potential Linear Velocity at Its End

In running, this principle is utilized in reverse. Thus, the knee of the recovery leg, and the arms as well, are bent in order to shorten these limb levers and bring them forward with less energy requirement.

Principle 4:
For Every Action There is a Reaction Equal in Amount but Opposite in Direction

With every running footstrike, the landing surface pushes back with a force equal to the impact force, driving the runner upward and forward in a direction opposite to that of impact.

There are, of course, additional biomechanical principles that describe the kinds of activities runners engage in during training. In chapter 4 we shall consider some of these, particularly those relating to development of leverage for the various aspects of strength training that comprise a total body conditioning program.

Sequence of Activity During A Running Cycle

Let us briefly describe what occurs as our limbs proceed through one running cycle. The relevant terminology and concepts are familiar to podiatrists, biomechanists, and orthopedists interested in gait, but they comprise a body of knowledge useful for coaches and athletes as well. Several good reviews describe rather precisely what occurs during running. These include Slocum and Bowerman, 1962; Slocum and James, 1968; James and Brubaker, 1972; Mann, Moran, and Dougherty, 1986; and Adelaar, 1986. More than one set of descriptive terms exist for identifying the various aspects of gait cycle for running; we will use that of Slocum and James.

Running and walking are both fundamental skills, but they differ from many other such skills in that the movement pattern is designed to be continuous, without interruption. We move one foot in front of the other, with the arms on each side moving synchronously but in opposite direction to the legs. Thus, as the left leg and right arm are moving forward, the right leg and left arm are moving backward. In both walking and running the trunk should have minimum forward lean. This reduces the load on postural muscles, which will be stressed least if they keep the large percentage of body weight that is made up by the trunk and head (60%) directly over the point of ground support.

The most important feature that distinguishes between running and walking is that in running there is a period during which we are airborne. Figures 1.3e, 1.3f, 1.3i, and 1.3j illustrate this. Both walking and running have two separate phases: support (or stance) and forward recovery (or swing). During walking, the support phase accounts for perhaps 65% of the total cycle time, with both limbs on the ground simultaneously for part of its duration. With running, the support phase is reduced in duration to as little as 30%, and the period of double-limb support disappears. If the support phase occupies 40% of a running cycle, then the free-floating forward recovery phase occupies about 60%.

There are, of course, other differences, but the period of free float is the most noticeable. In walking, the forward foot touches down heel first, before the toe of the other foot has pushed off. During running, the pushoff becomes so strong that the body is launched into the air; running is thus a kind of bounding. This causes other differences between running and walking. First, in running the arms are bent more acutely due to elbow flexion, which shortens the arm lever and thereby allows more rapid arm swing as stride rate increases. In contrast, during walking the arms are nearly extended. Second, greater vertical displacement of the trunk (the bounding aspect) occurs with running than with walking. Finally, there is more hip, knee, and ankle activity to accommodate the greater stresses that occur when running. At landing, a runner experiences a rapid knee and hip flexion, as well as ankle dorsiflexion, in response to the need for greater shock absorption. With walking there is ankle plantar flexion, not dorsiflexion.

We have already explained the difference between cycle and stride in running. Running velocity is the product of stride length and stride frequency. To measure stride length, it is best to measure from the toe of the landing shoe rather than from the back of the heel. Whereas walking is almost universally a heel-to-toe action, some runners do not land on their heels. Among talented runners, the majority (60%) land on the forefoot, a sizable number land on the midfoot (30%), and the remaining 10% are rearfoot strikers (Cavanagh, Pollock, & Landa, 1977). This is probably good, for the forefoot is better able to absorb stress than the rearfoot.

The support phase of running consists of three distinct periods: *footstrike*, *midsupport*, and *takeoff* (sometimes called contact, midstance, and toeoff). During forward recovery there are also three periods: *follow-through*, *forward swing*, and *foot descent*. Follow-through and foot descent are also known as the periods of float. These various periods are all identified in the photo sequence that comprises Figure 1.3, which shows 1986 U.S. 1,500m champion Linda Sheskey running at a pace of approximately 69 sec/400 m. By referring to this photo sequence, we can briefly describe what is occurring.

A few important podiatric and biomechanical concepts need introduction at this point to make this description more meaningful. Both walking and running are integrated series of rotations that propel the body through space. The so-called kinetic chain of structures that copes with the impact forces upon landing and the pushoff forces upon takeoff includes, in sequence, the lumbar spine, pelvis, proximal lower limb (femur), distal lower limb (tibia and fibula), rearfoot (calcaneus and talus), midfoot (navicular and

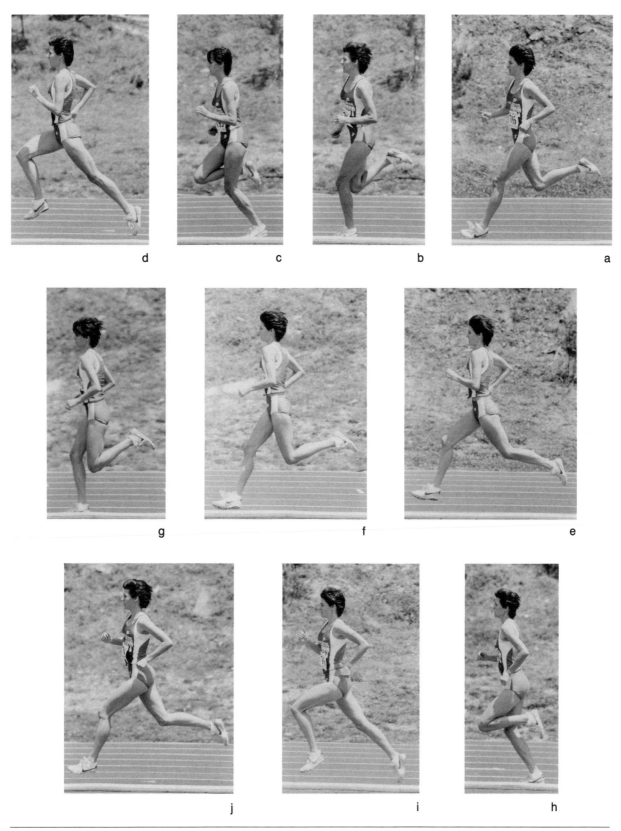

Figure 1.3 Photo sequence of one running cycle for the left leg. There are two phases: support (a-c), which occupies 40% of the cycle, and forward recovery (d-j), accounting for 60%. Each phase has three periods. Support phase periods are (a) footstrike, (b) midsupport, and (c) takeoff. Forward recovery phase periods are (d) follow-through (float), (e-h) forward swing, and (i-j) foot descent (float).

cuboid), and forefoot (cuneiforms, metatarsals, and phalanges). Joints connect each of these various links: pelvis (hip to femur), knee (femur to tibia), ankle (tibia to talus), subtalar (talus to calcaneus), and so on, through the midtarsal and tarsometatarsal to the metatarsophalangeal.

Muscles, tendons, ligaments, bones, and joint capsules work together to dissipate and manage the rotatory, angulatory, and compressive forces that occur during a gait cycle. Muscles are particularly important because they initiate movement, stabilize bones, and decelerate or dampen movement forces resulting from sudden weight-bearing. Muscle fatigue reduces this protective function, increasing the risk of injury to the other tissues in the kinetic chain.

The body has three axes of rotation: frontal, sagittal, and transverse. Relative to the foot, frontal plane rotation represents inversion and eversion, sagittal plane rotation represents dorsiflexion and plantar flexion, and transverse plane rotation represents abduction (external rotation) and adduction (internal rotation). A complication in foot mechanics is that the ankle, subtalar, and midtarsal joints have axes of rotation that are oblique to these three body movement planes. These joint movements have components of all three motions. Thus, pronation consists of dorsiflexion, calcaneal eversion, and external rotation, whereas supination consists of plantar flexion, calcaneal inversion, and internal rotation. The talus bone lies just below the tibia and above the calcaneus, and thus is a pivotal structure in linking the movements of the lower leg and foot. When it articulates with the tibia to form the ankle joint, it works as part of the foot to permit dorsiflexion and plantar flexion. When it articulates with the calcaneus at the subtalar joint, it works as part of the leg to permit pronation and supination.

Figure 1.4 illustrates the neutral (or intrinsically stable) foot position (a) in comparison to pronation (b) and supination (c). When one stands barefoot in the neutral position, the tibia, talus, and calcaneus are aligned perfectly, with neither pronation nor supination at the subtalar joint. As seen by surface anatomy, the thick, dark vertical bars drawn above and below the lateral malleolus are aligned. Although not pictured, the heads of all the metatarsal bones should also rest on the standing surface. The arch of the foot should require no support from muscles and tendons in addition to that provided by the foot bones. Pronation is illustrated in Figure 1.4b, where the curve below the lateral malleolus is even more everted than the curve above it. In Figure 1.4c the foot is supinated at the subtalar joint, and this is easily seen using surface anatomy by noticing that the surface curve below

the lateral malleolus is in the opposite (inverted) direction to the curve above (everted).

Now let's follow Linda Sheskey through one of her running gait cycles. We will follow her left leg as it moves through its support and nonsupport phases. In Figure 1.3a her foot is about to touch the ground, initiating footstrike. Her foot is still in flight and will have a certain amount of supination as it approaches footstrike. As she touches the ground, her foot is slightly ahead of her center of mass, to minimize braking and preserve linear momentum forward. Her subtalar joint plays the major role in converting the rotatory forces of her lower extremity into forward motion. In the split second from foot contact to full support on the running surface (Figures 1.3a and 1.3b), the knee flexes, the tibia internally rotates, the ankle plantar flexes, and the subtalar joint pronates, causing heel eversion (seen from behind in Figure 1.4e). This pronation permits absorption of compressive shock forces, torque conversion, adjustment to uneven ground contours, and maintenance of balance. The foot is a nonrigid, supple structure during this time, thus suited admirably for its role. Knee flexion is controlled by eccentric tension in the vastus medialis, vastus lateralis, rectus femoris, and sartorius of the thigh (shown nicely in the anterior view of a runner landing in Figure 1.5). The posterior tibialis, soleus, and gastrocnemius muscles by eccentric tension decelerate subtalar joint pronation and lower extremity internal rotation. Pronation reaches its maximum during this time, with sufficient resupination then occurring to permit the foot to pass through its neutral position (shown from behind in Figure 1.4d) at midsupport.

A certain amount of pronation is thus desirable to disseminate the energy of footstrike over the mid- and forefoot. Too little pronation transfers too much impact to the rearfoot, and excessive subtalar joint pronation causes too much calcaneal eversion, putting undue strain on the longitudinal arch. The plantar fascia restrains the extent to which this arch can depress and thus absorbs much of this landing force. Too little supination at takeoff also stresses this fascia. It originates from a tubercle on the bottom of the calcaneus (Figure 1.6) and divides into three bands as it continues forward along the plantar surface of the foot and attaches to the proximal parts of the toes. If microtears occur in this fascia from overuse, the resulting painful, localized inflammation (plantar fasciitis) can be quite debilitating. Careful footwear selection is thus important to minimize excessive pronation.

The period of midsupport continues until the heel starts to rise upward into takeoff (Figure 1.3c). During this time Linda's foot must convert from a supple,

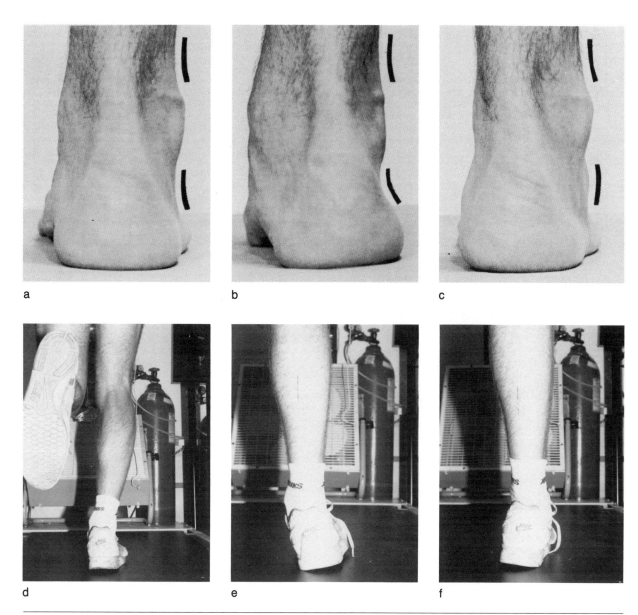

Figure 1.4 Comparison of (a, d) neutral, (b, e) pronated, and (c, f) supinated foot positions. *Note.* From *Normal and Abnormal Function of the Foot: Clinical Biomechanics–Volume II* (p. 157) by M.L. Root, W.P. Orien, and J.H. Weed, 1977, Los Angeles: Clinical Biomechanics Corporation. Copyright 1977 by Clinical Biomechanics Corporation. Reprinted by permission.

mobile structure to a rigid lever to adequately support many times her body weight (4 times at her pace as illustrated). This change is not so much dependent on muscle action as on change in position of the subtalar and midtarsal joints of the foot, the anatomical shape of the bones involved, and tension on the various ligaments. Supination of the subtalar joint establishes this rigid lever for forward propulsion. Thus, the knee joint extends, the lower extremity rotates externally, the calcaneus inverts, the midtarsal joint locks, and the foot becomes a rigid lever. The propulsive force is a thrust backward and downward,

resulting from a combination of hip extension (gluteal and hamstring muscles), knee extension (quadriceps group), and ankle plantar flexion (soleus and gastrocnemius). The end result is a rise in the center of mass as the body becomes airborne. The wider forefoot than rearfoot helps to provide balance and also increases the weight-bearing surface area.

As soon as the foot leaves the ground, Linda is in the initial floating period of the forward recovery phase, called follow-through (Figure 1.3d). Her left limb movement will be counteracted (slowed) by the action of the hamstrings. Simultaneously, footstrike

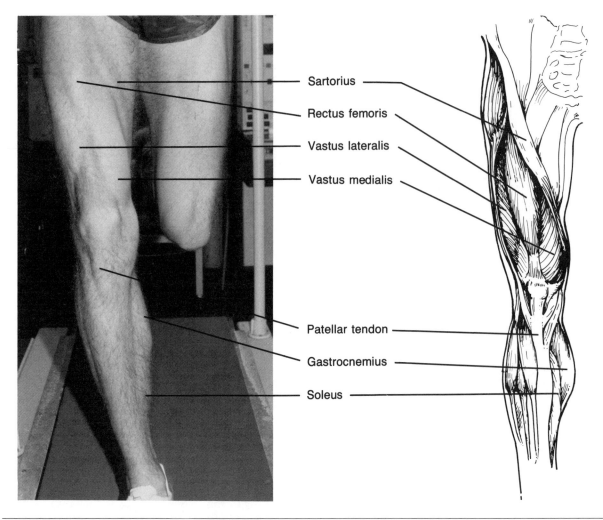

Sartorius

Rectus femoris

Vastus lateralis

Vastus medialis

Patellar tendon

Gastrocnemius

Soleus

Figure 1.5 Anterior view of major superficial muscles of the thigh.

Figure 1.6 The plantar fascia of the foot. Sometimes called the *plantar aponeurosis*, this is a glistening white fibrous membrane that resembles a flattened tendon. Just as with tendons, circulation of blood is very poor. Its collagen-containing bundles of fibers are tightly packed and arranged in parallel, giving great strength. It attaches to the medial process of the tuberosity of the heelbone and eventually becomes broader and more flattened. Near the metatarsal heads it divides into five processes, one going to each of the toes.

by the opposite limb is about to occur. The trailing leg then decelerates, and the hip, knee, and ankle reach maximum extension. That limb then begins to move forward, initiating forward swing (Figure 1.3e).

This reversal of limb direction requires time and energy. Hip flexion and forward rotation of the pelvis start moving the thigh forward (Figure 1.3f–h). Studies by Mann, Moran, and Dougherty (1986) suggest that hip flexion, achieved through action of the iliacus and psoas muscles, is probably the single most important contributor to forward limb movement (Figure 1.7). Whereas the iliacus muscle has its origin at the base of the sacrum and the anterior surface of the ilium, the psoas originates on the bodies and intervertebral cartilages of the last thoracic and all the lumbar vertebrae, as well as the transverse bony processes of the lumbar vertebrae. Both muscles then

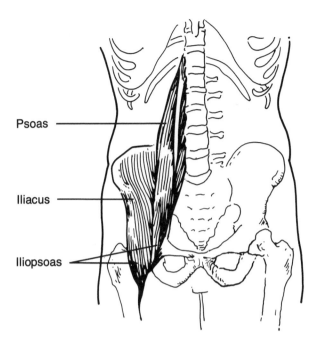

Figure 1.7 The iliacus and psoas muscles, important hip flexors for forward movement of the lower limbs. The psoas arises from the lower thoracic vertebra and first five lumbar vertebrae, whereas the iliacus arises from the ilium. The two muscles join together and proceed as the iliopsoas to insert on the lesser trochanter of the femur.

attach by the same tendon to that portion of the femur known as the lesser trochanter.

Knee flexion, which is mainly passive, assists this hip flexion by shortening the lever arm, thus permitting the thigh to move forward at a velocity considerably faster than the body's forward velocity. As soon as maximum hip flexion has been reached and the thigh is farthest off the ground, the final float period, called foot descent, begins (Figure 1.3i, j). Final preparations are made for the footstrike that will initiate the next cycle. Quadriceps muscle activity promotes knee extension for maximum forward movement of the lower limb. The hamstrings then slow the forward movement of the foot and leg by generating tension, antagonizing any additional knee extension. In slowing this limb movement, the hamstrings lengthen. Movement of the limb now slows to that of the trunk. When the next footstrike occurs, ideally the foot will be moving backward with a velocity equal to the forward movement of the trunk.

Practical Considerations About Running Biomechanics

The technical information presented in the preceding section typically stimulates a wide variety of practical questions.

How does running velocity influence stride frequency and stride length? Both increase as we run faster, with stride length increasing more than frequency (Figure 1.8). The exact combination of length and frequency at a given velocity may differ slightly for each runner due to such variables as leg length, hip flexion, breathing rate, and state of fatigue. Considerable current knowledge about biomechanics of runners stems from the elegant studies done over the past 12 years by Peter Cavanagh and Keith Williams with their associates (Cavanagh et al., 1985; Cavanagh & Kram, 1990; Williams & Cavanagh, 1987).

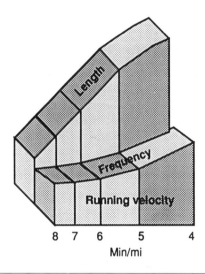

Figure 1.8 The relationship between stride frequency and stride length. As running velocity increases, stride frequency increases, but stride length increases even more, most likely from recruitment of additional skeletal muscle fibers. *Note*. From "Should You Change Your Stride Length?" by P. Cavanagh and K.R. Williams, 1979, *Runners World*, **14**(7), p. 64. Copyright 1979 by *Runners World*. Adapted by permission.

How do runners know when they are taking the optimum stride length for a particular running velocity? Unless runners are trying consciously to take longer or shorter strides than normal, this optimum stride length is probably occurring subconsciously. The more skilled the runner, the more precise this relationship. It develops with practice over time, from cerebellar integration of incoming information from joint receptors. Figure 1.9 indicates the relationship between O_2 cost at stride lengths on either side of and at the most optimum value. A lengthening or shortening of stride length would predispose the runner to premature exhaustion due to excessive energy requirements.

How do the back and pelvis interact with the legs in running? It must be remembered that, although it is the foot that strikes the ground, the actual pivot point

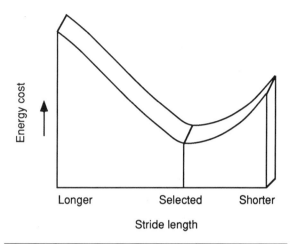

Figure 1.9 The relationship between O₂ cost and stride length, showing how a deviation from the selected stride length (typically minimal in energy cost) is less efficient. Depending upon individual differences, it may be more energy costly to shorten or to lengthen stride. *Note.* From ''Should You Change Your Stride Length?'' by P. Cavanagh and K.R. Williams, 1979, *Runners World*, **14**(7), p. 64. Copyright 1979 by *Runners World*. Adapted by permission.

for the lever system that provides movement is really the lumbar spine and pelvis. During midsupport and takeoff, the pelvis tilts forward through action of the lumbar muscles, and this helps provide greater backward thrust of the leg (Figure 1.3b, c). To minimize swaying from side to side, the entire trunk turns in a counterbalancing direction, that is, opposite to the direction of thrust. Major hip muscles such as the gluteus maximus and gluteus medius are important in this regard. The lumbar spine reaches maximum extension during follow-through (Figure 1.3d) and maximum flexion during forward swing (Figure 1.3g).

How can stride efficiency be increased? The most efficient runner will probably decelerate least at footstrike, have the least vertical oscillation, and get maximum forward movement with every stride. Footstrike deceleration will increase by overstriding, that is, landing well in front of the body's center of mass. Vertical oscillation relates to the combination of trunk length and leg length, determined by their state of extension or flexion. Running efficiency increases as a result of subtle adjustments in these variables directed toward energy conservation. Depending on inherent running skill, some runners, even after years of training, have measurably more vertical oscillation than others. Maximum forward movement relates in large measure to the torque-generating abilities of the primary muscles involved. In turn, this is developed through increased motor unit recruitment and strengthening of lower limb and hip muscles.

Do taller runners have similar biomechanical characteristics to shorter runners? Although the answer is probably yes, there are some disadvantages to being a tall runner. As we get taller, we get heavier. But the relationship is exponential; that is, we get heavier at a faster rate than we get taller. A survey of nearly 1,500 New York City marathoners (Stipe, 1982) suggested that as height increases linearly, body weight increases exponentially (to the 2.5 power). Thus, if Runner A is 66 in. (167.6 cm) tall, and Runner B is 72.6 in. (184.4 cm)—a 1.1-fold difference—Runner B's expected body weight (156 lb, or 70.9 kg) would be 1.3 times that of Runner A (120 lb, or 54.5 kg). This relationship suggests exponentially greater impact forces on landing. Do feet increase in size appropriately, that is, by 1.3 times? No. Overall foot size, as well as the impact-absorbing surface area on the bottom of the foot, does not increase relative to the increase in body weight. Thus, taller runners have greater running loads to support but a relatively lesser margin of safety for managing the impact stress of those loads. Cushioning or energy-absorption characteristics of shoes thus need to be increased appropriately as shoe sizes increase to accommodate these greater stresses.

Are there any notable differences between men and women in their running mechanics? This question is in its infancy in terms of resolution. Only recently has a study of elite female runners been completed (Williams, Cavanagh, & Ziff, 1987) as a companion to earlier work done with elite men (Cavanagh et al., 1977). Although these studies do not represent a huge data base, nevertheless some gender differences seem identifiable. Elite male runners appear to have less hip flexion, shorter stride lengths in relation to leg length, and more vertical oscillation than elite female runners. Although it has been widely reported that women in general have a wider pelvis, this appears not to be clearly demonstrable and seems dependent more on exactly how one measures pelvic dimensions.

Can a knowledge of biomechanics improve our understanding of running injuries? Yes indeed, and there are many examples. Let's consider one. What happens when runners pull a hamstring? Recall in our discussion of the running cycle that there is a brief moment when both quadriceps and hamstrings groups are generating tension simultaneously. The quadriceps group permits hip joint flexion and knee joint extension for increased forward limb movement in preparation for foot descent and footstrike. The hamstrings attempt to restrain the extent of hip flexion and knee extension, true to their role as antagonistic muscles, and thus serve to decelerate the thigh and lower leg (Stanton & Purdam, 1989). During early footstrike, the hamstrings are maximally stretched across the hip and knee joints and generate tension together with the quadriceps and gluteals in a team effort to absorb the downward force of body weight as it impacts on the running surface. The net effect of the two antagonistic muscle groups acting simultaneously will be determined by their relative tension-generating abilities. The quadriceps group typically is stronger than the hamstrings group. If the hamstrings group has a limited range of motion due to inflexibility (e.g., from inadequate stretching) or has inadequate strength in the tendons that connect these muscles to the pelvis, tearing of tissue may occur during that brief period when both muscle groups are generating tension. The risk is greater with faster running velocities, as both the forces generated and the stretching required are increased. Although this kind of injury is thus more common in sprinters, it can still affect middle- and long-distance runners who include shorter intervals of running at near-maximum velocity during their peaking periods for important competitions.

Evaluation and Improvement of Running Biomechanics

Good running style is a blending of all the separate movements of the trunk and limbs so that along with optimum mechanical efficiency we also have the visual appearance of minimum effort for the task required. Thus, running style suggests a combination of biomechanics and visual appearance, or form. When judging running style with a view toward its improvement, we search for improvements in biomechanics that will help reduce the cost of movement; the end result is probably a smoother appearance as the individual runs. One element of good running style, for example, is an optimum combination of cadence and stride length. This will vary not only for each event but also for each runner's height and flexibility. Both overstriding and understriding are energy costly (Figures 1.8, 1.9). Running style for one event may be entirely inappropriate for another: The marathon cannot be run using a style that is appropriate for the 100m dash or the 1,500m run. To do so would require a pace that could not be sustained for 42,195 m.

A good running style does not automatically guarantee a great running performance, but poor running style can certainly be detrimental. Exceptions to this concept may exist, but there aren't many. Emil Zatopek has often been used as an example to illustrate that style is really not all that important, and doing what comes naturally (with little attempt at refinement)

is best. After all, his record at the 1952 Helsinki Olympic Games speaks for itself—gold medals in the 5,000m, the 10,000m, and the marathon.

Our response to this argument is that with some improvements in his running style, he probably would have run faster. Without the excessive counterrotation of his shoulders, his stiff and high arm action, and his strained facial and neck muscles that produced a characteristically agonizing countenance as he rolled his head from side to side, Zatopek might have conserved considerable energy. The brutal fact is that Zatopek triumphed because he trained harder than the rest. He pioneered volumes of distance running coupled with massive sets of short-distance repetitions. Compared to his contemporaries, his stamina was unmatched—as evidenced by his medals—but he never developed anything like the basic speed of today's long-distance runners. His best 1,500m time was 3:52, which today can be matched by 16-year-old boys. Many of his 400m repetitions were at paces no faster than the over-distance paces used by many of today's elite-level male runners.

To us, the school of thought that argues that one's "natural" style is not only best but unchangeable represents a defeatist attitude. It ignores the reality that the nervous system has great adaptive capabilities to incorporate subtle changes in data input that create an improved movement pattern. In so many sports—golf, tennis, swimming, gymnastics, and more—coaches expert in design of corrective exercises and instructional commands can bring observable changes in style that contribute to improved performance. The same can occur in running.

We see examples of this plasticity of nervous system development when we observe the changes that occur in running style over time, as children mature. Marjorie Beck (1966) studied young American boys in elementary school grades 1 through 6, noting carefully the changes that occurred in their running as they matured. These changes represent improvements in running biomechanics and form. Good coaching ought to assist more mature runners in refining their form in a similar manner. Beck observed five improvements:

1. Longer running strides
2. Footstrike coming closer to a point under the center of gravity
3. More float time
4. Decreased vertical oscillation
5. Increased knee flexion at the end of forward swing

Seb Coe's style of running has been described by sportswriters and commentators as "poetry in motion," but it was not always so. He had a cramped, high arm action and excessive shoulder movement when he began training during his early teens. After a little more than 3 years of corrective effort through coaching, these faults were reduced, and the new version became his "natural" style. The true measure of success in correcting faults is when they fail to return when the athlete is under pressure. Obviously, the earlier in an athlete's career that attention is paid to correcting faults the better, as movement patterns are less ingrained. But there is always time to attempt improvements in style if it is perceived that useful benefits in efficiency will accrue. Of course, the contrary side of this argument is equally apropos. In pursuit of perfection, seldom if ever is it reached, and coaching judgment should permit identification of when further attempts at correction will be counterproductive. Even today, the purists can see that one of Seb Coe's elbows is slightly wingy when he is moving quickly, but after 20 years of competitive running there wouldn't be much benefit in constantly picking away at him with corrective exercises to improve it.

An analysis of style involves assessing the principal parts of a running cycle with a view toward identifying aspects of excellence as well as areas for improvement. Let us begin with the feet. When an athlete runs in a straight line, successive foot placements should be in parallel with each other (or very nearly so) and in the direction of running. This will help to reduce rotational torque about the ankles and knees as well as minimize stride shortening from turning out (splaying) of the feet. Because the hip, knee, and ankle joints are all subjected to severe loads during running, it is best to minimize rotatory torques, in favor of emphasis on torque generation that optimizes forward movement.

Figure 1.10 illustrates good and not-so-good foot placement in this regard. The photo was taken very near the finish of the 800m final at the 1986 European Athletics Championships in Stuttgart and shows the exciting British sweep of the medal positions. Seb Coe (#326) and Tom McKean (#351) took the gold and silver respectively, and their foot placement parallel to the direction of movement is fairly obvious. With the bronze medalist, however (Steve Cram, #328), his left foot is markedly turned out, as well as his left knee, giving that leg a reduced forward force vector as it generates propulsive thrust. More of Cram's propulsive energy is being absorbed by the knee and ankle joints in resisting the torsional stresses generated by his splayed foot plant. This style of foot plant not only increases the risk of lower limb injuries but also reduces his stride length by more than 1 cm. At his race pace and stride length in Stuttgart, Cram was losing a little more than 50 cm every 100 m. In today's races, this is an enormous disadvantage to overcome. Here is an excellent example in which an

Figure 1.10 Lower-limb running mechanics in three of Britain's best 1500m runners. Note the optimum foot orientation parallel to the path of movement in Seb Coe (326) and Tom McKean (351), but excessive lower limb rotation in Steve Cram (328).

athlete's potential performance abilities might be enhanced considerably by an ongoing program of corrective strengthening exercises designed to improve foot placement.

An important feature to examine in assessing the ankle joint is its flexibility. Improved flexibility has a payoff in stride length. Ankle flexibility seems best to be displayed at major international track meets by the African runners, particularly those who grew up as children running barefoot. Their style shows the knee of the supporting leg well in front of the ankle, giving the foot a greater range of motion throughout takeoff. It is a well-known physiological fact that a muscle can generate greater shortening if it has been prestretched before tension generation begins. The longer the heel is left in contact with the ground while the knee moves forward, the greater the prestretch on the calf muscles. This will increase both stride length and power. Figure 1.11 illustrates this effect of early and late takeoff caused by lesser or greater ankle flexibility.

Concerning the knee, here again velocity determines style. High-velocity running requires a high knee lift, marathon running does not, and there is a pro rata accommodation in between. Sprint-oriented runners have such a rapid ballistic stroke during forward swing that the heel of the swing leg very nearly touches the buttock; in coaching jargon this increased knee flexion is often termed "heel flick." Sprinters thus have both a high knee lift and a high heel flick as a result of

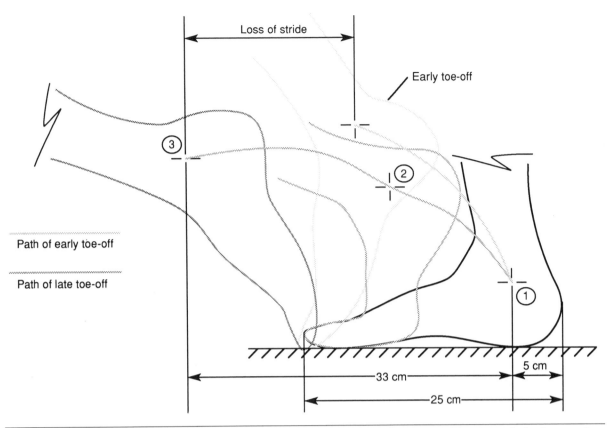

Loss of stride

Early toe-off

Path of early toe-off

Path of late toe-off

33 cm

25 cm

5 cm

Figure 1.11 Effect of early and late takeoff (also known as toe-off) on stride length caused by, respectively, lesser and greater ankle flexibility. Early takeoff results in a shorter stride and more vertical displacement of the center of mass, creating a less efficient running style than later takeoff, which enhances stride length and lessens vertical displacement.

the rapid forward leg movement required. Long-distance runners do not need to employ such motion. If they do, their vertical oscillation rises. This is inefficient because energy that should be directed toward forward movement is not utilized usefully.

Runners should not attempt to increase stride length beyond that which seems natural for them. Increasing leg muscle strength will increase stride length naturally because of an increased propulsive thrust. Landing in front of the center of gravity, as mentioned earlier, applies a decelerating force and thus is counterproductive. Increase in stride length comes from increased rate of forward swing of the rear leg, which in the process increases knee lift. Increased strengthening and joint mobility (range of motion) are the keys to improved stride length.

The pelvis is the next joint along the kinetic chain, and it too has a unique and crucial role in running. Its large size accommodates large muscles, which generate the powerful propulsive forward thrust of the plant foot as well as the flexor thrust of the forward-swinging leg. Lack of hip joint mobility also limits stride length. The muscles that stabilize the hip against rotatory torque must be especially strong to prevent injury if they are strained excessively. Ad-

ductor muscle injuries are particularly slow to heal due to their small attachment areas. We have already mentioned the importance of the iliopsoas muscle group in hip flexion. Those, together with the large gluteal muscles and adductor muscles, require specific strengthening and stretching to ensure the athlete's ability to complete long powerful strides when fast running is required. The great Australian distance runner Ron Clarke often mentioned in conversations with athletes and coaches that a runner could never be too strong around the middle, and his idea is sensible. Forward trunk lean often occurs as compensation for a lack of hip mobility. Thus, an increase in hip flexibility can often lead to a more vertical, energy-efficient running style.

The shoulders and upper arms are also important in running. Though they primarily provide balance at relatively slow speeds, they increase in importance in assisting the leg muscles as running velocity increases and as a runner climbs hills. Adequate arm and shoulder interaction reduces the need for counterrotation of the trunk musculature, which is more energy-wasteful. Good running style suggests that the arms swing fairly loose and be held quite naturally, never hunched. Neither should the shoulders be pulled back and the chest thrust out in front. Unnecessarily tensed muscles suggest an unnecessary waste of energy. The shoulders should be carried vertically above the hips.

Arm action varies with running velocity; it is much more vigorous at faster velocities than slower. Elbows kept close in toward the body minimize the tendency for the hands and lower arms to cross the midline of the chest. They normally should only approach the midline. At a wide range of running velocities the elbow joint is flexed at about 90 degrees and remains that way through the range of arm swing. However, at very fast racing velocities, this elbow flexion angle unlocks and varies on either side of 90 degrees to provide more fluidity. Arm swing and leg action are inextricably interwoven. If arm swing tends toward the erratic, it detracts from good style and is energy-costly.

At all times the hands should be kept loose and relaxed. Notice in Figure 1.10 that this is occurring even in the final moments of the race as these 800m runners are racing at top speed toward the finish line. Their thumbs are not sticking up like spikes, their wrists are fairly loose, and their fingers are slightly bent. Without flopping about like limp lettuce, their hands are still relaxed, again minimizing energy consumption.

Except for making a desperate dip at the finish of a race, the head must be poised well above the shoulders. It is a very heavy piece of anatomy, and if it is not positioned properly it can cause either of two problems, both bad. If it is too far backward it places an unnecessary strain on the neck muscles. If it is too far forward it can restrict the airways and make breathing difficult.

Figure 1.12 illustrates three well-known runners—Seb Coe, Said Aouita, and Ingrid Kristiansen—at different race paces: 400m, 5,000m, and 10,000m. Some comments are provided to assist readers in making their own style analyses. Runners are encouraged to have a friend take similar snapshots (or videos) for analysis. Utilizing the information provided here, athletes may be able to identify individual areas for improvement. Although such tasks as keeping elbows in or relaxing the hands must be practiced consciously at first, over time they can become automatic instead of voluntary movements and then an inherent part of improved form. Flexibility, stretching, or strengthening exercises appropriate to improve mechanics can also be designed if required.

a   b   c

Figure 1.12 Assessment of various features of running style in contemporary elite athletes running at various paces. In Figure 1.12a Sebastian Coe (Great Britain) is running at 50 sec/400m pace during training. In Figure 1.12b Said Aouita (Morocco) is running at 64 sec/400m pace during a 5,000m race. In Figure 1.12c Ingrid Kristiansen (Norway) is running at 75 sec/400m pace during a 10,000m race. Both races were at the 1987 Rome World Championships. Each athlete has the hands relaxed, with a 90-degree angle at the elbow joint. Stride length varies with pace; Coe requires a more powerful leg drive than the others, resulting in a more extended rear leg. The trunk is maintained in a vertical position, the head well poised. Kristiansen exhibits more tension in the muscles of her forehead than the others. Each is in the inside of the lane, conserving distance.

PHYSIOLOGY OF SKELETAL MUSCLES

Every organ system in the body contributes in its own way to the coordination of movement that permits daily activities. Skeletal muscles could be a prime candidate for the one organ system that contributes most to athletic performance. They typically comprise about 40% of the total body mass in a male of average stature (a little less in women). This mass of tissue at rest may consume as much as 15% to 30% of the total O_2 intake. It is the largest tissue mass devoted to a single function, namely, movement of the skeleton. These muscles, however, cannot function alone. They also require a functional innervation, good perfusion by blood to provide nutrition as well as cooling, and good provision of metabolic dynamics in the form of energy reserves and fuel-metabolizing enzymes.

Training distance runners involves to a large extent training skeletal muscles to perform optimally when challenged. Coaches and athletes are inundated with literature from various manufacturers of training equipment, all of whom suggest that their equipment or strategy is best for developing optimum performance. Terms such as fast-twitch and slow-twitch muscle fibers, fiber interconversion, motor unit recruitment, hypertrophy, and many more provide

frustration to those with nontechnical backgrounds but keen athletic interests. So much has been learned in the past few years, making muscle physiology a rather labile science: Today's hypotheses may be tomorrow's facts or fallacies. A brief synthesis of what seems correct at the moment should again not only help enhance communication among athletes, coaches, and scientists but also allow more intelligent assessment of training concepts for improving skeletal muscle function.

Anatomic Aspects of Neuromuscular Integration

Estimates of the number of skeletal muscles in the human body range from 435 (Gregor, 1989) to around 650 (Thomas, 1989), depending on the system of nomenclature. Most of these occur in pairs, and a runner in competition will actively involve the majority of them. Muscles come in a wide variety of sizes. The stapedius muscle of the middle ear is but 2 to 3 millimeters (mm) in length, whereas the sartorius of the upper leg (Figure 1.5) can be more than half a meter long in a tall individual. Skeletal muscles are typically surrounded by a thin layer of connective tissue. This is their epimysium (Figure 1.13). Each skeletal muscle is made up of dozens to hundreds of

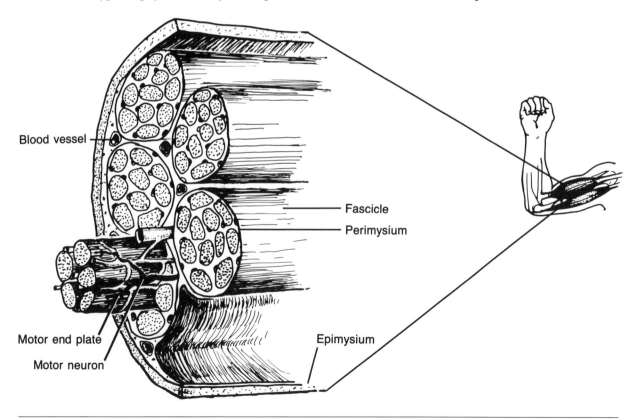

Blood vessel

Fascicle
Perimysium

Motor end plate

Motor neuron

Epimysium

Figure 1.13 General arrangement of skeletal muscle into small groups of muscle cells, called fascicles, with each fascicle surrounded by a connective tissue perimysium. Each muscle cell is innervated by a branch of a motor neuron.

muscle cells, also called muscle *fibers*. These muscle fibers attach to bones by tendons. The epimysium extends into the body of each muscle, encircling small groups of perhaps a dozen muscle fibers. This surrounding connective tissue is now called the *perimysium*, and the bundles of muscle fibers are called *fascicles*. They are sometimes large enough to be seen without a microscope.

Muscles are also often covered by glistening white, dense fibrous connective tissue called *fascia*. We see this fibrous connective tissue in other places as well: Tendons connect bones to muscles, and ligaments connect bones to each other. The term *fascia* derives from the Latin word for band, and it might be useful to think of fascia around muscles as a kind of bandage that assists in postural stability. Perhaps the most well-known example of fascia to runners is the iliotibial band located within the fascia lata, illustrated in Figure 1.14. The fascia lata begins at the iliac crest as a broad fibrous connective tissue

sheath along the lateral aspect of the leg, continues to and past the knee, and attaches to the lateral tibial tubercle. Two muscles, the tensor fasciae latae (a thigh flexor) and gluteus maximus (a thigh extensor), insert into the iliotibial band, a thicker lateral tendon within this fascia. This band is a stabilizing ligament between the tibia and the lateral femoral condyle of the knee. Tension in this fascia helps stabilize the knee joint.

The arrangement of fascicles in skeletal muscles in part determines muscle power and the range of motion of the joint to which they connect. Considerable variation exists in the arrangement of fibers in skeletal muscles. Figures 1.4, 1.15, and 1.16 illustrate some of these possibilities, using a combination of sketches and photographs of elite runners' muscles to provide the best practical view of these arrangements. One of the muscles of the quadriceps group (the rectus femoris) has its fascicles arranged much like a feather plume, with the tendon in the middle and fascicles converging toward it from two sides

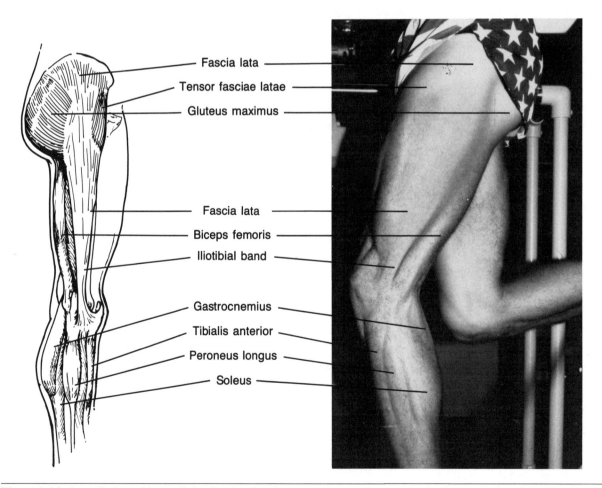

Figure 1.14 Lateral view of lower limb, showing the gluteus maximus and tensor fasciae latae muscles of the hip, the lateral fascia of the upper limb (fascia lata and iliotibial band), and some of the lower limb muscles.

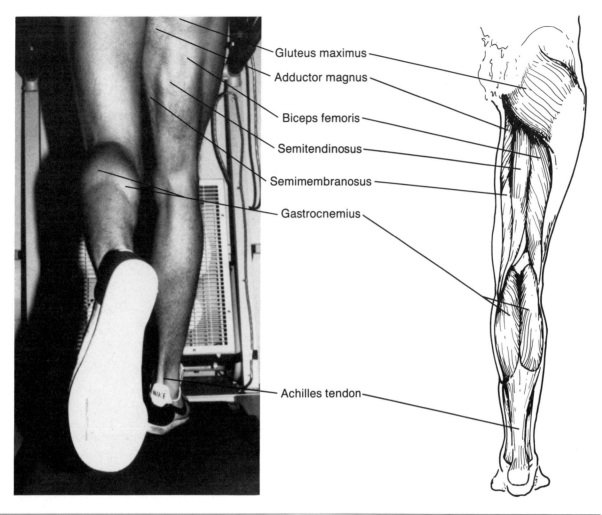

Gluteus maximus

Adductor magnus

Biceps femoris

Semitendinosus

Semimembranosus

Gastrocnemius

Achilles tendon

Figure 1.15 Posterior view of muscles of the hip and lower limb, showing in particular the three muscles of the hamstrings group.

(Figure 1.4). It is called a bipenniform muscle. A few muscles of the hamstrings group (such as the semimembranosus and semitendinosus) have a feather-plume arrangement as well, but with their tendon running along one side (Figure 1.15). These are penniform muscles. The longitudinal muscles, best exemplified by the sartorius (Figure 1.4), are strap-like and thin, with fibers arranged in parallel along the full length of the muscle.

Figure 1.16 illustrates the pectoralis major and deltoid muscles, which have several different actions. The pectoralis is known as a triangular muscle because of its fan-shaped appearance; muscle fibers radiate outward from the narrow attachment at the humerus toward the sternum and collarbone (clavicle). The middle portion of the deltoid muscle is multipenniform, with several tendons present and muscle fibers extending diagonally between them. Other parts of the deltoid are fusiform, or spindle-shaped. Another

multipennate muscle is the gluteus maximus (Figures 1.14, 1.15). The gluteus medius and minimus are fan-shaped. The fiber arrangement of all these various muscles is optimally advantageous for their special functions. Thus, penniform muscles typically are more powerful in relation to their size but have less range of motion than nonpenniform muscles.

The two attachment points of a muscle to the skeleton are called the origin and insertion. The **origin** is the less movable end, closer to the body, whereas the **insertion** is the more movable end, farther away. Virtually all muscles connected to joints have actions that are opposed by the actions of other muscles. In such pairs of muscles, if one is the agonist—that is, it initiates the movement in question—the other muscle is the antagonist providing a stabilizing action for the involved joint, remaining relaxed while the agonist is active or permitting the opposite motion to occur. One of the most familiar pairs is the biceps and triceps

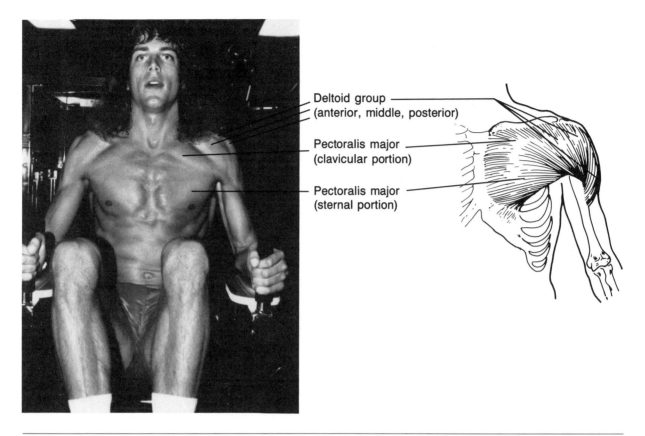

Deltoid group (anterior, middle, posterior)

Pectoralis major (clavicular portion)

Pectoralis major (sternal portion)

Figure 1.16 Anterior view of superficial muscles of the shoulder joint, including the pectoralis major and deltoids.

of the upper arm; the former flexes the elbow, and the latter extends it.

Motor innervation is the key to muscle function. A **motor nerve** is made up of many dozens of individual *nerve cells* (*neurons*), each of which will branch and connect to variable numbers of muscle fibers. The **motor point** is the site of entry of the nerve into the muscle. Such sites are well known to physical therapists, who are trained to evaluate muscle function by examining the dynamics of muscle tension generation using electrical stimulation. At the motor point, a minimum amount of electrical current will excite the muscle.

One **motor unit** is defined as a single motor neuron along with all the skeletal muscle fibers innervated by it. These fibers are dispersed throughout the muscle rather than closely adjacent to each other, permitting a more uniform change in muscle shape when they are activated. Also, this prevents having a large number of active muscle fibers all competing for the same blood supply, except of course when the entire muscle is extremely active. Figure 1.17 illustrates several neuron branches, each connecting to a muscle fiber via a neuromuscular junction (see also Figure 1.13). The number of muscle fibers per motor neuron varies widely, depending on specificity of muscle activity. The medial head of the human gastrocnemius

muscle, for example, has as many as 1,900 muscle fibers per motor unit and nearly 580 motor units (Gregor, 1989). This muscle can perform only gross, relatively nonspecific activity. By contrast, laryngeal muscles have only two to three muscle fibers per neuron and are very precise in their action. There is very little overlapping of muscle fibers in any given motor unit; that is, the fibers are well dispersed throughout the muscle.

Generation of Muscle Tension

Normally, neuron and muscle cell membranes are electrically polarized. When a motor nerve is stimulated sufficiently, a very brief wave of depolarization (called a neuron action potential) travels along its various neurons (and along their branches) until it reaches each neuromuscular junction. The depolarization wave crosses these junctions and is reinitiated as a muscle cell action potential along its surface. At certain points this wave will be carried deep within the muscle cell as well by means of transverse (T) tubules that serve as inward extensions of the cell membrane (Figure 1.18).

Notice that each muscle cell has dozens of myofibrils arranged in parallel (Figures 1.18, 1.19) with several types of cellular organelles in between. The

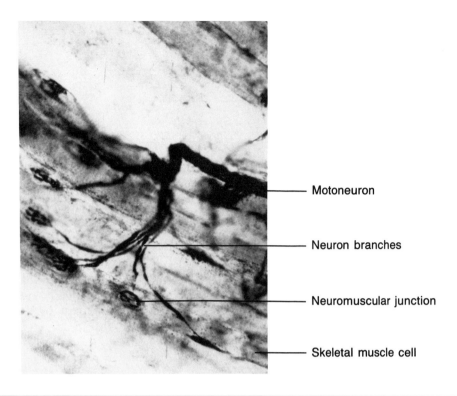

Figure 1.17 Components of a motor unit: a motorneuron, with its many branches, connecting to individual muscle fibers via neuromuscular junctions.

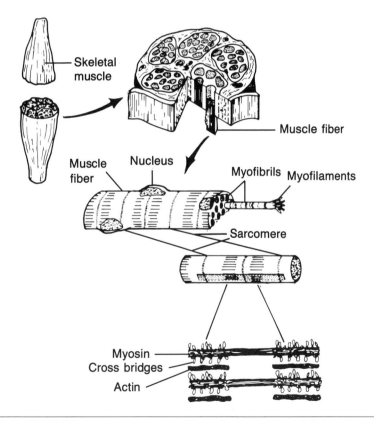

Figure 1.18 Microscopic details of skeletal muscle structure, illustrating sequential subdivision into myofibrils and myofilaments. The two major types of myofilaments are actin and myosin. Myosin molecules are thicker and heavier and have enzymatic activity at localized sites known as cross bridges. At rest, actin and myosin are prevented from interacting by the presence of other protein molecules, the troponin-tropomyosin complex, located between them but not shown here.

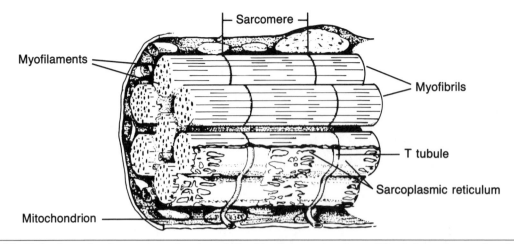

Figure 1.19 Skeletal muscle ultrastructure, showing relationships between transverse (T) tubules and sarcoplasmic reticulum around myofibrils. The muscle cell action potential travels down the T tubule membrane, eventually affecting the calcium-ion-containing sarcoplasmic reticulum through close contact points. Influence of the action potential causes liberation of calcium ions from the sarcoplasmic reticulum into the surrounding myofibrillar area, permitting actin and myosin molecules to interact (slide past each other) and produce muscle cell shortening.

organelles perform many specialized functions required to keep cells alive and functional. The nucleus, for example, is responsible for cellular division. Each myofibril is composed of many parallel myofilaments, which include the two primary tension-generating proteins actin and myosin. Thicker myosin filaments are arranged around thinner actin filaments in such a manner that measured segments, called sarcomeres, result. Another organelle, called the sarcoplasmic reticulum, is a storehouse for calcium (Ca^{++}) ions, which are required for the physicochemical interaction of actin and myosin.

From the standpoint of energy and movement, mitochondria are the organelles of greatest importance (Figure 1.19, 1.20). In these organelles are found the enzyme systems that permit complete breakdown of fuels by eventual interaction with O_2, with liberation of large amounts of energy available to provide movement. The energy released from such breakdown is stored in a molecule called *adenosine triphosphate (ATP)*, which will be described in greater detail shortly. Because of their role, mitochondria are often thought of as the powerhouses of the cell. Typically they are 1 to 2 micrometers (μm) long and 0.3 to 0.7 μm wide, but can vary considerably in size and shape depending on their tissue location and its metabolic state. They have a peculiar double-membrane structure with the inner membrane folded into leaves called *cristae*, which increases its surface area. As much as 25% of the total protein content of this inner mitochondrial membrane comprises all the various enzymes required for aerobic fuel breakdown. Adaptation of skeletal muscle to permit increased metabolic abilities involves an increase in both the size and number of mitochondria.

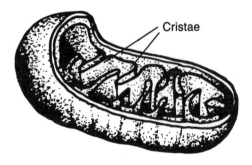

Figure 1.20 Anatomical structure of a mitochondrion. These organelles are ovoid in shape, roughly 2 μm long and 0.7 μm wide, and have two very different membrane structures. The inner mitochondrial membrane is greatly folded, forming cristae. The enzymes, which are responsible for oxidative metabolism of fuels, are an integral part of the cristae.

Actin molecules have ATP bound to them. Myosin molecules have enzymatic activity so that they can break down ATP; that is, they are ATPases. Normally these two molecules are blocked from interacting and generating tension due to the presence of several proteins that for simplicity we can group together as the *troponin-tropomyosin complex* (Figure 1.18). In this state, the muscle is resting, that is, generating minimum tension. One function of the electrical stimulus wave that passes along the cell membrane is to release Ca^{++} ions from their storage sites within the sarcoplasmic reticulum. Calcium ions temporarily remove the blockade by the troponin-tropomyosin complex, permitting actin and myosin interaction to occur, thanks to the energy release available through enzymatic breakdown of ATP. The interactions between actin and myosin molecules are referred to as *cross-bridge linkages* and form the basis for muscles to generate tension. A sliding filament theory for muscle tension generation, whereby the actin and myosin molecules simply slide past each other as their cross-bridge linkages are rapidly formed and broken, was proposed about 36 years ago by two separate groups of investigators (Huxley & Hanson, 1954; Huxley & Niedergerke, 1954). This shortening or lengthening of sarcomeres causes corresponding changes in muscle length. Their theory has been proved essentially correct.

Tension may be maintained with no change in muscle length (called *isometric* or *static tension*) or may result in the myofilaments sliding past each other (Figure 1.18). This sliding may cause lengthening (eccentric tension) or shortening (concentric tension), depending on the arrangement of the muscle and its load. Once tension generation has occurred, reaccumulation of Ca^{++} ions back into their storage sites promotes relaxation. Increasing the frequency of stimulation as well as the magnitude of stimulation (increasing the number of motor units activated) increases the total muscle tension.

A specific relationship exists between the amount of tension (and thus force) that a muscle can develop and the velocity with which shortening or lengthen-

ing occurs. The faster the rate of cross-bridge linking between actin and myosin myofilaments, the faster they can slide past each other, and the faster the rate of tension generation in the muscle. However, the faster the rate of cross-bridge linking, the smaller the number of linkages in place at any given moment, and thus the smaller the net tension generated.

This situation provides a real dilemma for sprinters, who must be both quick and strong (i.e., very powerful) at the same time. The only way they can achieve this is to recruit large numbers of muscle fibers and develop them through prior training that increases the amount of protein in each cell. This explains in part why excellent sprinters typically have large leg muscles. Figure 1.21 depicts this force-velocity relationship. On the vertical axis (ordinate) is plotted muscle force, and on the horizontal axis (abscissa) is plotted velocity of muscle movement. As velocity of muscle shortening or lengthening increases, the tolerable work load decreases. Training increases the tolerable work load at any given velocity (point Y on the graph) due to an increase in muscle protein as well as an ability to recruit more fibers into action. For whole muscle, extreme force production at very slow velocities is prevented by neurological inhibition; this is not seen when single muscle fiber preparations are stimulated experimentally.

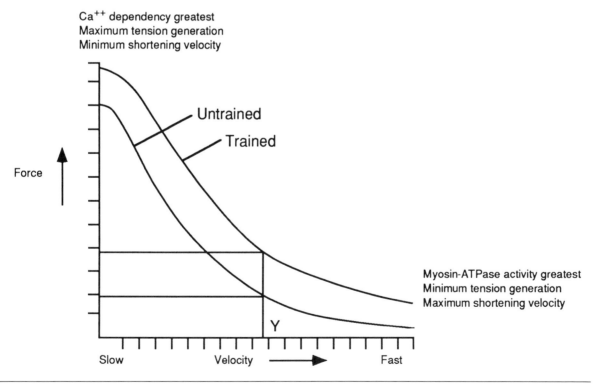

Figure 1.21 Relationship between muscular force developed (also conceptualized as work load, or muscle tension, or torque) and velocity of muscle shortening. Training a muscle for greater work load tolerance brings adaptations within the muscle cells to permit, at submaximum velocities, greater work output.

Skeletal Muscle Fiber Types

As far back as the late 19th century, gross differences in coloration of skeletal muscles within species as well as among different species were noted in the scientific literature (Ranvier, 1873). We need only visit the meat department of a grocery store and compare the white and dark meat of chicken or the red cuts of beef and grayish cuts of pork to realize that considerable variation occurs. Such obvious individual differences in muscles prompted what has become an extremely detailed study of this tissue in an attempt to learn how such color differences might help explain the properties of individual tension-generating muscle cells. As a result, we probably know more about the functioning of skeletal muscle—even down to the molecular level—than about any other organ system. The explanation for the color difference has been reasonably easy to solve. Each of two different types of red-pigmented substances plays an important role in the complete metabolism of fuels. One is myoglobin, an O_2-binding pigment similar to hemoglobin in its function. The other is a series of molecules called cytochrome enzymes, which we shall find later to be associated with the metabolic interaction between complete fuel breakdown, energy release, and interaction with O_2.

Thus, muscles appearing grossly to be almost white in appearance are composed of cells with considerably less myoglobin and cytochrome enzymes than those that are brillant red. Those muscles intermediate in coloration are heterogeneous in their fiber composition, having a mixture of both cell types. The important question for those interested in work and exercise is the relationship between color and performance.

Early physiological investigations of muscle function suggested some general relationships between structure and function. In general, muscles with a major role in posture (the antigravity muscles) were more of the red variety, whereas the gravity-assisted muscles often were lighter colored. This brought the terms *tonic* (or fatigue-resistant) into use for the red fibers, with *phasic* (or fatigue-susceptible) best describing the white fibers.

During the late 1960s and early 1970s, particularly with the advent of laboratory methods of enzyme histochemistry, continuing interest in understanding the details of muscle structure and function directed investigational focus not only on specific enzymes related to metabolism but also on different types of myofibrillar proteins. Muscle tissue was obtained in the form of needle biopsy specimens from willing volunteers. In a needle biopsy, local anesthetic around the biopsy site minimizes pain. Once obtained, the piece of muscle tissue is immediately deep-frozen and kept for later sectioning and study using a variety of laboratory procedures. The results of these refined analyses brought a few new fiber classification schemes into the scientific literature. Unfortunately, not all of these schemes are exactly interchangeable, for various technical reasons. Excellent reviews of progress made in these areas exist (Gollnick & Hodgson, 1986; Rice, Pettigrew, Noble, & Taylor, 1988; Saltin & Gollnick, 1983). Our purpose here is to provide only some of the most useful basic information—terms, concepts, and conclusions—that will permit us to better appreciate the significance of muscle fiber types from the viewpoint of exercise performance.

One set of terminology stems from the work of Brooke and Engle (1969). These workers studied the behavior of myosin ATPase in the myofibrils and divided muscle fibers into two groups, which they arbitrarily termed Type I and Type II. Their Type I fibers roughly corresponded to fatigue-resistant fibers, with Type II equating to the fatigue-susceptible fibers. Then, Edstrom and Nystrom (1969) labeled the Type I fibers as red and the Type II fibers as white. The Type II fibers, however, were soon found to fit two different categories, depending on whether, in addition, they demonstrated high (Type IIa) or low (Type IIb) oxidative enzyme activity (Brooke & Kaiser, 1970).

Subsequent physiological studies by Gollnick, Armstrong, Saubert, Piehl, and Saltin (1972) showed that the Type I muscle cells require a longer time to reach peak tension when stimulated than do the Type II cells (75 versus 35 milliseconds). This is illustrated in Figure 1.22. The terms *slow-twitch* (ST) and *fast-twitch* (FT) thus came into vogue to describe, respectively, Type I and Type II fibers. Table 1.1 indicates some of the basic differences between these two primary fiber types, although we should emphasize that this is an oversimplification.

At about this same time J.B. Peter and his group (Peter, Barnard, Edgerton, Gillespie, & Stempel, 1972) further studied the properties of the two categories of Type II fibers. They offered another set of terminology that combined tension-generating and metabolic properties to identify the various fiber types. Type I cells were termed *slow oxidative (SO)*, the term oxidative referring to complete fuel metabolism, which utilizes O_2. Type II cells were either *fast glycolytic (FG)*, the term glycolytic referring to an emphasis on glycogen and glucose breakdown to pyruvic acid, which does not require O_2, or *fast oxidative-glycolytic (FOG)*, suggesting good capability for complete (oxidative, or aerobic) metabolism as well as incomplete (glycolytic, or anaerobic) metabolism. FG fibers thus are similar to Type IIb fibers, with FOG fibers similar to Type IIa fibers.

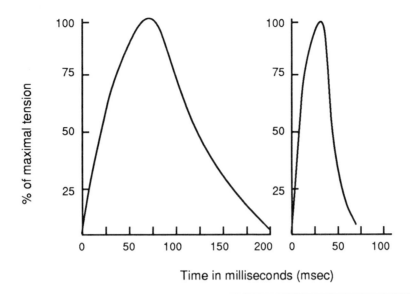

Figure 1.22   Difference between the twitch characteristics of fast-twitch and slow-twitch skeletal muscle fibers. Slow-twitch fibers, on the left, reach their maximum tension in about 75 msec after stimulation and have fully recovered after about 200 msec. Fast-twitch fibers, however, reach peak tension more quickly (30 to 35 msec) and recover very quickly (by about 70 msec). *Note.* From "Relationship of Strength and Endurance With Skeletal Muscle Structure and Metabolic Potential" by P.D. Gollnick, 1982, *International Journal of Sports Medicine*, **3** (Suppl. 1), p. 26. Copyright 1982 by Georg Thieme Verlag. Reprinted by permission.

With these details in mind, let us consider human skeletal muscles from the viewpoint of fiber type and performance.

How are the various fiber types arranged in human muscles?   Unlike the situation in certain mammals, human skeletal muscles are never solely FT or ST. Most are quite heterogeneous. Even within any muscle, there is a variation in fiber arrangement in different regions. As an example, Bengt Saltin and his colleagues (Saltin, Henriksson, Nygaard, & Andersen, 1977) showed that muscles such as the gastrocnemius in the lower leg, the vastus lateralis and rectus femoris in the upper leg, and the biceps brachii in the arm in untrained subjects are about 50:50 FT:ST. The soleus (an antigravity muscle) is predominantly ST (75%–90%), however, and the triceps brachii is primarily FT (60%–80%).

Do elite athletes, proficient in endurance- or strength-oriented events, have larger numbers of one or another fiber type?   Considerable evidence suggests that the answer is yes. Unfortunately, these athletes were not biopsied before they began their serious training. Thus, the interaction between genetics and training is still not well understood. Did they find their particular event an easy one in which to excel in relation to other people because in addition to their hard training, they had a genetic predisposition toward that event as a result of the appropriate fiber-type

preference? We just do not know this unequivocally. As an example, the lateral head of the gastrocnemius muscle of 14 elite male long-distance runners showed a range of from 50% to 98% ST fibers (Fink, Costill, & Pollock, 1977) compared to the range of 50% to 64% among the untrained population (Rice et al., 1988). However, in the elite runners, because the ST fibers were 29% larger than the FT fibers, on the average 82% of the muscle cross-sectional area was composed of ST muscle. Thus, training can selectively increase the size of muscle fibers, and we shall shortly describe some of the changes that can occur with training.

Within this group of elite runners, however, individual ST:FT ratios correlated poorly as a predictor of running success as judged by personal best performance time. This poor correlation has been reported elsewhere (Gollnick & Matoba, 1984). Additional factors all contribute to successful athlete preparation, such as the desire to endure long years of difficult training, a proper training plan to permit development without injury, and improved running efficiency. Many variables also set the stage for an excellent competitive performance, such as achievement of peak physical fitness when it counts most, a psychological profile and readiness that is optimal for success, and near-perfect competitive circumstances. Finally, there is considerable overlap in the extent to which various fiber type combinations can explain sport performance. Consider, for example, the following set of six performances by Morocco's Said Aouita during 2 months of 1986:

Event	Time	Date	Rank of performance in the world in 1986
1 mile	3:50.33	Aug.	4th fastest performer
2,000m	4:51.98	Sept.	Fastest performer
3,000m	7:32.23	Aug.	Fastest performer
2 miles	8:14.08	Sept.	Fastest performer
5,000m	13:00.86	Aug.	Fastest performer
10,000m	27:26.11	July	2nd fastest performer

Table 1.1   Characteristics of Slow Oxidative and Fast Glycolytic Fibers

Slow-twitch (ST) muscle fibers	Fast-twitch (FT) muscle fibers
Loosely referred to as red or tonic fibers	Loosely referred to as white or phasic fibers
Example of predominant ST muscle in human: soleus	Example of predominant FT muscle in human: triceps brachii
Longer muscle fibers, therefore a greater total length change capability	Shorter fibers, therefore a smaller total length change capability
Maintenance of posture	More rapid, voluntary movements
Quicker recruitability; lower threshold for stimulation (-70 mV) and smaller connecting neuron	Slower recruitability; higher threshold for stimulation (-85 mV) and larger connecting neuron
Longer time to reach peak tension (75 msec)	Shorter time to reach peak tension (35 msec)
Fewer muscle cells per motor unit; less strength capability	More muscle cells per motor unit; greater strength capability
Good endurance, slow fatigability	Poor endurance, rapid fatigability
Oxidative enzymes predominate	Glycolytic enzymes predominate
More mitochondria	Fewer mitochondria
Contain H form of lactic dehydrogenase	Contain M form of lactic dehydrogenase
Greater surrounding capillarization	Lesser surrounding capillarization
No change in glycogen content after repeated stimulation for 2 hr at 10/sec	Stimulation at relatively low frequencies (5/sec) reduces stored glycogen
Greater myoglobin content	Larger stored calcium pool for interaction with tension-generating proteins

Uniform excellence over quite a wide range of events is clearly evident. On the short-distance side, a generous FT endowment is essential, but the 10,000m cannot be raced without a sizable ST endowment to provide the aerobic capabilities. In view of the variability found among published studies relating performance with fiber type, the suggestion could thus be plausibly offered that if Aouita had several of his major running muscles biopsied, percentage ratios of FT:ST fibers ranging anywhere from 60:40 through 50:50 to 40:60 might all be appropriate to explain the preceding track performances.

How are muscle fiber types arranged in motor units, and how are they recruited during exercise?
Motor units are either all FT or all ST; there is no fiber intermixing. There are two available mechanisms for increasing the tension generated by skeletal muscle. One is termed *rate coding*—the intensity of activity of stimulated neurons increases. The other is termed *recruitment*—additional motor neurons are brought into action. As reviewed recently by Deschenes (1989), the principle of recruitment (on the basis of neuron size) seems the predominant mechanism, although rate coding may come into play during higher intensity work loads. At relatively low work rates, the ST fibers are utilized predominantly. This is because their innervation is primarily by smaller neurons that are activated by low-level stimulation. Increasing loads require activation of more muscle protein, achieved by recruitment of additional motor units.

Figure 1.23 depicts this relationship more clearly. ST motor units will respond to meet the needs of all the easier submaximum work loads, with FT Type IIa and FT Type IIb motor units contributing as work loads become more challenging and approach maximum intensity. This is a beautifully designed system to provide optimum use of muscle fibers specialized for complete metabolism during lighter work loads, minimize the anaerobic metabolite accumulation (such as lactic acid) that would result if FT Type IIa (and particularly FT Type IIb) fibers were mobilized, and permit use of both types of fuels (carbohydrates and fatty acids). Then, as work loads become more intense, instead of a substitution of FT for ST fibers there is an additional contribution by FT fibers, in teamwork fashion, to the output of ST fibers already activated. The practical significance of this for endurance runners is that, if months pass by without any training at higher work intensities, a sizable number of muscle fibers—the entire FT complement—will have only a minimal training stimulus to improve their performance potential. This is a physiological explanation for a training tenet that will be continually emphasized later in this book: Never get too far

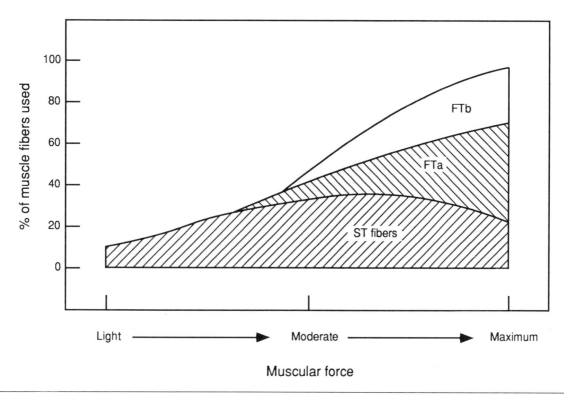

Figure 1.23 Relationship between exercise intensity and utilization of fast-twitch and slow-twitch muscle fibers. Assuming a hypothetical instance of an individual having roughly 45% slow-twitch fibers, 40% fast-twitch Type IIa fibers, and 15% fast-twitch Type IIb fibers, at maximum work loads more than half the total number of fibers in use will be of the fast-twitch variety. However, their relatively high threshold of stimulation makes the influence of slow-twitch fibers dominant during light and even moderate work intensities. *Note.* From "Weight Training for Swimmers—A Practical Approach" by R. Uebel, 1987, *National Strength and Conditioning Association Journal,* **9**(3), p. 39. Copyright 1987 by National Strength and Conditioning Association Journal. Reprinted by permission, National Strength and Conditioning Association, Lincoln, Nebraska.

away from periodic inclusion of fast running to ensure maintenance of the performance capabilities of FT fibers.

What determines the percentage of the various fiber types? Studies done by Komi et al. (1977) with identical twins suggests that genetic endowment determines fiber type in skeletal muscles. Additional elegant work by Buller, Eccles, and Eccles (1960) indicates that the nervous system determines whether a muscle cell is FT or ST. Subsequent studies by Close in 1969 and Barany and Close in 1971 using laboratory animals and involving cross-reinnervation (i.e., the sectioning of nerves innervating predominantly FT and ST muscles followed by rejoining opposite ends) demonstrated this even more strikingly. In the rat and the cat, FT muscles became ST after cross-reinnervation, not only in their myosin characteristics but also in other physiological features such as mitochondrial density, enzyme composition, and even the number of capillaries around individual muscle cells (ST fibers have more than FT).

Are there any differences between male and female endurance runners with regard to fiber types? Apparently not, on the basis of the few data available. Two well-known studies of elite male (Fink et al., 1977) and female (Costill, Fink, Flynn, & Kirwan, 1987) distance runners, carried out by some of the same investigators, revealed quite similar fiber ratios and fiber composition (mitochondrial size and enzyme activity profiles) for athletes specializing in similar events. Thus, marathoners tended to have a higher ST endowment than middle-distance runners. However, one consistently observed gender difference occurring among runners regardless of event specialty is a larger muscle fiber cross-sectional area in males, especially the FT fibers. This is probably a result of the muscle protein-building action of testosterone which exists in higher concentration among males than females.

Can the stimulus of serious endurance- or strength-oriented training convert FT fibers to ST, and vice versa? This has been studied carefully for many years in controlled longitudinal studies involving both humans and laboratory animals (Pette, 1984). The evidence is still inconclusive that a complete fiber interconversion (FT to ST or ST to FT) with enzymatic changes, myofibrillar protein changes, and other physiological aspects can occur. A change in the relative numbers of FG and FOG fibers, however, has been rather clearly demonstrated (Henriksson & Reitman, 1976; Ingjer, 1979; Prince, Hikida & Hagerman, 1976). Thus, FG (Type IIb) fibers can preferentially take on the characteristics of FOG (Type IIa) fibers in response to the stimulus of the chronic submaximal-pace training stimulus of distance running, providing a greater oxidative capacity for the working muscles. This maintains the anaerobic aspects of cell function while enhancing the aerobic aspects, thereby improving competitive capabilities. The reverse change can also occur with strength training.

Effects of Training on Skeletal Muscle Performance

Skeletal muscle tissue has an enormous capacity for adapting to increased exercise loads, both strength- and endurance-oriented. The changes involve structural, biochemical, nutritional, and cardiovascular improvements in working capacity. The resulting improved strength and tolerance to submaximum work increases performance capabilities, in turn permitting continued resistance (within reasonable limits) to injury. Two good reports of progress in this area have been published by Holloszy and Coyle (1984) and Nadel (1985).

One beneficial adaptation to endurance training is as much as an 80% increase in myoglobin content in skeletal muscles (Pattengale & Holloszy, 1967). This report confirmed what had been more or less assumed ever since G.H. Whipple showed back in 1926 that hunting dogs had more myoglobin in their working leg muscles than sedentary dogs. This increased myoglobin provides a larger O_2 reservoir within the working cells for use when circulatory O_2 supplies are inadequate.

Along with an improved intracellular O_2 reservoir, there is also an improved O_2 delivery capability. The studies of Brodal, Ingjer, and Hermansen (1977) have shown a more extensive capillarization in the working muscles of endurance-trained men compared to untrained men. Notice in Table 1.1 that untrained skeletal muscles reveal fewer capillaries around the FT fibers than around the ST—typically about four around ST and FT Type IIa fibers and three around FT Type IIb cells, according to the studies of Saltin

et al. (1977). Endurance training brings a significant increase in the number of capillaries around ST fibers. This decreases the diffusion distance for O_2 as it moves from capillary blood into the working muscle cells. As illustrated in Figure 1.24, Karlsson (1986) has shown a positive relationship between percent ST fibers in working muscles and the maximum volume of O_2 (called $\dot{V}O_2max$) that can be taken up during exercise. Similarly, Saltin et al. (1977) demonstrated a similar relationship between skeletal muscle fiber capillarization and VO_2max. The cardiopulmonary aspects of O_2 delivery and capillarization as they relate to endurance performance will be discussed in chapter 2.

Holloszy (1967) also demonstrated that during endurance training, many more fuel-metabolizing enzymes are found in what now are larger mitochondria of both FT Type IIa and ST cells. Thus, an increase in the rate of replenishment of ATP—the storage form of energy in cells—can occur. There is also an increase in the number of mitochondria (Hoppeler, Luthi, Claassen, Weibel, & Howald, 1973). The net effect of these adaptations is somewhat akin to putting a larger engine inside an automobile. Or, in the context of the body, trained skeletal muscles become more similar to heart muscle in their ability to sustain prolonged submaximal work loads. Only those muscles affected by the training show these increased mitochondrial dynamics. The explanation for this lies partly in the important principle of **symmorphosis** (Taylor & Weibel, 1981), which states that adaptation will be only as extensive as the requirement provided by the stimulus. That is, over-adaptation will probably never occur; it is metabolically too costly. All this adaptation takes time, dictated by the limits of intracellular turnover and manufacture of materials. (A bricklayer working at his fastest pace will not likely lay more bricks if he is paid more, simply because the increased recompense doesn't increase the dexterity with which he performs his skilled task.) The more prolonged this intense period of system challenge, the greater the extent of adaptive response, reflected in muscle fiber performance characteristics.

Muscle glycogen supplies in the working muscles can also increase. In part this is due to increased enzymatic activity in these cells, which promotes more glycogen synthesis for storage. But the majority of the increase occurs as a result of the stimulus of exercise, which through depletion of muscle carbohydrate stores stimulates enhanced storage during the recovery phase (Saltin & Gollnick, 1983). In chapter 5 we will discuss further the techniques that runners can use to enhance their carbohydrate stores. Although

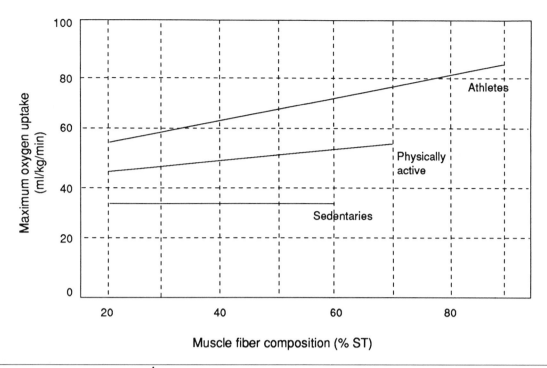

Figure 1.24 Relationship between V̇O₂max and percent slow-twitch skeletal muscles in primary muscle movers. Endurance training improves the work capacities of these muscles. People with a greater percentage of slow-twitch fibers respond more than those with fewer slow-twitch fibers and increase their maximum oxygen uptake capacity to a greater extent. *Note.* From ''Muscle Fiber Composition, Metabolic Potentials, Oxygen Transport and Exercise Performance in Man'' by J. Karlsson. In *Biochemical Aspects of Physical Exercise* (p. 4) by G. Benzi, L. Packer, N. Siliprandi (Eds.), 1986, Amsterdam: Elsevier Science. Copyright 1986 by Elsevier Science. Reprinted by permission.

lipid stores are adequate for even the longest of competitive exercise events, this increased carbohydrate storage is of great benefit in delaying the onset of fatigue. The reason for this relates to the interesting interrelationship between the use of these two major fuels during exercise. This will be discussed shortly.

Strength training can also improve muscle function along with endurance training. In particular, strength training has an important nervous system stimulus that isn't as evident with endurance training. Motor units become better synchronized and recruitable (Sale, MacDougall, Upton, & McComas, 1983). Thus, there is better teamwork among motor units, with more contributing to the task at a given work load and each functioning at a lower intensity.

Changes in cross-sectional area of skeletal muscle cells, resulting in skeletal muscle enlargement (hypertrophy), tend to occur with high-intensity resistance training, initiated by increased muscle strain itself (McDonagh & Davies, 1984). The cross-sectional area of FT fibers seems to increase more than that of ST fibers, however, even though both types are stimulated. This may be determined by a different responsiveness of the two types of myosin in these cells to quite different intracellular levels of acidity. This

might explain why elite long-distance runners, with their increased numbers of ST fibers, do not experience the accompanying muscle cell hypertrophy of athletes endowed with a majority of FT cells, even though they may include serious strength training as part of their development (to increase joint strength and thereby reduce injury risk).

Thus, the body has the potential to adapt in many ways to the stimulus of serious training. Each organ system responds in its own particular way, with the ultimate goal of accommodating to a sizable training stress and making it more easily tolerable. Then, an even greater stress can be applied, permitting further adaptation and, it is hoped, better performance in training and competition. It is essential to realize that the adaptation takes time (one does not get fit overnight) and that the stimuli must be reasonable as well as appropriate—that is, not excessive. Chapters 3 and 4 will consider the various training modalities, and chapter 6 will consider the challenge of keeping training within manageable limits.

Whatever the specific details of training plan design, they must always remain within the limits of energy availability for the muscles being challenged. Thus, energy fuel dynamics within the working muscle cells must be acceptable: sufficient to provide movement but not prevent it. It is thus appropriate to turn our attention briefly to the metabolic aspects of this relationship and consider the biochemical principles that ensure that energy is provided for movement to occur.

BIOCHEMICAL ASPECTS OF RUNNING

Sizable quantities of chemical energy are involved in muscle tension generation. This is in contrast to most man-made devices for doing mechanical work, which typically utilize heat or electrical energy. The metabolic rate of skeletal muscle can undergo a greater increase from its resting level than any other body tissue, and enormous mechanical work can be done. Study of these performance dynamics at the cellular level becomes, in a real sense, a study of applied biochemistry. Understanding these chemical energy dynamics in the context of the tension-generating processes of muscle permits a more complete impression of how the body can accomplish mechanical work.

It is not essential to understand the precise details of every chemical reaction involved in the conversion of foodstuffs into energy, but it is important to comprehend the concepts. Thus, to analogize, it is more essential to know the rules of soccer than knowing the names of the players if we truly desire to understand how the game is played. Once we understand the game, then knowing some personal details about the players and the various teams adds delightful subtleties that increase satisfaction in watching the game. It is the same with running and biochemistry. Knowledge of the general principles of metabolism—the fuels that are used, how much energy can be produced, and how energy production is regulated—permits a good understanding of the limitations and capabilities of the body for providing energy. Once these are clearly in mind, we are in a better position to apply these principles to suit our purpose, which is performance enhancement.

Thermodynamic Perspectives

The laws of thermodynamics govern metabolism. Two of these laws are appropriate for our consideration. The first law states simply that the total energy of the universe remains constant. We can define **energy** as all forms of work and heat. The second law states, again very simply, that the entropy of the universe increases. And we will define **entropy** as disorder

or randomness. How do these two laws relate to running? Very simply, running requires energy, which is obtained by the breakdown of energy-containing fuel. Of the total energy released in fuel breakdown, not all is available to produce movement. A large portion is in the form of heat, as runners soon discover when they train! Our stored fuel reserves are assimilated from the foods we eat. Thus, our understanding of metabolism needs to include fuel intake, processing, and storage as well as fuel breakdown and utilization.

Solar energy is the source of all biological energy. The energy from sunlight actually arises from nuclear energy. Because of the immensely high temperature of the sun, a part of the enormous energy locked within the nucleus of hydrogen atoms is released as they are converted into helium atoms and electrons by nuclear fusion. The world of green plants utilizes this energy. Plants have a pigment, chlorophyll, that can convert the radiant light energy into chemical energy. This chemical energy, in turn, is utilized to produce glucose by chemical reduction of atmospheric carbon dioxide (CO_2). The process is termed *photosynthesis*. Molecular O_2 is formed and given up to the atmosphere. The overall equation for this photosynthetic reaction is described as follows:

$$6\ CO_2 + 6\ H_2O \xrightarrow{\text{Energy}} C_6H_{12}O_6 + O_2$$

ΔG = free energy = +686 kcal/mol = +2,872 kJ/mol
ΔH = heat energy = +673 kcal/mol = +2,817 kJ/mol
ΔS = entropy = −43.6 cal/mol = −183 J/mol   (1.2)

All this thermodynamic jargon may at first appear almost incomprehensible even to those not too far away from their college chemistry and physics courses. Some additional explanation is thus appropriate. The ΔG, ΔH, and ΔS terms written below the general equation describe the details of the energy relationships about the photosynthesis reaction. To better understand these, realize first that, when energy is measured, it is quantified either in units of calories (cal) or joules (J). These can be interconverted as follows:

$$1\text{ cal} = 4.186\text{ J};\ 1\text{ J} = 0.24\text{ cal} \qquad (1.3)$$
$$1,000\text{ cal} = 1\text{ kilocalorie (kcal)};\ 1,000\text{ J} = 1\text{ kilojoule (kJ)} \qquad (1.4)$$

The ΔG term refers to *free energy*, or that portion of the total energy of the system available to perform work. Its + sign indicates that energy was used for synthesis (not breakdown). The quantity ΔH refers to *heat energy*, and its + sign indicates that heat energy was used or absorbed in the process of forming glucose. Finally, the quantity ΔS refers to *entropy*. Its $-$ sign indicates that there is less randomness in having the CO_2 and water (H_2O) molecules chemically linked together as glucose.

Our own cells require the complex energy-rich products of photosynthesis as fuel and as a carbon source. This is because we are unable to use such simple molecules as CO_2 either as fuel or as building blocks for synthesizing the components of our cells. We rely on the plant world as the ultimate source of our food and energy, providing us with fatty acids (stored as triglycerides), sugars (stored as complex carbohydrates such as glycogen), and amino acids (bound together into proteins). We ingest these fuels, and the next grand step in the flow of biological energy is the breakdown of such stored fuels by the digestive system back to their smallest component parts: simple sugars, fatty acids, and amino acids. Then, by absorption into our circulation and reassimilation *(anabolism)* by the cells in our tissues, fuel supplies in the form of complex carbohydrates and fats are stored in various quantities, along with the stored energy in their molecular structure. Subsequent fuel breakdown, or *catabolism*, with release of stored energy, provides for the particular needs of all of the various cell types. For muscle cells, of course, some of the stored energy goes to produce movement. Assuming that complete fuel breakdown results from this so-called cellular respiration, the stable end products of CO_2 and H_2O result. The equation for cellular respiration in its simplest form is thus virtually the opposite of the equation for photosynthesis. Using glucose, a simple carbohydrate, as an example, we may write:

$$C_6H_{12}O_6 + 6\,O_2 \longrightarrow 6\,CO_2 + 6\,H_2O + \text{energy}$$

$\Delta G = \text{free energy} = -686 \text{ kcal/mol} = -2,872 \text{ kJ/mol}$

$\Delta H = \text{heat energy} = -673 \text{ kcal/mol} = -2,817 \text{ kJ/mol}$

$\Delta S = \text{entropy} = +43.6 \text{ cal/mol} = +183 \text{ J/mol}$

(1.5)

Again, considering this equation in thermodynamic perspective, the ΔG term is $-$, indicating a large amount of free energy output available for storage and later use. Considerable heat is released, as seen by the $-\Delta H$ value. The entropy of the system is positive, as seen by the $+\Delta S$ term, showing that glucose breakdown has brought more disorder to the universe.

Several important observations should be made at this point. First, protein typically is not a primary fuel source, although protein breakdown and reassimilation may occur with hard work. Carbohydrates (represented by glucose) and fats (represented by fatty acids) are our primary fuel sources. Many of the details of

both synthesis and breakdown of these two fuel sources are similar, as we shall see, although some important differences exist as well. Table 1.2 compares glucose (a typical carbohydrate) and palmitic acid (a fatty acid) as cellular fuels. It can be seen that the energy value of palmitic acid is nearly 2-1/2 times greater on a per-gram basis than that of glucose.

Second, the heat production that accompanies metabolism should be familiar to everyone. Our resting body temperature is about 37 degrees C (98 degrees F). We have evolved mechanisms for getting rid of this heat, through sweating and dilation of skin blood vessels. During exercise, body temperature rises, and the accompanying blood diversion to permit sweating and cutaneous dilation diminishes the flow available for working muscles. This explains the typically slower competitive performances in very warm weather.

Third, the free energy values that we have been quoting are only theoretical maximum values if the metabolic processes were 100% efficient. This doesn't occur, and there is a loss of between 40% and 60% of this theoretically available free energy. Fourth, although the equation for breakdown of glucose as a typical fuel appears simple, this is deceptive, because there are a few dozen separate, sequential, enzymatically controlled steps required in the chemical breakdown of glucose to CO_2 and H_2O (see Figures 1.36 and 1.38). We do not plan to describe the details of these reactions here, nor will we do so for fatty acid metabolism; that is the substance of college courses in biochemistry. We can, however, identify some of the most important steps in these metabolic pathways, particularly those that are relevant for performance enhancement during training or competition. Before doing that, however, we should describe briefly how the free energy produced from fuel breakdown is actually harvested and stored in chemical form for eventual use in permitting movement.

Energy Storage in Tissues: ATP and CP

We have already mentioned that the energy released from complete cellular breakdown of fuels is conserved in the form of ATP. Oxygen is required for this complete catabolism, and thus the phrase *oxidative metabolism* is commonly used to describe the reactions involved. Figure 1.25 shows the structure of the parent molecule called adenosine monophosphate (AMP), to which additional phosphate ($PO_4^{\equiv}$) groups can bind, forming first adenosine diphosphate (ADP) and then ATP itself. This chemical binding, however, requires considerably more energy than that found

Table 1.2   Metabolic Aspects of Carbohydrates and Fatty Acids as Fuels

	Carbohydrate (glucose)		Fatty acid (palmitic acid)	
Structure	*(glucose ring structure: CH₂OH, O, H, OH groups)*		$CH_3(CH_2)_{14}COOH$	
Molecular weight, gm	180		256	
% carbon and hydrogen	47		88	
% oxygen	53		12	
Relative stored energy				
kcal/gm kJ/gm	3.81	15.9	9.1	38.1
Total stored energy				
kcal KJ	686	2,872	2,340	9,795
Energy generated as ATP				
kcal kJ	360	1,507	1,300	5,442
Energy value				
kcal/ATP kJ/ATP	19	79.5	18	75.4
O_2 needed for catabolism, L	130		515	
Energy production per L of O_2				
kcal kJ	5.28	22.1	4.54	19.0
CO_2 produced in catabolism, L	130		358	
Energy production per L of CO_2				
kcal kJ	5.28	22.1	6.54	27.4
CO_2 produced/O_2 used (Respiratory Exchange Ratio)	1.00		0.71	

Note. From "Dynamics of pulmonary gas exchange" by B.J. Whipp, 1987, *Circulation*, **76** (Suppl. VI), VI-19. Reprinted by permission of the American Heart Association, Inc.

in the other bonds linking the various atoms together. The wavy line denotes these so-called *high-energy bonds*, in contrast to the straight-line notation for lower-energy bonding. High-energy $PO_4^{\equiv}$ bonds are thus a kind of gold standard of metabolic energy currency in the biological world. The free energy available from oxidation of food is utilized to link together a $PO_4^{\equiv}$ group to adenosine diphosphate (ADP), thereby forming a molecule of ATP. When cells require energy for biosynthesis of other substances or for chemical interactions, such as those of actin and myosin in muscle for tension generation, ATP is used. By the coupling of oxidation (the use of O_2 to permit complete breakdown of fuels with release of energy) to phosphorylation (the storage of this energy as ATP), the free energy available from breakdown of fuels can thus be used for mechanical work.

Historically, the realization that phosphates were the storage form of the free energy from fuel oxidation dates back to 1925. Gustav Embden, a German biochemist, observed that much more $PO_4^{\equiv}$ would diffuse into the solution bathing an isolated, twitching skeletal muscle preparation than around a resting muscle. Two years later, in 1927, two groups of investigators simultaneously discovered a substance called *creatine phosphate* (CP), a very unstable derivative of a nitrogen-containing substance called *creatine* (Figure 1.26). Creatine exists in sizable concentrations in muscle and nerve cells, with skeletal muscles having the largest supplies. Then in 1929, ATP and ADP were discovered independently by Karl Lohmann in Germany and by two American scientists. The ensuing few years saw work proceed toward the unraveling of how these various $PO_4^{\equiv}$-containing substances

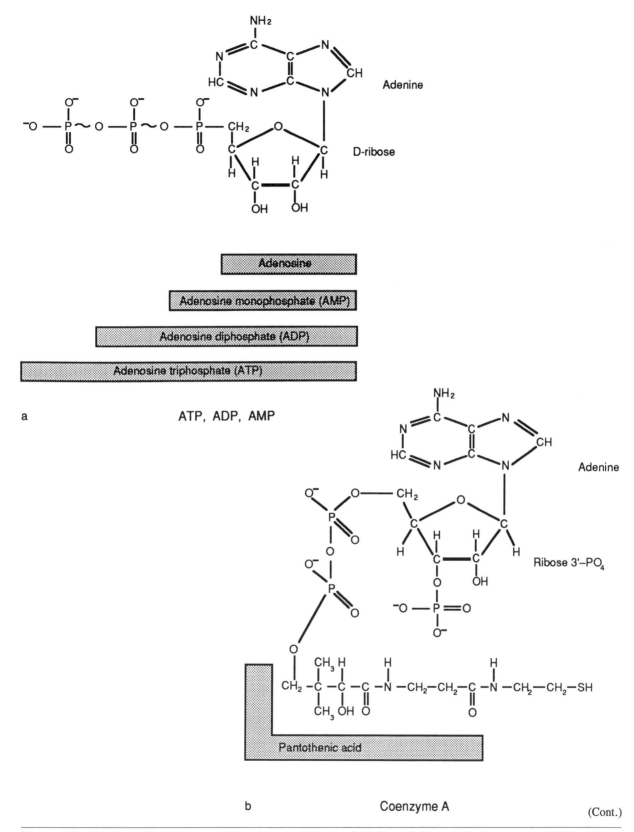

a   ATP, ADP, AMP

b   Coenzyme A   (Cont.)

Figure 1.25 Structures of vitamin-containing substances important in fuel metabolism: ATP, Coenzyme A, NAD, and FAD. Notice that all molecules contain adenosine and a sugar, ribose. ATP is the simplest of these substances, containing only phosphate groups in addition to adenosine and ribose. The others all have a vitamin incorporated as well: pantothenic acid for Coenzyme A, nicotinic acid for NAD, and riboflavin for FAD.

Figure 1.25 (Continued)

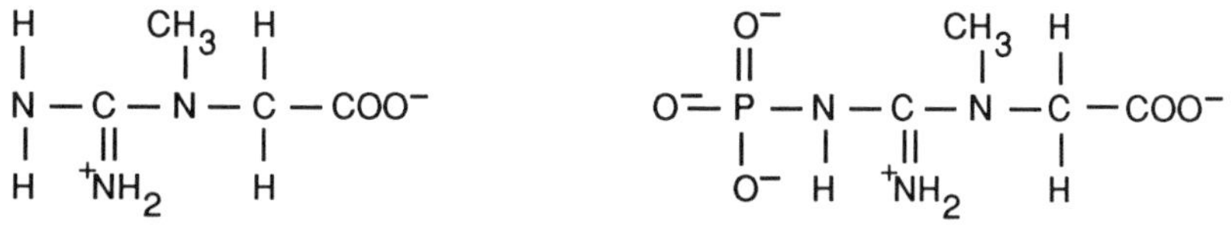

$$
\begin{array}{c}
\text{H} \qquad\quad \text{CH}_3 \;\; \text{H} \\
| \qquad\qquad | \qquad\; | \\
\text{N} - \text{C} - \text{N} - \text{C} - \text{COO}^- \\
| \qquad\quad \| \qquad\quad | \\
\text{H} \quad\; {}^+\text{NH}_2 \qquad \text{H}
\end{array}
\qquad\qquad
\begin{array}{c}
\text{O}^- \qquad\qquad\;\; \text{CH}_3 \;\; \text{H} \\
\| \qquad\qquad\qquad | \qquad\; | \\
\text{O} = \text{P} - \text{N} - \text{C} - \text{N} - \text{C} - \text{COO}^- \\
| \qquad\; | \qquad \| \qquad\quad | \\
\text{O}^- \;\; \text{H} \quad {}^+\text{NH}_2 \qquad \text{H}
\end{array}
$$

Creatine   Creatine phosphate

Figure 1.26 Structures of creatine and creatine phosphate.

interacted in energy storage and release (Lehninger, 1982).

The classic study came in 1934 when Lohmann demonstrated that cell-free muscle extracts of CP would split $PO_4^{\equiv}$ from creatine only in the presence of ADP, with the resulting formation of ATP. His explanation of the situation was simple. CP is a reservoir of $PO_4^{\equiv}$ (in effect a reservoir of energy), utilizable only if there is first a need for ATP. Lohmann envisioned muscle tension generation as somehow involving ATP breakdown directly into ADP. As soon as ADP was formed, available CP would rephosphorylate it back into ATP. Subsequent research proved him correct, and equations 1.6 and 1.7 are often termed the Lohmann equations to recognize his brillance in identifying what was occurring.

$$
\text{ATP} + \text{H}_2\text{O} \xrightarrow{\text{myosin-ATPase}} \text{ADP} + \text{H}_3\text{PO}_4
$$
$$(1.6)$$

$$
\text{creatine phosphate} + \text{ADP} \underset{\text{kinase}}{\overset{\text{creatine}}{\rightleftharpoons}} \text{creatine} + \text{ATP} \quad (1.7)
$$

Equation 1.7 is reversible, as shown. That is, it can proceed in either direction, but its equilibrium normally is shifted toward the right, keeping the ADP phosphorylated as ATP at all times by use of CP. Thus, the CP pool represents a small but labile reservoir of high-energy $PO_4^{\equiv}$ groups. When ATP is plentiful, so also is CP. If a sudden, enormous ATP requirement occurs in muscle cells, such that metabolism of carbohydrates and fats cannot occur in the available time period to provide the needed energy, CP can provide it. In sprinting, for example, whether it be the 100m dash or the final 50m rush to victory in a 10,000m run, CP will play an important role. Skeletal muscle is thus biochemically capable of generating tension for brief periods (perhaps 20 sec) even without any energy derived from ongoing carbohydrate or fat breakdown. A CP shuttle exists between the cytoplasm and mitochondria, as shown in Figure 1.27. In the myofibrillar region of the cytoplasm, $PO_4^{\equiv}$ is taken from CP to allow ADP conversion to ATP. This provides a ready source of ATP for muscle tension generation. When CP arrives back to the mitochondrial membrane, creatine becomes rephosphorylated.

The *creatine kinase* (CK) enzyme shown in Equation 1.7 occurs in three forms, known as isoenzymes. These are restricted to skeletal muscle (CK-MM), cardiac muscle (CK-MB), and brain tissue (CK-BB), although skeletal muscle also produces some CK-MB. When these tissues are challenged by trauma (such as in a boxing match), circulatory shutdown (as with a clot in a coronary artery of the heart), or fuel exhaustion (during and following a marathon race), for several days following these insults clinically elevated levels of the appropriate CK isoenzymes will appear in the bloodstream (Rogers, Stull, & Apple, 1985). Thus, particularly for distance runners, measurement of serum CK levels can serve as a marker for excessive training or competitive stress, indicating the need for temporary training reduction and increased use of appropriate therapeutic modalities to enhance recovery.

Thus, the essence of metabolism is in the conversion of fuels to end products, with appropriate storage of the energy as a usable form (ATP) for cellular function (Figure 1.28). It is interesting that ATP is present in only very small quantities in cells. A warm-blooded skeletal muscle may have typically about 6 μmoles of ATP/gm, compared to between 20 and 30 μmoles of CP/gm. According to Lehninger (1982), a reasonably sedentary 70-kg male has only about 50 gm ATP in his entire body, yet he would probably require the equivalent of 190 kg of ATP to provide his daily energy requirements!

The ATP content of muscle and other cells is thus recycled between ATP and ADP many times per minute, with $PO_4^{\equiv}$ groups alternating from CP to ADP to ATP. Extremely heavy work loads reduce the CP supply, but following this, CP is rapidly regenerated by continued metabolism. This CP-ATP

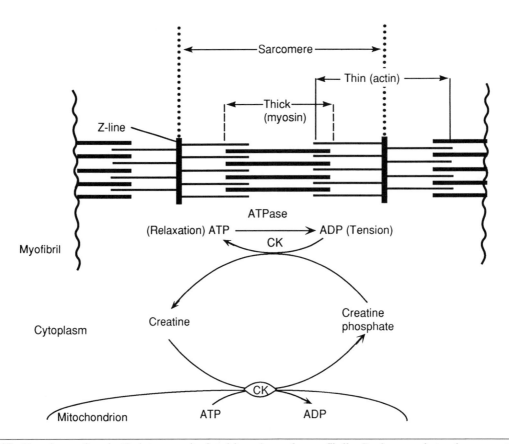

Figure 1.27 Phosphocreatine shuttle between mitochondria and muscle myofibrils. During muscle tension generation, ATP contributes energy, forming ADP, and this energy supply must be regenerated. Creatine kinase (CK), in the vicinity of the tension-generating proteins (myosin and actin), permits regeneration of ATP. Similarly, at the mitochondrial membrane, CK provides for regeneration of phosphocreatine using energy provided from fuel metabolism.

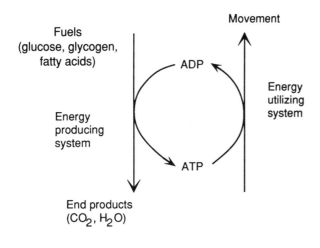

Figure 1.28 The essence of metabolism. Available fuels are broken down, and the energy resulting is stored as a usable form (ATP) for purposes such as skeletal muscle tension generation and thus the production of movement.

system can provide energy needs without any breakdown of fuels such as glucose or fatty acids for perhaps 15 to 20 sec of intense work. This is sometimes called the sprinters' energy system because of its major role in energy provision for the short sprints. Distance runners by contrast require a superbly developed metabolic engine capable of harnessing not quite as much energy per unit time (except perhaps for an exciting race finish), but instead the much greater total quantities of energy that can be made available from fats and carbohydrates. Figure 1.29 provides a graphic summary of the relative contribution of various energy sources for running: CP and ATP, the latter being produced either with or without the presence of O_2. Before discussing the details of metabolism of the various fuels, we should clarify in general terms the specific role of O_2 in metabolism. Its availability determines primarily whether the body will completely break down fuels, thereby releasing

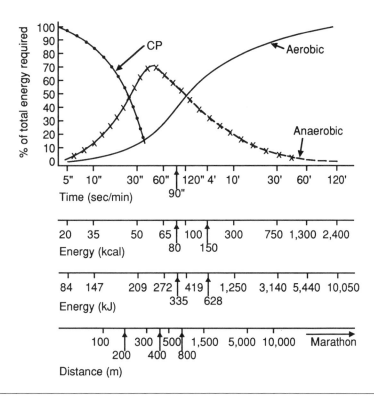

Figure 1.29 Graphic summary of the relative contribution of various energy sources for maximum effort over the spectrum of distances from the sprints through the marathon. For the short sprints, creatine phosphate (CP) is the primary energy supplier, with an increasingly substantial contribution from anaerobic glycolysis up through events lasting about 1 min. For events requiring longer than 1 min, CP supplies would have already been depleted, and aerobic (complete) breakdown of fuels (fatty acids and glucose) becomes increasingly important; for marathon racing, aerobic metabolism is by far the predominant energy source.

enormous quantities of energy, or whether such breakdown will be restricted, with only minimal energy release.

Aerobic Versus Anaerobic Metabolism

The complete catabolism of carbohydrates and fatty acids in mitochondria involves an interaction with O_2. The term *aerobic metabolism* is used to describe this chemical breakdown sequence and signifies "in the presence of O_2." If the O_2 supply to mitochondria is insufficient to meet the rate at which it is required for ongoing metabolism, cells can still produce energy for movement, although in limited supply. The term *anaerobic metabolism* is used to describe this process. Its presence in skeletal muscles has earned them the nickname of "twitch-now, pay-later" muscles. By contrast, cardiac muscle, which can never afford to fall behind in its O_2 supply for tension generation, is often referred to as "twitch-now, pay-now" muscle.

Oxygen provision may be limited by any of several circumstances. There may be insufficient circulation of blood, or the rate of physical activity may be so

great as to challenge the ability of even an optimally functioning circulatory system to provide adequate O_2. The inability to respond when the mind says "go" and the body says "no," as we try to increase speed in a race or a training session when already fatigued from prior effort, attests to the very definite limits of aerobic and anaerobic metabolism. An important goal of training is to extend these aerobic and anaerobic limits as far as possible.

For O_2 to be available in mitochondria, it must be brought from the outside environment into metabolizing cells. This movement requires an intricate pathway through the respiratory passageways, then through the bloodstream, into and through the interstitial fluid, and finally into the cytoplasm of individual cells. Along each step of the way, O_2 moves by diffusion down its concentration gradient—that is, from a region of higher concentration to successive regions of lower concentration. The term *O_2 cascade* is often used to suggest this stepwise movement of O_2 toward cells awaiting its arrival. The partial pressure exerted by O_2 (its PO_2), both in the atmosphere and in dissolved fluids such as blood and cell cytoplasm, is typically expressed in units of millimeters of mercury (mm Hg). Figure 1.30 shows the various PO_2 values that are found between the external environment and mitochondria.

The generalized equation for aerobic breakdown of a carbohydrate such as glucose results in enormous amounts of energy for work, as shown here:

$$C_6H_{12}O_6 + 6\,O_2 \longrightarrow 6\,CO_2 + 6\,H_2O + 36\,ATP \tag{1.8}$$

For fatty acid breakdown, the reaction is similar in principle, also with plenty of energy release. It is summarized by the following equation, using palmitic acid as an example:

$$C_{16}H_{32}O_2 + 23\,O_2 \longrightarrow 16\,CO_2 + 16\,H_2O + 130\,ATP \tag{1.9}$$

If insufficient O_2 is available for complete fuel breakdown, a small amount of energy release can occur with glucose conversion to an intermediate substance—pyruvic acid. This can be converted into lactic acid, and these reactions occur in the cytoplasm with no involvement of mitochondria. By contrast, no such anaerobic energy release is possible with fatty acids; their stored energy can be accessed only once they are completely broken down. Under physio-

logical conditions the lactic acid produced from anaerobic carbohydrate metabolism dissociates almost immediately and completely (Gladden, 1989) into lactate (Lac^-) ions and hydrogen (H^+) ions. The same is true for a large number of other metabolic acids that we will encounter in fuel metabolism. It is accepted biochemical jargon to refer to these acids by the name of their negative ion; for example, lactate (Lac^-) for lactic acid, oxalacetate for oxalacetic acid, and so forth. We will use this convention here as well.

A summary equation for the anaerobic conversion of glucose to lactate is given in Equation 1.10:

$$C_6H_{12}O_6 \longrightarrow 2\,ATP +$$
$$2\,\text{Lactic acid} \rightleftharpoons 2\,H^+ + 2\,Lac^- \tag{1.10}$$

By comparing the ATP generated in Equations 1.8 and 1.10, we can see that anaerobic metabolism provides only 1/18—about 5.5%—as much energy as aerobic metabolism (2 ATP as compared to 36). Thus, anaerobic fuel metabolism is extremely substrate-costly, meaning that large amounts of glucose are consumed with minimum energy return. Also, the rapid accumulation of H^+ ions (commonly called protons) as a result of lactic acid dissociation eventually inhibits the enzymatic breakdown sequence. The

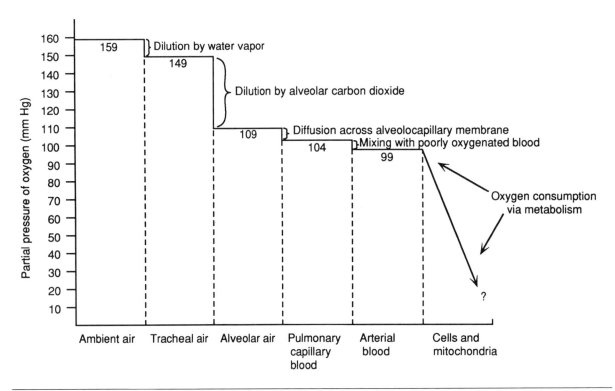

Figure 1.30 The oxygen cascade, showing how oxygen moves down its concentration gradient from environmental air to the mitochondria of living cells. Dilution steadily lowers its partial pressure, and then its utilization in metabolism decreases its concentration enormously within cells.

enzymes of glycolysis operate best within a specific narrow range of acidity. Acidity is determined by the number of available protons. Excessive tissue acidity (acidosis) inhibits the activity of many of the enzyme reactions for fuel metabolism. Thus, optimum cell function depends upon adequate O_2 to maximize energy (ATP) production via aerobic metabolism. Improving performance fitness in skeletal muscles involves adaptation in any and all ways to provide a higher level of ATP-derived energy release with minimum tissue or blood acidification.

Carbon dioxide is also an acid. An acid is defined as a substance that donates H^+ ions to its surrounding solution. When CO_2 dissolves in body water, it becomes hydrated to form carbonic acid (H_2CO_3), which then dissociates into H^+ ions and bicarbonate (HCO_3^-) ions according to the following equation:

$$CO_2 + H_2O \rightleftharpoons H_2CO_3 \rightleftharpoons H^+ + HCO_3^-$$

(1.11)

Carbon dioxide is called a volatile acid because it can be eliminated as a gas through the lungs. This elimination occurs as blood returning from the body is distributed through the lungs for reoxygenation. The lungs thus are the body's most powerful organ for acid excretion. Lactate, on the other hand, is a nonvolatile acid and is not eliminated via the lungs. Although the lactate ion itself can be used by many tissues as a fuel, the inhibitory effects of its H^+ ion on metabolism must be minimized. One substance playing an important role in this regard is sodium bicarbonate ($NaHCO_3$), which circulates in the bloodstream and interstitial fluid that bathes cells. Equation 1.12 illustrates the so-called buffer action of $NaHCO_3$ in the blood perfusing working tissue, whereby many of the H^+ ions resulting from lactate production can combine with HCO_3^- to form H_2CO_3. Only the H^+ ions themselves contribute to acidity.

$$Na^+ + HCO_3^- + H^+ + Lac^- \longrightarrow NaLactate +$$
$$H_2CO_3 \longrightarrow H_2O + CO_2 \qquad (1.12)$$

Athletes desiring to increase their performance potential by minimizing blood and tissue acidosis when training and competing should use the following suggestions based upon the preceding concepts. First, ensure adequate recovery after exercise by cool-down exercise and postexercise massage to enhance blood and lymphatic drainage through the challenged muscles. This helps to restore normal fluid and acid/base status in these tissues. Second, ensure adequate fluid and energy-rich nutritional intake soon after the hard training session, to restore blood volume for adequate tissue perfusion, and to permit rejuvenation of muscle energy stores and a recovered aerobic metabolic state.

Excessive acidity in tissues has several undesirable effects. We have already mentioned its inhibitory effects on optimum enzyme functioning for efficient metabolism. Another is its destabilization of cell membranes, allowing some of their vital enzymes to leak out, into either the bloodstream or the interstitial fluid. A third is its tendency to cause H_2O to enter cells in an attempt to maintain osmotic equilibrium between the cells and their surrounding fluid environment. An acidotic cell cytoplasm has excessive numbers of ions (electrolytes) dissolved in its fluid portion (H^+, Lac^-, Na^+, HCO_3^-, etc.). As a result, there are relatively fewer H_2O molecules per unit volume than in surrounding solutions such as blood or extracellular fluid. An osmotic inflow of H_2O attempts to restore fluid-electrolyte balance. When this occurs in highly active muscle cells, which normally are elongated and thin, the increase in fluid content makes them shorter and thicker. Functionally, athletes sense this after a hard training session as a decreased joint range of motion.

Maintenance of increased circulation following such training, typically in the form of easy running, will enhance recovery. This is often referred to simply as *cool-down*, because during this process the body temperature gradually decreases from its maximum during exercise back toward its resting level. It is an important intermediate step in the activity continuum from the highly active state on one end to the resting condition on the other. The enhanced circulation, maintained aerobically and at little energy expense, helps restore fluid and electrolyte balance in the working muscles. It also provides continued perfusion of O_2-rich blood into the working muscles, which facilitates complete breakdown of metabolic acids still remaining.

Carbohydrates and Fatty Acids as Fuels

Table 1.3 provides a quantitative idea of the available energy substrates in the body. The principal storage form of carbohydrate is glycogen. Glycogen is essentially polymerized glucose—long chains, sometimes branching, as depicted in Figure 1.31. These glycogen polymers are sometimes so large that histologic sections of tissue, when stained appropriately, will reveal them as cytoplasmic glycogen particles, larger in the liver than in skeletal muscle. When glycogen is broken down to glucose (a process called *glycogenolysis*), one ATP is produced per mole of glucose removed.

Adipose tissue and the liver provide the greatest reservoir of fat-related energy. The much greater reservoir of fat in contrast to carbohydrate can be seen in Table 1.3. Muscle cells have a large capacity to

Table 1.3   Energy Substrates Available for Metabolism

	kg	kcal	kJ
Tissues			
Fat	15	141,000	590,000
Protein	6	24,000	100,500
Muscle glycogen	0.35	1,400	5,900
Liver glycogen	0.085	340	1,400
	21.435	166,740	697,800
Circulating Fuels			
Extracellular fluid glucose	0.020	80	335
Fatty acids	0.0004	4	17
Triglycerides	0.003	30	126
	0.0234	114	478

utilize fat, and it can diffuse in easily across cell membranes. Endurance training increases both carbohydrate and fat supplies in skeletal muscle. Cardiac muscle, with its never-ending activity in generating upward of 100,000 heartbeats every day, is specially endowed with fat stores and mitochondria to satisfy its needs.

Fats are essentially water-insoluble and exist in the body as triglycerides. These result from the linking together of glycerol with three fatty acid molecules—a process called esterification and illustrated in Figure 1.32. Fat found in food (e.g., butter, bacon, marga-

rine, oils) is chiefly in the form of triglycerides. Those fats that are liquid at room temperature tend to be of plant origin, whereas the solid fats are principally animal-derived. The number of H^+ ions bound to fatty acids (known as its extent of hydrogenation or saturation) determines their melting point and thus whether they will be liquid or solid at room temperature. Cooking oils, such as safflower or corn oil, are polyunsaturated, that is, not very extensively hydrogenated. Animal fat, such as lard, is much more saturated.

When fats are ingested, they are first broken down from triglycerides into fatty acids (sometimes called nonesterified fatty acids because they are not bound to glycerol). These are absorbed into the bloodstream and then bind to albumin, our most common plasma protein, for transport. Because the plasma fatty acid concentration is typically higher than that in such tissues as liver, adipose, and muscle cells, this gradient permits a steady fatty acid influx into these cells. No active transport mechanism for fatty acids is known, and as they enter, the freed albumin is now available for assistance in transport of other fatty acids. As shown in Figure 1.33, the fatty acids are eventually bound again as triglycerides and stored for later use by these metabolizing cells.

By studying Equations 1.8 and 1.9 along with Table 1.2, several interesting differences between carbohydrates and fats as fuels can be seen. First, note that fat is a more efficient form of stored energy than carbohydrate. Fats are 88% carbon and hydrogen with 12% O_2, compared to 47% carbon and hydrogen and

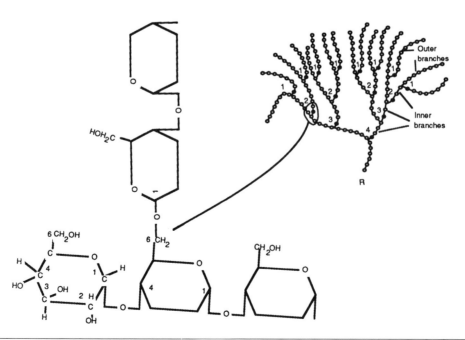

Figure 1.31   The glycogen molecule, showing branches made up of glucose subunits.

$$
\begin{array}{c}
\underset{\displaystyle\text{Triglyceride}}{
\text{H}_2\text{C - O - }\overset{\displaystyle\text{O}}{\overset{\displaystyle\|}{\text{C}}}\text{ - R}_1 \\
\text{HC - O - }\overset{\displaystyle\text{O}}{\overset{\displaystyle\|}{\text{C}}}\text{ - R}_2 \quad + 3\,\text{H}_2\text{O} \\
\text{H}_2\text{C - O - }\overset{\displaystyle\text{O}}{\overset{\displaystyle\|}{\text{C}}}\text{ - R}_3
}
\end{array}
\;\underset{\text{Esterase}}{\overset{\text{Lipase}}{\rightleftharpoons}}\;
\begin{array}{cc}
\underset{\text{3 Fatty acids}}{
\text{OH - }\overset{\text{O}}{\overset{\|}{\text{C}}}\text{ - R}_1 \\
\text{OH - }\overset{\text{O}}{\overset{\|}{\text{C}}}\text{ - R}_2 \\
\text{OH - }\overset{\text{O}}{\overset{\|}{\text{C}}}\text{ - R}_3
} &
\underset{\text{Glycerol}}{
+ \;\; \text{H}_2\text{C - OH} \\
\text{HC - OH} \\
\text{H}_2\text{C - OH}
}
\end{array}
$$

Figure 1.32 Breakdown of a triglyceride into three fatty acids. A lipase enzyme permits removal of fatty acids from the glycerol molecule to which they were bound. An esterase enzyme permits the storage of fatty acids, bound to glycerol as a triglyceride; this storage process is called esterification.

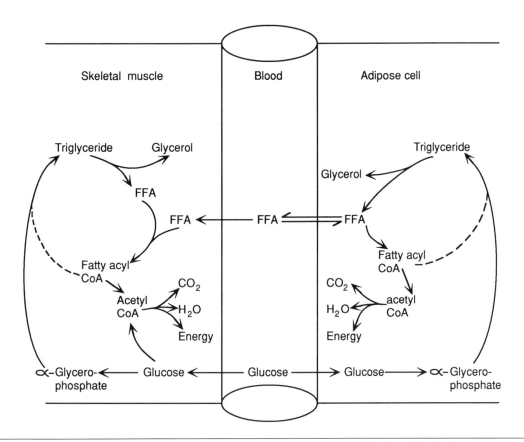

Figure 1.33 Summary of interrelationships between fatty acids and glucose in metabolism. Blood glucose can enter either skeletal muscle cells, for eventual breakdown, or adipose cells, for eventual conversion to triglyceride. Fatty acids can also enter either skeletal muscle cells or adipose cells. In the former, they are typically metabolized for energy; in the latter they can be stored for later release and transport to muscle tissue.

53% O_2 for carbohydrates. Oxygen atoms in a molecule of stored energy merely add more bulk, as they generally can be obtained from the environment as needed. However, as exercise intensity increases, this can be a liability, making carbohydrates a preferred fuel over fats as O_2 requirements begin to approach O_2 supply capabilities. Also, carbohydrates require less O_2 for metabolism than fats. Thus, for glucose, 36 ATP are produced per 6 O_2 utilized (36/6 = 6). With palmitic acid, it is 130 ATP per 23 O_2 utilized (130/23 = 5.7).

Second, it can be seen that fats are less acidic than carbohydrates; that is, less CO_2 is produced per quantity of O_2 used in fuel breakdown. This ratio of CO_2 produced by cells to O_2 consumed by cells is termed the *respiratory quotient* (RQ). More practically, we measure the volumes of O_2 and CO_2 exchanged by the lungs. Here, the ratio of CO_2 to O_2 is referred to as the *respiratory exchange ratio* (R). For glucose,

$$R = 6\ CO_2/6\ O_2 = 1.00. \qquad (1.13)$$

For palmitic acid,

$$R = 16\ CO_2/23\ O_2 = 0.70. \qquad (1.14)$$

Third, fat is less bulky than carbohydrate; that is, fats are higher in energy content per unit mass than are carbohydrates. Oxidation of 1 gram of fat will form 508 moles of ATP as compared to only 211 for an equal weight of carbohydrate.

An individual at rest consuming a normal diet will have a resting R value of about 0.80, indicating that the majority of ongoing energy requirements is met by fat oxidation, with perhaps one third by carbohydrate. If this person now begins to exercise at a steadily increasing work rate, carbohydrate metabolism increasingly becomes the dominant energy source. We could follow the course of this change by monitoring the rise in R. Table 1.4 shows this nicely as part of a set of data obtained when one of our elite-level women runners underwent a performance evaluation, using treadmill running, to allow estimation of

$\dot{V}O_2$max. The data point marked *Rest* indicates baseline values before her test began. The next four data points show the progressive rise in R values as well as other accompanying physiological responses to the steadily increasing work load. The final five data points were obtained during the few minutes just prior to voluntary exhaustion. Not only has R equalled 1.00, but it has actually gone beyond it. The explanation for this resides in the high level of acidosis, which provided an additional stimulus to ventilation. CO_2 production was in excess of that explainable by pure carbohydrate metabolism. In chapter 2 we will discuss how this occurred.

Glycogenolysis: Breakdown of Glycogen to Glucose

It is well known that a progressive fall in working muscle glycogen occurs during vigorous exercise, and when fatigue is noticeable in those muscles, glycogen depletion is a likely explanation (Costill, Bowers, Branam, & Sparks, 1971). Higher exercise intensities reduce available glycogen supplies much more quickly than low-level exercise. How is glycogen mobilized to permit exercise? And how can glycogen be stored and replenished in working muscles? The glycogen content of tissues varies considerably, depending upon nutritional status, level of physical training, premeasurement exercise level, and the influence of several hormones. Cortisone (from the adrenal cortex) and insulin (from the pancreas) elevate the glycogen content in tissues by increasing its synthesis from glucose. Adrenaline (from the adrenal

Table 1.4   Effect of Increasing Work Load During a Treadmill Stress Test on Oxygen Consumption, Carbon Dioxide Production, and Elevation of Respiratory Exchange Ratio (R)

Elapsed time (min)	Heart rate (beats/min)	Respiratory rate (breaths/min)	Oxygen consumption (ml/min)	Oxygen consumption (ml/kg/min)	Carbon dioxide production (ml/min)	Respiratory exchange ratio (R)
Rest	60	14	320	6.8	260	0.79
1/2	136	32	1,522	29.4	1,293	0.84
1	136	33	1,612	31.2	1,364	0.85
1-1/2	140	33	1,904	36.8	1,625	0.86
2	145	35	1,914	37.0	1,634	0.86
14-1/2	167	46	3,220	62.3	3,053	0.95
15	170	46	3,353	64.9	3,206	0.96
15-1/2	176	47	3,414	66.0	3,329	0.97
16	180	47	3,474	67.2	3,503	1.02
16-1/2 End	188	48	3,691	71.4	3,862	1.04

medulla) and glucagon (from the pancreas) reduce the glycogen content of tissues such as the liver and muscle by stimulating its breakdown to glucose.

The release of noradrenaline (from the sympathetic nervous system) and adrenaline stimulate glycogen mobilization during exercise. Statements made by athletes referring to "a surge of adrenaline" and "getting the juices flowing" in a real sense have some truth to them and suggest the "fight, flight, or fright" syndrome that characterizes sympathetic nervous system activation. In addition to mobilizing glucose reserves through glycogen breakdown, these substances also raise the heart rate and blood pressure, thereby increasing blood flow to working tissues.

Glycogen breakdown occurs through the action of an enzyme called *phosphorylase*, as shown in Figure 1.34. Not all of the steps are shown, but the end result is the formation of glucose-1-PO$_4$. The phosphorylase enzyme typically exists in an inactive form. Its activation results from a rather complex series of chemical events. Any of three circulating blood substances—two hormones (adrenaline and glucagon) and noradrenaline from the sympathetic

nervous system—have the ability to interact with a specific enzyme located in cell membranes called *adenyl cyclase*. This interaction permits breakdown of intracellular ATP to a substance called *cyclic 3',5'-AMP*. Magnesium ions are also required for this reaction to proceed. Cyclic AMP in turn activates the phosphorylase enzyme, permitting cleavage of a glucose fragment from glycogen.

Continued supplies of adrenaline, glucagon, or noradrenaline will extend cyclic AMP production in both liver and muscle cells, providing both with supplies of glucose. However, there is an important basic difference between these two cell types in terms of how this glucose is utilized. In liver cells, glucose-1-PO$_4$ can either be metabolized completely to CO$_2$, H$_2$O, and ATP to satisfy the energy needs of the cell, or be converted back to free glucose (i.e., glucose unbound to PO$_4^{\equiv}$). This free glucose can diffuse out of the cell, whereas the phosphorylated form cannot. Thus, as illustrated in Figure 1.35, liver cells have two important enzymes, hexokinase and glucose-6-phosphatase. The former permits glucose to enter into cellular metabolic pathways, and the latter

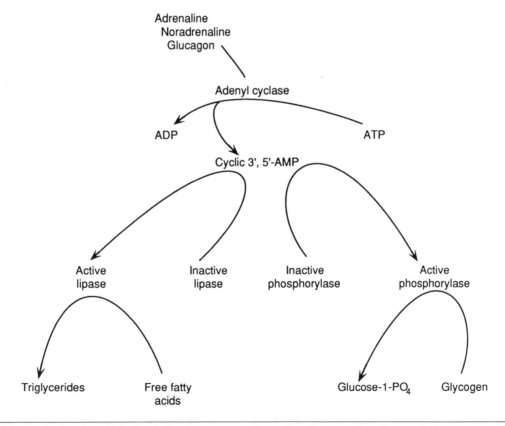

Figure 1.34 Mechanism by which circulating hormones, such as adrenaline, noradrenaline, and glucagon, can promote mobilization of both free fatty acids and glucose when required for energy metabolism. In each instance an inactive fuel breakdown enzyme is activated by the presence of cyclic 3', 5'-AMP, which in turn is produced by the action of adenyl cyclase on ATP. The three involved hormones when bound to adenyl cyclase permit this enzyme to function.

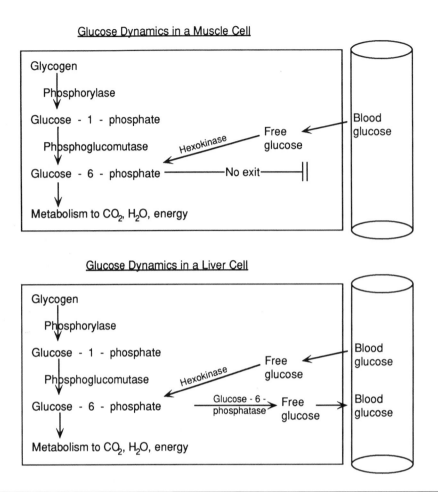

Figure 1.35 Glucose dynamics in muscle as compared to liver cells.

allows glucose the option of returning to the bloodstream. Once in the bloodstream, the glucose can be transported to muscle cells.

Muscle cells do not possess glucose-6-phosphatase and thus cannot release their glucose, when cleaved from glycogen, back into circulation. This situation creates an interesting dilemma. Glycogen reserves of nonworking muscles cannot be transferred to the working muscles, because once inside a muscle cell, glucose must remain there and be metabolized within that cell. Thus, in a long endurance event such as marathon running, a partial explanation why competitors often prefer courses with periodic slight elevation changes may be that the accompanying variation in muscle activation permits the sharing of glycogen reserves among a larger number of working muscles.

For every gram of glycogen stored, approximately 3.0 gm of H_2O are stored with it to maintain osmotic equilibrium (Costill & Miller, 1980). This contributes in part to the total weight gain as marathon runners taper for a race and continue their carbo-hydrate intake. In fact, such weight monitoring is done commonly by such athletes as they attempt to maximize their carbohydrate stores a few days prerace. As glycogen is metabolized during the race, this bound H_2O, together with the H_2O released from fuel breakdown, can serve as an important contribution to available body H_2O supplies. On a warm day, when H_2O is being lost from perspiration, this can be an asset.

Anaerobic Glycolysis: Breakdown of Glucose to Pyruvate

Both glycogen and glucose are metabolized in the fluid portion of cells—the cytoplasm, or as it is called in muscle, the sarcoplasm. The entire process, from breakdown of glycogen to glucose to pyruvic acid, can proceed without O_2 involvement; hence it is termed anaerobic. The term glycolysis refers to the portion of this metabolic pathway from glucose through pyruvate. The major chemical reactions involved in this conversion are summarized in Figure 1.36.

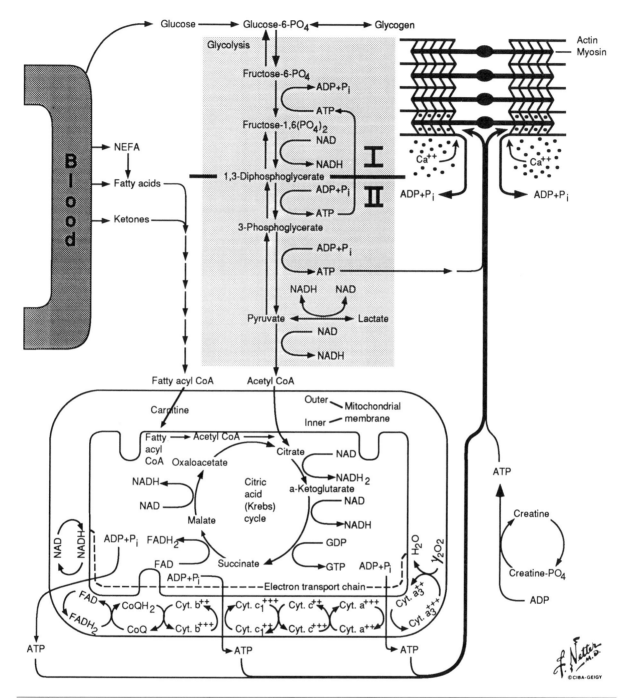

Figure 1.36 Outline of chemical reactions involved in breakdown of glucose and fatty acids for energy. For glucose, initial breakdown occurs in the cytoplasm (anaerobically), with eventual formation of small 2-carbon (acetyl) fragments that combine with Coenzyme A for entry into the mitochondria as acetyl-Coenzyme A. Some energy is released. Fatty acids, however, must first enter the mitochondria, where they then are cleaved into similar acetyl-Coenzyme A units. Each acetyl group can combine with oxalacetate to form citrate, which then is further degraded in a series of reactions collectively known as the citric acid (Krebs) cycle. Hydrogen atoms released by this breakdown sequence (or their corresponding electrons) are eventually transferred by way of the electron transport chain to oxygen. Energy released by this transfer is directed toward formation of ATP from ADP. In this manner, energy from fuel breakdown is available for crucial cellular functions such as tension generation in muscle cells, which utilizes energy stored as ATP. *Note.* From *Musculoskeletal System, Part I* (The Ciba Collection of Medical Illustrations, Vol. 8) (p. 162) by F.H. Netter, 1987, Summit, NJ: CIBA-GEIGY. Reproduced with permission from the CIBA Collection of Medical Illustrations by Frank H. Netter, MD. All rights reserved.

Notice that we have divided glycolysis into two phases. The initial phase requires an input of ATP and eventually splits the 6-carbon-atom glucose molecule into two 3-carbon units. Each of these is then broken down to pyruvate, with generation of small quantities of ATP. We must subtract the energy input in this initial phase from the energy output obtained during the second phase to determine the net energy production. This is an interesting task, because there is a difference in the energy dynamics of glucose derived from muscle glycogen breakdown versus glucose derived from the liver and sent through the blood to that same muscle. Figure 1.37 illustrates this.

Marathoners, however, have some logistical problems regarding their energy dynamics, which will be discussed in chapter 5 in connection with their prerace training preparations.

In Phase I of glycolysis shown in Figure 1.36, notice the substance labeled *NAD*, permitting conversion of 3-phosphoglyceraldehyde to 1,3-diphosphoglycerate. This substance is called *nicotinamide adenine dinucleotide* (NAD), and its structure is outlined in Figure 1.25. Biochemists call it a coenzyme, of which several can be identified. Notice that an integral part of its structure is nicotinic acid; this is vitamin B_5. We shall see that several water-soluble vitamins are essential to the success of glucose metabolism. This supports the need for adequate dietary vitamin intake. The oxidized form of NAD is required to catalyze the reaction that produces 1,3-diphosphoglycerate. In the process, NAD is reduced (or hydrogenated); this is written as $NADH_2$. Under aerobic conditions, O_2 eventually permits the removal of H^+ ions from this coenzyme, regenerating NAD and permitting more substrate (glucose) breakdown to occur. Thus, adequate O_2 implies adequate NAD, which permits continuing glycolysis.

But we know that glycolysis can occur anaerobically. How do we produce NAD in the absence of adequate O_2? The answer is relatively simple. Pyruvate already available is converted to lactate, using $NADH_2$ and the enzyme lactic dehydrogenase (LDH). The equation for this reaction is

Figure 1.37 gives:

Muscle cell -derived

Glycogen ⟶ glucose-1-PO_4 : no ATP needed

Glucose-1-PO_4 ⟶ pyruvate : one ATP needed

Glucose-1-PO_4 ⟶ pyruvate : 4 ATPs produced

Net gain: 3 ATPs

Liver cell -derived

Free glucose (from liver via blood) ⟶ glucose-1-PO_4 : one ATP needed

Glucose-1-PO_4 ⟶ pyruvate : one ATP needed

Glucose-1-PO_4 ⟶ pyruvate : 4 ATPs produced

Net gain: 2 ATPs

Figure 1.37 Summary of the energy dynamics of muscle-derived versus liver-derived glucose in metabolism.

$$
\begin{array}{ccc}
COO^- & & COO^- \\
| & \text{lactic dehydrogenase} & | \\
C{=}O & \rightleftharpoons & H{-}C{-}OH. \\
| & NADH_2 \quad NAD & | \\
CH_3 & & CH_3 \\
\text{pyruvate} & & \text{lactate}
\end{array}
$$

(1.15)

When glucose *within* a muscle cell is obtained from glycogen, one ATP is required to provide energy and initiate the breakdown process. Enough energy to create four ATPs will be generated. The net gain is three ATPs. Glucose *entering* a muscle cell from the liver via the blood requires two ATPs to initiate breakdown, with four ATPs again generated. This is a net gain of only two ATPs. The implication of this is that, for purposes of metabolic efficiency, muscle cells should rely on their own stored glycogen instead of on glucose mobilized from the liver. Indeed, for distance races through 21,000m, and for training runs under 18 mi (29 km), this is not a problem, because muscle glycogen stores are more than adequate.

This, then, is the biochemical reasoning that can explain lactate production in muscles when O_2 supplies are inadequate. It provides a mechanism for NAD production, which in turn allows glycolysis to continue. The LDH enzyme occurs in two forms, depending upon location. In the heart, as well as in ST skeletal muscles, the so-called H-LDH isoenzyme (H for heart) exists, and its action shifts the direction of the reaction toward the left, thereby minimizing lactate formation. In FT skeletal muscles, the so-called M-LDH isoenzyme (M for muscle) favors a right-shifted equilibrium, thereby permitting more lactate to form.

Runners attempting to race or train at near-maximum velocities over distances between 200 m and 800 m cannot continue for very long at those paces. Despite the excellent adaptations with training for aerobic metabolism (increased myoglobin and hemoglobin for O_2 storage and transport, increased capillarization, increased CO_2 excretion and acid buffering, and increased reservoirs of high-energy $PO_4^{\equiv}$), O_2 demand still exceeds O_2 supply. Anaerobic metabolism adds to the total energy supply available, but the process is both inefficient and self-limiting. How is this process inefficient? Recall Equations 1.8 and 1.10, which indicate that anaerobic metabolism of glucose requires 18 times more substrate than aerobic metabolism to produce an equivalent amount of ATP.

How is it self-limiting? As the acidity within working muscle cells increases, the functional capability of certain key glycolytic enzymes decreases, thereby slowing the rate of fuel breakdown. This is a safety mechanism to prevent cell destruction. Should acidosis become excessive, it could be catastrophic for muscle cell activity due to the presence of intracellular organelles called *lysosomes*. These contain a variety of enzymes capable of causing digestion of the muscle cells themselves. Their outer membrane is unstable under acidic conditions. If rupture occurs, cell death will result. Thus, anaerobic metabolism must be a powerfully self-limiting process that shuts itself off when it produces such "environmental" pollution that its own existence is threatened.

The need for such an all-powerful inhibition is obvious when we observe runners in events such as the 400m dash and the 800m run, particularly the final stages. They struggle valiantly to maintain pace, more than willing to endure almost any amount of discomfort if it will assure victory. Gradual inhibition of metabolism in their prime movers brings an inevitable slowing of pace unless other accessory muscles can be implemented to provide additional energy output. This is often seen as they start to toe out, thereby utilizing some leg muscles that still have aerobic capabilities. Biomechanically this may not appear very stylish, but it just may make the difference between winning and losing. If these runners didn't have metabolic inhibition to shut down their excessively acidotic cells, extensive cell death and dissolution of their leg muscles could occur. Indeed, this does occur in certain pathological situations and is termed *rhabdomyolysis*.

Are there any precautions athletes can take prior to beginning their intensive training sessions or races to manage excessive muscle acidity? There certainly are, and one of them is the familiar prerun *warm-up*, defined as a period prior to more intense activity when mild exercise is performed. Along with cool-down following hard work, warm-up is another necessary step in the energy continuum. Enzymes work optimally at temperatures slightly above our normal core temperature of about 37 degrees C (98 degrees F). Initial easy jogging, with transition into faster but still easy running, raises metabolism, and thus body temperature, and improves circulation. Not only is enzyme-controlled fuel breakdown enhanced, but the muscles also improve their elasticity, permitting greater range of joint movement.

Aerobic Glucose Metabolism

If glucose metabolism is to continue beyond the formation of pyruvate and lactate with eventual release of large amounts of energy, then adequate O_2 must be available. Also, because the majority of these chemical reactions will occur in the mitochondria, pyruvate must be transported across the mitochondrial membrane. Let us examine how this occurs (see Figures 1.36 and 1.38).

Instead of being converted to lactate, pyruvate is degraded further to a metabolic fragment called an *acetyl group*, with a loss of CO_2 in the process. This acetyl group combines with a molecule called Coenzyme A, forming *acetyl Coenzyme A*. Figure 1.25 illustrates the structure of this coenzyme, and its resemblance both to NAD and ATP can be seen. All three molecules have adenine coupled to a sugar called ribose. NAD and Coenzyme A have vitamins attached to the sugar—NAD has nicotinic acid and Coenzyme A has pantothenic acid (vitamin B_3). In Figure 1.38 the acetyl group of pyruvate is circled, allowing us to observe how Coenzyme A participates in transferring this group to oxalacetic acid (oxalacetate), forming citric acid (citrate). Coenzyme A thus serves to transfer cytoplasmic glucose fragments into the mitochondria without itself being altered. The renowned British biochemist Sir Hans Krebs first delineated the complete set of reactions whereby citrate is subsequently broken down to oxalacetate, permitting a repetitive cycle whereby additional acetyl groups from pyruvate can be utilized to form more citrate (Krebs, 1970). This series of reactions is commonly referred to as the *Krebs cycle* or *citric acid cycle*.

Through subsequent degradation involving several intermediate steps indicated in Figure 1.36, the 2-carbon acetyl group is degraded to CO_2 and H^+ ions. Each step is enzymatically controlled, and no O_2 is consumed directly in the process. For glucose, eight H^+ ions are generated (four for each 2-carbon acetyl group). The steps in which H^+ ions are removed are called dehydrogenation steps. Notice that NAD serves as the hydrogen acceptor in three of them. In the fourth, FAD does this. FAD is *flavin adenine dinucleotide*, a relative of NAD except that still another vitamin, riboflavin (B_2), is substituted for

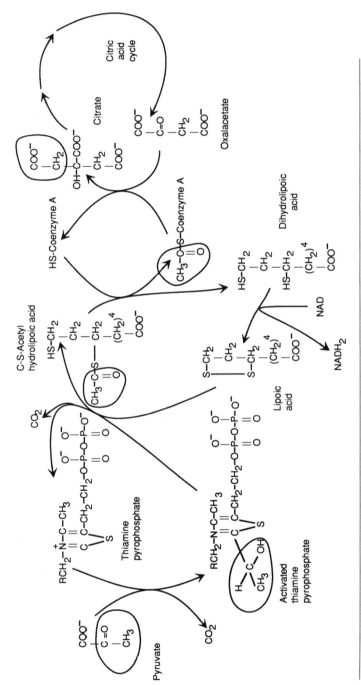

Figure 1.38 Chemical reaction sequence for transporting the acetyl group of pyruvic acid into mitochondria for linking to the citric acid cycle and further breakdown.

nicotinamide. Figure 1.25 depicts the structure of FAD.

Four important points are appropriate concerning this Krebs cycle reaction sequence. First, O_2 plays only an indirect role, because its presence in the cell permits oxidation of $NADH_2$ to NAD (through removal of 2 H^+ ions to form H_2O). Without the existence of NAD, permitting conversion of dihydrolipoic acid to lipoic acid (lipoate), acetyl Coenzyme A production could not occur (Figure 1.38). Second, this series of reactions is the connecting link between the anaerobic and aerobic aspects of carbohydrate breakdown. Metabolism of glucose through the formation of acetyl Coenzyme A occurs in the cell cytoplasm, but further degradation of the acetyl group can occur only in mitochondria.

Third, note that this reaction sequence, from pyruvate to acetyl Coenzyme A, marks the first instance where a glucose-derived carbon atom is lost (in the form of CO_2). Thus, this sequence is irreversible and for that reason alone exceedingly important. This is a key transition from a biochemical viewpoint in terms of glucose utilization. Fourth, notice in Figure 1.38 that an additional vitamin, thiamine (B_1), plays a vital role in this sequence by mediating the transfer of the acetyl group of pyruvate to lipoate.

A comment is germane at this point concerning vitamins. These are organic substances that the body cannot synthesize but that are required for metabolic reactions. We have, through evolution, lost the genes required for their synthesis, and thus they must be ingested as part of our normal food intake pattern. The **minimum daily requirement** (MDR) is the quantity of each of these essential nutrients required to permit normal physiological function without signs of deficiency. The **recommended dietary allowance** (RDA) is the level of daily intake considered in the judgment of members of the U.S. Food and Nutrition Board as adequate to meet the known nutritional needs of practically all healthy persons. RDA values are usually higher than MDR values.

A common interest among exercise-conscious people is to ensure that they have enough vitamins. Fair enough, as they're important in metabolism. But how much is enough? Glowing testimonials by health food product manufacturers in over-the-counter fitness magazines suggest improved capability to train or race following the use of specific brands of megavitamin supplements or individual vitamin preparations available only from mail-order outlets or specialty shops often referred to as health food stores (Jarvis, 1983). Proprietors of such establishments argue for the people's right to freedom of choice and urge the correct choice (obviously, their specific product). The alternative, of course, is the more acceptable mode of

consuming nutritious fresh foods that have plenty of vitamins in wide variety, along with other essentials such as energy fuels, H_2O, and trace elements.

Because metabolism proceeds in a precise fashion, specific quantities of each vitamin are required. Water-soluble vitamins, such as the B series described previously, that are ingested through megadose supplementation but are not required in such excess will be excreted through the urine. This seems a waste of money. In terms of the B vitamins, excellent non-manufactured sources include green leafy vegetables, nuts, and yeast. This explains why many so-called health food stores emphasize specialized mixtures of yeasts or nuts and seeds. The cost of these mixtures typically exceeds that of equally excellent and tasty sources of these vitamins such as a tossed salad of fresh vegetables obtained from a local grocery store or farmer's market (both of which, incidentally, also are "health food stores").

There is no sensible justification for megavitamin ingestion in terms of performance enhancement (Weight, Myburgh, & Noakes, 1988). Even athletes devoting several hours each day to their training do not require as much nutrition or energy as is often suspected. A marathon run by a 132-lb (60 kg) runner requires approximately 2,600 kcal (10,880 kJ), roughly equivalent to that individual's daily energy requirement without training. In other words, that runner has gained a day's requirement in meals. True, this is a sizably increased energy requirement. But we are dealing with perhaps twice the normal required vitamin intake, not the many-times-greater-than-RDA often provided in megavitamin preparations. And seldom do runners engage in the equivalent of a marathon's energy requirement in a day's training. The suggestion is often made that large supplemental vitamin ingestion may be required if an athlete is so busy that meals are skipped. This practice in itself should be reevaluated in terms of priorities. Adequate nutritional intake is essential if supplies of energy fuels, minerals, and vitamins are to be maintained. Nutritious and tasty meals are both essential and enjoyable and assure proper food balance. They should be a top priority for any athlete; this is an important (and delightful) part of the training process.

Electron Transport Chain

Although the Krebs cycle indeed describes the fate of the carbon skeleton of the acetyl portion of pyruvate, the cycle itself is not concerned directly with the mechanism of energy conservation. This involves the H^+ ions (with their electrons) that have been gathered up and bound to NAD or FAD (Figure 1.36). These reduced molecules, $NADH_2$ and $FADH_2$, will donate their electrons to another series of enzymes, collectively termed the *electron transport chain*, illustrated at the bottom of Figure 1.36. This is the final common pathway by which energy derived from the various cellular fuels—fatty acids, carbohydrates, and even proteins—is harvested, ultimately through interaction with O_2, the final oxidant or electron acceptor in aerobic cells. This phase of fuel breakdown is thus the "financial end" of the business of cellular metabolism, for this is where the metabolic currency (ATP) is produced.

The complex sequence of reactions in the electron transport system involves several molecules of quite diverse structure, of which only a few are illustrated in Figure 1.36. A group of proteins, known collectively as cytochromes and abbreviated as *cyt*, have a molecular similarity to hemoglobin; one important difference is in the oxidation state of iron within their molecular structure. In hemoglobin, iron exists in the ferrous (Fe^{++}) state, but in cytochromes it is in the ferric (Fe^{+++}) state. Each cytochrome in its oxidized form (i.e., with Fe^{+++}) can accept an electron from a hydrogen atom and become reduced (Fe^{+++} becomes Fe^{++}). The hydrogen atom becomes a H^+ ion and thus contributes to the acidity of the medium. In turn, this cytochrome can then donate its electron to the next carrier in its oxidized form, and so on, almost as with the children's game of tossing a hot potato. Notice, for example, how cytochrome b^{+++} transfers an electron to cytochrome c_1^{++}, forming cytochrome c_1^{+++} and cytochrome b^{++}. The final cytochrome, called cytochrome a_3^{+++} or cytochrome oxidase, gives up its electron to molecular O_2 directly. As two electrons attach to an oxygen atom, two H^+ ions also bind, and H_2O forms as a result. Each electron transfer releases considerable free energy, which is harvested as ATP. Figure 1.36 represents only a simplified version of a much more complex system. As well as the cytochrome pigments, other substances (one of which is indicated as Coenzyme Q [CoQ]), including FAD and NAD as well, are involved.

We may now write an energy balance sheet for glucose oxidation, as shown in Figure 1.39, and summarize how much energy is produced and from where, in the overall metabolic pathway (Figure 1.36). We need 2 ATPs to initiate glycolysis, and 4 ATPs are recovered. Four hydrogen atoms are released in the anaerobic phase of glycolysis, bound as $NADH_2$. For every two hydrogen atoms carried, 3 ATPs are produced if delivery into the electron transport system is via NAD. Thus, these four hydrogen atoms yield 6 ATPs of energy. Four hydrogen atoms are released in the transfer of pyruvate to Coenzyme A; this yields 6 ATPs because NAD is again the carrier. In the Krebs cycle, six sets of two hydrogen atoms are released to NAD, yielding 18 ATPs. Two sets of hydrogen atoms are released to FAD, and here only 4 ATPs are generated (2 ATPs per hydrogen atom pair). Thus, the Krebs cycle production of ATP is 11 ATPs per acetyl group, or 22 ATPs per mole of glucose. The processes preceding the Krebs cycle produce 16 ATPs, with 2 ATPs lost in sequence initiation. The net ATP production, therefore, tallies $22 + 16 - 2 = 36$.

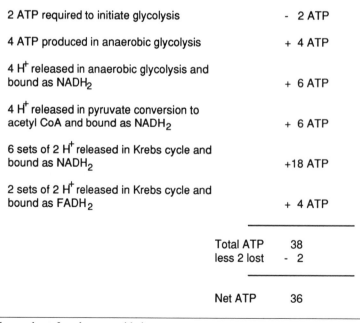

2 ATP required to initiate glycolysis	- 2 ATP
4 ATP produced in anaerobic glycolysis	+ 4 ATP
4 H^+ released in anaerobic glycolysis and bound as $NADH_2$	+ 6 ATP
4 H^+ released in pyruvate conversion to acetyl CoA and bound as $NADH_2$	+ 6 ATP
6 sets of 2 H^+ released in Krebs cycle and bound as $NADH_2$	+18 ATP
2 sets of 2 H^+ released in Krebs cycle and bound as $FADH_2$	+ 4 ATP
Total ATP	38
less 2 lost	- 2
Net ATP	36

Figure 1.39 Energy balance sheet for glucose oxidation.

Metabolism of Fat as a Fuel

We have thus far emphasized carbohydrate metabolism, and we must realize that we have accomplished only part of the task of providing energy for metabolism. Far less stored energy is available in carbohydrates than in fats, which provide the mainstay of energy supply for the entire continuum ranging from rest through marathon racing and beyond. Trained skeletal muscles, just as cardiac muscles, have more stored fats, fat-metabolizing enzymes (the same Krebs cycle enzymes that break down glucose), and more as well as larger mitochondria. The higher the potential for fatty acid oxidation in muscle, the better the endurance performance capacity of that muscle. In the heart this capacity is enormous.

Glycogen and triglycerides have a similar initial pattern of catabolism. An activated phosphorylase and lipase, respectively, interacts with cyclic 3',5'-AMP to initiate the fuel breakdown sequence (Figure 1.34). Fatty acids released by this process must then enter the mitochondria for subsequent catabolism. Movement across the double mitochondrial membrane requires coupling to a substance called *carnitine*. This occurs in a three-step process. First, coupling of acetyl Coenzyme A to the fatty acid molecule produces a *fatty acyl-Coenzyme A*, which crosses the outer mitochondrial membrane (Figure 1.36). Then, the enzyme carnitine acyltransferase I exchanges carnitine for Coenzyme A, forming *fatty acyl-carnitine*. This crosses the inner mitochondrial membrane. Finally, carnitine acyltransferase II exchanges carnitine for intramitochondrial Coenzyme A, re-forming fatty acyl-Coenzyme A. The coupling of carnitine to fatty acyl-Coenzyme A is thus the rate-limiting step for the speed of fatty acid oxidation. This may also explain why endurance-trained runners have more carnitine in their skeletal muscles—it indicates a greater adaptation to their ability for utilizing fatty acids as fuel (de Palo et al., 1986).

Now, a systematic, enzyme-directed cleavage of 2-carbon units begins from the multicarbon fatty acid skeleton. This reaction sequence is called *beta oxidation*, because cleavage occurs at the second (beta) carbon instead of the first (alpha). With the 16-carbon palmitic acid, for example, seven cleavages of acetyl groups would achieve complete breakdown. Each 2-carbon acetyl fragment combines with Coenzyme A inside the mitochondrion to form acetyl Coenzyme A (Figure 1.36). Interaction with oxalacetate and formation of citrate, as with carbohydrate breakdown, permits eventual energy release in accordance with principles that we have already discussed regarding the Krebs cycle and electron transport chain.

Reciprocal Regulation of Fatty Acid and Carbohydrate Metabolism

At rest, fats are our dominant energy source, with carbohydrates playing only a minor role. Because we take in plenty of O_2 for our metabolic needs, fuel breakdown is completely aerobic. Fatty acids cannot be metabolized without sufficient O_2 to guarantee complete breakdown. When we begin to exercise and encounter situations in which O_2 demand exceeds O_2 supply, what causes the shift in emphasis toward carbohydrate metabolism? The answer lies in a kind of reciprocal regulation: Each fuel regulates the other. The complete explanation is complex, but a few of the major concepts can be mentioned. One primary regulator of glucose metabolism resides in available quantities of citrate. Ongoing fatty acid metabolism provides ample quantities of citrate, which has an inhibitory effect on the activity of a key glycolytic enzyme, phosphofructokinase. This keeps glycolysis proceeding at a low level and explains the usual dominance of fatty acid metabolism.

As we start exercise, an initial brief period of hypoxia develops in the working skeletal muscles because the increase in circulation does not quite parallel the immediate increase in elevated O_2 requirements. Some anaerobic metabolism occurs, with lactate formation and an increasing tissue acidity. This developing intracellular acidosis decreases the activity of the carnitine acyl-transferase enzyme. For a brief period, a decrease in citrate occurs as fewer acetyl groups from fatty acid breakdown are available for combination with oxalacetate to form citrate. Because citrate level regulates glycolysis, this brief decrease in citrate supply removes the inhibition of glucose breakdown, permitting it to increase. Hypoxia also increases the activity of phosphorylase, increasing breakdown of additional glucose units from glycogen. It also increases the activity of hexokinase, increasing the rate of conversion of free glucose to glucose-6-PO_4.

Running velocity and length of time that this velocity can be maintained are related inversely. Running too fast for too long soon begins to limit continued performance at that pace. The H^+ ions from excessive lactate accumulation also inhibit the action of phosphofructokinase, thereby decreasing glycolysis. These H^+ ions also compete with Ca^{++} ions for the binding sites that regulate actin-myosin interaction (Katz, 1970). Thus, although H^+ ions seem to be "metabolic monsters" in causing such inhibition of fuel breakdown, their presence is beneficial from several points of view. By slowing the rate of metabolism, they keep acidity levels above the critical point where lysosome-mediated cell destruction could occur. Also, they directly inhibit smooth muscle tone in adjacent arterioles delivering blood to the region, thereby enhancing perfusion and with it the distribution of fuel, O_2, and buffers.

SUMMARY

1. Running is one of our fundamental movement patterns, practiced from childhood, improved upon in terms of biomechanical efficiency during our growing years, and refined so well that as adults we usually take an optimum combination of stride frequency and stride length that gives us the greatest gains (in movement) for the least cost (in metabolic energy). Thus, mature athletes interested in becoming competitively competent performers find it functionally more useful to concentrate on improving their fitness than on improving their biomechanics. Understanding some of the principles of the biomechanics of running provides an avenue for communication with experts who can provide advice on optimizing strengths and minimizing weaknesses for improved performance with less risk of injury.

2. The details of which muscles we use as we complete the two strides (landing on each foot) that comprise a running cycle have been reasonably well worked out and are briefly described. As we run faster, we impact on the ground with greater force, causing more stress on the entire musculoskeletal system. It thus becomes the challenge of a proper training plan to improve the performance capabilities of these tissues.

3. To ensure an intelligent approach to the application of a training stress on those tissues most susceptible to injury—namely the muscles, and in part also the connective tissues—a decent understanding of their structure and function is appropriate. An appreciation for muscle structure at both the gross and microscopic levels, as well as the mechanism by which tension is generated, has been described. The adaptations that various kinds of training bring to the different skeletal muscle cell types (slow-twitch fibers and the two major forms of fast-twitch fibers) have also been outlined.

4. From a metabolic (biochemical) point of view, we are not adapted for the rigors of competition over the middle and long distances, although we do have the capability of completing such distances without much specialized training when time for completion is unimportant. Thus, to "go the distance" faster and faster, we must indulge in specific activities, called training, that will make it biochemically more feasible for the winning desires of athletes to be approached. More work must be done in a smaller unit of time if one is to race more effectively. The energy currency for muscular work is ATP (one mole of which represents about 46 kJ, or 11 kcal of energy). ATP is provided in several ways, depending upon the intensity with which training or competitive work is carried out. Some of these energy dynamics were discussed.

5. Short bursts of high-speed sprinting, lasting for about 20 sec, can be managed entirely by available stores of creatine phosphate in the muscles. These stores will be replenished during this brief space of time by ATP without the need for other types of metabolism. Such explosiveness, however, is more in the world of sprinting than in middle- and long-distance running.

6. Work at high intensity carried out over a longer time period—that is, between 20 sec and about 8 min—demands more energy than can be provided by complete (aerobic) fuel metabolism. In other words, the energy requirements are far greater than can be met by the intake of O_2 to provide complete fuel breakdown. The O_2 consumption for racing distances such as 200 m to 400 m, for example, is in excess of 100 ml/kg/min. The primary fuel supply for work loads approaching and exceeding $\dot{V}O_2$max intensity is carbohydrate. However, this process is extremely fuel-consumptive and self-limiting because of the effects of acidosis. As racing distances lengthen from 800 m through 10,000 m, acid accumulation

again slows performance, but it becomes increasingly more feasible to provide O_2 supplies that approach requirements. Adequate muscle glycogen and triglyceride are available for fuels, as well as blood glucose. The longer the distance, the slower the maximum pace that can be maintained, because we must rely more and more on complete (aerobic) metabolism that minimizes H^+ ion accumulation. Fat metabolism assumes greater and greater importance, as does adequate provision of O_2.

7. The purpose of training, then, is to improve the ability of muscle cells to manage (buffer) the effects of acidosis, and to increase O_2 utilization so that, at any particular pace, the anaerobic contribution is smaller than before. How we manage to shift the relative dominance between these various fuel sources to match the energy requirements at particular performance intensities requires a good basic knowledge of the principles of fuel breakdown by the body. The essentials of this topic were discussed.

8. Long-term adaptation through training and short-term increases in stored fuels by a combination of rest with continued fuel intake should provide increased abilities to produce energy. A thorough process of warm-up before exercise should increase muscle circulation gradually and adequately to ensure that an elevated level of metabolism is already occurring prior to the assigned work load (be it training or competition). This should provide an environment for both fat and carbohydrate metabolism in a ratio appropriate to the intensity of the competitive or training effort. Similarly, when training is completed, a period of easy running to begin the process of restoring metabolic equilibrium (perfusion of stressed muscles with nutrition for energy replenishment and O_2 for complete metabolism of anaerobic metabolites such as lactate) quickens recovery. An optimum combination of training, prerace preparation, and race plan, then, is a good example of better living through chemistry.

REFERENCES

Adelaar, R.S. (1986). The practical biomechanics of running. *American Journal of Sports Medicine*, **14**, 497-500.

Barany, M., & Close, R.I. (1971). The transformation of myosin in cross-innervated rat muscle. *Journal of Physiology*, **213**, 455-474.

Beck, M. (1966). The path of the center of gravity during running in boys grade one to six. Unpublished doctoral dissertation, University of Wisconsin, Madison.

Brodal, P., Ingjer, F., & Hermansen, L. (1977). Capillary supply of skeletal muscle fibers in untrained and endurance-trained men. *American Journal of Physiology*, **232**, H705-H712.

Brooke, M.H., & Engel, W.K. (1969). The histographic analysis of human muscle biopsies with regard to fiber types. I. Adult males and females. *Neurology*, **19**, 221-233.

Brooke, M.H., & Kaiser, K.K. (1970). Muscle fiber types: How many and what kind? *Archives of Neurology*, **23**, 369-379.

Buller, A.J., Eccles, J.C., & Eccles, R.M. (1960). Interaction between motoneurones and muscles in respect of the characteristic speeds of their response. *Journal of Physiology (London)*, **150**, 417-439.

Cavanagh, P.R., Andrew, G.C., Kram, R., Rodgers, M.M., Sanderson, D.J., & Hennig, E.M. (1985). An approach to biomechanical profiling of distance runners. *The International Journal of Sports Biomechanics*, **1**, 36-62.

Cavanagh, P.R., Kram, R. (1990). Stride length in distance running: Velocity, body dimensions, and added mass effects. In P.R. Cavanagh (Ed.), *Biomechanics of Distance Running* (pp. 35-60). Champaign, IL: Human Kinetics.

Cavanagh, P.R., Pollock, M.L., & Landa, J. (1977). A biomechanical comparison of elite and good distance runners. *Annals of the New York Academy of Sciences*, **301**, 328-345.

Close, R.I. (1969). Dynamic properties of fast and slow skeletal muscle after nerve cross-union. *Journal of Physiology*, **204**, 331-346.

Costill, D.L., Bowers, R., Branam, G., & Sparks, K. (1971). Muscle glycogen utilization during prolonged exercise on consecutive days. *Journal of Applied Physiology*, **31**, 834-838.

Costill, D.L., Fink, W.J., Flynn, M., & Kirwan, J. (1987). Muscle fiber composition and enzyme activities in elite female distance runners. *International Journal of Sports Medicine*, **8**, 103-106.

Costill, D.L., & Miller, J.M. (1980). Nutrition for endurance sport: Carbohydrate and fluid balance. *International Journal of Sports Medicine*, **1**, 2-14.

de Palo, E., de Palo, C., Macor, C., Gatti, R., Federspil, G., & Scandellari, C. (1986). Plasma free fatty acid, carnitine and acetylcarnitine levels as useful biochemical parameters in muscular exercise. In G. Benzi, L. Packer, & N. Siliprandi (Eds.), *Biochemical aspects of physical exercise* (pp. 461-467). Amsterdam: Elsevier Science.

Deschenes, M. (1989). Short review: Rate coding and motor unit recruitment patterns. *Journal of Applied Sport Science Research*, **3**, 34-39.

Eccles, J.C., Eccles, R.M., & Kozak, W. (1962). Further investigations on the influence of motoneurones on the speed of muscle contraction. *Journal of Physiology*, **163**, 324-339.

Edstrom, L., & Nystrom, B. (1969). Histochemical types and sizes of fibers in normal human muscles. *Acta Neurologica Scandinavica*, **45**, 257-269.

Fink, W.J., Costill, D.L., & Pollock, M.L. (1977). Submaximum and maximum working capacity of elite distance runners. Part II. Muscle fiber composition and enzyme activities. *Proceedings of the New York Academy of Sciences*, **301**, 323-327.

Gladden, L.B. (1989). Lactate uptake by skeletal muscle. *Exercise and Sports Sciences Reviews*, **17**, 115-155.

Gollnick, P., Armstrong, R., Saubert, C., Piehl, K., & Saltin, B. (1972). Enzyme activity and fiber composition in skeletal muscle of untrained and trained men. *Journal of Applied Physiology*, **33**, 312-319.

Gollnick, P.D., & Hodgson, D.R. (1986). The identification of fiber types in skeletal muscle: A continual dilemma. *Exercise and Sports Sciences Reviews*, **14**, 81-104.

Gollnick, P.D., & Matoba, H. (1984). The muscle fibre composition of muscle as a predictor of athletic success. *American Journal of Sports Medicine*, **12**, 212-217.

Gregor, R.J. (1989). The structure and function of skeletal muscles. In P.J. Rasch (Ed.), *Kinesiology and applied anatomy* (7th ed., pp. 32-47). Philadelphia: Lea & Febiger.

Henatsch, H.-D., & Langer, H.H. (1985). Basic neurophysiology of motor skills in sport: A review. *International Journal of Sports Medicine*, **6**, 2-14.

Henriksson, J., & Reitman, J.S. (1976). Quantitative measure of enzyme activities in type I and type II muscle fibers of man after training. *Acta Physiologica Scandinavica*, **97**, 392-397.

Holloszy, J.O. (1967). Biochemical adaptation in muscle. Effects of exercise on mitochondrial oxygen uptake and respiratory enzyme activity in skeletal muscle. *Journal of Biological Chemistry*, **242**, 2278-2282.

Holloszy, J.O., & Coyle, E.F. (1984). Adaptation of skeletal muscles to endurance exercise and their metabolic consequences. *Journal of Applied Physiology*, **56**, 831-838.

Hoppeler, H., Luthi, P., Claassen, H., Weibel, E.R., & Howald, H. (1973). The ultrastructure of the normal human skeletal muscle. A morphometric analysis on untrained men, women, and well-trained orienteers. *Pflugers Archiv für die gesamte Physiologie*, **344**, 217-232.

Huxley, H.E., & Hanson, J. (1954). Changes in the cross-striations of muscle during contraction and stretch and their structural interpretation. *Nature*, **173**, 973-976.

Huxley, A.F., & Niedergerke, R. (1954). Structural changes in muscle during contraction. *Nature*, **173**, 971-973.

Ingjer, F. (1979). Effects of endurance training on muscle fibre ATPase inactivity, capillary supply and mitochondrial content in man. *Journal of Physiology*, **294**, 419-432.

James, S.L., & Brubaker, C.E. (1972). Running mechanics. *Journal of the American Medical Association*, **221**, 1014-1016.

Jarvis, W.T. (1983). Food: faddism, cultism, and quackery. *Annual Review of Nutrition*, **52**, 3-35.

Kaggestad, J. (1987). So trainiert Ingrid Kristiansen 1986. *Leichtathletik*, **38**, 831-834.

Karlsson, J. (1986). Muscle exercise, energy metabolism and blood lactate. *Advances in Cardiology*, **35**, 35-46.

Katz, A.M. (1970). Contractile proteins of the heart. *Physiological Reviews*, **50**, 63-158.

Komi, P.V., Viitasalo, J.H.T., Havu, M., Thorstensson, A., Sjodin, B., & Karlsson, J. (1977). Skeletal muscle fibers and muscle enzyme activities in monozygous and dizygous twins of both sexes. *Acta Physiologica Scandinavica*, **100**, 385-392.

Krebs, H. (1970). The history of the tricarboxylic acid cycle. *Perspectives in Biology and Medicine*, **14**, 154-170.

Lehninger, A.L. (1982). *Principles of biochemistry*. New York: Worth.

Mann, R.A. (1982). Foot problems in adults. *Instructional Course Lectures*, **31**, 167-180.

Mann, R.A., Moran, G.T., & Dougherty, S.E. (1986). Comparative electromyography of the lower extremity in jogging, running, and sprinting. *The American Journal of Sports Medicine,* **14,** 501-510.

McDonagh, M.J.N., & Davies, C.T.M. (1984). Adaptive response of mammalian muscle to exercise with high loads. *European Journal of Applied Physiology,* **52,** 139-155.

Nadel, E.R. (1985). Physiological adaptation to aerobic exercise. *American Scientist,* **73,** 334-343.

Pattengale, P.K., & Holloszy, J.O. (1967). Augmentation of skeletal muscle myoglobin by a program of treadmill running. *American Journal of Physiology,* **213,** 783-785.

Peter, J.B., Barnard, R.J., Edgerton, V.R., Gillespie, C.A., & Stempel, K.E. (1972). Metabolic profiles of three fiber types of skeletal muscles in guinea pigs and rabbits. *Biochemistry,* **11,** 2627-2633.

Pette, D. (1984). Activity-induced fast to slow transitions in mammalian muscle. *Medicine and Science in Sports and Exercise,* **16,** 517-528.

Prince, F.P., Hikida, R.S., & Hagerman, F.C. (1976). Human muscle fiber types in power lifters, distance runners, and untrained subjects. *Pflugers Archiv,* **363,** 19-26.

Ranvier, L. (1873). Propriétés et structures différentes des muscles rouges et des muscles blancs chez les lapins et chez les raies. *Compte Rendu Hebdomadaire des Séances de l'Académie des Sciences (D) Paris,* **77,** 1030-1034.

Rice, C.L., Pettigrew, F.P., Noble, E.G., & Taylor, A.W. (1988). The fibre composition of skeletal muscle. *Medicine and Sport Science,* **27,** 22-39.

Rogers, M.A., Stull, G.A., & Apple, F.S. (1985). Creatine kinase isoenzyme activities in men and women following a marathon race. *Medicine and Science in Sports and Exercise,* **17,** 679-682.

Root, M.L., Orien, W.P., & Weed, J.H. (1977). *Normal and abnormal function of the foot* (p. 157). Los Angeles: Clinical Biomechanics Corp.

Sale, D.G., MacDougall, J.D., Upton, A.R.M., & McComas, A.J. (1983). Effect of strength training upon motoneuron excitability in man. *Medicine and Science in Sports and Exercise,* **15,** 57-62.

Saltin, B., & Gollnick, P.D. (1983). Skeletal muscle adaptability: Significance for metabolism and performance. In L.D. Peachey, R.H. Adrian, & S.R. Geiger (Eds.), *Handbook of physiology: Sec. 10. Skeletal muscle* (pp. 555-663). Washington, DC: American Physiological Society.

Saltin, B., Henriksson, J., Nygaard, E., & Andersen, P. (1977). Fiber type and metabolic potentials of skeletal muscles in sedentary man and endurance runners. *Annals of the New York Academy of Sciences,* **301,** 3-29.

Slocum, D.B., & Bowerman, W. (1962). The biomechanics of running. *Clinical Orthopedics,* **23,** 39-45.

Slocum, D.B., & James, S.L. (1968). Biomechanics of running. *Journal of the American Medical Association,* **205,** 721-728.

Stanton, P., & Purdam, C. (1989). Hamstring injuries in sprinting—the role of eccentric exercise. *Journal of Orthopaedic and Sports Physical Therapy,* **10,** 343-349.

Stipe, P. (1982). Scaling of body size and cushioning in running shoes. *NIKE Research Newsletter,* **1**(2), 3-4.

Taylor, C.R., & Weibel, E.R. (1981). Design of the mammalian respiratory system. I. Problem and strategy. *Respiration Physiology,* **44,** 1-10.

Thomas, C.L. (1989). *Tabor's cyclopedic medical dictionary* (16th ed.). Philadelphia: Lea & Febiger.

Weight, L.M., Myburgh, K.H., & Noakes, T.D. (1988). Vitamin and mineral supplementation: Effect on the running performance of trained athletes. *American Journal of Clinical Nutrition,* **47,** 192-195.

Whipp, B.J. (1987). Dynamics of pulmonary gas exchange. *Circulation,* 76(Suppl. 6), 18-28.

Whipple, G.H. (1926). The hemoglobin of striated muscle. I. Variations due to age and exercise. *American Journal of Physiology,* **76,** 693-707.

Williams, K.R., & Cavanagh, P.R. (1987). Relationship between distance running mechanics, running economy, and performance. *Journal of Applied Physiology,* **63,** 1236-1245.

Williams, K.R., Cavanagh, P.R., & Ziff, J.L. (1987). Biomechanical studies of elite female distance runners. *International Journal of Sports Medicine,* **8**(Suppl. 2), 107-118.

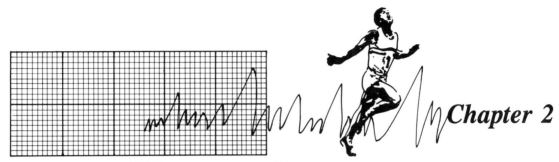

Heart, Lung, and Blood Dynamics During Exercise

Observing a group of elite distance runners warming up before an important race is much like seeing a diesel locomotive idling in a railroad yard, its 100 or so freight cars being connected in preparation for its next trip. There is no way that a person can really appreciate the enormous work capabilities of these two types of "engines" until we see them in action—runners competing at a near-world-record pace and the locomotive ascending a mountain grade with relative ease.

The primary organs involved in running are the heart and blood vessels, lungs, and blood flowing through the highly active tissues. They respond magnificently to the challenge of permitting high-intensity work to occur. The overall concept of the cardiopulmonary system involves a pump that can vary its output (the heart), and a given volume of fluid (the blood) that is contained within a space that can vary in its volume (the vascular capacity of the blood vessels). This blood interfaces with a gas exchanger (the lungs) each time it circulates through the body. The pressure on the blood vessel walls is determined by the existing blood volume and the variable muscle tone in those vessel walls. This tends to make the vascular capacity larger or smaller. Thus, blood flow, blood volume, blood gas (O_2 and CO_2) concentration, blood pressure, and blood distribution all exist within a framework of variability to meet ongoing needs and

cope with developing demands. Lung blood flow will increase along with lung ventilation, and the venous blood returning to the lungs from the rest of the body will exit the lungs almost fully oxygenated and free of excess CO_2.

We can begin to comprehend the magnitude of the performance increase from the idling to the competing state of an elite distance runner by comparing values for a few physiological variables at rest and during all-out exercise. One of the most impressive increases is in the amount of O_2 utilizable by the tissues. At rest this averages 3.5 ml per kilogram of body weight per minute; for a 60-kg athlete this is 210 ml/min. But this O_2 uptake can increase to as much as 85 ml/kg/min and more in highly trained male runners—more than 5 L/min. This so-called $\dot{V}O_2max$ for trained endurance athletes is more than twice that typically found among untrained people. Clearly, an enormously successful teamwork occurs among the various tissues identified previously to make possible this movement of O_2 from mouth to mitochondria. There is a functional coupling of external respiration (breathing O_2 into the body) with internal respiration (cellular O_2 utilization) in meeting the challenge of exercise (Wasserman, 1984). Breathing rate can increase to 45 or 50 breaths/min, compared with roughly 12 at rest. Total expired airflow can increase 30 times, from 6 to 180 L/min. Blood pumped out of the heart (the cardiac output) may increase eightfold, from 5 L/min at rest to more than 40 L/min in highly trained endurance athletes during maximum exercise (Ekblom & Hermansen, 1968). The working skeletal muscles may increase their bloodflow requirements from 20% of the output of the heart at rest to more than 85% during maximum exercise. Skeletal muscle blood flow may increase from 1.2 L/min to more than 22 L/min (Figure 2.1). This means that many other tissues, notably the viscera, will have blood shunted away from them; there just isn't enough to go around. But they still will receive sufficient flow so that their function will not be compromised.

Along with O_2 delivery to working muscles at rates that are as much as 20 times higher than at rest, the body must manage the dynamics of transporting all the products of metabolism. Two major types of metabolic acids result: volatile acids such as CO_2 (which is excreted as a gas via the lungs) and nonvolatile acids (the best example of which is lactate). Fuels need mobilization from storage sites in the liver and fat tissue, with transport through the bloodstream to supplement fuel reserves in the highly active working muscles. Finally, heat production will increase by as much as 100-fold, to 5,000 kJ/hr (1,194 kcal/hr) and higher. This must be eliminated, and primarily this occurs through evaporation of sweat, production of which can reach 2 L/hr. The other major source of heat loss is through convection from dilated skin surface blood vessels. Fluid losses through perspiration will be derived from body water everywhere but primarily from blood plasma. If sweat losses are excessive, the eventual decrease in blood volume can compromise effective tissue perfusion.

The ultimate goal of training is to increase the functional capacity of the organ systems most concerned with generating movement. Primarily these are cardiac and skeletal muscle tissues. We have already seen in chapter 1 how this functional capacity from a biochemical viewpoint involves the use of O_2 to permit complete fuel breakdown, with subsequent removal of the CO_2 produced and harnessing of energy as ATP. It becomes the integrated role of the lungs, blood, and blood vessels to satisfy the goal of getting the necessary O_2 and fuels to the skeletal muscles and heart for their use in generating movement and maintaining blood flow. The purpose of this chapter is to permit a better understanding of how these systems interact, how genetic endowment as well as the effect of proper training contribute to maximum performance abilities for improving athletic performance, and how these abilities can be measured and monitored using laboratory evaluation.

AEROBIC AND ANAEROBIC CONTRIBUTIONS TO PERFORMANCE

In chapter 1 we explained how, as we transition from rest to hard exercise, O_2 demands for complete metabolism in the working muscles are not always met with available O_2 supply. Let us now consider some of the metabolic and cardiopulmonary interactions that occur as an athlete proceeds through a continuum of activity starting from the resting level, increasing stepwise in intensity, and ending about 20 min later with voluntary cessation due to exhaustion and work load intolerance. This is often done using treadmill stress testing protocols. We will collect the expired air from this trained athlete for analysis of O_2 uptake and CO_2 production, and as well we will have an indwelling catheter inserted in an arm vessel from which we can collect small samples of blood for measurement of lactic acid as exercise proceeds. Finger-tip blood sampling and uphill running near the end of the test are often substituted for a vessel catheterization and a level-running protocol to satisfy athlete preference and yield higher $\dot{V}O_2$max values.

In Figure 2.2, on the horizontal axis is plotted running pace values to fit those within the ability level of our talented, trained male runner prepared for hard competition. After a pretest warm-up run, our athlete starts from a standing, resting situation (point P) and begins to run at what for him is an easy initial pace of 7:30/mi (4:40/km), which is a velocity of 215 m/min (12.9 km/hr). Note that coaches and athletes typically think of movement in terms of pace (the time elapsed in covering a specific distance), whereas scientists usually think in terms of velocity (distance traversed during a specific time period). His O_2 consumption at this pace, plotted along the vertical axis, is about 35 ml/kg/min, already ten times greater than at rest. Runners not quite so talented or fit would start their runs at a slower pace, but this sudden increase in energy requirement exists for them as well, so the same physiological response will occur. Through such a gradual but steadily increasing exercise protocol we can observe this runner's changing responses to progressive exercise, and note the paces at which these changes occur.

One response known to all athletes is that breathing, heart rate, and blood flow do not immediately speed up to ensure circulation to the working muscles sufficient for keeping metabolism completely aerobic. And movements are not as efficient as they will be later on. There is a time lag, represented by the distance between points P and Q, during which O_2

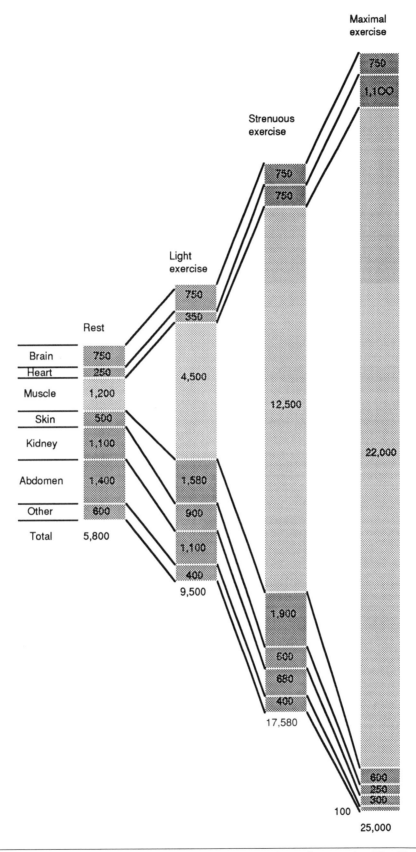

Figure 2.1 Redistribution of blood flow to working skeletal muscles with increasing exercise. Bloodflow in ml/min is shown for the various organs. *Note.* From "The Physiology of Exercise" by C.B. Chapman and J.H. Mitchell, 1965, *Scientific American*, **212**(5), p. 91. Copyright 1965 by Scientific American, Inc. Adapted by permission.

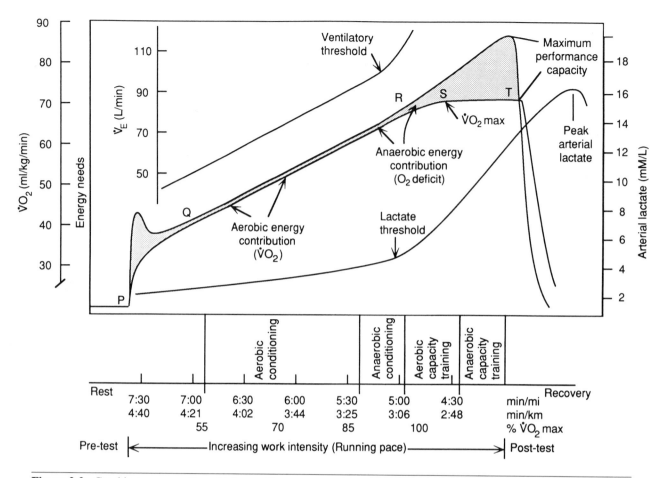

Figure 2.2 Graphic summary of aerobic/anaerobic energy provision, O₂ consumption, and blood lactic acid during a treadmill test of an elite male runner's performance abilities. The exercise intensity steadily increased until voluntary exhaustion at about 20 min. Starting pace was 7:30/mi (P). Initially, O₂ demand exceeded uptake, with anaerobic mechanisms providing needed energy. By Q aerobic metabolism was providing almost all required additional energy, and this continued until R. Aerobic metabolism could no longer match energy needs, and effects of increasing anaerobic metabolism were seen as more rapid blood lactate accumulation. V̇O₂max was reached a 4:35/mi pace (S), but additional work could be performed using more anaerobic reserves. When maximum work tolerance was reached (T), the test was stopped, with cooldown accompanied by continued elevated breathing and heart rates until recovery was complete. Blood lactate level peaked at about 5 min posttest.

demands are greater than O₂ supply. Anaerobic glycolysis in the skeletal muscles provides the additional required ATP-derived energy for this initially elevated activity. Recalling the essentials of anaerobic fuel metabolism from chapter 1, as glucose is catabolized to pyruvate, some of the accumulating H⁺ ions are available to convert pyruvate to lactate through interaction with lactic dehydrogenase (LDH) and NADH₂. At this relatively easy initial pace, primarily ST skeletal muscle fibers are utilized. LDH exists in two different isoenzyme forms. In ST muscle fibers the H-LDH isoenzyme form (H for heart) maintains the equilibrium shown here preferentially shifted toward pyruvate, which minimizes lactate formation and permits H⁺ ions to accumulate:

$$\text{Pyruvate} + \text{NADH}_2 \underset{\text{M-LDH}}{\overset{\text{H-LDH}}{\rightleftarrows}} \text{Lactate} + \text{NAD}. \tag{2.1}$$

Interestingly, it is the very presence of accumulating H⁺ ions that helps to initiate a marked increase in local blood flow to the working muscles and enhance their O₂ supply. Both H⁺ ions (from anaerobic glycolysis) and CO₂ (from mitochondrial oxidation) are potent inhibitors of smooth muscle tension generation in blood vessels. This action dilates the small local blood vessels, which increases local blood flow. Greater O₂ availability from increased circulation and breathing permits more aerobic metabolism. Removal of CO₂, lactate, and H⁺ ions helps to restore and maintain appropriate acid-base balance in the active tissues. Eventually, increases in circulation and respiration permit O₂ delivery to catch up with demand almost completely (point Q). It has been thought by some that the so-called **second-wind phenomenon**, which we may define as a sudden improvement in general comfort and ability to tolerate pace following several minutes of running, may correlate with initial achievement of this initial aerobic metabolic dominance (point Q), where external respiration now has caught up with internal respiration. No one really knows for sure.

Once our athlete has achieved a predominantly aerobic metabolic state in his working muscles, although he is still gradually quickening his pace, the work load increase is slow enough to permit a steady increase in O_2 uptake, circulation, and utilization to meet metabolic demands. A near-balance situation is achieved between acidic metabolite production and removal. CO_2 is excreted through the lungs and does not accumulate. Nearly all lactate is metabolized or converted back to glucose by other tissues, and during the range of pace increase from point Q to point R, blood lactate concentration will rise a small amount. Although both fatty acids and glucose are the major fuel sources, the latter is becoming increasingly important.

Eventually, the continuing pace increase results in a work load (point R) where again aerobic metabolism by itself can no longer meet the additional energy requirements. In part, this is caused by the increased recruitment of skeletal muscle fibers that are predominantly of the FT variety. These are specialized more for anaerobic than for aerobic metabolism, converting glucose rapidly to pyruvate. In these fibers, the M-LDH isoenzyme form (M for muscle) directs Equation 2.1 preferentially toward the right, permitting formation of additional lactate. At this exercise intensity (point R), blood lactate starts to accumulate at a faster rate because increased lactate production by working muscles and release into the blood is greater than its utilization (as a fuel) by other tissues. This can be termed the *lactate threshold*. Ongoing measurements of the increasing ventilation during exercise usually also show a change in ventilatory pattern here as well. In Figure 2.2, point R indicates this *ventilatory threshold* along with the lactate threshold. The change in breathing intensity at this workload can often be sensed by runners.

Despite these various metabolic changes with increasing pace, our athlete manages the situation well and continues to run faster and faster, eventually reaching his maximum O_2 power or $\dot{V}O_2max$ (point S). Although this work load is quite stressful, being similar to 5,000m race pace, if we continue to give him encouragement, and if he as well is possessed with good racing fitness and a desire to do his very best, he will be able to run even faster for as long as a minute or two. Anaerobic glycolysis now provides all of the additional energy requirements for whatever work load he can manage beyond point S, and blood lactate level rises exponentially. Voluntary exhaustion occurs at point T, and our athlete has completely "run out of reasons for running," achieving his maximum performance capacity.

Upon termination of this test run to voluntary exhaustion, our athlete quickly slows his pace to an easy jog for a cool-down, and recovery begins. Breathing and heart rate quickly return toward their resting levels but remain elevated for a variable period as metabolic recovery proceeds. This increased circulation provides O_2 to the working tissues that fell behind in their ability to completely metabolize their available fuels and also permits removal of CO_2. Blood lactate will continue to rise for about 5 minutes, and then start to fall (Gollnick, Bayly, & Hodgson, 1986). In chapter 1 we identified the benefits of such a cool-down following hard exercise, for maintaining an enhanced circulation to speed these recovery processes.

PHYSIOLOGICAL INDICATORS OF PERFORMANCE

We identified in Figure 2.2 three exercise intensities of physiologic significance. One of these, which we have termed the **maximum performance capacity**, is very easy to sense because it is the exercise termination point, but it is much less easy to quantify. It is the sum of the effects of maximum anaerobic metabolism superimposed on maximum aerobic metabolism. Continued anaerobic glycolysis occurs after $\dot{V}O_2max$ is achieved, and because $\dot{V}O_2max$ has plateaued, the additional increase in energy provision is solely from anaerobic sources, with the end product, lactate, diffusing out of the working muscle cells into the blood. This increased energy production by anaerobic glycolysis is as enormous as it is inefficient—18 times more fuel breakdown required than with aerobic glycolysis to produce the same amount of ATP. The rapid buildup of H^+ ions in muscle tissue, even though much of it can diffuse into the bloodstream, soon limits further effort. Margaria, Cerretelli, and Mangili (1964) reported that such exercise beyond the achievement of $\dot{V}O_2max$ could occur for no more than 30 to 40 sec, depending on fitness. Our experience with Olympic-caliber middle-distance runners evaluated close to their peak period of competition when they have enormous tolerance to the stress of intense anaerobic work suggests that this can exceed 2 min. When we consider techniques for fitness profiling, we shall identify some measured quantities that can help to describe the magnitude of this maximum performance capacity.

The other two exercise indicators of performance identified in Figure 2.2 are $\dot{V}O_2max$ and the lactate/

ventilatory threshold. These can be quantified rather easily in the laboratory, although they may not be so easily sensed. The interaction of the heart, lungs, blood vessels, and blood provides the transport capabilities for fuel and O_2 to the working muscles. The dynamics of this fuel and O_2 availability determine how large $\dot{V}O_2$max can become and at what work intensity the lactate/ventilatory threshold will occur. Before we discuss just how these organ systems adapt with training to increase $\dot{V}O_2$max and lactate/ventilatory threshold, it is appropriate to further describe these two important variables at least in general terms. When quantified, they can serve as the basis for defining appropriate training paces to further improve aerobic and anaerobic fitness.

Maximum Aerobic Power ($\dot{V}O_2$max)

$\dot{V}O_2$max functionally represents the maximum amount of oxygen that can be removed from circulating blood and used by the working tissues during a specified period (Mitchell & Blomqvist, 1971; Mitchell, Sproule, & Chapman, 1958). Whether the relationship between increasing O_2 consumption and running speed is linear or curvilinear has been a subject of great interest and varying opinion ever since the early experiments of Hill and Lupton in the 1920s. The studies of Rodolfo Margaria and his colleagues during the 1960s, showing that the submaximal aerobic energy demand for running was approximately 1 kcal per kilogram of body weight per kilometer of distance covered, provided a basis for estimating energy utilization for a variety of other activites. This was also the basis for the aerobic exercise programs popularized by Cooper (1968) for maintaining fitness and optimum body weight. Although Figure 2.2 illustrates a linearity in O_2 consumption with increasing submaximum work until $\dot{V}O_2$ max is reached, this by no means represents the final word. The American College of Sports Medicine (1986) has developed an equation for estimating the $\dot{V}O_2$ used at any given velocity while running over level ground, assuming that a linear relationship exists:

$$\dot{V}O_2 = (\text{velocity} \times 0.2) + 3.5, \qquad (2.2)$$

where $\dot{V}O_2$ is in ml/kg/min, velocity is in m/min, and 0.2 ml O_2/kg/min are consumed for every m/min increase in velocity. The value of 3.5 ml/kg/min represents the typical resting metabolic energy level without exercise (often referred to as 1 MET). There is no difference in O_2 consumption between level treadmill and overground running. When running up a grade, however, treadmill running is less energy-demanding than overground running. The equations for the additional O_2 consumption that must be added to the horizontal component are as follows, with grade expressed as a decimal (for example, $2\% = 0.02$):

$$\dot{V}O_2 = \text{velocity} \times \text{grade} \times 0.9 \text{ } or \text{ } 1.8, \qquad (2.3)$$

where 0.9 and 1.8 ml O_2/kg/min are consumed for every m/min velocity increase, respectively, for treadmill and overground running.

Influence of Training, Genetics, and Aging.
Whereas a young female (20-29 yr) of average fitness has a $\dot{V}O_2$max of 35 to 43 ml/kg/min (Nagle, 1973), an elite-level female distance runner similar in age would have a $\dot{V}O_2$ max of 61 to 73 ml/kg/min (Pate, Sparling, Wilson, Cureton, & Miller, 1987). Similarly, for a man of average fitness the $\dot{V}O_2$max value ranges from 44 to 51 ml/kg/min (Nagle, 1973); an elite male athlete has a $\dot{V}O_2$max ranging from 71 to 84 ml/kg/min (Pollock, 1977).

A large portion of this difference, anywhere from 30% to 50%, can be attributable to training (Klissouras, 1972; Shephard, 1984). As either active or sedentary people undertake serious aerobic training, their $\dot{V}O_2$max typically increases. Thus, the capacity to adapt to increased endurance work loads is a trainable attribute of healthy people, and $\dot{V}O_2$max is an appropriate indicator of the improved aerobic fitness.

The extent to which quantities such as $\dot{V}O_2$max can improve with training is not the same in everyone, however. As Claude Bouchard et al. (1988) put it, there are high and low responders to training, and this is hereditary. There is also a genetic variability in the determinants of endurance performance (Bouchard & Lortie, 1984), probably the most notable being the differing composition of skeletal muscles with regard to FT and ST fibers. In addition, not everyone begins to respond to training at the same age; some are more responsive at an early age, others later. Olympic gold medal prospects thus are most likely those who have

- an interest in training,
- a high endowment of physiological attributes related to good running performance,
- a high sensitivity of response to training, and
- a well-designed training program.

Thus, in the words of Per-Olof Astrand (1982): "Top athletes in endurance events are only partly products of a tough training program" (p. 193).

Another important factor that changes $\dot{V}O_2$max is the aging process. As we get older, performance gradually deteriorates; aging is the price we pay for living. Astrand and Rodahl (1977) suggest that $\dot{V}O_2$max declines about 1% per year from around age 25 onward among individuals who lead relatively sedentary lifestyles. Many changes occurring as part of the aging process contribute to the gradual decline in $\dot{V}O_2$max during later years. The maximum attainable heart rate in beats/min declines at a rate of about six beats per decade, and this is an important component of $\dot{V}O_2$max. Unless stroke volume increases appropriately, maximum cardiac output declines. After age 60, muscle cells seem to deteriorate more rapidly than previously, contributing to a gradual decrease in skeletal muscle strength. Campbell, McComas, and Petito (1973) have suggested that these changes may be induced by accelerated nervous system degeneration during these later years, especially in sedentary people.

The addition of serious fitness training as an integral part of lifestyle can substantially slow these processes. Athletes during their second and third decades of life probably will experience very little reduction in $\dot{V}O_2$max, provided they continue in serious training. The coupling of genetic trainability with continued effective aerobic training can provide a rather extended period of comparably superlative performances provided that interruption does not occur due to injury. The marathon is the most aerobically dependent Olympic running event and has contributed several well-known athlete examples of such interaction. Many will recall the 1984 Los Angeles Olympic gold medal marathon performance (2:09:21) by 37-year-old Carlos Lopes of Portugal. (His 2:07:12 at Rotterdam the following April was a new world best.) The 1990 Boston marathon world best performance of 2:11:04 by New Zealander John Campbell at the age of 41 is equally outstanding. Among the women, two of the more brilliant marathoners include Priscilla Welch, with her British record of 2:26:51 at age 42 in 1987, and Sweden's Evy Palm, who at age 47 set a new national record of 2:31:05 in 1989. Both of these records were established over the fast London marathon course.

It does become difficult to quantify exactly how $\dot{V}O_2$max and other performance criteria of such athletes change over time. This is because as athletes grow older, their lifestyles also change, giving them less time to devote to training. Moreover, a greater requirement for recovery following hard training decreases their manageable weekly training volume, slowing the rate of adaptation possible.

Male-Female Differences. There is a gender difference in that women as a group have smaller $\dot{V}O_2$max values than men. Typically, men are taller (and thus heavier) than women, but if values are expressed in ml/kg/min, the difference still remains. It is assumed, of course, in studies reporting such differences that both groups are comparably trained, but ensuring this has been difficult. Inclusion as study subjects those men and women athletes specializing in similar events and performing at a similar competitive level has often provided the basis for that assumption, but still the idea of whether they have been doing comparable training can be debated. Because men have been competing at distance running events longer than women, the top standard for women may not be quite as refined as that for men.

Some have suggested that it might be better to express $\dot{V}O_2$max values as ml/kg/min of fat-free body mass when comparing men to women (Astrand, 1984). Women have a larger percent body fat than men as a result of their higher concentration of fat-storing estrogen hormones. Also, men have a larger amount of skeletal muscle mass than women as a result of their higher circulating testosterone levels. Fat tissue consumes O_2 but does not contribute to providing the ability to increase work rate. If anything, it impedes maximum work output, because it must be transported during running. When such comparisons are made using fat-free body mass measurements, the difference between men and women diminishes somewhat but still remains.

One factor contributing to the gender difference relates to the larger quantity of hemoglobin circulating in men than in women of similar fitness and absolute body weight. This is also in part due to the anabolic (protein-building) effects of testosterone. In men this hormone not only stimulates production of higher levels of erythropoietin, the glycoprotein hormone that stimulates the bone marrow to release more red blood cells, but it also promotes the production of more hemoglobin, also a protein. Because 98.5% of the blood-borne O_2 is transported by hemoglobin, more hemoglobin means a greater O_2-carrying capability. For men, a hemoglobin level of 15 gm per deciliter (dl) of blood, multiplied by 77 ml blood volume/kg of body weight, results in 11.6 gm hemoglobin/kg. For women, 14 gm hemoglobin/dl × 66 ml blood volume/kg = 9.2 gm hemoglobin/kg. Thus, women have roughly 21% less hemoglobin/kg than men. In the bloodstream, similar calculations that will be illustrated later reveal that women have about 11% less circulating O_2/dl than men.

Influence of Economy. Almost all of the highly trained elite-level distance runners that we have tested have lower O_2 consumption values at submaximum running paces than those predicted by the ACSM formula (Equations 2.2 and 2.3). This has been reported by others as well (Bransford & Howley, 1977; Conley & Krahenbuhl, 1980). Thus, either genetic factors or the enormous volumes of training that these runners have indulged in over the years have provided them with sufficient thriftiness in O_2 consumption that they have become more economical. To help quantify this concept, Daniels (1974) defined **running economy** as the O_2 required for an individual to maintain any particular submaximum running pace.

To an extent, we become more economical at running simply through running. For example, we tend naturally to develop an optimum balance between stride length and frequency that requires minimum O_2 cost (better tuned aerobic demand). Fatigue, however, affects economy in a negative way, increasing aerobic demand due to the use of tired prime movers plus others brought into action to help us maintain pace. Well-coached runners, when it is time to race, ensure that they are fresh and completely recovered from the performance-slowing effects of prior hard training. In this manner they keep aerobic demand as low as possible at their race pace. As they approach exhaustion toward the end of the race, their economy likely will decrease.

Just as we can see variations in economy within populations, we can determine whether a runner has improved economy from training over a period of time by comparing the aerobic demand at the beginning and end of this period. As an example, if we determined a runner's O_2 consumption in November at a 6 min/mile pace (268 m/min; 3:44/km) as 47 ml/kg/min, and then, 5 months later, with no change in the runner's percent body fat or body weight, remeasured and found the O_2 consumption at the same pace to be 41 ml/kg/min, we might (correctly) conclude that this runner was now performing more economically in April than in November.

Ideally, we are most concerned with being optimally economical at race pace. The longer the race, and thus the smaller the anaerobic racing component, the greater will be the influence of running economy on performance quality. Thus, the marathoners can probably benefit most from either above-average running economy through genetic factors or specific training to improve it. This has been offered as an explanation for the rather low $\dot{V}O_2$max values recorded among some top-level marathon runners.

Some notable examples fall into this category. One includes the former Australian world-record holder Derek Clayton (personal best of 2:08:34), who was studied by Costill, Thomason, and Roberts (1973) and found to have a $\dot{V}O_2$max of 69.7 ml/kg/min. Another is the Swedish marathoner Kjell-Erik Stahl (personal best of 2:10:38 with more than 60 sub-2:20:00 marathons), studied by Sjodin and Svendenhag (1985) and found to have a $\dot{V}O_2$max of 66.8. Both had exceptionally low aerobic demands when measured at selected submaximal work rates—for example, Clayton 59.5 and Stahl 59.7 ml/kg/min at 20 km/hr (3:00/km; 333 m/min; 4:50/mi). But we (as well as others) have studied marathon runners with performance credentials just as excellent and who possess considerably higher O_2 consumption rates at submaximal and maximal loads than those described here. We are reminded of the words of Mark Twain: "Few things are harder to put up with than the annoyance of a good example!"

Clearly, the influence of running economy interacts with other performance characteristics in the total analysis of athletic excellence. This chapter explains what is physiologically required to optimize both running economy and $\dot{V}O_2$max, and chapter 3 gives the practical details.

Threshold of Increases in Blood Lactate and Ventilation

It was probably Hill and Lupton (1923) who first suggested that when skeletal muscles are subjected to gradually increasing work loads, eventually their metabolic demands exceed those that can be served solely by complete (aerobic) metabolism. To meet these increased needs, anaerobic metabolism occurs, with glucose being converted to pyruvate and lactate. In 1930, W. Harding Owles provided the first catchphrase that seemed to encapsulate this concept. He referred to a *critical metabolic level* of exercise intensity (using walking, not running) beyond which the blood lactate level would increase above that found in the resting state. Also in 1930, Harrison and Pilcher found that patients with heart disease produced more CO_2 during exercise than normal healthy subjects doing the same exercise. These scientists hypothesized that the excess CO_2 was released from plasma HCO_3^- as a result of chemical buffering of increased lactate being produced from a failing heart.

For many years it was technologically difficult to analyze, simultaneously and on line during exercise, both O_2 and CO_2 to measure changes in exercise responsiveness. Such pioneers as Issekutz, Birkhead, & Rodahl (1962) made great strides in this technology, as did the team headed by Karlman Wasserman in California. It was Wasserman and McIlroy (1964) who first used the term **anaerobic threshold** to define a particular work load, during a test to measure exercise tolerance, where blood lactate levels first began to rise above their resting levels. An increase in the rate of rise in expired ventilatory volume ($\dot{V}_E$) also began to occur that was greater than the rate of ongoing increase in O_2 uptake. The term seemed logical to suggest the notion that anaerobic metabolic processes had begun to increase their role in supplementing aerobic processes to provide energy for movement. The term *anaerobic* literally means "without O_2," but refers here to anaerobic metabolism.

The term *threshold* refers to a region of change. As we shall describe shortly, this is not the same lactate/ventilatory threshold that we identified in Figure 2.2. That depicted threshold is one of rapid blood lactate accumulation rather than one of moderate rise. The anaerobic threshold of Wasserman occurred in our athlete in Figure 2.2 somewhere between points P and Q.

An enormous controversy began shortly following the appearance of Wasserman's paper and shows little sign of abating after 25 years! It wasn't the quality of Wasserman's research that was in doubt; that has always been superb. But as scientists around the world attempted to confirm his work, using diverse groups of subjects (patients, sedentary controls, and athletes) and diverse kinds of methodology (varying test durations and intensities, use of treadmill vs. bicycle ergometers for evaluation, blood lactate vs. measurements of ventilatory changes, and more), great confusion arose. A major reason for the controversy is the existence of two thresholds where anaerobic influences can be observed: one seen initially with mild work (accompanied by breathing changes and a small rise in blood lactate), the other observed with more intense exercise (accompanied by breathing changes and a rapid accumulation of blood lactate). The exact details of what causes the ventilatory and blood lactate changes and whether these are closely coupled have still not been completely explained. Most of the general concepts, however, have been identified, and we will attempt to describe these in the context of practical application for development of distance runners.

Lactate has a varied role in metabolism that is appropriate to review here, as part of the anaerobic threshold controversy has revolved around the notion by some that no anaerobic metabolism (and thus no lactate production) occurs at rest. This is incorrect, because lactic acid is being produced even during the quietest of resting states, and this gives rise to the baseline lactate concentration in the blood. An untrained individual who has a sample of blood collected in the morning from an arm vein, after a 12-hr postabsorptive period and before any exercise, has a lactate level ranging from about 4 to 15 mg/dl (because 1 mg/dl = 0.1112 millimole per liter [mM/L], this is 0.44 to 1.7 mM/L). Our trained elite distance runners, when examined in a similar manner, typically have a lactate level near the low end of this range (around 3 to 5 mg/dl, or 0.3 to 0.6 mM/L). Lactate can be produced and released into the bloodstream by the intestines and skeletal muscle. Red blood cells are another source, as they are capable of glycolysis, but have no mitochondria. Thus, pyruvate and lactate, instead of accumulating, diffuse out into the plasma.

Nonexercising skeletal muscle will metabolize lactate (Essen, Pernow, Gollnick, & Saltin, 1975). So will the liver (Wahren, Hagenfeld, & Felig, 1975), the kidneys (Yudkin & Cohen, 1975), and also the heart (Welch, 1973).

Even exercising skeletal muscle can metabolize lactate. We know it is an important energy source, being released from both FT and ST skeletal muscle cells and usable as a fuel by especially ST muscle cells. Thus, lactate is not some kind of gremlin molecule to be maligned as an internal poison but is produced in a well-understood manner and usable as an important energy source. The blood lactate level measured at rest or at any particular level of exercise represents a balance between its rate of production and release into the blood, and its removal.

The Two Thresholds of Change in Ventilation and Blood Lactate. As runners begin a training session, gradually increasing their pace to a comfortable aerobic level (e.g., transitioning from points P to Q in Figure 2.2), their arterial blood lactate level typically increases into the range of 15 to 22 mg/dl (1.7 to 2.4 mM/L), and then remains relatively unchanged despite subsequent reasonable submaximum pace increases. The particular threshold of work intensity that initiates such a small elevation of blood lactate beyond resting baseline levels was termed the *anaerobic threshold* (Wasserman & McIlroy, 1964), as described previously. Others have given it a different name: the *aerobic threshold* (Skinner & McLellan, 1980); the *lactate threshold* (Ivy, Withers, Van Handel, Elger, & Costill, 1980); the *onset of plasma lactate accumulation* (Farrell, Wilmore, Coyle, Billing, & Costill, 1979); the *first threshold* (Heck et al., 1985); the *aerobic threshold (2 mM)* (Kindermann, Simon, & Keul, 1979); and on and on.

Both ventilatory and blood lactate increases can be observed at this first threshold. The ventilatory rise is explainable on the basis of blood HCO_3^- buffering mechanisms. The H^+ ion resulting from lactate dissociation combines with available HCO_3^- to form H_2CO_3. By action of the enzyme carbonic anhydrase, H_2CO_3 is converted into H_2O and CO_2. As hypothesized by Harrison and Pilcher (1930), these changes are stoichiometrically equivalent; that is, one H^+ ion from lactic acid combines with one HCO_3^- from the bicarbonate buffer supply to form CO_2 via carbonic acid. Recall equation 1.12 in chapter 1 where this relationship was introduced.

This additional CO_2 beyond that normally produced by aerobic metabolism—22 ml of CO_2 for every millimole of lactate buffered—provides an additional ventilatory stimulus. Thus, there is a disproportionate rise in expired ventilation (V_E) in comparison to the ongoing rise in $\dot{V}O_2$ uptake. Therefore the $\dot{V}_E/\dot{V}O_2$ (ventilatory equivalent for O_2) increases without an accompanying increase in $\dot{V}_E/\dot{V}CO_2$ (ventilatory equivalent for CO_2). $\dot{V}CO_2$ continues to rise at a rate similar to $\dot{V}_E$, however. The term *isocapnic buffering* is often used to describe this phenomenon—*isocapnic* referring to the relatively equal rate of rise of CO_2 with $\dot{V}_E$, and *buffering* referring to the relatively stable acidity during this period. More than 90% of the buffering of lactate is carried out by the action of $NaHCO_3$. This threshold usually occurs at 35% to 60% $\dot{V}O_2$max when R is between 0.85 and 0.90.

Once this threshold is reached, the work load can increase rather sizably (e.g., from points Q to R in Figure 2.2) with only gradual and relatively small increases in circulating lactate. Trained male marathon runners, as an example, can maintain reasonably stable arterial lactate levels (ranging from around 26 mg/dl [2.9 mM/L] to 44 mg/dl [4.9 mM/L]) during running work loads reaching paces exceeding 5:00/mi (19.4 km/hr; 3:06/km; 322 m/min). Women marathoners can retain this blood lactate stability at faster than 5:50/mi (16.5 km/hr; 3:38/km; 276 m/min). For less fit or less talented runners, this pace range for stable blood lactate is considerably slower.

At work loads greater than those described or at comparable paces for other runners (75% to 90% of $\dot{V}O_2$max when R is around 1.0), the blood lactate level then begins a more rapid rise (occurring at point R in Figure 2.2). The threshold at which this sudden rise occurs can also be termed an *anaerobic threshold* (Skinner & McLellan, 1980), but it has also been termed the *respiratory compensation for metabolic acidosis* (Wasserman, 1984); the *lactate turnpoint* (Davis et al., 1983); the *onset of blood lactate accumulation to 4 mM* (Sjodin & Jacobs, 1981); the *individual anaerobic threshold* (Stegmann, Kindermann, & Schnabel, 1981); the *second threshold* (Heck et al., 1985); and the *anaerobic threshold (4mM)* (Kindermann et al., 1979).

Both ventilatory and blood lactate changes occur at the second threshold as well. At the work intensity where the blood lactate concentration begins to accumulate rapidly, elevated ventilatory removal of CO_2 can no longer maintain blood acidity (measured as pH) within reasonable limits. As blood lactate levels rapidly rise, blood pH begins to fall, and this rising H^+ ion concentration (remember that a decrease in pH implies an increase in H^+ ions) provides an additional powerful ventilatory stimulus.

Perhaps the saddest part of this controversy is that no universal satisfaction exists with any of these terms to this day, showing perhaps that the competitiveness of scientists in defending their varying terminologies as "the best" is matched only by the aggressive as-

sault on first place by athletes in a race. Not even anaerobic threshold is considered an acceptable term anymore (Walsh & Banister, 1988). In this book we will be referring primarily to the second threshold, as it is the one of greatest interest to training of athletes. When we are referring to the threshold as determined by blood lactate measurements, we shall use *lactate threshold*, and we shall use *ventilatory threshold* to refer to this region of metabolic change when determined by respiratory changes. Otherwise, we shall use the combined term *lactate/ventilatory threshold*. Doll and Keul (1968) reported that during an incremental exercise test, similar in principle to that described earlier, untrained healthy people demonstrated this sudden rapid increase in blood lactate concentration beginning at about 50% of their $\dot{V}O_2$max. For trained distance runners this occurs considerably closer to $\dot{V}O_2$max, being measured (using ventilatory changes) at typically between 80% and 90% (Martin, Vroon, May, & Pilbeam, 1986).

Two of the previously mentioned synonyms for the lactate threshold refer to a 4 mM/L value. The significance of this dates back to the work of Mader et al. (1976), who reported on a group of subjects in whom the threshold for rapid lactate accumulation typically occurred at a level of 4 mM/L (36 mg/dl). Because of this report, it became popular to assume that this was true for all endurance athletes and therefore that those athletes interested in identifying a training intensity to further raise this threshold should train at the 4 mM/L running pace. Stegmann et al. in 1981 reported that this simply was not universally true, either logically or in fact. They found that the threshold at which blood lactate begins to rise had considerable individual variation, from around 2 to 7 mM/L (18 to 63 mg/dl). It can only be imagined how many elite-level distance runners have suffered training misfortunes over the years as a result of following advice for training paces that were assigned arbitrarily upon a 4 mM/L work intensity as unequivocally representing their lactate threshold. Some doubtless were overtrained, incurring needless fatigue and staleness, whereas others were undertrained and did not achieve their intended goals in quickening the pace at which their lactate threshold occurred.

Interaction of Variables in Determining Athletic Performance

Four components contribute to an individual's maximum sustainable pace:

1. The genetic composition of skeletal muscle cells (i.e., a large percentage of ST cells)
2. A gradual lowering (with proper training) of the

aerobic demand to run at any submaximal pace (implying greater economy of movement)

3. An improvement in the O_2 consumption capabilities of the working muscles (more intracellular mitochondria, better blood perfusion, etc.)

4. A gradual improvement in ability to buffer the effects of increasing acidosis as increased numbers of FT fibers are recruited to manage the work load at higher intensities

We attempt to quantitate these components by measuring such variables as $\dot{V}O_2$max, lactate/ventilatory threshold, and running economy and describing maximum performance capacity. The athlete who has the highest $\dot{V}O_2$max plus the highest lactate/ventilatory threshold plus the greatest running economy plus the greatest ability to tolerate metabolic acidosis has the greatest potential for winning. The combination of hereditary endowment and training emphasis determine which of these variables will be higher or lower in any given athlete.

There is no doubt that a high $\dot{V}O_2$max constitutes a kind of membership card required for entrance into the world of top-level middle- and long-distance running excellence. But anaerobic aspects of performance also contribute to the difference between finishing first and second in a race, because these interact with $\dot{V}O_2$max. However, because $\dot{V}O_2$max has been relatively much easier to quantify, it has perhaps received an undue share of credit as the major contributor to endurance running performance. Probably the most important physiological variable for distance running success is the **maximum sustainable pace**. This has both aerobic and anaerobic aspects; it is defined as the fastest pace at which one can race a given distance without suffering the performance-slowing effects of developing acidosis. This concept is perhaps discussed most frequently among those interested in marathon racing. The great length of this event precludes accumulation of blood lactate except at the end. Indeed, it has been shown clearly that the performance potential for a marathoner among a homogeneous population (i.e., all very talented marathon specialists) correlates better with the pace at lactate/ventilatory threshold (expressed either by itself or as a percentage of $\dot{V}O_2$max pace) than to $\dot{V}O_2$max (Farrell et al., 1979; Sjodin & Svedenhag, 1985). Costill et al. (1973) have referred to this relationship between lactate/ventilatory threshold and $\dot{V}O_2$max as the fractional use of the aerobic capacity.

Let's take a practical example and see how this concept applies. Jim and John both have $\dot{V}O_2$max values of 75 ml/kg/min. If they have identical running economy and they are running over a level surface at $\dot{V}O_2$max pace, they will be side by side. Jim, how-

ever, can sustain 85% of this pace for a marathon, but John is limited to 81%. Other aspects being equal, Jim will run faster over the marathon distance. This principle holds true over the entire spectrum of distance racing, from the marathon, where athletes attempt to compete at the fastest sustainable aerobic pace, through to the 800m, where they must cope with additional large anaerobic accumulations over a few minutes' time. The larger their $\dot{V}O_2$max, the smaller their total anaerobic contribution will be at any given pace, or the faster they can run before anaerobic effects start to impair performance. But once $\dot{V}O_2$max has been elevated about as high as it can be without inordinate additional training volumes, anaerobic development will make the additional difference between being optimally fit (i.e., able to use all trainable performance characteristics) and marginally fit (i.e., not fully trained).

Athletes and coaches are always interested in applying physiological data in a meaningful way to improve training or racing effectiveness. Figure 2.3 provides a graphic summary of how the fitness variables that we have just identified can increase performance when trained. In a fashion similar to Figure 2.2, we have plotted O_2 uptake and blood lactate concentration on the vertical axis and increasing exercise load (represented by running pace) on the horizontal axis. Consider Runner A who has attempted to improve his performance by appropriate training to increase $\dot{V}O_2$max and running economy, and Runner B who has attempted to raise lactate threshold. Runner A trained effectively between February and June 1986 and experienced a measurable improvement in running economy but no change in $\dot{V}O_2$max, which remained stable at 73 ml/kg/min. If this athlete competed at 92% of $\dot{V}O_2$max for a 10,000m race, his race finish time would clearly be faster in June than in February.

Between June 1986 and June 1987, Runner A's $\dot{V}O_2$max improved from 73 to 78 ml/kg/min, with no changes in body weight. However, in this training year from 1986 to 1987, Runner A experienced no improvement in running economy. As shown, if this athlete races at 92% of $\dot{V}O_2$max pace, as with a 10,000m race, his June 1987 finish time would also be considerably faster than that of June 1986 as a result of the improvement in $\dot{V}O_2$max. Runner B engaged in a training program that provided greater tolerance to anaerobic work. Whereas initially the pace at which blood lactate levels began to markedly rise was at 5:00/mi (3:06/km), now, upon retesting several months later, this pace has quickened to about 4:45/mi (2:57/km). Again, this is a sizable performance improvement.

The interesting question at this point relates to the

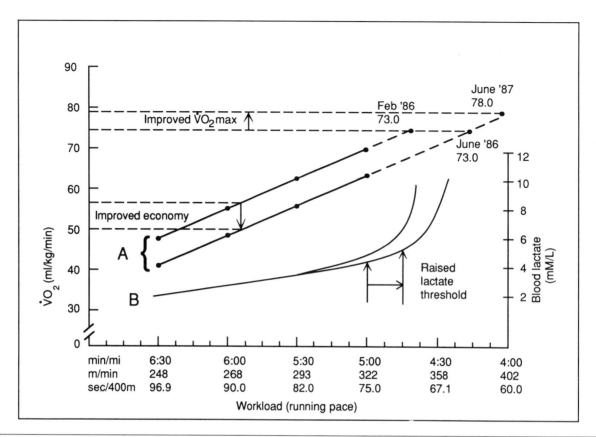

Figure 2.3 Graphic plot of O_2 consumption and blood lactate as a function of running velocity to show that a higher $\dot{V}O_2$max, an improved running economy, and a higher lactate/ventilatory threshold can increase performance potential in racing.

kind of training that will provide such noticeable improvements in $\dot{V}O_2$max, running economy, and lactate/ventilatory threshold. Running solely long distances at a manageable pace stimulates FT muscle fibers little, and thus is an incomplete training stimulus. Various patterns of faster running are thus essential to provide the necessary stimulus for the adaptations that permit successful competitive racing. But such training must be done correctly in terms of distance, pace, and recovery. Returning to Figure 2.2, we have used the lactate/ventilatory threshold and $\dot{V}O_2$max points to help delineate four zones, or pace ranges, named for the predominant physiological benefit resulting from training in each. In chapter 3 we will describe in detail both the kinds of training appropriate to each zone and the physiological adaptations resulting. Before considering these practical training details, however, it is appropriate to summarize the major concepts of cardiopulmonary and blood physiology that explain the kinds of possible adaptations that can occur, as well as how some of these can be measured using laboratory performance profiling or field tests such as time trials.

EXERCISE AS A CHALLENGE TO THE HEART, LUNGS, AND BLOOD

Of all the vital signs that anyone considers in evaluation of health, surely to a runner the pulse or heartbeat must be the one most symbolic of working capacity. The pounding heartbeat felt as the apex of the heart thumps the inside of the chest wall just following all-out exercise is familiar to all. An elevated pulse rate during the few days following difficult training sessions is a sure sign of the need for some additional recovery time. Measuring heart rate as an indicator of exercise intensity or adequacy of recovery before beginning another interval of higher-speed running is done commonly in training. Gradual reduction in resting heart rate following a successful endurance training program—a decrease from between 60 to 80 beats/min down to as low as 30 to 40 beats/min—is common among endurance athletes. How does a runner's heart adapt to the stress of exercise? Surely it must become a more functional pump, but how is this accomplished? How are its needs met for providing more and more blood through its own circulation (the coronary vessels) to ensure that its cells are properly supplied with O_2 and fuel? Some familiarization with function of the cardiovascular system can help us appreciate how this system adapts remarkably well to the needs of exercise and how its own limitations in turn limit exercise capacity.

The Challenge of Exercise to the Heart and Its Circulation

Functionally, we have two hearts: the right delivering blood to the lungs and the left delivering blood everywhere else. Each heart has two primary operating variables: its beat frequency or *heart rate* (HR) and the volume pumped out per beat, or *stroke volume* (SV). The product of the two equals the *cardiac output* (CO), typically measured in ml or L of blood. Thus,

$$HR \times SV = CO. \qquad (2.4)$$

As an example using untrained resting values, a heart rate of 70 beats/min and a stroke volume of 70 ml/beat provides a cardiac output of 4,900 ml/min. Using trained maximum values, a heart rate of 190 beats/min and a stroke volume of 190 ml/beat yields 36,100 ml/min.

The heart can deliver to the arterial side of the body only that blood which returns to it from the venous side. Thus, cardiac output must equal venous return. In an individual who is at rest, four principal factors control venous return:

1. The tone or caliber of the venous vessels
2. The position of the body in space
3. The total body blood volume
4. The depth of breathing

As exercise begins, a fifth factor becomes important, and that is the milking action of skeletal muscles that helps push blood through the veins back toward the heart.

The interaction of these factors should be easily understandable and can be illustrated using three examples. First, if the blood volume is large, or if an individual has high blood pressure tending to force the incompressible blood into a smaller volume, venous return will be easily maintained or even increased. Second, as breathing produces alternately increased and decreased intrathoracic subatmospheric pressures, venous return will alternately rise and fall. Increased breathing during exercise makes such fluctuations greater. Third, if venous tone is reduced, blood will pool in the periphery, decreasing venous return. This can occur during heavy exercise as blood

flow increases to the working muscles. Sudden stopping reduces venous return because of diminished muscular activity, and fainting could occur from inadequate perfusion to the brain. The sight of runners bending over at the end of a hard, fast race is a familiar one (Figure 2.4) and readily explainable in light of this information. These runners would probably faint if they remained standing upright, because the large quantity of blood pooling in the periphery cannot be returned to the heart quickly enough to guarantee delivery of adequate blood flow to the brain. Bending at the waist lowers the head to the level of the heart, thereby reducing the pressure needed to maintain adequate cerebral blood flow.

Figure 2.4 Competitive middle-distance runners immediately following an 800m race. By bending forward, bringing the head closer to the level of the heart, less blood pressure is required to ensure adequate cerebral perfusion. Extreme vasodilation in the skeletal muscles, as well as an absence of milking action of skeletal muscles on enhancing venous return, contributes to a temporary reduction in blood pressure.

The heart muscle itself receives a substantial blood flow even at rest—about 80 ml/100 gm tissue/min, which is about 5% of the resting cardiac output. During exercise, this flow may increase as much as fivefold. If we recall the anatomy of the coronary arteries, as diagrammed in Figure 2.5, we see that these vessels are embedded for a sizable portion of their length along the outer surface of the heart. The left coronary artery is very short and divides almost immediately into two branches. The large circumflex artery extends to the left in a groove between the left atrium and ventricle and continues as a large vessel that descends on the rear surface of the left ventricle.

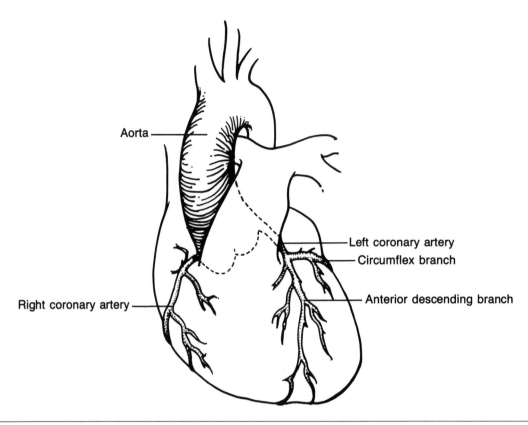

Figure 2.5 Position of right and left coronary arteries and their main branches on the surface of the heart.

It supplies the left atrium as well as the upper front and whole rear portion of the left ventricle. The other branch is the anterior descending artery, circling to the left of the pulmonary artery and then running downward in a furrow to the apex of the heart. It supplies the front wall of the left ventricle and a small part of the rear of the right ventricle. The right coronary artery, embedded in fat, runs to the right in a groove between the right atrium and ventricle and carries blood to both structures. It also has two branches, the posterior descending and the marginal arteries. Four specific characteristics of cardiac muscle and its perfusion via the coronary circulation contribute to the heart's ability to adapt to exercise stress.

Characteristic I:
Oxygen Extraction From Perfusing Blood

When blood is sampled from the coronary arteries and from the coronary venous sinus and analyzed for its O_2 content, it is found that an exceedingly large amount of O_2 has been removed. Coronary sinus O_2 content may be only 1 to 2 ml/dl of blood, compared to 4 to 5 ml/dl of blood from the veins draining the skeletal muscles of exercising athletes or 15 ml/dl found on the average in blood returning to the heart

of a resting individual. Coronary artery blood O_2 concentration averages 20 ml/dl, so the coronary arteriovenous O_2 difference is 18 to 19 ml/dl. This O_2 extraction capability in the heart is so enormous that almost no additional removal occurs during increased exercise. Any additional increase in O_2 uptake by cardiac muscle can result only from an increased blood flow through its perfusing vessels.

Characteristic II:
Increased Coronary Blood Flow by Dilation

As the heart enlarges with training, the coronary vessels also enlarge. Coronary flow increases as a logical consequence of these larger vessels. However, the powerful vasodilator effect of CO_2 is effective here just as in other actively metabolizing tissue beds. Thus, as metabolism in the heart increases during exercise, compensatory vasodilation from this important metabolite also enhances coronary flow.

Postmortem examination of the heart of accomplished long-distance runners has seldom been done, but in those instances where this has been possible the findings have often been very interesting. Probably the most famous case involves Clarence DeMar, veteran of more than 100 marathons, seven-time winner of the Boston marathon, and a lifelong runner who between the ages of 21 and 69 participated in more than 1,000 long-distance races.

DeMar was a willing subject in some of the earliest treadmill studies conducted at the Harvard Fatigue Laboratory during the mid-1920s. His willingness allowed significant inroads into the cardiovascular adaptations of runners with abilities such as his. He died in 1958 of metastatic rectal carcinoma. An autopsy was conducted and reported in the scientific literature by the famed cardiologist Paul Dudley White (Currens & White, 1961). DeMar's heart weighed a normal 340 gm, but his left ventricular wall was 18 mm thick, compared to the normal thickness of 10 to 12 mm. His right ventricle was 8 mm thick, twice the normal value. His heart valves were normal, but his coronary arteries were estimated to be two to three times normal size. He had visible signs of developing arteriosclerosis in his coronary vessels, as do most people at his age. His very large coronary arteries, however, gave him a large margin of safety to protect against loss of functional coronary flow and as well allowed his heart an enormous blood flow during the many years of his racing career.

Characteristic III:
Protection Against Developing an O_2 Debt

An increased coronary artery flow and increased O_2 extraction from the blood are both desirable features for an exercising heart. A primary reason for the elevated O_2 extraction involves the third adaptive characteristic of the heart, namely a maintained high gradient for O_2 movement into the cardiac muscle cells from the coronary vessel blood. Within the heart cells themselves there are adaptations to utilize large quantities of O_2. The heart simply cannot, under any circumstances, incur an O_2 debt. It is constantly very active, and there would never be a time when such a debt could be repaid effectively. Thus, cardiac muscle is the supreme example of a "twitch now, pay now" muscle.

Cardiac cells represent the extreme adaptive characteristics of ST muscle cells, with adaptations so extensive that if skeletal muscle cells had personalities, the ST members of this population would be extremely envious. Any adaptation possessed by the ST muscle cells is present to a greater extent in cardiac muscle cells. There is an increase in the amount of myoglobin, the O_2-storing pigment. Huge numbers of mitochondria are present, and the cells can metabolize lactate very effectively in addition to fatty acids and glucose. During exercise, this lactate uptake is so great that it is the preferred fuel even above fatty acids. This ability has obvious value in delaying the onset of metabolic acidosis during intense physical activity.

Characteristic IV:
Increased Diastolic Perfusion Time

An interesting challenge to providing adequate blood flow to the cardiac muscle is discovered when we consider the circulation of blood through this muscle during the entire cycle of cardiac muscle tension generation (known as *systole*) and relaxation (called *diastole*). The longer each diastolic interval, the more thorough the perfusion can be. Thus, it is better to have fewer but longer perfusion periods than more but shorter perfusion periods. This is exactly what occurs in the trained heart. As a result of cardiac chamber enlargement, stroke volume of any given work load is larger, with heart rate lower, increasing the available perfusion time. During systole, muscle tension generation is so powerful that coronary artery flow slows dramatically and may even temporarily stop. This action of the cardiac muscle on its blood vessels is termed *extravascular compression*.

The flow situation is different with the left and right heart. A higher left ventricular systolic pressure causes enough extravascular compression to almost stop the left coronary artery flow at the point where this vessel penetrates into the heart muscle tissue. Flow through the tissues perfused by the right coronary artery is less affected and continues, although reduced, all through systole.

During exercise, the left ventricular systolic pressure rises, thus increasing aortic pressure. Because the coronary arteries are the first to branch off from the aorta, their perfusion rises as well. Remember, of course, that because these vessels have their openings just behind the aortic semilunar valves, flow into them occurs primarily during diastole. Even with the extended diastolic perfusion time in a trained heart, the left ventricle can develop signs of hypoxia during exhaustive exercise (and especially in individuals with developing coronary artery disease). The right ventricular systolic pressure shows much less increase during exercise, and hence perfusion of the right heart muscle via that coronary artery generally proceeds effectively.

Cardiovascular Determinants of Maximum Aerobic Power

We have already discussed the measurement and importance of $\dot{V}O_2$max as a determinant of performance excellence. $\dot{V}O_2$max and $\dot{V}O_2$submax can be expressed mathematically in terms of the cardiovascular dynamics of O_2 transport. $\dot{V}O_2$ is equal to the product of cardiac output times O_2 extracted from the blood. O_2 extraction is measured by subtracting the mixed venous blood O_2 concentration from the arterial blood O_2 concentration. The term used for this O_2 extraction is *arteriovenous O_2 difference*, or *a-$\overline{v}O_2$ difference*. Therefore we can write the following equation:

$$\dot{V}O_2max = (HR_{max} \times SV_{max}) \times max \ a\text{-}\overline{v}O_2 \ difference \tag{2.5}$$

Cardiac output is graphed as a function of a-$\overline{v}O_2$ difference in Figure 2.6. The typical resting $\dot{V}O_2$ and also $\dot{V}O_2max$ in a trained runner are depicted. Changes in any of these variables, as might occur with training or during exercise, can alter $\dot{V}O_2$. Changes in heart rate and stroke volume comprise the so-called central circulatory adjustments, in contrast to changes in blood O_2 extraction in the tissues, which is a peripheral adjustment. It is of great interest, therefore, to understand how training can improve the capacity of these variables in their response to exercise and to appreciate the magnitude of possible changes in these variables with exercise at varying intensities. We shall see that maximum heart rate is either unchanged or slightly reduced by endurance training, and max a-$\overline{v}O_2$ difference peaks at about

16 ml/dl. Thus, it is primarily increases in maximum stroke volume that improve the heart's capacity to increase the body's aerobic power.

Heart Rate.   All of the various cell types in the heart are functionally connected anatomically by microscopic structures called intercalated discs. Thus, activity in one cell can be transmitted quickly to all other cells. Certain regions of the heart have nodes of tissue that are not specialized for tension generation but are composed of cells that are neither muscle nor nerve. Their cell membranes are rather unstable, particularly regarding the maintenance of a stable ionic equilibrium between the surrounding fluid and their cytoplasm. A slow, ongoing inward Ca^{++} ion leakage across the cell membrane brings a gradual depolarization until a sudden, almost explosive membrane-oriented ionic disruption occurs. This so-called action potential is transmitted all through the heart and results in depolarization, with momentary sudden tension generation (systole), in all of the muscular cells in the heart. Very rapid recovery occurs, and it is this ongoing repeated process of cellular depolarization and repolarization, causing tension generation and relaxation, that forms the basis for the ongoing heart rhythm. The sinoatrial node is the primary tissue responsible for this periodic cardiac depolarization and as such is often termed the pacemaker of the heart.

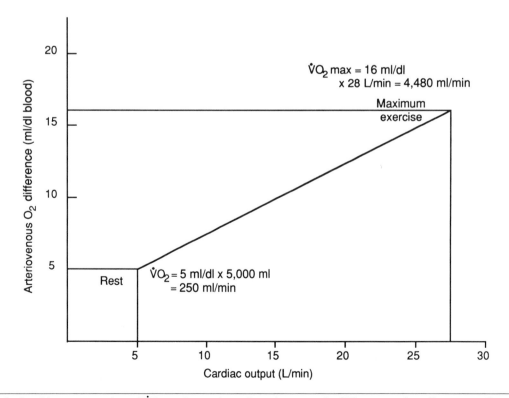

Figure 2.6 Graphic representation of $\dot{V}O_2$ as the product of arteriovenous O_2 difference and cardiac output. In turn, cardiac output is the product of heart rate $\times$ stroke volume.

It has an intrinsic, basal rhythm of about 105 depolarizations each minute. Systole thus represents the period during the cardiac cycle in which blood is ejected from the ventricles, whereas diastole represents ventricular filling.

Transmitter chemicals from the two divisions of the autonomic nervous system (parasympathetic and sympathetic) each affect this intrinsic rate of depolarization of sinoatrial node tissue, thus changing the heart rate. Figure 2.7 depicts these two innervations to the heart. Acetylcholine, released from the vagus nerves (parasympathetic system), increases the stability of the nodal cell membranes, thereby decreasing the rate of depolarization and lowering the heart rate. When we are at rest, and particularly during sleep, the parasympathetic nervous system dominates. Its stimulation of the heart via the vagus nerve keeps the heart rate at its lowest value. Apprehension or arousal as

the time approaches for a training session or competition brings an increase in sympathetic nervous system activity (with its noradrenaline release from the cardiac accelerator nerves) as well as adrenaline release from the adrenal medulla, and heart rate begins to rise. Thus the heart rate determined at any moment reflects a balance between the relative activity of these three physiological influences on the basal intrinsic rhythm. At rest, parasympathetic tone dominates over sympathetic, giving a net resting heart rate of about 60 to 70 beats/min in sedentary people. As exercise begins, this vagal tone is gradually released, up to about 100 beats/min; sympathetic tone then increases significantly.

Breathing also influences heart rate by mechanisms involving blood pressure receptors located in the carotid arteries. These pressure receptors (called carotid sinus baroreceptors) are admirably located to

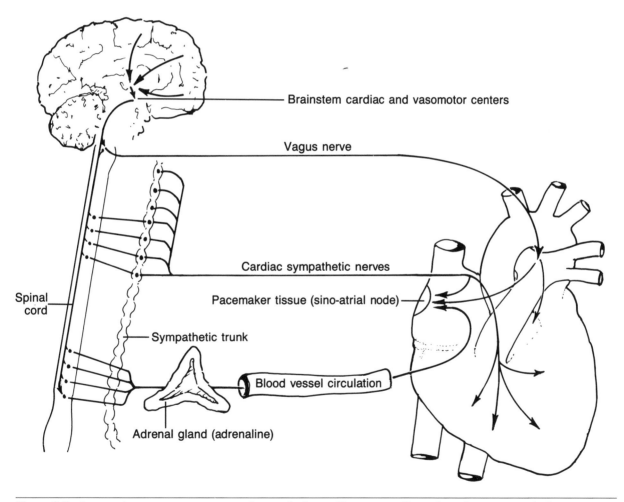

Figure 2.7 Autonomic nervous system connections to the heart. Vagus nerve fibers, from the parasympathetic nervous system, connect primarily to the pacemaker tissue. Their stimulation decreases the heart rate. Cardiac accelerator nerve fibers, from the sympathetic nervous system, extend from the spinal cord through the adjacent sympathetic trunk, and then to the heart. Stimulation of these accelerates heart rate. Sympathetic nervous system activation can also increase adrenaline release from the adrenal medulla, which also increases heart rate.

monitor blood pressure generated by the heart as it pumps blood toward the brain. The slightest decrease in perfusion pressure to these receptors will be sensed, with an appropriate increase in nervous impulse traffic to the brain centers for regulating blood pressure and heart rate. As we inspire, the increased volume occupied by the lungs in the thoracic cavity temporarily impedes venous return, lowering cardiac output, illustrated in Figure 2.8. This slight reduction in aortic blood flow is sensed by the baroreceptors, and a brief reflex increase in heart rate occurs by increased nervous activity to the cardiac centers in the brain. In turn this reduces parasympathetic nervous activity (via the vagus nerve); the heart rate rises and blood pressure is maintained. By that time, however, expiration has occurred, with venous return and cardiac output increasing as a result of a decreased lung volume in the thoracic cavity. This too is sensed by the baroreceptors as an increased blood flow and pressure in the carotid arteries. The resulting increase and decrease in heart rate caused by breathing is sometimes termed a *respiratory* or *rhythmic arrhythmia.*

Thus, a delicate interplay between the activity of the nervous and respiratory systems keeps the resting pulse changing in a rhythmic fashion. In the electrocardiogram tracing from a trained marathon runner in Figure 2.8, the varying time intervals between each heartbeat are clearly evident. This athlete has a lower resting heart rate (in the range of 45 to 55 beats/min) than the norm of 70 beats/min seen in the sedentary population. The respiratory arrhythmia is more pronounced in athletes and is truly striking among those highly trained runners who have resting heart rates as low as 30 beats/min! The electrocardiographic tracing illustrated shows the difficulty in attempting to determine an individual's resting heart rate solely on the basis of time difference between two beats. Typically a series of beats is recorded over a time frame of 10 or 20 sec (and then multiplied by, respectively, 6 or 3) to give the heartbeat rate per minute.

What causes the decrease in resting heart rate observable in trained endurance runners? The possible mechanisms are twofold: an increase in parasympathetic nervous system activity or a decrease in sympathetic nervous system activity (Frick, Elovainio, & Somer, 1967). Increased vagus nerve stimulation decreases the rate of spontaneous depolarization of the specialized cells in the sinoatrial node, which, when activated sufficiently, triggers a myocardial depolarization that initiates a heartbeat. Decrease in the activity of these cells thus decreases the frequency of heartbeat generation. The reverse occurs with cardiac accelerator nerve activation. Available evidence suggests that both sympathetic decreases and parasympathetic increases occur in cardiac function as a result

of training. But exactly what triggers these adaptive changes in distance runners isn't clear. The end result is the often-seen decreased resting heart rate (*bradycardia)* and decreased maximum heart rate as well.

Stroke Volume.   Trained distance runners have an increased stroke volume both at rest and during exercise. What causes this increase in stroke volume? There are several possible contributing factors. One is the end-diastolic volume, sometimes called ventricular preload. This is the amount of blood in the ventricles just prior to the next heartbeat. One study (Rerych, Scholz, Sabiston, & Jones, 1980), involving 18 college endurance athletes who trained for 6 months, did show such a change. But the exact explanation for how it is brought about isn't clear.

One possibility is simply an increased circulating blood volume as an adaptation to endurance training. This has indeed been demonstrated, as an increase in both plasma volume and red blood cell mass (Brotherhood, Brozovic, & Pugh, 1975). These workers found a 16% increase in blood volume, which involved a 13% increase in red-cell mass and 18% increase in plasma volume. This lowered hematocrit (percent of blood that is red cells) decreases blood viscosity, making it flow more easily through the vessels. Because the total red cell mass in trained runners is actually increased, the term *dilutional pseudoanemia* is used to describe this altered blood volume relationship (Eichner, 1986).

A second factor involves increased cardiac dimensions. A larger ventricular chamber should provide greater stroke volume upon emptying. In 1927 an English translation of a book published in German in 1924 by Felix Deutsch and Emil Kauf provided the most detailed study ever attempted to document heart size among athletes. No study has matched it, and the authors' conclusions are still significant today. In comparing athletes to sedentary subjects, they showed that serious athletes engaged in such sports as rowing, cycling, skiing, swimming, and running had a statistically large incidence of enlarged hearts. The cardiac enlargement involves an increase in size of the heart chambers (dilatation) as well as an increase in the mass of heart muscle. Both chambers of the right and left heart are affected.

The increase in heart muscle mass is the result of an increase in size of existing myocardial cells (hypertrophy) and not an increase in the number of cells (hyperplasia). An increase in the number of mitochondria and myofilaments increases the diameter of each cell. There is also an increase in the number of sarcomeres, which increases the length of these muscle cells. Unfortunately, very little data exist on heart sizes

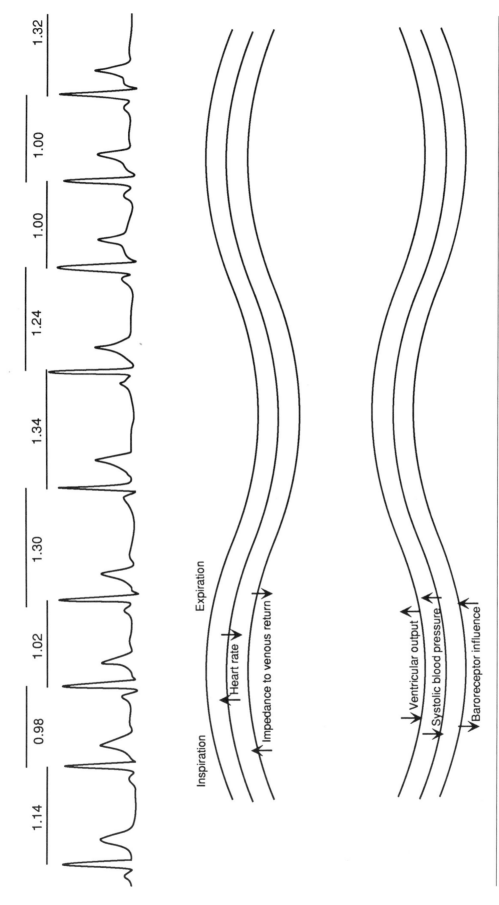

Figure 2.8 Effect of changes in intrathoracic pressure during breathing on cardiac output and electrocardiographic pattern. Inspiration impedes venous return toward the heart, briefly decreasing cardiac output. This brings an equally brief reflex increase in heart rate. Expiration does the reverse. In this athlete, mean heart rate was 53 beats/min; breathing frequency, 10/min. Numbers given at the top are time intervals (sec) between heartbeats.

in these athletes *before* they began to engage in the training that gave them their status as trained athletes. Do certain athletes, born with larger-than-usual hearts, find endurance athletics easier than those athletes less endowed and hence participate in those activites, enlarging their hearts even more? Or is it solely the great devotion of these individuals to endurance athletics together with the adaptive abilities of the heart to enlarge with stress that produce the observed result? We just do not know at present.

The response of the heart to exercise is specific to the type of loading to which it is subjected. Echocardiographic studies comparing the hearts of endurance-trained athletes (swimmers and runners) with strength-trained athletes (wrestlers and shot-putters) have been especially informative (Morganroth, Maron, Henry, & Epstein, 1975). Table 2.1 compares the net effects of these two training emphases on four aspects of cardiac adaptation. Endurance athletes devote most of their training to submaximum work and thus present their hearts with long periods of increased venous return. We call this *volume loading* of the heart. The cardiac response to such an exercise challenge is lengthened ventricular muscle fibers and thus an increased ventricular chamber volume, with no appreciable change in ventricular wall thickness. This produces a larger stroke volume both at rest and during exercise. In turn, a slower heart rate is needed at any given work load to maintain cardiac output, thereby enhancing perfusion of the cardiac muscle during the diastolic (rest) period. Because the maximum achievable heart rate changes very little, endurance training increases the maximum cardiac output, which contributes to an increased VO$_2$max.

Table 2.1   Comparison of the Effects of Isotonic (Endurance-Oriented) Versus Isometric (Strength-Oriented) Training on Cardiac Adaptation to Exercise

Variable	Isotonic	Isometric
Heart wall thickness	Unchanged	Increased
End-diastolic ventricular volume	Increased	Unchanged
Cardiac mass	Increased	Increased
Cardiac output	Increased	Unchanged

In contrast, athletes engaged in strength-oriented training have a left ventricular response that is an adaptation to short-term high pressure loading. During periods of maximum or near-maximum activity, the working skeletal muscles provide such large compressive force against the blood vessels within them that flow is essentially stopped. In turn, the heart generates enormous muscular tension in an attempt to overcome this high resistance to blood flow. As summarized in Table 2.1, the heart's adaptation to permit this is an increased left ventricular wall thickness in an attempt to provide the additional tension-generating protein. There is thus minimum change in maximum stroke volume and cardiac output and minimum improvement in VO$_2$ max.

A third factor involves *myocardial contractility*. There is little doubt that exercising people have greater myocardial vigor; that is, an increased speed and force of cardiac muscle tension generation. However, there is little evidence that training itself makes the heart more vigorous in its abilities to function, which are already honed virtually to perfection. Each beat pumps virtually all of the blood out of the heart, leaving a very small residual volume. During exercise, this residual volume gets even smaller, contributing to the increase in stroke volume. Very little room exists for any further increase in tension-generating efficiency. If endurance training does increase vigor, it hasn't yet been detectable.

A fourth possible factor is *arterial blood pressure*, sometimes referred to as ventricular afterload. Again, as with myocardial vigor, no evidence exists that endurance training brings changes in arterial blood pressure that would contribute to an increased stroke volume. If anything, at VO$_2$max among athletes, mean arterial blood pressure is a little reduced. We know, of course, that skeletal muscle blood flow increases with training, and thus in the face of no real increase in blood pressure, this blood pressure reduction is explainable by an increased skeletal muscle vascular conductance. This means that there are more small skeletal muscle blood vessels (capillaries) open to permit more flow.

Development of this combined bradycardia and increased stroke volume form some of the most crucial adaptations to the higher-speed training that is an integral part of the advanced preparation of all middle- and long-distance runners. Anaerobic conditioning sustainable for between 15 and 20 min and done at lactate/ventilatory threshold pace provides the kind of volume overload stimulus that eventually increases ventricular chamber size. At the same time, by a small increment the intrinsic pacemaker rhythm decreases, in turn lowering the maximum attainable heart rate. Table 2.2 summarizes these changes in cardiac dynamics—decreased heart rate and increased stroke volume—that can occur both at rest and at maximum exercise among elite distance runners as compared to sedentary people. Figure 2.9 summa-

Table 2.2   Changes in Heart Rate and Stroke Volume at Rest and Maximum Exercise in Sedentary People and Endurance-Trained Runners[a]

Variable	Resting conditions		Maximum exercise	
	Nonathlete	Elite runner	Nonathlete	Elite runner
Cardiac output (ml/min)	4,900	4,515	22,800	36,100
Stroke volume (ml)	70	105	120	190
Heart rate (beats/min)	70	43	190	190
$\dot{V}O_2$ (ml/kg/min)	3.5	3.5	46	85

[a]Data are from two 60-kg male subjects.

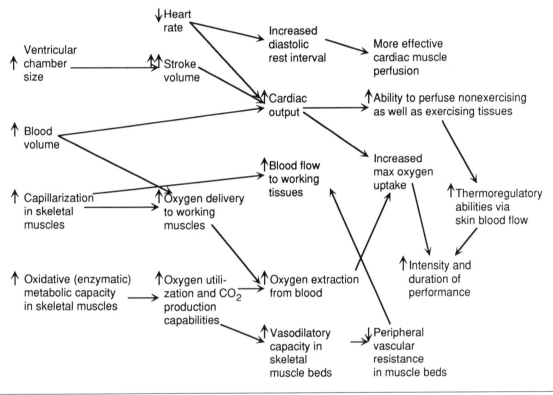

Figure 2.9 Flow scheme illustrating how major adaptations occurring with endurance training (increases in ventricular chamber size, blood volume, skeletal muscle capillarization, intracellular enzyme content, and a decrease in heart rate) all contribute to the potential for improved performance.

rizes the means by which the primary adaptations seen with endurance training all contribute to improved performance potential: a decrease in heart rate and increases in ventricular chamber size, blood volume, skeletal muscle capillarization, and muscle cell enzyme content.

Arteriovenous O_2 Difference.   Figure 2.10 shows the changes in arterial and venous O_2 content of blood observable as athletes increase their intensity of exercise. Whereas arterial O_2 content may rise slightly

due to the movement of fluid into the active muscle cells and fluid space outside the capillaries, mean venous O_2 content decreases dramatically. Saltin and Gollnick (1983) explained that a major reason for this increased O_2 extraction comes from an increase in skeletal muscle capillary density with training. More capillaries around each skeletal muscle fiber reduce the diffusion distance for O_2 as it moves from the circulatory system to muscle tissues. Also, there is an increased mean transit time for blood moving through working muscle.

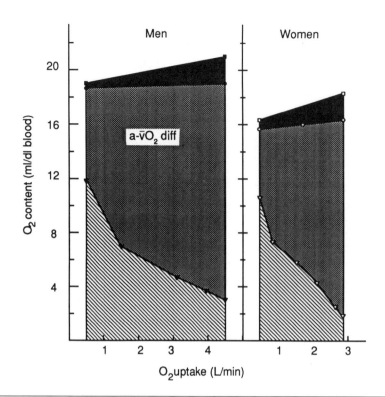

Figure 2.10 Changes in arterial and venous O_2 content of blood (a-$\bar{v}O_2$ difference) during increasing exercise intensity. For both men (left) and women (right), the response is similar. The darkest shaded area at the top represents the difference between calculated O_2-binding capacity and actual O_2 content in arterial blood. The lower hatched area represents calculated mixed venous blood O_2 content, which decreases as work load (measured in L/min of O_2 uptake) increases. The middle stippled area indicates the increasing arteriovenous O_2 difference. *Note.* From *Textbook of Work Physiology* (2nd ed.) (p. 183) by P.-O. Astrand and K. Rodahl, 1977, New York: McGraw-Hill. Copyright 1977 by McGraw-Hill, Inc. Adapted by permission.

Interestingly, the total blood volume in the skeletal muscles does not increase as a result of the observed increase in capillary blood volume. Physiologically, this would be unwise, because more blood would be in the periphery, decreasing stroke volume and ventricular filling pressure. It appears that skeletal muscle blood volume is maintained by a combination of increased capillary volume and reduced venous volume.

Other factors contributing to the a-$\bar{v}O_2$ difference exist. Skeletal muscle myoglobin levels increase with endurance training. This O_2-binding pigment provides an effective O_2 reservoir when the partial pressure of O_2 in muscle begins to fall to low levels. There is also an increase in the total mitochondrial enzyme content in trained skeletal muscles, permitting greater O_2 usage. An additional possible contributory factor could involve greater shunting of blood away from all the nonexercising tissues and into the working muscles. Endurance exercise training, however, does not appear to change this, because near-maximum vasoconstriction occurs in these tissues even among untrained individuals. Thus, in these lesser perfused

tissues, their ongoing metabolism results in an increased O_2 extraction from their diminished blood flow. This contributes to the increased overall a-$\bar{v}O_2$ difference. The maximum a-$\bar{v}O_2$ difference found in healthy people is about 16 ml/dl, which represents extraction of about 85% of available O_2 from blood into tissues.

The Challenge of Exercise to the Pulmonary System

The pulmonary system plays a critical role in permitting exercise because it is the primary site for both O_2 delivery to the blood perfusing the working tissues and CO_2 removal from those tissues. Thus, not only do the lungs permit aerobic metabolism in working tissues because of their O_2 delivery capabilities, but also they serve as the body's primary organ for acid (CO_2) excretion. In contrast to organ systems such as the heart and skeletal muscles, extensive morphological adaptations by the pulmonary system to the rigors of long-term endurance exercise do not develop. Instead, there are accommodative changes in response to the demands of exercise. This means that the pulmonary system is essentially already equipped as a result of its existing structure to deal reasonably well with demands placed upon it to maintain unchanging O_2 (iso-oxic) and CO_2 (isocapnic) concentrations in the arterial blood perfusing the working tissues.

Oxygen Transport From the Lungs to the Blood.

Our normal breathing rate of about 12 breaths/min, with about half a liter per breath, permits a resting respiratory minute volume (RMV)—or expired ventilation ($\dot{V}_E$)—of about 6 L/min. This air swirls through a complex series of breathing tubes, beginning with the mouth and continuing through the pharynx, larynx, trachea, bronchi, and bronchioles to eventually circulate in about 300 million tiny air sacs that we call *alveoli*. Thirty percent of the total airflow remains in the tubes above the alveoli, where no exchange with blood occurs; this is termed dead space ventilation ($\dot{V}_D$). Immediately adjacent to the alveoli are the pulmonary capillaries. Each of these associated cell membranes has a thickness of about 0.5 μm. It is across this so-called *alveolocapillary membrane* that the respiratory gases (O_2 and CO_2) flow in opposite directions (Figure 2.11). Assuming a resting cardiac output of 4,900 ml/min and a pulmonary capillary blood volume of about 70 ml, these capillaries are emptied and refilled 70 times every minute! During maximum exercise, the respiratory minute volume can exceed 170 L/min, and cardiac output can exceed 40 L/min. It thus becomes quite intriguing to consider how gas exchange is managed under such circumstances.

The primary task of the pulmonary system in accommodating the needs of a distance runner in either hard training or competition is to provide adequate gas exchange between alveoli and arterial blood with minimum work required by the lungs and chest. Otherwise, the added O_2 cost would not justify the O_2 gain. Two challenging problems are presented to the lungs as exercise becomes more intense: One involves the need to increase the amount of blood flowing through the pulmonary capillaries without increasing pulmonary system blood pressure. Such an increase would cause fluid to leak into and accumulate within the alveoli or the interstitial space between alveoli and capillaries, producing edema. This problem is managed nicely in two ways. First, exercise increases the filling of capillaries that were essentially nonperfused at rest, thereby providing a passive expansion of the pulmonary blood volume without increases in pulmonary blood vessel resistance. Second, if any tendency toward extravascular fluid accumulation does occur, the lungs are equipped with a very extensive lymphatic drainage system (Staub, Nagano, & Pearce, 1967), ensuring prompt fluid removal and maintenance of effective lung function.

A second problem involves the movement of ever-increasing quantities of O_2 from ambient air into the blood. A greatly increased O_2 extraction from tissue capillary blood during exercise makes the returning venous blood considerably less oxygenated than during the resting state. This so-called *mixed venous*

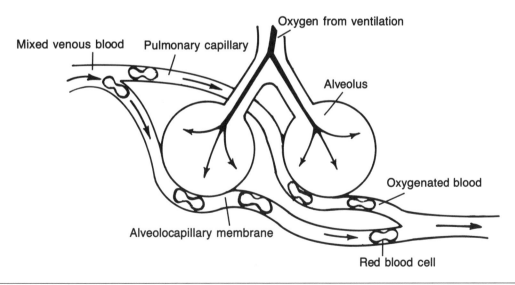

Figure 2.11 Gas exchange across the alveolocapillary membrane. Normally, the fusion of capillary endothelium with alveolar epithelium provides a membrane of about 1.0 μm in thickness, ideal for rapid exchange of gases (O_2 and CO_2) between pulmonary capillary blood and alveolar gas. Red blood cells, being about the same or greater diameter as the capillaries through which they move, may twist and bend as they proceed.

blood flows from the right heart into the lungs via the pulmonary artery and then into the smaller arterioles that eventually empty into lung capillaries. Oxygen flows down its concentration gradient from the air-filled alveoli across the alveolocapillary membranes and into the pulmonary capillaries during the brief period that the blood in the lungs flows through those capillaries (Figure 2.11). Only across the alveolocapillary membranes can gas exchange with the blood occur.

Oxygen movement from the atmosphere into blood is determined by its concentration difference between alveolus and pulmonary capillary, its solubility in blood, and the amount of hemoglobin to which it can bind once inside the bloodstream. The air we breathe is a mixture of gases, O_2 comprising about 20.9% of the total. Physical laws explaining gas movement tell us that each gas in the atmosphere behaves independently, without chemical interaction with the others. Thus, each gas contributes independently to the total pressure exerted by the gas mixture as it moves down its concentration gradient from one place to another. If sea-level barometric pressure, for example, is 760 mm Hg, with O_2 comprising 20.9% of the atmosphere, then the partial pressure exerted by O_2 (written as PO_2) can be calculated as follows:

$$PO_2 = 760 \times 0.209 = 158.8 \text{ mm Hg.} \quad (2.6)$$

The air we inhale gets completely humidified as it moves into the alveoli. This dilution with water vapor helps to lower the alveolar O_2 partial pressure (P_AO_2) down to about 100 mm Hg. As pulmonary arteriolar blood enters the capillaries, a very rapid O_2 transfer into the blood begins, along with CO_2 transfer from blood into the alveoli. Normally, a complete equilibrium is nearly reached, and the arterial blood O_2 partial pressure (P_aO_2) varies between about 90 and 98 mm Hg. Thus, at rest the alveolo-arterial O_2 gradient (written as [A-a]PO_2 gradient) is between about 2 and 10 mm Hg (Table 2.3).

This seeming imperfection in the equilibrium of O_2, even at rest, is relatively unimportant. The difference between the total quantity of O_2 carried in arterial blood with a P_aO_2 of 90 mm Hg as compared to 98 mm Hg is very small. This is because in addition to the total quantity of O_2 *dissolved* in the blood (measured as PO_2), a very much larger quantity of O_2 is *bound* to hemoglobin. Oxygen has a very strong affinity for hemoglobin. When O_2 enters the bloodstream it diffuses through the plasma across the red blood cell membranes and attaches to hemoglobin molecules contained within. We can calculate the total O_2 content of arterial blood as the sum of the dissolved plus the bound forms. As an example, let us consider

Table 2.3   Values for Selected Cardiopulmonary Variables at Rest and During Hard Exercise in Trained Male Runners

Variable	Rest	Hard exercise
Alveolar ventilation ($\dot{V}_A$) (L/min)	4.2	140
Tidal volume (V_T) (L)	0.5	3
Breathing rate (f) (per min)	12	55
Expired ventilation ($\dot{V}_E$) (L/min)	6	180
O_2 consumption ($\dot{V}O_2$) (ml/min)	270	5,500
O_2 consumption ($\dot{V}O_2$) (ml/kg/min)	3.8	85
Alveolar PO_2 (P_AO_2) (mm Hg)	100	120
Arterial PO_2 (P_aO_2) (mm Hg)	97	90
(A-a) PO_2 difference (mm Hg)	2-10	30
Mixed venous PO_2 ($P_{\bar{v}}O_2$)	40	20
Arterial PCO_2 (P_aCO_2) (mm Hg)	40	25-32
Arterial pH	7.4	7.2-7.3
Pulmonary blood flow (L/min)	5	30
Lung capillary blood volume (ml)	70	250
Mean rbc transit time (sec)	0.75	0.5

a male runner with a hemoglobin concentration of 16 gm/dl and a P_aO_2 of 90 mm Hg. The binding affinity of O_2 for hemoglobin is 1.31 ml/gm, and O_2 is attached to 96% of the available sites (this is referred to as 96% saturation). At a P_aO_2 of 90 mmHg, the dissolved O_2 is (0.27 ml/dl). The bound O_2 is determined by the product of hemoglobin concentration times O_2 binding affinity times percent O_2 saturation (16 × 1.31 × 0.96). Thus,

$$O_2 \text{ content} = 0.27 + (16 \times 1.31 \times 0.96) = 20.39 \text{ ml/dl.} \quad (2.7)$$

Similarly, if the P_aO_2 were 98 mm Hg (giving a dissolved O_2 value of 0.29 ml/dl) and the hemoglobin saturation 98%, then the total O_2 content would be calculated as

$$O_2 \text{ content} = 0.29 + (16 \times 1.31 \times 0.98) = 20.83 \text{ ml/dl.} \quad (2.8)$$

For a woman runner with a hemoglobin concentration of 14 gm/dl and assuming a dissolved O_2 level of 0.27 ml/dl as well as 96% hemoglobin saturation with O_2, O_2 content would be as follows:

$$O_2 \text{ content} = 0.27 + (14 \times 1.31 \times 0.98) = 18.24 \text{ ml/dl.} \quad (2.9)$$

Thus, women have about 11% less O_2/dl of blood than men.

Figure 2.12 illustrates the relationship between blood PO_2 and the percentage of potential O_2 bind-

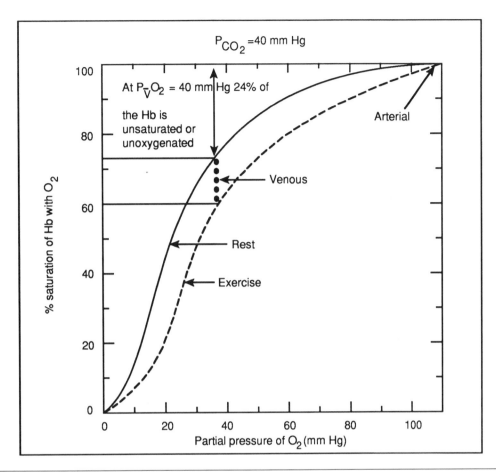

Figure 2.12 The oxyhemoglobin dissociation curve. A sigmoid relationship exists in relation to the binding of oxygen to hemoglobin when hemoglobin is exposed to increasing quantities of oxygen dissolved in red blood cell water. Arterial saturation (P_aO_2 = 100 mm Hg) is nearly 100%; mixed venous saturation ($P_{\bar{V}}O_2$ = 40 mm Hg) is about 75%. Increasing blood PCO_2 decreases binding affinity of hemoglobin for O_2, as seen by the right shift of the curve (dashed line). This occurs with exercise. As shown, at any given P_aCO_2 this decreased affinity permits release of sizable quantities of additional O_2 into the fluid portion of blood (as dissolved O_2), thereby ensuring a gradient of O_2 movement from blood into working tissues. *Note.* From *Respiratory Anatomy and Physiology* (p. 190) by D.E. Martin and J.W. Youtsey, 1988, St. Louis: C.V. Mosby. Copyright 1988 by C.V. Mosby. Reprinted by permission.

ing sites on hemoglobin that are saturated with O_2. The sigmoid shape of the binding relationship, as well as the fact that arterial blood hemoglobin is very nearly saturated with O_2 under normally existing PO_2 conditions, means that a considerable reduction in P_aO_2 can occur without much reduction in total arterial O_2 content.

When blood reaches the systemic capillaries, dissolved O_2 diffuses rapidly across the capillary membrane and into the adjacent tissues. This reduces the capillary PO_2, which in turn promotes the release of a portion of the O_2 reservoir of hemoglobin out into the surrounding plasma to help raise the capillary PO_2. Typically, as blood leaves the systemic capillaries, a sizable part of the O_2 reservoir of hemoglobin has been depleted, and the PO_2 is somewhat reduced.

Notice in Figure 2.12 that the PO_2 of mixed venous blood (the mixture of blood returning to the lungs from all the various tissue beds) has fallen from just under 100 mm Hg to about 40 mm Hg. At this $P_{\bar{V}}O_2$, there still remains about 75% of the total blood O_2 reservoir bound to hemoglobin. During intense exercise, the $P_{\bar{V}}O_2$ can fall to as low as 20 mm Hg.

During high-intensity exercise, does the (A-a)PO_2 gradient of 2 to 10 mm Hg remain? No, and this points out one limitation of the pulmonary system to exercise. Dempsey, Hanson, and Henderson (1984) have reported a steady reduction in dissolved arterial O_2 (called arterial hypoxemia) as highly trained distance runners approach their maximum performance capacities. At O_2 consumption values of 4,000 ml/min this (A-a)PO_2 gradient can be 20 to 30 mm Hg and as high as 40 mm Hg at O_2 consumption values of 5,000 ml/min (Table 2.2). Still, although this so-called *diffusion disequilibrium* is developing at these high work rates, adequate O_2 is available for the working tissues. It has not yet been accurately determined whether this disequilibrium is actually performance-limiting for these highly trained athletes.

What is the explanation for the decrease in P_aO_2 (and decreased hemoglobin saturation with O_2) seen with near-maximum exercise in trained runners? It is caused by a combination of two factors: the need to add much more than the usual quantity of O_2 to blood perfusing the lung capillaries, and the reduced amount of time that blood has in contact with the alveolar surface. Figure 2.13 shows us that normally a red blood cell will be in a pulmonary capillary for about 0.75 sec, well within the time required for nearly complete oxygenation to occur. Only about 0.6 sec is required. As exercise increases in intensity, blood flow through pulmonary capillaries increases and eventually is so rapid that only about 0.45 sec exists for alveolar gas exchange. Though this may

be adequate for CO_2 removal, it probably isn't for O_2 uptake.

Breathing During Progressively Increasing Exercise. The ventilatory system is self-optimizing in its efficiency of providing airflow. Just as with blood flow, where $CO = HR \times SV$, so also with breathing; expired ventilation ($\dot{V}_E$) is the product of breathing rate (f_R) and the volume expired per breath (tidal volume, or V_T). Thus,

$$\dot{V}_E = f_R \times V_T. \qquad (2.10)$$

Excessively deep breaths, few in number, would be too energy-costly. Very many breaths, each small in volume (as observed when dogs pant to rid themselves of heat by evaporative cooling) would not provide effective alveolar gas exchange. And so we optimize, with V_T never more than about 60% to 65% of the **vital capacity**, defined as the maximum amount of air that can be exhaled after a maximum inspiration. Thus, among our highly trained athletes undergoing a maximum exercise evaluation, we commonly record

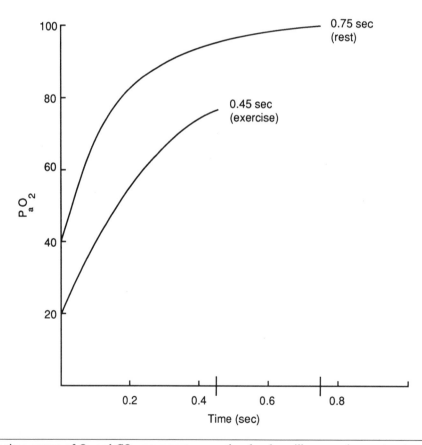

Figure 2.13 The time course of O_2 and CO_2 movement across the alveolocapillary membrane at rest and during exercise. At rest, with 0.75 sec available, only about 0.6 sec is required to achieve an acceptable arterial PO_2 of 95 mm Hg. However, during maximum exercise in very highly trained distance runners, only 0.45 sec may be available due to increased blood transit time through pulmonary capillaries. Thus, PO_2 values of not much more than 85 mm Hg may be reached in blood destined for the systemic arterial circulation.

maximum f_R values no greater than about 55/min. If each breath (V_T) is about 3,000 ml, this gives a $\dot{V}_E$ of about 165 L/min. Quite often, runners synchronize their f_R to stride frequency. Thus, if two footstrikes occur during the time required for both inhalation and exhalation, a commonly seen cadence of 196 footstrikes/min would permit 49 breaths/min. One practical implication of this information involves the shortening of stride and quickening of cadence when climbing hills. This coupling of f_R with increased stride frequency helps increase O_2 intake.

The primary respiratory muscle during resting breathing is the diaphragm, but exercise recruits a large number of accessory muscles to assist with ventilation. Some, such as the abdominal muscles, are primarily expiratory in their contribution. Their powerful expiratory force helps optimize the available inspiratory time as breathing depth increases. This also helps to lengthen the diaphragm, increasing the tension it can exert when it is stimulated. Other muscles, notably the intercostals, scalenes, and sternocleidomastoids, provide marked inspiratory assistance. Subtle but important activity in other muscles also makes breathing easier. Stimulation of laryngeal abductor muscles, for example, increases the diameter of this narrowest portion of the respiratory tract, thereby decreasing resistance to flow through it (Dempsey, Aaron, & Martin, 1988).

As we begin to exercise, and our V_T increases, the portion going into the alveoli (the so-called alveolar ventilation or $\dot{V}_A$) increases more than does the remaining dead space ventilation (V_D). Pulmonary physiologists thus say that the V_D/V_T ratio decreases with increasing exercise, at least initially. A steady-state level of elevated breathing depth and rate will match increased metabolic needs. This increased breathing to meet metabolic requirements is termed *exercise hyperpnea* and will continue until V_T reaches a plateau that corresponds to the first (ventilatory) threshold. As exercise intensity continues to increase beyond this threshold, the most efficient means for maintaining an increasing alveolar ventilation ($\dot{V}_A$) is to increase f_R.

During long-duration exercise at relatively low work intensities, such as between 50% and 60% of $\dot{V}O_2$max for about 2 hr, a gradual but measurable rise in breathing rate (15% to 40%) occurs, accompanied by a reduction in V_T (by about 10% to 15%). This is termed a *tachypneic ventilatory drift*. The decrease in V_T does not exactly compensate for the increased frequency because $\dot{V}_E$ increases as well. This drift is not observed during the short-duration runs (1 hr or less) that characterize most training sessions.

This slight increase in frequency is more energy-wasteful than resting breathing because of greater net air movement in relation to actual alveolar ventilation. Typically, about 70% of each V_T goes into the alveoli, with the remaining dead space ventilation filling the nonalveolar portion of the respiratory tract (from mouth through all the small lung passageways above the alveoli). With ventilatory drift, the small net decrease in alveolar ventilation causes a slight accumulation of CO_2 in arterial blood. We know that CO_2 is a powerful ventilatory stimulant, and this small rise in P_aCO_2 probably causes the gradual increase in $\dot{V}_E$ (by 10% to 30%). The level of $\dot{V}_E$, with its removal of CO_2, thereby serves as the major determinant of arterial H^+ ion concentration during this submaximum long-term work (i.e., at work loads ranging from a long training run to marathon-pace training or racing). These subtle changes in volume and rate dynamics are controlled automatically to optimize mechanical efficiency while maintaining normal blood O_2 and CO_2 concentrations. Thus, it is unwise for coaches or athletes to attempt voluntary regulation of breathing patterns during running, because it is unlikely that such changes will improve upon an already optimized regulatory pattern.

Body temperature modifies the hyperventilatory response. As body temperature increases, for example, with running on a warm and humid day, ventilation increases (MacDougall, Reddan, Layton, & Dempsey, 1974). Cooling, as permitted by running in conditions of low humidity that permit evaporative heat loss, in turn reduces the magnitude of hyperventilation.

Physically fit individuals typically can maintain a steady-state ventilation and blood acid-base equilibrium over a long period at exercise loads that do not exceed about 50% of their $\dot{V}O_2$max. Endurance training can raise this capability to more than 80% of $\dot{V}O_2$max. Because $\dot{V}O_2$max will also likely rise with such training, this represents a remarkable accommodation capability of the pulmonary system. When exercise intensity exceeds these values, for example, >50% of $\dot{V}O_2$max in fit individuals and >80% of $\dot{V}O_2$max in well-trained runners, then the steady state is no longer maintainable. The tachypneic ventilatory drift is observable, and a definite time limitation for prolonged exercise at such intensities exists.

These limitations in part explain the intensity at which various competitive distance events can be managed. As an example, the 10,000m event is raced by a trained athlete typically at roughly 90% to 92% of $\dot{V}O_2$max and the marathon at just below lactate/ventilatory threshold pace. Accumulating metabolic acidosis from the faster pace limits the time that 10,000m runners can race effectively at that intensity. Developing fatigue (from acidosis in 10,000m runners, fuel depletion in marathoners) decreases running efficiency, thereby increasing the metabolic rate required to maintain pace. In turn, heat production increases, raising core temperature. Increasing dehydration from fluid loss provides a smaller reservoir for perspiration, decreasing evaporative potential and also increasing body temperature. Both of these factors (dehydration and fatigue) contribute to the tachypneic ventilatory drift. Increased diversion of blood to maintain ventilatory muscle function occurs. Dempsey et al. (1988) refer to this as a ''stealing'' by the ventilatory muscles of blood flow from the pool available for the limb muscles. The extent of energy drain for maintaining effective ventilatory muscle activity during vigorous exercise has not been accurately quantified because of measurement difficulties, but it could be as high as 25% during hard work (Pardy, Hussain, & Macklem, 1984).

Trained endurance runners tend to exhibit a reduced ventilatory response to very intense exercise. Teleologically one could suggest that, because dyspnea is a limiting symptom for exercise tolerance, removing it might permit greater tolerance. Particularly in view of the reservoir of O_2 bound to hemoglobin, it might be possible for trained runners to optimize between a slightly reduced ventilation at the expense of greater arterial hemoglobin desaturation, thereby permitting increased high-level work tolerance. Indeed, such arterial hemoglobin desaturation does occur, as described in the literature (Dempsey et al., 1984) and seen in our own experience with trained runners.

One advantage of a decreased ventilation during heavy work loads would be a decreased ventilatory stealing of blood from the highly active limb muscles. Or it would prolong these maximum effects from occurring until an even greater work load had been reached, thereby helping to characterize the physiological greatness of an elite runner.

Thus, athletes undergoing arduous endurance training have been invaluable in identifying some of the limitations of the pulmonary system to high-level performance. There are limitations in gas exchange between alveoli and blood, increases in ventilatory cost, and an inability to sustain breathing at high rates. This same training has also provided a means for us to observe some of the temporary overrides for permitting such extremely intense exercise that might never be observed by studying the responses of less-trained people.

Changes in Pulmonary Function Among Trained Runners. Do trained distance runners have improved pulmonary function? When they are compared, in cross-sectional fashion, to age-, height-, and sex-matched untrained controls, there are improvements in some aspects. But because these same athletes were not evaluated before they began training, it is not

exactly certain to what extent hereditary components may also affect consideration of this matter. Are these subjects excellent runners because they possess pulmonary function capabilities greater than generally observed, or has training actually brought specific beneficial changes? We do not know.

Clinically, a *pulmonary function test* (PFT) assesses three different aspects of system performance: the size of the lungs, the dynamics of flow through the pulmonary system, and the ability of O_2 to diffuse from the environment through the lungs into the bloodstream. Figure 2.14 illustrates one of our athletes undergoing a PFT evaluation. Standard guidelines were published by the American Thoracic Society in 1979 for quantification of various lung volume and flow rate values, as well as for diffusing capacity. Using such guidelines, we have done PFT evaluations on a sizable population of trained distance runners, both men (Martin, May, & Pilbeam, 1986) and women (Martin & May, 1987) in an attempt to identify possible differences from an age-, height-, and sex-matched untrained control group. There is little statistical difference among the two population means due to considerable individual variation within each group, but quite large differences do exist among individual athletes. Another reason for conducting PFT evaluations is to screen for disease or quantify the extent of disease processes that do occur. Some of our athletes have varying degrees of exercise-induced asthma. PFT evaluation (illustrated in Figure 2.14 with Keith Brantly as the test subject) allows better identification of the extent of this breathing disorder as well as evaluation of the effectiveness of approved medication for treatment.

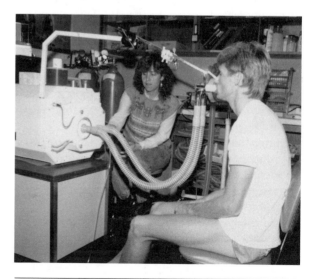

Figure 2.14 Pulmonary function evaluation of a trained distance runner. Typically, such studies include assessment of lung volume, flow rate, and diffusing capacity.

Among the various flow rate variables, one that we frequently find elevated among both trained men and women runners is *maximum voluntary ventilation* (MVV). This is determined as a 12- to 15-sec test of maximum airflow generation. One might predict such increased performance, as distance running requires that the muscles of breathing be moderately active during long runs and highly active during fast-paced sessions. Although MVV may be an indicator of short-term endurance, however, it may not be a good indicator of maximum sustainable ventilation (MSV). MSV can be measured during the final moments of treadmill testing as athletes are approaching their performance limits. MSV is also elevated among trained runners when compared to matched untrained controls. MVV is typically larger than MSV, by about 35%.

One complicating factor in appreciating pulmonary system performance is that runners nearing their MSV in treadmill tests to determine maximum performance are operating at a lower remaining lung volume at the end of each breath than they are when performing the MVV clinical test. The former condition is more efficient than the latter because the diaphragm is longer and able to generate tension more efficiently. We don't understand the mechanism explaining how these athletes respond to their clinical evaluation in a physiologically different manner than their natural breathing style during running. It may relate to how they perceive and perform their assigned task. During the MVV test athletes are seated, at rest, and encouraged to blow into and out of the collecting tube as rapidly and deeply as possible. The forced time urgency of the clinical test is likely greater than that of maintaining breathing during a stress test, and this may stimulate a slightly earlier inspiratory effort.

One of the variables related to lung volumes that seems consistently increased in trained runners is the inspiratory capacity (IC). This is the largest volume of air that can be inspired after one has taken a normal expiration (i.e., starting at the so-called end-expiratory position). Whereas an improvement in MVV could be ascribable to both inspiratory and expiratory muscle function, the increased IC suggests a measurable training effect among the inspiratory muscles, particularly the diaphragm. Stronger inspiratory muscles ought to be able to overcome more effectively the resistance of the chest and lungs at high volumes, permitting greater capacity.

Lung diffusing capacity represents the largest amount of O_2 that can transfer across the alveolo-capillary membrane and bind to hemoglobin molecules in the pulmonary capillary blood adjacent to that membrane. There is thus a *membrane component* (related to the thickness, surface area, and physicochemical properties of the alveolocapillary membrane) as well as a *perfusion component* (determined by pulmonary capillary blood volume and hematocrit). We find rather consistent increases in resting diffusing capacity among highly trained runners as compared to their matched sedentary controls, and the reason for this has not yet been clearly identified. The actual size of the lungs doesn't seem to increase with endurance training. But resting cardiac output (Henderson, Haggard, & Dolley, 1927) and total blood volume (Brotherhood et al., 1975) tend to be increased. This should bring more extensive lung perfusion with possibly a greater pulmonary blood volume, and thus an increased diffusing capacity. Active investigation of this interesting topic is underway in several laboratories around the world.

The Challenge of O_2 Transport by the Blood

Metabolizing tissues require O_2 in quantities far in excess of those solely dissolved in the bloodstream. Thus, an additional reservoir of O_2 is mandatory. Hemoglobin binds to O_2 and thus serves this need admirably. In fact, it carries 98.5% of all the O_2 in the bloodstream, only 1.5% being dissolved. Although hemoglobin has additional important roles in the transport of CO_2 and H^+ ions, which makes it a major buffer against acidosis, its role as an O_2 reservoir is primary.

On every pass through the circulatory system during resting conditions, each 100 ml (1 dl) of blood typically loses between 5 and 6 ml O_2 to meet the body's metabolic needs. If hemoglobin did not exist, insufficient O_2 would be available in the dissolved form to provide this requirement. Under resting conditions of blood flow (about 5 L/min flowing out of each of the right and left heart), the dissolved arterial O_2 partial pressure (P_aO_2) would need to be 2,000 mm Hg. But our resting sea-level P_aO_2 approaches only 100 mm Hg, limited by existing atmospheric conditions. Apart from breathing high concentrations of O_2 from a tank of pure O_2, the only other possibility to meet O_2 demands by dissolved O_2 alone would be to increase blood flow, but then we would need 80 L/min to provide enough O_2 to meet just resting needs. This is impossible, because even during maximum exercise the human heart isn't capable of permitting more than about 40 L/min of blood flow! Clearly, hemoglobin is a crucial molecule in solving the body's needs for a large quantity of available bound O_2.

The structure of hemoglobin gives many clues as to how it acts in carrying respiratory gases. It is a roughly spherical molecule consisting of four units, each of which in turn has a long protein chain (called globin), composed of about 150 amino acids, linked to a complex organic chemical ring structure (called a porphyrin). Whereas CO_2 and H^+ ions binds to the globin portion of the molecule, O_2 binds to *heme*, which is the term given to the porphyrin ring plus an iron atom bound to its center.

Many molecules resembling hemoglobin exist in the living world. Chlorophyll, for example, closely resembles heme. It was the substitution of iron for the magnesium found in chlorophyll that allowed heme to form, thus paving the way for the organic evolution of animals. Recall that the cytochrome enzymes of the electron transport chain have a heme structure as well, but with iron in the ferric (Fe^{+++}) oxidation state instead of the ferrous (Fe^{++}) state found in hemoglobin.

Myoglobin is an O_2-carrying pigment related to hemoglobin but different in several ways. It has only one heme moiety and one globin chain, and thus is only one fourth as large as hemoglobin. Myoglobin binds only one O_2 molecule (hemoglobin binds four), but its affinity for O_2 is much greater than that of hemoglobin. Whereas hemoglobin is fully saturated with O_2 at a PO_2 of about 100 mm Hg (which we typically approach in arterial blood), myoglobin is saturated at a PO_2 of only 27 mm Hg. Myoglobin is found in muscle tissue, not blood, and serves as a muscle O_2 reservoir. The two pigments interact very nicely, hemoglobin serving to transport O_2 from the lungs through blood to the working tissues and myoglobin maintaining an O_2 supply in the muscle tissue to meet metabolic needs during high demand, as with exercise. Myoglobin is thus an integral part of the so-called *O_2 cascade* as O_2 moves down its concentration gradient, from lungs to blood to tissues and finally to mitochondria.

The precise nature of the interrelationships between hemoglobin, O_2, and CO_2 were discovered at the turn of this century. In 1904, Christian Bohr, one of Denmark's leading physiologists, and two of his students, August Krogh and Karl Hasselbalch, described the nature of the O_2-binding relationship to hemoglobin that was illustrated in Figure 2.12. They hadn't planned, however, on also discovering a strong influence of CO_2 on the binding of O_2 to hemoglobin. If the PCO_2 was increased, the entire curve displaced, or shifted, to the right. If PCO_2 was lowered, the curve shifted to the left. These phenomena are often referred to as the *Bohr effect*. The increased PCO_2 can occur by fever or exercise; both are situations of increased metabolic needs. During exercise, the body temperature also rises, up to as high as 40 degrees C (104 degrees F) in active muscles. Thus, in the tissues, CO_2 entering capillary blood assists hemoglobin with its unloading of O_2, maintaining the gradient of O_2 flow from blood toward skeletal muscle mitochondria.

In the lungs, the reverse occurs. There, the blood PO_2 rapidly increases as O_2 moves from alveolus into capillary blood. Does this increased PO_2 decrease the amount of CO_2 that the blood can carry, which would be the opposite of the Bohr effect existing in metabolizing tissues? Yes, it does, because the increased oxygenation of hemoglobin decreases the amount of CO_2 that can be bound to it. Of course, in the pulmonary capillary CO_2 can quickly diffuse into adjacent alveoli. The influx of O_2 thus actually helps CO_2 leave the blood by favoring the movement of hemoglobin-bound CO_2 into solution. These relationships in the lung were reported in 1914 by John Scott Haldane at Oxford, together with his colleagues Charles Douglas and Joanne Christiansen.

The Critical Role of Iron in O_2 Transport and Utilization.

Of all the substances in metabolism contributing to the beneficial adaptations seen with endurance training, a powerful case could be made for iron as the most critical, for at least four reasons. One relates to hemoglobin. We have already described the increased circulating blood plasma volume and red cell mass that occur as an adaptation to endurance training (Brotherhood et al., 1975). Hemoglobin fills about one third of the volume of each red blood cell, so an increase in red cell mass results in an increased total hemoglobin. Without iron, hemoglobin cannot be manufactured.

An increased red cell mass means that the rate of production of red blood cells must be stepped up in endurance-trained athletes. In untrained people, typical dynamics of the red blood cell synthesis-breakdown continuum are such that about 233 million cells are released from the bone marrow into the bloodstream each second, with an equal number destroyed (Cronkite, 1973). This is increased even further among trained runners. A red blood cell has no nucleus and thus divides no further, but because all its precursor cells do, this cellular division requires enormous DNA turnover. The rate-limiting enzyme for DNA synthesis, ribonucleotide reductase, is iron-containing (Hoffbrand, Ganeshaguru, Hooton, & Tattersall, 1976). Without adequate iron, this enzyme cannot be produced in quantities required.

Endurance training is characterized among other things by an increased skeletal muscle content of myoglobin (Pattengale & Holloszy, 1967). As we mentioned previously, myoglobin is iron-containing; limitations in iron supply should reduce its availability as an O_2 storage reservoir in skeletal muscle.

We mentioned in chapter 1 that the volume and quantity of mitochondria increase in the skeletal muscles of trained endurance runners. The enzymes for oxidative phosphorylation are located in these organelles. Among these enzymes are those of the Krebs cycle, more than half of which are iron-containing (Dallman, Beutler, & Finch, 1978). So are the cytochrome proteins, which allow eventual interaction of O_2 with H^+ ions to form H_2O, completing the large-scale energy release from fuel breakdown.

Thus, although even at rest there is a varied and essential iron requirement to ensure blood O_2 transport, intracellular muscle O_2 storage, and complete fuel breakdown, for athletes undergoing high-volume endurance training this requirement is increased. Realizing this, the hypothesis could be advanced that this challenges the body's ability to acquire and store adequate iron reserves, and that this limit may compromise the magnitude of adaptations to the training response.

To examine this hypothesis, it is appropriate to ask the following seemingly simple question: "Do elite-level endurance runners exhibit definable indications of reduced iron stores?" The best answer is that they apparently do, and rather commonly (Haymes & Lamanca, 1989). Given this, then several other questions follow. First, what are the characteristics of this reduction? Second, could iron inadequacy compromise training effectiveness, and how? Third, is the inadequacy caused by iron intake problems? Fourth, can strenuous training contribute to an increased loss of iron stores? Fifth, could dietary iron supplementation be useful in maintaining optimum iron stores in runners with diminished supplies? Sixth, what are the mechanisms by which reduced iron availability might impair training effectiveness? Particularly this latter question has brought controversy (Newhouse & Clement, 1988) because of its very practical relevance to athletes striving toward successful long-term adaptation to training.

Iron Depletion as a Potential Problem for Distance Runners. When we first began to evaluate the performance characteristics of highly trained distance runners, we were intrigued by literature reports of what seemed to be an increased incidence of anemia among Olympic team endurance athletes. The Dutch team was surveyed in 1968 (DeWijn, deJongste, Mosterd, & Willebrand, 1971), the Australian team in 1972 (Stewart, Steel, Tayne, & Stewart, 1972), and the Canadian team in 1976 (Clement, Asmundson, & Medhurst, 1977). Hemoglobin levels were frequently lower than among the general population, particularly in distance runners. We know now, of course, that this decrease is likely a result of their increased plasma volume caused by endurance training. It is now well-known that such training increases the release by the body of such hormones as aldosterone, vasopressin, and renin, causing a net

retention of Na^+ and H_2O and thus a volume expansion of the blood and a dilutional pseudoanemia. We did not observe this decrease in blood hemoglobin in the athletes we profiled, which led to our continuing interest in better understanding the importance of iron in the dynamics of oxygen transport and fuel metabolism.

Table 2.4 summarizes blood chemistry data collected from 15 of our male athletes whose specialty at the time was marathon training and racing. Their range of personal best race performances certainly attests to their status as talented athletes, but it by no means suggests that they had consistently good health or race performances. On the contrary, they were more often fraught with downtime due to injury or periods of profound fatigue, and they wanted to learn how to turn this situation around. We gained some helpful clues about their tendency for breakdown and how to prevent it as we began to better appreciate the importance of each of the blood chemistry variables that we profiled.

Table 2.4 Selected Erythrocytic and Hematologic Variables in Elite Male Marathoners[a]

Variable	Reference range		Athlete mean[b]	
Erythrocytes (billion/ml)	4.5 -	6.2	5.08 ±	0.27
Hematocrit (%)	38 -	45	44.9 ±	2.1
Hemoglobin (gm/dl)	14 -	17	15.7 ±	0.74
Serum iron (μgm/dl)	50 -	165	97 ±	39.2
Ferritin (ng/ml)	50 -	150	30.1 ±	12.7
Haptoglobin (mg/dl)	27 -	139	27.6 ±	21.4
Reticulocytes (thousand/μl)	10 -	50	55.3 ±	36.8

[a]n = 15; mean age = 27 yr (range 24 - 30); mean best marathon time 2:13:41 ± 2:13.

[b]All values ± 1 standard deviation.

Hemoglobin levels among these athletes were, as mentioned, entirely within the normal reference range, and all but two were within the normal mean range of 15 to 16 gm/dl. Hemoglobin is contained within the red blood cells, and the athletes' red cell count was also within the normal reference range, as was their hematocrit. Assuming that our runners had the plasma volume increase characteristic of this population, they must have been using additional iron from their available stores to produce the extra hemoglobin required to keep its concentration unchanged.

Ferritin is the body's primary iron-storage molecule in all cells. The mean serum ferritin level, as well as most of the individual values, was significantly lower than the accepted range for healthy untrained people. Only two athletes were as high as the low-normal range; the rest were lower. In adults, most red blood cells are produced in the bone marrow. The level of circulating blood ferritin correlates quite well with bone marrow iron stores. Four of the 15 ferritin values were below 20 nanograms per milliliter (ng/ml). In our assay, a ferritin level of 20 ng/ml or lower in the blood indicates zero bone marrow iron stores. Interestingly, those athletes with the lowest ferritin levels also had the lowest blood hemoglobin and red blood cell concentrations.

We continue to find this trend among both middle- and long-distance runners engaged in hard training. Instead of observing routinely in endurance runners a dilutional pseudoanemia with lower-than-normal hemoglobin values, we find normal hemoglobin levels accompanied by low ferritin levels. In these highly fit athletes, the body's top priority for iron utilization seems to be the capability for adequate oxygen transport (via hemoglobin). This may leave inadequate iron available for the increased requirements in producing iron-containing enzymes as skeletal muscles attempt to adapt to training.

Four of these runners demonstrated an increased bone marrow response to the stress of training, as shown by greater bone marrow activity to produce more red blood cells (their ferritin levels were > 25 ng/ml). This response was seen as an elevation in the blood level of reticulocytes and the presence of shift cells. Reticulocytes are immature red blood cells, and shift cells (also called stress reticulocytes) are slightly more immature cells normally restricted to the bone marrow. The increased presence of these cells in blood is a clinical indication that the marrow is responding to the need for additional O_2 carrying capacity. The high end of the reference range for reticulocytes is 50,000/μl, and in our laboratory > 75,000/μl indicates a vigorous response. However, four athletes were in the low-normal range (< 20,000/μl), and their ferritin levels were < 20 ng/ml. The remaining five athletes fell between these extremes but had ferritin levels > 20 ng/ml. The suggestion from these data is that only when iron stores are adequate is bone marrow activity responsive to meet increased O_2 delivery requirements by producing more hemoglobin-containing red blood cells.

The clinical picture, then, for many of these runners is iron depletion (low body stores of iron) rather than iron deficiency (low hemoglobin levels, or anemia, in addition to iron depletion). Similar findings have been published by others studying distance runners (Clement & Admundson, 1982; Dufaux, Hoederath, Streitberger, Hollmann, & Assman, 1981).

Serum haptoglobin levels in our 15 runners also averaged below the lower normal limit of 50 mg/dl in untrained people. Our reference range is 27 to 139 mg/dl, and 7 of the 13 runners were below this limit. Haptoglobin is a normally circulating plasma protein whose function is to bind to free hemoglobin that gets released into the plasma when red blood cells break down, either after their normal life span of about 120 days or for other reasons. This haptoglobin-hemoglobin complex is captured either by the liver (Magnusson, Hallberg, Rossander, & Swolin, 1984) or by specialized cells located along the linings of blood vessels (called the reticuloendothelial system), where iron is reclaimed and redistributed. Serum ferritin reflects metabolism of iron stores from either of these routes (Letsky, Miller, Worwood, & Flynn, 1974). A decrease in available haptoglobin suggests that red blood cell breakdown (hemolysis) is elevated, because only unbound haptoglobin is quantified by the assay procedure. When enough hemoglobin is liberated by intravascular hemolysis, the haptoglobin concentration falls quickly and can reach zero within 8 to 12 hours. Return toward normal then begins due to the continued release of haptoglobin into the circulation from the liver. Should the haptoglobin level fall to zero, remaining unbound hemoglobin may be filtered by the kidneys, resulting in a loss of iron from the bloodstream (Allison, 1957).

A recent study has confirmed that the major cause of hemolysis during running is mechanical trauma to red blood cells from increased foot impact forces (Miller, Pate, & Burgess, 1988), as illustrated in Figure 2.15. Running shoe technology has brought marvelous improvements in impact shock absorption, but athletes training 15 miles a day (24 km/day) still subject themselves to over 15,000 footstrikes with more than twice their body weight impacting on plantar surfaces. Hemolysis is thus inevitable in the plantar capillaries of the feet. This is an extension of the so-called "march hemoglobinuria" first observed in soldiers more than a century ago (Fleischer, 1881) and later observed in apparently healthy athletes after they ran long distances (Attlee, 1937).

There are other causes of hemolysis, also illustrated in Figure 2.15. One is an increased red blood cell membrane instability caused by acidosis (Yoshimura, Inoue, Yamada, & Shiraki, 1980), which results from faster-paced anaerobic training. Red blood cells on the slightly more acidic venous side are more fragile and susceptible to hemolysis. Another cause of hemolysis is mechanical trauma from an increased velocity of movement. As the cardiac output rises during intense training or racing, movement velocity of blood increases. Red blood cells are barely small enough to pass through capillaries, and often they must bend

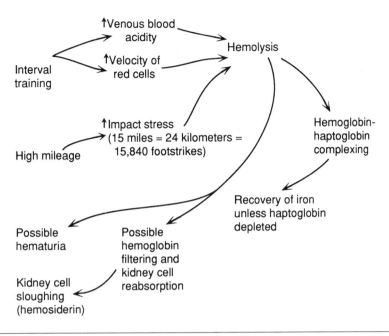

Figure 2.15 Increased blood acidity, red cell velocity, and impact stress can all increase the red blood cell destruction rate, with a risk for increased urinary iron loss unless hemoglobin can be recovered.

and twist to do so. Flow through larger vessels may become turbulent instead of laminar, which also increases the susceptibility to damage. Extravascular compression by skeletal muscles generating tension also makes blood vessels smaller and can even force them completely shut, causing additional trauma to the cells within.

Because of the time course of haptoglobin decline and return following training hemolysis, the timing of blood evaluation to observe such changes is important to assess maximum-effect responses of specific training sessions. Our blood collections with athletes are in the early morning, fully 15 or more hours after their previous training. Thus, although we often see values below 10 mg/dl among those athletes as a residual effect of very hard training, we have never seen levels that are so low as to be unmeasureable. We do suspect that this occurs, however, because of information we have gained through urine analysis. The kidney tubules have a maximum absorption rate for iron, after which any excess filtered hemoglobin is excreted in the urine (this is called *hematuria*). Iron stored in these tubule cells is bound to an insoluble protein called *hemosiderin*. As part of kidney cell homeostasis and normal sloughing of cells, hemosiderin appears in the urine and can be visualized using appropriate staining techniques. Among athletes with low haptoglobin, we commonly find a positive urine hemosiderin test.

Clearly, the greater an individual's level of endurance fitness, the greater the O_2 demands and the more

extensive the body's system of iron storage and utilization must be to ensure that these demands are met, but there are other demands as well. It is tempting to suggest that the body manages iron supplies so as to give top priority to providing adequate O_2 carrying abilities via hemoglobin and secondarily to distributing iron to the many iron-containing enzymes essential for aerobic metabolism. Whereas clinically normal or moderately low hemoglobin values may not constitute functional anemia in sedentary populations, they may indeed do so in physically active populations (Pate, 1983). However, as more iron-containing enzymes are required for increasing metabolic demands, such synthesis draws even more heavily upon existing iron reserves. If adequate iron is not available, this synthesis likely will not occur, and the athlete essentially does not progress in cellular adaptation to training. If the athlete then begins to increase the intensity or volume of training load as part of the continuing phase of development, inadequate prior adaptation typically brings either fatigue, illness, or injury.

The increased loss of iron from hemolysis and inadequate iron recapture stimulates other questions concerning iron availability, some of which were mentioned earlier. It turns out that decreased dietary iron intake and increased iron loss are important considerations in understanding the dynamics of iron availability in such athletes. Each of these aspects can be discussed briefly.

There are two primary dietary sources of iron. One

is through consumption of red meat, with its accompanying hemoglobin and myoglobin; this is called heme iron because of the iron attachment to the heme portion of these molecules. Of all the available dietary forms of iron, heme iron is the most easily absorbed (Conrad, Benjamin, Williams, & Fox, 1967). The human species evolved as an omnivorous hunter-gatherer and thus has maintained a hereditary preference for heme iron.

The other source of iron is via a variety of non-heme-containing foods. Iron is plentiful in egg yolks, dates, baked or boiled potatoes, dried fruits, baked beans with molasses, broccoli, brussel sprouts, and soybeans. Cooking with iron pots and skillets also provides a source of elemental iron, but our current trend toward plastic-coated utensils has decreased the availability of iron from that route. Absorption of nonheme iron depends on the presence of accompanying ligands in food that will either enhance or inhibit conversion of iron from the Fe^{+++} to the Fe^{++} oxidation state. For inhibition of absorption, egg yolk has a phosphoprotein, polyphenols such as tannin are prevalent in coffee and tea, and bran fiber is present in wheat and cereals. Also, calcium and zinc compete with iron for the same receptor site, decreasing iron absorption if these other two atoms are also present in sizable quantity. Enhancement of iron absorption occurs in the presence of ascorbic acid and citric acid in fruits and amino acids derived from the digestion of red meat and fish. This underscores the importance of at least a modest portion of lean red meat in the diet as both a source of heme iron and an enhancer of nonheme iron absorption (Snyder, Dvorak, & Roepke, 1989). The prevalence of nutritional iron deficiency rises as the amount of dietary animal protein diminishes.

Current dietary practices for elite runners in many parts of the world as well as for much of American society emphasize low saturated fats and cholesterol, which implies a minimum of red meat intake, and a greater emphasis on vegetable protein and complex carbohydrates. For athletes scheduling two training sessions per day and who require a high energy intake that can be assimilated easily and quickly, such emphasis is useful. However, this diet is likely to have a lowered iron content.

As athletes increase their intensity of training, particularly regarding anaerobic interval sessions, the accompanying gastrointestinal tract ischemia, with blood flow being reduced by as much as 80% (Clausen, 1977), commonly decreases appetite. Stored fat reserves are then used for required energy needs, typically observed over time as a decreased percent body fat. Though this decrease may enhance performance as there is less body mass to transport, an extended

period of decreased iron intake may reduce the total amount of iron assimilation into the enzymes of aerobic metabolism. And the decrease in energy intake as well as intake of other nutritional elements may also compromise performance if prolonged. A side effect of the ischemia from intense training may be an increased rate of cell sloughing in the gastrointestinal tract, causing loss of already absorbed iron that has not yet entered the bloodstream (Green et al., 1968). It is suspected that hypoxia is the ultimate cause of the increased cell sloughing. These aspects of physiology all need closer investigative scrutiny in distance runners before the full practical extent of this problem of dietary iron intake and loss is realized.

Runners also appear to have elevated iron losses in comparison to the sedentary population. At least three possible routes exist for iron loss from the body: via perspiration, the gastrointestinal tract, and the urinary tract. The final story has certainly not been synthesized on this subject either, and more research should provide a better basis for deciding which routes may be most important in iron loss. Early studies of iron losses in perspiration (Paulev, Jordal, & Pedersen, 1983; Vellar, 1968) suggested that this route was of considerable importance, but a more recent study (Brune, Magnusson, Persson, & Hallberg, 1986) concluded that iron losses in sweat (obtained from people in a sauna) are minor. The differences in composition of sweat from exercising athletes and that from people in a sauna need to be quantified.

Although it has been suggested that runners may lose iron from the gastrointestinal tract during hard races (Stewart et al., 1984), a more routine loss can occur from the use of aspirin. It is common for elite runners to ingest therapeutic doses of aspirin as both an analgesic and an anti-inflammatory agent during periods of particularly intense training. One gram of aspirin per day causes about 1 ml of blood loss, which represents anywhere from 0.5 mg (Wintrobe et al., 1981) to 1.5 mg (Stewart et al., 1984) of iron loss.

Perspectives for Maintaining a Healthy Blood O_2 Transport Status. In applying the concepts described previously to a coach and an athlete aspiring to a successful college championship or other track season peak, which typically occur during early to late summer, one can envision a sad scenario. The athlete has successfully endured many months of hard work in preparation for a superlative competitive result. However, training and lifestyle patterns favor a net iron loss rather than a balance between iron intake and output, and the stage is set for an eventual inadequacy in iron availability. Let us take the example of late spring and early summer training. The days get warmer, and losses of iron through sweat increase. Training gets more intensive, and thus hemolysis from both impact stress and blood acidosis increases. Gastrointestinal ischemia from such higher intensity training, as well as an accompanying decrease in appetite, result in lowered iron intake.

It is almost an occupational hazard of such a lifestyle for progressive depletion of available iron supplies to occur when they are most needed. The athlete progresses very well through the middle of the season, with several weeks remaining before championship time, but then takes a turn for the worse. For no apparent reason, a state best characterized as "burnout" develops, with sleepless nights, more fatigue than usual, and decreased ability to manage even less intense training than was easily tolerated a few weeks before. Training continues, because the championships are impending, but the athlete never recovers, instead experiencing progressively poorer quality training, a developing bad attitude, and a dismal showing at the championships. This happens all too often, and when we are contacted (typically too late) by an athlete in such a state, a blood chemistry evaluation shows acceptable hemoglobin but very low ferritin, haptoglobin, and reticulocyte levels and a positive hemosiderin test. This athlete's iron stores may not have been adequate to meet the various metabolic adaptations required beyond adequate O_2 transport.

We have had many opportunities to take blood chemistry profiles from runners in the middle of such late-spring warm-weather buildups to important championships, and we have found the same pattern of values. We have suggested that the athlete attempt to improve iron stores by taking an oral supplement (0.5 to 1.0 mg/kg body weight) in the form of ferrous sulfate, gluconate, or fumarate. For a 60-kg athlete, this would be 30 to 60 mg, compared to the recommended dietary iron allowance of 15 mg/day for adult women and 10 mg/day for adult men (Food and Nutrition Board, 1989). Because even a small amount of iron supplementation can cause side effects ranging from constipation to gut aches to dark stools, evening intake is optimal because training does not occur again for many hours. Also, substances that inhibit iron absorption are typically absent from the evening meal. For most athletes, a turnaround in tolerance to training occurs within 2 weeks—they can manage comparable work loads, they lose the sensation of profound fatigue, and they regain a positive attitude to training. One might consider the explanation simply a placebo effect, but this is not likely the case, because taking a pill becomes a simple daily habit. (This has been difficult to specifically assess, because the side effects of iron supplementation are difficult to duplicate in a placebo pill to be used in a double-blind randomized trial study design.)

We never suggest such supplementation without continued blood chemistry monitoring. Just as fast-paced running sessions typically are timed precisely, with records kept to examine progress, periodic blood chemistry evaluation is also important when dietary iron supplementation is considered. Such supplementation should not be considered unless needed. A small percentage (about 5% to 10%) of the population is subject to iron overload, which causes symptoms of extreme fatigue and malaise (Herbert, 1987) similar to those with iron inadequacy. Our common experience with such subsequent blood profiling is that reticulocyte count increases, a small increase in hemoglobin occurs, ferritin rises, and both haptoglobin and hemosiderin data remain unchanged unless training changes. We certainly are not stating that iron supplementation is the instant and permanent cure for illness and fatigue in seriously training endurance runners. Inappropriately excessive training will eventually prove disastrous to any athlete. We do suggest, however, that over the time course of training sessions, athletes enduring high-volume and high-intensity training have considerably increased needs for iron above the requirement for hemoglobin, and unless these are satisfied, symptoms of performance reduction similar to those found with iron deficiency are likely even though only iron depletion exists.

This point is emphasized because recent articles (Eichner, 1988; Peota, 1989) suggest that the notion of performance impairment in athletes as a result of iron store depletion may be more fallacy than fact. Unfortunately, a generalization is being made; conclusions from study subjects who fit the category of "active people" or athletic individuals with moderate training schedules cannot be applied to elite-level endurance runners managing distance running training schedules requiring 80-plus miles (130-plus km) per week on a continual basis. Such extension of conclusions from one subject group to another is inappropriate here. Highly trained distance runners are athletes with performance requirements quite different from people engaged in serious fitness programs.

Even more important than the consideration of iron supplementation are suggestions for improving the training environment in a manner that helps to reduce iron loss and enhance iron acquisition.

1. Train as often as possible on packed dirt trails or low-cut, smooth grass surfaces.
2. Eliminate unnecessary volumes of low-intensity running that simply burn fuel without improving aerobic fitness, add impact stress, and give the logbook a high number for weekly completed distance.
3. Train during the cool parts of the day.

4. Eat a modest amount of lean red meat.
5. Stay away from beverages such as coffee and tea, which reduce iron absorption and contribute to dehydration due to their diuretic effect.
6. Plan occasional days with no running to permit dietary replenishment, mental refreshment, and physical recovery.

MEASURING CARDIOPULMONARY PERFORMANCE USING LABORATORY TESTING

We have now identified the major kinds of cardiopulmonary and blood responses and adaptations that occur with training, and we have also indicated that it is useful to identify specific training pace ranges that will best permit these kinds of adaptations. Scientists for many years have been devising various test protocols to evaluate individual responsiveness to exercise tolerance. Coaches and athletes have also been doing this in a less specific manner, using time trials over a measured distance or race simulations. It is quite possible, and indeed in vogue, to devise laboratory test protocols that satisfy everyone: Scientists obtain interesting data concerning the physiological response of the tested individual to exercise, and athletes and coaches can directly apply the results to training. Sets of data from a large athlete population of comparable fitness can be contrasted with similar results from an age-matched untrained population; scientists call this a *cross-sectional study*. Athletes and coaches tend instead to prefer *longitudinal studies*—sets of data obtained several times during the course of a training season and then from year to year, with the athlete serving as his or her own control—to identify changes in such variables as $\dot{V}O_2$max, lactate/ventilatory threshold, and running economy and also to develop suggested training paces based upon these data.

Coaches unaware of the benefits of laboratory monitoring sometimes question the worth of such testing: "It doesn't mimic a race," they say. "My athlete does not race or train on a treadmill, and in addition, in a race situation so many other extraneous variables contribute to the outcome." Though all this is true, these coaches are missing the underlying rationale for laboratory profiling. We specifically attempt to remove as many extraneous variables as possible, such as weather, terrain, and tactics, because then changes observed are more likely to be caused by a physiological adaptation to training. Useful information in any or all of three important areas can be obtained:

1. Improvements in training since the past evaluation are readily identifiable.
2. Suggestions for the next phase of development can be given more precisely.
3. Race strategies can be suggested that take advantage of the athlete's existing performance strengths.

All of this assists the athlete's development and fine-tuning. Also, treadmill training can help athletes develop a working knowledge of the effort sense or stress level required for running at specific paces, particularly the optimum sub–lactate/ventilatory threshold race pace for marathon runners. Then, as they train in varying weather and terrain, their overground pace can vary as they instinctively maintain effort sense. Prevention of overtraining in such circumstances is an important legacy of the intelligent use of such information. Particularly as athletes achieve greater excellence and require a stronger training stimulus for improvement, such specific training takes on added value.

Scientists first began to study the physiological capabilities of trained athletes during the early part of this century. Some of the best scientists of the day—Lindhard in Denmark (1915), Liljestrand and Stenstrom in Stockholm (1920), and Hill and Lupton in London (1923)—designed equipment and protocols that, although pioneering, were so sound that the principles underlying their use are still applied today. Equipment presently available for this purpose is sophisticated, although computerization has simplified much of the tedium of data collection and analysis. Because of the importance of O_2 in metabolism and because the amount of O_2 that can be taken up and used is an endpoint that can be identified easily, $\dot{V}O_2$max has long been the most widely used criterion for assessing maximum endurance performance. This value quantifies the net ability of the cardiorespiratory system to transport O_2 to all the active tissues and the ability of these tissues to use it (Astrand, 1976).

Many methods have been developed for quantifying $\dot{V}O_2$max, but treadmill running and bicycle ergometry are used most frequently (Hermansen & Saltin, 1969). Evaluation of untrained people who have had very little experience with either running or bicycling usually shows a higher $\dot{V}O_2$max value when using a treadmill than when using a bicycle ergometer. Treadmill testing can lead to higher values by as much as 4% to 23% (Astrand, 1976; Hermansen & Saltin, 1969; Kamon & Pandolf, 1972). Because a larger total muscle mass is active (the upper as well as the lower limbs), venous blood return to the heart is greater. Venous return typically equals cardiac output, which is an important variable affecting $\dot{V}O_2$max (Shephard et al., 1968).

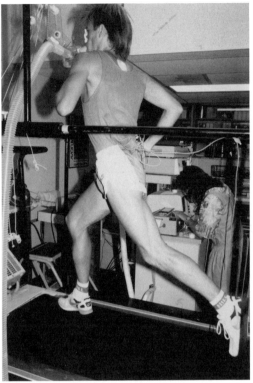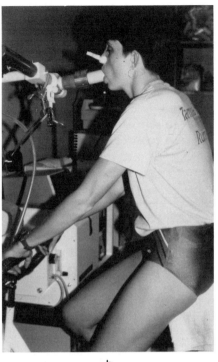

a   b

Figure 2.16   The two most popular modes of evaluating endurance exercise capabilities in the laboratory: a treadmill run (a) and bicycle ergometry (b).

Improvements in $\dot{V}O_2$max occur with training and are best identifiable using a test protocol that challenges the body in a manner most similar to the mode of training (Clausen, Klausen, Rasmussen, & Trap-Jensen, 1973; McArdle, Magel, Delio, Toner, & Chase, 1978). Trained cyclists thus are at a disadvantage using a treadmill test when compared to a bicycle ergometer (Hagberg, Giese, & Schneider, 1978). Analogously, runners are at a disadvantage when tested using a bicycle (Pannier, Vrijens, & Van Cauter, 1980). Thus, as demonstrated in Figure 2.16a by U.S. long-distance star Jon Sinclair, we use a treadmill for our maximum performance tests of runners. However, for certain specialized tests, such as cold-air challenge tests to evaluate exercise-induced asthma, as illustrated in Figure 2.16b by Britain's two-time Olympic 3,000m finalist Wendy Sly, a bicycle is perfectly acceptable because the purpose is to produce a mild exercise response rather than determine $\dot{V}O_2$max.

How high can one raise $\dot{V}O_2$max by training? In part the answer relates to inherent genetic endowment, but the level of fitness at which one begins the training program also plays a role. Recent studies have shown (Makrides, Heigenhauser, McCartney, &

Jones, 1986) that untrained people over a broad age range who embark upon a serious aerobic fitness development program can raise their sedentary lifestyle $\dot{V}O_2$max values as much as 40% or more (for example, from 35 to 50 ml/kg/min). Among already established top-level runners, this percentage increase is considerably less. Although some researchers claim that $\dot{V}O_2$max among elite-level runners changes little over the course of a year, we find quite distinct differences, determined according to varying emphasis in training. We have seen as much as 18% improvements in some of our top-level distance runners over the period of a successful training year, from 4,695 to 5,525 ml/min as an example, in one athlete over a 7-month period whose weight remained unchanged.

We mentioned very early in this chapter that the interaction of aerobic with anaerobic capabilities determines an individual's performance ability in an all-out competitive effort. Does aerobic power by itself relate to successful performance in competitive distance running? For any given competitive distance being considered, this relationship depends on the nature of the athlete population being studied. Unfortunately, the wide variation among research study populations has resulted in a wide range of correlation coefficients (from $r = 0.08$ to $r = 0.91$) relating VO_2max to race performance (McConnell, 1988). In statistical analysis, a correlation coefficient (r) of 0.91 suggests a rather strong linear relationship between the two compared variables. If the athlete population is heterogeneous; that is, made up of people comprising a broad spectrum of aerobic fitness (as demonstrated by a wide spread of VO_2max values, such as from 35 to 85 ml/kg/min), then there is a high statistical correlation between aerobic power and competitive performance. When considered together, those athletes at the top of world performance lists in middle- and long-distance events typically have a VO_2max averaging 77 ml/kg/min for males and 66 ml/kg/min for females. Those values are between 60% and 70% higher than the 48 and 39 ml/kg/min values observed commonly among untrained young adults whose performance times in running events would be far slower than those of the world's best endurance athletes.

If the group of people under consideration is homogeneous; that is, if we are considering the fastest 20 people in the world for a given distance-running event, then the correlation between performance and VO_2max is poorer. In other words, if we could determine VO_2max from all these athletes under similar laboratory conditions 1 week before a race and then have them all race under identical conditions, the order of finish would very likely not relate to the rank order of VO_2max values. The correlation between aerobic power and performance would be rather low.

Therefore, other variables must contribute to race performance along with VO_2max. We suggested early in this chapter that such a group of runners judged homogeneous simply by their competition results is probably rather heterogeneous in their aerobic and anaerobic performance capacities. Thus, those athletes with the most outstanding competitive results probably had the best combination of high aerobic *as well as* lactate/ventilatory capability. For example, the athletes with the very best performances may have had a high VO_2max, a high lactate/ventilatory threshold (both in absolute terms and as a percentage of VO_2max), a long test duration time beyond achievement of VO_2max, a high VCO_2max, and a tolerance to high tissue and blood acidity, whereas those farther back in the rankings most likely had fewer of these variables well developed.

A problem exists in attempting to steadily increase aerobic and anaerobic capabilities through training. The greater the increase in such performance indicators as VO_2max, lactate/ventilatory threshold pace, and whatever maximum anaerobic work indicators are used, the greater the subsequent intensity and volume of training required for any further increases. Thus,

higher volumes of aerobic running bring so little performance benefit that the increasing risks of overuse injury or development of symptoms of overtraining outweigh the potential performance gains. To use a medical expression, the *risk-benefit ratio* becomes excessively high. Sjodin and Svedenhag (1985) have seriously questioned the benefits of more than 115 to 120 km/week (71 to 75 mi/week) at lower intensity aerobic conditioning paces for distance runners seeking to improve their VO_2max values. Marathon runners are a special case in requiring very high training volumes in order to stimulate greater fuel storage abilities in their working muscles. They also realize that they must build greater connective tissue tolerance to prolonged impact stress, but they well know that this is done at the increased risk of overuse injury. As suggested earlier in this chapter, once aerobic conditioning has provided the initial stimulus, this should then be followed by higher intensity (quicker pace, shorter distance) aerobic capacity training sessions to bring VO_2max to its peak for that particular training season.

Graded Exercise Test (GXT) Design to Measure Fitness in Distance Runners

The term *graded exercise test* or GXT is commonly applied to a cardiopulmonary fitness evaluation in which the test subject is assigned a protocol involving a graded (i.e., gradual) increase in work load that produces either voluntary exhaustion or a level of submaximum exercise sufficient to permit observation of certain disease symptoms. Very often, such a test involves walking or running uphill, and this has caused some semantic confusion. The term "graded" does not refer to a specific percent grade (often several will be used) or rate of treadmill inclination.

Test protocols tend to vary widely, having been developed to fit available equipment, subjects studied, and investigator preferences. Our athletes prefer a single treadmill test to measure VO_2max, ventilatory threshold, submaximum running economy, and maximum performance capacity. This can essentially all be done by monitoring heart rate and expired air to determine minute ventilation, CO_2 production, and O_2 uptake. Collecting a blood specimen before and after the test allows determination of maximum achieved blood lactate concentration. Some laboratories prefer two separate tests, one for VO_2max and the other for running economy and some of the other variables, including intermittent blood sampling for identification of lactate threshold. If good technique is combined with sensible methodology, the actual values obtained for the measured variables are similar with each protocol.

Some general constraints in designing treadmill test protocols can be outlined here to help athletes and coaches better understand the logistics of test implementation. First, test length should optimize accurate data collection. Our tests measure

1. O_2 consumption at several submaximum training paces,
2. the threshold at which steady-state work can no longer be maintained, and
3. the absolute limits of performance.

Metabolic measuring systems use either mixing chambers (from which expired air collected over prescribed periods is sampled periodically) or breath-by-breath analyses of gas composition. Thus, our protocol is a stepwise series of steady-state pace increases every few minutes, changing to a rampwise format with steadily increasing work rates to optimize information collection in the shortest time possible. Taylor, Wang, Rowell, & Blomqvist (1963) concluded that all major physiological adaptations to permit such high-level exercise are functioning within about ten minutes. From a measurement viewpoint, a relatively short test is also advantageous because we desire physiological changes large enough to be identifiable. Variations in sequential measurements caused by analytical noise must be substantially less than the various threshold changes being studied. Thus, our athletes are on the treadmill for 18 to 22 minutes, with only the final 11 to 13 minutes being truly stressful.

Second, because a higher $\dot{V}O_2$max value is obtained by having subjects climb a grade rather than run on a solely level surface, uphill running should form the final portion of the test protocol. Saltin and Astrand (1967) recommended a 2.6% grade rise every 3 min. Shephard et al. (1968) suggested 2.5% grade increments every 2 min. In our studies of elite runners we use 2% grade rises every 2 min during the final portion of the test after completion of our O_2 cost studies using level-surface running.

Third, running velocities or paces for the GXT should be selected that fit comfortably within the training habits of the tested athletes (McConnell, 1988). Each work load should be a similar increment of intensity higher than the preceding in energy cost. Pollock (1977) suggested a range of 10.5 to 12 km/hr (9:12 to 8 min/mi) for sedentary controls and 16.1 to 19.4 km/hr (6 to 5 min/mi) for trained runners. Our GXT protocols have male athletes run from 14.5 to 19.4 km/hr (7:30 to 5 min/mi); the women have a smaller range, from 14.5 to 16.5 km/hr (7:30 to 5:50/mi).

Fourth, treadmill data collection conditions should be kept as constant as possible to optimize the detection of changes in fitness of the athletes tested from one session to the next. We keep relative humidity at less than 50% to ensure effective evaporative cooling. We also maintain our laboratory room temperature at a relatively cool 17 degrees C (64 degrees F) during testing as suggested by Rowell, Taylor, and Wang (1964). It is also appropriate to keep the treadmill running conditions as similar to overground running as possible. At least through velocities as fast as 6 min/mi (268 m/min), submaximum O_2 uptake as measured with treadmill running is insignificantly different from that measured with track running (McMiken & Daniels, 1976). Biomechanical differences in running stride between the moving treadmill belt and running overground are minimal. Although overground running creates air resistance, such resistance brings an added aerobic demand only at velocities considerably faster than those routinely used in our evaluations. According to the studies of Pugh (1970), the effect of air resistance starts to measurably increase O_2 consumption only at faster paces. As an example, at a velocity of 12 mph (4:36/mi; 350 m/min), the additional aerobic demand is 5.7 ml/kg/min. Indeed, this added energy demand to a front-runner in a fast-paced race is used to advantage as a tactical maneuver by runners who remain in that athlete's wind shadow. We position a variable-speed fan in front of our runners to provide evaporative cooling and to simulate as much as possible the conditions of a breeze being created by over-ground running.

Preparing Athletes to Deliver a Good GXT Effort

Athletes always want to deliver their best possible efforts when they train and compete, and this is equally true for time trials and GXT evaluations. They are interested in how they can best prepare themselves both in the days preceding and on the day of the test to help their technical colleagues get the most meaningful data from them. We find it useful to explain clearly the essentials of what will be done and how it will be done so that the athletes can best interface with these activities.

Athletes should already have made some preparations for their maximum performance GXT a few days before the day of the test. Neither very long-distance runs nor intense anaerobic interval sessions should be done in training during the 2 days preceding a test. These will decrease skeletal muscle glycogen stores and alter normal substrate balance, in turn decreasing both submaximum and maximum blood lactate concentrations during and following the performance test (Busse, Maassen, & Boning, 1987; Foster, Snyder, Thompson, & Kuettel, 1988; Fric et al., 1988; Jacobs, Sjodin, Kaiser, & Karlsson, 1981). Similarly, dramatic changes in dietary habits, such as carbohydrate loading or increased lipid intake, will respectively elevate or lower the blood lactate response to hard work (Ivy, Costill, Van Handel, Essig, & Lower, 1981). Thus, a normal diet is recommended. Because we want the athletes to work to their absolute voluntary performance limits, we suggest that they treat the test as a time trial or race effort and schedule a defined, repeatable, relatively easy training regimen during the 2 days preceding the test.

We schedule each athlete's GXT at a similar biological clock time to minimize the effects of circadian fluctuations in physiological variables, such as heart rate (Reilly, Robinson, & Minors, 1984), basal metabolism (Aschoff & Pohl, 1970), and body temperature (Roe, Goldberg, Blaw, & Kinney, 1966) that may alter performance. Thus, the actual time during the day that we test athletes varies depending on the number of time zones they crossed in coming for evaluation; we attempt to test everyone at a time that is late morning for them. This precludes testing several athletes as a group. One might suspect that dealing with all of these varied constraints adds too much complexity to such performance evaluations. We do not consider this a problem; if accurate data are desired, then taking appropriate reasonable steps to reduce the impact of confounding variables is simply good science.

Before our athletes undergo a GXT for data collection purposes, we ensure that they have all gained prior experience of at least 30 min of treadmill running as well as experience at running hard with headgear and/or gas collection mouthpiece affixed. This develops the confidence and experience essential for a successful test, ensures practice in maintaining a natural running style, provides a review of test protocols, and allows experience at getting on and off the moving belt at varying speeds. Thorough familiarization of the test protocol minimizes the unexpected.

Typically, we assess the resting metabolic status of each athlete before beginning the GXT. This is easily accomplished; the athlete sits comfortably in a chair and breathes normally through the gas collection equipment for about 10 min. Analyses typically show a resting O_2 consumption of between 250 and 300 ml/kg/min. During this same period, resting heart rate and blood pressure can be determined. We typically do not utilize the complete 12-lead electrocardiographic (EKG) monitoring system that would be considered essential for evaluating patients with known cardiac risk or unknown physical fitness.

Instead, a simpler EKG system is employed to provide accurate measurement of heart rate as well as detection of the primary arrhythmias observed occasionally in trained athletes (Huston et al., 1985). As illustrated in Figure 2.17a by U.S. marathoner Don Janicki, common practice in many laboratories is to affix EKG electrodes on bony parts of the chest to minimize background interference from skeletal

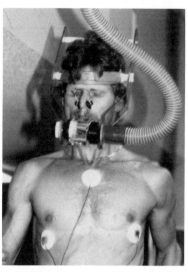

a

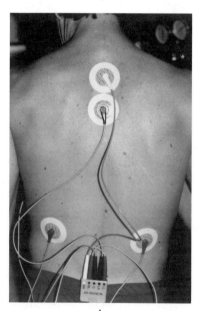

b

Figure 2.17 Suggested positioning of electrocardiographic electrodes for treadmill testing of distance runners. In each photo, RA = right arm, LA = left arm, LL = left leg, and RL = right leg ground. In Figure 2.17a chest limb lead II is monitored, whereas in Figure 2.17b all six limb leads can be monitored. In addition, placement of one chest electrode (the cable can be seen at the left) also permits monitoring of lead V5.

muscle activity. We prefer, as do our athletes, to affix EKG electrodes to the back (Figure 2.17b) because it interferes less with arm motion during running.

A thorough warm-up period, similar to that done in preparation for a competition, should be provided before the test. This is important because in functional terms an evaluation of maximum performance is a serious competitive effort with the best possible result desired. Considerable motivation and mental preparedness is required for athletes to deliver a best result. Such a warm-up may include from 15 to 30 min of running, with stretching exercises done before or following. We affix EKG electrodes (and perform our resting metabolic studies) before this warm-up period so that the GXT can begin very shortly after warm-up has been completed.

We find that it is also useful to explain some of the technical details of gas collection and analysis to the athletes. This helps them become more "user-friendly" with items such as nose clips and breathing valves, which can be sources of distraction unless their need is appreciated. The nose clip ensures that air intake occurs only through the mouth. We desire to collect and chemically analyze samples of the athlete's expired air during the test and quantify the magnitude of increasing O_2 consumption and CO_2 production with increasing work loads. Upon inhalation, air enters the mouth through one side of the valve, with exhaled air entering a tube connected to the other side of the valve en route to a mixing chamber and then to the gas analyzers. This is known as an *open-circuit spirometry system*.

Typically, rather bulky headgear is used to keep the breathing valve in place, as demonstrated by marathoner Anthony Sandoval in Figure 2.18a. The headgear should fit snugly enough so as not to come loose during the test but not so tight as to cause discomfort. This dilemma is routinely a source of frustration to both athlete and technician. The ingenuity of one of our colleagues, Meryl Sheard, has permitted the design and use of a "floating gas collection valve" positioned at an appropriate spot above the treadmill surface directly in front of the athlete's face and suspended by an ingenious pulley arrangement. As demonstrated by Jon Sinclair in Figure 2.18b, the athlete then simply connects him- or herself to the gas collection valve via its mouthpiece. The athlete has both freedom of movement and no distraction from bulky headgear. Soon even this will be replaced by a small tube with all appropriate instrumentation affixed for breath-by-breath gas analysis and improved performance evaluation. Some athletes desire verbal encouragement during the test; others do not. Such requests are respected and consistently followed to minimize variability.

a

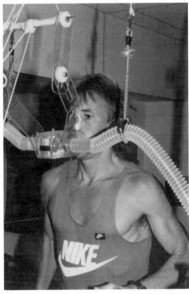

b

Figure 2.18 Equipment worn during exercise testing of elite endurance runners (a) Anthony Sandoval and (b) Jon Sinclair. Both athletes have a nose clip affixed to ensure that all expired air passes through the mouth. This air then moves through a low-resistance breathing valve, visible in these photos, and then into a collection tube that eventually directs it to O_2 and CO_2 analyzers. In Figure 2.18a Sandoval's breathing valve is kept in place by a fitted headgear, which many find distracting. Our improved technology, being used here by Sinclair in Figure 2.18b, eliminates the headgear, permitting the gas-collecting valve to float freely in front of the athlete during the test. Changing hemoglobin saturation can be measured using an earlobe oximeter, as illustrated in Figure 2.18a.

Some laboratories attempt to obtain a subjective estimation of effort sense from athletes being tested as an accompaniment to the physiological data acquisition. One means for assessing effort sense has involved the development of *ratings of perceived exertion* (RPE). Gunnar Borg (1973) was instrumental in developing scales that are usable for quantifying effort sense during performance evaluation of athletes. Particularly when the lactate/ventilatory threshold is reached, there is a noticeable effort-sense breakpoint. Beyond this work intensity, effort sense is too great to permit the kind of almost indefinite performance that characterizes marathon running. Below this level, athletes feel quite confident that the work load can be maintained. The Borg scale in its various formats consists of a dozen or more verbal labels describing effort. Terms such as "hard," "very hard," and "very, very hard" are used. Numerical codes beside each label permit exercising subjects when requested to call out the number corresponding to their perception of effort. Of course, this becomes impossible if the athlete has a mouthpiece and headgear affixed to collect expired air samples. Pointing to appropriate numbers painted on the front treadmill guardrail provides a convenient substitute system of communication.

One study involving a mixture of active people and trained athletes suggested an RPE value of "somewhat hard" as equivalent to the stress at the onset of blood lactate accumulation (Purvis & Cureton, 1981). The effectiveness of such a rating system relies on the premise that everyone perceives "very hard" work equivalently, and this is most likely not universally true. In part there are semantic variations, and there are also differences in work effort tolerance among individuals. Accuracy of such reporting is based on the presumption that during a performance test the athlete not only is willing to interrupt concentration to categorize feelings, but also can objectively compare present effort sense with effort sense yet to be experienced because the test is still in progress. At present we are still uncertain that, with highly trained athletes, including such documentation during treadmill tests provides information of sufficient value for athlete and coach in training to justify the intrusion upon the athlete's concentrated competitive effort and to ensure that the intrusion does not influence the attainment of maximum performance capacity.

Our athletes themselves terminate their tests due to voluntary exhaustion, step off to the side of the treadmill, and then begin their recovery according to prearranged plans. Varying protocols exist in different laboratories for transitioning back to the resting state after test completion. Continued easy jogging, walking, or complete rest through either sitting or recumbency are all used. We routinely measure peak blood lactate levels after this maximum exercise test and observe how quickly such variables as heart rate, respiratory exchange ratio, and $\dot{V}_E$ return toward baseline levels. Such monitoring demands a standardized pattern of posttest activity (Fujitsuka, Yamamoto,

Ohkuwa, Saito, & Miyamura, 1982; Ohkuwa, Kato, Katsumata, Nakao, & Miyamura, 1984). Our experience, coupled with that of the Japanese investigators, suggests that as soon as the treadmill can be slowed and leveled, an immediate slowdown to an easy walk maintained for 3 minutes to permit continued collection of metabolic recovery data provides a safe, acceptable, and repeatable posttest protocol. Such data, therefore, is also of considerable value and should be collected in a consistent and repeatable manner. Blood for maximum lactate determination is then collected immediately after this cool-down which is 5 minutes after test termination (Gollnick et al., 1986).

Computer-interfaced instrumentation permits rapid analysis, calculation, and display of results while the test is in progress. This is not always used or available, however. For example, if data are to be collected from athletes running around a 400m track, as shown in Figure 2.19, it becomes more appropriate to collect the expired air in large balloons for temporary storage and transport to gas analyzers located in a nearby laboratory setting. Regardless of the mode of collection, because the inspired concentrations of O_2 and CO_2 are known (O_2 typically is 20.93%, CO_2 almost negligible at 0.04%), measurement of expired

Figure 2.19 Field-test collection of expired gases using meteorological balloons. Elite-level United States marathoner Ken Martin is shown here at the U.S. Olympic Training Center. Note the gas collection equipment monitoring from the golf cart.

volumes of O_2 and CO_2 permits calculation of O_2 utilized and CO_2 produced with relative ease. From these values, the respiratory exchange ratio (R) can be calculated as $\dot{V}CO_2/\dot{V}O_2$.

Interpreting the Data From a GXT

Table 2.5 summarizes the kinds of data that can be obtained during an incremental treadmill test. These data were obtained from an elite male distance runner (a specialist in the 3,000m to 10,000m range), peaked for an excellent performance in the 1988 United States Olympic trials. At the top of each column appear abbreviations for the various data that were collected and reported at 20-sec sampling intervals. Some values are probably familiar: O_2 consumption ($\dot{V}O_2$, in ml/min); CO_2 production ($\dot{V}CO_2$, also in ml/min); and heart rate (HR, in beats/min). Breathing frequency (f_R, in breaths/min) and total expired ventilation ($\dot{V}_E$,

in L/min) are also measured. From these data, other variables have been calculated. Recall the respiratory exchange ratio, or R, from chapter 1, calculated as $\dot{V}CO_2/\dot{V}O_2$ (no units). Tidal volume (V_T), the size of each breath, is equal to $\dot{V}_E/f_R$ (ml/min).

Oxygen pulse is calculated as $\dot{V}O_2$ extracted per heart beat, and can be used to estimate maximum stroke volume at peak exercise. We can rearrange Equation 2.5 as follows:

$$\dot{V}O_2max/HR = SV \times max\ a\text{-}\bar{v}O_2\ diff. \quad (2.11)$$

Remembering that max a-$\bar{v}O_2$ difference is at about 16 ml/100 ml, SV can then be estimated. Using the data in Table 2.5, for several minutes O_2 pulse was between 29 and 30 ml/beat, with maximum SV approaching 190 ml. The beginnings of cardiac limitation in the final 40 seconds of exercise (seen by the decrease in O_2 pulse to 28.5 ml/beat), suggest an SV reduction to about 178 ml.

Table 2.5   Treadmill Evaluation of a Distance Runner—Physiological Data

	Elapsed time	Heart rate (beats/min)	O_2 pulse (ml/beat)	$\dot{V}_E$ (L/min)	$\dot{V}O_2$ (ml/min)	$\dot{V}O_2$ (ml/kg/min)	$\dot{V}CO_2$ (ml/min)	R	$\dfrac{\dot{V}_E}{\dot{V}O_2}$	$\dfrac{\dot{V}_E}{\dot{V}CO_2}$	f_R (br/min)	V_T (ml)	Hb (sat. %)
7:30 pace	:20	125	21.9	70	2,739	40.3	2,418	.88	26	29	37	1,890	95
	:40	125	21.0	68	2,624	38.6	2,288	.88	26	30	42	1,610	94
	1:00	125	20.1	63	2,518	37.0	2,171	.85	25	29	42	1,500	94
	1:20	125	18.4	55	2,302	33.9	1,953	.85	24	28	33	1,660	95
	1:40	125	22.3	70	2,793	41.1	2,423	.86	25	29	42	1,670	93
	2:00	125	19.6	57	2,444	35.9	2,070	.84	23	27	33	1,730	94
6:40 pace	2:20	125	21.4	63	2,673	39.3	2,247	.84	24	28	44	1,440	95
	2:40	125	21.6	64	2,695	39.6	2,289	.84	24	28	37	1,710	94
	3:00	125	23.0	70	2,869	42.2	2,525	.88	25	28	38	1,850	93
	3:20	125	22.5	67	2,815	41.4	2,433	.87	24	28	40	1,680	94
	3:40	130	23.1	71	3,005	44.2	2,607	.87	24	27	40	1,770	94
	4:00	135	22.0	72	2,967	43.6	2,580	.88	24	28	41	1,780	93
	4:20	135	22.2	73	3,000	44.1	2,630	.88	24	28	44	1,860	93
	4:40	136	22.3	74	3,034	44.6	2,649	.87	25	28	42	1,770	93
	5:00	136	22.5	74	3,061	45.0	2,691	.88	24	28	36	2,060	93
6:00 pace	5:20	136	23.2	77	3,157	46.4	2,795	.88	24	28	45	1,740	94
	5:40	136	21.7	75	2,952	43.4	2,652	.90	25	28	43	1,760	94
	6:00	140	22.6	81	3,159	46.5	2,835	.90	26	29	45	1,810	94
	6:20	140	22.0	74	3,085	45.4	2,707	.87	24	27	40	1,870	93
	6:40	145	23.6	88	3,427	50.4	3,093	.91	26	29	44	1,990	93
	7:00	145	22.3	80	3,235	47.6	2,931	.91	25	27	36	2,230	93
	7:20	145	24.3	89	3,526	51.9	3,161	.90	25	28	42	2,130	94
	7:40	145	22.9	85	3,314	48.7	2,984	.89	26	28	42	2,020	92
	8:00	145	23.9	88	3,464	50.9	3,130	.90	25	28	40	2,190	92

(Cont.)

Table 2.5 (Continued)

	Elapsed time	Heart rate (beats/min)	O₂ pulse (ml/beat)	$\dot{V}_E$ (L/min)	$\dot{V}O_2$ (ml/min)	$\dot{V}O_2$ (ml/kg/min)	$\dot{V}CO_2$ (ml/min)	R	$\dfrac{\dot{V}_E}{\dot{V}O_2}$	$\dfrac{\dot{V}_E}{\dot{V}CO_2}$	f_R	V_T (ml)	Hb (sat. %)
5:30 pace	8:20	145	22.6	85	3,277	48.2	2,946	.90	26	29	44	1,940	92
	8:40	145	23.3	86	3,372	49.6	3,037	.90	26	28	41	2,080	92
	9:00	148	23.3	91	3,445	50.7	3,154	.91	27	29	43	2,140	94
	9:20	148	24.0	93	3,545	52.1	3,221	.92	26	29	42	2,210	92
	9:40	150	24.8	97	3,717	54.7	3,447	.92	26	28	42	2,300	93
	10:00	150	25.4	103	3,803	55.9	3,547	.93	27	29	45	2,280	91
	10:20	155	23.0	92	3,568	52.5	3,311	.93	26	28	39	2,350	93
	10:40	155	25.5	102	3,951	58.1	3,657	.93	26	28	39	2,620	92
	11:00	160	24.7	107	3,947	58.0	3,701	.93	27	29	45	2,400	92
5:00 pace	11:20	160	22.5	99	3,602	53.0	3,414	.95	28	29	42	2,350	91
	11:40	160	23.9	103	3,828	56.3	3,540	.93	27	29	48	2,130	90
	12:00	167	23.0	106	3,848	56.6	3,595	.94	27	29	45	2,370	90
	12:20	167	23.0	106	3,849	56.6	3,628	.95	27	29	45	2,350	90
	12:40	167	24.9	113	4,159	61.2	3,956	.94	27	29	45	2,520	89
	13:00	167	25.0	119	4,177	61.4	4,093	.99	29	29	45	2,650	89
	13:20	167	23.6	108	3,941	58.0	3,800	.97	28	29	41	2,650	88
	13:40	167	24.5	120	4,084	60.1	3,989	.98	29	30	46	2,590	89
	14:00	167	25.2	113	4,206	61.9	4,005	.96	27	28	42	2,680	89
6:00 4%	14:20	167	25.8	122	4,313	63.4	4,143	.96	28	29	45	2,700	88
	14:40	167	23.9	114	3,989	58.7	3,853	.96	28	29	42	2,720	87
	15:00	167	24.7	117	4,130	60.7	3,978	.96	28	29	42	2,770	88
	15:20	167	25.2	112	4,207	61.9	3,938	.93	27	29	42	2,680	88
	15:40	167	25.1	114	4,192	61.7	3,942	.93	27	29	41	2,750	87
	16:00	167	23.9	111	3,987	58.6	3,789	.95	28	29	41	2,700	87
6:00 6%	16:20	167	25.7	121	4,299	63.2	4,130	.96	28	29	46	2,650	86
	16:40	167	26.2	120	4,377	64.4	4,210	.97	27	28	46	2,620	87
	17:00	167	28.1	129	4,694	69.0	4,501	.96	27	29	45	2,860	88
	17:20	170	26.7	128	4,534	66.7	4,458	.99	28	29	43	2,990	87
	17:40	170	27.6	131	4,700	69.1	4,622	.99	28	28	45	2,920	86
	18:00	170	28.4	138	4,826	71.0	4,785	1.00	29	29	47	2,930	85
6:00 8%	18:20	170	26.8	122	4,549	66.9	4,464	.99	27	27	45	2,690	85
	18:40	170	29.5	145	5,010	73.7	5,025	1.00	29	29	48	3,020	86
	19:00	170	28.9	142	4,921	72.4	5,006	1.02	29	28	47	3,050	87
	19:20	180	28.2	151	5,083	74.8	5,249	1.02	30	29	50	3,060	87
	19:40	180	29.0	154	5,216	76.7	5,431	1.04	30	28	51	3,040	84
	20:00	180	28.0	149	5,044	74.2	5,238	1.03	30	29	48	3,100	84
6:00 10%	20:20	180	29.0	159	5,219	76.8	5,489	1.04	31	29	53	3,040	85
	20:40	180	29.3	162	5,266	77.4	5,589	1.07	31	29	53	3,080	84
	21:00	180	29.1	165	5,229	76.9	5,672	1.09	31	29	54	3,050	84
	21:20	180	29.2	164	5,251	77.2	5,659	1.07	31	29	54	3,030	83
	21:40	180	30.7	175	5,532	81.4	6,054	1.10	32	29	57	3,070	85
	22:00	180	29.7	172	5,354	78.7	5,935	1.10	32	29	57	3,000	84

	Elapsed time	Heart rate (beats/min)	O_2 pulse (ml/beat)	$\dot{V}_E$ (L/min)	$\dot{V}O_2$ (ml/min)	$\dot{V}O_2$ (ml/kg/min)	$\dot{V}CO_2$ (ml/min)	R	$\dfrac{\dot{V}_E}{\dot{V}O_2}$	$\dfrac{\dot{V}_E}{\dot{V}CO_2}$	f_R	V_T (ml)	Hb (sat. %)
11%	22:20	180	29.5	170	5,307	78.0	5,918	1.10	32	29	57	2,990	82
	22:40	188	28.6	177	5,377	79.1	6,119	1.15	33	29	60	2,960	80
	23:00	188	28.4	176	5,332	78.4	6,070	1.15	33	29	62	2,850	76
Recovery	23:20	188	26.6	172	5,006	73.6	5,744	1.14	34	30	61	2,820	78
	23:40	188	17.0	130	3,192	46.9	3,747	1.18	41	35	50	2,600	86
	24:00	150	18.0	114	2,707	39.8	3,218	1.19	42	35	51	2,250	88
	24:20	150	18.2	123	2,735	40.2	3,618	1.33	45	34	50	2,460	88
	24:40	125	18.8	93	2,344	34.5	3,330	1.42	40	28	32	2,900	89
	25:00	125	16.6	97	2,071	30.5	2,987	1.45	47	32	39	2,470	93
	25:20	115	17.8	97	2,045	30.1	2,991	1.45	47	32	39	2,500	92
	25:40	115	15.7	87	1,802	26.5	2,544	1.43	48	34	39	2,200	91
	26:00	115	14.5	82	1,670	24.6	2,343	1.39	49	35	41	2,020	93

Oxygen Consumption. We can express $\dot{V}O_2$ data both in absolute terms (L/min) and relative to body weight (ml/kg/min). Expression in absolute terms is least ambiguous (Astrand, 1984), preventing changes in body weight from being confused as changes in $\dot{V}O_2$. Table 2.6 shows some of the difficulties that can occur in interpreting data expressed in the two formats. We use the example of a talented male runner who had three physiological performance evaluations done in October, February, and June as a training plan progressed to bring him toward a fitness peak during June. Notice that between October and late February his weight remained constant at 60 kg. His relative $\dot{V}O_2$max improved from 78 to 82 ml/kg/min, an increase of $(4/78) \times 100 = 5.1\%$. But his absolute $\dot{V}O_2$max was raised by $(200/4700) \times 100 = 4.3\%$, an increase of from 4,700 to 4,900 ml/min. Between March and June, his training gradually shifted toward maintaining $\dot{V}O_2$max and increasing anaerobic capabilities. This was reflected in the form of an essentially unchanged $\dot{V}O_2$max in absolute terms—from

4,900 to 4,950 (an insignificant 1% increase). However, his weight decreased from 60 to 57 kg, a reduction of $(3/60) \times 100 = 5\%$. Relative $\dot{V}O_2$max, calculated as $4,950/57 = 87$ ml/kg/min, increased by $(5/82) \times 100 = 6\%$. When we express the improvement in $\dot{V}O_2$max during the entire training period from October to June, in relative terms this was $(9/78) \times 100 = 11.5\%$, whereas the absolute increase was only $(250/4700) \times 100 = 5.3\%$.

We could consider the $\dot{V}O_2$max of our runner in Table 2.5 as the largest observed $\dot{V}O_2$ value, which is 81.4 ml/kg/min. Or by averaging that value with the four subsequent values, we obtain what we term a mean sustainable $\dot{V}O_2$max of 79.1 ml/kg/min. The duration of this plateau becomes an important indicator of anaerobic work tolerance, since once $\dot{V}O_2$max is achieved, anaerobic metabolism provides the additional energy for continued work. What is the error associated with such $\dot{V}O_2$ measurements? Variability is a fact of life and measurement, and being able to identify changes in $\dot{V}O_2$submax as well as $\dot{V}O_2$max

Table 2.6 Expressing $\dot{V}O_2$max Data in Absolute and Relative Terms

Date of $\dot{V}O_2$max measurement	October	February	June
Body weight (kg)	60	60	57
Absolute $\dot{V}O_2$max (ml/min)	4,700	4,900	4,950
% change in absolute $\dot{V}O_2$max	⊢————— +4.3 ————→	⊢——— +1.0 ————→	
Relative $\dot{V}O_2$max (ml/kg/min)	78	82	87
% change in relative $\dot{V}O_2$max	⊢————— +5.1 ————→	⊢——— +6.0 ————→	

values that actually represent increases or decreases in fitness must be viewed in light of this constraint. In this era of excellent technology, most laboratories take great care to perform proper calibrations, maintain constant room temperature and humidity for repeat test procedures, and ensure consistency in technician competence. Even so, $\dot{V}O_2$max values obtained on different days from the same athlete will not be identical. No more than 10% of the variation should be caused by technological variability. The remaining 90% of the variability will be biological; that is, inherent within the individual being tested. Gibson, Harrison, and Wellcome (1979) suggested that the coefficient of variation of $\dot{V}O_2$max can be held within ±3%. Our laboratory experience is similar. Thus, using the $\dot{V}O_2$max value of 81.4 ml/kg/min as an example, values within 3% (that is, between 79.0 and 83.8) cannot be guaranteed as training-related because they fall within the expected error range of the measurement system.

Running Economy. The first part of the GXT evaluation is concerned largely with assessing oxygen consumption at a series of submaximum paces, which identifies running economy as defined by Daniels (1974). Notice in the data summary of Table 2.5 that there is an initial warm-up period at a pace of 7:30/mi (4:40/km). Following this warm-up, economy is assessed by collecting 3 min of $\dot{V}O_2$ data at the four level running paces of 6:40, 6:00, 5:30, and 5:00 per mi (4:09, 3:44, 3:25, and 3:06 per km). Using scientific rather than coaching jargon, this would be the four level running velocities of 241, 268, 293, and 322 m/min (14.5, 16.1, 17.6, and 19.4 km/hr). This pace (velocity) range encompasses the aerobic range of this athlete during all but higher speed track-oriented training sessions. For our female runners, we use running paces of 7:00, 6:30, 6:10, and 5:50 per mi to measure running economy. Those desiring to develop their own test protocols that best match their athletes' fitness can do so using convenient guidelines developed by the American College of Sports Medicine (1986), based on Equations 2.2 and 2.3.

Note in Table 2.5 that adaptation to each work load is not instantaneous, and a measurable upward creep in results of expired gas analyses occurs. Our experience with these work loads for highly trained runners has been that for the paces indicated, adaptation is sufficient by the end of 3 min so that continued running at each pace for a 4th min or longer does not reveal $\dot{V}O_2$ or $\dot{V}CO_2$ values significantly different from those obtained during the 3rd min. Having our athletes run at these submaximal test paces for only as long as necessary thus minimizes boredom during the test and also decreases total sweat loss.

We estimate the submaximal O_2 demand (economy) at each pace as the average of the three 20-sec samples collected during the final minute of running at that pace. Using the statistical technique of regression analysis, an equation can be written using these four pairs of pace and $\dot{V}O_2$ data that best describes each runner's O_2 consumption with increasing work load. For example, using linear regression, an equation of the type

$$y = mx + b \qquad (2.12)$$

would be generated, where y = O_2 demand, b = the y ordinate intercept, x = velocity, and m = slope of the line of best fit of the data.

This regression equation determined from data obtained during level running permits extrapolation to the level-ground pace at which the athlete would be running at $\dot{V}O_2$max intensity. One need only insert the $\dot{V}O_2$max value into the equation, rearrange, and solve for velocity. This is called the velocity at $\dot{V}O_2$max, or v-$\dot{V}O_2$max. This value can be quite useful from a coaching viewpoint because, as described earlier, when coupled with other values such as the pace for the lactate/ventilatory threshold, pace ranges can be identified for the four training zones identified in Figure 2.2 (which will be described more fully in chapter 3). Such extrapolation is valid, however, only if the rate of change in O_2 consumption outside the range of measured data points follows the same mathematical relationship as it did within the range. As an example, let us hypothesize that the relationship between O_2 consumption and velocity is not linear, but curvilinear instead. If the pace range used for producing the regression equation involves relatively slow running velocities and is not wide enough to fully characterize the curvilinearity at the other end, where $\dot{V}O_2$max occurs, then the extrapolated v-$\dot{V}O_2$max pace will be overestimated. If, however, the relationship between running velocity and O_2 consumption is linear throughout, then the extrapolated v-$\dot{V}O_2$max pace will be accurate.

Is the relationship between running velocity and O_2 consumption linear or curvilinear? Daniels (1985, p. 333) hedges the answer by stating that "work done since 1950 *generally* supports the concept of a linear or *very nearly* linear relationship . . . during *submaximal* running, where energy demands are met aerobically and where the range of running speeds is *rather limited*" (emphasis added). Thus, whereas one study generated performance tables using a curvilinear relationship between $\dot{V}O_2$ and velocity (Daniels & Gilbert, 1979), subsequent reports, typified by a study of female middle- and long-distance runners (Daniels,

Scardina, Hayes, & Foley, 1986), used linear regression to describe the same relationship. This inconsistency in data analysis even among individual investigators suggests that the final conclusion is still unknown as to whether this relationship between $\dot{V}O_2$ and running velocity is linear or curvilinear across its entire range in humans. The present evidence seems almost in favor of curvilinearity. If the relationship was linear throughout, the slope of the regression lines obtained by most workers who evaluate the economy of distance runners should all be essentially parallel, differing only in that the more efficient runners are positioned lower than the less efficient runners due to their decreased O_2 cost at submaximum paces. Such appears not to be true; both Daniels (1985), and Kearney and Van Handel (1989) state or summarize information from other published studies suggesting that a range of faster running velocities results in a steeper slope than a range of lower running velocities.

One plausible explanation is that the several sets of data have been obtained from different parts of a relationship between $\dot{V}O_2$ and work load, which varies according to the influence of other factors (such as the effects of anaerobic energy demands and running mechanics). The frequently reported suggestions of a linear relationship between O_2 consumption and work load may thus be based on data collected from a rather narrow submaximal range of work intensities. Thus, although the studies of Cavagna and Margaria are quoted frequently regarding the relationship whereby 1 kcal of energy is required per kilogram of body weight per kilometer of distance covered submaximally (Cavagna, Saibene, & Margaria, 1964; Margaria, Cerretelli, Aghemo, & Sassi, 1963), this linearity may not necessarily be true for energy demands beyond the lactate/ventilatory threshold and approaching $\dot{V}O_2$max.

Clearly, additional work is needed in this area to elucidate more fully the details of this relationship between O_2 consumption and work load. For best accuracy in preparing useful regression equations to extrapolate v-$\dot{V}O_2$max pace when linear regression is to be used, the fast end of the level-ground submaximum pace range should not be too far away from $\dot{V}O_2$max. If curvilinear regression is to be used, then a sufficiently wide pace range is needed (including higher intensity work loads) to ensure identification of the extent of curvilinearity. Coaches may want to have their athletes perform a track time trial that lasts somewhere between 10 and 12 min, which is the longest period of time that $\dot{V}O_2$max can be sustained. Knowing the distance covered and the elapsed time provides a good estimate of v-$\dot{V}O_2$max. This can serve as a check on the accuracy of treadmill test data interpretation.

What factors can alter running economy, and can training improve running economy? There has been the suggestion that anaerobic capacity training (repeated intervals of shorter faster running) improves running economy (Daniels, 1985), but the same author states elsewhere (Daniels, 1986) that "training seems to play a minimal, if any, role in running economy" (p. 66). Thus the specific kinds of training that may improve running economy have yet to be clearly identified. Intuition suggests that the larger volumes of aerobic conditioning, which begin to develop in a runner the ability to manage elevated training loads as a development season begins, would provide an improvement in fitness, strength, and coordination that is reflected in an improved economy of O_2 consumption. But it hasn't been as easy to document this. The studies of Scrimgeour, Noakes, Adams, and Myburgh (1986), which report that athletes training less than 60 km/wk have as much as 19% less running economy than athletes training more than 100 km/wk, might support this suggestion. But those running less than 60 km/wk were not asked to average more than 100 km/wk for a prolonged period to determine whether aerobic running in that particular group of individuals actually *caused* an improvement in economy. Those athletes doing the high-volume training might simply have found the training easier to manage than the lower volume athletes because their economy was greater before they began training.

There seems to be no difference in running economy between men and women who are comparably trained (Davies & Thompson, 1979), but the question of how one determines comparable training between the two sexes is still under consideration. Many factors extraneous to training can also affect economy. Rainy weather, for example, increases the weight of socks and shoes, thereby increasing O_2 cost and decreasing economy. Wearing lighter racing flats instead of heavier training shoes decreases O_2 consumption at submaximal paces and thus improves economy. For our GXT evaluation of athletes, we recommend that they run in racing flats, primarily for consistency but also because they wear them in competitive racing situations.

Lactate/Ventilatory Threshold. A complete explanation of the possible interrelationships between the exercise-induced ventilatory changes and lactate production by working muscle has still not been developed. The threshold rises in blood lactate and ventilation (familiar to most as the lactate/ventilatory threshold) occur together with high correlation among metabolically normal people (Caiozzo et al., 1982; Clode & Campbell, 1969; Davis, Vodak, Wilmore, & Kurtz, 1976). If one of the factors limiting exercise from the athlete's perspective is an increasing subjective ventilatory discomfort, this heightened respiratory stress may be a more important variable to measure than a blood chemistry variable such as lactate, although it is presumably the acidosis that initiates the increased ventilatory drive. Laboratories specializing in studies of human performance often can measure both lactate and ventilatory thresholds. The problems inherent in quantifying blood lactate, which will be described shortly, may make its measurement less informative than that of ventilatory changes. Individual subject variability sometimes makes one or the other threshold less easy to discern. This is another reason that both variables are sometimes determined during a GXT. The preferred measurement seems to depend on the fundamental research bent of the investigators as well as the nature of the exercise test protocol (i.e., bicycle or treadmill and laboratory or field study).

The ventilatory threshold can be estimated best using graphic plots of $\dot{V}_E$ versus increasing workload, to identify the change in linear rate of rise in $\dot{V}_E$. Often, at about this same time, $\dot{V}CO_2$ produced exceeds $\dot{V}O_2$ utilized, and this crossover can also be graphed. Using such plots, we estimated that our athlete's ventilatory threshold in Table 2.5 occurred at about 72 ml/kg/min. This is at about 88.5% of his absolute $\dot{V}O_2$max and 91% of his mean sustainable $\dot{V}O_2$max.

The ventilatory equivalents have also been used to suggest that, certainly at sea level, ventilation in athletes with healthy lungs is probably not a limiting factor in running performance. Let us compare healthy resting values of $\dot{V}_E$ and $\dot{V}O_2$ (5 L/min and 0.25 L/min) to the $\dot{V}_E$ and $\dot{V}O_2$ of our trained male runner in Table 2.5 at maximum effort (177 L/min and 5.5 L/min). We can compute $\dot{V}_E/\dot{V}O_2$ as rising from 5/0.25 = 20 to 177/5.5 = 32. Notice the greater rise in ventilation than in O_2 consumption. The limitations to maximum exercise are thus more likely those of cardiovascular O_2 transport or tissue utilization than they are of ventilatory effectiveness.

Measuring Blood Lactate. Analysis of blood lactate was simplified in the 1980s with the advent of reasonably accurate and rapid enzymatic microassay techniques, requiring only a lancet puncture of a fingertip or earlobe to obtain a small aliquot of peripheral blood. For sequential collection of blood at various work loads during a treadmill test or after field-test runs around a track, such collection is preferred by athletes to blood collection via syringe or indwelling vessel catheter. It is this simplicity that has most likely stimulated the enormous wealth of scientific literature concerning the quantitation of onset of blood lactate accumulation during exercise.

We see a number of difficulties with such analyses. To start, athletes prefer a racelike, uninterrupted treadmill protocol, which obviously cannot be maintained with such analyses. Also, concerning the liabilities in analyzing capillary as opposed to venous blood, capillary blood collected following lancet puncture will certainly be contaminated with interstitial fluid and possibly with sweat as well. Finally, only if the lancet puncture is firm enough to provide plenty of free-flowing blood will it be essentialized arterialized (meaning that arterioles hve been severed) rather than predominantly capillary blood. The first drop will be contaminated with interstitial fluid and so must be wiped away. Then, collection must be rapid to prevent clotting at the puncture site. Massaging the site to enhance flow must not be done; it will alter the blood composition. Third, along with the lactate sample, a second sample must be collected and analyzed for hemoglobin and hematocrit.

Why is it necessary to measure hemoglobin if the blood lactate changes are of interest? The answer is simply that there are sizable fluid movements out of the bloodstream during exercise, and we need to measure hemoglobin to quantify the extent of this hemoconcentration. During a treadmill test, which lasts at best around 20 min, the plasma volume loss is due primarily to sweat (up to 3 pounds) (Martin, Vroon, & Sheard, 1989). During more prolonged exercise, particularly in warm weather, both sweat loss and osmolar movement of water out of the bloodstream because of increased electrolyte accumulation in the plasma and plasma protein movement into the interstitial fluid can amount to as much as 15% of plasma volume (Nadel, 1988). Because of this hemoconcentration, even if there were no increases in lactate derived from anaerobic metabolism during exercise, the blood lactate concentration in a postexercise sample would appear larger than in a sample obtained near the beginning of exercise, because the latter lactate value is being expressed as millimoles or milligrams per unit of a now-decreased blood volume. This hemoconcentration varies among runners from 5% or less to as high as 13% (Martin et al., 1989). It does not appear to relate to fitness level or sex, and it can vary considerably even among individuals whose treadmill test endurance times are similar.

Dill and Costill (1974) described how correction for hemoconcentration can be made using measurements of hemoglobin made on the two collected blood samples (preexercise and during or after exercise). To ensure consistent analysis and adequate sample volume, venipuncture is appropriate. Percentage hemoconcentration of a during- or posttest blood sample as a result of volume loss is given by the following equation:

% Hemoconcentration = 100 −
[(pretest Hb/posttest Hb) × 100]   (2.13)

To correct the during- or posttest lactate value for hemoconcentration, the following equation is appropriate:

Corrected lactate = (pretest Hb/posttest Hb) × posttest lactate
(2.14)

An example from our own unpublished data can help illustrate this concept. One of our elite female marathoners ran for slightly longer than 20 min during a treadmill test. Her $\dot{V}O_2$max was 72 ml/kg/min. Her pre- and posttest hemoglobin values were 13.3 and 15.0 mg/dl, respectively. Her posttest maximum blood lactate was 88 mg/dl (9.8 mM/L). Her percent hemoconcentration can be calculated as

% Hemoconcentration = 100 − [(13.3/15.0) × 100] = 11.3%
(2.15)

If we correct for this hemoconcentration, her posttest maximal lactate is given by

Corrected lactate = (13.3/15.0) × 88 =
78.0 mg/dl (8.7 mM/L)   (2.16)

Typically, in published reports describing blood lactate concentrations during or after exercise in runners, such volume corrections for hemoconcentration appear not to have been made (e.g., Fay, Londeree, LaFontaine, & Volek, 1989; Sjodin & Jacobs, 1981; Sjodin & Svedenhag, 1985). This prevents an accurate appreciation for the actual magnitude of blood lactate rise as a result of varying intensities of exercise; it also adds to the error involved in estimating training paces based on preset blood lactate concentrations such as 4 mM/L.

Maximum Performance Capacity. Although O_2 consumption eventually peaks and plateaus, in trained distance runners anaerobic contributions from additional recruited FT fibers at high work rates both extend and increase total work output. This anaerobic capability is a crucial part of an athlete's physiological competitiveness, and is thus deserving of careful assessment. This is why we encourage our athletes to endure absolutely as long as possible during their treadmill tests. Recall from chapter 1 that it is the H^+-ion-induced inhibition of Ca^{++} binding to troponin in the muscle filaments, as well as a reduced production of ATP due to the H^+-ion-induced blockade of the phosphofructokinase enzyme in the glycolytic pathway, that shuts down not only tension generation but also the means to produce it. Studies have indicated that intracellular muscle pH may fall as low as 6.2 during heavy exercise, with plasma levels as low as 6.8 (Hermansen & Osnes, 1972). We sense this acidosis subjectively. Thus, the increasing metabolic acidosis becomes an intolerable stress. Exactly what limits exercise is therefore probably more easily answered subjectively as a symptom-limiting situation involving an intolerable effort sense in either the limb muscles or the breathing muscles (Jones, 1988). We can evaluate anaerobic responsiveness from one test to another in several ways. Perhaps the most quantitative is to measure the accumulated O_2 deficit using a protocol described by Medbø et al. (1988). But there are other observations that can be made from data such as that in Table 2.5. One is to note the length of time the $\dot{V}O_2$max plateau is maintained. Another is to compare the length of time the athlete is working with a respiratory exchange ratio greater than 1.0, which indicates a respiratory compensation to increasing metabolic acidosis, and to identify the maximum achieved R value during the test. A third is to compare the $\dot{V}CO_2$max value between tests just as we assess $\dot{V}O_2$max. A fourth is to compare the 5-min posttest maximum blood lactate level. Whereas effective endurance training ought to lower blood lactate concentrations observed at any given submaximum work load, a higher maximum lactate suggests greater tolerance to anaerobic work (Holloszy & Coyle, 1984). Finally, a fifth observation is to evaluate subjectively athlete stability during the final few moments prior to test termination: Is running form maintainable throughout the test or beginning to deteriorate?

For our athlete whose data are summarized in Table 2.5, it can be seen that

- his sustainable $\dot{V}O_2$max plateau lasted 80 sec;
- his maximum R during the test was 1.15, and he was above R > 1.0 for 4:40;
- his $\dot{V}CO_2$ max was 6,119 ml/min, or 96 ml/kg/min; and
- his maximum blood lactate was 119 mg/dl (13.2 mM/L), after correction for a 9.1% hemoconcentration during the test.

SUMMARY

1. Two important tasks of the cardiovascular system, the pulmonary system, and the blood are to transport fuels to the working muscles, including O_2 for their complete metabolism, and remove the resulting products of metabolism. These products include volatile acids such as CO_2 and nonvolatile acids such as lactate.

2. Such factors as maximum oxygen consumption ($\dot{V}O_2$max), the ability to work for long periods at near-$\dot{V}O_2$max intensity with minimum lactate accumulation, and the capacity to work for short periods at intensities far in excess of $\dot{V}O_2$max are all trainable to a varying extent (depending on fitness level) by means of specific stimuli to the cardiopulmonary and musculoskeletal systems, although there is a hereditary component as well. Their net effects couple with psychological readiness and knowledge of tactics to produce a good competitor.

3. The interaction of all of these factors explains why, in a homogeneous population of gifted and trained endurance runners all with excellent competitive credentials, no one of these physiological aspects of performance by itself explains very well the superiority of one athlete rather than another.

4. Training brings specific adaptations in the cardiovascular system, the pulmonary system, and the blood that can improve the maximum oxygen uptake ability ($\dot{V}O_2$max), raise the lactate/ventilatory threshold, and improve running economy and maximum anaerobic capacity. Such improvements directly increase aerobic and anaerobic performance capabilities. There is an increased blood volume, which permits better perfusion of tissues, and a larger fluid reservoir for sweat production and dilution of metabolic acids. The ventricular chambers of the heart expand to permit more stroke volume per beat. This in turn permits an adequate cardiac output with minimum increase in heart rate, thereby ensuring optimum time between beats for perfusion of the heart tissue with blood through the coronary vessels. Greater perfusion permits increased O_2 extraction from blood, seen as an increased a-$\bar{v}O_2$ difference. The lungs are capable of oxygenating blood as completely as at rest during all but the most intense work loads.

5. $\dot{V}O_2$max is determined by heart rate, stroke volume, and rate of extraction of O_2 from blood. It is lower in women than in men, because women have less O_2-carrying capacity. It decreases with age. Elite-level and trained distance runners can have $\dot{V}O_2$max values more than twice those of untrained controls. Both training and heredity contribute to the observed difference.

6. Lactate/ventilatory threshold can refer to either of two work intensities where changing influences of anaerobic metabolism in supplementing aerobic metabolism are observed. For distance runners, the work intensity marked by the onset of blood lactate accumulation, typically accompanied by an increase in ventilation, is commonly used as part of the training regimen intended to improve competitiveness at longer distances. This threshold does not always occur at a blood lactate level of 4 mM/L as often suggested but varies among individuals and also within individuals as a result of training. As a runner becomes better trained, not only does the $\dot{V}O_2$max rise, but so does the lactate/ventilatory threshold, both in absolute terms and when expressed as a percentage of $\dot{V}O_2$max.

7. The multifaceted importance of iron in aerobic metabolism makes adequate iron supply crucial to long-term endurance performance success. It is a part of the hemoglobin and myoglobin molecules, a part of the enzymes that metabolize fuels aerobically, and a part of the enzyme that controls division of the several precursors of red blood cells. Hard training as well as dietary preferences while in training can decrease iron intake. Hemolysis from footstrike impact and the acidosis of intense training predisposes an athlete to iron loss via the urine. Iron losses through sweat are measurable. Monitoring of blood variables such as ferritin (to assess iron stores), haptoglobin (to evaluate hemolysis), reticulocytes (to assess red blood cell production), as well as urinary hemosiderin (to identify urinary loss), in addition to monitoring hemoglobin levels, can all be useful for assessing the extent to which an athlete is managing the stress of training from the standpoint of O_2 transport and fuel metabolism. Dietary iron supplementation (coupled with measurement of iron-related blood chemistry variables) may be appropriate to restore adequate iron stores if they become depleted.

8. Repeated GXT evaluation at various points over a training year provides knowledge of which aspects of performance—$\dot{V}O_2$max, lactate/ventilatory threshold, running economy, and maximum performance capacity—have changed as a result of training. This provides

a fine-tuning mechanism for assignment of subsequent training or a best estimate of strengths for best race strategies. Running economy as the aerobic demand of running at submaximum paces can be determined for a series of such paces. By using a regression equation constructed from these data, we can calculate training paces at $\dot{V}O_2$max and lactate/ventilatory threshold as well as pace ranges for each of four identified training zones: aerobic and anaerobic conditioning, and aerobic and anaerobic capacity training.

9. Athletes desiring to obtain the best results from a GXT should (a) mentally consider the test as a competitive event; (b) taper their training a few days prior to the test, ensuring freshness and minimal metabolic effects of very long or very intense runs; (c) ensure familiarity with both treadmill running and the test protocol; (d) ensure a thorough warm-up similar to that done before a competition; and (e) strive to work as hard as possible until voluntary exhaustion to ensure not only $\dot{V}O_2$max determination but also maximum anaerobic performance aspects.

10. Good test-retest reliability is obtained by (a) keeping laboratory conditions (temperature, humidity, test equipment, and test decorum) as constant as possible; (b) minimizing circadian fluctuations by testing at the same time of day; and (c) using a protocol that is of appropriate length to provide exhaustion without more than about 10 min of intense effort.

11. Blood sampling is often used in GXT evaluation, either after the test to measure maximum lactate or at intermittent points during the test to identify the work load at which lactate accumulation begins. Hemoconcentration occurs primarily due to sweat losses. Lactate measurements thus should be accompanied by measurements of hemoglobin and hematocrit to correct lactate values for this hemoconcentration. Values obtained by venipuncture must not be confused with values obtained by fingertip or earlobe puncture.

REFERENCES

Allison, A.C. (1957). The binding of haemoglobin by plasma proteins (haptoglobins): Its bearing on the "renal threshold" for haemoglobin and aetiology of haemoglobinuria. *British Medical Journal*, **2**, 1137.

American College of Sports Medicine. (1986). *Guidelines for exercise testing and prescription* (3rd ed.). Philadelphia: Lea & Febiger.

American Thoracic Society. (1979). ATS statement—Snowbird workshop on standardization of spirometry. *American Review of Respiratory Diseases*, **119**, 831-838.

Aschoff, J., & Pohl, H. (1970). Rhythm variation in energy metabolism. *Federation Proceedings*, **154**, 29-35.

Astrand, P.-O. (1976). Quantification of exercise capability and evaluation of physical capacity in man. *Progress in Cardiovascular Disease*, **19**, 51-67.

Astrand, P.-O. (1982). Muscle oxygen supply in exercise. In J.A. Loeppky & M.L. Riedesel (Eds.), *Oxygen transport to human tissues* (pp. 187-194). New York: Elsevier/North Holland.

Astrand, P.-O. (1984). Principles in ergometry and their implication in sports practice. *International Journal of Sports Medicine*, **5**, S102-S105.

Astrand, P.-O., & Rodahl, K. (1977). *Textbook of work physiology*. New York: McGraw-Hill.

Attlee, W.H.W. (1937). Hemoglobinuria following exertion. *Lancet*, 1: 1400.

Bohr, C., Hasselbalch, K.A., & Krogh, A. (1904). Uber einen in biologisches Beziehung wichtigen Einfluss den die Kohlensaurespannung des Blutes auf dessen Sauerstoffbindung ubt [Concerning an important influence in the biological relationship which the CO_2 tension of blood has on its O_2 binding]. *Skandinavisches Archiv für Physiologie*, **16**, 402-412.

Borg, G. (1973). Perceived exertion: A note on history and methods. *Medicine and Science in Sports*, **5**, 90-93.

Bouchard, C., Boulay, M.R., Simoneau, J.-A., Lortie, G., & Perusse, L. (1988). Heredity and trainability of aerobic and anaerobic performances. *Sports Medicine*, **5**, 69-73.

Bouchard, C., & Lortie, G. (1984). Heredity and endurance performance. *Sports Medicine*, **1**, 38-64.

Bransford, D.R., & Howley, E.T. (1977). Oxygen cost of running in trained and untrained men and women. *Medicine and Science in Sports*, **9**, 41-44.

Brooks, G.A. (1985). Anaerobic threshold: Review of the concept and directions for future research. *Medicine and Science in Sports and Exercise*, **17**, 23-31.

Brotherhood, J., Brozovic, B., & Pugh, L.G.C. (1975). Haematological status of middle and long distance runners. *Clinical Science and Molecular Medicine, 48*, 139-145.

Brune, M., Magnusson, B., Persson, H., & Hallberg, L. (1986). Iron losses in sweat. *American Journal of Clinical Nutrition, 43*, 438-443.

Busse, M.W., Maassen, N., & Boning, D. (1987). The work load-lactate curve: Measure of endurance capacity or criterion of muscle glycogen storage? I. Glycogen depletion. *International Journal of Sports Medicine, 8*, 140.

Caiozzo, V.J., Davis, J.A., Ellis, J.F., Azus, J.L., Vandagriff, R., Prietto, C.A., & McMaster, W.L. (1982). A comparison of gas exchange indices used to detect the anaerobic threshold. *Journal of Applied Physiology, 53*, 1184-1189.

Campbell, M.J., McComas, A.J., & Petito, F. (1973). Physiological changes in aging muscles. *Journal of Neurology, Neurosurgery, and Neuropsychiatry, 36*, 174-182.

Cavagna, G.A., Saibene, F.B., & Margaria, R. (1964). Mechanical work in running. *Journal of Applied Physiology, 19*, 249-256.

Christiansen, J., Douglas, C.C., & Haldane, J.S. (1914). The absorption and disassociation of carbon dioxide by human blood. *Journal of Physiology, 48*, 244.

Clausen, J.P. (1977). Effect of physical training on cardiovascular adjustments to exercise in man. *Physiological Reviews, 57*, 779-815.

Clausen, J.P., Klausen, K., Rasmussen, B., & Trap-Jensen, J. (1973). Central and peripheral circulatory changes after training of the arms or legs. *American Journal of Physiology, 225*, 675-682.

Clement, D.B., & Asmundson, R.C. (1982). Nutritional intake and hematological parameters in endurance runners. *Physician and Sportsmedicine, 10*(3), 37-43.

Clement, D.B., Asmundson, R.C., & Medhurst, C.W. (1977). Hemoglobin values: Comparative survey of the 1976 Canadian Olympic Team. *Canadian Medical Association Journal, 117*, 614-616.

Clode, M., & Campbell, E.J.M. (1969). The relationship between gas exchange and changes in blood lactate concentrations during exercise. *Clinical Science, 37*, 263-272.

Conley, D.L., & Krahenbuhl, G.S. (1980). Running economy and distance running performance of highly trained athletes. *Medicine and Science in Sports, 12*, 357-360.

Conrad, M.E., Benjamin, B.I., Williams, H.L., & Fox, A.L. (1967). Human absorption of hemoglobin-iron. *Gastroenterology, 53*, 5-10.

Cooper, K. (1968). *Aerobics*. New York: Bantam.

Costill, D.L., Thomason, H., & Roberts, E. (1973). Fractional utilization of the aerobic capacity during distance running. *Medicine and Science in Sports, 5*, 248-252.

Cronkite, E.P. (1973). The erythrocyte. In J.R. Brobeck (Ed.), *Best and Taylor's physiological basis of medical practice* (9th ed., pp. 4-24). Baltimore: Williams & Wilkins.

Currens, J.H., & White, P.D. (1961). Half a century of running. *New England Journal of Medicine, 265*, 988-993.

Dallman, P.R., Beutler, E., & Finch, B.A. (1978). Effects of iron deficiency exclusive of anemia. *British Journal of Haematology, 40*, 179-184.

Daniels, J. (1974). Physiological characteristics of champion male athletes. *Research Quarterly, 45*, 342-348.

Daniels, J.T. (1985). A physiologist's view of running economy. *Medicine and Science in Sports and Exercise, 17*, 332-338.

Daniels, J.T., & Gilbert, J. (1979). *Oxygen power: Performance tables for distance runners*. Tempe, AZ: Oxygen Power.

Daniels, J.T., Scardina, N., Hayes, J., & Foley, P. (1986). Elite and subelite female middle- and long-distance runners. In D.M. Landers (Ed.), *The 1984 Olympic Scientific Congress proceedings: Vol. 3. Sport and elite performers* (pp. 57-72). Champaign, IL: Human Kinetics.

Davies, C.T.M., & Thompson, M.W. (1979). Aerobic performance of female marathon and male ultramarathon athletes. *European Journal of Applied Physiology, 41*, 233-245.

Davis, J.A., Caiozzo, V.J., Lamarra, N., Ellis, J.F., Vandagriff, R., Prietto, C.A., & McMaster, W.C. (1983). Does the gas exchange threshold occur at a fixed blood lactate concentration of 2 or 4 mM? *International Journal of Sports Medicine, 4*, 89-93.

Davis, J.A., Vodak, P., Wilmore, J.H., & Kurtz, P. (1976). Anaerobic threshold and maximal aerobic power for three modes of exercise. *Journal of Applied Physiology, 41*, 544-550.

Dempsey, J.A., Aaron, E., & Martin, B.J. (1988). Pulmonary function and prolonged exercise. In D.R. Lamb & R.R. Murray (Eds.), *Perspectives in exercise science and sports medicine: Vol. I: Prolonged exercise* (pp. 75-124). Indianapolis: Benchmark Press.

Dempsey, J.A., Hanson, P., & Henderson, K. (1984). Exercise-induced arterial hypoxemia in healthy human subjects at sea level. *Journal of Physiology (London), 355*, 161-175.

Deutsch, F., & Kauf, E. (1927). *Heart and athletics*

(L.M. Warfield, Trans.). St. Louis: C.V. Mosby. (Original work published 1924)

DeWijn, J.F., deJongste, J.L., Mosterd, W., & Willebrand, D. (1971). Hemoglobin, packed cell volume, serum iron, and iron-binding capacity of selected athletes during training. *Nutrition and Metabolism*, **13**, 129-139.

Dill, D.B., & Costill, D.L. (1974). Calculation of percentage changes in volumes of blood, plasma, and red cells in dehydration. *Journal of Applied Physiology*, **37**, 247-248.

Doll, E., & Keul, J. (1968). Zum Stoffwechsel des Skeletmuskels. II. *Pfluger's Archiv für die gesamte Physiologie*, **301**, 214-229.

Dufaux, B., Hoederath, A., Streitberger, I., Hollmann, W., & Assman, G. (1981). Serum ferritin, transferrin, haptoglobin, and iron in middle- and long-distance runners, elite rowers, and professional racing cyclists. *International Journal of Sports Medicine*, **2**, 43-46.

Eichner, E. (1986). The anemias of athletes. *Physician and Sportsmedicine*, **14**(9), 122-130.

Eichner, E. (1988). Other medical considerations in prolonged exercise. *Perspectives in Exercise Science and Sports Medicine*, **1**, 415-442.

Ekblom, B., & Hermansen, L. (1968). Cardiac output in athletes. *Journal of Applied Physiology*, **25**, 619-625.

Essen, B., Pernow, B., Gollnick, P.D., & Saltin, B. (1975). Muscle glycogen content and lactate uptake in exercising muscles. In H. Howald & J.R. Poortmans (Eds.), *Metabolic adaptations to prolonged physical exercise* (pp. 130-134). Basel: Birkhauser.

Farrell, P.A., Wilmore, J.H., Coyle, E.F., Billing, J.E., & Costill, D.L. (1979). Plasma lactate accumulation and distance running performance. *Medicine and Science in Sports and Exercise*, **11**, 338-344.

Fay, L., Londeree, B.R., LaFontaine, T.P., & Volek, M.R. (1989). Physiological parameters related to distance running performance in female athletes. *Medicine and Science in Sports and Exercise*, **21**, 319-324.

Fleischer, R. (1881). Uber eine neue form von Haemoglobinurie beim Menschen [Concerning a new form of hemoglobinuria in people]. *Berliner Klinische Wochenschrift*, **18**, 691-694.

Food and Nutrition Board. (1989). *Recommended dietary allowances* (10th ed.). Washington, DC: National Academy of Sciences.

Foster, C., Snyder, A.C., Thompson, N.N., & Kuettel, K. (1988). Normalization of the blood lactate profile in athletes. *International Journal of Sports Medicine*, **9**, 198-200.

Fric, J., Jr., Fric, J., Boldt, F., Stoboy, H., Meller, W., Feldt, F., & Drygas, W. (1988). Reproducibility of post-exercise lactate and anaerobic threshold. *International Journal of Sports Medicine*, **9**, 310-312.

Frick, M.R., Elovainio, R.O., & Somer, T. (1967). The mechanism of bradycardia evolved by physical training. *Cardiologia*, **51**, 46-54.

Fujitsuka, N., Yamamoto, T., Ohkuwa, T., Saito, M., & Miyamura, M. (1982). Peak blood lactate after short periods of maximum treadmill running. *European Journal of Applied Physiology*, **48**, 289-296.

Gibson, T.M., Harrison, M.H., & Wellcome, R.M. (1979). An evaluation of a treadmill work test. *British Journal of Sports Medicine*, **13**, 6-11.

Gollnick, P.D., Bayly, W.M., & Hodgson, D.R. (1986). Exercise intensity, training, diet, and lactate concentration in muscle and blood. *Medicine and Science in Sports and Exercise*, **18**, 334-340.

Green, R., Charlton, R.W., Seftel, H., Bothwell, T., Mayet, F., Adams, B., Finch, C., & Layrisse, M. (1968). Body iron excretion in man. A collaborative study. *American Journal of Medicine*, **45**, 336-353.

Hagberg, J.M., Giese, M.D., & Schneider, R.B. (1978). Comparison of the three procedures for measuring VO$_2$max in competitive cyclists. *European Journal of Applied Physiology*, **39**, 47-52.

Harrison, T.R., & Pilcher, C. (1930). Studies in congestive heart failure. II. The respiratory exchange during and after exercise. *Journal of Clinical Investigation*, **8**, 291.

Haymes, E.M., & Lamanca, J.J. (1989). Iron loss in runners during exercise: Implications and recommendations. *Sports Medicine*, **7**, 277-285.

Heck, H., Mader, A., Hess, G., Mucke, S., Muller, R., & Hollmann, W. (1985). Justification of the 4-mmol/L lactate threshold. *International Journal of Sports Medicine*, **6**, 117-130.

Henderson, Y., Haggard, H.W., & Dolley, F.S. (1927). The efficiency of the heart and the significance of rapid and slow pulse rates. *American Journal of Physiology*, **82**, 512-524.

Herbert, V. (1987). Recommended dietary intakes (RDI) of iron in humans. *American Journal of Clinical Nutrition*, **45**, 679-686.

Hermansen, L., & Osnes, J.B. (1972). Blood and muscle pH after maximal exercise in man. *Journal of Applied Physiology*, **32**, 304-308.

Hermansen, L., & Saltin, B. (1969). Oxygen uptake during maximal treadmill and bicycle exercise. *Journal of Applied Physiology*, **26**, 31-37.

Hill, A.V., & Lupton, H. (1923). Muscular exercise,

lactic acid, and the supply and utilization of oxygen. *Quarterly Medical Journal*, **16**, 135-171.

Hoffbrand, A.V., Ganeshaguru, K., Hooton, J.W.L., & Tattersall, M.H.N. (1976). Effects of iron deficiency and desferrioxamine on DNA synthesis in human cells. *British Journal of Haematology*, **33**, 517-520.

Holloszy, J.O., & Coyle, E.F. (1984). Adaptations of skeletal muscle to endurance exercise and their metabolic consequences. *Journal of Applied Physiology*, **56**, 831-838.

Huston, T.P., Puffer, J.C., & Rodney, W.M. (1985). The athletic heart syndrome. *New England Journal of Medicine*, **313**, 24-32.

Issekutz, B., Jr., Birkhead, N.C., & Rodahl, K. (1962). Use of respiratory quotients in assessment of aerobic work capacity. *Journal of Applied Physiology*, **17**, 47-50.

Ivy, J.L., Costill, D.L., Van Handel, P.J., Essig, D.A., & Lower, R.W. (1981). Alterations in the lactate threshold with changes in substrate availability. *International Journal of Sports Medicine*, **2**, 139-142.

Ivy, J.L., Withers, R.T., Van Handel, P.J., Elger, D.H., & Costill, D.L. (1980). Muscle respiratory capacity and fiber type as determinants of the lactate threshold. *Journal of Applied Physiology*, **48**, 523-527.

Jacobs, I., Sjodin, B., Kaiser, P., & Karlsson, J. (1981). Onset of blood lactate accumulation after prolonged exercise. *Acta Physiologica Scandinavica*, **112**, 215-217.

Jones, N.L. (1988). *Clinical exercise testing*. Philadelphia: W.B. Saunders Co.

Kamon, E., & Pandolf, K.B. (1972). Maximal aerobic power during laddermill climbing, uphill running, and cycling. *Journal of Applied Physiology*, **2**, 467-473.

Kearney, J.T., & Van Handel, P.J. (1989). Economy: A physiologic perspective. *Advances in Sports Medicine and Fitness*, **2**, 57-89.

Kindermann, W., Simon, G., & Keul, J. (1979). The significance of the aerobic-anaerobic transition for the determination of work load intensities during endurance training. *European Journal of Applied Physiology*, **42**, 25-34.

Klissouras, V. (1972). Genetic limit of functional adaptability. *Internationale Zeitschrift für angewandte Physiologie*, **30**, 85-94.

Letsky, E.A., Miller, F., Worwood, M., & Flynn, D.M. (1974). Serum ferritin in children with thalassaemia regularly transfused. *Journal of Clinical Pathology*, **27**, 652-655.

Liljestrand, G., & Stenstrom, N. (1920). Respirationsversuche beim gehen, laufen, ski- und schlittschuhlaufen [Gas exchange experimentation with walking, running, skiing, and skating]. *Skandinavisches Archiv für Physiologie*, **39**, 167-206.

Lindhard, J. (1915). Uber das minutenvolum des herzens bei ruhe und bei muskelarbeit [Concerning the cardiac output at rest and with exercise]. *Pflugers Archiv für die gesamte Physiologie*, **161**, 233-283.

MacDougall, J.D., Reddan, W.G., Layton, C.R., & Dempsey, J.A. (1974). Effects of metabolic hyperthermia on performance during heavy prolonged exercise. *Journal of Applied Physiology*, **36**, 538-544.

Mader, A., Liesen, H., Heck, H., Philippi, H., Rost, R., Schuerch, P., & Hollmann, W. (1976). Zur Beurteilung der sportartspecifischen Ausdauerleistungsfahigkeit im Labor [Estimation of sport-event-specific endurance work capacity during exercise]. *Sportarzt und Sportmedizin*, **4**, 80-88.

Magnusson, B., Hallberg, L., Rossander, L., & Swolin, B. (1984). Iron metabolism and "sports anemia." *Acta Medica Scandinavica*, **216**, 149-164.

Makrides, L., Heigenhauser, G.J.F., McCartney, N., & Jones, N.L. (1986). Physical training in young and older healthy subjects. In J.R. Sutton & R.M. Brock (Eds.), *Sports medicine for the mature athlete* (pp. 363-372). Indianapolis: Benchmark Press.

Margaria, R., Cerretelli, P., Aghemo, P., & Sassi, J. (1963). Energy cost of running. *Journal of Applied Physiology*, **8**, 367-370.

Margaria, R., Cerretelli, P., & Mangili, F. (1964). Balance and kinetics of anaerobic energy release during strenuous exercise in man. *Journal of Applied Physiology*, **19**, 623-628.

Martin, D.E. (1988). *Respiratory anatomy and physiology*. St. Louis: Mosby.

Martin, D.E., & May, D.F. (1987). Pulmonary function in elite women distance runners. *International Journal of Sports Medicine*, **8**, S84-S90.

Martin, D.E., May, D.F., & Pilbeam, S.P. (1986). Ventilation limitations to performance among elite male distance runners. In D.M. Landers (Ed.), *The 1984 Scientific Congress proceedings: Vol. 3. Sport and elite performers* (pp. 121-131). Champaign, IL: Human Kinetics.

Martin, D.E., Vroon, D.H., May, D.F., & Pilbeam, S.P. (1986). Physiological changes in elite male distance runners training for Olympic competition. *Physician and Sportsmedicine*, **14**(1), 152-171.

Martin, D.E., Vroon, D.H., & Sheard, M.M. (1989). Effects of hemoconcentration during maximum-effort treadmill tests on blood lactate levels in trained distance runners. *Proceedings, First IOC World Congress on Sport Sciences* (pp. 37-38). Colorado Springs: United States Olympic Committee.

McArdle, W.D., Magel, J.R., Delio, D.J., Toner, M., & Chase, J.M. (1978). Specificity of run training on VO₂max and heart rate changes during running and swimming. *Medicine and Science in Sports*, **10**, 16-20.

McConnell, T.R. (1988). Practical considerations in the testing of VO₂-max in runners. *Sports Medicine*, **5**, 57-68.

McMiken, D.F., & Daniels, J.T. (1976). Aerobic requirements and maximum aerobic power in treadmill and track running. *Medicine and Science in Sports*, **8**, 14-17.

Medbo, J.I., Mohn, A.C., Tabala, I., Bahr, R., Vaage, O., & Sejersted, O.M. (1988). Anaerobic capacity determined by maximal accumulated O₂ deficit. *Journal of Applied Physiology*, **64**, 50-60.

Miller, B.J., Pate, R.R., & Burgess, W. (1988). Foot impact force and intravascular hemolysis during distance running. *International Journal of Sports Medicine*, **9**, 56-60.

Mitchell, J.H., & Blomqvist, C.G. (1971). Maximal oxygen uptake. *New England Journal of Medicine*, **284**, 1018-1022.

Mitchell, J.H., Sproule, B.J., & Chapman, C.B. (1958). The physiological meaning of the maximal oxygen uptake test. *Journal of Clinical Investigation*, **37**, 538-547.

Morganroth, J., Maron, B.J., Henry, W.L., & Epstein, S.E. (1975). Comparative left ventricular dimensions in trained athletes. *Annals of Internal Medicine*, **82**, 521-524.

Nagle, F.J. (1973). Physiological assessment of maximal performance. *Exercise and Sports Science Reviews*, **1**, 313-338.

Nadel, E.R. (1988). Temperature regulation and prolonged exercise. *Perspectives in Exercise Science and Sports Medicine*, **1**, 125-151.

Newhouse, I.J., & Clement, D.B. (1988). Iron status in athletes. *Sports Medicine*, **5**, 337-352.

Ohkuwa, T., Kato, Y., Katsumata, K., Nakao, T., & Miyamura, M. (1984). Blood lactate and glycerol after 400 m and 3,000 m runs in sprinters and long distance runners. *European Journal of Applied Physiology*, **53**, 213-218.

Owles, W.H. (1930). Alterations in the lactic acid content of the blood as a result of light exercise, and associated changes in the CO₂-combining power of the blood and in the alveolar CO₂ pressure. *Journal of Physiology*, **69**, 214-237.

Pannier, J.L., Vrijens, J., & Van Cauter, C. (1980). Cardiorespiratory response to treadmill and bicycle exercise in runners. *European Journal of Applied Physiology*, **43**, 243-251.

Pardy, R.L., Hussain, S.N., & Macklem, P.T. (1984). The ventilatory pump in exercise. *Clinics in Chest Medicine*, **5**, 35-49.

Pate, R.R. (1983). Sports anemia: A review of the current research literature. *Physician and Sportsmedicine*, **11**(2), 115-131.

Pate, R.R., Sparling, P.B., Wilson, G.E., Cureton, K.J., & Miller, B.J. (1987). Cardiorespiratory and metabolic responses to submaximal and maximal exercise in elite women distance runners. *International Journal of Sports Medicine*, **8**(Suppl. 2), 91-95.

Pattengale, P.K., & Holloszy, J.O. (1967). Augmentation of skeletal muscle myoglobin by a program of treadmill running. *American Journal of Physiology*, **213**, 783-785.

Paulev, P.E., Jordal, R., & Pedersen, N.S. (1983). Dermal excretion of iron in intensely training athletes. *Clinica Chimica Acta*, **127**, 19-27.

Peota, C. (1989). Studies counter myths about iron in athletes. *Physician and Sportsmedicine*, **17**(11), 26-27.

Peronnet, F., & Thibault, G. (1989). Mathematical analysis of running performance and world running records. *Journal of Applied Physiology*, **67**, 453-465.

Pollock, M.L. (1977). Submaximal and maximal working capacity of elite distance runners. Part I: Cardiorespiratory aspects. *Annals of the New York Academy of Sciences*, **301**, 310-321.

Pugh, L.G.C.E. (1970). Oxygen intake in track and treadmill running with observations on the effect of air resistance. *Journal of Physiology (London)*, **207**, 823-835.

Purvis, J.W., & Cureton, K.J. (1981). Ratings of perceived exertion at the anaerobic threshold. *Ergonomics*, **24**, 295-300.

Reilly, T., Robinson, G., & Minors, D.S. (1984). Some circulatory responses to exercise at different times of day. *Medicine and Science in Sports and Exercise*, **16**, 477-482.

Rerych, S.K., Scholz, P.M., Sabiston, D.C., & Jones, R.H. (1980). Effects of exercise training on left ventricular function in normal subjects: A longitudinal study by radionuclide angiography. *American Journal of Cardiology*, **45**, 244-252.

Roe, C.F., Goldberg, M.J., Blaw, C.S., & Kinney, J.M. (1966). The influence of body temperature on early postoperative oxygen consumption. *Surgery*, **60**, 85-92.

Rowell, L.B., Taylor, H.L., & Wang, Y. (1964). Limitations to the prediction of maximum oxygen uptake. *Journal of Applied Physiology*, **19**, 919-927.

Saltin, B., & Astrand, P.-O. (1967). Maximal oxygen uptake in athletes. *Journal of Applied Physiology*, **23**, 353-358.

Saltin, B., & Gollnick, P.D. (1983). Skeletal muscle adaptability: Significance for metabolism and performance. In L.D. Peachy, R.H. Adrian, & S.R. Geiger (Eds.), *Handbook of physiology: Sect. 10. Skeletal muscle* (pp. 555-631). Washington, DC: American Physiological Society.

Scrimgeour, A.G., Noakes, T.D., Adams, B., & Myburgh, K. (1986). The influence of weekly training distance on fractional utilization of maximum aerobic capactiy in marathon and ultramarathon runners. *European Journal of Applied Physiology*, **55**, 202-209.

Shephard, R.J. (1984). Tests of maximum oxygen uptake: A critical review. *Sports Medicine*, **1**, 99-124.

Shephard, R.J., Allen, C., Benade, A.J.S., Davies, C.T.M., di Prampero, P.E., Hedman, R., Merriman, J.E., Myhre, K., & Simmons, R. (1968). The maximal oxygen uptake. *Bulletin of the World Health Organization*, **38**, 757-764.

Sjodin, B., & Jacobs, I. (1981). Onset of blood lactate accumulation and marathon running performance. *International Journal of Sports Medicine*, **2**, 23-26.

Sjodin, B., & Svedenhag, J. (1985). Applied physiology of marathon running. *Sports Medicine*, **2**, 83-99.

Skinner, J.S., & McLellan, T.M. (1980). The transition from aerobic to anaerobic metabolism. *Research Quarterly for Exercise and Sport*, **51**, 234-248.

Snyder, A.C., Dvorak, L.L., & Roepke, J.B. (1989). Influence of dietary iron source on measures of iron status among female runners. *Medicine and Science in Sports and Exercise*, **21**, 7-10.

Staub, N.C., Nagano, H., & Pearce, M.L. (1967). Pulmonary edema in dogs, especially the sequence of fluid accumulation in lungs. *Journal of Applied Physiology*, **22**, 227-240.

Stegmann, H., Kindermann, W., & Schnabel, A. (1981). Lactate kinetics and individual anaerobic threshold. *International Journal of Sports Medicine*, **2**, 160-165.

Stewart, G.A., Steel, J.E., Tayne, M.B., & Stewart, M.H. (1972). Observations on the hematology and the iron and protein intake of Australian Olympic athletes. *Medical Journal of Australia*, **2**, 1339-1342.

Stewart, J.G., Ahlquist, D.A., McGill, D.B., Ilstrup, D.M., Schwartz, S., & Owen, R.A. (1984). Gastrointestinal blood loss and anemia in runners. *Annals of Internal Medicine*, **100**, 843-845.

Taylor, H.L., Wang, Y., Rowell, L., & Blomqvist, G. (1963). The standardization and interpretation of submaximal and maximal tests of working capacity. *Pediatrics*, **32**, 703-715.

Vellar, O.D. (1968). Studies on sweat losses of nutrients. *Scandinavian Journal of Clinical and Laboratory Investigation*, **21**, 157-167.

Wahren, J., Hagenfeld, L., & Felig, P. (1975). Glucose and free fatty acid utilization in exercise: Studies in normal and diabetic man. *Israeli Journal of Medical Science*, **11**, 551-559.

Walsh, M.L., & Banister, E.W. (1988). Possible mechanisms of the anaerobic threshold. *Sports Medicine*, **5**, 269-302.

Wasserman, K. (1984). Coupling of external to internal respiration. *American Review of Respiratory Diseases*, **129**, S21-S24.

Wasserman, K., & McIlroy, M.B. (1964). Detecting the threshold of anaerobic metabolism in cardiac patients during exercise. *American Journal of Cardiology*, **14**, 844-852.

Wasserman, K., Whipp, B.J., Koyal, S.N., & Beaver, W.L. (1973). Anaerobic threshold and respiratory gas exchange during exercise. *Journal of Applied Physiology*, **5**, 236-243.

Welch, H.G. (1973). Substrate utilization in muscle—adaptations to physical effort. In J.P. Naughton & H.K. Hellerstein (Eds.), *Exercise testing and exercise training in coronary heart disease* (pp. 193-197). New York: Academic Press.

Wilmore, J.H., & Norton, A.C. (1974). *The heart and lungs at work: A primer of exercise physiology*. Schiller Park, IL: Beckman Instruments.

Wintrobe, M.W., Lee, G.R., Boggs, D.R., Bithell, T.C., Foerster, J., Athens, J.W., & Lukens, J.N. (1981). Iron deficiency and iron-deficiency anemia. In *Clinical hematology* (8th ed., pp. 617-645). Philadelphia: Lea & Febiger.

Yoshimura, H., Inoue, T., Yamada, T., & Shiraki, K. (1980). Anemia during hard physical training (sports anemia) and its causal mechanism, with special reference to protein nutrition. *World Review of Nutrition and Dietetics*, **35**, 1-86.

Yudkin, J., & Cohen, R.D. (1975). The contribution of the kidney to the removal of a lactic acid load under normal and acidotic conditions in the conscious rat. *Clinical Science and Molecular Biology*, **48**, 121-131.

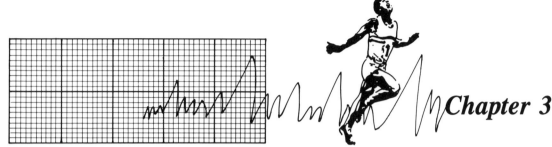

A Unified Strategy for Training Distance Runners

Chapter 3

I keep six honest serving men,
They taught me all I knew;
Their names are What and Why and When
And How and Where and Who.

This old rhyme of Rudyard Kipling echoes down through the years and is the foundation upon which any logical system of achievement is based. In athlete development, just as in the design and building of a piece of precision equipment, these "six serving men" allow completion of the job with relative ease and certainty. They represent the six most searching questions that must be answered in the construction of an effective training plan:

1. What should be done?
2. Why is it being done?
3. When should it be done?
4. How is it done best?
5. Where should it be done?
6. Who should do it?

The answers to these questions may not be perfectly obvious at first glance as athlete and coach try to design a more specific training plan. "What" defines the details of each session—for example, running repetitions (a given number and distance), up a hill (of a specific grade) or on a track, with a specific recovery time. It also defines the overall goals of the entire training plan. "Why" identifies the reason for the specific physiological training zone, or muscle groups, being challenged in a training session. "When" addresses the time of day or the point during a particular training cycle when development of the system being challenged is most sensible or safest. "Where" demands a decision as to the best site to get the job done—a track versus a grassy hill, or a gymnasium versus a weight room. It also can refer to scheduling training camp situations in various parts of the country (or elsewhere) to take advantage of weather or special facilities. "How" demands a decision as to the best method for developing the system in question—level or uphill sprinting versus free weight exercises (or both) for building strength (or power, or endurance) in the leg extensor muscles, for example. "Who" refers to event specialty or level of development—is the athlete an 800m runner or a marathon runner; a runner at the beginning or near the end of a development year?

By continually seeking answers to these questions, the training plan will become ever more reasoned and finely tuned. And so will the quality of the finished product, namely, an athlete honed into a very fit and able competitor. Always ask these questions—they will "concentrate the mind wonderfully" (in the words of the venerable lexicographer, Samuel Johnson), and ensure that no stone has been left unturned in a quest to produce an athlete who is both injury-free and in the best condition at the appropriate moment.

GOAL SETTING

Athletes who strive to compete at the highest levels must realize that it will take time to build the excellence required. This in turn will require effective planning directed at steady improvement. Logically, the coach of such athletes is in charge of engineering these plans. Good planning mandates achievable intermediate goals along the way to a larger, more ultimate goal, such as a personal best, a championship victory, or an Olympic medal. Goal setting is crucial at the outset because it demands an answer to a very important question to each athlete: "What do you want from running?" Once this answer is identified, this becomes the ultimate goal; working backward from that goal to the present is then much easier.

Goal Achievement Requires Long-Term Planning

Anyone desiring instant gratification—and probably we all do—will by now have sensed that the goals we are identifying are not achieved quickly. We are discussing goals over years or a career. A cycle of training, recovery, focusing, and competing is not a cycle of activity that repeats frequently. When we discuss training concepts themselves, we shall see that shorter term goals—those extending only a few weeks into the future—will also be an important part of the plan. Short-term goals delineate desired outcomes of day-to-day training and are thus the building blocks for the overall plan to reach toward long-term goals. For most athletes, it is difficult to put an entire year's training into a functional perspective unless these day-to-day building blocks are laid out to show the path toward progress. An old adage has great meaning here: "The hunting dog must see the rabbit for an effective chase." The long-term goals allow short-term goals to be outlined more easily.

Not only must goals be seen on the horizon, but also there must be some success along the way. Staying enthusiastic for 6 to 10 months of a developmental season or 6 to 10 years in a career is not easy when so many sacrifices are required in the life of a dedicated athlete. Fortunately, in most countries where athletics exists, many variably competitive opportunities,

if scheduled optimally, can serve as stepping-stones toward a major championship (again, short-term goals help in the achievement of a long-term objective).

In the United States, for example, each state typically has county and regional championships in the high school–age divisions prior to the state championship. In colleges and universities, the same concept exists: dual or triangular meets (with neighboring schools), conference meets, and finally the national collegiate division championships. For athletes not attending educational institutions, track meets as well as road race opportunities exist throughout the nation, conducted most often under the aegis of the national governing body for athletics, The Athletics Congress (TAC) or the Road Runner's Club of America (RRCA). Because no real rational plan exists for these postcollegiate activities, athletes and coaches must decide for themselves what has the greatest significance—again an example of goal setting. The TAC outdoor championships, for example, is often the selection meet for major international traveling teams, making it an important goal for track-oriented distance runners.

In Britain the athletics scene is rooted firmly in the club system, with relatively little actual school competition. Thus, in contrast to the United States, where high schools and colleges schedule frequent and important competitions far in advance as part of the academic program, in Britain the number of "required" or scheduled competitions that demand good performance is far smaller. These few can be given greater focus, scheduled comfortably as intermediate goals between blocks of time that allow for adequate training on the way to major competitive efforts.

In Table 3.1 we summarize Seb Coe's major event titles as a good example of how longevity can occur in an athlete's career when careful attention is given to prevention of overtraining and overracing. The table represents a span of 19 years as he progressed from a junior to a senior athlete. To add more insight to Seb's record progression, Figure 3.1 depicts the administrative areas of England's Amateur Athletic Association (AAA). Strong emphasis was always placed on being ready for the various administrative championships, because these were the logical stepping-stones for progression up the ranks of sport in the world. Thus, during any given year Seb competed initially in the city (Sheffield) school championships, then progressed through the county (Yorkshire) championships and into the national championships. Good performances along the way as a junior athlete could (and did) lead to Seb's selection for the European junior championships and eventually into higher

Table 3.1   Sebastian Coe's Major Championship Performances

Age	Meeting	Rank	Event	Class
14	Yorkshire County Championship	1	1,500m	Boy
16	Northern Counties Championship	1	1,500m	Youth
	UK Championship	1	1,500m	Youth
	English Schools Championship	1	3,000m	Youth
18	UK Championship	1	1,500m	Junior
	European Outdoor Championship	3	1,500m	Junior
20	UK Indoor Championship	1	800m (CBP)[a]	Senior
	European Indoor Championship	1	800m (UKR-CWR)	Senior
21	Memorial Ivo Van Damme	1	800m (UKR)	Senior
	European Outdoor Championship	3	800m	Senior
	Coca-Cola	1	800m (UKR)	Senior
22	UK Indoor Championship	1	3,000m	Senior
	UK Outdoor Championship	2	400m	Senior
	Europa Cup	1	800m	Senior
	Bislett Games	1	800m (WOR)	Senior
	Weltklasse	1	1,500m (WOR)	Senior
	IAAF Golden Mile	1	mile (WOR)	Senior
23	Bislett Games	1	1,000m (WOR)	Senior
	Olympic Games	2	800m	Senior
	Olympic Games	1	1,500m	Senior
24	UK vs. GDR Indoor	1	800m (WIR)	Senior
	Florence International	1	800m (WOR)	Senior
	Oslo Games	1	1,000m (WOR)	Senior
	Weltklasse	1	mile (WOR)	Senior
	IAAF Golden Mile	1	mile (WOR)	Senior
	World Cup	1	800m	Senior
25	European Outdoor Championship	2	800m	Senior
	4 × 800m relay	Fastest leg (WOR)		Senior
26	UK vs. USA Indoor	1	800m (WIR)	Senior
	Oslo Indoor	1	1,000m (WIR)	Senior
27	Olympic Games	2	800m	Senior
	Olympic Games	1	1,500m (OR)	Senior
28	European Outdoor Championship	1	800m	Senior
	European Outdoor Championship	2	1,500m	Senior
	Rieti	1	1,500m (PR)	Senior
32	AAA UK Championships	1	1,500m	Senior
	World Cup	2	1,500m	Senior

[a]CBP, championship best performance; UKR, United Kingdom record; WIR, world indoor record; PR, personal record; CWR, commonwealth record; OR, Olympic Games record; WOR, World outdoor record.

level European track and field meetings. Not always could perfect preparation be guaranteed, even with these relatively few periodic meetings; the exigencies of life didn't permit it. But long-term and short-term goals set on paper well in advance allowed construction of a development plan to provide as close a match as possible of good fitness on the given day of competition.

Effective Goal Setting Optimizes Racing Effectiveness

The essential specialization required for success at the top level mandates that runners not spread their energies too thin. Otherwise, they may be decent competitors all year long but never achieve real excellence at any specific point. Long-term goal setting

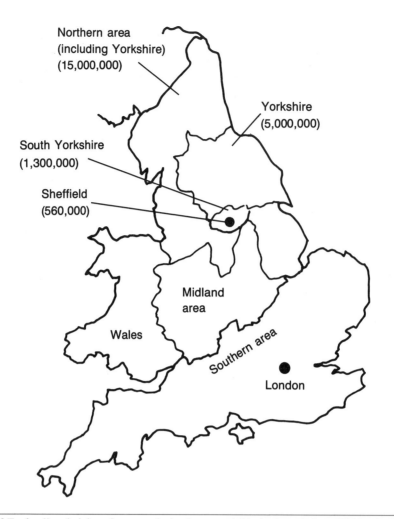

Figure 3.1 Division of England's administrative areas in its Amateur Athletic Association. Within the United Kingdom, the normal progression for an athlete is from city (schools) to county (analogous to a state in the U.S.) to area (analogous to a region in the U.S.) and finally to the national championships. Such progress will always elevate the level of competition since the catchment population for athlete selection increases. With Sebastian Coe, starting upward from Sheffield (population 560,000), moving through the South Yorkshire (1,300,000), Yorkshire (5,000,000), and eventually the Northern Counties championships (15,000,000), this was a 30-fold increase in population base for athlete selection. Moving toward the national championships represented another three-fold increase beyond that (the population of England is 46,500,000).

permits an athlete to assign relative importance to the various aspects of a training year. This in turn provides the variation in focus that can yield winning results at some periods and good performances during other periods.

As an example, running cross-country or road races during the fall and winter may be perfectly acceptable for a track racer who desires the summertime months as an ultimate peak. However, unless the athlete is unusually gifted, winning performances in these cross-country and road racing encounters may come very seldom. If they do come often, either the competition is not very stiff, or the athlete will have focused so completely on these events that burnout may occur before the summer season arrives. Typi-

cally, top-level road races and cross-country races are highly contested by many talented athletes for whom this season is, in fact, their focal point. To recall an adage oft-used by runners themselves, "There are only so many races when one can go to the brink."

We believe that it is unwise for athletes to be urged to "train through" a higher-level competition—that is, schedule a competition without making a serious attempt to perform well. The need to simply score points for the team or to be seen in a sponsoring firm's new line of sportswear removes some of the athlete's consistency in becoming optimally motivated to perform well in competitions. Racing and training are very different entities and demand different mental attitudes. It is unwise to develop a habit of coming to the starting line of a race with only a haphazard interest in attempting to run well; it may occur again when least desired! A better approach is to give the event a meaning different from that of a race. One example might be to define the event as a time trial—a run for time to obtain an indicator of fitness rather than a race against other people even for a mediocre placing. Points for the team (or perks from the athlete's sponsor) may thus be earned, but the athlete still considers the event a meaningful competitive situation.

An important point here relates to using excessive racing in the school setting as intermediate goals. The coach-athlete relationship ought to exist with the aim of long-term benefit to the athlete (i.e., post–high school, postcollegiate) rather than solely immediate (school- or college-oriented gratification via the coach's win-loss record). Demanding pressures placed on young athletes to perform at their maximum too often can be more debilitating to the spirit than beneficial to improvement. And it can produce injury.

Long-term goals permit a focus on the overall design of a yearlong season; each phase of the program can benefit the other phases sensibly. The United States' Craig Virgin is a good example of a track-oriented athlete who for many years was also excellent at cross-country competition internationally. His yearly philosophy was to use the fall and winter to build strength and endurance, with the World Cross Country Championships during March providing his ultimate test of progress. As a result, he earned berths on 10 USA World Cross Country teams in 11 years, winning the world title on two occasions. Following cross-country, Craig either continued in a racing mode for a few more weeks followed by a break or took his break immediately. Then upon this well-developed base of endurance fitness he began the kind of faster endurance and speed training needed for the fluidity and finesse required of a potential track champion at his June national championships. Again, he either followed those championships with a brief racing period on the early summer European circuit and then took a break, or inserted a break immediately in preparation for a later summer peak during August or September. By identifying these goals well in advance, Craig arranged the details of training, racing, and recovery in their proper context for meaningful development.

Nowadays extreme pressures are placed on top-level athletes to disrupt their development and overall goals by traveling to far-flung destinations and racing for huge sums of money to satisfy the whims of meet directors trying to establish or maintain the integrity of their particular competitive events. Similar financial pressures (so great that athletes can become rich almost beyond their imaginations) are exerted by meet directors to entice athletes to change events—the 10,000m runner being urged by huge financial incentives to debut in the marathon is one of the saddest examples.

An enormous amount of time is required for athletes to prepare properly for 10,000m or marathon racing, particularly in accommodating to each event's unique requirements. Should the switch in emphasis be forced as a result of ill-timed incentive propositions thrust upon the athlete that do not allow proper preparation, the athlete may very likely end up having a disastrous competitive experience. This is especially true for the marathon. Even if injury does not occur, the profound exhaustion will make the athlete require several weeks of recovery before resuming normal training. The more challenging the race, the less the athlete's chances of winning, simply because of the larger size of the invited competitive field. The race organization benefits regardless of the performance of the athlete in question. Prior to the race, it benefits from the publicity of having well-known athletes in the field, and after the race the story is how the battle at the front unfolded. One could argue well whether such infusion of money into the sport is for the athlete's (or the sport's) ultimate good when the athlete is relegated to the role of a short-lived tool in corporate machinations. Still, when faced with these challenges, the athlete and coach with well-defined goals are far better off in terms of at least considering workable ways to accommodate some of these opportunities than if their planning is limited to day-by-day guesswork with little organized basis for logical forward progress.

Examples of Setting Long-Term Goals

Let us consider two examples, one conceptual and the other real, in this game of goal setting to learn more about how it can be effective in organizing an athlete's career. The thought of running 5,000 m in 13 minutes may sound a bit audacious even to consider for any aspiring male distance runner just turning 20 years old. But if he is talented, then that talent should be nurtured, methodically and sensibly. Why not aim for the best, if that's really a desired goal? Is he dreaming? Yes, perhaps. But if he does not dream, then there is no hope of that dream ever becoming reality. Such is the essence of breaking records. So how does one logically identify goals for achieving such a performance?

The main coordinates of a career plan are the competitive event for which specialization is desired and the age at which athletes typically will be at their best for that distance. Using this knowledge, annual best-time achievements can be estimated on paper. For the men's 5,000m event, the average age at which the present top-ten runners have achieved their career best is 27 years (see Table 3.2). Let us outline goals for our 20-year-old athlete, whose birthday is January 1 and who has a personal best 5,000m time of 14 min. Essentially he needs to lower his time by 1 min in seven years, starting with the day he reaches 21 and ending with his 28th birthday. His peak performances will be during the northern hemisphere summer track circuit. Assuming that improvements in his performance will become more difficult as he reaches his peak, a weighted per-year time reduction is more realistic than an unweighted 10 sec/year. The weighting is determined as follows: With each passing year a diminishing age difference will occur as the athlete approaches the target year ($27 - 20 = 7$; $27 - 21 = 6$, etc., the last being $27 - 26 = 1$). The sum of all these differences (28) is then divided into the total time to be removed from the initial performance best (here, 60 sec). Thus, $60/28 = 2.14$. Multiplying this value by each yearly age difference gives the weighted reduction in number of seconds as a goal for that year. Thus, for the 21st year, $2.14 \times 7 = 15$ sec improvement over 14 minutes, or 13:45. Table 3.3 illustrates a more logical expected annual progression of yearly best times, if progress goes according to plan.

When we view Table 3.3, particularly the yearly best goals, we see that 13 min may now seem a little more achievable. Each year the desired improvement is sensible—for example, a 15-sec improvement over the space of the first year is not really so huge, and neither athlete nor coach need even consider performances such as 13:12 for 4 years! A crucial requirement over this 7-year development scheme, however,

Table 3.2   Average Age of Career-Best-Outdoor Performance for the Fastest 10 Athletes in Olympic Distance Running Events[a]

Event	Men	Women
800m	24.3 ± 1.8	25.6 ± 3.3
1,500m	27.7 ± 1.4	28.2 ± 2.0
3,000m	26.9 ± 2.1[b]	28.2 ± 4.2
5,000m	26.9 ± 2.5	26.7 ± 3.7[b]
10,000m	28.5 ± 4.2	26.1 ± 4.6
Marathon	28.6 ± 4.6	29.2 ± 3.6

[a]Performance marks as of 31 December 1989; all values in years $\pm$ 1 standard deviation.

[b]Not contested in the Olympic Games.

Table 3.3   Setting Goals Toward a Predicted Improvement From 14:00 to 13:00 for 5,000m

Present personal best	14:00	Present age	20
Desired personal best	13:00	Target age	27

Age difference	Improvement (sec)	Annual target
$27 - 20 = 7$	$7/28 \times 60 = 15$	14:00
$27 - 21 = 6$	$6/28 \times 60 = 13$	13:45
$27 - 22 = 5$	$5/28 \times 60 = 11$	13:32
$27 - 23 = 4$	$4/28 \times 60 = 9$	13:21
$27 - 24 = 3$	$3/28 \times 60 = 6$	13:12
$27 - 25 = 2$	$2/28 \times 60 = 4$	13:06
$27 - 26 = 1$	$1/28 \times 60 = 2$	13:02
Goal = 27	60	13:00

will be protecting the athlete from overuse injuries, thus creating an optimum environment for steady improvement.

What should be done if, for example, during the second year a breakthrough allows the athlete to reach the third year's target? Our opinion is quite clear. Additional progress should not necessarily be sought that year or even the next. The athlete is on schedule. However, if *several* races during the year are each consistently ahead of the planned program, this is grounds for careful reconsideration. As we shall detail in the specifics of training, goals are best achieved by doing the least amount of work necessary, not the most, because we want injury freedom as well as continued improvement over the next several years. The greedier an athlete becomes, the sooner he or she is spent.

Now let us consider a real example of long-term goal setting. Seb Coe started running as a school-lad at age 12. By age 13 his coach had constructed a plan shaped around relevant age-related minor championships initially but culminating with the 1980 Olympic Games. The plan was specific enough to set achievable goals yet flexible enough to cater to all the nuances of academic life from early schooling through postgraduate university work. By shifting emphases to fit examination periods, minor illnesses, and the like, the plan was kept intact.

The concept of the plan was relatively simple. In 1972 Seb's coach estimated on paper what he believed the world records in the 800m, 1,500m, and mile would be when Seb was ready to attack them, roughly by 1980 or 1981. The prediction was 1:43 for the 800m; Seb's first 800m world record (in 1979) was 1:42.33 at age 22. The prediction was 3:48 for the mile; Seb's first mile world record (also in 1979) was

3:48.95. Thus, the accuracy of estimation was good, but an element of surprise came in their arrival a year or so ahead of schedule. The forecasted 1,500m time, however, was delayed by 7 years—the estimate of 3:30 was achieved (3:29.77) only in 1986. Thus, no system is perfect, but this one was close.

PERIODIZATION AND THE CATEGORIZATION OF TRAINING

In athletic circles worldwide, one word is mentioned more frequently than any other when athletes and coaches discuss goals and plans: **periodization**. This impressive-sounding term refers simply to the specific time scale and format for all the various parts of a training plan. Such a format takes into consideration the four primary aspects of adaptation to training:

1. Initial breakdown and reduction in immediate performance capabilities
2. Adaptation to the stress of training as a result of physiological and psychological changes in the direction of improved performance potential
3. Retention of such performance characteristics following a tapering of training
4. Reduction in performance if training volume is decreased for too long a period.

Thus, the training life of an athlete is a constant cycling of hard work (with fatigue), recovery (with regeneration), improvement in performance (for a brief period), and brief layoff (for mental and physical rest) to permit another cycle to repeat.

Preparing a training outline involves the delineation of several kinds of information. First, all the units needed to achieve the various goals must be identified. By **units** we mean *general training assignments*. Some examples might include longer distance runs at moderate speed, upper body strength training, and shorter distance, faster runs. Second, training schedules need to identify the sessions appropriate to each unit. A **session** is a specific training assignment which identifies the volume, intensity, and density of effort that should provide a beneficial training effect. A session might include six 800m runs at 80% maximum effort up a 4% hill with a 2-min rest between runs. Another might include eight 1,500m runs at 90% of VO₂max pace, with a 3-min recovery between runs. Still another might include three sets of 15 split squats with a 20-kg weight on the shoulders. Finally, specific intermediate test situations (small races, time trials, a treadmill stress test, etc.) need scheduling as training proceeds to evaluate progress in achieving the ultimate goal of being ready for the major competitive period at the proper time.

In short, the value of periodization is that it permits a documented, methodical, incremental, and logical growth and development outline for athlete and coach. Both must consider carefully what will be done. Their ideas are thrust into the spotlight of reason. The objective of training is to bring an athlete to a peak fitness level at the proper time, with all the requirements for good performance brought along in balance. Periodization permits this balanced progression by ensuring that the appropriate mix is put together into a unified plan. Much has been written about this topic because it is essential for organizing athlete development (Bompa, 1988; Charniga, Gambetta, Kraemer, Newton, O'Bryant, Palmieri, Pedemonte, Pfaff, & Stone, 1986-87; Dick, 1975; Freeman, 1989).

Now that we've identified the need for a comprehensive master plan, it may seem contradictory to state that the essence of a good master plan is its malleability—its ability to be changed as required to ensure its optimum effectiveness. In a periodization scheme, it is unnecessary and impractical to write initially the exact details of each day's training on a day-to-day basis for a year in advance. Some coaches do, and their athletes become locked into (and victims of) a plan that becomes less appropriate over time. Continual adjustment of a training scheme is required to recognize (and take advantage of)

- variable rates of adaptation to specific training,
- small setbacks such as a minor injury, and
- personal life vicissitudes that demand temporary increased attention.

Thus, a generalized but well-thought-out master plan with all its parts laid out in perspective provides a reference point from which an intelligent beginning and reasoned continuity can occur. Without such a plan, athlete and coach are perpetually adrift, not knowing what to do or why and thus selecting training by whim.

Starting a Training Plan: Recovery From the Previous Plan

Although one year by itself as an expanse of time may not appear very long, a year of hard physical training is. The athlete therefore has a genuine need for full recovery from the previous training period to permit a fresh attack at another year of similar dedicated effort. Complete physical rest and mental refreshment can do wonders, particularly if it is allowed to last as long as a month. Considerable persuasion is needed to get an athlete to "hang up the shoes" for that long, but those who do are better for it, particularly as such a rest permits complete musculoskeletal repair from the accumulated stresses of the macrocycle just completed. Experienced runners most likely will suffer withdrawal symptoms from removal of the once- or twice-daily "fix" of running. Alternative exercises (swimming, biking, hiking, sailing, etc.) will never satisfy mentally this training hunger, although they can maintain cardiorespiratory fitness and joint mobility reasonably well. But then, they shouldn't be a total replacement; no habit that is so important a part of one's lifestyle can be extinguished over a period of a month and casually replaced by something else. But oh, how the mind will gain in its enormous desire to begin serious development again!

Resuming training too early is much like pulling an onion out of the garden and discovering that it is not yet fully grown. One cannot thrust it back in and expect more growth. Physiological and psychological fatigue must be fully resolved if the total approach to beginning another training cycle is to be one of excitement, anticipation, and willingness to rededicate one's life to training. Time does heal everything, it is said, but that requires time off!

When various types of mild active rest are continued, performance fitness does not deteriorate drastically. An interesting recent study by Cullinane, Sady, Vadeboncoeur, Burke, and Thompson (1986) reported that 10 days of rest reduced plasma volume by 5% and raised resting heart rate by 9 beats/min, but $\dot{V}O_2$max was unchanged in 15 distance runners averaging 80 km/week regularly prior to voluntary cessation from training. Probably the decrease in $\dot{V}O_2$max that should accompany decreased perfusion to the working muscles was offset by optimum recruitment of motor neurons and replenishment of muscle energy supplies as a result of the complete recovery. Mitochondrial size, enzyme concentrations, and energy storage capabilities in skeletal muscles were not evaluated, but the unchanged $\dot{V}O_2$max also suggests minor changes, if any, in these variables.

Because this recovery period is the first phase in a periodization scheme, coach and athlete need to discuss carefully the goals and objectives for the coming year, the strengths and weaknesses identified during the year just passed, and the possible inclusion of specific strategies during the coming year to remove or reduce weaknesses (increased flexibility exercises, for example, or increased focus on upper-body strengthening). A useful analogy is seen in annual one-month full-factory shutdowns that often occur in European industry. A factory overhaul, review of procedures, and incorporation of improvements set the stage for improved productivity during the next year.

Following a several-week layoff, easy and gradual aerobic running is important initially to readapt to impact stress. But not all is lost. When training is resumed, remarkably little time is required—as little as 2 to 3 weeks—for distance runners to again be able to handle 8- to 10-mi runs at 90% to 95% of earlier training paces. This is primarily due to an increase in blood volume since skeletal muscle mitochondrial content and capillarization are relatively unchanged unless the layoff has been many months of complete rest due to injury (Coyle, 1990). Attention to adequate rest, nutrition, fluid replacement, and flexibility maintenance will optimize the adaptive process. More formal training can then begin. The major question is how to structure this training.

Definitions: The Terminology of Periodization and Training

Good communication is easiest when clear understanding exists between communicator and listener—hence the origin of the familiar phrase "Say what you mean and mean what you say." Reasonably specific terminology is in use for describing the periodization of training and the kinds of adaptation that occur. To familiarize readers with these concepts, we will summarize their definitions.

Training is a sequence of activities done for the purpose of increasing efficiency and effectiveness in sport performance. In this instance, **performance** refers to quality of training and racing. Training improves several performance variables, identified many years ago by Nett (1965), including **strength**, defined as the quantity of muscular force exerted against resistance, and **speed**, which is the ability to perform body movements quickly, successively, and successfully. A good sprinter has excellent speed.

Endurance is also required for good running and racing; this is simply the ability to sustain submaximum activity for a prolonged period. A good marathoner has enormous endurance. **Fatigue** is a sensation of increasing difficulty to perform at a given work load and still maintain previous efficiency. (These definitions will receive closer scrutiny in chapter 6 when we discuss overtraining.) There are two types of endurance. **Aerobic endurance**, or **stamina**, is the ability to cope with fatigue while working primarily aerobically at a high effort load over a sizable (but not indefinite) period. Stamina is sometimes thought of as the ability to handle speed over time. A male 10,000m runner doing a session of 2 × 3,000m at 85% of his 5,000m race pace is developing stamina. So is a female 3,000m runner coping with a track session of 3 × 2,000m runs at 85% of her

3,000m race pace. **Anaerobic endurance**, or **speed endurance**, is the ability to tolerate fatigue and maintain both pace and form while running at near-maximum intensities for relatively short distances. Repeat 400m training is one example of work that will develop speed endurance.

Three terms—macrocycle, mesocycle, and microcycle—describe various phases of a training period. A **macrocycle** is a developmental period of considerable length directed toward achievement of a peak of maximum performance fitness. For many athletes, particularly the track-oriented middle-distance runners, this may require nearly a year. As an example, an athlete may begin training during the fall and aim ultimately for best performance at the national championships the following late spring or early summer (or even later; for example, at a summer major regional competition such as the Pan American Games or European Championships). For others, such a long period may not be required. For example, top-level marathon runners who remain injury-free with excellent general fitness can work well with a cycle that repeats every 4 to 5 months. There are 10 to 12 weeks of intense preparation, a few weeks of tapering, then the race, and a month of mental and physical recovery (Lenzi, 1987). This is why the world's fastest marathoners typically compete no more than two to three times a year.

A training macrocycle is compartmentalized into several smaller developmental periods. A **mesocycle** lasts anywhere from a few weeks to a few months and typically has a specific developmental objective, different from the mesocycle preceding and following it. One may emphasize development of an endurance base; another may represent a period of fine-tuning. Each mesocycle consists of at least one **microcycle**—a period of roughly one to two weeks during which a meaningful block of training can be completed that provides balanced athlete development. Figure 3.2 illustrates the use of these terms during a hypothetical training period. Intermediate-level competitive events or time trials may be scheduled along the way, typically at the end of a microcycle or mesocycle, to permit the assessment of developing fitness.

After goal identification has permitted the outline of a training macrocycle, the next task is to delineate the mesocycles and identify the work to be done during each microcycle. A wide variety of activities should be planned: Running and comprehensive conditioning form the backbone of the training plan, with other aspects included as well, such as a stretching program, recuperative modalities (e.g., massage), and periodic health evaluation. But how do we categorize the quality of these units that comprise this so-called training goal?

Several terms permit specific description of each day's training sessions. They relate closely to the classic questions that athletes ask their coaches when they meet for a training period. We'll use the running portion of training as an example.

- "How far must I run?" That's volume (The answer to the athlete might be "Ten runs of 200 m on the track.").
- "When are we going to do these again?" That's frequency ("Once more this microcycle, 6 days from now.").
- "How fast must I run them?" That's intensity, or duration ("Start at 33 seconds, eventually quickening to 30.").
- "How much recovery [rest] can I have between each run?" That's density ("One-and-a-half minutes in jogging back to the 200m mark on the track.").

Jogging for talented runners ages 20 to 30 is defined as very slow running—7 to 9 min/mi for men (4:21 to 5:36/km) and 8 to 10 min/mi for women (4:58 to 6:13/km). Jogging is more energy-costly than walking.

Now let's define more formally these descriptors of training load. Training **volume** is simply the quantity of training done during a given time period—work done per microcycle, total push-ups done on a given day, total weight lifted in one session, total distance run on a day of repeat 200m runs, and so on. It is a specific quantity that can be expressed in any of several time frames. Training **frequency** refers to the number of sessions completed during a particular time period or to the recurrence of a given training session during such a period, be it macrocycle, mesocycle, or microcycle. Some microcycles, for example, will have a training frequency of two sessions each day. On the other hand, repeat 1,000m runs may be assigned with a frequency of once every two weeks. Some exercises may be done nearly every day, such as sit-ups, push-ups, or aerobic conditioning runs. Other exercises, such as upper body strengthening in the weight room, may be done once or perhaps twice each week.

Training **intensity** identifies the quality of completed effort and is related inversely to volume. Thus, as training intensity rises, the volume assigned decreases. A medium-intensity, high-volume run might be 10 mi at a 6:15/mi pace (3:53/km) for a good female 10,000m runner. However, five repeat-mile runs at a 5:00/mi pace (3:06/km) for that athlete would represent a far more intense training stimulus, but with

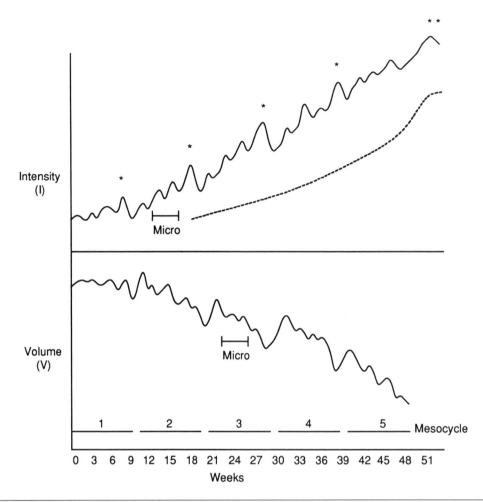

Figure 3.2 Hypothetical representation of a training period (here, 52 weeks), termed a macrocycle, divided into five smaller phases called mesocycles. During each successive mesocycle, the volume (V) of work done may either gradually lessen (as shown here) or be stable for a few mesocycles and eventually decrease. The intensity (I) of effort gradually increases as easier aerobic work is supplemented and/or replaced by more difficult anaerobic loads. The * symbols suggest periodic test points to determine progress at the end of mesocycles. The ** symbol indicates the major peak of that macrocycle. The dotted line (···) suggests competitive performance abilities, which should increase steadily as development proceeds but rapidly improve near the final week or two of tapering and rest. Each mesocycle is divided into a few training blocks, or microcycles, that permit appropriate cycling of training work loads.

reduced volume. The analog in strength training (weight lifting) would be the relationship of the load lifted with each repetition to that athlete's one-repetition maximum.

Figure 3.2 illustrates the interrelationship between volume and intensity as conceptualized by Matveyev (1981) and Bondarchuk (1988) in their descriptions of the periodization process. As a macrocycle progresses, although the net weekly training load may remain the same, total volume decreases because intensity increases. Also, more event-specific special exercises are emphasized as the eventual final peak is approached. For each event specialty, these exercises may be quite different, but they typically also involve shorter, more intense training sessions.

Training **density** defines the rest pause between work bouts. The shorter the rest pause, the greater the stimulus density. Two 300m runs on a track, each done in 44 sec with a 2-min rest between, are a stimulus of greater density than two 300m runs at the same speed but with a 3-min rest between each run. The rest pause can vary from a few seconds to several minutes, depending on the purpose of the session. Confusing jargon has developed among coaches in categorizing or identifying daily training sessions. It would be far preferable to be specific and informative, but such seems not to be in vogue, the result being worldwide difficulty in communication. Thus, one reads or hears about "cut-downs," but there is no knife or scissors involved. There are "breakdowns,'' but no one wants to really break down an athlete. There are "go's," meaning that after a specific recovery time (e.g., 2 min), the athlete begins the next run (a 2-min "go"). There are "ladders" (but no one is climbing), "clocks," "pyramids," and many more. All are simply variations on the theme of runs and rests, but they cause needless confusion since acceptable terminology is already established. Then there are phrases such as "tempo running," "interval running," and "repetition running" (Daniels & Scardina, 1984; Wilt, 1968), whose meanings are quite variant not only around the English-speaking world but also among middle-distance as compared to long-distance coaches. For example, some correctly refer to the term "interval" as the distance run, but others consider it the recovery time between runs. If any single factor has prevented effective coaching interchange in the sporting world, it is this all-too-frequent use of jargon that has different meanings to different people and event specialties. This is particularly exasperating because existing terms permit a simple and clear delineation of the details of a training session.

Such complexity and confusion is unnecessary. Any running assignment should include specific logical directions, using terms that have clear meanings in common usage. Assignments given by one coach to a group of athletes should be unambiguous to another group of athletes being tutored by a different coach. The terminology is as follows. We run a specific distance or for a specific period of time; this is the **interval** of running. Chances are that we'll do this more than once. Several intervals of the same distance are referred to as **repetitions** (reps). Following each running interval, a specified **recovery** time permits a varying amount of rest, complete or incomplete. Groups of intervals are called **sets**, and the recovery time between sets is typically longer than the recovery time between runs within a set. Finally, each run is done at an assigned velocity or pace; that's the **tempo**. It's as simple as that.

Using the preceding terminology, one example of a training session could be 10 intervals of 200 m at a 28-sec tempo with a 55-sec jog between repetitions. In coaches' shorthand, this might be written as 10 × 200 m @ 28 sec (55-sec jog). This session would be quite difficult—the athlete is running quickly and has very little recovery rest. Another might be a series of fast interval runs at 85% of maximum pace, the first lasting 5 min, the second 4 min, the third 3 min, the fourth 2 min, and finishing with four 1-min runs. The first two recovery times are 4 min, the next two are, respectively, 3 and 2 min, and there is 1 min of recovery between each of the 1-min efforts. Again, using coaching shorthand, this session could be written

as 5 min (4 min rec) + 4 min (4 rec) + 3 min (3 rec) + 2 min (2 rec) + (4 × 1 min) (1 min rec each).

The examples of training assignments given here represent only two of a myriad combination of higher intensity, good-quality repetitions of an interval of distance run at a given tempo. Typically, such runs fit into the physiological performance zones of anaerobic conditioning or aerobic and anaerobic capacity training. Later in this chapter we will provide guidelines for more exact categorization of training assignments into these various zones. In turn this will provide a basis for intelligent structuring and manipulation of such assignments to best fit developmental needs.

A Good Training Plan Must Have Balance and Specificity

One good method for injury-free performance progress over the course of a macrocycle involves harmonious interdevelopment of strength, speed, stamina, and endurance all during the year, never eliminating any of these entirely from the overall training plan. We thus define **multi-pace training** as the inclusion of training assignments at a variety of different paces over the entire training year. We tend not to agree with coaches who prescribe large volumes of solely longer distance running over a period of weeks followed by a similar concentrated bolus of solely higher intensity speed sessions over succeeding weeks. Instead, we view such training as a hunt for injuries due to overuse and maladaptation.

We also prefer to provide a smooth transition from a lower level of fitness to big-meet readiness by using a variety of training modalities (running, strength-training, mobility exercises, etc.), the combination of which is changed periodically to meet the changing focus on development. We thus define **multi-tier training** as the organization of training around several levels, or tiers, each of which builds upon the preceding one, and each of which has a focus of development intended to contribute to well-rounded performance improvement.

The most valuable ingredients in the pursuit of any objective include the correct assessment of what is required and the proper pursuit of those requirements. The fundamental rationale for our belief in the effectiveness of multi-tier training is scientifically based. It is the experience of orthopedic and podiatric experts in sports medicine that lower-limb musculoskeletal injuries of the overuse variety are more likely to occur when athletes suddenly change their ongoing load emphasis—for example, from flat surfaces to hills, from training flats to track spikes, or from slower over-distance sessions to quick short sessions. The explanation is simply that the musculoskeletal system needs time to adapt gradually to changing stimuli. If adequate time is not provided, a high-volume or high-intensity training stress will likely be excessive and provoke injury. We are uninterested in developing injury-prone athletes. Multi-tier training continually exposes athletes to a wide range of training stimuli but with varying emphasis during the year.

There is a practical rationale as well. It makes little sense, in our view, for athletes to permit their FT Type IIb skeletal muscle fibers to detrain due to little use during the long initial portion of a macrocycle. Such would occur if only low-intensity over-distance training was done for that period, because the FT Type IIb motor units are stimulated only at higher work rates. This would decrease mobilizable speed that when challenged suddenly can bring injury from a reduction in readiness of such motor units for use. When we refer to speed, we mean the repeatable sustained speed for a 400m runner, not the explosive short-lived speed of a sprinter. Both aerobic and anaerobic components are involved. Middle- and long-distance racing is about endurance and speed *together*. Endurance will get a runner to the finish line, but endurance with speed will get a runner there first. One of our maxims, first and foremost, has been that if speed is so important, then never venture very far away from it. Practically, this means that because speed must be practiced to be done well (to improve neural recruitment and permit cardiac and skeletal muscle strength adaptations), speed practice should continue, with varied degree, all through a macrocycle.

Notice that we emphasize speed *with* endurance for winning races. This is true from the 800m through to the marathon. There is little satisfaction for a marathoner to run the equivalent of a hundred and four 400m laps at a 76 sec/400m pace only to be outkicked in the final 595 m and lose the race. In 1987 the fastest male and female marathon runners also turned in very creditable 10,000m race performances during the same year (Takeyuki Nakayama lowered his national record to 27:35.33—the fourth fastest performance of the year. Ingrid Kristiansen's 31:08.85 was the year's fastest time). Similarly, an 800m or 1,500m runner may need to endure back-to-back racing for 3 to 4 days in a major championship; the final race will be the most difficult. Doing an 800m/1,500m double—as Seb Coe has managed with good success in two Olympic Games—may require seven races in 9 days. Yes, racing is indeed about endurance and speed together!

Except for the majority of a marathon race, virtually all Olympic-event distance racing is done at a pace that mandates a steady accumulation of anaerobic metabolites. The shorter the distance, the greater the relative percentage of anaerobic effort required. Table 3.4 illustrates this transition from aerobic to anaerobic emphasis as the race distance shortens; this is merely a tabular presentation of Figure 1.29. Each race must be run at the proper pace for the runner in question. Too much anaerobic accumulation and the race will be lost due to fatigue. An excessive premature anaerobic accumulation can occur from three possibilities:

1. Beginning too quickly due to a poor sense of pace
2. Utilizing tactics that were metabolically too costly
3. Being insufficiently fit to race at the required pace

Records in running continue to be broken. Records are broken because runners race ever faster. Over the past 60 to 70 years this rate of improvement has been enormous, yet it is a mere split second in the evolutionary span of our development as a species. In that short split second, we have not suddenly become biomechanically and physiologically more anaerobic or aerobic. Rather, greater participation and larger adaptive training loads produce athletes with greater aerobic and anaerobic abilities. As an example, Don Lash, an outstanding American distance runner of the 1930s (world record holder for the 2-mi in 8:58.4; personal best of 31:06.9 for the 10,000m, both in 1936), had a $\dot{V}O_2$max of 81.5 ml/kg/min (Robinson, Edwards, & Dill, 1937). Our elite-level male 10,000m athletes with personal bests faster than 28:00 all have $\dot{V}O_2$max values well in excess of 81 ml/kg/min.

What has caused this quickening of pace? One factor surely is the replacement of cinder tracks with artificial surfaces. Another likely factor is technical advances in shoe construction. A third is an unprecedented period of relative freedom from global strife, so that young men are able to turn their thoughts toward sport rather than war; and of course, women's opportunities for competitive distance running are finally beginning to improve. A fourth is a great increase in the number of competitive opportunities, both financial and athletic, that permit a larger gene pool of athletic talent to remain competitively active for a longer time. A fifth is an improvement in health care provision—nutrition, rehabilitative and restorative modalities, and injury prevention—that permits athletes to train more effectively at a higher level. This in turn permits the addition of an increased anaerobic work tolerance on top of an already highly developed aerobic tolerance; those who buffer acidosis the best will beat the rest!

How can a judicious inclusion of marginally to distinctly anaerobic work be added each week to an already generous diet of aerobic long-distance running? Quite simple. Use caution not to make the diet of dis-

Table 3.4 The Difference in Energy Sources That Contribute to Racing Performances in Olympic Distance Events

Event	World record		Approx. % $\dot{V}O_2$max	Race characteristic	% Energy contribution		
	Men	Women			Phosphate	Lactate	Aerobic
100m	9.83	10.76	NA	All-out; short speed	70	22	8
200m	19.75	21.71	NA	All-out; short speed	40	46	14
400m	43.29	47.60	NA	All-out; long speed	10	60	30
800m	1:41.73	1:53.28	135	95%-100% all-out; endurance speed	5	38	57
1,500m	3:29.46	3:52.47	112	95% all-out; speed endurance	2	22	76
3,000m	7:29.45	8:22.62	102	90% all-out; endurance with speed	<1	12	88
5,000m	12:58.39	14:37.33	97	85% all-out; endurance speed	<1	7	93
10,000m	27:08.23	30:13.74	92	Long endurance with some speed	<1	3	97
Marathon	2:06:50	2:21:06	82	Paced aerobic; long endurance; possibly speed	<1	<1	99

Note. NA = not applicable. Data adapted from Matthews (1990, pp. 265-270); Péronnet and Thibault (1989, pp. 453-465); and Leger, Mercier, and Gauvin (1986, pp. 113-120).

tance volume too excessive. Depending on the extent of ST muscle fiber type dominance in the prime movers, no measurable cardiorespiratory improvement (measured as $\dot{V}O_2$max) will occur beyond more than between 60 and 90 mi/week (96 to 145 km) of aerobic conditioning in elite-level long-distance runners (Costill, 1986). Especially for young developing runners, the quantity of aerobic conditioning should be kept considerably below this volume until their working muscles and connective tissues develop the tolerance to such work. Including a well-designed program of comprehensive conditioning (see chapter 4) and some faster paced running in addition to the endurance base produces a more balanced athlete with many well-developed talents: strength, speed, good range of joint mobility, and anaerobic work tolerance. Our concept of multi-tier training promotes this kind of development.

Tables 3.5 and 3.6 show an aerobic/anaerobic breakdown of Seb Coe's training early in his running career, when he was 16 and 18 years old. It can be seen that Seb's aerobic/anaerobic ratio in terms of training was roughly 65%/35%. Seb's coach felt that his performance expertise resided on the distance side of the 800m/1,500m events rather than on the sprint side, and thus Seb's training focus was directed accordingly. These two very successful years for Seb, which resulted in national titles and a bronze medal in the European Junior Championships, suggest that his relative training emphasis was suited precisely to his racing needs. Total weekly aerobic distance running was kept to a minimum, with quality speed work included to provide a complete training stimulus. This event-specific anaerobic training was required to com-

pensate for the aerobic dominance that characterized Seb's (and most distance runners') fitness prior to competitive training.

Practical knowledge about the concepts of FT and ST muscle fibers and their various properties relating to performance had not reached the lay press in the early to mid-1970s. Even knowledge about various events' energy requirements was not generally available in the coaching literature. We know now, of course, that long, slow distance running provides little training stimulus to the FT muscle fibers, leaving any distance runner trained on such a diet unprepared for high-speed racing. But middle-distance runners need to develop endurance through such longer runs if they are to manage multiple high-speed races in a top-level championship. The longer runs help to provide the overall fitness base on which speed training can be placed for specialization. It thus seemed logical in Seb's development to train him specifically for both speed and endurance, keeping the total training load as small as possible to get the job done and having all systems in a progressively greater state of responsiveness. Only later was the beneficial connection between intuition and scientific logic discovered. Even for the longer distances, such as the 5,000m and the 10,000m, an appropriate combination of speed and endurance is mandated if races are to be won at any competitive level.

MULTI-TIER TRAINING AS A BASIS FOR PERIODIZATION

Training is much like constructing a multistory building. We need various kinds of building materials

Table 3.5 Training Summary and Analysis: Seb Coe, 1973, Age 16

Week #	# Training days		# Miles	# km	% Effort (aerobic)	% Effort (anaerobic)	Races
5	5		11	18	100	0	
6	7		15	24	50	50	XC
7	6		24	29	75	25	
8	6		35	56	82	18	
9	7		47	75	87	13	
10	6		21	34	55	45	
11	5		27	43	49	51	Indoors 800m
12	3		25	40	80	20	
13	6		34	55	57	43	XC
14	6		30	48	66	34	
15	6		14	22	33	67	
16	5		26	42	23	77	
17 (Apr.)	7		36	58	54	46	100m; 800m
18 (May)	6	↑	20	32	75	25	800m; 1,500m
19	7		23	37	38	62	800m in 1:56.0
20	6		21	34	28	72	
21	6		24	38	50	50	3,000m city ch.
22	6	T	24	39	77	23	
23	7	r	39	63	36	64	3,000m county ch.
24	6	a	9	14	0	100	1,500m NCAA
25	6	c	29	46	73	27	
26	6	k	23	37	82	18	
27	5		28	45	59	41	3,000m English schools ch.
28	7	s	28	45	64	36	
29	7	e	21	34	50	50	
30	7	a	29	41	46	54	
31	4	s	17	27	35	65	1,500m youth
32	7	o	24	39	79	21	
33	3	n	7	11	0	100	3,000m senior
34	5		26	46	100	0	
35	5		11	17	91	9	
36 (Sept.)	7		20	32	50	50	
37	4	↓	8	13	0	100	1,500m
38	4		15	24	75	25	
39	5		13	21	88	12	XC
40	5		20	32	100	0	
41	6		21	35	100	0	XC
42	5		23	37	100	0	XC
43	6		13	21	77	23	
44	5		7	11	55	45	
45	5		17	27	17	83	XC
46	4		16	26	100	0	XC
47	6		14	22	50	50	
48	6		26	42	81	19	XC
49	4		14	22	62	38	
50	1		2	3	0	100	

Week #	# Training days	# Miles	# km	% Effort (aerobic)	% Effort (anaerobic)	Races
51	5	27	43	100	0	Road race
52	5	21	35	81	19	XC
48 weeks	264/336 days Average = 5.5 days/week	1,021 21.3 mi/week	1,635 34.3 km/week	61%	39%	23 races, not including heats

Note. XC = cross-country; NCAA = Northern Counties Athletic Association.

Table 3.6 Training Summary and Analysis: Seb Coe, 1975, Age 18

Week #	# Training days		# Miles	# km	% Effort (aerobic)	% Effort (anaerobic)	Races
1 (Jan.)	7		41	66	50	50	
2	6		16	26	70	30	
3	7		47	76	82	18	7km XC
4	6		34	55	50	50	
5	7		33	53	55	45	7km XC
6	4		26	42	55	45	
7 (inj)	5		23	37	100	0	
8 (inj)	6		41	66	51	49	
9	7		39	63	45	55	
10	6		28	45	64	36	
11	7		42	68	50	50	
12	6		31	50	61	39	3,000m indoor
13 (Mar.)	7	↑	47	76	53	47	
14 (Apr.)	6		36	58	91	9	
15	7		31	50	58	42	1,500m
16	6		28	45	78	22	
17	7		29	47	50	50	
18	6	T	38	61	100	0	1,500m
19	6	r	19	31	75	25	
20 (inj)	0	a	0	0	—	—	
21 (inj)	0	c	0	0	—	—	
22	5	k	16	26	60	40	1,500m
23	7		33	53	55	45	800m
24	7	s	39	63	54	46	
25	6	e	25	40	56	44	1,500m NCAA
26	7	a	31	50	50	50	3,000m NCAA
27	7	s	37	60	40	60	
28	7	o	39	63	69	31	
29	6	n	36	58	61	39	

(Cont.)

Table 3.6 (Continued)

Week #	# Training days	# Miles	# km	% Effort (aerobic)	% Effort (anaerobic)	Races
30	7	25	40	60	40	1,500m AAA
31	6	29	47	60	40	
32	7	33	53	55	45	1,500m
33	6	37	60	57	43	
34	7	22	35	89	11	1,500m 3:45.2
35 (Aug.)	5	22	35	78	22	
36 (Sept.)	5	37	60	100	0	
37	6	29	29	89	11	
38	7	38	61	81	19	
39	2	10	10	90	10	
39 weeks	229/273 days Average = 5.9 days/week	1,266 32.5 mi/week	1,858 47.6 km/week	66%	34%	12 races, not including heats

Note. XC = cross-country; NCAA = Northern Counties Athletic Association; AAA = Amateur Athletic Association. Higher goals require a sharper focus on fewer targets. Note the reduction in number of races here as opposed to the number in Table 3.5. This change reflects the maturing athlete's realization that bigger events require greater concentration and focus.

(aerobic and anaerobic running, comprehensive conditioning, flexibility, etc.). Several kinds of materials (training intensities and modalities) should be utilized in an ongoing fashion to complete the goal of a finished building—or a competitively fit athlete. Depending on progress in the construction plan, the relative mix of all these materials will vary. As a training season develops, for example, comprehensive conditioning work for strength and endurance will gradually transition into an emphasis on power, with a substitution of intensity for volume in determining the total training load. Similar transitions occur with the pattern of running. An expert in periodization of training thus has a job similar to that of a good building contractor: Both are responsible for arranging the availability, quantity, and pattern of use of all the various components for completing the task at hand.

Training over a broad range of paces—those appropriate for distances on either side of as well as at the athlete's primary event—provides optimum preparation for that primary event. Thus, the concept of multi-pace training is interwoven into the fabric of multi-tier training. Longer distance runs of moderate intensity build aerobic endurance. Fast-paced longer distance running improves stamina whereas very fast shorter distance running improves strength and quickness. A 1,500m specialist needs 5,000m distance training as well as 800m speed training. A 10,000m specialist can benefit by a periodic very long run, done more frequently by marathon specialists, but needs 5,000m speed training as well. Primary-event race-pace training teaches awareness of the event itself.

Table 3.4 shows us that the best event specialty around which to focus training for year-round development of mature runners is the 5,000m (3,000m for younger athletes). Both are raced at just under 100% of VO_2max pace. Thus, stamina is the central developmental focus for such a runner, enhanced on one hand by a strong speed component and on the other by sustainable endurance running. Upon a sizable (but not overdone) endurance base is superimposed the ability to run quickly and to sustain that quick pace. As specialization becomes more appropriate, the focus can be switched to shorter or longer events with minimum injury risk and minimum learning of new skills. Moving up to the 10,000m event simply requires a subtle shift regarding more emphasis on endurance work. Moving down to the 1,500m event requires an appropriate shift of emphasis toward more anaerobic work. When both speed and endurance are developed simultaneously, as occurs with multi-pace training even early into the macrocycle, it is easy for the coach to learn where an athlete's natural capabilities reside, because genetic predisposition will soon reveal that one or the other is developing more easily. Then the task of deciding on a likely best event for the final focus is simplified for both athlete and coach.

Running assignments, however, are only one facet of the overall development of distance runners. Because runners are specialists at running, of course the running portion of training will occupy the bulk of a training plan and provide the specific stimulus for greatest improvement in competitive excellence. Comprehensive conditioning through circuit and specific strength training along with flexibility exercises are also crucial for the consistency and longevity of an athletic career. In addition, the use of recuperative and restorative modalities, proper nutrition, and adequate rest are all part of this building process. The coach should be a key facilitator in helping athletes develop effective working relationships with experts who can provide assistance in these various developmental areas.

The Mesocycles of Multi-Tier Training

Figure 3.3 illustrates our concept of training using a multi-tier framework. We can continue our earlier

analogy to constructing a building. During one macrocycle (or complete training period, typically approximating one year) the building will be constructed (i.e., the training will be completed). Each level of the building represents a mesocycle (or tier), indicated by X. Thus, multi-tier training is a training plan with several mesocycles, or levels, each of which has a different assigned goal for athlete development. The length of each mesocycle may vary depending on event requirements, athlete fitness, and the time available.

The recovery mesocycle (X_0) has already been identified as a restorative period of general activity that produces an athlete who has recovered from the previous training macrocycle and is committed to beginning the new one. The first training mesocycle (X_1) establishes an extensive aerobic conditioning base, and in our suggested time scale for a hypothetical distance runner, this may require 12 weeks. Then, through the next two mesocycles (X_2, X_3) there is an increasing emphasis upon higher intensity stimuli—faster aerobic work as well as anaerobic training. This training load must be regulated carefully, and as adaptation occurs it must be varied in volume, intensity, and density

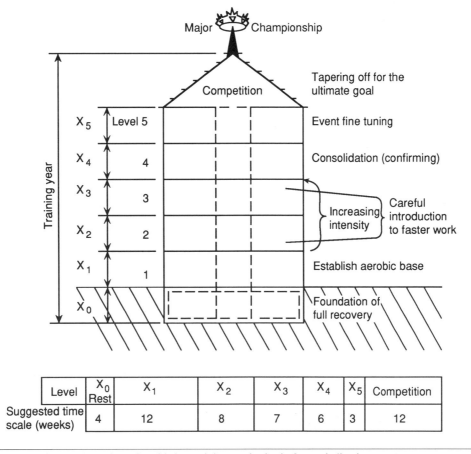

Level	X_0 Rest	X_1	X_2	X_3	X_4	X_5	Competition
Suggested time scale (weeks)	4	12	8	7	6	3	12

Figure 3.3 Diagrammatic representation of multi-tier training as the basis for periodization.

to ensure progress without fatigue. Typically, the volume of aerobic work is either maintained or reduced appropriately to keep the total load slowly increasing but always manageable.

An example from the training log of Florida distance runner Keith Brantly may serve as an illustration of mesocycle X_1. Following his University Games gold medal performance at 10,000m in Kobe in late August 1985, he ended his season and took a month of active non-running rest before starting his new training macrocycle near the end of September. After a few weeks of reorientation, he averaged more than 80 mi/week for 2 weeks—primarily aerobic conditioning with a single session each week of quick, short intervals. During the 3rd week he reduced his training to 49 mi, including a 10km road race in which he placed second. Following 3 additional weeks averaging 80 mi/week, his next week was only 46 mi, including another 10km road race. Following this was a transition into 5 weeks of slightly less aerobic conditioning but with the substitution of a weekly session of long intervals (2,000 to 3,000m) run at 5km to 10km race pace. Three more road races of varying quality were included during this period, each preceded by a few days of ample rest. The combination of long but easy aerobic sessions, a few aerobic capacity training sessions, plenty of recovery, and road racing when fresh to ensure positive challenging experiences gave him four victories, enough income to pay his bills, and a completed 11-week aerobic endurance mesocycle. He was healthy, happy, fit, secure, and had developed an adequate base to begin his next training mesocycle.

It should be clear from the description of mesocycle X_1, and is true for all mesocycles as well, that occasional recovery days *must* be included for both physiological and psychological reasons. Although arduous training has its ultimate positive benefits, it is very difficult. It isn't wise or necessary for athletes to feel that they are on a kind of never-ending training treadmill, committed to weeks and weeks of daily hard work with no letup. Only during the recovery periods will the regeneration of body processes occur that makes continued training possible.

During the consolidation mesocycle (X_4), careful assessment is given to the quality of progress in each of the many kinds of training modalities during the previous mesocycles. It is expected that not every phase of the athlete's development will have progressed precisely at the rate expected. One or two consolidating microcycles during this mesocycle should provide the optimum balance of additional training to improve speed, stamina, or endurance. Time is provided here for this "rounding out" to occur, whether it be an additional improvement in $\dot{V}O_2$max or greater

anaerobic work tolerance. A remarkably small amount of such higher-intensity training is required to provide substantial additional gains in fitness (Knuttgen, Nordesjo, Ollander, & Saltin, 1973). Each athlete's own genetic endowment and training success will have permitted better adaptation to faster or slower running over the shorter or longer distances.

Benchmarks of progress are required at reasonable points during each mesocycle to verify for coach and athlete that they are still on target for completing their goals. These benchmarks can include races, time trials, and laboratory physiological evaluations (such as a treadmill graded exercise test [GXT] and blood chemistry profiling). Target times for a variety of track distances (from 400m through 3,000m) should already have been defined as goals at various points during the year, based upon experience during previous macrocycles. For long-distance runners, road or track races of appropriate quality can also serve as indicators, provided the weather is comparable from year to year.

The athlete should not make elaborate attempts to actually peak for these impending tests. We are uninterested in eliciting the athlete's absolute best "rested performance." It is expected that the performance should indeed be slower than if complete recovery and the emotion of a top-level competition were included. These are simply timely indicators occurring in an environment of hard training and nothing more. To be sure, it may not be wise to enter such test situations in a profoundly fatigued state; an injury might occur, or the performance may be so poor that the athlete may be unable to maintain a proper mental attitude. Some subtle shifting in the daily training plan within a microcycle should handle this dilemma nicely. With these benchmarks of progress, whether in the laboratory or in the field, the athlete is serving as his or her own control over time. As progress is made through the macrocycle, the compared results of these with other indicators along the way characterize the extent and nature of the athlete's progress (for example, faster performance times at a given distance raced earlier, or a similar track session pace now manageable over a longer distance).

Mesocycle X_5 is the fine-tuning phase: The construction of our house (the development of our athlete) is virtually complete, and now the finishing touches must be added. If there is ever to be a departure from an emphasis on balanced development, this is the period. We have scheduled 3 weeks for our hypothetical athlete. Emphasis now involves developing any specialized performance abilities germane to the event or honing particular skills that are a special asset to this athlete. Following completion of this mesocycle there is a tapering period for the ultimate goal of a major championship performance or racing series.

During the final portions of the mesocycle X_5 and on into the competition mesocycle (shown here as extending for 12 weeks), training by no means ceases completely. As in levels X_1 through X_4, work continues in each room of the building (i.e., all aspects of training are still included). However, the volume of work is greatly decreased, leaving a freshness of both body and mind. A true peak, with best performances accompanied by very little maintenance effort, can be held for only about 3 weeks. However, during the other portion of this competition period, low-volume, moderate- to high-intensity training is arranged to fit around competition. (In contrast, during the previous mesocycles any small race or test situations would have been arranged around training, which was higher in volume and variable in intensity.) Such continued low-level, "quality maintenance" training prolongs the time during which the athlete can be successful competitively. For those athletes who schedule four to six competitions during their peak competitive level, this integration of "tapering training" fits nicely into this portion of the mesocycle.

If tapering and regeneration are timed properly, then the results of competitive performance will likely be exceptional (i.e., greater than predicted on the basis of previous ongoing evaluations). Yakovlev (1967) termed this phenomenon *supercompensation*, and Figure 3.4 illustrates it. The concept explaining supercompensation is simple; timing racing performance to coincide with it is more difficult. The phenomenon has three components. There is physiological adaptation to the training just completed (more and bigger mitochondria, more blood volume, greater skeletal muscle protein, more stored muscle fuels, etc.); there is a neurological recruitment effect, caused by a reduction in neural fatigue from the continued high-level training stimulus. Finally, an increased psychological readiness comes from a combination of rest from training, the motivation to perform well, the confidence that preparation has been optimal, a focus on competition, and a full stadium ready to enjoy the drama. This supercompensation response has been likened to the adaptive recovery response of bone following a stress fracture. Repair is so good at the fracture site that the recovered part of the bone is actually stronger than the part surrounding it. It is crucial in tapering, as with bone repair, that adequate time be permitted for attainment of this additional performance capacity.

The Yakovlev model can also be applied to a single training session, a microcycle, or a mesocycle. For example, a given day of hard training will produce

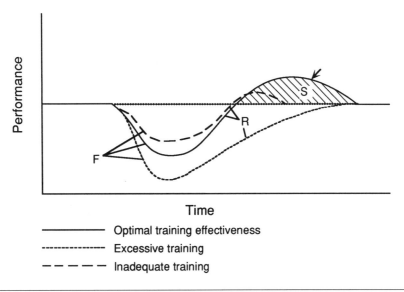

Figure 3.4 The Yakovlev model of supercompensation (S). Training places a physiological load on the body, resulting in fatigue (F) and a decrease in maximum performance abilities. Following a training load, improvement in performance can occur only with adequate recovery (R). Inadequate training may bring only small short-lived improvements. Overtraining requires excessive recovery time and may not bring any improvements in overall performance. An appropriate recovery period can bring temporarily improved performance abilities due to increased metabolic potential (more fuel reserves, cardiovascular adaptation, etc.). If coupled with a tapering phase, the additional reduction in neural fatigue and increased psychological readiness for competition can bring a more extended period of excellent performance—a supercompensation (S). This model is viable for both short- and long-term blocks of training.

fatigue, with a temporary decline in performance, and regeneration occurring during the ensuing hours or days, depending on the training volume. Success in daily training resides in the optimum timing of each training stimulus so as to prevent excessive fatigue and to permit the most difficult sessions to occur when regeneration is optimal.

In keeping with the philosophy that athletes cannot generally be successful at simultaneously training hard and competing well, during the competitive period athletes must acquire the confidence that they indeed have done the work required during their previous mesocycles and that it is absolutely appropriate to turn off the focal emphasis on training and tune in to competing. Such a switch is crucial in order to bring on, as dominant emotions, the excitement to race, the yearning to win, and the striving to plow new turf by attempting personal best performances. These kinds of attitudes provide the proper beginning for athletes to start on a roll toward success. A few races that are longer or shorter than the athlete's event specialty against athletes of varying (but probably known) abilities will create a mental framework conducive to competing again. Racing well and winning both create such an emotional high that the athlete desires overwhelmingly to experience it again. The trick is to start this process at the proper moment. Peaking at the appropriate race is one of the most elusive quests in the art and science of physical training. Training, recovery, and mental preparation all combine with environmental distractions or synergists. Thus, there are no guarantees because not all contributing factors are positive and controllable. The athlete works hard and hopes everything else comes together properly.

When the ultimate goal has been contested, then it may be appropriate to enter into the recovery phase and "shut down the engines." This may not always be done immediately. Often, other sport meetings will be scheduled just following the major competition; they provide the athlete with lesser total stress but still offer enormous performance quality, because the field of talent will all be at nearly their best performance levels. The athlete's emotional relief from the hype of a major competition combined with excellent fitness has often provided an environment for personal best performances and world records. It isn't wise, however, to overdo such a competitive streak because the effects of reduced training will result eventually in performance decrements. This increases the risk of injury and can be mentally discouraging.

If the results of the major championship or competitive season have been satisfying, then it is quite easy for athlete and coach to relax and enjoy a rest. If disappointment occurred, the sense of nonachieve-

ment or failure can be heartbreaking at best, disastrous at worst. But failure must always be handled with positive thinking; this provides a meaningful opportunity to determine what might have gone wrong. When instances of performance disaster are studied carefully, it can frequently be seen that the athlete pursued a development plan that was geared poorly toward improvement. The athlete trained and enjoyed training, but it was either overdone, or else improvement in all areas was simply not adequate, and these were either overlooked or not identified soon enough. Unfortunately, at the big competition, the other athletes were either better rested or far better prepared, and they performed better. This kind of floundering among athletes with ill-defined goals or a poorly-designed plan is so sad to see. It's much like shooting at a flock of ducks without aiming carefully—there is enjoyment from the blast and the kick of the gun (the training itself was enjoyable), but no birds are bagged (the results of racing are poor). There is no substitute for knowledgeable organization in increasing the odds for an excellent end result.

The Specifics of Multi-Tier Training

Categorization of Training Into Meaningful Domains. We mentioned earlier that multi-tier training includes multi-pace running as well as a variety of other activities that contribute to total body fitness during each level of development (throughout mesocycles X_1 through X_5). Table 3.7 illustrates this in greater detail. On each floor (tier) of our building (i.e., during each mesocycle), the same number of rooms (or training domains) exist (i.e., the same basic kinds of training and developmental modalities are utilized). Two domains include comprehensive conditioning, which will be described in chapter 4. Another domain, analogous to a maintenance service shaft in our building, will always be accessible from any level. This represents ongoing health-care delivery, recuperative modalities such as massage and various forms of therapy, and laboratory performance evaluation to assess progress. The other four domains involve various intensities and volumes of running that stimulate development in the four training zones identified in Figure 2.2, which we shall describe in greater detail shortly.

As we progress from mesocycle X_1 toward X_5, the training load (intensity or volume) will increase gradually. Careful integration of daily sessions will provide optimum stimulation of the various energy systems to ensure progress without breakdown. To complete our construction analogy, any particular room (domain) on any tier (mesocycle) may be larger or smaller and may be entered more than once.

Table 3.7   The Seven Domains of Multi-Tier Training

Floor Plan

Room 1—Aerobic conditioning
- Distance runs: long/medium typically done on roads, trails, or grass
- Primary means of cardiovascular adaptation to running
- Heart rates of 70% to 80% of maximum

Room 2—Anaerobic conditioning
- 15 to 20 min of medium-intensity steady runs at or near estimated lactate/ventilatory threshold pace
- Can be done on road, track, or trails
- Emphasis on comfortable and quick fluidity and rhythm with marginal anaerobic accumulation, thereby promoting anaerobic tolerance
- Increasing adaptation should quicken lactate/ventilatory threshold pace

Room 6—Circuits and weights
- General and specific strength development using free weights, machines
- Strength and stamina development using circuit training
- Emphasis on total body fitness

Room 7—Health maintenance
- Massage, ultrasound
- Nutritional assessment
- Blood chemistry profiling
- Treadmill runs to identify training paces and quantify fitness differences over time
- Anthropometric measurements
- Psychometric profiling to identify overtraining
- Pulmonary function evaluation

Room 3—Aerobic capacity training
- 2 to about 8 min of fast running at or near estimated $\dot{V}O_2$max pace
- Recovery should be complete or nearly complete to minimize anaerobic inhibition
- Can be done on road, track, trails, or grass
- Can include hill training
- Emphasis on maintained good running form throughout

Room 5—General mobility
- General stretching exercises
- Specific flexibility exercises
- Gymnastics, plyometrics, swimming

Room 4—Anaerobic capacity training
- 200m to 800m fast runs at 95% or more of maximum effort
- Done at >100% $\dot{V}O_2$max pace
- Marginal to complete recovery
- Will be considerably slower early in a macrocycle, done to preserve inherent speed and style
- Of greatest importance for shorter distance specialists
- Can be done on hills and flats

As mentioned earlier, multi-tier training suggests that a developmental plan for all distance runners should have similar components over the entire training year. This seems not in keeping with the concept of event specificity; an 800m runner is indeed not a marathon expert. Thus, the paradox. A paradox has no solution, only a resolution. Here, it is simple: Depending on the athlete, the event, and the time frame within the macrocycle, we vary the emphasis on any of the types of training identified. Varying the emphasis refers not only to how many units from each training domain might be assigned during a given microcycle, but also to their intensity. In this manner, none of the components of training is ignored or eliminated. All are included because all are important. In fact, the risk of injury increases if such balance is not maintained or if specific modalities are inserted suddenly following neglect. Varying the mix of activities selected from the groups identified as training domains according to event specialty as well as the mesocycle of development optimizes training specificity.

The specificity of optimum development for each individual athlete mandates individuality of training plans; this requires time, thought, and dedication. Ensuring this proper mix is the task of a competent coach. Athletes often are too close to their training to complete this task objectively. Because considerable work is involved, it is possible for a coach to work effectively with only a relatively few athletes, or else gamble that a few will always run well in spite of inadequate supervision (which isn't really fair to the athletes being coached). Athletes desiring long-term success ought to seek out coaches who are dedicated to working well with a few athletes rather than those who have an unmanageable number.

Each specific assigned running interval—easy long run, short fast run, or something in between—provides a different physiological stimulus. If the stimulus is sizable and adequate recovery occurs, the physiological adaptation will also be sizable. We want the best adaptation appropriate for our event specialty. We do not want the athlete to train excessively (due to the increased injury risk) or inadequately (because optimum adaptation will not occur). By understanding the kinds of physiological adaptation that occur in each of the four training zones identified in Figure 2.2 and then viewing this from the perspective of what is required for performance excellence in each competitive running event, we are in the best possible position to develop meaningful training assignments. They will make good biological as well as athletic sense.

Table 3.7 and Figure 3.5 also summarize some of the physiological characteristics of performance within each of the four zones. In Figure 3.5 we have constructed a pyramid with several levels. The width of each level represents both the distance run (interval) and the running pace (tempo). Thus, the greater the width, the longer the interval and the slower the pace. Recovery times will vary. Longer distance intervals at slower tempos require less recovery time than shorter distance intervals at a fast tempo. As fitness improves, recovery times following all intervals will likely decrease.

The uppermost portion of the pyramid in Figure 3.5 represents the pure sprint speed of the 100m through 400m specialists (speed strength). This facet of performance isn't emphasized particularly for middle- and long-distance training, although some fast running over very short distances is indeed important. The other tiers of the pyramid, however, represent the four primary training zones in which middle- and long-distance runners do their daily work. Figure 3.5 can serve as a companion diagram with Figure 2.2, the former providing more of a coaching (practical) perspective, the latter more of a physiological (scientific) perspective. Let us now describe each of these four training zones in greater detail.

Aerobic Conditioning. Aerobic conditioning represents the bulk of a distance runner's training. The lowermost level of the training pyramid for running illustrated in Figure 3.5 is the foundation upon which other running is superimposed. The mainstay of such a program is sizable volumes of continuous, longer-distance running at below race pace for any of the middle- and long-distance running events. It is often referred to as "base work," and sometimes called "conversational running," because it is slow enough to permit conversation during the run. The relatively easy nature of such training makes it appropriate for athletes of comparable ability to train together, providing camaraderie and adding enjoyment to sessions that for marathoners may last 2 hours or more.

It is convenient to express the intensity of running pace appropriate for each of these four training zones as a percentage of VO_2max pace. Thus, aerobic conditioning runs typically are done at 55% to 75% of VO_2max pace, depending on distance covered and level of fitness. In Figure 2.2, for the male runner whose treadmill test data are graphed, the appropriate pace range is between 5:40 and 6:50 per mile. How can one determine VO_2max pace? It can be easily identified using treadmill testing, but this is not always available. It can also be estimated from a track time trial, recognizing that 100% VO_2max pace can be maintained for no more than 10 min. As an example, let's use the same athlete whose data were

Physiological adaptations	Blood lactate	Heart rate	%V̇O₂ max	Training interval run time	Systems challenged	Common jargon describing sessions	Training interval distance	Race pace for
Speed and strength; ST and FT fiber development; Increased neurological recruitment; Improved blood buffering ability; Tolerance to stress of acidosis	>9 mM/L 8 mM/L	200 190	130 100	Sprint — 30 sec 2 min (V̇O₂ max)	Anaerobic-capacity training	Short interval; Repetitions; Short speed	200m → 1,000m	800m 1,500m
Speed; ST and FT fiber development; Some increase in neurological recruitment; Some increase in blood buffering ability; Increased glycolytic enzymes	8 mM/L 7 mM/L 5 mM/L	190 180	100 98 90	8 min	Aerobic-capacity training	Long interval; Long speed	800m → 3,000m	3,000m 5,000m 10,000m
Stamina; ST and some FT Type IIa development; Increased heart chamber size; Increased stroke volume; Increased oxidative/glycolytic enzymes; Increased blood volume	5 mM/L 4 mM/L 3.5 mM/L	180 160	90 75	20 min (Lactate/ventilatory threshold)	Anaerobic conditioning	Tempo training; Pace training; Marathon training	Marathon race pace 15-20 min	Marathon
Endurance; ST fiber development; Increased blood volume; Increased connective tissue development; Increased muscle fuel storage; Increased oxidative/glycolytic enzymes; Increased capillarization	3.5 mM/L 2 mM/L	160 140	75 60 55	2 hr	Aerobic conditioning	Over-distance running; Base work	All longer distances	

Figure 3.5 The primary training zones of performance during running.

graphed in Figure 2.2. If he covers 3,500 m in 10 min (600 sec), an equation can be written using simple arithmetic where

$$3{,}500 \text{ m}/600 \text{ sec} = 1{,}609 \text{ m}/x \text{ sec.} \qquad (3.1)$$

Solving Equation 3.1 for x, we obtain

$$3{,}500x = 965{,}400 \text{ and } x = 275.8 \text{ sec} = 4{:}35.8/\text{mi} \qquad (3.2)$$

for $\dot{V}O_2$max pace. Or, using the metric system,

$$600 \text{ sec}/3{,}500 \text{ m} = x \text{ sec}/1{,}000 \text{ m.} \qquad (3.3)$$

Solving Equation 3.3 for x, we obtain

$$3{,}500x = 600{,}000 \text{ and } x = 171 \text{ sec/km} = 2{:}51/\text{km.} \qquad (3.4)$$

Running slower than 55% $\dot{V}O_2$max pace brings little measureable aerobic improvement and merely adds to impact stress. Running faster than 75% $\dot{V}O_2$max pace causes excessive glycolytic activity, and it is preferentially fatty acid metabolism that is desired for emphasis in this zone. Shorter distance runs might range from 8 to 15 km (5 to 9 mi), depending on event specialty and years of experience, and longer runs might range from 10 to 35 km (6 to 22 mi). A talented 16-year-old high school boy averaging 30 mi/week (48 km/week), with a racing interest in 1,500 m or 1,600 m, may find a 6-mi (10-km) run at a 7:30/mi (4:40/km) pace an appropriate aerobic conditioning stimulus. A top-quality collegiate male 10,000m runner averaging 75 mi/week (121 km/week) may find it more appropriate to cover 10 mi (16 km) at a 6:30/mi (4:02/km) pace to achieve a comparable conditioning stimulus. The explanation for this difference is that the young athlete's $\dot{V}O_2$max is considerably lower than it will be after he has continued to develop and has attained the overall maturation and tolerance to chronic elevated training loads that characterize the collegiate athlete.

Heart rate values between 70% and 80% of maximum (Karvonen, Kentala, & Mustala, 1957) are typical for aerobic conditioning. Maximum heart rate varies considerably among individuals, depending on heredity and prior training. Thus, specific heart rate values are best calculated by athletes after they determine their own maximum values. For example, if a runner's maximum heart rate is 188 beats/min, 70% to 80% of this as an aerobic conditioning heart rate range would be 132 to 150 beats/min in men and a little higher in women (a woman's heart is smaller in relation to body size than a man's).

Aerobic conditioning serves to improve oxidative metabolic capabilities in cardiac muscle and in those skeletal muscle cells that are activated. It also provides a stimulus for improving joint and tendon strength without excessive impact stress, which would result at faster paces. Increases occur in the quantity of stored fuels (carbohydrates and fatty acids) as well as number and size of mitochondria in the stimulated muscle cells. Increasing blood volume and capillary density in trained muscles improve O_2 delivery and CO_2 removal by increasing the net transit time of blood through these working tissues and decreasing the diffusion distance between the interior of capillaries and the mitochondria in adjacent muscle cells.

Because aerobic conditioning is not a very intense training stimulus, it should form the mainstay of the initial return to training among those athletes who periodically take complete breaks from formal conditioning. It provides a gentle, yet sizable and important, adaptation to the work load provided, with both cardiovascular and musculoskeletal improvements. All during a training year aerobic conditioning still forms much of the total work load, because it can serve as a maintenance stimulus for cardiovascular conditioning (on which more intense training will stimulate further development) and a continuing developmental stimulus for connective tissue adaptation. The sustained increased venous return to the heart, particularly during longer runs, provides an initial stimulus toward enlarging ventricular chambers, eventually increasing stroke volume and permitting a given volume of blood to be pumped at a lower heart rate than if this training effect was not present. This cardiac adaptation is first noticed as a lower resting (morning) heart rate.

Aerobic conditioning stimulates primarily the ST skeletal muscle motor units because their motor neurons are more responsive to lower intensity activity than those of FT motor units. The adaptations in muscle cell and cardiovascular working capabilities occurring with training permit each ST motor unit to work at any given submaximum intensity with less fatigability. Thus, fewer motor units are required for maintaining a given pace, or those activated do not need to work as hard as before (in relation to their maximum output). Improved conditioning among specific muscle groups serving as the prime movers reduces the need for contributions by accessory muscles for producing movement. This helps to improve running economy because less muscle activity is involved (and less O_2 consumption is required) in producing movement. Runners perceive this, often remarking that they "feel smoother and stronger." In actuality, this change isn't as much a strength increase (meaning more force production) as it is greater endurance (better fatigue resistance caused by better perfusion and less anaerobic metabolic influences at typical training paces).

The primary liability of such overdistance training is the relatively slower and less complete adaptation of connective tissue. Tendons and ligaments do not improve their circulation or increase their size as muscles do to permit appropriately increasing tolerance to their chronic work load. This probably accounts for the greater incidence of debilitation from inflammation and injury in connective tissue than in the muscles. Runners should avoid training on crowned road surfaces because the left and right foot-strike surfaces are at slightly (but importantly) different elevations, giving asymmetric impact stress. Sidewalks, trails, or grassy surfaces such as firm, flat pastures or golf courses are preferable to cambered or rough, uneven surfaces.

Anaerobic Conditioning. A proper balance of greater volume–oriented, slower-paced work with greater intensity–oriented, faster-paced work all through the training year permits a large base of endurance fitness, on top of which is an essential element of raw sustainable speed. Higher intensity training falls into three categories, as diagrammed in Figures 2.2 and 3.5, one of which is anaerobic conditioning. Training at a higher intensity than aerobic conditioning brings appropriate adaptations in those muscle cells that are only stimulated by such higher intensity stimuli, and also increases the adaptational response of the heart and cardiovascular system. Thus, judicious inclusion of higher intensity training (below the limits that produce injury from excessive connective tissue overloading) are both beneficial and essential for the competitive athlete interested in training to race rather than simply training to train.

An effective anaerobic conditioning pace should range from just slower than marathon race pace to just beyond lactate/ventilatory threshold pace. This pace is marginally too fast for maintaining conversation and is best described as "comfortably hard" (although some runners who call aerobic conditioning "moderate" often use the term "steady" for lactate/ventilatory threshold running). The lactate/ventilatory threshold is the work intensity beyond which blood lactic acid begins to accumulate at an increasing rate. Because acidosis has a stimulatory effect on ventilation, typically this increased ventilation can be both measured in the laboratory and sensed by runners. This increased rate and depth as well as eventual rise in working tissue acidity contributes to the subjective sensation of an increased work load that cannot be maintained indefinitely. Hence, selecting an appropriate length of run as well as running pace is impor-

tant in planning manageable training sessions. Working at a pace slightly faster than lactate/ventilatory threshold pace optimally stimulates the kinds of adaptive physiological changes that will eventually quicken the pace at which this threshold occurs. Although aerobic aspects of performance also improve with training in this pace range, the anaerobic conditioning response is the predominant training benefit with the type of work typically assigned.

If it is not possible to specifically identify this threshold using treadmill testing, we suggest that athletes make an initial arbitrary assumption that the threshold occurs at 80% of $\dot{V}O_2$max pace. Thus, $\dot{V}O_2$max pace should be reduced by 20% and then two 20-min runs tried at that pace with a 5-min recovery at an aerobic conditioning pace in between. The training session should be "comfortably hard," not so easily manageable that it really is aerobic conditioning, but also not so difficult that it is inordinately stressful. Depending on outcome, the training pace can be slightly increased or decreased to better match fitness.

Depending on heredity and fitness level, the threshold pace may vary from about 75% to as high as 90% of $\dot{V}O_2$max pace. This may represent a heart rate from about 80% to as high as 95% of its maximum value in men and closer to maximum in women. With our runner in Figure 2.2, this pace occurred at 86% of $\dot{V}O_2$max pace, or 5:12/mi (3:14/km), and $\dot{V}O_2$max pace was 4:36/mi (2:51/km). The faster paced training in this region can be maintained with minimum accumulating discomfort for anywhere from 15 to 25 min before it is appropriate to slow the pace and permit recovery before starting no more than one additional repetition. For the athlete described in Figure 2.2, an appropriate anaerobic conditioning session might include a few kilometers of warm-up, then a 20-min run at lactate/ventilatory threshold pace (5:12/mi, or 3:14/km), 1 recovery mile at 6:00/mi (3:44/km), and a 15-min run at 5:00/mi (3:06/km).

Although ST fiber stimulation is emphasized with such training, as well as during aerobic conditioning, increased activity among FT Type IIa (and perhaps even some FT Type IIb) motor units now occurs in the working muscles. Increased glycolytic as well as oxidative enzyme utilization promotes an increased number of such enzymes as part of the adaptation process, along with additional increases in capillarization and plasma volume. The increased metabolic rate in all of these fibers does stimulate glycolysis, but there is minimum blood lactate accumulation, making the training load reasonably well tolerated. The ST fibers utilize their specialized form of lactic dehydrogenase to minimize lactate formation, and the small amount of lactate formed by the FT fibers can be used as fuel by nearby oxidative muscle fibers or by other tissues. The relatively high submaximum work load, sustained for a somewhat prolonged period, promotes adaptive changes in cardiac function most noticeable as an increase in ventricular chamber size, thereby increasing stroke volume. The end result of all these adaptations is that submaximum prolonged training becomes more easily manageable.

The most effective marathon race pace is ever so slightly slower than lactate/ventilatory threshold pace. This permits the fastest long-term sustainable running pace without requiring increasing anaerobic energy contributions until near the end of the race, when anaerobic reserves can help initiate a quick finish (Lenzi, 1987). Race pace at shorter distances (10,000m and less), however, is typically faster than the pace at which this threshold occurs. Athletes with a quicker lactate/ventilatory threshold pace have the advantage in that their anaerobic energy contribution during the race is less. The best method for introducing an initial training stimulus to raise this lactate/ventilatory threshold pace is faster paced training sustained for a period long enough to initiate physiological adaptation, yet not so long that needless training discomfort occurs. The reward is a faster sustainable marathon race pace.

One method for determining lactate/ventilatory threshold heart rate has been based on the hypothesis that the rate of heart rate rise during increasing-intensity exercise decreases at the lactate/ventilatory threshold. This has been termed the *Conconi test* (after Francesco Conconi, who initially described it) (Conconi, Ferrari, Ziglio, Droghetti, & Codeca, 1982). Figure 3.6 illustrates the use of this test with a set of data obtained from an elite male marathon runner. The athlete wears a portable heart-rate monitor and runs around a 400m track, beginning with a very easily manageable aerobic pace (e.g., a heart rate of about 130 to 135 beats/min). At each 200m interval, the pace is increased, perceptibly but not greatly (ideally no more than 1 sec/200 m). Heart rate values can be either called out at the end of each 200m by the athlete or stored by the monitor (depending upon its sophistication). The coach or an assistant carefully times each 200m interval and provides feedback to the athlete regarding whether the pace increases are appropriate. Ideally, by about 12 to 16 pace increases, the running pace will have increased sufficiently so that the linear rate of heart rate rise will change to a still linear but now perceptibly slower increase. When graphed, this change in slope can be seen easily. The pace at which the rate changed can be determined from the 200m time just previous to

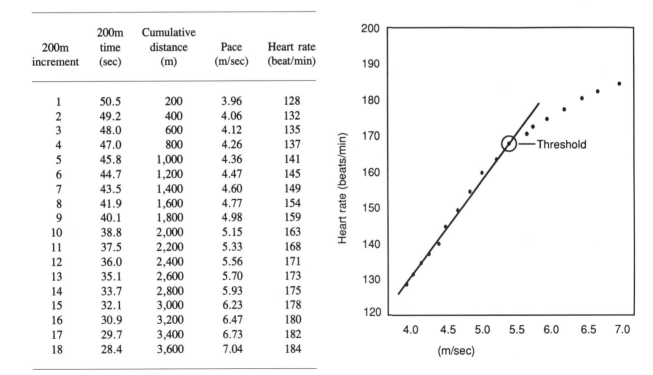

200m increment	200m time (sec)	Cumulative distance (m)	Pace (m/sec)	Heart rate (beat/min)
1	50.5	200	3.96	128
2	49.2	400	4.06	132
3	48.0	600	4.12	135
4	47.0	800	4.26	137
5	45.8	1,000	4.36	141
6	44.7	1,200	4.47	145
7	43.5	1,400	4.60	149
8	41.9	1,600	4.77	154
9	40.1	1,800	4.98	159
10	38.8	2,000	5.15	163
11	37.5	2,200	5.33	168
12	36.0	2,400	5.56	171
13	35.1	2,600	5.70	173
14	33.7	2,800	5.93	175
15	32.1	3,000	6.23	178
16	30.9	3,200	6.47	180
17	29.7	3,400	6.73	182
18	28.4	3,600	7.04	184

Figure 3.6 Use of the Conconi test to determine lactate/ventilatory threshold heart rate.

its occurrence. Training sessions can then be designed specifically for this athlete.

For several reasons, the use of this proposed method has not become very popular. First, other investigators attempting to duplicate Conconi's observations (Lacour, Padilla, & Denis, 1987; Tokmakidis & Leger, 1988) have not been very successful. We find the kind of clear relationship graphed in Figure 3.6 more of a rarity than a common result. Typically the heart rate response does not exhibit a measureable change in a rate of rise. Second, we find quite frequently that the heart rate of elite-level women distance runners at lactate/ventilatory threshold pace is the same as their maximum heart rate; thus no deflection in rate of rise could occur. Third, there doesn't yet appear to be any good physiological rationale to explain how either the increase in ventilation or the onset of blood lactate accumulation, which characterize lactate/ventilatory threshold, should be functionally linked to an increase in heart rate.

Aerobic Capacity Training. Once there is a sizable foundation of musculoskeletal and cardiopulmonary development, it is appropriate to insert periodic training sessions intense enough to provide a stimulus to the ST and FT skeletal muscle cells, and thus provide a vigorous but not maximum challenge to both aerobic and anaerobic capabilities. Aerobic capacity training challenges the maximum aerobic capabilities (although a sizable anaerobic working component occurs as well) and is carried out at paces similar to those found in racing events from 3,000 m through the half-marathon. The intensity is about 90% to 100% of $\dot{V}O_2$max pace. Because this is fast running, each interval cannot be too long or the higher level anaerobic energy contribution brings excessive fatigue. The first few minutes of each run will be largely anaerobic before circulation and breathing increase to permit regaining of aerobic dominance. Then, about 5 or 6 minutes of aerobically dominant training can occur before the session begins to feel too stressful.

Adequate recovery and rest between running intervals is essential to permit restoration of blood acidity to near-resting levels. Otherwise, premature performance debilitation will affect the subsequent running interval. Early exhaustion will require recruitment of additional (accessory) muscles. This not only costs more in fuel usage, because these muscles are not those optimally intended for the movement pattern, but also increases risk of overuse injury. The tendons of these accessory muscles may not be conditioned sufficiently to accommodate such stress. As fitness improves during a training session, experienced runners find that their required rest between running in-

tervals decreases even though pace is maintained. This is a sure sign of beneficial training.

Depending on event orientation (middle-distance vs. long-distance), the acceptable running interval time should not exceed 6 to 9 minutes, with the pace being quicker or slower depending upon time run. Recovery will be quite rapid because blood acidity is not excessive, and it is appropriate to make the recovery period no longer than the length of the run. The typical distance covered during aerobic capacity training ranges from 1,000 m to 3,000 m, depending in part on the athlete's specialty. The entire training session load can range from about 6,000 m to 8,000 m. In our coaching of longer distance runners, we find it quite effective to cycle such aerobic capacity sessions around a 5-week block, including one session per week. For example, we might use a sequence of 2 × 3,000 m, 3 × 2,000 m, 4 × 1,600 m, and 6 × 1,000 m, returning to 2 × 3,000 m the 5th week. The longer runs will be more similar to 10,000m race pace, with the shorter runs more similar to 5,000m or 3,000m pace. If physiological adaptation to such training has occurred, the 5th-week session should be more easily tolerable than the same session done 4 weeks previous. As improvement occurs, it is not appropriate to quicken the pace beyond 100% $\dot{V}O_2$max intensity because this merely increases the anaerobic component, and that is not the purpose of aerobic capacity training. Instead, lengthen the running interval.

The physiological adaptations resulting from this kind of training include

- an increase in oxidative and glycolytic enzymes in working muscles,
- activation of additional FT muscle fibers that were not stimulated by less intense training, and
- a small increase in blood buffering capacity.

This is in keeping with the results of work by Fox, Bartels, Billings, Matthews, Bason, and Webb (1973), who suggested that intensity rather than volume of training provides the most complete stimulus for raising $\dot{V}O_2$max to its limits. Near-maximum aerobic metabolism is emphasized in both ST and FT fibers, with anaerobic metabolism providing the additional energy requirements for pace maintenance. The nature of the training stimulus (moderate running time, adequate recovery) keeps blood acidity at a tolerable level. The increased blood acidity does, however, bring a noticeable increase in ventilation, adding to the subjective training stress.

In addition to track-oriented level running, where pace, distance, and time can be controlled precisely, hill running sessions can also be done as aerobic capacity training. However, with longer distance hill runs, the deviation from level-ground running cannot be very large. Also, the pace needs reduction from that maintained over level ground to compensate for the ascent. As an example, a 5:00/mi pace (3:06/km) over level ground is roughly equal to a 6:00/mi pace (3:44/km) at a 4% elevation (2.3 degrees). The exaggerated arm/shoulder and hip-flexor/high-knee-lift actions not seen during level-ground running both require added energy. This further increases energy requirements, causing excessive anaerobic metabolite accumulation unless pace is appropriately reduced.

Anaerobic Capacity Training. This is very intense training, at anywhere from 100% to 130% of VO_2max pace and at 95% or more of maximum (all-out) pace. The primary goal of anaerobic capacity training is to improve pure racing speed and strength. Particularly for athletes specializing in events where it is essential to change pace quickly and effectively, to sustain long, fast end-of-race maximum-intensity running, or to run an entire race faster than VO_2max pace, anaerobic capacity and high tolerance to acidity must be well developed. Neural capacity to recruit more skeletal muscle fibers is also mandatory. The middle-distance events (800m, 1,500m, 3,000m, and 3,000m steeplechase) are all contested at paces faster than 100% VO_2max pace, requiring tolerance to steadily accumulating blood and working muscle tissue lactate levels. The longer distance events, particularly 5,000m and 10,000m, will also be raced best by those who can maintain the fastest possible pace with the least lactate accumulation until near the end, and then add a large sustained anaerobic component during the final stretch to the finish. Such racing demands that all skeletal muscle fibers (ST and FT) be as well trained as possible to perform. When we study the physiological characteristics of middle-distance runners, we thus find that they have not only relatively high VO_2max values but also quite high maximum blood lactate values, suggesting a generous FT endowment, well-developed neural recruitability, and a high tolerance to tissue acidosis.

Training sessions that increase anaerobic capacity are done at a very fast pace, and thus the distances covered must be fairly short—typically 200 m through 800 m with a training session ranging from 2,400 m to 4,000 m. Using our runner whose VO_2max pace is 4:36/mi as an example, 120% faster than this for a high-end anaerobic capacity training session = 1:50 for 800 m = 55 sec/400 m = 27 sec/200 m. Because this athlete's best 800m time is 1:49, it is inappropriate to ask him to attempt repeated 800m intervals at es-

sentially his personal best pace. However, the 400m and 200m intervals ought to be within his grasp. They are run at a pace that he must learn to tolerate longer and longer if he desires to improve his 800m personal best. A session of two or three sets of $(1 \times 200$ m at 27 sec$) + (1 \times 400$ m at 55 sec$) + (2 \times 200$ m at 27 sec$)$ with, respectively, 1:30, 3:00, and 1:30 of recovery might be a useful anaerobic capacity training stimulus for this runner during the mid-to-later stages of his seasonal development. Use ten minute recovery between sets.

A characteristic feature of a properly controlled aerobic and anaerobic capacity training session is that the final repetition is manageable at a considerably faster pace than the previous repetitions. For example, a world-class male 1,500m/mile runner with a good aerobic base needs to develop the ability to manage 20 x 200m in 28 to 29 sec with a 60-sec recovery before a racing season begins. Each year Seb Coe regained the ability to run 30×200 m in 27 or 28 sec with a 45-sec recovery. Toward the end of that session, however, he could also manage to run one or two intervals in the 23- to 24-sec range. If he was not able, then he was doing the session too intensively. This inserted fast-pace repetition is the test of excessive anaerobic buildup during such an interval session.

Special emphasis should be given to maintaining excellent form throughout each run, despite coping with the effects of increasing fatigue. Blood lactate levels continue to rise during the recovery period, and they remain high as the next interval begins, despite the relatively long recovery period. This prolonged high blood lactate level is helpful for improving the body's buffering capacity. A strong developmental stimulus is provided to FT Type IIa fibers, and these seem to have the greatest capability to increase their total tension-generating protein as a training adaptation. This provides a strength-building stimulus, and runners often perceive after several such sessions that submaximum paces now seem considerably easier to maintain. This ease is probably due in part to the additional strength, along with improved blood buffering ability, even greater blood volume, and an improvement in neuromuscular recruitment characteristics.

Glycogen and phosphate energy supplies will be utilized extensively in the stimulated skeletal muscle fibers during such high-speed training. Whereas ATP reserves will be regenerated rather quickly (within minutes), carbohydrate reserves will require anywhere from 24 to 72 hr to replace, depending on intensity and volume of the session. Along with energy supply replacement, restitution of muscle cell electrolyte and osmotic balance and connective tissue breakdown products must occur—for both aerobic and anaerobic capacity training. Therapeutic modalities of a wide variety all have their proper place in the hours and days following such sessions. Gentle as well as deep muscle massage, ice water baths, anti-inflammatory medications such as aspirin or ibuprofen, and stretching sessions can be useful to enhance an athlete's timely recovery.

Distribution of Work Load Throughout a Macrocycle.

General Concepts of Work Load Organization.
The precise details of training plan construction soon come to haunt any coach or athlete; these are the keys to achieving meaningful long-term development. How do longer distance running, all the various faster running sessions, and comprehensive conditioning fit into a given time frame that ensures complete development and adequate recovery without undue fatigue? The most important part of any training plan is designing its details to match the needs and abilities of each athlete. Differing abilities to tolerate training stress may cause microcycles to vary in length anywhere between 1 and 2 weeks.

All too frequently coaches and athletes yearn to mimic specific day-to-day training plans of other athletes who have been successful. There is, of course, the notion of quality by association; if the training brought success for that other athlete, then it must be good for them as well. Also, there is the notion that another athlete and coach may have thought of some element of development that is so different from typical training routines that this in itself accounts for the excellence in the athlete's performance. We suggest that copying such training strategies is not in the best interests of either coach or athlete. First, their own creativity is stifled, and they are no longer masters of their own destiny. Second, virtually never do two training athletes have such similar training environments, competitive racing goals, basic fitness, genetic gifts, and practiced ability to handle each other's training sessions.

Running magazines abound with excerpts of "a week in the training diary of . . .", as if to suggest that "You too can run well—just do this!" Using such brief training plans out of context is seldom meaningful unless they describe a general weekly or fortnightly format that repeats in cyclic fashion for many weeks. (The injury can be sizable if runners have not done the necessary prior training to tolerate the stress involved.) Studying what others have done can certainly be useful, but such study should focus on development of a general picture of training strategy over weeks or months. The net effect of months of training is more important than the temporary effects of a week-long summary in bringing measurable fitness at the end of a training period. It is always tempting to consider some modifications of training to include new sessions, but it will always be difficult to assess whether these alterations were the specific cause of any notable performance or fitness changes.

Table 3.8 provides our view of one suggested format for the distribution of work load, expressed in units/week, that might be appropriate for a middle-distance (1,500m) and long-distance (10,000m) runner, progressing through the first four training mesocycles (X_1 through X_4). Some caveats are appropriate to give this table proper perspective. First, recall our definition of training unit as a general assigned modality. Second, realize that any given training period may contain more than one unit. A 40-min run of alternating fast and slow miles performed on grass, for example, will involve work in both the aerobic and anaerobic conditioning zones. This comprises two units of training. Such a session might be followed by a gradual cool-down and then a session of upper-body strength training in the weight room, adding a third unit to that day's training load.

Second, the schedules outlined in Table 3.8 assume that a macrocycle lasts about one year. Starting with 4 weeks of recovery (X_0), then progressing through the 33 weeks of work outlined (X_1 through X_4) and finishing with 3 weeks of fine-tuning (X_5) and 12 weeks of competition (X_6), this is 52 weeks. Is it possible to shorten this macrocycle and have two major peaks? Perhaps, but the rhetorical question could be asked whether either peak could match that single peak in excellence. To perform superbly at the level of today's major world competitions, multiple peaks of equal excellence may not always be possible. To achieve them, we would have to shorten the number of weeks in each microcycle, thus providing less total training and probably inadequate fitness to compete successfully at the highest level. We mentioned earlier the situation of the elite-level, already well-conditioned, uninjured marathon runner who may be able to begin a new macrocycle every 4 to 5 months. The slightest deviation in this runner's harmonious balance—a small injury, a bout with the flu, the need for additional mental rest from the unending strain of focusing on training and competing—can all disrupt this rhythm, adding weeks or months of additional preparation time until the next expected peak. Proper development simply cannot be hurried.

Athletes must decide their preference. Would they like to provide the sporting world with a few command performances of enormous quality when the time is ripe as a result of a profoundly effective building period requiring most of a year? Or would they prefer to be somewhat successful year-round as a result of minor emphases here and there on a generalized plan

Table 3.8   Distribution of Training Load for a Middle- and Long-Distance Runner During a Training Macrocycle

A. Middle distance

Room / Period	Weeks	1 Aerobic conditioning	2 Lactate/ventilatory threshold	3 Aerobic capacity training	4 Anaerobic capacity training	Total running units	Total distance Miles	km	5 Mobility	6 Circs & wts	Total units
x_1 (12 weeks) Establish aerobic base	4	5-6	0-1	0	0	5-7	30-40	48-64	4	0-1	9-12
	4	4-5	1-2	1-2	1	7-10	45-60	72-96	4	1-2	12-16
	4	4-5	2-3	2	2	10	65-75	104-120	4	2-3	16-19
x_2 (8 weeks) Increasing intensity	4	3	3	2	3	11	70-75	112-120	4	3	18
	4	3-4	4	2	3	12-13	75-80	120-128	4	3	19-20
x_3 (7 weeks) Harder tempo	4	3	5	2	3	13	70	112	5	2	18
	3	3	5	3	3	14	65	104	5	2	21
x_4 (6 weeks) Consolidate	3	3-2	4	3	4	14-13	60	96	4	1	18-19
	3	3-2	4	3	4	14-13	55	88	4	1	18-19

B. Long distance

Room / Period	Weeks	1 Aerobic conditioning	2 Lactate/ventilatory threshold	3 Aerobic capacity training	4 Anaerobic capacity training	Total running units	Total distance Miles	km	5 Mobility	6 Circs & wts	Total units
x_1 (12 weeks) Establish aerobic base	4	4-5	0-1	0	0	4-6	30-50	48-81	3	0-1	7-10
	4	4-5	1-2	1-2	1	7-10	55-70	89-112	3	1-2	11-15
	4	5-6	3-4	1	1	10-12	75-90	120-145	3	2-3	15-18
x_2 (8 weeks) Increasing intensity	4	4-5	3-4	2	1	10-12	80-95	128-153	3	3	16-18
	4	4-5	4-5	2	1	11-13	80-95	128-153	3	3	17-19
x_3 (7 weeks) Harder tempo	4	4-5	4-5	2	2	12-14	80	128	4	2	18-20
	3	4-5	4-5	3	2	13-15	75	120	4	2	19-21
x_4 (6 weeks) Consolidate	3	4-5	4-5	4	2	14-16	70	112	3	1	18-20
	3	4	4	3-4	2-3	13-15	70	112	3	1	17-19

of training that provides fitness without much substantial improvement? Increasingly, at the highest levels of sport, the demands of television, corporate sponsors, and team selection races create the need for more competitive appearances with more performance peaks required to permit eventual qualification into major championships. Producing a few truly great performances instead of simply competing at a high level requires both a physical and an emotional peak which in turn can only be achieved by uncluttered nurturing of talent.

Third, note the attention given to development of strength, power, joint mobility, and kinesthetic awareness by inclusion of several units each week that are labeled simply as ''mobility'' and ''circuits and weights.'' This relates to development of comprehensive conditioning, which is the subject of chapter 4—training for total body fitness that is different from actual running. It is assumed that runners will include appropriate joint-mobility and muscle-stretching exercises each day, particularly after running and before units of weight-room or circuit training, to ensure adequate joint range of motion and muscle length.

Fourth, marathon runners have a somewhat unique necessity for specific emphasis on high-volume aerobic conditioning each week. Thus, their total training distance will often be higher than outlined in Table 3.8. These details are discussed further in chapter 5 in relation to strategies for marathon race preparation. A sizable increase in susceptibility to overuse injuries, however, occurs in this attempt to build additional aerobic capabilities. Plenty of rest, adequate nutrition to offset the energy losses, training on flat, soft surfaces with shoes that provide good support and impact absorption, and routine use of recuperative modalities such as massage all assume increased importance.

Fifth, training sessions that fit within a particular training zone for one athlete may be so much more difficult (or easy) to tolerate for another athlete that they really belong in a different zone. This may also be true with sessions for particular athletes as they increase their fitness. As one example, consider a session of 5 × 800 m @ 2:20, 2:16, 2:12, 2:08, 2:04 (2 min rec), or a session of 5 × 800 m @ 2:16 with recovery times of 2:00, 1:50, 1:40, 1:30, and 1:20. Such an intensity may be anaerobic conditioning or aerobic capacity training for an 800m runner but in the zone of aerobic capacity training or even anaerobic capacity training for a marathon runner. Alternatively, these work loads may be anaerobic capacity training (i.e., faster than $\dot{V}O_2$max pace) for a 1,500m runner early in a macrocycle but aerobic capacity training (i.e., around $\dot{V}O_2$max pace) after several

months of quality development. By reviewing previous training diaries, using time trials or treadmill testing, and carefully monitoring sessions repeated throughout a development sequence, these changing fitness levels can be best identified. If there is ever doubt about optimum training intensity, recovery times should be overestimated and running speeds underestimated; this minimizes the risks of injury and overtraining.

Specific Concepts of Training Plan Construction. We have already presented several examples of individual training sessions and how their intensity will be determined by the combination of natural and developed skills as well as position within a training macrocycle. Thus, no two coaches or athletes will be able to use identical training plans with similar effectiveness. In addition, varying terrain, weather, and availability of facilities all require additional individualization for the athlete to achieve the desired training stimulus. A variety of recently published books have suggested specific weekly and monthly training schedules for athletes of varying abilities and event ambitions. Some of these are quite good and can serve as a source of variations for daily training plan design (Dellinger & Freeman, 1984; Galloway, 1984; Humphreys & Holman, 1985; Wilt, 1968). The optimal development plan will use available training facilities, strike a balance between intensity and volume of training, be sensitive to individual abilities, use valid scientific concepts relative to progressively increasing training loads, and contain ingenuity to provide a continually stimulating and challenging training stimulus.

Table 3.9 provides a specific outline of a 12-day training block for a middle-distance (1,500m) athlete and a 14-day block for a long-distance (10,000m) athlete. Though specific in nature, it permits identification of several key principles. One principle involves the inclusion of rest. Note that there are one or two potential rest days, which can be positioned as needed. An essential part of training is regeneration, both mental and physical, from prior training. If this is best achieved by an entire day off, so be it. Training ought not to consume every single day of any runner's sport career. This puts the runner into a very deep rut indeed, and there is little difference between a rut and a grave, save for the depth. If easy training (mentally low-key as well as physically manageable) is appropriate, that's fine as well. Typically, the day off (or off-day) serves to invigorate body and soul for good-quality training in the few days following.

A second principle involves use of the multi-pace concept—training at both faster and slower than race pace for the athlete's primary event. Notice how the middle-distance runner's 12- to 14-day block is constructed around a framework in which the faster sessions steadily get shorter in total distance and quicker in pace as the block progresses. Thus, as seen in Table 3.9a, the total distance covered on Day 10 (1,580m) is much less (but more intense) than the 3,800 to 5,100m done on Day 8. For the long-distance athlete as well, multi-pace training is implemented but with a different overall pattern.

Tables 3.10 and 3.11 provide some specific examples of how training plans can be constructed using the aforementioned guidelines. They have been extracted from Seb Coe's early training diaries and were selected particularly for the benefit of younger athletes and their coaches. Seb was 16 years old in 1973 (Table 3.10), 18 in 1975 (Table 3.11). Realize, of course, that many months of prior training had preceded these few-week blocks leading up to his important competitions, and he was in a tapering phase. Nevertheless, even then the multi-pace development scheme permitted continuity in all aspects of competitive excellence, thereby providing a well-rounded athlete for competition.

Table 3.9 Generalized 12- to 14-Day Training Blocks

(a) Middle distance

Day	Session	Pace
1	3 × 2,000m or [(2 × 1,200m) + (1 × 800m) + (2 × 400m)]a	5,000m
2	Over-distance fartlek	
3	6 to 8 × 800ma	3,000m
4	Distance running on roads	
5	16 to 30 × 200m alternating with 10 × 400ma	1,500m
6	Potential rest day (if race); if not, fartlek	
7	Race or time trial	
8	4 to 6 × 400m alternating with 6 to 9 × 300m	800m
9	Distance running on roads	
10	(1 × 300m + 2 × 200m + 4 × 100m + 8 × 60m)	400m
11	Over-distance fartlek	
12	Rest if racing next day; if not, choose pace for next race	

(b) Long distance

Day	Session	Pace
1	A.M. long run of 12-20 miles, easy	
2	A.M. no run; P.M. 7 miles easy	
3	A.M. 7 miles steady; P.M. (4 × 200m with 200m jog) + (4 × 2,000m with 3 min jog) + (4 × 200m with 200m jog)	1,500/5,000m
4	A.M. 7 miles easy; P.M. 10 miles easy with occasional accelerations to 10 km race pace, sustained for 2 min	
5	A.M. 15 miles easy; P.M. no run	
6	A.M. no run; P.M. (4 × 300m with 300m jog) + (6 × 800m with 3 min jog) + (4 × 200m with 200m jog)	1,500/5,000m
7	A.M. 9 miles easy; P.M. no run	
8	A.M. long run of 12-17 miles easy	
9	A.M. 5 miles steady; P.M. no run	
10	A.M. 9 miles easy; P.M. (4 × 200m with 200m jog) + (5 × 1,000m with 2 min jog) + (4 × 200m with 200m jog)	1,500/5,000m
11	A.M. no run; P.M. 7 miles easy	
12	A.M. 5 miles steady with several accelerations to 10 km race pace, sustained for 2 min	10,000m
13	Single easy run if race the next day; if not, 2 distance runs, 5-7 miles and 7-10 miles, the latter with fartlek	
14	Race; if not, 2 × 15-20 min at lactate/ventilatory threshold pace	Marathon

aWill be run at a faster pace when in peaking stages for major races.

Identifying Strengths and Weaknesses in Performance.   For any given athlete, it will be much easier to complete training at some paces than at others. There are a few reasons for this. One relates to varying genetic predisposition. Athletes with a genetic emphasis for ST motor units may likely find short-distance, fast-speed training relatively more difficult than their friends with a majority of FT motor units. As the adaptive effects of training bring greater fitness, the running paces will quicken, and recovery

Table 3.10   Prechampionship Buildup to Illustrate Multi-Tier Training: Seb Coe, Age 16

Day	English Schools Championships 3,000m - July 1973	AAA Youth Championships 1,500m - Aug. 1973
1	3 km steady warm-up (10 × 100m) + (6 × 200m) + (2 × 300m) + (1 × 400m)	School races, 800m and 1,500m
2	10 km cross-country running	15 km on road; first 7.5 km fast, second 7.5 km steady
3	7 × 800m on road (2:15 per 800m)	(4 × 400m) + (4 × 150m)
4	(1 × 300m) + (2 × 200m) + (4 × 100m)	3 × (10 × 200m) with 5 min recovery between sets
5	(4 × 400m) in 56, 55, 57, 60 sec	7 × 800m (avg. 2:15 per 800m)
6	Rest day	(2 × 150m) + (6 × 100m) + (2 × 200m) + (8 × 80m)
7	A.M. 10 km cross-country P.M. 5 × 200m	(2 × 200m) + (4 × 400m) + (4 × 200m)
	Week total = 25 miles (40 km)	Week total = 30 miles (48 km)
8	(20 × 200m) with 45 sec recovery	14 km cross-country running
9	A.M. 4 km fast; (4 × 800m) + (1 × 400m) P.M. (6 × 800m)	Rest day
10	A.M. (30 × 100m) up 10 degree hill P.M. 1,000m + 400m + 300m + (4 × 200m)	(7 × 800m)
11	A.M. 10 km on roads P.M. (2 × 400m) + (2 × 200m)	(10 × 400m)
12	A.M. 8 km P.M. 15 × 200m	A.M. 8 km P.M. (5 × 200m) + (2 × 300m) + (3 × 100m)
13	Rest day	(30 × 100m) up 10-degree hill with jog-back recovery
14	Race 3,000m (first place)	1,500m heats
15		1,500m final (first, in 3:55 with last 300m in 42 sec)
	Week total = 28 miles (45 km)	Week total = 17 miles (27 km)

times can decrease. The athlete will gradually increase fitness over the entire range of running paces. This subtle manipulation of intensity, volume, and recovery is the running world's version of the progressive resistance/overload concept that weight lifters have used in strength training since the 1940s. This concept will be more fully discussed in chapter 4.

Another reason relates to the varying rates of adaptation in different tissues. Acquisition of endurance typically takes longer than acquisition of speed, primarily because cardiovascular adaptations are slower to develop than neuromuscular adaptations. But speed training is more difficult due to its greater intensity. For this reason, speed training sessions during the earlier mesocycles will by necessity be at slower paces, although the relative intensity of such training may be comparable to faster sessions later on. It is important for athletes and coaches to know whether a greater need for improvement exists on the quickness end or the endurance end of the chosen dis-

tance specialty. Once this is known, some specialization in that direction can bring proper consolidation of overall skill. But how does one determine these so-called equivalent multiple-event paces? Table 3.12 provides one mechanism for answering this question.

We have constructed three sets of formulas for determining equivalent race performances over several distances when the performance for one distance is known. Three tables are better than one because of each individual runner's specific event and ability to manage speed and endurance. To utilize a single table for all athletes would counter our concepts of individual and event specificity. Table 3.12a is primarily for the longer distance specialists—those with competence at 8 km, 10 km, and 15 km who may also run marathons (or have an interest in doing so) but who also actively compete at 5,000m for speed development. Table 3.12b is primarily for the 3,000m and 5,000m specialists who have an interest in the shorter races as well as the 10,000m event but for

Table 3.11 Prechampionship Buildup to Illustrate Multi-Tier Training: Seb Coe, Age 18

Day	NCAA 1,500m/3,000m Championships[a]	European Junior Championships
1	11 km distance running	A.M. weights P.M. 14 km distance running
2	Raced 800m	A.M. 6.5 km distance running P.M. 20 × 200m (28 sec)
3	A.M. 8 km distance running P.M. 30 × 100m (10-degree hill)	A.M. 6.5 km distance running P.M. (4 × 400m) + (1 × 1,600m)
4	7 miles distance running	4 × 150m @ 18 sec/150m, 3 × 300m @ 41 sec, 1 × 400m
5	7 × 800m	A.M. 6.5 km distance running P.M. 10 × 400m @ 60 sec
6	11 miles distance running	Light weight training
7	A.M. 1 × (400m + 300m + 200m + 150m) P.M. 5 km recovery run	7 × 800m (avg. 2:10 per 800m)
8	4 × 1,200m	1 × (200m + 400m + 200m + 300m) + 4 × 100m
9	10 × 150m	10 km distance running
10	A.M. 30 × 100m (10-degree hill) P.M. 6.5 km distance running	6.5 km distance running
11	7 × 400m	A.M. 6.5 km distance running P.M. strides and accelerations
12	11 km distance running	Raced 1,500m heats
13	A.M. 6.5 km distance running P.M. 10 × 100m	Raced 1,500m final (3:45)
14	5 km distance running	11-day total = 33 miles (53 km)
15	Raced 1,500m heat and final (3:50) 14-day total = 70 miles (112 km)	
16	Rest	
17	A.M. 6.5 km distance running P.M. 1 × (200m + 400m + 300m + 200m)	
18	A.M. 7 km distance running P.M. 20 × 200m	
19	1 × (100m + 300m) + (2 × 400m)	
20	A.M./P.M. 8 km distance running	
21	8 km easy pace running	
22	Raced 3,000m final (8:14.2) 6-day total = 28 miles (45km)	

[a]NCAA = Northern Counties Athletic Association.

whom the 800m is seldom contested. Table 3.12c serves the needs of the 800m and 1,500m runner who does not consider longer distances like the 10,000m as a yardstick to evaluate endurance or stamina. The stippled areas represent distances contested less frequently by each group.

An example showing the use of this table can be given using data from one of our own athletes. Keith Brantly's best 10,000m time (28:02) is a road mark set in February 1989 over a flat, certified loop course in a highly competitive race run under cool conditions. His best performance in the 1,500m (3:45.49) occurred in late May in very warm and humid weather (in Florida) as a tune-up for a personal-best 5,000m effort of 13:40.20 at his national championships 3 weeks later in similarly difficult conditions (in Houston). Using Table 3.12a, on the basis of his 10,000m effort Keith's 1,500m and 5,000m personal

Table 3.12   Suggested Formulas for Estimating Equivalent Times Over Five Race Distances

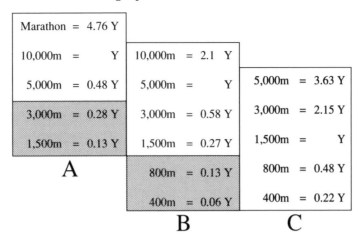

bests should be 3:39 and 13:27 if the races were run under similar conditions to the 10,000m. These are faster than Keith has achieved but are reasonable expectations and show that the effect of weather slowed these performances by 2% to 3%. Keith considers himself a 5,000m/10,000m specialist and thus could utilize either Table 3.12a or 3.12b for estimating comparable performances. In this present instance, Figure 3.12b would not provide a meaningful estimate, as his 5,000m personal best was slowed by weather. (Those calculations, for example, suggest a personal best at 10,000m as 28:42, which is far too slow.)

Helping Younger Runners Chart Racing Progress Over Time

Achieving personal best times is always enjoyable and an unequivocal indicator of improvement. As younger runners develop expertise over a range of distances, it becomes useful to learn whether developing excellence at one distance is comparable to doing so at another distance. As an athlete's strength and endurance increase from growth as well as from training, such monitoring is important. At this younger end of the fitness continuum, the equations presented in Table 3.12 may not be quite as accurate. One method that has gained popularity in Britain for profiling such performance improvement is the Esso-sponsored Amateur Athletic Association Five-Star Award Scheme. Youngsters convert results from track and field (athletics) performances into a point score modified by inclusion of bonus points. In Table 3.13 we reprint a portion of one of these award schemes and superimpose data for Seb Coe over various distances as he developed from age 12 through age 18. Though such tables permit comparison of relative quality of performances over various running dis-

tances, they also permit analysis of improvement over time. Such improvements have a greater point value and when graphed show a rise toward the top of the table.

A practical example of intelligent use of information from such performance ranking systems explains some fundamental decisions made early in Seb Coe's athletic development. When he was 12 years old, Seb joined an athletics club, and along with his school sports he had the opportunity to run occasional short sprint races. Although he was quite nimble because of his slim physique, his running showed a significant lack of endurance. To remedy this, some distance training and participation in boys' cross-country were included. The combined beneficial effect was marked indeed, as seen in Table 3.13. Seb's age-13 performance results soared in the longer track events yet remained relatively static in the shorter events. The best interpretation of these data, we believe, was not to suggest that Seb should have stopped his short-distance sprint training, decided that he was a "born marathoner," and begun to so specialize. The proper interpretation was that the improvement in endurance was caused by a shift in training specificity, the adaptation being appropriate to the stimulus applied.

As Seb progressed through his 14th year, a positive effort was made to improve the balance between speed work and endurance work—neither one at the expense of the other. As can be seen in Table 3.13, improvements occurred over the entire spectrum of tested distances, from 100 m through 3,000 m. After that, his training was adjusted with a view toward maintaining a straight-line relationship between the various test distances, anticipating that the line extended through all of them would slope in a manner that indicated the event range for which he was naturally gifted. For Seb, it was easier to adapt to the training

Table 3.13   Esso Five-Star Award Scheme for Evaluating Athletic Performance Over Several Distances

Points	Sprints			Distance			Age
	100m	200m	400m	800m	1,500m	3,000m	18 years
Amount per extra point	0.05	0.1	0.2	1 sec	2 sec	4 sec	16 years
100		22.6	50.3	1.57	4.02	8.48	
99	11.0	22.7	50.6	1.58	4.04	8.52	15 years
98		22.8	50.9	1.59	4.06	8.56	
97	11.1	22.9	51.2	2.00	4.08	9.00	
96		23.0	51.5	2.01	4.10	9.04	
95	11.2	23.1	51.8	2.02	4.12	9.08	
94		23.2	52.2	2.03	4.14	9.12	
93	11.3	23.3	52.6	2.04	4.16	9.16	
92		23.4	53.0	2.05	4.18	9.20	
91	11.4	23.5	53.4	2.06	4.20	9.24	14 years
90		23.6	53.8	2.07	4.22	9.28	
89	11.5	23.7	54.2	2.08	4.24	9.32	
88		23.8	54.6	2.09	4.26	9.36	
87	11.6	23.9	55.0	2.10	4.28	9.40	
86		24.1	55.5	2.11	4.30	9.44	
85	11.7	24.3	56.0	2.12	4.32	9.48	
84		24.5	56.5	2.13	4.34	9.52	13 years
83	11.8	24.7	57.0	2.14	4.36	9.56	
82	11.9	24.9	57.5	2.15	4.38	10.00	
81	12.0	25.1	58.0	2.16	4.40	10.05	
80	12.1	25.3	58.5	2.17	4.42	10.10	
79	12.2	25.5	59.0	2.18	4.45	10.15	
78	12.3	25.7	59.5	2.19	4.48	10.20	
77	12.4	25.9	60.0	2.20	4.51	10.25	
76	12.5	26.2	60.5	2.21	4.54	10.30	
75	12.6	26.5	61.0	2.22	4.57	10.35	
74	12.7	26.8	61.5	2.23	5.00	10.40	
73	12.8	27.1	62.0	2.24	5.03	10.45	
72	12.9	27.4	62.5	2.25	5.06	10.50	
71	13.0	27.7	63.0	2.26	5.09	10.55	
70	13.1	28.0	63.5	2.27	5.12	11.00	
69	13.2	28.3	64.0	2.28	5.15	11.05	
68	13.3	28.6	64.5	2.29	5.18	11.10	
67	13.4	28.9	65.0	2.30	5.21	11.15	
66	13.5	29.2	65.5	2.32	5.24	11.20	12 years
65	13.6	29.5	66.0	2.34	5.27	11.25	
64	13.7	29.8	66.5	2.36	5.30	11.30	
63	13.8	30.1	67.0	2.37	5.33	11.35	
62	13.9	30.4	67.5	2.39	5.36	11.40	
61	14.0	30.7	68.0	2.40	5.39	11.45	
60	14.1	31.0	68.5	2.42	5.42	11.50	
59	14.2	31.3	69.0	2.43	5.45	11.55	
58	14.3	31.6	69.5	2.45	5.48	12.00	
57	14.4	31.9	70.0	2.46	5.51	12.10	
56	14.5	32.2	70.5	2.48	5.54	12.20	

Data for Seb Coe are plotted from ages 12 through 18 to illustrate how progression in performance can be plotted over time. Some performances for ages 16 and 18 years are off the chart but are still plotted and illustrate the emphasis on attempting to maintain the performance line horizontal.

required for the 800m and the 1,500m than to the 400m, indicating that he most likely had a generous endowment of both FT and ST skeletal muscle fibers rather than a predisposition toward FT as is more typical among sprinters. An attempt to maintain the performance line in Table 3.13 as horizontal as possible ensured that neither the speed nor the endurance components of his training were unduly overemphasized.

Another way of profiling athletic performances across several events is to use the International Amateur Athletic Federation (IAAF) Scoring Tables (which presently exist only for men's track and field events). These can be useful in suggesting possible performance shortfalls as an athlete moves up the performance success ladder. We have found the 1962 (Belgrade) edition preferable to more recent versions, as the latter are intended more for the combined-event competitions. Again, examples from athletes with whom we are familiar can serve to illustrate, although runners and coaches will doubtless find examples from their own experience. Depicted in Figure 3.7a are the performances (with their appropriate point values) that Seb Coe delivered for the 800m, the 1,000m, and the mile during his exciting summer of 1981—all world records. Though the world marveled at how he could manage to run so well in race after race, the fact was that the 1,000m and mile efforts corresponded well in terms of fitness quality to his earlier 800m performance.

A simple interpolation, however, also indicates that Seb should have been capable of running 3:29 for 1,500 m, but optimum racing conditions just never materialized. These finally occurred 5 years later, 3 weeks short of his 30th birthday, in Rieti after the European Championships of 1986. The time was ripe; his fitness was appropriate as judged by his 800m/1,500m Championships double at Stuttgart. Following that double, it was a simple decision to attempt to bring home the long-deserved mark in the 1,500m rather than experiment with other events. Again, the world marveled, but the victory simply made logical sense.

A similar kind of assessment is effective for evaluating the performance of long-distance runners. During the summer of 1987, for example, Mexico's Arturo Barrios set as a goal to lower his personal best performances in shorter distance events in preparation for the Rome World Championships. His major competitive asset was his highly developed endurance capability, but his liability was less-well-developed raw speed. If he could improve his speed, then this combined with his endurance fitness could give him optimum preparation for Rome. True to his desires, on the European track circuit during July he achieved

personal bests in the 5,000m (13:13.52), the 3,000m (7:44.63), and the 1,500m (3:39.38). Were these results comparable in quality? And what might he have expected as a possible goal for the Rome 10,000m race under good conditions? Use of the IAAF Scoring Tables provides insight into these questions, and Figure 3.7b graphs Arturo's performances in relation to their equivalent point values.

His longer distance performances were of the greatest quality, the 5,000m and 3,000m being similar in point value (1,106 and 1,083, respectively). His 1,500m performance was slightly slower by comparison (1,008 points) but was still an improvement for him in the middle-distance range. Comparable 10,000m performances to the 5,000m and 3,000m results would be, respectively, 27:48 and 28:05. He placed fourth at Rome with 27:59.66 despite stopping temporarily at the end of 24 laps due to reigning confusion among participants regarding elapsed laps.

During the summer of 1989 Arturo returned to Europe with the similar goal of improving his best track performances. His three major races are also graphed in Figure 3.7b. The first effort (13:32.63) was at 5,000m and was slowed by time zone acclimatization and less-than-ideal racing circumstances. Eight days later he was ready to challenge his best 10,000m time. In Stockholm, his 27:18.45 victory (1,145 points) was outstanding indeed—nearly a 7-sec personal-best improvement. He followed this 7 days later in Nice with a 7:35.71 for the 3,000m (1,129 points), again a personal-best improvement (by nearly 9 sec). The Stockholm race was slightly better in quality using the IAAF point system, but the two were comparable. Five days later, in London, he lowered his 1987 5,000m personal best by nearly 5 sec to 13:07.79 (1,123 points). Such consistency at the highest level led Arturo to believe that a brief period of rest followed by a modest additional dose of very high quality training to provide fine-tuning could give him the mental and physical preparedness for an assault on the world 10,000m record.

His preparations proceeded optimally—recovery, training, travel back to Europe, a few tune-up races (one of which gave him a personal best of 3:37.61 for 1,500 m and proved that his speed was well honed), and he was ready. On the evening of August 18, 6 days after his 1,500m best, with favorable racing conditions (good-quality athletes to set the initial pace and a supportive audience at Berlin's Olympic stadium), Arturo thrilled the world with a wonderful run of 27:08.23. This was a clear testament to the value of an athlete carefully planning a peak, racing seldom but under meaningful circumstances, and realizing that a foreign environment and

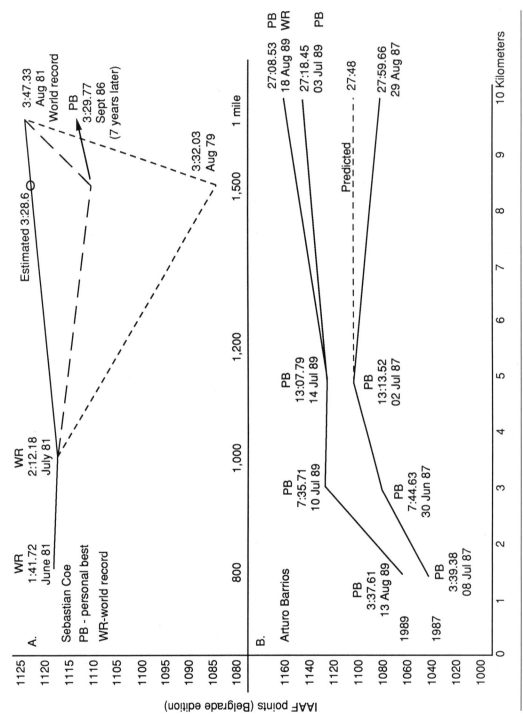

Figure 3.7 Use of IAAF scoring tables to assess quality of competitive race performances.

challenging races both require time for physical and mental regeneration as well as preparation. We would thus urge those who read this book to become familiar enough with the formular (Table 3.12) and tabular (Table 3.14) systems for performance evaluation so they can be used informatively. The investment in effort is well worth the returns in ability to better assess competitive capabilities.

A few other assessment systems exist for estimating performance potential in individual running events. One example is the Kosmin test for projecting performance in the 800m. The athlete must run all-out for 1 min, followed by a 3-min recovery. The distance covered is measured accurately. Then, another 1-min all-out run is done; again, the distance covered is measured. By using the formula

$$T(800 \text{ m}) = 217.4 - 0.199D \qquad 3.5$$

where D = the distance run, the expected 800m race time can be estimated. Table 3.14 gives projected 800m times based upon 2×60-sec test-run distances between 805 m and 950 m.

Multi-Tier Training in the Context of Other Systems

Many training systems for developing distance runners have evolved during this century. Various athletes have immortalized themselves by their superb middle- and long-distance running achievements, setting world records and earning Olympic and other major championship medals. In chronicling these marvelous achievements, the media have traditionally asked two major questions to the athlete and his or her coach: to the athlete, "What was the secret to your successful performances?" and to the coach, "Tell us about his (or her) training."

To examine how multi-tier training fits into the broad picture of training plan design, it is useful to examine a few of the more well-known athlete/coach relationships and their unique characteristics. In the 1920s and early 30s, the legendary Paavo Nurmi (22 world records between 1,500m and 10,000m; 12 Olympic medals) and his Finnish distance coach Lauri Pikkala placed a significant emphasis on more training periods of shorter duration with adequate rest instead of longer, slower distance running. The details of skeletal muscle physiology and cellular biochemistry were in their infancy during that period, so no one realized specifically that Nurmi's greater emphasis on faster training was providing a good training stimulus for his FT skeletal muscle fibers, which required a more intense stimulus to respond (see Figure 1.23). Many subsequent training systems have been

Table 3.14 Use of the Kosmin Test to Project 800m Race Times

Distance run in 2×60 sec (m)	Projected 800m time
805	2:01.6
810	2:01.0
815	2:00.4
820	1:59.8
825	1:59.2
830	1:58.6
835	1:58.0
840	1:57.4
845	1:56.8
850	1:56.2
855	1:55.7
860	1:55.1
865	1:54.5
870	1:53.9
875	1:53.5
880	1:52.7
885	1:52.1
890	1:51.3
895	1:50.9
900	1:50.3
905	1:49.7
910	1:49.1
915	1:48.5
920	1:47.9
925	1:47.3
930	1:46.6
935	1:46.0
940	1:45.4
945	1:44.8
950	1:44.2

Note. Recovery time between runs = 3 min; 800m time (sec) = $217.4 - (0.119 \times \text{distance run})$.

little more than modifications of the principle that "Those who race fast train fast"—provided that the companion requirement of recovery is also incorporated appropriately.

During the early 1940s, Woldemar Gerschler (coach of Rudolf Harbig) proposed that rest periods between short running intervals (100m to 200m) be determined by monitoring the heart rate (waiting until the pulse returns to about 120 beats/min). Mihaly Igloi (coach of Sandor Iharos during the 1950s) developed the concept of sets of short distances run quickly (in any set the recovery time between runs is minimal, with a longer rest between sets) to permit (unknowingly) a greater total FT Type IIb and FT Type IIa muscle fiber stimulus. Arthur Lydiard (coach of the 1960 Rome Olympic gold medalists Peter Snell [800m] and Murray Halberg [5,000m]) preached the initial development of a profound aerobic (endurance) base upon which to place faster running as well as emphasis on total body development. This included hill running to improve arm and shoulder action. A subsequent brief period of short-distance, fast-speed training permitted development of anaerobic stamina. Over the years, the pendulum seems to have swung between the extremes of speed emphasis and endurance emphasis. But there is often little logic to fashion, and such extremes lack a sensible rationale. As with arguments, once both sides have been presented, the best solution is often an incorporation of an appropriate mix of each.

Our view is that two elements have been missing from these various training systems. One needed element is an inclusion of training over a rather wide range of running paces all through the year, with continual and careful assessment of the extent to which adaptation occurs to paces slower and faster than the race pace. This ensures rapid identification of the liability aspects of performance—those aspects (aerobic or anaerobic) for which the athlete is less genetically gifted and for which a more careful developmental emphasis must be given. The other needed element is consideration of the running portion of an athlete's training as only one aspect of a program of total body conditioning. To ensure health maintenance and injury or staleness prevention requires that all facets contributing to performance adaptation—positive mental attitude, strength, speed, endurance, stamina, flexibility, and recovery—must be developed optimally. Our multi-tier training concept has attempted to incorporate these. We do not consider our system revolutionary or new because we have been using it for years. Recently published articles describing the views of well-established coaches of distance runners (Bondarchuk, 1988; Daniels, 1989; Vigil, 1987) and experts on periodization (Bompa, 1988; Freeman, 1989; McInnis, 1981) describe concepts that have certain similar features.

Our system for training athletes is holistic in that we realize that all parts of the system must be fully operational to ensure long-term success. Using an analogy to biological ecosystems, disruption of even a small facet of the ongoing order can bring profound decrements in performance because a harmonious interdependence of all systems provides the balance for system survival. So often this occurs when athletes deemphasize one aspect of development in favor of an excess of another. It is possible for athletes to be quite fit but not healthy—nonfunctional from a competitive point of view. They may be injured as a result of overtraining and left to languish in an ath-

letic purgatory while they recover. Being in excellent health sets the stage for becoming totally fit. Extraordinary fitness sets the stage for competitive excellence and is achieved only after complete adaptation to rigorous training.

Objective Evidence for the Value of Multi-Pace Training

It could be asked whether there is any objective evidence that a mixture of both aerobic and anaerobic (distance and speed) training is more effective at building an athlete for better racing performance than simply a steady diet of long-distance running. There is such evidence available, and to illustrate it is useful to review two particularly noteworthy studies presented at the Twelfth European Coaches Association annual meeting at Acoteias, Portugal, in 1983. Both were the work of Danish investigators.

One study was conducted by Henrik Larsen and Henning Bentzen from the August Krogh Institute at the University of Copenhagen. These scientists worked with a group of nine male athletes, each of whom had several years of experience in middle- and long-distance running. The first part of the study required that all nine athletes run an average of 100 km (62-1/2 mi) per week at a speed of between 60% and 80% of $\dot{V}O_2max$ (i.e., aerobically) for 26 weeks. After this period, a GXT was performed and a gastrocnemius muscle biopsy was obtained to assess physiological fitness prior to the next phase of the study. The GXT involved running against a steadily increasing work load to voluntary exhaustion to determine $\dot{V}O_2max$. These athletes were then divided into two groups. Five athletes reduced their total weekly running distance to 50 km (31-1/4 mi), but half of their training was made up of anaerobic efforts over a distance range of 60 to 1,000 m. This program was maintained for 14 weeks. The other four athletes continued their routine of 100 km/week for the 14-week period.

Following this training regimen, the same evaluative tests were repeated to assess possible changes in fitness characteristics. The anaerobically trained athletes averaged a 7% increase in $\dot{V}O_2max$ with a significant increase in maximum heart rate, whereas those with only aerobic training showed no change. Another evaluation involved two track races over distances of 1,000 m and 10,000 m. Those athletes with the anaerobic component added to their training improved an average of 4 sec in the 1,000m race, but the aerobically trained athletes showed no change. Neither group changed their 10,000m race performance times significantly, although the trend was for the 10,000m race times among the anaerobically trained athletes to improve.

Skeletal muscle biopsies were evaluated for biochemical changes that might better describe cellular adaptive specialization after training. None of the athletes had very many FT Type IIb fibers (specialized primarily for glycolytic [anaerobic] activity); most of the FT fibers were Type IIa (specialized for both glycolytic [anaerobic] and oxidative [aerobic] activity). The anaerobically trained runners increased the volume of their FT Type IIa fibers, however, suggesting an adaptive increase in anaerobic responsiveness.

In summary, this study by Larsen and Bentzen suggests that VO_2max can be improved better by a combination of aerobic and anaerobic training than by aerobic training alone. The greater the aerobic reserve, the more intense can be the levels of performance when anaerobic performance begins to supplement (lactate/ventilatory threshold) and when the aerobic limit (VO_2max) is reached. Because there is an anaerobic as well as an aerobic limit of work performance, it is optimal to train both, ensuring that aerobic capability is the highest possible at the time when performance requirements are greatest.

The second study was conducted by Thomas Okkels, also at the August Krogh Institute. Its purpose was to study the effectiveness of two intensities of anaerobic training upon performance. Again, a group of experienced runners (16) was subjected to an initial, manageable, extended aerobic training period averaging 90 to 120 km/week (54 to 72 mi/week) for between 16 and 20 weeks. Accompanying this was a mix of circuit training, hill running, and fartlek running to provide a well-rounded developmental stimulus. Then baseline physiological performance evaluations (GXT and muscle biopsy) were carried out before the group was divided into two subgroups for specialized anaerobic training.

The total weekly aerobic training for all 16 runners was then reduced from 90 to 120 km/week down to 60 to 90 km/week (36 to 54 mi/week), for a 7-week period. Seven runners scheduled 3 days/week of anaerobic capacity training (Okkels termed it "interval training," which is rather meaningless). These runners ran short-distance sessions (200m to 600m) at maximum or near-maximum intensity, with recovery limited to what would allow the runner to complete the session while still maintaining proper running form. The anaerobic capacity training aspects of such sessions were evidenced by capillary blood lactate concentrations of between 15 and 23 mM/L (135 and 207 mg/dl) after the final repetition. (These lactate values were not corrected for hemoconcentration and thus lose considerable value in helping to explain adaptive changes.) The other nine runners scheduled 3 days/week of what we would term aerobic capacity training—800m to 1,500m intervals done at a fast pace with recovery adequate to permit completion of the session with good running form. Blood lactate levels (uncorrected) following the final repetition were in the range of 10 to 11 mM/L (89 to 99 mg/dl).

Results of the treadmill GXT to voluntary exhaustion revealed a 4% increase in VO_2max among those athletes completing the anaerobic capacity training period but no change in VO_2max for those runners doing aerobic capacity training. An additional treadmill test was conducted to examine anaerobic performance; it was a short-duration all-out run at each athlete's maximum 800m speed, again to voluntary exhaustion. Both groups of runners improved their anaerobic performance abilities, as measured using this test, by increasing their treadmill run time about 15%. Following this anaerobic treadmill test, blood lactate values measured at 1 min and 4 min posttest were increased by an average of 14% among the runners trained with aerobic capacity training but were not changed significantly among the runners trained using anaerobic overload. This suggests that the sustained nature of the aerobic capacity training aspect seems better for improving anaerobic output capabilities than are short-term, high-intensity work bouts at an even higher (but shorter) anaerobic work load.

Muscle biopsy studies (again from the gastrocnemius muscle) included evaluation of enzyme profiles. Glycolytic enzyme activity increased between 11% and 22% in the runners who included aerobic capacity training, whereas it either did not change or actually decreased in those doing anaerobic capacity training. Okkels did not discuss the implications of these findings, but several practical suggestions seem appropriate. First, the value of anaerobic capacity training for its ability to stimulate maximum neuromuscular recruitment should not be forgotten, and this is likely a beneficial effect. It probably contributed to the increase in VO_2max seen in these subjects. However, the results described here suggest that anaerobic capacity training should not be overdone; if it is, the likely consequence is a diminution of glycolytic (anaerobic) performance potential. The cellular explanation for this may involve a combination of decreased available muscle carbohydrates as well as the inhibitory effects of extremely high acid levels on glycolysis itself.

These studies seem to confirm the scientific conclusions summarized in chapter 1 regarding the mobilization of skeletal muscle fibers. Higher intensity (faster paced) training will maintain a high level of adaptation in those fibers that are recruited only at higher work loads and may as well stimulate accumulation of more muscle protein. Both of these increase an athlete's strength capabilities, paving the way for increased speed and a decrease in perceived (and real) effort sense at given submaximum paces. Not including such higher intensity training thus deprives athletes of developing their full potential by promoting detraining in muscle fibers that are not activated.

USING VARIOUS MODALITIES SUCCESSFULLY IN MULTI-TIER TRAINING

The Many Aspects of Recovery

Five recovery periods are important in training: four physical, one mental. They can be identified as follows:

1. The recovery between intervals
2. The recovery between sets of intervals
3. The recovery between hard training days
4. The recovery required following injury or overtraining
5. The pause needed for mental refreshment

For two reasons, any good system of training must be flexible in its provision for recovery. First, we can never determine in advance exactly how much recovery time is optimal. Second, inadequate recovery carries with it a sizable injury risk, and this should be minimized. Just as challenging sessions have a critical purpose in providing an overload stimulus (putting the working muscles awash in lactates and initiating adaptive responses), so also the recovery period allows the adaptive regeneration to occur.

Recovery between intervals is related to the level of adaptation already achieved and should be only as long as required to permit performance of the next interval at the target pace. Thus, determining recovery time between intervals is important, because we desire a good performance from each interval. As a particular mesocycle or microcycle progresses, the combination of running time and recovery time changes in such a way that training intensity is increased. Interval times and recovery times must both be estimated carefully to bring steady adaptation without undue stress. Again using Seb Coe's earlier diaries as an example, sessions of 300m will change from an early macrocycle work load of 9 to 10 @ 41 to 42 sec with a 3-min recovery to a subsequent stimulus of 6 @ 38

sec with a 90-sec recovery, and finally to 8 @ 38 sec with a 45-sec recovery. The last 300 m are always done at maximum velocity.

Recovery between sets is not quite as critical in exact terms. It must be long enough to ensure that target paces are achieved during the next set, yet not so long that excessive physiological cool-down occurs or mental commitment is lost. In the early part of a macrocycle, it may not be possible to handle the pace required for these intervals without this periodic longer recovery between sets. Dividing intervals into sets (for example, 12×400 m into $3 \times 4 \times 400$ m) allows enough intervals at a brisk pace to provide a training stimulus for muscular strength and speed. Both recoveries (between sets and intervals) should be active, such as easy jogging, to maintain circulation through the milking action of skeletal muscles on blood vessels located within them.

Recovery between days of hard sessions is sometimes difficult to quantitate, but the concepts for assessment are simple enough. Any athlete who feels the aching tiredness in muscles and joints that follows a hard session, even during inactivity, knows without a doubt that recovery time is needed to rebuild muscle energy supplies and connective tissue integrity. This requirement applies to circuit/weight-room sessions as well as to all major running interval sessions at higher intensities. Variability among athletes and with training intensity will make it appropriate to set a hard/easy/hard day pattern, or hard/hard/easy, or hard/easy/easy, and so forth. Recovery days programmed into each microcycle thus permit the rearrangement of trainings within that microcycle so that no sessions are missed.

Coping with a mild injury or overtraining will be discussed more thoroughly in chapter 6. Should such an event occur, the healing processes of the body require considerable time and the results of recovery are typically excellent, but it is difficult to increase the rate at which recovery processes occur. Premature resumption of training in a manner that has the slightest chance of causing a relapse into an injured or overtrained state is unwise. When an athlete is faced with the need for downtime, the important question should not be, ''How quickly can I get back to training seriously again?'' but rather, ''How long should I remain away from serious training?'' The difference may appear subtle, but the emphasis is important. The recovery, not the training, is of greatest importance at this point.

A pause for mental refreshment can either be programmed into the training process or be inserted if it appears necessary. It can be very temporary, such as a day off from training, or it can be incorporated into an entire mesocycle in other ways. Athletic success comes only with great dedication and considerable sacrifice of many social pleasures. Thus, when possible, it is desirable to try to ensure an optimum mental attitude whenever possible in addition to a good physical environment. Depending on resources, several possibilities exist. Particularly for athletes living in a winter climate, moving to a warmer climate for an entire mesocycle can permit quality work in a mentally satisfying situation. Double Olympian Wendy Sly, one of our most talented female athletes, has used such a plan effectively for several years, combining a mesocycle of wintertime training in Florida with a judicious selection of indoor track or outdoor road races as periodic performance tests along the way. In the United States, where northern winters are even more severe than in Europe, athletes tend to migrate southward during the winter to Arizona, California, or Florida. We must be careful, however, to program the athlete's return to the home climate at a period when weather is tolerable. Coming back to winter weather can be dismal, particularly if it slows continued development or brings illness.

Choosing the Best Recovery Times

A question asked frequently by athletes once they have devised training paces is, "How much recovery should I require?" The simplest answer, of course, is enough to ensure that the athlete can complete each interval in the training session at the assigned pace while maintaining good form. In turn, this will be determined by the combined effect of the length of the assigned running interval, the weather (temperature and humidity), and the athlete's level of fitness. It makes little sense to begin the second or third or any subsequent run during an interval session in such a state of exhaustion that form cannot be maintained. Mental composure will probably disappear as well. Thus, recovery needs to be adequate to permit the maintenance of good form for the succeeding interval. For longer runs at a slower pace, this recovery will be considerably shorter than the length of time run. For very short intervals, a far longer time than that required to run the interval distance may be appropriate. Table 3.15 establishes a basis for estimating recovery times between running intervals expressed as fractions or multiples of the time spent running.

As can be seen from this table, required recovery time increases systematically as running intensity increases. Physiologically, this makes good sense. We should recall the three major aspects of development and potential adaptation that occur with running. There

Table 3.15 Estimation of Recovery Times Between Running Intervals

Loading	Running time (RT)	Recovery time	Recovery activity
Short speed (all-out) (anaerobic capacity training)	10 sec	3 × RT	Walking and/or stretching
	20 sec	3 × RT	Jogging
	30 sec		
Long speed (95%-100% of maximal effort) (anaerobic capacity training)	30 sec	3 × RT	Jogging
	60 sec	2 × RT	Jogging
	80 sec		
Speed + endurance (90%-95% of maximal effort) ($\dot{V}O_2$max to aerobic capacity training)	80 sec	2 × RT	Jogging
	2 min 40 sec	1 × RT	Rest
	3 min		
Endurance (80%-90% of maximal effort) (anaerobic conditioning)	3 min	1 × RT	Rest
	4 min	0.5 × RT	Rest
	20 min		

is neuromuscular recruitment: Increasing intensity of effort stimulates more and more motor units, bringing FT as well as ST motor units into action. Second, there is myocardial efficiency: Increasing ventricular chamber size produces an increased stroke volume and decreased heart rate at submaximum work loads. The increased volume of blood returning to the heart distends the ventricular chambers with each beat, eventually initiating their enlargement. Finally, there is a management of lactate dynamics: The anaerobic stimulus increases lactate production in skeletal muscles, which diffuses out into the blood. Its effects must be dealt with: Some tissues can use lactate as a fuel, but the accompanying H^+ ions also provide a direct stimulus to increase breathing. Tolerance to the discomfort of acidosis can be developed only through experience with it. As adaptation occurs, the stress of such training decreases, the distance at which the pace can be sustained increases, and the required recovery before the athlete can begin again decreases.

Determining the recovery time is only half the challenge, however. We need to identify the optimum run time, which serves as the basis for determining the recovery time. This is determined by distance; shorter distances can be run more quickly. We recommend a simple and fairly practical method to construct a plan for a fast-paced ($\dot{V}O_2$max or aerobic capacity training) session. We'll assume that the coach and athlete have made a rational decision about the interval distance to be run and the number of repetitions. We need to know the pace and the recovery. Take the athlete's best time for that distance and make it slower by 25%—that's the interval time. Then use Table 3.15 to determine recovery time.

For example, we have a female runner whose expertise is at the 3,000m. Her $\dot{V}O_2$max pace is at 5:21.8/mi (80 sec/400m), her personal best for 400 m is 63 sec, and she desires to do a session of 10 × 400 m at 100% of her $\dot{V}O_2$max. She should complete each run in 63 + (63 × 0.25) = 63 + 17.75 = 81 sec, with a recovery time of 80 × 2 = 160 sec = 2:40. As adaptation to this work load occurs, the run time should be shortened (i.e., the pace should be quickened) to the point where now the athlete's best time is increased by only 20% (this would be an anaerobic capacity training pace corresponding to 110% of $\dot{V}O_2$max unless $\dot{V}O_2$max also had increased). In our example, 63 + (63 × 0.20) = 72 sec, with a recovery time of 72 × 2 = 144 sec = 2:24. When a session like this is being done for the first time, plenty of coach/athlete feedback is essential to give an impression of just how well the athlete's assignment fits the formula. No formula fits all individuals with 100% satisfaction. If slightly more or less rest is appropriate, this information goes into the logbook and serves as the basis for implementation of the next session.

Whether we are working with high school–level athletes or world champions, the emphasis should be on quality work that at the same time is manageable. As performance quality improves, the pace required to maintain that quality will quicken, or the length of time at which that pace can be maintained will increase. For 5,000m/10,000m specialists the emphasis is initially on increasing·the length of repetitions as development occurs and decreasing the recovery time more than on increasing the tempo. With 800m/1,500m specialists, the emphasis is typically on decreasing the recovery time and increasing the tempo. Also remember when planning a session that it is a mistake to consider only the total distance run. At any given pace, the intensity of effort is not directly proportional to the distance run. Thus, 30 × 200 m at 32 sec is easier than 15 × 400 m at 64 sec, although the total distance is the same.

Fartlek

Fartlek is a Scandinavian term roughly translating as "speed-play." In the past, it was part of Sweden's military training, and it consists of runs over mixed terrain at varied paces. The Swedish coach Gosta Holmer applied this concept of "go-as-you-please" training to the development of distance runners. On first consideration, it sounds delightful. Training out in the forest, on wooded trails, and on back roads, runners who combined inventiveness, motivation, and self-discipline could run together or alone at varying paces initiated by arrival at some selected object (a telephone pole or large rock or tree). The constant pace-changing, varied terrain, and soft footing provide a good combination of safety and fitness development in the context of the natural beauty of the wilderness.

Though this may be a good training system for experienced athletes, younger and less experienced runners may require more structured assistance to achieve proper value from this style of training. Also, there is a risk of some problems if fartlek is carried out with a group of runners of mixed abilities. Some will push the pace and tire less quickly than others, leaving those less fit hanging on for dear life. For the tiring runners, this is not training; it is hell and a risk for injury, overtraining, and negative mental attitudes. Unless the coach of such a group is out on the course, he or she will most likely not learn who has profited well by the training and who has suffered until it is too late. We wonder whether the benefits of such an unstructured session outweigh the potential hazards.

A controlled version of fartlek training can be done on a golf course or in a park that has loops within earshot of a centrally placed coach. A grassy terrain with some hilly slopes and a quality running surface is really best. The athlete runs at an easy pace, according to individual fitness, ability, age, and so on, and takes an adequate 20- to 30-min warm-up. When the coach blows the whistle, the athlete immediately quickens pace to between 80% and 90% of maximum, continuing as fast as can be sustained until the next whistle blast.

There are both assets and liabilities to this kind of session. What are the assets? The athlete must respond to an outside signal and surge hard, not necessarily when ready but rather when required; in the context of racing, when a competitor makes a move. Also, the athlete will not know in advance when it will be okay to back off and recover; this will not be known in a race either. So the simulation to a racing environment is excellent.

Now, what are the liabilities? This kind of session is advisable only for coaches who are masters of restraint, who understand their athletes very well, and who are in complete control of their own egos. The athlete is strongly controlled by the coach in this situation. The training load must be adjusted closely to the athlete's fitness level. If long sprints with short recoveries are demanded, then the session cannot last very long. Whether short or long, fast runs are stressful and must be appropriate to the total training load of that microcycle. In other words, the coach must plan in advance what is intended for development rather than thoughtlessly blasting inappropriate training demands through capricious use of a commanding whistle. Such a session is also inappropriate for a group of runners of mixed abilities, because as the group strings out, some may be running too quickly up a hard hill whereas others may be dashing downhill even faster. Neither of these practices makes good developmental sense.

Hill Running

Three kinds of hill running are useful for distance runners. One is a series of gentle uphills and downhills as part of a road or cross-country distance run. Another is a series of runs up a long but manageable hill. The third is a speed session up a short steep hill. Not only does hill running increase the stress at any given pace due to the increased work necessary to counter the elevation change, but it also requires the use of arms, legs, and trunk musculature in ways that are different than in level running. This different style is beneficial for improved racing abilities. When running hilly long-distance courses, it is most beneficial to run steadily on the flat portion and vigorously up the hill. This optimizes the benefits of including the hills in that particular training session. The vigorous arm, shoulder, and trunk muscle activation from hill running just cannot be duplicated on flat surfaces. It closely mimics the muscular activity that occurs when a runner changes pace suddenly; thus, hill running is akin to an exaggerated pace-change session.

The downhills can serve as a respite for the cardiopulmonary system from the more vigorous flat and uphill portions of the run. The downhill portions should be treated with respect, however, for two reasons. First, the eccentric loading of muscles that occurs with such training activates fewer motor units at any given pace, placing more stress on those that are activated. Second, there is a greater impact force on the hip and knee joints due to increased gravitational loading. Few runners have the luxury of a chauffeur accompanying them out on a long run, but it would actually be ideal if the runner could have a ride to the bottom of long, steep downhill portions of road training courses. Seb Coe did get such attention during his first 5 years of running. Training in the mountainous, sparsely populated Yorkshire countryside likely contributed to his longevity in the sport. His father followed behind him in the family car, letting him jump in at the crest of high plateaus for a quick lift to the bottom where he would resume his run.

Attacking hills during a long run provides a constantly recurring challenge. Each hill is a fresh obstacle to be overcome, testing an athlete's resolve and building mental toughness. Distance racing requires a similar resolve to counter other runners' attempts to break away from the field. In road and cross-country races some competitors will make a strong surge forward specifically at a hill to initiate the break. Hill training thus is a simulator for conditioning the mind and the body in a specific and practical manner. Of course, not all distance runs should be on hilly courses run in the manner described. A session emphasizing hill running is just that: a specific kind of training stimulus to be used judiciously.

Long repetitions run up hills of around 800m to 1,000m done at a level anaerobic conditioning pace may be equivalent physiologically to aerobic capacity interval runs due to the added stress of the incline. The gradient of such hills ought to be in the neighborhood of 1 in 14 (7%, or 4 degrees). This is an excellent means for improving both aerobic and anaerobic power. However, unlike a track run, where it is relatively easy to jog back to the start and keep the rest as small as appropriate, a long run up an incline may require a jog back that provides too much recovery. The ideal, of course, would be a rising but mildly curving path that then continues back to the start. With a little searching, such courses can often be located.

Longer hill runs are even more useful (i.e., challenging) when there are slight changes of gradient along the way—one or two short level sections or a slight dip. Neither the dip nor the level stretches should be used to snatch a brief respite. Instead, the athlete should maintain running effort, allowing these places to be for acceleration. Again, the change of pace and the lack of regular rhythm are excellent race simulations performed under difficult conditions. If this is done well, the specific adaptations, both mental and physical, will be useful.

Seb Coe has for years run on a traffic-free cycle path, that includes a challenging 800m section. After a steady 400m climb, it levels off for another 100 m only to climb still more steeply for another 250 m, finishing with 50 m slightly downhill. When preceded by a 3-mi warm-up and followed by a 2-mi cooldown, six to eight laps on this course completes a major workout for the day, one that is finished relatively quickly and that challenges many aspects of competitive running in a very specific manner. Figure 3.8 shows another of Seb's favorite hills, very steep and only 180 m long, but with a varying gradient. Every serious distance runner should have one of these courses designed for use when a hill session comes due on the schedule.

Short hill sessions run very quickly need require only about 100m of hill; a gradient of about 1 in 6 (17%, 9.6 degrees) is ideal. The short jog-back recoveries make these runs predominantly anaerobic. An exaggerated running style is required to maximize speed, as this spreads the energy requirement to large muscle groups other than the legs. Once again, the vigorous arm action, a quick and powerful knee lift by action of the hip flexors, and the powerful toe-off from each driving leg are all important elements for sudden dramatic pace changing and for continued

Figure 3.8 Illustration of a smooth-surface, traffic-free, aesthetically pleasing, somewhat steep 180 m long hill suitable for running lactate/ventilatory threshold and $\dot{V}O_2$max sessions. The river Thames is in the background.

dash-to-the-finish long sprinting. Figure 3.9 depicts a steep slope together with a suggested program to build gradually an ability to do many repetitions. It isn't wise to run up such hills aiming for specific transit times. Although these times may be kept for reference, the real reason for this kind of training is to build powerful and controllable (and therefore wondrous to behold!) hill-running ability. Excellent form

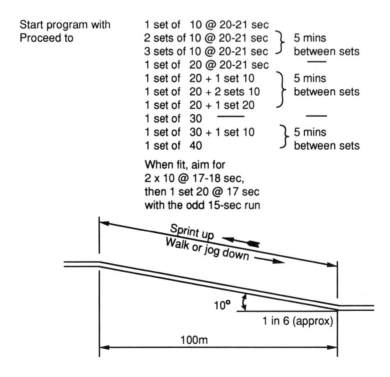

Figure 3.9 Suggested model for developing a hill running program.

should always be the watchword; achievement of specific paces is secondary.

Learning to Accelerate

How can an athlete develop the ability to tolerate a steadily increasing running pace—gradual acceleration? All athletes realize that the finale of races is run faster than the earlier portions; this is achieved through an additional increase in anaerobic energy output added to that already being provided by aerobic and some anaerobic energy sources. Also, with the end of the race near, it isn't as necessary to keep anaerobic energy production at a minimum for preservation of good racing form. Those runners who have such a large aerobic potential that they have incurred minimum anaerobic accumulation up to the moment of this pace increase will have an edge over their opponents who aren't so well endowed. But those who can mentally tolerate the stress of anaerobic accumulation will have an edge as well over those who are not as well prepared. Once again, the interaction of speed and endurance sets the stage for racing to win.

Two types of shorter-distance interval sessions will help build the ability to accelerate during races. Figures 3.10 and 3.11 present the pace systems for permitting this. We have drawn lines through both figures to provide a specific illustration. The example shown is for a male runner wanting to run 1,500m in 3:45 (approximately a 4:01 mile). We will also characterize him as more of a 400m/800m specialist,

with a fast 400m time but somewhat short on stamina. It is stamina that we desire to improve. The first session involves running a series of steadily *lengthening* distances, each at a slightly *faster* pace. Recovery time *increases* because it involves a return to the start over the distance run. As illustrated in Figure 3.10, we begin with a 100m interval and increase each repetition by 10m, the final interval being for 200 m. Each interval is followed by a jogged recovery at the distance just run.

The time for his first (100m) interval is 15 sec, which is at the race pace (60 sec/400 m) of his target 1,500m race time. The pace for his final (200m) interval is that of his best 400m time (47 sec), thus giving him 23.5 sec for his 200m distance. The next task is to determine the increase in time required for each successive intermediate interval. There will be 11 intervals of running but only 10 increases in distance. Thus, we need to determine the difference between the 100m and 200m interval times and divide this by 10. This will give us the time increment by which each interval should be lengthened. Thus, 23.5 sec − 15 sec = 8.5 sec/10 = 0.85 sec. Using this increment, the 110m interval will be covered in 15.0 + 0.85 = 15.85 sec, the 120m interval in 15.8 + 0.85 = 16.70 sec, and so forth.

The pace session illustrated in Figure 3.11 is more difficult and should be begun only when the session in Figure 3.10 has been practiced and mastered. Here the first interval is 200 m, increasing to 300 m in increments of 20. We use the same starting and finishing

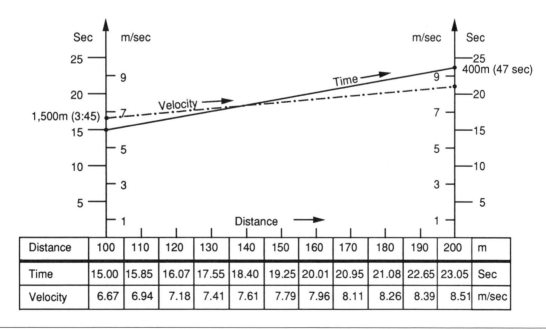

Distance	100	110	120	130	140	150	160	170	180	190	200	m
Time	15.00	15.85	16.07	17.55	18.40	19.25	20.01	20.95	21.08	22.65	23.05	Sec
Velocity	6.67	6.94	7.18	7.41	7.61	7.79	7.96	8.11	8.26	8.39	8.51	m/sec

Figure 3.10 Plan for systematic increase of velocity and distance for a session of 11 repetitions run from 100 m to 200 m. Total distance run is 1,650 m (recovery period is a walk straight back to the start).

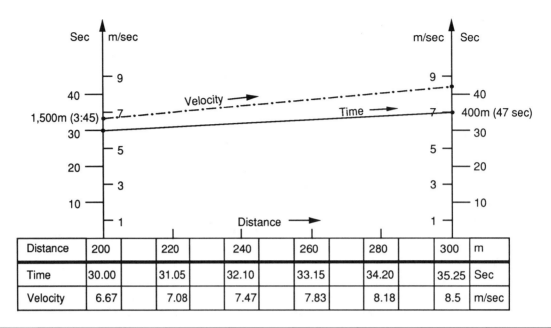

Distance	200		220		240		260		280		300	m
Time	30.00		31.05		32.10		33.15		34.20		35.25	Sec
Velocity	6.67		7.08		7.47		7.83		8.18		8.5	m/sec

Figure 3.11 Plan for systematic increase of velocity and distance for a session of six repetitions run from 200 m to 300 m. Total distance run is 1,500 m, with recovery starting at a 3-min walk and reducing with development.

paces as before because this is the same runner doing the training. Thus, his 200m interval will be at his 1,500m pace (30 sec), and his 300m interval will be at a 47 sec/400m pace (35.25 sec). There are five pace increases and six intervals. We can calculate the required time increase for each increment as the following: 35.25 sec − 30 sec = 5.25 sec/5 = 1.05 sec. Thus, the 220m interval will be covered in 31.05 sec, the 240m interval in 32.10 sec, and so forth.

The second type of repetition running also involves an increase in pace with an increase in distance, but now the recovery time is reduced. Again, mastery of the sessions described previously is essential before the athlete moves on to this session. Here, we use the data calculated from Figure 3.11. Our runner will start at the 200m mark and finish at the 400m track finish line. He then will jog or walk around the track to the 200m mark, which will remain the starting point for each successive interval. The second interval, however, will finish 20 m beyond the track finish line, giving him 20 m less recovery distance (and an appropriately reduced recovery rest) until the starting point for running is again reached. By the end of this session, athletes will have just completed a fast 280 m and will have a recovery distance of only 120 m before beginning again! To prevent this session from becoming too frustrating to complete initially, athletes may prefer to lengthen the recovery—slow down the jog or walk. Athletes should make notes in their logbooks about what they found difficult and when they first noticed improvement. The object is to improve speed and speed endurance, not bring undue

duress in the athlete's development. Again, always err initially on the side of doing such sessions too slowly, so as to identify what can be managed, rather than beginning initially with a session so difficult that the athlete is floundering.

Speed Drills

Fast running is vastly different from easy aerobic distance running. Running stride is lengthened. Arm and shoulder action contribute more to the act of producing forward movement instead of primarily maintaining balance. All the various skeletal muscle motor units are now active—FT as well as ST. An athlete must develop tolerance to the discomfort of such stress, and this discomfort cannot be allowed to hinder the athlete's desire to perform.

There is a paradox in learning how to cope with speed. Consolidation of all the various facets that permit fast running—biomechanical, biochemical, and physiological—is required, and this can be achieved only through a large number of running repetitions. But this brings fatigue, a state in which the ability to tolerate the repetitions—and thus to learn— deteriorates rapidly. In such a state an athlete tends to replace correct technique with poorer technique, including the use of assisting muscle groups. Resolving this paradox requires the development of sufficient general conditioning and total body fitness during the earlier mesocycles so that the anaerobic and neurological challenge provided by the speed stimulus can be managed effectively. Once the techniques of speed running have been mastered, there is all the more reason for runners to include such work throughout their training macrocycle, with appropriate pace management.

Several drills to enhance speed development can be incorporated judiciously into the training plan, particularly during the later mesocycles (X_4 and X_5). One of these drills emphasizes rapid knee flexions and can be done during the warm-up period. We mentioned in chapter 1 the term heel flick, where the heel nearly touches the buttock during the rapid forward-swing phase of the running stride. During the warm-up period, in a series of rapid short steps, initially every third or fourth step can include a smoothly executed high heel flick. Gradual reduction of steps between high heel flicks, ending with a brief sequence of continuous running with a high flick of each heel, permits an easy and gradual transition into a sense of lower limb quickness, even though the forward speed is quite slow.

A second speed drill emphasizes hip flexions using a sequence of from 10 to 20 high knee lifts. Good iliopsoas muscle strength and endurance is important for these exercises. Forward movement again is quite slow, and arms must be moved vigorously through a wide range of motion. Elbows should be unlocked from their typical 90-degree position. A coaching suggestion is that the knees should lift as high as if they were en route to touching the chest. This is essentially an exaggeration of sprinting style, but the slow forward movement adds considerably more vertical oscillation (bounce). Plenty of recovery time should occur between each set to minimize mental and physical fatigue; these exercises are energy costly and demand concentration if they are to be done well.

Short accelerations are another effective speed drill. Figure 3.12 shows a series of seven markers placed at 30m intervals in a zigzag pattern. Beginning at Point A, six sprint accelerations are made, with five 90-degree turns around the outside of each marker. Being forced to slow down to negotiate these turns without stopping requires the athlete to develop a combination of agility and acceleration/deceleration skills.

Another short acceleration drill consists of 30m to 50m straight intervals beginning with a standing start three paces back from the sprint start line on a standard track. Crouch starts should not be used, as they represent an unnecessary risk for middle- and long-distance runners. These are anaerobic sessions, and thus the interval distance is purposely short. Middle-distance runners tend toward the shorter sprint accelerations (30 m), emphasizing quickness. Long-distance runners can opt for the longer distance (50 m), running not quite so quickly but still at high intensity to acquire an equivalent training stimulus. The tendency

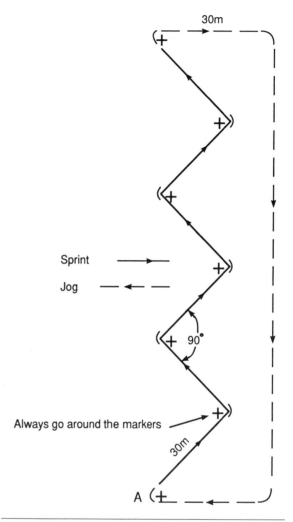

Figure 3.12 Suggested course layout to permit 30m zigzag sprint accelerations as a speed drill. **A** is the starting point.

for most athletes is to take inadequate recovery, which brings premature fatigue. Unhurried walking recoveries ensure the fastest possible runs.

These straight acceleration drills are best done in sets of three or four runs, each set at increasing pace. An example would be the following, written in coaches' shorthand, which by now should be familiar:

4 × 30 m (85% max intensity); 2 min rec between intervals

5 min rec before the next set

4 × 30 m (90% max intensity); 2 min rec between intervals

5 min rec before the next set

4 × 30 m (95% max intensity); 2 min rec between intervals

5 min rec before the next set

4 × 30 m (100% max intensity)

When an athlete is training for maximum speed development, the demands of each running interval require that the recovery time between them be lengthened if pace and intensity are to be maintained. A better method is to reduce the length of each interval, keeping the intensity and recovery time the same. Two examples using a series of four fixed-distance intervals at 95% maximum intensity follow:

150 m, 120 m, 90 m, 60 m, with 3 min walked recovery

120 m, 100 m, 80 m, 60 m, with 2-1/2 min walked recovery

Some perspective is appropriate here, particularly for the longer-distance people contemplating such short-distance work. First, athletes specializing in the 5,000m and longer will discover that such nearly all-out sprinting is very fatiguing when practiced hard for the first time. As always with specific training, the maxim is to run easy at first, become familiar with and adapted to the stress, and then raise the tempo as appropriate. The faster an individual's maximum sustainable pace for even relatively short distances, the higher will be his or her sustainable submaximum longer paces. Primarily this is due to improved neurological recruitment abilities.

Second, preceding such speed drills with plenty of warm-up and flexibility exercises and following them with a cool-down, stretching session, and massage are all essential parts of this high-level training process. Third, these sessions are not intended as a one- or two-time event done the week before an important race. These sessions can begin to be inserted near the end of mesocycle X_4 and on into mesocycle X_5, done initially at the lower intensities and with fewer total repetitions and progressing through the remainder of the macrocycle to provide a firmly developed speed stimulus. The end result will be the athlete's unusually fine ability to suddenly surge forward for several strides during a race at a point when such tactics are essential for positioning. Examples of where this is appropriate will be provided in chapter 5.

Pace Judgment

Very simply, there are two kinds of pace. One is maximum, all-out, as fast as one can run. A runner requires no judgment to realize that he or she cannot run any more quickly. The second is submaximum, which encompasses all the other possible paces. The runner's judgment of submaximum pace can be altered by everything from fatigue or level of freshness to environmental temperature and humidity. Even a breeze—not a strong wind—can confuse judgment because it changes the effort required to maintain a given pace. Daylight versus nighttime illumination also affects pace judgment. A car being driven at night seems to be moving more quickly than in daylight even though the two velocities may be the same. This is because a person's limit of vision is closer at night from poorer illumination. Similarly in running, when nighttime track meets are held under artificial light, pace sense is altered so that runners seem to be running more quickly than they actually are.

Pace sense to an extent is a gift; that is, even with practice, some 5,000m or 10,000m runners find it difficult to maintain pace consistency when fresh or tired, in warm weather or cool. Others do it with seeming ease. When the pace is increased in a race, however, a runner needs a well-developed ability to realize functionally the size of the change. For example, a runner who increases the pace and takes the lead with the intention of breaking the field may estimate that it will take four laps at this pace to do so. If this estimate turns out to be wrong (with several athletes still alongside), the confidence of knowing that sustaining this pace for a little longer should be adequate to achieve the purpose will prevent him or her from increasing the pace again, out of panic, to a level that may be unsustainable. Thus, pace sense and pace change are two valuable elements in a runner's racing armamentarium. Both need to be honed through practice.

How can pace practice be included in training? If training routes have one or more sections accurately measured as one kilometer or one mile, pace can be checked easily against a watch worn during the run. Also, if the course involves the same route up to that particular measured segment, cumulative time can be estimated and compared to previous runs. Pace sensing should not need incessant attention, because it isn't useful to have each training session serve as an intense cross-examination of pace detection abilities. A microcycle is a long period of time, and a few pace checks each week will provide plenty of practice. Keith Brantly includes a 400m track as part of his running routes through the city of Gainesville, Florida. Easy access to the track and the ability to still maintain his training pace permits a hassle-free means of accurate pace assessment and mentally divides his longer distance runs into shorter segments.

Maintaining a sense of constant pace under changing track conditions can be developed by mixed-distance VO_2max pace runs done with different accompanying runners who are entering the workout in various degrees of freshness. One of Seb Coe's favorite summertime track challenges included careful lap-time recording during a (2 × 1,200 m) + (1 × 800 m) + (2 × 400 m) session, with various other club runners coming in alongside to accompany him. As an example, if his VO_2max pace was 4:12/mi, his goal paces would be 3:08 for 1,200 m, 2:05 for 800 m, and 62.6 sec for 400 m. As each lap is run, deviations from the prescribed intended pace can be determined. Maintaining pace when tired and not speeding up when fresh runners begin is an essential part of learning, ensuring, and refreshing pace judgment.

Can race-pace practice be included in training? The answer is a very definite yes, although we have thus far been suggesting that intervals of less than race distance ought to be done faster than at race pace, whereas intervals longer than race distance ought to be done slower than at race pace. One example of the use of race-pace training includes what we call incremental race-distance running. In our experience, we believe that many more women could get under the 2-min barrier for 800 m if they used this kind of training. A simple series of training sessions over several weeks might include the following to get them there:

Stage 1. Run 8 ×100 m in 14.75 sec, with a 30 sec recovery between each interval, remaining at this level until each 100m interval can be run consistently at this pace.

Stage 2. Repeat with slightly reduced recovery times, staying again at each training intensity level until the pace is perfectly identified.

Stage 3. Repeat Stage 2, using four 200m runs, with ever-shortening recovery times until a nonstop 800 m is recorded.

Training at actual race pace and also over the race distance can best be done by athletes specializing in the shorter events. During most of his youth and even afterward, Seb Coe used an undulating valley road as a test course. On this road, observed by his coach from a following car, Seb would run 6 to 8 × 800m runs with short recoveries (as short as 1-1/2 minutes), all at his 800m race pace. Apart from undergoing very tough anaerobic work, Seb was learning to judge race pace when he was both fresh and very tired, and not over limited distances but over his full race distance. Pace judgment at all levels of fatigue is an important sense to be developed.

Changing Pace

In any race longer than 400 m, the ability to initiate a change of pace is very important. It must be done properly to be effective. Changing pace is different from sprinting and puts different demands on a runner. It is not initiated from a stationary start but occurs as a sequel to an already rather fast pace. Because it is a tactical maneuver, it may be called upon more than once and not always for the same reason. Pace changing can and should be learned and practiced during training.

Three kinds of pace changes are used in racing. One is termed a *gradual*, or *economical*, change of pace. It is most frequently used in races from the 3,000m through the marathon and occurs during the bulk of the race; that is, not during the final few laps (when other kinds of pace changing occur). This is simply a firm and steady, but not necessarily rapid, increase in the pace, which typically will split the field or open up a gap from the entire field. It can usually be achieved simply by a slight increase in stride length with no change in running cadence. Emphasis is on maintaining form and relaxation. The smoother and more steadily this is achieved, the more economical it is on energy reserves. It can be practiced in training during longer interval runs, such as 1,000 m to 3,000 m. Split times are recorded every 200 m or 300 m to determine the rate of the pace increase. The athlete is typically instructed to begin a steady increase in pace approximately midway through the interval until a subsequent signal, at which time running remains at that assigned pace. Too rapid a change will bring exhaustion because there is considerable distance yet to be covered. The purpose of this kind of training is to teach sensible pace increase as well as the ability to maintain good form despite steadily more challenging circumstances.

Another kind of pace changing is called *intermittent*. Varying amounts of acceleration will be required, but the effort is submaximal and quite brief. It may be repeated during a race, and its effects should not affect the athlete's ability to maintain the ongoing race pace because there isn't sufficient anaerobic buildup to impair performance. One good example of the need for such pace changing occurs in the 800m and 1,500m races when it becomes appropriate for the runner to remedy a poor race position. The runner may find it useful to accelerate quickly and pass three or four runners to reach a desired location. In this instance, it is most efficient for the runner to increase cadence fairly quickly but maintain stride length. One method for developing this ability is for a group of four or five runners of similar abilities to run at a 5,000m or 10,000m race pace for a long-interval track run of 2,000 m to 3,000 m. As the runners stay in single file, at each 200m mark the rearmost runner quickly accelerates to take the lead and then slows to the group pace. Thus, if five runners are doing this session, every 1,000 m would see an acceleration by each of the runners moving into the lead.

The third change of pace is used only once, near the end of a race, and is termed a *sprint acceleration*. When making a final assault on the finish line, the athlete's effort must be total and the effect instantaneous. This is an important strategy in the sport of cycling and can win running races as well. For runners, the key to success in sprint accelerations is to quicken the cadence. Arm swing depends on cadence, and as cadence quickens, the arms will naturally come up into their full sprinting-cycle carriage to provide the increased upper-body accompaniment to the higher knee lift and pronounced toe-off. As soon as maximum cadence is achieved, stride is again lengthened for maximum velocity. All of this is done smoothly and quickly. In a race the runner typically begins this final effort from one of two places. One is from the end of the back straight, so the runner can obtain the lead and be able to fight off anyone attacking around the bend. This will ensure unobstructed running toward the finish. The second is the final kick at the start of the finishing straight as the runner is leaving the bend, for a late short drive to the tape. In chapter 5 we will use these principles in suggesting strategies for specific event racing.

In these two attacks, the runner is either entering or leaving a curve. To provide practice for this in training, bend running is essential, but it is important that athletes include this practice only when they are relatively fresh. Thus it is best for them to run individual laps beginning at the start/finish line, using the first bend and the back straight to build into a pace about 90% of maximum 400m speed. For into-the-bend practice, at about 250 m out from the finish, an acceleration signaled by a hand clap, shout, or whistle brings the runner into the back turn at full effort, which is sustained until he or she is at least halfway around the bend. In an actual racing situation, this may be required when the pace must be maintained in a field still bunched together with about 200 m remaining to the finish. Thus, in some practice runs, it is wise to include an occasional maximum effort actually maintained to the end.

For out-of-bend practice, acceleration to near-maximum running pace need not be achieved until the runner is about 150 m from the finish. Then the pace can be maintained or even increased slightly through the bend until he or she reaches the finishing straight. From a point between 80 m and 100 m from the finish, the final do-or-die kick is launched. As can be imagined, it is not the quantity of these bend-run repeats that improves racing effectiveness as much as it is the preservation of excellent running

form and learning the technique of sudden pace change. A few such repetitions can provide an effective learning stimulus.

Therapeutic Runs

At times all runners begin to develop thoughts that they may not or cannot run well in an upcoming competition. Their attitude seems more negative than positive, and they often complain of tiredness or fatigue. The coach should not dismiss these feelings, because as we shall learn in chapter 6, some of these emotions may indeed be suggestive of overtraining. Loss of vigor and the will to win often go hand in hand with excessive fatigue. The coach, in a supportive role, should on one hand offer positive words of comfort directed toward reviewing the good aspects of the athlete's recent development but on the other attempt to elicit objective reasons as to why the feelings of doubt exist (is it fear of a particular competitor, real symptoms of overtraining, or rumors of what a competitor has been doing during training?). At such moments the runner can benefit from a brief respite from hard work and also by some positive physical evidence that indeed running can be enjoyable and can be done quickly and easily.

One approach to this problem is to find a suitable training course, preferably one that is very slightly downhill, the distance of which is compatible with training for the forthcoming race, and, even better, with a slight prevailing wind in the running direction. The athlete's task is to run the course, not hard but quickly. It will be easy to do and not exhausting. The athlete should preferably run it alone, moving at a pace that feels satisfying. At the end the athlete's feeling of strength and well-being and the ability to have good turnover should put to rest any doubts about being competent to perform. Of course, if the athlete attempts such a run and barely finishes it, this may indeed be good evidence of developing overtraining or a bout of the flu or a head cold. This objective evidence may then allow a better informed decision about perhaps canceling the upcoming race.

Sixteen years ago Seb Coe found himself in just such an unhappy situation, wondering whether he was really ready for a scheduled competition. A run that met the previously described criteria was selected; it was just outside and high above the city of Sheffield (in a spot called Moscar Top). From this point the road gently descended toward the city, with exhilarating views. With a brisk swinging stride, Seb covered those 5 miles quickly and easily, feeling very fresh at the finish. He slept that evening with his doubts and fears far up on the moors where they belonged.

Long after having figured out the reasoning behind this rather sly coaching tactic, Seb still found that such a run had almost a magic "battery-recharging" effect. And far more than once since, when the moment has been ripe, either Seb or his coach would query the other with, "How about going out for a therapeutic?"

Anthony Sandoval had such a run in Los Alamos, New Mexico, often done in the middle of hard training weeks during the X_1 and X_2 mesocycles when he was preparing for the USA Olympic marathon trials of 1980 and 1984. (He won the trials in 1980, was sixth in 1984, and fourth in 1976, and his personal best for a loop marathon course stands at 2:10:20). It's a 10-mile jaunt down Bandelier Canyon. After a short jog into the forest outside the city and onto a narrow trail, a sharp switchback descent of several hundred feet down into the bottom of the canyon put Anthony into a world of his own. Paralleling a rushing stream that flows through the canyon, a scarcely used hiking trail of packed dirt provided a steady downhill run. The noise of the bubbling water as well as its cool spray, the green ferns and other lush vegetation along the way, and the incredible ease of dashing along miles of trail at a 6:00/mi pace with scarcely elevated breathing allowed Anthony's love of running to return undiminished. Of course, a breakfast of fresh blueberry muffins and juice brought by his wife and a few hugs from his children who drove to the mouth of the canyon to pick him up completed the picture of a runner in tune with his environment. That's a therapeutic!

KEEPING A TRAINING DIARY

Considerable emphasis in this chapter has been on the necessity of planning and managing an athlete's career. It is impossible to do this effectively without the proper records needed to assess, in long-term perspective, the results of training. Very often yesterday's comments point to the answers for today's and tomorrow's questions. A good training log forms a unique educational base from which it often becomes extremely obvious what needs yet to be done, or how what is being done is affecting performance (whether positively or negatively). Winston Churchill once remarked that people "occasionally stumble over the truth, but most of them pick themselves up and hurry off as if nothing had happened." A good log makes it more difficult to stumble without realizing what caused it and easier to identify how the truth can be achieved without falling at all.

We have seen many printed examples of training logs and diaries; they are for sale seemingly every-

where. And we have devoted countless hours to poring over the training logs of the runners with whom we have worked closely. It is interesting how the two seem to differ. Relatively few elite runners with whom we have worked use these fine-looking but ever-so-regimented formats. There is so much diversity in training details that no real regimented format is possible. Specifics of track sessions, unique and novel names given to specific running routes, mental notes about the effort sense of a session, details of weather or daily activities that may have added frustration or spirit to the training, and much more all have varying importance on different days. The staunchly independent and free-spirited mental framework of most runners demands that the simplest, most adaptable system be the basis for noting the appropriate details that make each training day unique and noteworthy.

We have urged our athletes to document some details precisely on a consistent basis. For interval sessions, include the sets, the repetitions, the recovery times, the distances run, the feelings of perceived exertion, and the nuances that gave bother or pleasure at the moment. For aerobic conditioning (longer runs), include the time and distance and an indicator of effort sense (with an established communicated agreement that such terms as "easy," "steady," and "hard" have rough physiological equivalents; e.g., a heart rate of roughly 135, 145, and >160 beats/min). Physiological observations such as morning heart rate, hours of sleep, weight measured at a meaningful time (for repeatability), and aches and pains ought to be recorded, but not in such day-to-day, regimented fashion that it becomes a drudge. Finally, comments after the day's training to give a perspective for ease of recovery, lasting fatigue, findings after massage, and so on can be very useful to provide a sense for developing fatigue or malaise that ought to be corrected by inserting a few days of rest. Essays need not be written; shorter, almost cryptic but still understandable comments make it much more likely that the athlete will maintain a daily record-keeping routine. Table 3.16 suggests a format for such a training log. Notice that the space provided for each section is purposely small, to emphasize thoughtful, succinct, specific comments that stimulate all the recall necessary to put that day's training into conversational form for discussion.

A similar format needs implementation for competitions or time trials. Several important considerations need recording. First, record the specific details, including split times if possible. Second, was preparation okay? What could have been done to prepare better? Or did everything go well according to plan? Third, what were the immediate primary impressions about the competition and the entire experience? So often athletes write very little if they performed well; their thoughts are on celebrating. And similarly if they raced poorly, they would prefer to forget the whole thing. Such emotional responses may be understandable, but still an objective postmortem assessment of the event is of inestimable value. First thoughts and impressions, honestly written, can be very useful later on in helping to recall the entire event in a more reasoned light. Table 3.16 also gives a suggested race summary format, again with most space devoted to room for short, cryptic, but capturing commentary that lays bare the essentials of that important moment.

Table 3.16   A Sample Training Summary

Date _____ Total distance run _____

Morning pulse _____ Sleep _____ Weight _____

Morning session:

Description _____

_____

_____

Afternoon session:

Description _____

_____

_____

Comments:

_____

_____

Items:

Course
sets
reps
Tempo
Recovery
Conditions
Perceived exertion
Nuances

Competitions/Time Trials

Date _____ Event _____

Distance _____ Time _____

Splits _____

Notes on final preparation: _____

_____

Notes on the race: _____

_____

Notes for the future: _____

_____

SUMMARY

1. Hard work over a long period of time is the primary route to developing athletic performance potential. The art of coaching is to identify the smallest amount of the most specific work needed to ensure continual upward progress in performance ability. All other training is overtraining and risks injury, excessive fatigue, or the problems of staleness. There is also a science to coaching in that it is now well known that the body responds to the stress

of training in specific ways, with either physiological adaptation that brings performance improvement or pathological deterioration that precipitates illness or injury.

2. The training process has a stimulus and a response. The response is physiological breakdown caused by the work done and the body's adaptation during the rest period following recovery. Unless there is recovery, there is no chance even for performance restitution, let alone performance improvement. Thus, regenerative rest is absolutely essential to the training process. Good nutrition, fluid replacement, adequate sleep, use of recuperative modalities such as warm and cold baths and massage, and enjoyment of activities that contribute to the wholeness of life beyond simply being a runner are all important.

3. Both coaches and athletes must have goals, short-term and long-term. With goals, training plans can be easily designed. With no goals, no plans make sense. Periodization is the term given to this reasoned division of a training season (macrocycle) into long time blocks (mesocycles), which have a broad focus of improvement, and short time blocks (microcycles), which contain daily training assignments for specific development.

4. All training sessions should be performed with a desire for perfection, pride in achievement, variety, and purpose. Every training session should end with the athlete being capable of doing more. If there is ever a question of whether to do more, do less. And keep good records, realizing that although no training program can be utilized exactly more than once, knowledge gained from progress and development during one season can serve as fine-tuning for more effective improvement during a subsequent season.

5. The primary goals of training are to improve strength (muscular force capacity), speed or power (quick mobilization of strength), stamina (management of speed for sizable periods of time), and endurance (long-term resistance to submaximum effort fatigue). Training sessions involving running consist of a given distance traversed (that's the volume, or interval) a specific number of times (the frequency, or repetitions) at a specific pace (the intensity, or tempo). If there is more than one repetition, there is a specific recovery period (the density, or rest).

6. Any training program must reflect an athlete's beginning fitness level. The athlete must take the time to recover completely from the previous training and competition season—both physically and mentally—and then begin again reasonably, realizing that all good things take time. Athletic excellence requires months of steady and proper preparation, when the body's homeostatic processes adapt at their own rate. For this reason, it is preferable to train around individual excellence and needs. Particularly with more challenging training sessions, work load tolerance too often is specific only to a few individuals; for the others it is too fast or too slow. In a race one must go it alone, and training itself is a good place to become callous to the challenge of high-level performance.

7. The running portion of training can be divided into four performance intensity zones, named for the predominant physiological benefit resulting from a manageable training session in each. The running pace in each zone is based on a percentage of the pace at which one reaches maximum O_2 consumption ($\dot{V}O_2$max pace). This pace can be determined easily using results obtained from treadmill testing or from a track time trial (given that 100% $\dot{V}O_2$max pace can be maintained for 10 to 12 minutes). Aerobic conditioning involves conversational-pace longer-distance runs and forms the bulk of the volume of most distance runners' training. Anaerobic conditioning consists of comfortably hard distance runs from 15 to 25 minutes at approximately lactate/ventilatory threshold pace. Aerobic capacity training consists of shorter-distance intervals of running done essentially at 5,000m to half-marathon race pace. Anaerobic capacity training involves even shorter intervals at faster-than-5,000m race pace. As the intensity of running increases, so does the amount of recovery rest required between intervals, although improving fitness can tend to reduce the time needed.

8. Important physiological adaptations occur with such training: increased blood volume, larger ventricular chambers, more stored fuels in muscle cells, increased enzyme capability in muscle cells for metabolizing fuel, increased effectiveness of the nervous system

in recruiting more muscle fibers, stronger muscles, and increased tolerance of supporting connective tissues to the chronic impact stress of thousands of miles or kilometers of running each year. A carefully designed plan of development, where the training load is regulated to ensure steady improvement, will provide satisfying rewards in the form of a healthy, happy athlete with a much-improved ability to perform. Both athlete and coach will be delighted.

REFERENCES

Bompa, T. (1988). Physiological intensity values employed to plan endurance training. *New Studies in Athletics*, **3**(4), 37-52.

Bondarchuk, A. (1988). Constructing a training system. *Track Technique*, **102**, 3254-3268.

Charniga, A., Jr., Gambetta, V., Kraemer, W., Newton, H., O'Bryant, H.S., Palmieri, G., Pedemonte, J., Pfaff, D., & Stone, M.H. (1986-1987). Periodization. *National Strength and Conditioning Association Journal*, **8**(5), 12-22; **8**(6), 17-24; **9**(1), 16-26.

Conconi, F., Ferrari, M., Ziglio, P.G., Droghetti, P., & Codeca, L. (1982). Determination of the anaerobic threshold by a noninvasive field test in runners. *Journal of Applied Physiology*, **52**, 869-873.

Costill, D.L. (1986). *Inside running*. Indianapolis: Benchmark Press.

Coyle, E.F. (1990). Detraining and retention of training-induced adaptations. *Sports Science Exchange*, **2**(23), 1-4.

Cullinane, E.M., Sady, S.P., Vadeboncoeur, L., Burke, M., & Thompson, P.D. (1986). Cardiac size and VO_2max do not decrease after short-term exercise cessation. *Medicine and Science in Sports and Exercise*, **18**, 420-421.

Daniels, J. (1989). Training distance runners—A primer. *Sports Science Exchange*, **1**(11), 1-4.

Daniels, J., & Scardina, N. (1984). Interval training and performance. *Sports Medicine*, **1**, 327-334.

Dellinger, B., & Freeman, B. (1984). *The competitive runner's training book*. New York: Macmillan.

Dick, F.W. (1975). Periodization: An approach to the training year. *Track Technique*, **62**, 1968-1970.

Fox, E.L., Bartels, R.L., Billings, C.E., Matthews, D.K., Bason, R., & Webb, W.M. (1973). Intensity and distance of interval training programs and changes in aerobic power. *Medicine and Science in Sports*, **5**, 18-22.

Freeman, W.H. (1989). *Peak when it counts*. Los Altos, CA: Tafnews Press.

Galloway, J. (1984). *Galloway's book on running*. Bolinas, CA: Shelter.

Humphreys, J., & Holman, R. (1985). *Focus on middle distance running*. London: Adam & Charles Black.

Karvonen, M.J., Kentala, E., & Mustala, O. (1957). The effects of training on heart rate. *Annales Medicinae Experimentalis Biologicae Fennicae*, **35**, 307-315.

Knuttgen, H.G., Nordesjo, L.-O., Ollander, B., & Saltin, B. (1973). Physical conditioning through interval training with young male adults. *Medicine and Science in Sports*, **5**, 220-226.

Lacour, J.R., Padilla, S., & Denis, S. (1987). L'inflexion de la courbe fréquence cardiaque-puissance n'est pas un témoin du seuil anaerobic [The inflection on the graph of heart rate versus work is not a proof of the anaerobic threshold.]. *Science et Motricité*, **1**, 3-6.

Larsen, H., & Bentzen, H. (1983). The effect of distance training and interval training on aerobic and anaerobic capacity, muscle fiber characteristics and performance in endurance trained runners. *Twelfth European Track Coaches Congress*, Acoteias, Portugal, pp. 10-16.

Leger, L., Mercier, D., & Gauvin, L. (1986). The relationship between % VO_2max and running performance time. In D.M. Landers (Ed.), *Sport and Elite Performers*, vol. 3., (pp. 113-120). Champaign, IL: Human Kinetics.

Lenzi, G. (1987). The marathon race: Modern training methodology. *New Studies in Athletics*, **2**, 41-50.

Matthews, P. (Ed.) (1990). *Athletics 1990*. London: Sports World.

Matveyev, L. (1981). *Fundamentals of sports training*. Moscow: Progress Publishing.

McInnis, A. (1981). Systematized approaches to peaking. In V. Gambetta (Ed.), *Track Technique Annual* (pp. 25-30). Los Altos, CA: Tafnews Press.

Nett, T. (1965). Die Lehre der Leichtathletik [The teaching of athletics]. *Leichtathletik*, **16**, 1023.

Okkels, T. (1983). The effect of interval- and tempo-training on performance and skeletal muscle in well-trained runners. *Twelfth European Track Coaches Congress*, Acoteias, Portugal, pp. 1-9.

Péronnet, F. & Thibault, G. (1989). Mathematical analysis of running performance and world running records. *Journal of Applied Physiology*, **67**, 453-465.

Robinson, S., Edwards, H.T., & Dill, D.B. (1937). New records in human power. *Science*, **85**, 409-410.

Tokmakidis, S.P., & Leger, L. (Dotson, C.O., and

Humphrey, J.H., eds., 1988). *Exercise physiology: current selected research*, **5**, 43-58.

Vigil, J. (1987). Distance training. *Track Technique*, **100**, 3189-3192.

Wilt, F. (1968). Training for competitive running. In H.B. Falls (Ed.), *Exercise physiology* (pp. 395-414). New York: Academic Press.

Yakovlev, N.N. (1967). *Sports biochemistry*. Leipzig: Deutsche Hochschule für Korperkultur [German Institute for Physical Culture].

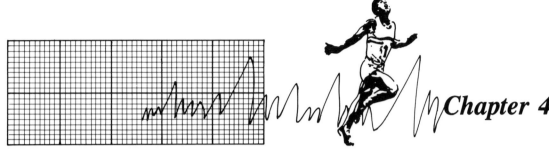

Comprehensive Conditioning for Runners

Running, though a relatively simple form of exercise, is also specific in that certain muscle groups are stimulated more than others. The greater the magnitude of this running stimulus, and it can indeed be sizable in athletes training 70 or more mi/week (110 km/week) for many months, the better developed certain muscles become. Examples are the posterior lower limb muscles (hamstrings) and lower back muscles. Other muscle groups, such as the anterior lower limb muscles (quadriceps) and abdominal muscles, are relatively less stimulated by running to improve in strength or endurance. Still other musculature, notably in the upper limbs and trunk, receives even less development. Runners who have been able to incorporate into their training plans what we might term a *comprehensive conditioning program* to improve the balance between the performance capabilities of all their various major muscle groups tend to have a sizable competitive advantage over those who have not done so. In part this is because when all-out competitive effort is required, those athletes with excellent total-body conditioning will have a greater total strength, power, and work output capability than those without such development. In part, however, it is also because athletes with a better balance between the performance capabilities of their major muscle groups tend to have fewer injuries. A longer period of injury freedom provides the opportunity for athletes to develop their talents more fully. After training, the single most important contributor to improved performance is remaining injury-free for long periods.

An important aspect of comprehensive conditioning relates to adequate flexibility. This is ensured by consistently and adequately stretching muscles prior to vigorous use in training. It is essential to have a joint range of motion greater than that required during the exercise; otherwise there is a real risk of muscle tears. Studies of hamstring muscle pulls suggest that muscles that are weak, inflexible, or both are the most susceptible to strain and injury (Christensen, 1972; Nicholas, 1970). A well-developed strength balance between the extensors and flexors of the hips and legs as well as adequate joint range of motion (greater than that required during the exercise) permits safe execution of the powerful strides essential for end-of-race sprints to the finish or shorter interval training sessions.

Total body fitness thus has three components:

1. Efficient cardiovascular and fuel-metabolizing systems developed by running, which provide specific aerobic and anaerobic fitness for running
2. A comprehensive conditioning program to provide adequate joint flexibility as well as strength, power, and endurance in all the major muscle groups, thereby ensuring the kind of structural balance that reduces the risk of musculoskeletal injury
3. An acceptable body composition (implying no excess body fat)

Table 4.1 presents a useful self-test of physiological performance and assessment that will give runners

Table 4.1   A Physiological Performance Evaluation of Total Body Fitness for Talented Distance Runners

Athlete's name _____ Height _____ Weight _____

I. Basic running ability

Stamina test: Run for 15 min around the track, covering as much distance as possible in that time.

    4,000m = 52.8 ml/kg/min $\dot{V}O_2$ = poor for elite men; fair for women

    4,500m = 61.1 ml/kg/min $\dot{V}O_2$ = fair for elite men; good for women

    5,000m = 69.5 ml/kg/min $\dot{V}O_2$ = good for elite men; world-class for women

Speed test: Sprint 40 yd (36.6 m) from a standing start. 6 sec = poor, 5.5 sec = fair, 5 sec = good, 4.5 sec = very good

II. Muscle performance ability—strength, power, stamina, agility

Muscular endurance test:

    a. Maximum number of press-ups in 1 min. 30 = poor, 40 = fair, 50 = good.

    b. Maximum squat thrusts in 1 min. Knees must reach level of arms. 30 = poor, 40 = fair, 50 = good.

    c. Maximum sit-ups in 1 min. Lying supine, legs outstretched, hands resting on thighs, head raised with chin pressed to chest, reach forward and touch hands to knees. 40 = poor, 50 = fair, 60 = good.

    d. Maximum pull-ups in 1 min, holding bar with palms forward, no leg assistance. Men: 3 = poor, 6 = fair, 9 = good. Women: 2 = poor, 3 = fair, 4 = good.

Muscular power tests for legs:

    a. Hop test: Hop 25m on each leg and count the hops required. 14 hops = poor, 12 = fair, 10 = good.

    b. Standing broad jump: Distance equal to own height = poor; distance equal to own height + 10% = fair; distance equal to own height + 25% = good.

    c. Sargeant jump: Face the wall, make the highest mark possible with chalk-dusted fingertips of an upstretched arm; now turn sideways, leap up, and again touch fingertips to the wall, making a mark with chalk dust; measure the distance between the 2 marks. 12 in. = poor, 18 in. = fair, 24 in. = good.

    d. Do a full squat with barbell weights. Half body weight = poor, 3/4 body weight = fair, body weight = good.

Strength/weight ratio:

    a. Standing medium grip barbell curl. 1/4 body weight = poor, 1/2 body weight = fair, 6/10 body weight = good.

    b. Standing barbell press, starting with the barbell placed either on the chest (military press), or on the upper back. 1/4 body weight = poor, 1/2 body weight = fair, 3/4 body weight = good.

III. Range of motion

Flexibility test:

    a. Attempt to touch toes with fingertips, keeping legs straight.

    b. Lying prone (on stomach), raise the chest off the ground and hold 10 sec.

    c. Lying supine (on back), legs raised and straight at a 45-degree angle with the ground, hold for 10 sec.

    d. Lying prone, raise chest and legs off the ground for 10 sec.

    e. Lying supine, knees well bent, hands behind the neck, rise to a sitting position.

    f. Lying prone, arms outstretched to the sides, bring right foot over to touch left hand, and vice versa, with minimum chest movement.

IV. Body composition

Percent Body Fat:

    If % body fat is > 8% for men and > 13% for women, fat weight is in excess for quality performance in running.

Height/weight ratio:

Men	Women
71.5 in. (182 cm)/138 lb (62.7 kg)	68.5 in. (174 cm)/116 lb (52.7 kg)
70.0 in. (178 cm)/135 lb (61.3 kg)	66.6 in. (169 cm)/113 lb (51.3 kg)
68.5 in. (174 cm)/132 lb (60.0 kg)[a]	64.9 in. (165 cm)/110 lb (50.0 kg)[a]
66.9 in. (170 cm)/129 lb (58.6 kg)	63.1 in. (160 cm)/107 lb (48.6 kg)
65.4 in. (166 cm)/126 lb (57.3 kg)	61.5 in. (156 cm)/104 lb (47.3 kg)

[a]Middle values represent means of top ten world-ranked athletes in 1989; values above and below are calculated based upon a metric height/weight ratio of 2.9 cm/kg for men and 3.3 cm/kg for women, or an Imperial ratio of 1.9 lb/in. for men and 1.7 lb/in. for women. For men, variations ± a few kg are common, with marathon runners tending to be lighter than runners from 800m through 10,000m. For women, variations are larger, with a more noticeable increase in weight from 10,000m toward 800m. Longer-distance runners of both sexes tend to be shorter, on the average, than shorter-distance runners.

an overview of where they fit in terms of high-level comprehensive conditioning for their sport. Distance runners find it relatively easy to hone the cardiovascular endurance component of fitness to a high standard, for that is their specialty area. Overall muscle development and joint flexibility, however, are often neglected but are also very important. Thus, runners who have not emphasized comprehensive conditioning in their training programs often perform poorly in this self-test. A low score should not be thought of negatively but rather as a stimulus for future development, with its accompanying rewards in improved performance.

It may be neither necessary nor desirable for distance runners to improve their strength enormously through the acquisition of more muscle mass. But there are at least three reasons to have a high level of general strength, particularly in the lower trunk and limbs. First, submaximal work loads of greater intensity can be managed more easily. Second, greater muscular strength decreases the risk of joint injury or overuse strain by minimizing stress on the connective tissue aspects of the musculoskeletal system (ligaments, tendons, and cartilage) that share in maintaining joint integrity. Third, a conditioning program will help strengthen these connective tissues, making the entire support system more durable. In a sport in which musculoskeletal injuries from overuse and overtraining are the dominant cause of lost time, giving attention to an effective conditioning program is a wise investment for improving an athlete's longevity.

Athletes seeking to develop and maintain a high standard of comprehensive fitness often find themselves confronted with a bewildering array of fundamental questions regarding an appropriate training plan. Even worse, the answers they receive from experts in various types of conditioning programs can range from appropriate to inappropriate to even contradictory. In part, this confusion occurs because considerable sales pitching occurs regarding the potentially greater benefits of one particular kind of conditioning equipment or regimen over another. Also, it results from our modern-day dilemma of overspecialization: A marathon runner querying a strength coach in the football program at a major American university may get advice more appropriate for a quarter-miler whose needs are more like those of a quarterback. However, the strength-building needs of a 400m or 800m runner are considerably different from those of a marathoner.

Serious runners want bottom-line answers to specific questions that will help them ultimately become better runners with greater longevity. How do strength, power, flexibility, and endurance interact to improve performance? Are increases in muscle mass really necessary for distance runners to become stronger? What kind of overall conditioning (and injury-prevention) suggestions would be helpful for all distance runners, and how can these be implemented using the many kinds of available modalities (free weights, machines, etc.)? How do circuit training and stage training contribute to conditioning? Of the three primary methods for strengthening muscles (identified by whether tension, length, or velocity is being held constant during training), which is best for runners attempting to improve their athletic performance? How do eccentric, concentric, and plyometric loading of muscles relate to these three strengthening methods? Similarly, how do flexibility and stretching exercises fit into the training process? With all this seeming complexity, it is understandable why distance runners often neglect to develop a comprehensive conditioning program and concentrate simply on running. Such a decision is a real error. This chapter should provide a better understanding of and solution to the challenge of developing a comprehensive conditioning plan. In turn, this should help prevent injuries and provide the kind of balanced fitness an athlete requires to move toward the goal of extended competitive excellence.

MUSCLE RESPONSE AND ADAPTATION TO STRESS LOADING

Basic Definitions: Strength, Work, Torque, Power, and Speed

In chapter 1 we outlined some of the important anatomical and physiological principles explaining skeletal muscle function. Now let us apply some of this knowledge practically to improvement of the various components of muscular performance through specialized training. **Strength** is often defined as the maximum force that can be developed during muscle activation (tension generation). If we think of strength as equivalent to force, its units of measurement would be the newton (n) in the metric system or the pound (lb) in the Imperial system, where 1 n = 0.225 lb and 1 lb = 4.4 n. Commonly, the term "contraction" is used as an alternative to "activation" or "tension generation," implying that the muscle shortens. But depending on circumstances, the muscle could also lengthen or remain unchanged in length and still produce tension and exert force. Thus, contraction (i.e., shortening) does not always describe accurately what is happening. Tension generation is indeed occurring when force is being exerted regardless of whether the muscle is changing in length, so it is a more accurate phrase. By using appropriate descriptors such as lengthening or shortening tension, we can then characterize more clearly the kind of tension generation occurring.

Strength is often said to be influenced primarily by two components, muscular and neural, but there is a third as well (mechanical), which shall be discussed later. The muscular component of strength also has three aspects: cross-sectional area, muscle fiber length, and muscle architecture (McDonagh & Davies, 1984). The greater the cross-sectional area, as seen when muscles incorporate more protein and become larger, the greater their force production capability. The longer the muscle, as seen when muscle cells add sarcomeres on either end, the greater its potential shortening or lengthening capability. Force output will be greatest when the overlap among tension-generating proteins (actin and myosin) is maximal. In chapter 1 we illustrated the variety of possible architectural arrangements in muscle—fusiform, multipennate, and so on. These variations change the force development pattern during muscle shortening or lengthening as movement occurs.

The neural aspect has two components: stimulus frequency and recruitment. Recall that skeletal muscle cells are each influenced by their connecting motor neurons. As stimulus frequency increases, force production rises (Person & Kudina, 1972) because more and more motor units are activated. The relationship is sigmoidal rather than linear (Rack & Westbury, 1969). **Recruitment** refers to a predictable and sequential activation of motor units as work intensity increases (Denny-Brown, 1949). Low-threshold stimuli activate slow-twitch (ST) motor units preferentially. As the stimulus strength rises, those motor units with a higher threshold of response are gradually brought into action. Interestingly, however, the sequence of motor unit activation with a *natural* (neural) increase in the intensity of muscle stimulation is the opposite of that seen when *artificial* (electrical) stimulation occurs. Natural stimulation recruits motor units in the following sequence (Burke, 1981): ST with fatigue-resistant (slow oxidative) muscle cells, FT with intermediate fatigability (fast oxidative glycolytic muscle cells), and FT with rapidly fatigable (fast glycolytic) muscle cells. Because of considerable overlap, however, even at low work intensities some FT motor units will be activated.

Electromyostimulation produced simply by sending electrical current through a stimulating electrode placed on the skin over the surface of a muscle brings the opposite response in motor units. This is related to the response characteristics of the motor neurons to electrical stimulation. The largest nerve axons have the lowest threshold of stimulation, and thus the rapidly fatigable FT muscle cells are stimulated first (Eccles, Eccles, & Lundberg, 1958; Henneman,

1957). Only with higher intensity stimulation will the smaller neurons, which innervate the ST fatigue-resistant muscle cells, be activated. These differing responses have important implications in the rehabilitation of injured muscles as well as in normal function.

Various skeletal muscles differ in the relative combinations of stimulus frequency and motor unit recruitment that permit force production. Even at relatively low force outputs, some muscles will have nearly all their motor units active but stimulated at a rather low frequency. Other muscles will produce an equivalent force but rely initially on only a few fibers being stimulated at a higher frequency. Both stimulus frequency and recruitment are related to the level of outflow from the central nervous system. This is often termed the *central drive* and is determined in large measure by such ill-defined but powerful factors as motivation.

Technically, it becomes more correct to add a few additional constraints to our earlier definition of strength. John Atha (1981) defined **strength** as the maximum force exerted in a single effort of tension generation when (a) the muscle is not allowed to change length, and (b) time is not a factor in force production. Time, however, is a critical factor in distance running performance. The quicker an athlete runs, the faster he or she reaches the finish line. The concepts of velocity and speed thus become crucial. **Velocity** is a vector quantity (implying that it has both magnitude and direction) and is the rate of change in position over time. It can be expressed in a variety of units. For example, at the 1988 Seoul Olympic Games, when Morocco's Moulay Brahim Boutayeb won the 10,000m run in a new Olympic record time of 27:21.46, this represented an average running velocity around the track of 6.1 m/sec, or 13.6 mi/hr, or 65.7 sec/400 m. **Speed,** however, is a scalar quantity (it has only magnitude, with no direction implied). It thus is a more general term, relating to quickness; a runner with inherent speed can run quickly.

When we apply force to move a particular resistance through a given distance, work is done. Thus, **work** can be defined as the product of the force used for displacement times the distance the resistance is moved. It measures the energy output of activated muscles. The appropriate units for work measurement would be newton-meters (nm) in the metric system and foot-pounds (ft-lb) in the Imperial system. One nm = 1 j = 0.738 ft-lb, and 1 ft-lb = 1.356 j. If no movement occurs, regardless of the force exerted on a given resistance, no work is done.

Torque is defined as the effort of a force required to move an object around an axis of rotation (Laird & Rozier, 1979). Some find it useful to think of torque as angular work. It is calculated as the product of an exerted force and the length of the involved lever arm. In turn, **lever arm** is the distance of a line drawn perpendicular from the line indicating the direction of muscle force (called the muscle force vector) to the axis of rotation of the movable joint to which the muscle is connected (Figure 4.1). Thus, the units of torque are the same as those for work—nm or ft-lb. As the muscle shortens or lengthens, producing limb rotation around the joint, lever arm length also changes, producing a change in torque without a change in applied muscular force. Thus, in addition to the neural and muscular components of strength identified earlier, inclusion of this so-called *mechanical* component is essential. However, though a strength training program may improve the body's ability to neurally recruit more muscle fibers or increase the total available muscle protein, it has very little effect on changing lever arm relationships because these are structurally (i.e., mechanically) defined.

Power is the rate at which work is done. The metric unit for power is the watt (1 nm/sec or 0.7376 ft-lb/sec). Thus, power can be calculated as force times velocity, or as torque times angular velocity. A powerful athlete can produce force rapidly. An increase in power can occur either by increasing the rate at which a given work output occurs or by increasing the amount of work accomplished in a given time period. Thus, strength as well as the velocity of shortening or lengthening of muscle cells are important aspects of power output. Training in a manner that improves power output through modest gains in *both* strength and velocity may be less injurious and fundamentally more useful than attempting impressive gains in either strength or velocity alone.

Lever Systems: Their Relationship to Force and Movement

The extent to which we can move objects depends in part on the force we can generate and in part on the lever arrangement in the involved bones, muscles, and joints. Good leverage, which increases mechanical advantage, can permit more effective movement than

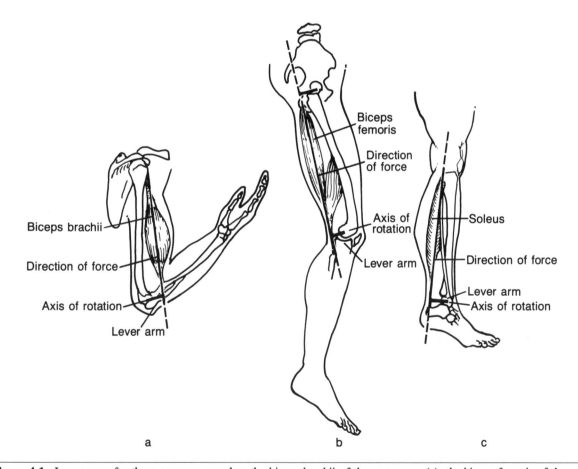

Figure 4.1 Lever arms for three common muscles: the biceps brachii of the upper arm (a), the biceps femoris of the upper leg (one of the hamstrings) (b), and the soleus of the lower leg (c). In each instance the lever arm extends from the axis of rotation of the distal (movable) joint attachment to the muscle force vector, indicating the muscle's direction of force output.

poor leverage. The simplest form of lever is nothing more than a rigid bar that can move about an axis. In the human body, bones represent the bar, and joints are the axes around which the bones move. The point of rotation is termed the *fulcrum*, and the long bones form the lever arms. When muscles (which attach to bones via ligaments) generate tension and exert force, one end of the bone will typically move more than the other.

Three classes of levers exist (Figure 4.2), determined by the relationship between the point where force is applied, the point where resistance is provided, and the point where rotation occurs. Most skeletal muscles function as third-class levers. As shown in Figure 4.2a, the axis of joint rotation is between the force-producing entity (the muscle) and the resistance entity (the barbell). In this example, the biceps brachii of the upper arm acts to raise the barbell by elbow flexion, resulting in rotation of the lower arm around the elbow joint. All levers have two arms. The force arm extends between the joint axis of rotation and the applied muscular force—here, the biceps insertion. The resistance arm extends from the axis of rotation to the resistance, which here is the barbell.

The product of the force arm times the force applied equals the product of the resistance arm and the resistance exerted. Notice in Figure 4.2a that the resistance arm is much longer than the force arm. Simple arithmetic suggests to us that the biceps will need to provide considerable force to support or move even a small resistance. However, notice also that just a small shortening tension in the biceps will bring about a very sizable movement of the hand as elbow flexion begins. It is well known that most sport-related actions involve high movement velocities. Third-class leverage relationships (a long resistance arm and a short force arm) permit this to occur. Similarly, in Figure 4.1b it can be seen that one of the hamstrings (biceps femoris), being a two-joint muscle, operates as a third-class lever at the knee joint. For knee flexion, the short force arm extends from the knee joint axis of rotation to the biceps insertion (the source of force). The long resistance arm extends from the knee joint to the ankle and foot. A small shortening of the biceps, although requiring great force, brings a very rapid flexion of the lower limb. Examples of third-class levers in the physical world include a set of fireplace tongs or a screen door with a spring to help keep it shut.

Interestingly, if our athlete lowers the barbell in Figure 4.2b instead of raising it, the biceps brachii will still be the active muscle, but it now will function as a second-class lever. In this lever system, the resistance entity (the muscle) is between the joint axis of rotation and the force-producing entity (the barbell). Muscular force production is not resisting the reversal of joint axis motion caused by the external force. Notice that, with second-class levers, enormous movement force can be managed and is favored over movement velocity. Other examples of second-class levers include lifting a wheelbarrow and plantar flexion of the foot.

Figure 4.2c provides an example of a first-class lever and its function. The axis of joint rotation is between the force-producing entity (the triceps brachii), attached to the olecranon (the large curved

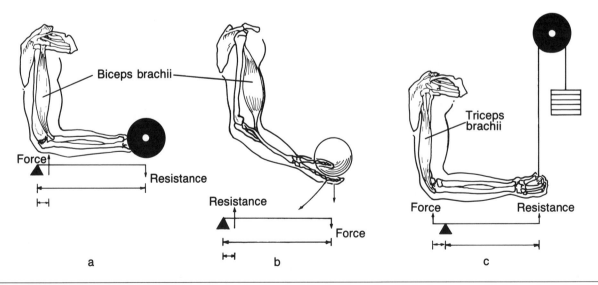

Figure 4.2 The three lever systems for force production. In 4.2a the biceps brachii is shown as a third-class lever in lifting a barbell (elbow flexion). In 4.2b it acts as a second-class lever in lowering it (elbow extension). In 4.2c the triceps brachii is shown as a first-class lever in raising the weight on a pulley during elbow extension.

prominence at the upper back of the ulna) and the resistance entity (the forearm and hand grasping the weighted pulley). Triceps muscle shortening produces elbow joint extension, and this force permits a downward pull on the weighted cable.

A few other concepts concerning the arrangement of muscles are important in understanding the function of bones and muscles in lever systems. In chapter 1 we referred to the more movable attachment (insertion) and the more fixed, or stabilized, attachment (origin) of muscles to bones. When a muscle generates tension, both attachments are affected equally. Typically, a distal bone moves more than the proximal bone. Thus, when doing a biceps curl, the forearm moves more than the upper arm. In contrast, however, when performing a forearm pull-up, the forearms are more stationary as the upper arms move toward them.

Another concept refers to the *angle of pull*. This is defined as the angle between the line of pull of a muscle (the force arm) and the mechanical axis of the bony part of the lever (the resistance, or stabilizing arm). When this angle of pull is at 90 degrees (Fig. 4.3a), the muscle is most effective at generating force for producing movement, because all of the available force goes toward joint rotation. Most muscles have an angle of pull well less than 90 degrees—typically in the neighborhood of 50 degrees (Figure 4.3b). Here the force produced contributes in part toward rotation (R) and in part toward stabilization (S). When the angle of pull is > 90 degrees (Figure 4.3c), force

distribution is divided between rotation and dislocation (D). Because of the greater mechanical advantage at 90 degrees, we commonly utilize this as the initial angle for starting exercises such as pull-ups.

Static Resistance Exercise— Isometric Training

When we attempt to push, pull, or lift a fixed or otherwise immovable object (referred to as an external force), our skeletal muscle fibers generate tension but cannot exert sufficient internal force to produce movement. Some fibrillar shortening within the muscle occurs, but the elastic components stretch, and the external length of the whole muscle remains unaltered. Because of this relatively unchanging length, the muscles are said to be under *isometric* or *static tension*. They can produce maximum tension or any amount of varying submaximum tension at essentially any joint angle.

Isometric training was brought to the forefront of the fitness world in 1953 when Hettinger and Muller announced their surprising finding that essentially a single isometric effort of only 6 sec duration at as little as two thirds of maximum intensity could be effective in improving muscular strength. Thus, hours of barbell lifting and other kinds of hard work might be unnecessary for strengthening muscles. Quite logically, as athletes have used other forms of strength training for centuries to build muscle size and strength, this report of the benefits of isometric training was

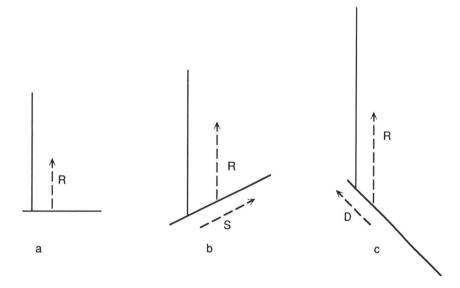

Figure 4.3 There are 2 force components, rotational (R) and stabilization (S), which promote stability when joint movement is < 90° or dislocation (D) when joint movement is > 90°. In Figure 4.3a, where the joint angle is at 90°, all force is directed toward rotation. In Figure 4.3b there is rotation and stabilization since the joint angle is < 90°. In Figure 4.3c muscular force is distributed between rotation and dislocation.

scrutinized carefully, and a large number of subsequent studies followed in the ensuing two decades. The current status of these studies has suggested that the initially reported 5% increase per week in strength was not very repeatable, but a smaller increase, approaching 2%, could be expected. Thus, isometric training does increase strength, and the initial gains are sizable, but they fall off rapidly after about 5 weeks. These gains typically are localized to within about 20 degrees of the training angle (Knapik, Mawdsley, & Ramos, 1983). Thus, several joint angles must be selected over a broad range to ensure reasonably uniform strength development over a joint's entire range of motion.

One of the most familiar examples of isometric tension generation in runners is seen when they lean toward and push against a wall or tree as a warm-up exercise before a training run or a race (look ahead to Figure 4.21, p. 206). Although the intent of the exercise may be to stretch the posterior lower limb muscles, the upper torso and upper limb muscles come under isometric tension. A second example of isometric stimulation involves training at specific joint angles where increased strength is required—for example, in the knee joint at takeoff in the high jump. In the weight room, athletes may use a power rack to produce isometric tension in their quadriceps muscles at this takeoff knee joint angle by pushing a bar upward against appropriately positioned restraining pins. Isometric activity is also used during rehabilitation of limbs that have been injured and immobilized as a result of recent surgery. Exercises that produce isometric tension can slow or prevent muscle cell atrophy.

A few problems occur with the performance of isometric exercises. The most important is a sizable increase in both systolic and diastolic blood pressures. This occurs even if the active muscles form a rather small fraction of the total muscle bulk. Another difficulty involves joint discomfort and stress occurring from excessive bone and joint compression. Some of the exercises used in isometric conditioning are ill advised for beginners until the vertebral column becomes well protected by associated musculotendinous development. For example, using a standard isometric squat rack can direct excessive force on the vertebral column, increasing the risk of lower back pain and possible injury.

A third difficulty involves the absence of natural ballistic action in body segments. Most sport activities require far more than simply isometric strength capabilities. They involve a high degree of automatic control of skilled ballistics movements. Neuromuscular coordination, effective utilization of multiple joints, and a broad range of movement of those joints are crucial for success. These movements have large initial accelerations that require considerable strength followed by fine-tuned control that requires split-second timing and optimum movement economy. As described in chapter 1, fast motion and multiple joint actions are the mainstay of distance running, integrated in a repetitive ballistic sequence of footstrike, midsupport, takeoff, follow-through, forward swing, foot descent, and then another footstrike. Although joint stability may be improved by static resistance training, the resulting increased muscle strength does not translate well to improved sport performance. Hence, if a runner has the option between static and dynamic strength training exercises, the latter would be preferred because they transfer more directly to running.

Dynamic Resistance Exercise

If an unchanging resistance such as a barbell or some other weighted object can be moved, either directly by lifting it or indirectly through action on cables and pulleys, then tension generation, force production, and length changes will all occur in the muscles utilized. This is called **dynamic resistance exercise**, and it refers to the training of skeletal muscles by application of loads of such magnitude that the muscles can lengthen or shorten within their normal movement limits. If the resistance is unchanging, as with lifting a barbell, the term *isotonic* is appropriate (suggesting constant tension or tone but actually referring to a constant load). Some familiar examples of working against a constant resistance include the use of one's own body weight to perform exercises such as push-ups (press-ups), chin-ups (pull-ups), or sit-ups. Another form of constant resistance exercise can be achieved through the use of free weights such as barbells. Plates of varying weights are placed at either end of a metal bar. As the athlete assumes various positions of standing, sitting, or lying, these weights are lifted, pushed, or maintained in position while some other part of the body is moved (see Figures 4.7, 4.10, 4.11, 4.12, 4.17, and 4.19 later in this chapter). The tension generated will vary in magnitude depending on leverage relationships, gravitational influences on inertial and velocity changes, and number of actomyosin cross-bridge connections. The term *dynamic tension* is often used to describe this continually changing tension.

By using certain specialized equipment to be described shortly, athletes can also train their muscles by moving them at a constant velocity (isokinetic tension) through their entire range of motion. Tension generation can be maximal or submaximal, and the equipment provides an accommodating resistance to permit constant velocity.

With either form of dynamic exercise training, the muscle fibers may lengthen (producing eccentric tension) or shorten (producing concentric tension). For example, when we do sit-ups, the abdominal muscles, particularly the rectus abdominus, are shortened as we sit up and then lengthened as we return to the supine position. During concentric tension generation, work is done by the muscles on the load, which here is overcoming the force of gravity in raising the head, upper limbs, and upper torso. This is termed *positive work*. During eccentric tension generation, work is done by the load on the muscles; this is called *negative work*. The energy cost of negative work is less than for positive work, and the muscles involved are under higher tension than during either positive work or isometric tension generation (Olson, Schmidt, & Johnson, 1972). Presumably, during eccentric work fewer motor units and thus fewer muscle cells are involved, but they are involved more intensely. This may explain the relatively greater postexercise soreness that accompanies eccentric work (e.g., long downhill runs) than other types of muscle activation.

Using the biceps brachii in the upper arm to lift the body in performing a chin-up is an example of isotonic concentric tension generation. The corresponding antagonist muscles (triceps) are relaxed during this activity. Returning to the starting position would involve isotonic eccentric tension generation in the biceps. The antagonists also remain relaxed. Similarly, the act of sitting or squatting involves negative work by the leg extensors; moving to the supine position from a sitting position requires negative work by the hip flexors. Standing from the squatting position, or sitting up from the recumbent position, involves positive work by these same muscles. Their antagonist muscles (leg flexors for sitting, hip extensors for lying) are inactive during this period of activation.

By Newton's **Second Law of Motion**, the force (F) developed by such dynamic exercise is determined by the sum of the downward pull of gravity (W) and the product of the mass (m) of the involved object (the weight of a barbell, for example) and its acceleration (a). Thus,

$$F = W + ma. \qquad (4.1)$$

Initially, considerable force is required to start the muscle movement, whether it be pushing, pulling, or lifting, because inertia must be overcome. Once movement begins, the same applied force can now maintain acceleration as the pace quickens. As a constant pace is achieved this rate of acceleration, of course, slows to zero. Fatigue will decrease the extent to which such initial accelerations are easily achieved.

Unchanging Resistance—Isotonic Training. The phenomenon of skeletal muscles getting bigger and stronger through a program of gradually more challenging isotonic loading is probably one of the oldest observations in physiology and is certainly as old as sport itself. Hardly a lecture or article describing the principles of strength training fails to mention the legendary feats of Milo of Crotona. Milo was a wrestler with a very long and successful career during the sixth century BC. He was an Olympian in terms of allegedly winning a victory wreath at those ancient games. But he could as well be called a Pythian, an Isthmian, and a Nemean, having been successful at those city games as well (Young, 1984). Some people erroneously refer to Milo as a weight lifter instead of a wrestler because of the exercises he used to develop enormous strength. The story is often recited of how as a sheepherder, he would hoist a small lamb across his back and shoulders, then squat down and return to his standing position several times in succession. As the lamb grew and gained weight, this provided a greater resistance, to which Milo gradually adapted over time. The legend becomes misty in suggesting that he could steadily increase his own strength development until the animal reached adulthood. Nevertheless, he eventually became so strong that no one could match him, and his enormous strength put him almost in a class by himself when he entered the wrestling arena.

It was the Romans, however, rather than the Greeks who developed and refined the techniques that form the basis of what we do today for systematically improving strength. The three fundamental principles of strength training date back so far that their originators have long been lost. One of these is the **principle of progressive resistance** which states that if skeletal muscles are overloaded, they will gradually adapt in such a manner that this new load will now be better tolerated. Then, progressively and over time, if the resistive load is again increased as a new level of overload, an eventual new level of adaptation will occur. Adaptation occurs in the skeletal and nervous systems as well as in the muscles. We may define **overload** as a substantially larger training load, consisting of either a larger resistance or an increased number of repetitions (reps) that the resistance is managed, or both.

The **principle of increasing intensity** states that it is not the frequency of muscle stimulation but the intensity that is important in strengthening muscle.

An interesting study by MacDougall, Wenger, and Green (1982) confirmed this rather nicely. Both body-builders and power lifters were studied in an attempt to learn more about the mechanism by which muscle training produces hypertrophy. These two types of athletes train quite differently, bodybuilders typically doing high repetitions at submaximum loads and power lifters generally doing only a few reps using very heavy loads. A common denominator of these two groups, however, is that both train to failure, that is, to the point of complete fatigue. Thus, they both provide a maximally intense stimulus to their muscles. Both types achieved a similar end result in terms of hypertrophy. The cellular mechanisms that trigger the hypertrophy have not yet been identified.

Two pioneering studies set the stage for the enormous interest in strength training that began shortly following World War II. Professor B. Morpurgo (1897) at the University of Siena verified that as muscles get bigger with training, it isn't the number of fibers that increases, but rather an increase in individual fiber size. Eyster (1927) later showed that the intensity of work performance rather than simply the work load managed is the stimulus for increasing muscle size and increasing its strength.

Thomas DeLorme in 1945 published one of the first scientific reports on the effects of dynamic (isotonic) resistance training on skeletal muscle development. If anyone can be identified as the originator of the phrase ''progressive-resistance exercise,'' it is he. Strength is improved best through high-resistance and low-rep exercise. Endurance, on the other hand, is developed through low-resistance and high-rep exercise without training to failure. Whereas strength increases in muscle accrue largely through an increase in intracellular muscle protein, endurance is improved by increased capillarization and intracellular mitochondrial dynamics. Strength training will not build the performance qualities that are developed by endurance training, and vice versa. This is the important **principle of specificity**: The adaptation to training is determined by the nature of the training stimulus. Thus, weeks and weeks of slow distance running do not improve our ability to run quickly as much as they provide an endurance base upon which fast running can then effectively improve racing capabilities.

A few years later (1948), DeLorme, together with Arthur Watkins, provided a systematized format for using progressive resistance exercise to increase gross muscle strength and endurance. They used an arrangement of cables and pulleys combined with the weight of the extremity to be trained (arms or legs) and counterbalancing weights. Their strength-building regimen required three sets of lifting, each set based on an amount of weight that could be lifted no more than 10 times (called a 10-rep maximum). The first two sets of 10 lifts were at 50% and 75% of maximum, thereby serving as a warm-up for the maximum effort that followed. This final third set contributed most as the actual strength-building stimulus. As strength gains occur, athletes can eventually manage easily more than 10 reps at the original 10-rep maximum. Arbitrarily, DeLorme and Watkins suggested that when 15 reps can be managed at the 10-rep maximum load, an increase in loading should then occur to permit a new strength-building challenge.

Subjects who used such a format often reported considerable fatigue, muscular pain, and inability to maintain full range of motion from doing so much work before the primary strength-building stimulus. Zinovieff suggested that instead of decreasing the volume of the two warm-up sets, the stimulus format be reversed. In 1951 he outlined a program of 10 sets of 10 reps, the very first to be done at the 10-rep maximum intensity when the muscles were fresh. Each set thereafter was done with decreasing resistance, the ideal situation being one in which increasing fatigue would be matched exactly by decreasing load so that all 100 reps would be at a functional maximum.

As one might imagine, these studies were followed over the next few decades by literally hundreds more, each suggesting a different variation on the same goal, namely, how to arrive at the best combination of sets, reps, interval of rest, and size of load that would bring the greatest gains in performance. At about this same time, the pioneering ultrastructural studies of muscle function began to reveal how muscle tension generation occurred. As we described in chapter 1, the sliding filament theory (A.F. Huxley & Niedergerke, 1954; H.E. Huxley & Hanson, 1954) postulated an enzyme-mediated movement of actin and myosin molecules past one another to permit shortening or lengthening. It provided a beautiful breakthrough of knowledge on the molecular level to accompany that occurring at the gross level regarding the mechanisms for improving muscular performance.

Depending on the athlete, performance aspirations will differ. Muscle hypertrophy is very important for a bodybuilder. A middle distance runner desires considerable strength and power but with a minimum increase in muscle size. For a long-distance runner, adequate overall joint strength and reasonable increases in both strength and power in the major muscle groups connecting to those joints is desirable, again with no need to increase muscle mass. No generic program is suitable for all athletes; based upon present fitness level, genetic predisposition regarding FT/ST fiber types, event specificity, past experience at comprehensive conditioning programs, and individual strengths and weaknesses, a workable plan can be designed for each individual.

During the early 1960s Richard Berger (1962) published a prodigious amount of work aimed at identifying the optimum mix of sets and reps to permit gains in muscular strength. His criterion for a strength gain was improvement in a one-rep maximum lift. His conclusion was that, for most people, three sets of four to eight reps done three times per week produced optimum strength gains. Unlike the DeLorme/Watkins system, however, where only the final set was at maximum, all three sets are done at maximum intensity. Thus, using a six-rep maximum load as an example, it may not be possible during the first training session to complete the assigned load. Instead of three sets of six reps at the six-rep maximum, the first may be six reps, the second five reps, the third only four or five reps. Gradually, however, increasing strength permits six reps at the six-rep maximum, showing nicely the adaptive improvement over time. When this work load can be tolerated routinely, then Berger's recommendation for load increase is to raise it by 5%.

In 1979 Wayne Westcott proposed a system of lifting that required less total effort yet provided gains in strength similar to those of other systems in use. Using an individual's one-rep maximum as the basis for identifying the training load, Westcott suggested three sets with decreasing reps (for example, 10 to 5 to 1) along with increasing resistance (55%, 75%, and 95% of maximum). The obvious conclusions when programs such as those of DeLorme, Berger, and Westcott are compared is that it isn't the total number of reps or the total weight lifted that is crucial for initiating a strength-building stimulus. Instead, as indicated earlier, it is the exercise intensity. The various combinations of submaximum efforts, either preceding or following the most intense (improvement-stimulating) part of the lifting session, merely vary the pattern of warm-up or cool-down as well as neural recruitment and total work output.

Because of individual differences in the FT/ST composition of skeletal muscles, the number of reps that can be managed at any work intensity will vary considerably. In chapter 1 we described the greater fatigue resistance in ST fibers. Although both FT and ST fibers will be recruited at high-intensity work loads (Lesmes, Benhain, Costill, & Fink, 1983), as is done during weight training or very fast running, athletes with a majority of FT fibers will fatigue more quickly. Thus, whereas one set of 8 to 12 reps may be com-

monly advocated, the ultimate decision regarding fewer or greater numbers of reps should be based on each individual athlete's predisposition toward endurance or strength excellence.

A typical result observed after several months of a strength-building program is a plateau in performance gains. The initial improvements are due largely to improved neurological recruitment abilities and gains in efficiency of performing each exercise. Skeletal muscle fiber adaptations, however, do contribute as well. Once recruitment and efficiency begin to plateau, however, continued gains in strength occur but are more specifically a result of intrinsic muscle cell adaptation (Hakkinen & Komi, 1983). For a runner relatively uninterested in producing muscle hypertrophy, this slowdown in improvement is not as important as the continued maintenance training effect that aids in injury prevention in the muscles and their associated connective tissues.

With constant-load (isotonic) training, the mechanical advantage of lever systems changes through the range of joint motion, particularly as the load is distributed among different muscle groups. Lifters are often limited to the weight they can manage at the weakest point in their range of motion—this is the sticking point. During the 1960s and 1970s a wide variety of so-called variable resistance machines appeared on the market as a preferable alternative to free weights. One type (Universal gym), developed by Harold Zimkin, had multiple stations, arranged around a central axis, using pulley and lever systems. An entirely different concept was pioneered by Arthur Jones (Nautilus Industries, Inc.), consisting of many separate machines utilizing eccentrically placed cams. In this way, the equipment's resistive load can be effectively lightened when the body's lever arms are working at their least mechanical advantage and maximized when the muscles are working most advantageously. A variety of investigative reports were published by one of Nautilus's technical specialists, Ellington Darden (1977).

The net effect of variable resistance provides a velocity profile through the range of motion that differs greatly, however, from that seen commonly in normal sport movements. In particular, the achievement of high acceleration is dampened. But the relatively slow training movements provide a high level of muscle fiber tension throughout the entire range of motion, and this is the preferred mode of training using this equipment. The consensus of individual experience with such equipment seems to indicate that one set of 8 to 12 reps using a sizable load is most successful for strength gains. Fast training movements are possible but often impractical because the ballistic movements cause problems with bouncing stacks of weights.

Accommodating Resistance—Isokinetic Training.

The commercial availability of machines in the 1970s that could essentially remove ballistic movement and permit overload training with maximum muscle tension generation at a constant velocity (isokinetic) throughout the full range of motion provided an entirely new dimension to fitness training. Probably the first isokinetic device was built in the 1920s (Levin & Wyman, 1927), using a needle valve to regulate oil flow between two connecting chambers. Forty-one years later, in 1968, Los Angeles bioengineer James J. Perrine published his research with a more sophisticated device eventually marketed commercially under the trade name of Cybex (Lumex Industries, Inc.). Since then, an expanding technology using everything from hydraulics to pneumatics and clutch-plates in tandem with flywheels has given us a wide variety of devices to provide resistance that is essentially a mirror image of the active force provided by the muscles. Thistle, Hislop, Moffroid, and Lohman (1967), in their first published study using the Cybex isokinetic dynamometer, pointed out that a so-called accommodating resistance is provided to the tension-generating muscles, and it matches almost exactly their force output. Because the velocity of muscle shortening is virtually unchanged throughout the movement range, the muscle cells are being isokinetically trained. The activated muscle cells are generating maximum tension at every point in their associated joint's range of motion.

Figure 4.4a illustrates an athlete (U.S. long-distance runner Bill Taylor) having his knee joint extension/flexion tested using the Cybex II isokinetic dynamometer. Before the test, the torque-measuring arm of the device is first aligned with his knee joint axis (Figure 4.4b). A wide range of angular velocities (we typically use nine, between 300 degrees/sec and 60 degrees/sec) permits evaluation of the dynamic properties of the involved muscles. Any additional force greater than that required to achieve these velocities is resisted (passively) by an equal and opposite force. This force can be quantified in various ways (Laird & Rozier, 1979; Moffroid & Kusiak, 1975). For example, peak torque, torque at specific joint angles, peak torque per body weight, work, and power can all be measured.

This isokinetic effort depicted in Figure 4.4a is considerably different from a knee extension and flexion maneuver with a weighted leg extension machine (similar to that in Figure 4.16a, b, later in this chap-

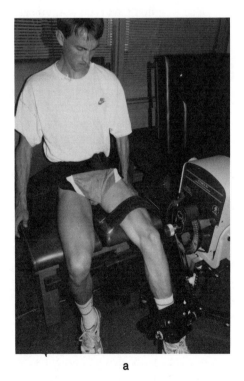

a

b

Figure 4.4 Evaluation of knee joint function using a Cybex isokinetic dynamometer (a). Prior to testing, the torque-measuring arm must be aligned with the subject's knee joint axis (b). In 4b the subject's left knee is in 90 degrees of joint flexion (and extension). Extending the knee, beginning in 4a, brings the knee toward 0 degrees of flexion.

ter). Isokinetically, movement from 90 degrees of knee joint flexion toward zero degrees requires concentric quadriceps tension, and movement from zero degrees of flexion back to 90 degrees requires concentric tension in the hamstrings and gastrosoleus muscles. Thus, the instructions given to our athlete were first to kick out as hard as possible (i.e., reduce knee flexion from 90 degrees toward zero degrees), and then pull back as hard as possible (i.e., increase knee flexion back toward 90 degrees). Using a leg extension machine, movement from 90 degrees of knee joint flexion to zero degrees requires concentric quadriceps tension, but movement back to 90 degrees requires eccentric quadriceps tension. Thus, eccentric tension generation is often not possible when using isokinetics and would need development using other devices, such as the isotonic leg extensor machine. Similarly, when an athlete uses an isotonic leg extension machine, knee joint flexor muscle development would need training by an additional dynamic resistance system such as a hamstring curl machine (see Figure 4.18 later in this chapter).

Figure 4.5a through c depicts graphically the maximum torque produced by knee extension as it proceeds from 90 degrees to zero degrees and returns by knee flexion to 90 degrees. Tracings are illustrated for three different movement velocities: 60 degrees, 180 degrees, and 300 degrees/sec. Each muscle or muscle group has its own unique force production curve in causing joint rotation; the difference between

knee extensors and flexors in Figure 4.5 can readily be seen. Notice also that maximum torque production varies not only with joint angle but with velocity of tension generation as well. This torque variation with different movement velocities relates to the number of cross-bridge linkages in place at any given moment in time. The faster the movement velocity, the fewer the number of cross bridges linked at any moment, resulting in less tension. Mary Moffroid and her colleagues (Moffroid & Whipple, 1970; Moffroid, Whipple, Hofkosh, Lowman, & Thistle, 1969) expanded on these early studies to provide a wealth of practical information concerning the value and utilization of isokinetic evaluation and training in clinical practice.

In nature, accommodating resistance can be imitated somewhat by exercising in water. Water surrounding a limb provides considerably more resistance than air, which tends to dampen or reduce the velocity of movement achievable. Thus, the limb will move at a more constant velocity throughout its range of motion.

Evaluating Training Responses to Isotonics and Isokinetics. One of the questions most commonly asked by athletes interested in designing an effective set of exercises to meet their particular conditioning requirements is simply "What works? What equipment should I use, and what is the best plan for me?" An indirect answer is that the kind of equipment isn't

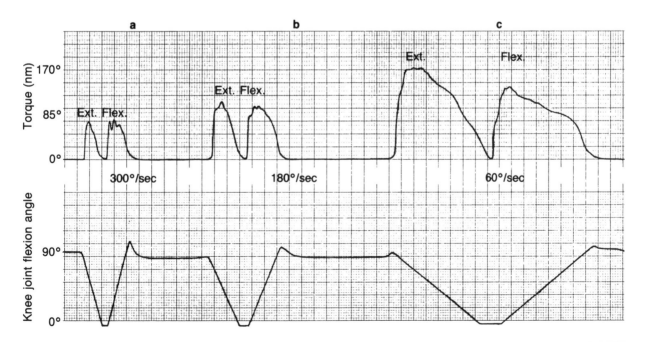

Figure 4.5 Tracings depicting the pattern of maximum torque output for isokinetic knee-joint extension and flexion at three different movement velocities: 300 degrees/sec (a), 180 degrees/sec (b), and 60 degrees/sec (c). Torque output varies with both specific joint angle and movement velocity.

necessarily as important as doing the training. All the various kinds of equipment—free weights, the use of one's own body weight, and machines—have the capability of increasing strength (with or without gains in muscle mass), power, and endurance. No single method has been shown to be unequivocally superior, although for athletes engaged in movement-oriented sports such as running, isometric training would definitely receive lower priority than isotonic and isokinetic training. The six keys to success are these:

1. Train regularly.
2. Train the muscle groups most in need of conditioning and that will be of greatest benefit to running.
3. Ensure muscle balance by training antagonists as well as agonists.
4. Provide a progressive overload stimulus.
5. Work the muscles through their full range of movement.
6. Allow adequate time between training sessions for recovery and physiological adaptation to occur.

For several reasons it has been difficult to compare effectively the various types of strength-training equipment available (Clarke, 1973; Kraemer, Deschenes, & Fleck, 1988; Pipes & Wilmore, 1975; Weltman & Stamford, 1982). First, untrained individuals will initially accrue sizable strength gains using any of several types of resistance work for training due to neurological adaptation and recruitment. The rate of the neurological aspect of these gains diminishes considerably as fitness increases, leaving a slower rate of improvement due to variable increases in muscle protein. Thus, to assess the relative benefits of one system or machine over another, subject groups that are all at the same level of initial training must first be identified. Then they must be assigned similarly stressful work loads. Both of these constraints are difficult to manage in scientific studies but must be managed if the conclusions are to have practical value for athletic training.

Second is the questionable credibility of the vast sales-oriented literature available from manufacturers of the more specialized machines for improving fitness. They have an intense desire to acquire even a small percentage of a very lucrative market. The more aggressive this promotion, the more slick the sales pitches suggesting that one or another piece of equipment is so revolutionary, so effective, so research-tested, and so ideal for the purpose that one would be a fool not to purchase it for spa or home. These companies commonly hire scientists to produce studies that characterize the performance capabilities of the particular equipment being marketed. This vested-interest relationship increases the need for caution in interpreting published reports.

Third is the problem of transferring fitness gains in improvement of performance on various machines to increased racing effectiveness. Machines that isolate individual muscle groups for development may not provide strength transfer as useful as that obtained from training modalities that stimulate multiple muscle groups, thereby improving agility and coordination and mimicking the individual sport activity. Comprehensive fitness training will indeed very likely improve general fitness, but it will be the total synergistic effect of this improved general fitness along with other specific training superimposed on it that provides sport-related performance gains. There is also the psychological component that accompanies such a comprehensive training program—the knowledge that nothing is being overlooked or that a winning edge may result from being just a little more completely prepared than a competitor is difficult to quantify.

Fourth is the phenomenon of specificity of adaptation to training. It is difficult to compare objectively the strength gains in groups of athletes who have trained using different types of equipment, because each type challenges the musculoskeletal system differently as a result of individual biomechanical variations. An exercise at a particular intensity for intended muscle groups using one piece of equipment may result in quite a different total work output compared to another piece of equipment, simply because either the same muscles are challenged using a different anatomic arrangement or additional muscles are involved. Though these differences may give each of the many kinds of variable resistance equipment its saleability (being touted as "better than the rest" or "unique"), they also prevent comparison of their functional effectiveness. Whereas these differences may be of great importance to a bodybuilder, they may make little difference to a runner who is using this equipment for the more general purpose of overall conditioning for musculoskeletal balance and injury protection.

Some examples of training specificity may serve to stimulate readers to think of additional examples germane to their own training programs. One example relates to the effect of the direction of a joint's movement on the training of muscles attached to that joint. Let us consider the act of pushing a barbell overhead. This requires activity in the pectoralis muscles, perhaps the most important chest muscles. When we stand and push the barbell overhead, primarily the portion of this muscle nearest the collarbone (clavicle) is activated. When we lie supine on a bench with trunk parallel to the floor, the middle portion of the muscle is most utilized. When we lie on an inclined bench with hips higher than the shoulders, mainly the lower portion of the pectoralis major is challenged.

Another example of specificity involves the consideration of linear versus rotary motion. Typically, muscles exert force in a straight line, but the effect of this shortening or lengthening is to produce rotary movement of a bone around a joint axis. Only if two joints are involved can linear motion be produced. In a squat, for example, the trunk moves up and down (linearly), due to rotary motion produced simultaneously at the ankles, knees, and hips. A leg extension involving only the knee joint, however, produces rotary movement.

A third example of specificity concerns the intricate interrelationships between skeletal muscles in permitting body movement to occur. We have been concerned primarily with those muscles directly involved in producing movement—the agonists or prime movers. Other muscles influence the function of these prime movers. There are at least four groups of these. We have already mentioned the antagonists, which typically act in the opposite direction to the agonists, but which, when the agonists are active, remain relaxed or else help stabilize the joints on which the agonists are acting. Synergistic muscles help the prime movers and may partially compensate for movement loss if paralysis or extreme fatigue occurs in the prime movers. Stabilizer muscles fix a relevant body part in such a way that motion can occur in the proper direction. Neutralizer muscles eliminate one of the two possible directions of movement by a prime mover.

A few examples to indicate the extent of skeletal muscle interaction may help illustrate these interrelationships. For knee joint flexion, the prime movers are the biceps femoris, semitendinosus, and semimembranosus. Synergists include the gracilis, sartorius, popliteus, and gastrocnemius. Neutralizers include the biceps femoris on one side and flexors on the other side. Stabilizers include flexors of the hip joint. For hip flexion, the prime movers are the iliopsoas group. Synergists include the adductors longus and brevis, sartorius, rectus femoris, tensor fasciae latae, parts of the gluteus medius and minimus, and pectineus. Neutralizers include the tensor fasciae latae and pectineus. Stabilizers include the extensors of the lumbar spine and the abdominal muscles. As a final example, for hip extension the prime movers are the gluteus maximus, biceps femoris, semitendinosus, and semimembranosus. Synergists include parts of the gluteus medius and minimus and the entire adductor magnus. Neutralizers include the gluteus medius and adductors. Stabilizers include the abdominal muscles and extensors of the lumbar spine.

From this it should be evident that during running much more is occurring than simply the activation of a few prime movers. Many other muscles are utilized, with different attachment points on several involved joints. These all must be adequately strengthened if they are to do their jobs of permitting distance runners to meet their competitive needs. These needs can vary from great strength or enormous quickness in short, fast races to prolonged performance at submaximum work loads in long-distance races. Though running itself provides the most specific development stimulus to the prime movers, conditioning programs should include exercises that effectively improve the performance abilities of these accessory muscles in assisting the prime movers.

Advantages and Disadvantages of Isotonics and Isokinetics. There are some identifiable advantages and disadvantages—good and bad points—regarding free weight systems and the myriad of variable and accommodating resistance devices available for use in a comprehensive conditioning program. Appreciating some of these differences may help athletes and coaches make the best decisions for their own needs. Free weights and the use of one's own body weight are particularly effective at improving strength and power while at the same time integrating balance and coordination of many major muscle groups in a manner that closely matches the neuromuscular patterns utilized in sport skills, particularly the ability to accelerate. Examples might include squats and power cleans using weights, and sit-ups and dips using one's body weight. Both eccentric and concentric tension can be developed, which seems to be better than developing either one alone. Although muscle group isolation can be achieved, it is easy as well to provide a strengthening stimulus for those muscles playing a stabilizing and assisting (synergizing) role in ensuring stable joint function.

With free weights, only the very sophisticated lifter needs more than relatively little specialized equipment. A bench and rack on which to position the weights can be purchased (or built) for relatively little expense and permits training in the privacy of one's basement or garage. An almost infinite combination of hand spacings on the bar, foot positions, and format of movements is possible, providing both variety and subtle stimulus variability from session to session. Identification of progress comes objectively by such measurements as the maximum manageable weight for one rep, the numbers of reps and sets that can be managed, subjective assessment of the effort required, and independent evaluation using a device (such as Cybex, Biodex, etc.) that can also quantify muscle performance characteristics. Free weights are relatively inexpensive and can be stored compactly. The use of one's body weight coupled with a chair, an overhead bar, and a box provides even greater simplicity.

Free weights have relatively few liabilities. One relates to the risk of injury unless the athlete learns proper technique before serious lifting. A spotter may be needed to provide assistance when required to minimize injury risk. If the free weight area of a training room is busy with many athletes of varying abilities attempting the same lifts, effective alternation between athletes may require the continual addition or removal of weight plates from the lifting bar to meet individual requirements. This can detract from athletes' concentration and can keep the activity level too high during the rest period. The best alternative may be to arrange a different time for training.

It is probably inappropriate to suggest assets and liabilities for fitness machines in general, due to their enormous variety in mode of operation. Essentially all of the variable resistance machines, however, have the user move a weight or resistance along some specific unchanging path. This permits greater isolation of individual muscles or specific muscle groups, providing localized overload. Both concentric and eccentric tension can be produced. Progress can be monitored by identifying how many plates or how much resistance is moved and by counting reps to reach fatigue. Machines with stacks of weights are typically safer than free weights because the weights slide up and down on metal bars, supported indirectly by the lifter (via cables or chains). The design of each piece of equipment provides for easy set-up in minimum time. With some equipment the athlete can perform a variety of exercises simply by moving from one station (position) to another around it.

Variable resistance equipment has some liabilities as well, however. Much of the equipment is so expensive that it is beyond the price appropriate for home purchase. Some brands are designed so that developing each major muscle group requires a separate machine. Caution is then necessary to ensure that for any agonist muscle group being trained, the appropriate machine is available for training the antagonist group. Very tall or very short individuals often cannot use these machines because most are constructed to fit the majority of people who are relatively close to the mean height for men and women. Finally, because many of these machines dampen acceleration

to ensure a slower speed for optimum strength development, the movement patterns have little direct transfer to sport skills. This is why these machines are tools to help develop comprehensive fitness rather than tools for specific sport skill development.

Accommodating (isokinetic) resistance equipment, marketed under such brand names as Cybex, Biodex, Kin-Com, and Lido, has provided an alternative to variable resistance equipment and free weights (Malone, 1988). Perhaps their greatest asset is that they provide the opportunity to develop maximum tension across the entire range of joint motion at a wide variety of velocities. In turn, this optimizes the development of strength, power, and work output. Injuries are minimal because the machines provide mainly passive resistance matching that initiated by the user. There are no free weights or stacks of plates that must be controlled. Newer versions often are equipped with video screens that graphically depict muscle responses. This can have considerable biofeedback value as it gives the user instantaneous visual display of force output or developing fatigue. On some models computerized data storage and retrieval can provide comparative and statistical analysis of responses from repeated sessions.

A variety of factors cause these machines to be less "user-friendly" than free weights and variable resistance machines. First, they too are quite expensive, making home use almost out of the question. Second, many joint testing functions are carried out on the same unit, requiring considerable machine readjustment for each joint tested. Professional assistance may be necessary to ensure proper joint alignment and calibration. Thus, their primary use seems to be either for diagnostic evaluation and rehabilitation or for specialized training for patients or athletes. With the former, the cost of the machine can be amortized through hospital-based third-party payment mechanisms. Similar cost-based utilization isn't always practical in a health spa or laboratory setting. In our work with elite-level distance runners, we find that isokinetic evaluation, particularly of lower limb muscles, can be very useful for identifying similarities or differences in right side versus left, extension versus flexion, and so on. The rate of recovery from an injury can be tracked in this manner, and the possibility of a developing imbalance that might predispose to injury can also be identified, along with the usual measurement of performance changes brought about by training.

Third, of the accommodating resistance machines on the market, only Cybex has been thoroughly validated as the result of a few decades of use by clinicians worldwide. The others are much less established and validated. Fourth, eccentric tension generation is not always possible with accommodating resistance equipment. Fifth, the newer machines are computer-controlled or computer-driven with already-programmed software packages. Individualized muscle testing or training sequences are not always easy to implement unless the existing software is modified or additional software is created. Sixth, testing and training are intended for relatively specific isolated muscle groups; multiple muscle group testing or training is difficult to accomplish. Thus, there is little of the integrative neuromuscular coordination that is so important in transfer to sport skills.

In summary, the bulk of experience over the past few decades suggests the following:

- Exercises that develop balance and coordination of many major muscle groups provide a better practical and total conditioning effect for runners than those that solely isolate one or a few muscle groups.
- Examples of such exercises typically include the use of free weights, one's own body weight, or arrangements of cams or pulleys connected to stacks of weights.
- The best plan is to identify the major muscle groups that need development and then create a training plan that best takes advantage of all the various kinds of equipment in a particular training facility.
- Keeping detailed records of amount of work done per rep or per sets of reps or records of more sophisticated aspects of left-right and agonist-antagonist similarities by use of accommodating resistance equipment (such as Cybex) provides methods for identifying both progress over time and deficits or imbalances that might indicate a predisposition to injury.

Combining hard work with a well-developed plan and specific monitoring will go far in providing an optimum level of comprehensive as well as specialized fitness.

Plyometrics—Eccentric/Concentric Tension Coupling

Bounding and jumping exercises involve isotonic tension generation but do so in a unique manner. As we strike the ground after having been in midair, an initial brief period of eccentric tension generation occurs as the landing legs absorb the impact effects of body weight and gravity by momentarily flexing at the knee. Forward momentum as well as body weight contribute to this eccentric tension. A split second later, this is followed by concentric tension generation. During concentric tension, forward and upward movement then occurs. As our feet strike the ground, every impact is accompanied by this eccentric-concentric tension-generation pattern. Bounding and jumping simply exaggerate it.

According to Matveyev (1981), the body's ability to improve the operational qualities of eccentric-concentric coupling with specialized training provides an enormous opportunity for improving power, particularly in jumping. Yuriy Verkhoshanskiy (1973) referred to exercises that improve tolerance to this kind of stress (typically jumping off boxes, landing, and then explosively leaping upward) as "shock-loading." Atha (1981) termed them "bounce-loading" exercises. The term **plyometrics** refers to training exercises that augment or increase concentric power output by means of a closely linked preceding eccentric (stretch) loading. The Greek word *pleythyein* means "to increase."

When eccentric-concentric coupling occurs, several phenomena interact to enhance power output. One of these is a muscle stretch reflex. As an example, let us consider a simple bounding exercise in which a lower limb is about to absorb landing shock and at the same time provide the pushoff that begins the next bound in the sequence. Lengthening tension in the quadriceps muscle cells stretches small receptor endings called *muscle spindles*. Activation of the sensory neurons connecting to these spindles produces a reflex stimulation of the motor neurons innervating the quadriceps muscle cells. An active generation of concentric tension occurs, producing a tendency for knee extension. If this reflex stimulation is timed perfectly with the nearly simultaneous volley of information from the cerebral cortex to voluntarily initiate takeoff, the two will summate, enhancing total neuromuscular output at the knee joint and providing a powerful knee extensor response.

A second phenomenon resulting from eccentric tension is the storage of energy in elastic components within the muscle cells (Thomas, 1988). These are arranged both in series with and parallel to the muscle cell proteins that slide past each other during tension generation. This elastic energy can be recovered during the subsequent shortening. The magnitude of recovery will be greatest when

- there is no time delay between lengthening and shortening tension (Komi & Bosco, 1978),
- the lengthening tension is not too great (Cavagna, 1977), and
- the velocity of lengthening tension is greatest (Burke, 1981).

Specific plyometric exercises are used actively by athletes in such disciplines as high jumping and triple jumping, where a major emphasis is developing maximum possible vertical or horizontal trajectories in flight. Plyometric exercises for leg muscles typically include various types of depth-jumping exercises using boxes or other gymnastics equipment. Receiving and immediately pushing back a medicine ball is an example of plyometric exercise challenging the upper body.

The kinds of equipment needed for plyometric exercises can be quite simple: sturdy boxes 10, 15, 20, 25, and 30 inches high, weighted vests (10, 15, 20, and 25 lb), a few adjustable hurdles, and a smooth grassy surface. Using these, an individualized program can be devised to provide a variety of challenging plyometric stimuli for developing muscle and joint strength and power. Exact numbers of reps and sets (and heights of hurdles or boxes) depend on the athlete's prior experience, position in a training macrocycle, and event specialty. We have found that for hurdle hops (jumping over five hurdles closely spaced to permit one 2-footed landing between them) or box jumping (jumping onto and off of four boxes closely spaced to permit one 2-footed landing between them), more than 20 to 25 bounds is excessive. If the athlete can easily manage sequences such as five sets of five bounds using low boxes or low hurdles, then the intensity can be increased gradually by increasing the athlete's body weight (using a weight vest) or the height to which the center of gravity must be lifted. The athlete can also do bounding exercises on a soft grassy surface, performing three sets of 10 elongated strides with the exaggerated knee lift used in the step phase of the triple jump.

On first consideration, it might not seem appropriate for distance runners to be interested in improving their jumping ability. Efficient running is characterized by, among other things, minimal vertical oscillation, thereby ensuring optimum conversion of energy into forward motion. A modest amount of plyometric training, however, particularly for middle-distance runners, will add a beneficial power component that would not be acquired through the more traditional isotonic training techniques. Such power can be beneficial in racing situations for sudden pace changes through effective use of the large hip and leg extensors. Additionally, any increase in joint strength resulting from such training would benefit the athlete in terms of injury prevention.

Plyometrics should be considered as highly specific exercises to be scheduled judiciously, and are potentially dangerous when done improperly or in a fatigued state. Six guidelines are therefore appropriate:

1. Because of their intensity and ballistic nature, plyometrics should be preceded by thorough warm-up and stretching exercises.
2. They should not be done after serious weight training or fast-speed running sessions, but rather should be scheduled as a first item on a training agenda, when muscles and joints are fresh.
3. Because these exercises have a large anaerobic component and require good technique and considerable concentration, nearly complete recovery should occur between sets.
4. Anaerobic running sesions should not be scheduled for the day following a quality plyometric session; one day of easy running is needed to ensure recovery.
5. Athletes should always use soft, resilient landing surfaces, such as grass or suitable mats, along with shoes that provide plenty of support.
6. Plyometrics should be introduced only after a substantial base of strengthening and conditioning; not all distance runners ought to consider plyometrics to be crucial or essential. They are an advanced form of specific training intended to provide middle-distance runners with an explosive component in their leg and hip extensors that can be beneficial during specific aspects of racing.

Circuit Training and Stage Training for Comprehensive Conditioning

During the 1950s, the pursuit of an active, health-oriented lifestyle became popular, and many people began to seek programs for building a high level of comprehensive fitness in its own right without pursuing the competitive aspects of bodybuilding, weight lifting, or other formally organized sports. The idea seemed plausible that a series of exercises could be designed and sequenced in such a manner that, when they were performed one after the other, a combination of strength, power, stamina, agility, flexibility, and cardiovascular conditioning could be stimulated. If such an exercise regimen were followed for a period of weeks, this would serve as an overload stimulus that would bring adaptive improvements in the performance variables challenged. At the University of Leeds, in England, Morgan and Adamson (1957) developed just such a routine and called it *circuit training*. Specific tasks were assigned for completion at a series of so-called exercise stations, some with simple pieces of equipment to assist with the exercise. These stations were arranged to fit available space. In this manner as many people as there were stations could train at the same time, each person moving from one station to another at a similar pace. The muscle groups stimulated at each adjacent station were quite different so as to minimize the chance for inappropriate localized fatigue.

Circuit work is now recognized as a useful means of both developing general conditioning as well as stimulating specific muscle groups. The number and intensity of reps can vary, and so can the rest interval between individual reps or sets of reps; the number of exercise stations; the emphasis on strength, power, or flexibility; and the extent of anaerobic as well as aerobic involvement. A large variety of circuit training regimens have been devised (Sorani, 1966), revealing considerable ingenuity and creativity to meet the needs of various athletic populations and workout environments. Some circuits consist solely of calisthenic exercises or exercises done against body weight that require no special equipment. These can be done either all in one place or at various sites; for example, around each of the four corners of a track with the athlete jogging or running from point to point to begin each new exercise. Other circuits can be done indoors, using the selection of wall bars, benches, and adjustable vaulting boxes commonly found in a gymnasium. Seb Coe's physical education instructor at Loughborough University, George Gandy, devised a plan during the mid-1970s that involved such varied exercises as a rope climb, depth jumps onto and off of a box, dips, burpees (sometimes called squatthrusts), leg raises, inclined push-ups (sometimes called press-ups), and step-ups onto a bench. This circuit merged plyometrics, strength training, flexibility, and cardiovascular development into a single program (Gandy, 1983). This is comprehensive conditioning at its finest.

Improvement in conditioning from such a program, done two to three times per week, can be measured in various ways (Wilmore et al., 1978). Subjectively, people sense that it becomes gradually less stressful to proceed through the circuit at a given volume and intensity of work. Careful observation by a coach or by other athletes can reveal greater or lesser performance competency in particular exercises. Objectively, measurements can be made of the number of reps, amount of weight managed, or total time required for completion of specific exercises. Motivation typically is high even from the beginning of such a program. Initially there is the satisfaction of learning new exercises. Later there is improvement of skill competency. Once this plateaus, further improvements occur with performance gains in strength or total work output.

Several simple guidelines can be outlined to assist athletes in constructing appropriate circuit training programs. First, schedule no more than between about 8 to 12 exercises (5 to 9 for beginners), and ensure through variety that all major muscle groups are exercised. Next assign an acceptable number of reps to permit completion of the circuit in about 12 to 15 minutes. This restricts each exercise to about half a minute in duration. The number of reps assigned can be determined through prior assessment. For more difficult exercises, the maximum number of reps achievable in 45 sec can be determined; for easier exercises, a 60-sec test period is appropriate. Then, half the total number of reps completed in each of these time limits can be assigned for the set. The intent is for athletes to remain continuously active, be at each station for about the same period of time, and not become excessively fatigued.

Second, plan to do from two to five reps of the circuit, depending on fitness level, which provides a training period lasting approximately an hour. Take no more than 2 to 3 minutes of rest between the completion of one circuit and the start of the next circuit repetition. Third, challenge different muscle groups at each adjacent station. Fourth, emphasize quality of performance output (good technique); do not rush through each exercise. Fifth, give special attention to the development of those muscles that are not emphasized during specialized event-related training. Sixth, incorporate all aspects of fitness into the circuit program: flexibility, agility, strength, and endurance, with additional emphasis on components of total fitness that are rather poorly developed in relation to others.

Two important variants to circuit training have developed that are quite different from simply changing the combination of basic exercises indicated previously. One involves the use of specific strength-training equipment such as free weights and machines (Allen, Byrd, & Smith, 1976). This approach is appropriately termed *circuit weight training*. In a prescribed short time limit (such as 30 sec), as many reps as can be managed are completed at a given station at about 50% of the one-rep maximum. Immediately the athlete moves to the next station, challenging different muscle groups in an equivalent manner. Stations that require push-ups, chin-ups, or sit-ups can also be inserted easily into such a routine.

The second variant is stage training. Here, a variety of exercises are arranged in circuit fashion, but the athlete proceeds through the circuit only once. At each stage, the athlete completes either several sets of reps—for example, one third of the maximum number that can be done in 45 or 60 sec with an appropriate rest period between each set—or one very long set. This permits specific and intense localized muscle loading as a stimulus to improve strength and endurance. Seb Coe has devised a stage training routine that can be done almost anywhere because it requires only a chair and a box or low table. Particularly during extended periods of travel away from his home training environment when workout facilities are not conveniently located, he can preserve a high level of overall conditioning that otherwise would tend to be neglected. Here is a brief summary of his stage-training routine:

Half-squats: Ranging from 2 sets of 5 x 200 to 2 sets of 500 each; recovery equal to the duration of one set.

Bent-knee sit-ups: Alternating straight trunk curls with oblique trunk curls, alternate elbows touching the opposite knee; one set of 200 to 250 reps.

Push-ups (press-ups): With feet elevated to incline the lower limbs; 5 sets of 20 reps.

Back extensions: Using a chair and either a friend or some immovable object to stabilize both legs; 3 to 4 x 20 to 30 reps; no more than 100 per session.

Step-ups: Done onto a box or a low sturdy table; 2 x 10 each with alternate legs; then 2 x 20 each with alternate legs; done as one continuous set.

Table 4.2 provides some suggestions for distance runners interested in devising circuit-, stage-, and free weight–training sessions. These exercises or lifts should be quite familiar to all readers, and a few are

Table 4.2 Suggestions for Comparing Light, Medium, and Hard Training Sessions Using Circuit, Stage, and Weight Training

The exercises to be performed in each set or circuit are marked with an X	Circuits[a] Number of circuits			Stage training[b] Number of stages		
	2-3 Easy	3-4 Medium	4-5 Hard	5-6 Easy	7-8 Medium	8-10 Hard
Dips		X	X			
Back extensions	X	X		X		
Back extensions over chair			X[c]		X	X[c]
Bent-knee sit-ups, straight raise	X			X		
Bent-knee sit-ups, twisting raise		X			X	
Bent-knee sit-ups, inclined			X			X
Press-ups (push-ups)	X	X		X		
Press-ups, feet elevated			X		X	X
Squat thrusts (frog jumps)	X		X	X		
Burpees		X	X		X	X
Leg raise			X			
Rope climb		X	X			
Chin-ups (pull-ups)	X	X				
Barbell step-ups			X	X	X	X

Strength + endurance weight training	Repetitions/set			Sets		
	Easy	Medium	Hard	Easy	Medium	Hard
Barbell curls	3	6	10	3	4	6
Bent-arm pullovers	2	5	8	3	3	2
Barbell bench press	2	4	6	4	4	4
Barbell half-squats	2	4	6	6	6	6
Barbell-alternated front lunge	2	4	6	3	3	6
Vertical rowing	2	3	5	4	5	6
Barbell step-ups (moderate load)	10	15	20	2	4	5-6

[a]Each circuit should consist of between about 8 and 12 exercises when athlete is fully accustomed to this kind of training.

[b]Each stage is a single exercise done a given number of repetitions.

[c]Use caution with this exercise if there is known low-back weakness; as with other exercises, initially always use care.

illustrated on the following pages (Figures 4.7 to 4.20) by three world-class runners: Seb Coe, Pat Porter, and Wendy Sly. An almost infinite variety of such exercises can be developed to fit the kinds of equipment available, whether in a gymnastics hall, a health spa, or a living room. Once a general outline of numbers of sets, reps, and rest breaks has been established, fine-tuning should provide the necessary alterations to optimize development and minimize unnecessary fatigue. Then this program can become an effective and integral part of the overall training plan. Figure 4.6 provides an overview of the interrelationships between comprehensive conditioning and the various aspects of running as they contribute not only to strength and speed but also to endurance and stamina. For distance running, total body conditioning is not as much a direct contributor to competitive success or failure as it is a tool toward achieving the goals of injury prevention and provision of a comprehensive fitness base for more event-specific training (i.e., running).

Comprehensive Conditioning Exercises

The exercises shown in Figures 4.7 through 4.20 can improve strength, power, and endurance in the major muscle groups that are important to distance runners. This sequence proceeds from upper to lower body; athletes will want to consider carefully the design of a training sequence that is best for them in terms of specific needs and well-rounded balance. Typically, an appropriate combination of exercises is selected to train those muscle groups that most need additional development. A training sequence is designed to prevent excessive fatigue by challenging different muscle groups at each station. Depending on an athlete's access to various kinds of equipment, for developing certain muscle groups it may be entirely appropriate to substitute another training modality for that illustrated here. Emphasis ought to be on good technique and an appropriate training stimulus for improving the strength, endurance, flexibility, and agility components of fitness.

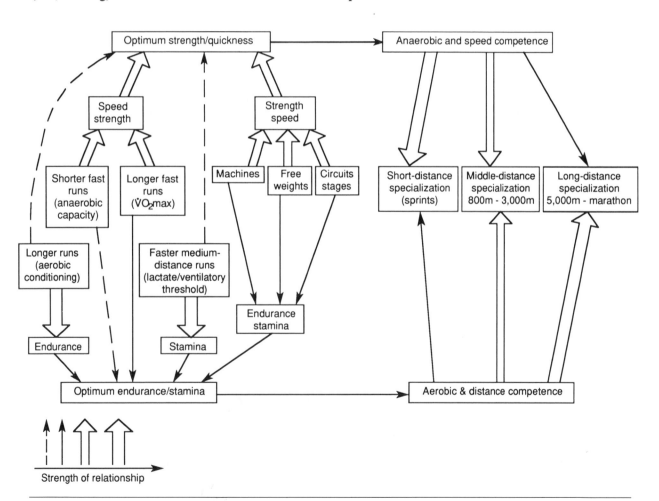

Figure 4.6 Summary of interrelationships between comprehensive conditioning and running in the development of strength/quickness and endurance/stamina in the three general groups of runners (sprinters, middle-distance, and long distance).

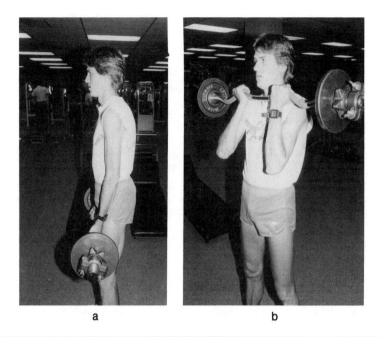

a   b

Figure 4.7 *Standing medium grip barbell curl* for developing the biceps brachii. Using a palms-up grip, hold the barbell at arm's length against the upper thighs, with feet and arms spaced about 15 inches apart (a). Inhale as the bar is curled up toward the top of the shoulders (b). Keep the back straight with legs and hips locked. Return to the starting position in a smooth, controlled manner using eccentric tension generation accompanied by exhalation.

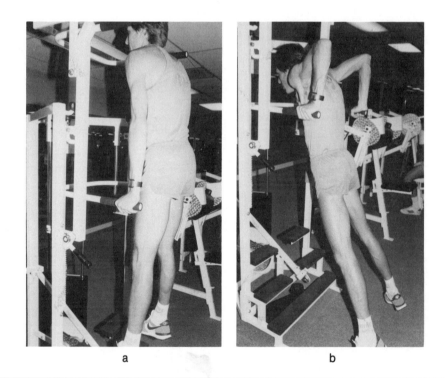

a   b

Figure 4.8 *Dips* to develop pectorals and triceps. Find a set of parallel bars or a dip stand built specifically for this purpose. The bars should be high enough to prevent the feet from touching the floor at the lowest point of the exercise. In the starting position (a), the athlete is supported in an erect position by the arms. With elbows at the sides as much as possible, the body is lowered by bending the arms until the biceps and the forearms come close together (b). An inhalation occurs during this descent. After a very brief pause, triceps shortening tension will permit the athlete to press back up to full arm's length, thereby allowing maximum activity in the triceps and pectoral muscles. Exhalation occurs during this return phase. The body will tend to swing to and fro during this exercise, but the athlete must develop control to minimize this movement.

Figure 4.9 *Push-ups (press-ups)* to develop pectorals and triceps. These exercises are very familiar to almost everyone, and there are many possible varieties. The simplest version is the medium-grip push-up with feet on the floor. When the hands are closer together, the inner pectorals receive more emphasis; hands spaced farther apart puts emphasis on the outer pectorals. The exercise is made even more difficult through increasing the resistance, as shown here by raising the position of the feet. Begin the exercise in the position shown, with the body rigid and the triceps and pectorals under tension but locked. From this position the body is lowered as far as possible. Following a very brief pause, the body is pushed upward again to return to the starting position. Inhalation with breath-holding occurs on the descent, with exhalation during ascent.

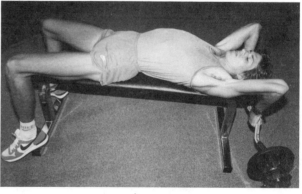

a   b

Figure 4.10 *Bent-arm barbell pullover* to develop upper pectorals and muscles of the rib cage. This exercise is begun in the position shown in Figure 4.10a, lying supine on a bench, shoulders near one end, head resting at the end, a barbell supported by the arms just above the chest and over the nipples using a palms-down handgrip a little wider than the width of the chest. Inhale as the weight is moved closely along and over the chest and face and finally lowered until it nearly touches the floor (Figure 4.10b). The return motion is essentially the reverse: exhalation as the bar is pulled upward, then past the face and back to the chest.

Whereas strength is increased by emphasizing higher intensity work with fewer reps, and endurance is best improved by the opposite format, that is, many reps of a submaximal stimulus, stamina bridges the gap between the two. Stamina represents a high level of strength sustainable for a considerable number of reps. Experience will dictate exactly how and when the athlete's emphasis needs directing more toward strength, stamina, or endurance to match personal needs. Although strength and stamina are typically stimulated in separate sessions, it is possible to incorporate both into single training sessions. Such patterns form the basis for sessions in which the number of reps per set decreases but the amount of weight

a   b

Figure 4.11 *Seated barbell press in front of and behind the neck* to develop the front and outer deltoid muscles. This exercise begins from a sitting position, with a barbell cleaned either to the front or the back of the shoulders, using a palms-down handgrip as shown in (a). The barbell is then pressed upward to arm's length overhead (b) and returned; if the starting position was behind the neck, return is in front of the neck. Inhalation is during the press; exhalation is during the eccentric return.

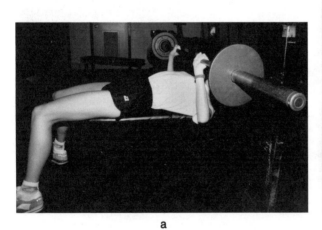
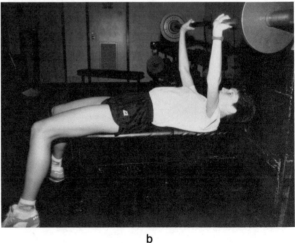

a   b

Figure 4.12 *Barbell bench press* to develop pectoral muscles. The outer pectorals will be best developed if the palms-out bar grip is wide; inner pectorals are best activated with a close grip. As the athlete lies supine on a flat bench with legs positioned on the sides of the bench and feet on the floor, the barbell is lifted off its rack, with inhalation occurring as the bar is being lowered (a) to the chest. Following a brief but definite pause, exhalation occurs as the bar is pressed upward to arm's length (b). The back may arch a little, but the hips (and the head as well) must remain on the bench.

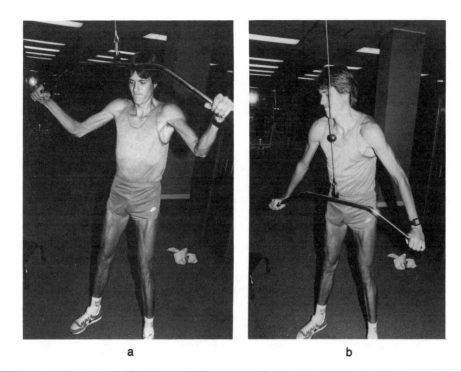

a   b

Figure 4.13 *Lat pull-down* to develop the latissimus dorsi. This exercise is best done using a machine with a bar attached to a cable, which in turn winds around a pulley arrangement and connects to a weight stack. With hands grasping the bar (either a wide palms-down handgrip as shown in Figure 4.13a or a close handgrip is possible) and supporting the weight stack, arms extended in front to head level, inhale and pull the bar straight down until the bar touches the top of the thighs (b). The more the arms are locked at the elbows, the greater the stimulus applied to the latissimi. Exhalation occurs with a return to the starting position. Variations of this exercise can be done in the kneeling position, beginning with the arms extended overhead, with a pull-down either in front to the top of the chest or in back to the neck.

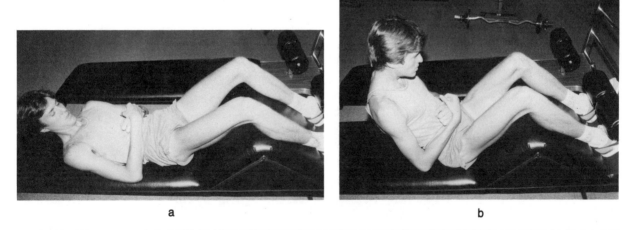

a   b

Figure 4.14 *Bent-knee simple and compound sit-up* to develop the four pairs of abdominal muscles. This exercise can be done using either a level sit-up board as illustrated or an inclined board. Some kind of strap or pad needs to be in place around which to restrain the feet. Thighs should make a 45° angle with floor (a). Hands may be placed behind the head, cradling it, or behind the head and extended, or held at chest or stomach level. For quite accomplished athletes, a weight may be held behind the neck. Upon inhalation, the torso is raised. The extent and direction of the raise is also variable; trunk flexion may be straight up to the mid-range of movement (b), at which point flexion can continue straight upward or be twisted right or left to promote oblique abdominal development. Trunk flexion can continue far enough so that the shoulders nearly touch the knees. When maximum flexion is reached, exhale and return to the original position. As abdominal muscle fatigue develops, hip flexors such as the iliopsoas become increasingly active, and lower back stress increases. Thus, high reps are neither necessary nor recommended (sets of 25 to 30 are adequate).

a   b

Figure 4.15 *Leg raise* to develop hip flexors. This exercise can be done using either dip bars or some other arrangement of parallel bars, or a single bar as shown here. The starting position can have the athlete hanging (a), or in the position to begin dips (see Figure 4.8a); in either situation, elbows are locked out. Inhale and bend at the waist, raising the legs until they are parallel to the floor (b). Try not to bend the knees. Exhale as the return to the starting position occurs. Primary hip flexors developed here are the psoas major and iliacus, but the rectus femoris, sartorius, and tensor fasciae latae are strengthened as well. Abdominal muscles are active as stabilizers.

a   b

Figure 4.16 *Quadriceps extension* to develop lower anterior thigh muscles (quadriceps group). Any of various leg extension machines may be used. The best sitting position is where the end of the seat is against the rear of the knees. The seat should be grasped with hands just behind the buttocks; usually handgrips are provided (a). Toes are pointed slightly downward. With inhalation, the weight stack is raised until legs are essentially parallel with the floor (b). The upper body should remain fixed during this activation of the thigh muscles. Return to the starting position is accompanied by exhalation.

a   b   c

Figure 4.17 *Barbell alternated front lunge* to develop anterior thigh muscles and biceps femoris of the posterior thigh (hamstrings group). A barbell is placed either on the rear shoulders as if in preparation for a barbell squat, using a palms-up grip (a), or held in position at the level of the upper chest as if in preparation for a barbell push press (again using a palms-up grip). The back is kept straight, the head up, and the feet planted firmly on the floor next to each other. The exercise is begun by inhaling and taking a step forward as far as possible until the thigh of the stepping leg is almost parallel with the floor (b, c). The rear leg should be as straight as possible; do not bend the knee any more than necessary. From here, two possibilities exist. The athlete can step back to the starting position (exhaling in the process) and either repeat the same movement with the other leg or repeat the movement with the same leg. A more intense training stimulus occurs if the set is completed using one particular leg stepping forward.

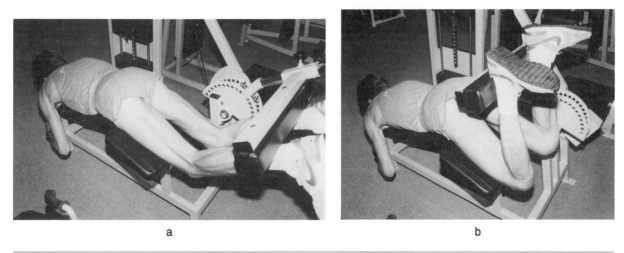

a   b

Figure 4.18 *Hamstrings curl* to develop posterior thigh muscles (hamstrings group), particularly the biceps femoris. Either a specific hamstrings curl machine or a leg extension machine can be used. Lie face down on the bench, straighten the legs, and place the heels under the appropriate foot pads (a). Grasp the front of the machine for support. On inhalation, curl the legs upward until the lower and upper legs nearly come together, lifting an appropriate stack of weight (b). Along with exhalation, return to the starting position.

a   b

c

Figure 4.19 *Barbell squat* for developing the entire body. The athlete begins this exercise in an erect standing position, with a barbell held on the shoulders using a palms-down handgrip (the photo in Figure 4.19a was taken a split-second after the squat portion began). The feet may be flat on the floor, or heels may be slightly raised. The chest is kept high, a deep inhalation occurs, and the athlete moves in a steady controlled fashion down to the squat position illustrated in Figures 4.19b and c. There is a definite momentary pause, with exhalation, followed by a second inhalation and return to the standing position and then exhalation. A fairly light weight can be used, because for distance runners it isn't muscle bulk that is important, but rather strength together with stamina. Five reps constitute a typical set. For the second or third set, three or four breaths may be appropriate instead of the initial two.

lifted per rep increases and will provide an equivalent stimulus to those muscle cells being recruited. Using Seb Coe (130-lb body weight) doing six sets of half-squats as an example, the number of reps per set will be 15, 15, 15, 10, 10, and 5, with the weight increasing by 10 lb per set from 140 to 190. Admittedly, this is a challenging session—more than 5 tons moved in 70 lifts—and it will be accompanied

a   b

Figure 4.20 *Total body conditioning* exercises need not be restricted to a formal setting in which specific muscle group development is emphasized. As illustrated here with leapfrogging (a) and partner-carries (b) done outside on a grassy but hilly surface, combining the principles of circuit work, stage training, and weight training can be carried out in an exhilarating and challenging atmosphere. Seb Coe emphasized such training for many of his developmental months, including one session each week that lasted as long as a few hours that gained the understandable nickname, "Sunday slogs."

by only easy running that day and the one following. The payoff in the development of local muscle stamina, however, is considerable.

Strong muscles in a distance runner (not necessarily large muscles) are a real asset to work tolerance and injury prevention. Stronger muscles can respond more effectively to the impact stress that occurs at footstrike during running. This is particularly valuable for stabilizing joints and for reducing fatigue during repetitive stress. Muscle injuries typically occur at the muscle end of musculotendinous junctions (Garrett, Safran, Seaber, Glisson, & Ribbeck, 1987). The muscle tissue attaching to the tendons has more connective tissue and fewer sarcomeres, and this difference apparently renders it weaker than the muscle tissue adjacent to it. Larger muscle mass at these junctions makes tears less likely to occur.

The fitness an athlete develops from such training can contribute to making the difference between winning and simply performing well, and between being injury-prone and injury-resistant. In a sense, this kind of work forms the real "secret training system" of a championship-caliber athlete—few people besides the coach see the athlete do this work. It provides the strength, suppleness, stamina, and potential for speed that other athletes will not develop unless they work equally hard. Once such complete conditioning begins to reward the athlete in terms of total fitness, the added mental confidence that develops from having done the

extra measure of effort makes this athlete just that much tougher to defeat in competition.

A few comments are appropriate at this point about the proper kind of breathing patterns during weight training (Austin, Roll, Kreis, Palmieri, & Lander, 1987). The traditional view is to exhale on the way out, down, or up (during the action phase) and inhale on return (during the recovery phase). Essentially, this strategy is correct. However, from a physiological and structural point of view, during the most difficult part of the pushing or pulling part of the movement—out, down, or up—it is entirely appropriate to breath-hold *briefly*. This permits a temporary increase in intrathoracic pressure, creating a rigid rib cage and thereby providing additional support for the thoracic spine. Breath-holding also produces tension in the abdominal muscles, contributing additional support for the lower spine.

The act of breath-holding when accompanied by tension generation in the abdominal muscles and an attempt to exhale against a closed glottis, is termed a *Valsalva maneuver* (after its original descriptor, the Italian anatomist Antonio Valsalva). If this maneuver is sustained for too long, the increase in intrathoracic pressure may reduce venous return to the heart, decreasing cardiac output. This could predispose the athlete to fainting. Thus, to have the best of both worlds—minimum reduction in venous return to the heart yet adequate support to the spine—it is suggested that athletes strive to develop an effective breathing pattern to accompany their own lifting patterns that takes advantage of the information provided here. As mentioned, a brief breath-hold at the moment of maximum tension seems ideal.

Some comments are also in order concerning training safety. Just as conditioning exercises are intended to reduce the injury risk from running by producing comprehensive musculoskeletal development, there is an injury risk in engaging in a conditioning program unless appropriate safety precautions are taken. First, sturdy shoes that give lift and support to the heels and arches are a must. Second, when the vertebral column is stressed, such as with squat exercises, a well-fitting leather waist belt is recommended. This belt teams up with the abdominal muscles that are developing tension at the same time. The belt helps to reduce some of the interarticular shearing force that is particularly stressful on the vertebrae of the lumbar spine.

How much time during any portion of a training macrocycle should be devoted to comprehensive conditioning? Remember that conditioning is merely an aid to running; it is not a substitute for it and must not be overdone. Thus, during any week of training, running will always occupy the majority of the total training effort. Three important observations should make it clear that an effective conditioning plan will very likely be different for each individual athlete. First, middle-distance runners will need more strength, power, and flexibility than the longer distance runners. Second, the athlete's individual strengths and weaknesses should be identified, with emphasis on developing those muscle groups that require greater conditioning and doing maintenance work for those groups already well conditioned.

Third, during the higher volume training portions of a macrocycle (e.g., during mesocycles X_2 and X_3 as illustrated in Figure 3.3), comprehensive conditioning should receive more emphasis than during other periods. Table 4.3 provides an overview of the varied intensity and pattern of circuit, stage, and weight training that Seb Coe found useful during his yearly training macrocycle. The accompanying hourglass-shaped figure alongside the table is an attempt to provide a dimensional image of the total conditioning work load. Its width represents volume, and its vertical dimension represents time. Notice that circuit and stage training form an initial conditioning base and account for a sizable volume of weekly work. Notice in A that as introductory training progresses, the volume of circuit and stage training increases. Then, this kind of training is gradually replaced by more intense weight training (B, C) as the midpoint of the training macrocycle is reached. Up to this point, as we described more fully in chapter 3, the running aspects

of training have been directed more toward increased volume, improving aerobic fitness. As running now includes more anaerobic components and the athlete transitions into the precompetitive sharpening phase, the intensity of total body conditioning will continue to decrease (D, E), with one additional brief period of increased volume (D) prior to a decrease (E) to permit recovery, regeneration, and freshness before the actual competitive phase begins.

FLEXIBILITY—ITS RELATIONSHIP TO JOINT MOBILITY

General Concepts: Flexibility, Range of Motion, and Stretching

During day-to-day activities, sedentary people typically do not move their joints through their maximum range of motion, except perhaps during a nice relaxing yawn accompanied by a stretch of the upper limbs. Only by more vigorous activities—calisthenics, sports, or a sudden burst of energy, for example, to bound up a flight of stairs—do people greatly increase the extent of joint movement. Muscular lengthening or shortening permits this to occur. If they are not periodically stretched, connective tissues within joints and muscles tend to become more dense and less stretchable over time, increasing the difficulty of achieving what earlier was considered the full range of joint motion. We can use the word **flexibility** to define a condition of suppleness characterized by the ability to move joints through their intended normal range of motion. The dictionary definition of flexibility is "a capability of being bent without breaking." In the body, breaking corresponds to a tearing of connective or muscle tissue.

The topic of joint flexibility receives discussion on almost an annual basis in lay running magazines (Anderson, 1989; Festa, 1988) and has been discussed frequently in the coaching/scientific literature (Alter, 1988; Anderson et al., 1984; Beaulieu, 1981; Cornelius, 1985). The benefits of adequate joint mobility (or flexibility) for athletes should already be evident. When an athlete is strong as well as flexible, more force is required to produce muscle or connective tissue tearing, and more stretch is required before tearing occurs. The greater these limits of strength or stretch, the greater the performance capacities of these tissues and the less liable the athlete to injury (Beaulieu, 1981; Corbin & Noble, 1960). When athletes remain uninjured for long periods, they can continue to make progress in their training, which permits them to more closely approach their performance

Table 4.3 Suggested Format to Incorporate Total Body Conditioning Into a Distance-Running Program[a]

Month	Wk	Activity	
Oct.		Complete rest, no running, only easy calisthenics and flexibility exercises	A
	4		
Nov.		One circuit training or easy stage training session each week	
	8		
Dec.		Two stage sessions, one easy, one hard, each week	
	12		
Jan.		Two stage training sessions, both hard, each week	
	16		
Feb.		One moderate stage session, one easy weight session using light weights for endurance each week	B
	20		
Mar.		One moderate stage session and one endurance weight session using heavier weights each week	
	24		
Apr.		One week with one hard endurance weight session alternating with one week with a pyramid lifting session @ 90%-95%	C
	28		
May		One easy endurance weight session, one easy stage session, each week	D
	32		
June		Alternating weeks of one easy endurance weight session with one easy stage or circuit session	
	36		
July		One easy circuit or stage session each week	E
	40		
Aug.		Mobility work only; competition period	
	44		
Sept.		Mobility work only; competition period	
	48		
		Mobility work only; competition period	
	52		

[a]As illustrated, this pattern is for a year-long macrocycle; appropriate rearrangement (but not increase in work load) would be required for shorter macrocycles.

potential. Losing such valuable development time from injury slows this process.

Individual differences make it inappropriate to compare one person's flexibility with another's, and it may very well be unwise to attempt to achieve or surpass the flexibility level of someone else who is better endowed. One difference involves variability in the positioning of muscle attachments to tendons and bones. Another involves the extent of recovery of muscles from intense anaerobic work. Inflow of H_2O into muscles to maintain osmotic equilibrium changes their shape, making them shorter and thus decreasing flexibility of the joints to which they attach. A third difference involves the effect of diurnal postural changes, particularly as we transition from sleeping to waking. The movement of water out of intervertebral discs as a person changes from the horizontal posture (during sleep) to the vertical posture (while moving about during the day) slowly decreases body length, thereby increasing back flexibility. This is one reason why we are more flexible in the evening than in the morning—as the day goes on we become shorter people (Martin, Vroon, May, & Pilbeam, 1986). A fourth difference involves the attention given to maintaining flexibility. People who routinely put their joints through a full range of motion on a daily basis will be blessed with considerably greater joint suppleness than those who do not. It is suggested that athletes be aware of and assess their own present state of flexibility and attempt in a reasonable manner to develop and maintain sufficient flexibility so that a margin of safety exists between the athlete's needs and the limits of joint range of motion.

There is less correlation between flexibility and such variables as body build (somatotype), age, and sport skill level than there is between the performance of exercises intended to develop flexibility and an actual improvement in joint range of motion. Adequate flexibility is almost guaranteed in those athletes who, in performing comprehensive conditioning exercises properly, emphasize activity through what for them is their full range of motion (Anderson et al., 1984). As an example, pull-ups should be started from an arms-outstretched hanging position (the same position as when doing leg-raises, illustrated in Figure 4.15a) to ensure full stretch as well as strength development through the movement range from 0 degrees of elbow flexion upward past 90 degrees as the exercise is completed. However, because it is quite difficult to complete this exercise through the initial phase, athletes often begin with the elbows closer to 90 degrees. One means of permitting a complete stretch of the biceps brachii until this strength deficit is overcome is to include a few reps beginning at 90 degrees of elbow flexion and proceed back toward 0 degrees using eccentric tension generation. In training jargon, this is often referred to as "doing negatives" (the concentric form of the exercise is termed a "positive"). In this manner, stretch is assured, and strength is gradually developed to permit full-range concentric movement.

Stretching exercises fit into several categories depending on how they permit achievement of range of joint motion. *Static stretching* exercises involve slow and gentle tissue lengthening as the athlete assumes certain specific postures, some of which are illustrated in Figures 4.21 to 4.30. These exercises can be active, that is, done by the athlete, or passive, with the athlete being assisted by a partner. *Ballistic stretching* exercises involve bouncing or swinging movements that are beyond the joint range of motion typically seen in sedentary living and that may equal or exceed the range of movement found in typical athletic endeavors. Such movement should not be so excessive that the joint's maximum range of motion is exceeded, because joint injury would occur. Finally, *proprioceptive neuromuscular facilitation* (PNF) exercises permit further lengthening of an agonist muscle beyond its normal maximum length by stimulating isometric tension in its antagonist counterpart. By appropriate inhibitory interneuronal connections involving both agonist and antagonist muscles via the spinal cord, increased relaxation of tone will occur in the agonist. These PNF exercises can be done either individually or with a partner assisting (Hatfield, 1982).

Two types of performance sessions involve running, and stretching exercises should be a part of both. Training sessions that involve easy to moderate or steady running do not vigorously challenge the maximum range of motion of the joints to which the major muscle groups attach. These sessions usually begin with easy jogging, gradually increase in intensity as the body warms up and metabolic reactions speed up their rate of operation, and culminate in completion of the training assignment for a particular distance over a specific pace range. Stretching is best left as the final activity of these sessions as part of the cooldown process. The still-elevated body temperature as well as the prior physical activity will have increased muscle stretchability, making it easier to do the exercises. In a reasonably short time, no more than 15 to 20 minutes, all of the exercises that will be described shortly in Figures 4.21 to 4.30 can be completed. This will permit a systematic physical assessment of right/left agonist/antagonist similarities and differences as well as provide the daily stimulus to achieve the usual maximum range of motion appropriate to that athlete.

Other running sessions will be more difficult—these are either actual competitions or higher speed training sessions with a sizable anaerobic component. Here an athlete's maximum joint range of motion may indeed be challenged, and stretching exercises are an important part of preparation. The usual sequence is an initial easy warm-up period of jogging or easy running followed by a comprehensive stretching session, and then a series of strides that take the athlete up to the pace anticipated during the racing or fast running portion of the day's activity. Following this, it is best to include again a period of easy running (cooldown) followed by a second stretching session to regain the usual maximum range of motion and to help restore body symmetry.

Establishing a Stretching Routine

The best stretching routine is one that is easy to complete, so repeatable that it becomes almost automatic, and includes the major muscle groups used in running. It should not be hurried, and thus it provides mental relaxation as well as the needed stretching and opportunity for physical assessment. The series of exercises shown in Figures 4.21 through 4.30 are certainly not unique; they have probably appeared in print dozens of times before, most likely because they are useful. Our model for these exercises is Bo Reed, a promising young U.S. long-distance runner (28:20 for 10,000m at age 22). He's not the most flexible athlete in the world, but he works consistently at maintaining an acceptable level of flexibility. He thus is a more preferable model than an aerobics instructor whose suppleness most runners can only dream of imitating (and which is probably not needed for running excellence).

A few cardinal rules apply for performing stretching exercises:

1. Stretch the muscles on both sides of the body.
2. Do not exceed the threshold for discomfort or pain.
3. Do not bounce or jerk, but rather gradually induce the stretch.
4. Maintain each stretch stimulus at or near maximum for anywhere between 20 and 40 sec to ensure optimum lengthening.
5. Be aware of whether one side is more or less flexible than the other—is this a result of structural differences, recovery from injury, or possible development of injury?

One of the most common hamstring and calf stretching exercises is illustrated in Figure 4.21. As shown here, with the left leg forward and the right leg supporting most of the body's weight, lean forward and balance with the hands against a sturdy object. Keep the head up and slowly bend the arms, thereby leaning further forward and increasing the stretch on the right hamstrings and calf. Reverse leg positions and repeat the exercise to stretch the left hamstrings and calf muscles.

Figure 4.22 adds two muscle groups to the posterior limb stretch maneuver just described. With hands on the hips for balance, raise the right leg upward and forward and step up to an adjacent raised object as shown. This stretches the adductor muscles in the right groin region as well as the hip flexors (iliopsoas group) on the left side. Again, keeping the head as well as the right rear foot directed straight ahead, increase the angle of flexion of the bent right knee, thereby moving the hips forward and slowly increasing the stretch. Return to the original position, and switch leg positions to complete the stretching exercise.

Another stretching exercise for the hamstrings is depicted in Figure 4.23. Lying in the supine position as shown, with the right leg partially bent at the knee, grab the left leg below the calf and pull it toward the shoulders, stopping and maintaining that position at the first detection of discomfort. After perhaps 10 or 15 sec, additional stretch can probably be applied. Switch leg positions and repeat the exericse.

An exercise similar in nature to Figure 4.22 done in the supine position adds a component of stretch to the iliopsoas group along with the hamstrings. As depicted in Figure 4.24, with the left leg (and left iliopsoas) outstretched, grasp the right knee and pull it slowly toward the chest. The left leg should remain outstretched if the iliopsoas on that side is adequately stretched, but if not, it will begin to rise up as the right leg is pulled farther. Maintain this stretch for 30 to 40 sec without forcing a stretch of any of these important muscles. Then switch sides.

In Figure 4.25 the quadriceps muscles are being stretched. Standing on the right foot, grab the left foot and pull it upward and toward the left hip. After a 10- to 20-sec stretch, repeat the exercise, standing on the left foot and pulling the right foot toward the right hip to stretch the quadriceps group on that side.

Figure 4.26 illustrates a useful stretching exercise for the neck, chest, abdominal, iliopsoas, and quadriceps muscles. From the recumbent position, use the arms to lift the upper torso, helping to increase the stretch by lifting the head back as far as possible. The sternocleidomastoid muscles are also stretched. These muscles originate on the sternum and collarbone and insert on the mastoid process of the temporal bone around the ear. They protect the carotid artery, jugular vein, and vagus nerve along either side of the neck, permitting chin elevation, head movement toward the shoulder, and flexion of the vertebral column.

Two exercises are useful for the back muscles and spine. Simply by rocking back and forth several times in the supine position with knees pulled gently toward the chest (Figure 4.27), a stretch of the back muscles can be produced. Figure 4.28 depicts what sometimes is called the Oriental squat position. By gently pulling forward with the arms and resisting this with the quadriceps group, using the body weight to keep from sliding forward, a gentle stretch will be applied to the lower back muscles, hips, and knees.

Figures 4.29a and b illustrate two methods for stretching adductor muscles. In Figure 4.29a, the hands are applying gentle downward pressure on the knees. In Figure 4.29b, the hands are being used to move the feet a little closer to the torso, with additional stretch applied to the legs by elbow pressure.

In Figure 4.30a and b, several muscle groups on both sides of the body are stretched. With the left hand on the ground and right arm clasped around the distal portion of the left upper leg, the left hip rotators, left abdominal obliques, and right-side back muscles can be stretched as depicted in Figure 4.30a. Also, turning the head to the left provides a stretch to the right trapezius and sternocleidomastoid muscles. When these positions are reversed, the corresponding muscles on the opposite side of the body will be stretched. In Figure 4.30b this exercise is repeated in the supine rather than sitting position. The left leg has been brought over toward the right side with gentle pressure by the right arm bringing the left leg toward (but not touching) the floor. The head is turned toward the left to enhance the stretch of the hip rotators and abdominal obliques. Again, remember to reverse this body position to complete the stretching routine.

We have deliberately omitted some stretching exercises from this routine because in some people, particularly those who have had specific muscle or joint injuries, a sizable element of reinjury risk exists. For those athletes who have not been injured and who can indeed complete these exercises successfully, they are both beneficial and acceptable. One exercise is the familiar reach down to touch the toes while keeping the legs straight. This can be excessively stressful to the lower back, particularly if done by overweight beginners or if accompanied by any bouncing. Another involves the so-called "hurdler's stretch," which is done in a sitting position. For athletes who have suffered rotational problems with the knee joints, hamstring pulls, or low back injuries, this exercise can be more injurious than beneficial. A third exercise is sometimes called the "plow," named because the position of the head, torso, and lower limbs resembles an old-style agricultural plow blade. The individual first lies supine, then raises the legs and brings them over the head and back far enough so that the toes touch the ground. The combination of body weight plus momentum can place excessive stress on the spine, even when the hands are used to provide partial back support. The exercises illustrated in Figure 4.21 to 4.30 are a more than adequate substitute for these three exercises to provide adequate flexibility for running at any intensity.

Figure 4.21 Hamstring and calf stretching exercise.

Figure 4.22 Adding a stretch of the groin muscles and hip flexors (iliopsoas) to the hamstrings/calf exercise.

Figure 4.23 Stretching the hamstrings from the supine position.

Figure 4.24 Adding a hip flexor (iliopsoas) stretch (keeping the left leg straight) to the supine hamstrings stretching exercise (pulling the right knee toward the chest).

Figure 4.25 Quadriceps muscle stretch.

Figure 4.26 Stretching exercise for the neck, chest, abdominal, iliopsoas, and quadriceps muscles.

Figure 4.27 Stretching the lower back and spine.

Figure 4.28 Using the Oriental squat position to stretch the low back, hips, and knees.

Figure 4.29   Stretching the major adductor (groin) muscles.

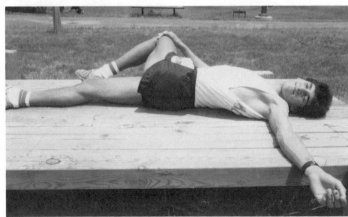

Figure 4.30   Stretching multiple muscle groups, including hip rotators and abdominal obliques.

BODY COMPOSITION

One of the more popular topics of interest to athletes and coaches as they query sport scientists about technical aspects of training and health maintenance concerns body fat: How much is optimal, is too much detrimental to performance, how can it be measured, and how accurate are the measurements? Along with lactate/ventilatory threshold, this is a topic in exercise physiology that has had more than its share of conceptual confusion and methodological mayhem. It seems a simple task to consider our total body weight as having fat and lean components. But beyond the fact that fat floats in H_2O and the rest of our tissue mass will sink, not much else regarding body composition is unequivocal. There are sex-related differences in fat storage and racial/ethnic differences as well—not only in sites of preferential fat storage but also in the density of various tissues.

When we measure such variables as body density and body fat, there are errors that, if too excessive, make the very act of measuring a waste of time because the information obtained has little use. Great care should be taken to reduce such errors. Such measurements are made for a variety of reasons. Scientists often do cross-sectional studies, collecting data from a large number of subjects to characterize body composition in a given population. Athletes usually prefer the longitudinal study approach in which they serve as their own controls and are measured several times each year over a period of years to identify the extent of change in body composition with different training patterns.

There is little doubt that the amount of fat we carry is an important topic, both in clinical medicine and in sport. When energy intake exceeds energy outgo, energy storage occurs, typically as fat. In technologically advanced societies where food is abundant and physical requirements of the working population are reduced, obesity is a chronic and important problem affecting that society's health. In turn, the desire to lose weight thus becomes a common motivating factor for many people to begin an exercise program.

The balance between training intensity (energy outgo) and nutritional status (energy intake) determines how much stored fat is present. Because protein turnover can increase during very intense training states, lean body mass can also change, increasing or decreasing depending on whether the training stimulus was appropriate or excessive. Thus, body weight, lean body mass, and body fat are all useful variables in assessing an athlete's changing body composition over time. Depending on how fat content is expressed, it can appear to change when in fact it is remaining stable. As an example, if a 60-kg male runner gains 2 kg of lean body mass through a serious strength-building program, although his *total fat content* may not change (we'll say he has 3.6 kg of body fat), his *percent body fat* will decrease from 6.0% to 5.8%.

Athletic performance can be affected in diverse ways by the presence of body fat. Swimmers, for example, find that a certain amount of fat beyond the minimum required for health maintenance is advantageous because it contributes to buoyancy. Competitive swimmers are still relatively lean people, however. Athletes in contact sports such as American football and English rugby find a certain amount of fat useful as a cushion against impact injury. Runners, though, discover that excess body fat is simply excess baggage. It increases inertia and mass and thus requires additional energy for its transport. A certain amount of fat is absolutely essential in everyone for life, however, so runners need reminding that an obsession for trying to become excessively thin can be as unhealthy as gaining too much weight. Many hormones, as well as vitamins A, D, E, and K, for example, are fat-soluble rather than water-soluble.

People with even a cursory interest in body composition have probably heard mention of (or have been measured by) such procedures as underwater weighing (densitometry), skinfold assessment (anthropometry) using calipers, or the newer technique of bioimpedance measurement (Wilmore, Buskirk, DiGirolamo, & Lohman, 1986). Densitometry determines body density directly, and anthropometry estimates it indirectly. Density measurement typically is the first step in quantifying leanness/fatness. Once density is determined, estimates can be made of percent fat and nonfat mass or lean body mass by use of regression equations. Both techniques are of considerable value, depending on the kind of information desired and the technological expertise available. An excellent review of this topic has been published recently (Brodie, 1988).

Densitometry

During the 1940s and 1950s several groups of scientists did the primary investigative work that led to the wide use of densitometry as the method of choice for evaluating human body composition. Brozek and Keys (1951) suggested that density differences in healthy people could be explained simply by differences in their relative amounts of lean and fat tissue. Detailed investigations of healthy young white adult subjects gave values for the density of body fat as 0.9007 gm/cc (Fidanza, Keys, & Anderson, 1953), with lean tissue mass averaging 1.100 gm/cc (Behnke, Osserman, & Welham, 1953). Because the human body's irregular shape makes accurate geometric volume measurement difficult and only fat tissue is less dense than H_2O, it is appropriate to determine body density by weighing underwater, using Archimedes' principle, and then converting this body density value into percent fat using a regression equation (Buskirk, 1961). **Archimedes' principle** states that a body immersed in water is buoyed up with a force equal to the weight of the water displaced. Two measurements of weight are made, one out of H_2O and the other when immersed, with a correction made for residual lung volume. Body density can then be calculated using the following equation, where

BD = Body density, OWBW = Out-of-water body weight, UWW = Underwater weight, RV = Residual volume, and WD = Water density:

$$BD = \frac{OWBW}{\frac{OWBW - UWW}{WD} - RV} \quad (4.2)$$

Two regression equations have gained popularity for converting body density values to percent body fat. The equation of Siri (1956) in which

$$\% \text{ fat} = [(4.95/\text{body density}) - 4.50] \times 100 \quad (4.3)$$

assumes fat density as 0.9 gm/cc and fat-free tissue density as 1.1 gm/cc. The equation of Brozek, Grande, Anderson, and Keys (1963) in which

$$\% \text{ fat} = [(4.57/\text{body density}) - 4.142] \times 100 \quad (4.4)$$

is based on values for the so-called reference man of 70 kg and 14% body fat.

Hydrostatic weighing is reasonably accurate but requires specialized equipment, several time-consuming repetitive measurements, and the subjects' willingness to be dunked into a tank of water. But the importance of obesity as a problem in clinical medicine as well as the interest of physical educators concerning the effect of body fat on physical performance has ensured the widespread use of this procedure. Table 4.4 provides some basic information concerning percent fat in various groups of men and women. There

Table 4.4 Selected Anthropometric Data for Men and Women

Category	% body fat Men	% body fat Women
Non-sex-specific essential body fat	2-3	2-3
Fat in trained distance runners	5-9	9-16
Fat in active healthy young adults	12-20	16-25
Clinical obesity	> 25	> 30

Category	Body mass index[a] Men	Body mass index[a] Women
Active healthy young adults	25	25
Trained distance runners	18-22	18-20
Clinical obesity	> 30	> 30

[a]Body mass index = weight in kilograms/square of height in meters.

is a certain amount of non-sex-specific essential fat in the body, which refers to lipids that are intimately associated with the life of our tissues—most cell membranes, the coverings of nerve cells, and in the brain. This is small in quantity, roughly between 2% and 3% of body weight. Usually, the term *lean body mass* includes this essential lipid (Buskirk & Mendez, 1984), with *storage fat* referring to the remainder. The term *fat weight* more accurately reflects what is measured hydrostatically, and this actually refers to all fat tissue, leaving the rest as *fat-free body weight*. Equations (4.5) and (4.6) summarize these relationships (BW = Body weight):

$$\text{Total BW} = \text{fat-free BW} + \text{fat weight} \quad (4.5)$$

and

$$\text{Total BW} = \text{(lean body mass with essential fat)} + \text{storage fat} \quad (4.6)$$

The presence of a certain amount of fat is hormonally determined. Estrogen hormones are higher in concentration in women's circulating blood than in men's. These have a hypolipemic (fat-storing) effect, with fat typically deposited in subcutaneous areas such as the buttocks and lower limbs. Men have lower circulating blood levels of estrogen than women and thus less stored fat, but men exhibit higher levels of protein-building hormones such as testosterone. Muscle tissue is more dense than adipose tissue, containing about 75% water as compared to only 10% for adipose tissue. Thus a 60-kg man at 8% fat will look smaller than a 60-kg man at 15% body fat.

Storage fat exists in such places as bone marrow, around the internal organs, and in the same subcutaneous regions where estrogen-related fat is deposited. The ideal is to have only as much stored fat as is required for normal health, which seems to range from about 4% to 8% for men and 8% to 12% for women. Unfortunately, some runners develop the erroneous belief that all fat can be dispensed with if they simply eat less and train harder. This is simply untrue and can cause a variety of nutritional disorders that will be detrimental to continued good health.

At least five technological sources of error contribute to our inability to measure body density precisely. Most of these can be controlled reasonably well. One is the dry-land weight obtained using a measuring scale. Another is the body volume measurement. A third is the weighing chamber water temperature; only at 39.2 degrees F (4 degrees C) does water have a density of 1 gm/cc. (This method would be even more unpopular with subjects if that were the water temperature used during submersion!) Water temperature at 85 degrees F (29.5 degrees C) has a density of 1.004 gm/cc. A fourth error comes from the presence of intestinal gas, which is more difficult to estimate than to reduce by using dietary guidelines the day before testing to minimize intestinal gas production. Finally, there is lung volume, which can be minimized (i.e., reduced to residual lung volume) by having the subject exhale maximally prior to submersion (Weltman & Katch, 1981). Using predicted nomographic values for residual volume based on age, sex, and height instead of measured values, however, can also add considerable error (Morrow, Jackson, Bradley, & Hartung, 1986) and should be avoided.

In addition to the five sources of technological error mentioned earlier, other constraints can and may cause problems in interpreting densitometric data accurately. We do not yet know precisely how an intense training program maintained over a period of months may change subtle aspects of body composition. MacDougall, Sale, Elder, and Sutton (1982) suggest that athletes may have denser bones and muscles than nonathletes. If true, this would cause an overestimation of percent fat using the equations that assume lesser body density.

Even when these technological sources of error are minimized, there is still a roughly 3% margin of error that represents the biological limitation of using only two components—fat weight and fat-free body weight —in our measurement model. There are individual variations in body water content and in lean tissue density, yet the assumption is made that body density is a fixed value. Thus, an athlete measured as having 6% body fat might actually have anywhere between 3% and 9% body fat depending on how closely his or her body density approaches the idealized value used in the equation. Such limitations might seem so large that coaches and athletes, who are accustomed to timing race performances in 100ths of a second, might consider measurements of percent fat a waste of time, especially if it means dunking an athlete in a tank of water each time the measurements are made. They shouldn't worry, however, because usually they are not interested in identifying the so-called *absolute value* for percent fat as much as they are in quantifying changes in the measured value over time as fatness and fitness vary. Sequential measurements made on a given individual over a period of time, particularly if the same instrument and measurer are used, will have much less error associated with them because of minimal technological variability and density changes in that individual between measurements.

We do not know precisely the extent to which variation in the density of various tissues occurs with racial/ethnic differences. By racial we refer to a group

of individuals with certain common biological features, and by ethnic we refer to a group distinguished by cultural differences such as language or religion. Often there is considerable overlap, but great diversity can occur as well. If such differences exist, then the equations of Siri (1956) and Brozek et al. (1963), validated for the healthy American white (European stock) young adult population, may not apply to these other groups. Data of Robert Malina (1973), for example, suggest that black American athletes when compared to white American athletes tend to display a more linear physique, smaller skinfolds, higher body density, and greater skeletal muscle mass and density. A more recent study by James Schutte et al. (1984) has extended some of these observations, comparing young healthy black and white American males. Certainly because of a greater bone mineral content in blacks, and perhaps also because of greater muscle density, blacks' body density has been estimated as 1.113 gm/cc, compared to the 1.100 gm/cc of Behnke et al. (1953). Schutte et al. thus suggest the following formula for converting density to body fat in blacks:

$$\% \text{ fat} = [(4.374/BD) - 3.928] \times 100 \qquad (4.7)$$

Anthropometry

As we attempt to minimize the logistic and other constraints of densitometry, it is not surprising to learn of alternative simpler methods considered to provide similar information regarding leanness and fatness. In physical education, where having an effective ongoing impression of changing body composition in sizable numbers of athletes during training is important, an emphasis has been placed on the development of methodology that can be implemented simply, conveniently, quickly, and inexpensively using techniques with good reliability. A number of anthropometric variables have been evaluated over the past few decades for their possible predictive value in estimating body density. Among these are bone diameters, height/weight indices such as the body mass index (Table 4.4), circumference of selected body parts, and skinfold thicknesses.

An effective interaction between the disciplines of physiology and biostatistics has produced a large variety of prediction equations for estimating body density from the kinds of variables mentioned previously. Evidence has gradually favored the use of several skinfold measurements alone rather than combinations with other anthropometric variables such as bone diameters and various circumferences. As a result, the seven-skinfold equations developed by Andrew Jackson and Michael Pollock for men (1978) and women (Jackson, Pollock, & Ward, 1980) have achieved considerable popularity. In a subsequent review of literature, Timothy Lohman (1981) agreed with this notion of using a variety of skinfold measures.

Jackson and Pollock (1978; Jackson et al., 1980) detailed the nature of some of the important problems that must be considered when using anthropometry to estimate body density. First, the relationship between body density and skinfold fat is nonlinear. Thus, quadratic rather than linear regression equations are needed for greatest accuracy. Second, skinfold fat is not distributed uniformly between the sexes; it is thicker at some sites than at others. The larger quantity of sex-specific essential fat in women means that a given skinfold thickness in women represents a greater quantity of fat.

Third, body composition is age-related; that is, beyond age 35 adults tend to increase their stored fat, and this relates in part to activity level. Fourth, sizable prediction errors can occur if equations are used that were created for one specific population (e.g., middle-aged sedentary men) and are then applied to data representing a different population (e.g., trained male distance runners). It is preferable to develop prediction equations that generalize from large populations rather than equations based upon specific populations. The equations of Jackson and Pollock (1978; Jackson et al., 1980) are just that—they best fit the data from a heterogeneous sample.

Racial/ethnic differences in skinfold thickness also occur, meaning that a prediction equation for one group may not apply to another (Robson, Bazin, & Soderstrom, 1971). Blacks and Mexican-Americans, when compared to whites, tend to have less subcutaneous fat on their extremities than on their trunk (Malina, 1973; Mueller, Shoup, & Malina, 1982). This has been observed by measuring thinner triceps and thicker subscapular skinfolds. Further work is needed to determine whether the skinfold sites chosen for anthropometry in whites are equally diagnostic for body density in other ethnic groups. Because of such variations in skinfold thickness and density as well as possible differences in tissue density caused by the training stimulus, some investigators prefer simply to assess changes in the numerical sum of skinfold thicknesses over a given time period. Though this does reduce the confounding influence of some of the possible errors identified here, it does not permit the evaluation of changes in leanness that may also occur with fluctuating body weight. Loss of storage fat from intense training and net energy outgo with no net change in leanness is an entirely differ-

ent energy picture than the reverse. Typically, both fatness and leanness changes occur, and in varying degrees. Thus, measuring the sum of skinfolds along with total body weight to permit calculation of percent fat as well as lean body mass is needed to give an adequate picture of ongoing metabolic dynamics.

Obtaining Accurate Skinfold Measurements

As in so many forms of data analysis, proper acquisition of data is crucial; a good analysis of poor-quality information is worse than a poor analysis of good-quality information. When using skinfold assessment for estimation of percent body fat, keep four primary considerations for valid data collection in mind. First, use a reliable measuring calipers, and use the same calipers from one measurement session to another. Second, make repeatable measurements at the proper site, using the correct technique. Third, have a trained (preferably the same) technician make the measurements. Fourth, once reliable data are obtained, use a regression equation that has been validated for the population group being studied. The equations published by Jackson and Pollock for men (1978) and Jackson et al. for women (1980) that are shown in Table 4.5 have been validated for trained white distance runners whose percent fat tends to be below the 12% and 16% values that might suggest the lower end of the normal range for healthy normal young men and women, respectively.

Guidelines for identifying and measuring the various skinfolds are best provided by a combination of illustrations (Figures 4.31 through 4.39) and written descriptions (Lohman, Roche, & Martorell, 1988). The following suggestions should help ensure good reliability and repeatability:

1. Use the right side of the body for all measurements.
2. Use the thumb and index finger of one hand to grasp the skin, and use the calipers, held in the other hand, to measure the skinfold thickness.
3. Have the calipers perpendicular to the skinfold when making the measurement.
4. Use the full caliper grip pressure (typically this is about 10 gm/mm²).
5. Make repeated measurements at each site until repeatability is ensured.
6. Practice measuring the entire series of skinfolds with at least 50 different subjects before considering that technical competency is minimally acceptable.

Table 4.5 Body Mass Index, Body Density, and Percent Body Fat

Athlete _____   Test date _____

Birth date _____   Exact age _____

Weight (kg) _____ (lb) _____   Height (cm) _____ (in.) _____

Body mass index = weight (kg)/square of height (m) = _____

Skinfold thicknesses (mm):

Triceps	_____	Biceps	_____ [a]
Pectoralis	_____	Midaxillary	_____
Subscapular	_____	Suprailiac	_____
Abdominal	_____	Thigh	_____
Calf	_____ [a]		

Sum of skinfolds = E = _____ (mm)   Sum squared = E^2 = _____

Calculated estimate of body density:

Women (Reference: Jackson, Pollock, & Ward, 1980):

BD = $[1.097 - 0.00046971 \times E] + [0.00000056 \times E^2] - [0.00012828 \times age]$

 = 1.097 − _____ + _____ − _____

 = _____

Men (Reference: Jackson & Pollock, 1978):

BD = $[1.112 - 0.00043499 \times E] + [0.00000055 \times E^2] - [0.00028826 \times age]$

 = 1.112 − _____ + _____ − _____

 = _____

Calculated estimates:

% body fat = $[4.57/BD - 4.142] \times 100$ = _____

Nonessential fat mass = weight × %BF = _____ (kg) _____ (lb)

Fat-free body mass = weight − fat mass = _____ (kg) _____ (lb)

[a]Biceps and calf not used in calculations.

7. Make sure these measurements are taken when the athlete is in a normal hydrated state, typically as part of preliminary data acquisition before a treadmill stress test to measure fitness or before a training session. Dehydration will decrease skinfold thickness, thus decreasing the value calculated for percent fat.

SUMMARY

1. Successful runners do more than simply run when developing their expertise. They use a comprehensive conditioning program intended to improve the output capabilities of those

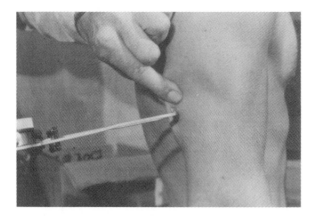

Figure 4.31 *Triceps:* A vertical fold is taken over the muscle belly, midway between the olecranon and the tip of the acromion processes of the humerus; the elbow is extended and the entire limb is relaxed.

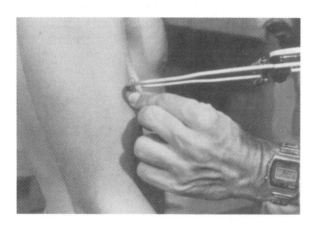

Figure 4.32 *Biceps:* A vertical fold is taken over the midpoint of the muscle belly, midway between the anterior axillary fold (above) and the antecubital space (below); the elbow is extended and the entire limb is relaxed.

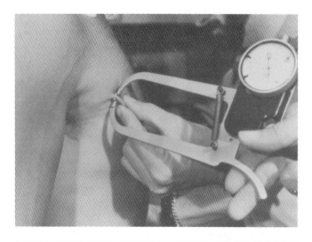

Figure 4.33 *Pectoralis:* A diagonal fold is taken halfway between the nipple and anterior axillary line for men, and two thirds of the distance toward this anterior axillary line for women.

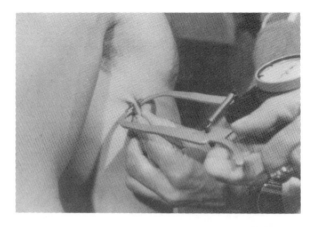

Figure 4.34 *Midaxillary:* A vertical fold is taken at the level of the xiphoid process of the sternum, on the midaxillary line.

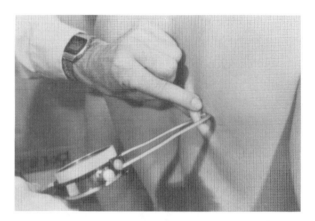

Figure 4.35 *Subscapular:* A diagonal fold is taken no more than 2 cm below the inferior angle of the scapula.

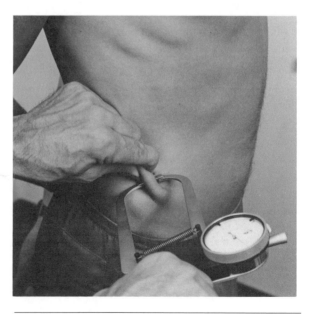

Figure 4.36 *Suprailiac:* A diagonal fold is taken just above the iliac crest at the midaxillary line.

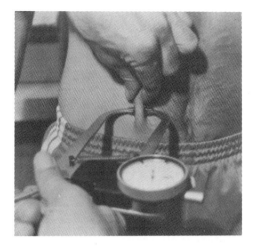

Figure 4.37 *Abdominal*: A vertical fold is taken about 2 cm to the right of the umbilicus.

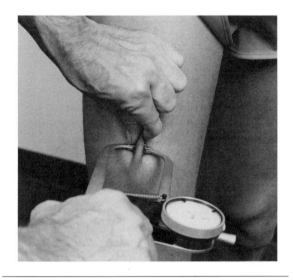

Figure 4.38 *Thigh*: A vertical fold is taken at the anterior midline of the non-weight-bearing lower limb, halfway between the hip and knee joints.

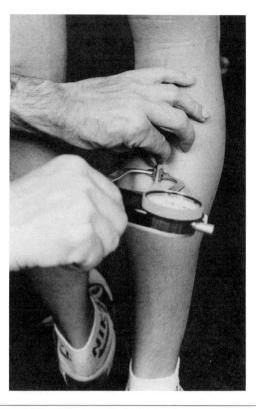

Figure 4.39 *Calf*: A vertical fold is taken at the largest portion of the posterior non-weight-bearing lower limb, over the belly of the gastrocnemius.

muscle groups that are not specifically challenged by running but that assist in that regard and that also contribute to overall joint strength for injury prevention. This also includes an adequate program of stretching exercises to maintain effective joint range of motion. They must take care, however, not to overdo either conditioning or stretching. Runners should not experience such ongoing residual fatigue from conditioning that their ability to manage the running aspects of their training plan is compromised. Similarly, they should not strive so diligently for improved flexibility that stretching injuries result.

2. Strength (force-generating capability) is determined by muscular factors (cross-sectional area of working muscle, fiber length, and muscle architecture) as well as neural factors (stimulus frequency and recruitment). A strengthening program will improve the functional capabilities of ligaments, tendons, cartilage, and bone as well as working muscle. Bones move as a result of muscle-directed rotation around the axis of the joint to which they connect. The torque generated by a limb as it moves around its axis of rotation is given by the product of force and the distance between axis of movement and point of contact (force arm).

3. Varying lever arrangements determine the magnitude of torque generation that can be achieved. Three classes of levers can be identified, but the majority of running-related movements are examples of third-class levers. A long resistance arm and a short force arm provide fast movement speeds in preference to large torques. Improved strength increases quickness and safety, with submaximum work loads being more easily tolerable.

4. When muscles generate tension, they can either lengthen (eccentric movement), shorten (concentric movement), or not change length at all. Muscles can be strengthened using principles that maintain relatively constant tension (isotonic training), length (isometric training), or velocity (isokinetic training). The principle of specific training for sport suggests that dynamic (i.e., movement) training is preferable to static (isometric) training, with isotonic training having more direct transfer to running than isokinetic training.

5. Athletes can improve their muscle strength through a program of gradually increasing the intensity of the load applied. A stimulus requiring at least 80% maximum effort and involving about 3 sets of 6 to 8 reps is required to stimulate muscle growth. As adaptation occurs, the size of the stimulus is appropriately increased. A wide variety of training equipment and techniques is available for implementing such a program. When possible, muscle groups that can play a synergistic, stabilizing, and neutralizing role in running should be developed in addition to the prime movers. The equipment used can include one's own body weight, free weights (such as barbells), and specialized machines that provide variable or accommodating resistance. The techniques can include several types of muscle activation (isokinetic, isotonic, and isometric) as well as variable sequencing of multiple activities to provide a comprehensive conditioning stimulus (circuit and stage training).

6. Skeletal muscles respond to the intensity of their training overload rather than to the actual method of the overload. Thus, relatively nonchallenging activities will provide generalized conditioning, whereas more intense exercises that simulate movement patterns, velocities, and forces characteristic of the chosen event will contribute to specialized performance enhancement. By progressively increasing the resistance provided by an overloading stimulus, continued performance improvement should occur. A wide variety of training equipment and techniques is available for implementing such a program. In this chapter we have provided a brief introduction to some of them.

7. Performance of exercise in any form requires adequate joint range of motion. The longer the stride, as with faster running, or the more uneven the terrain, as with cross-country running or the steeplechase, the more important becomes maintenance of adequate flexibility. An athlete who does not achieve this adequate range risks injury or impaired performance in competition. Thus, stretching exercises should be an essential part of any athletic training regimen, not only to ensure minimum movement potential in all joints but also to provide the margin of safety required for excellence in a given event specialty.

8. In sports activities such as running, where the body weight is transported, it becomes important to have the minimum nonfunctional weight present. Thus, body composition analysis for determining body fat and nonfat body mass has become popular. Densitometry (underwater weighing) will provide the most accurate value for density, from which percent fat can be estimated. With anthropometry (skinfold measurements), we attempt to predict the percent body fat that would exist if hydrostatic weighing were done. Percent fat measured by the two techniques often yields very similar results, and it is not uncommon for both to be used at least once for comparison. For practical reasons, it is generally preferable to use skinfold assessment with athletes, as it is less time-consuming and uses more easily accessible equipment. Also, athletes are more interested in knowing whether changes in fatness or leanness have occurred over time in relation to diet and training rather than knowing absolute values.

REFERENCES

Allen, T.E., Byrd, R.J., & Smith, D.P. (1976). Hemodynamic consequences of circuit weight training. *Research Quarterly*, **47**, 299-306.

Alter, M.J. (1988). *Science of stretching*. Champaign, IL: Human Kinetics.

Anderson, B. (1989). The flex factor. *Runner's World*, **24**(2), 38-43.

Anderson, B., Beaulieu, J.E., Cornelius, W.L., Dominguez, R.H., Prentice, W.E., & Wallace, L. (1984). Coaches roundtable: Flexibility. *National Strength and Conditioning Association Journal*, **6**(4), 10-22.

Atha, J. (1981). Strengthening muscle. *Exercise and Sport Sciences Reviews*, **9**, 1-73.

Austin, D., Roll, F., Kreis, E.J., Palmieri, J., & Lander, J. (1987). Roundtable: Breathing during weight training. *National Strength and Conditioning Association Journal*, **9**(5), 17-25.

Beaulieu, J.E. (1981). Developing a stretching program. *Physician and Sportsmedicine*, **9**(11), 59-69.

Behnke, A.R., Osserman, E.F., & Welham, W.L. (1953). Lean body mass. *Archives of Internal Medicine*, **91**, 585-601.

Berger, R.A. (1962). Effects of varied weight training programs on strength. *Research Quarterly*, **33**, 168-181.

Brodie, D.A. (1988). Techniques of measurement of body composition. *Sports Medicine*, **5**, 11-40, 74-98.

Brozek, J., Grande, F., Anderson, J.T., & Keys, A. (1963). Densitometric analysis of body composition: Revision of some quantitative assumptions. *Annals of the New York Academy of Sciences*, **110**, 113-140.

Brozek, J., & Keys, A. (1951). The evaluation of leanness-fatness in man: Norms and intercorrelations. *British Journal of Nutrition*, **5**, 194-205.

Burke, R.E. (1981). Motor units: Anatomy, physiology, and functional organization. In V.B. Brooks (Ed.), *Handbook of physiology: Sec. 1. The Nervous System: Vol. II. Motor control, Part I* (pp. 345-422). Bethesda, MD: American Physiological Society.

Buskirk, E.R. (1961). Underwater weighing and body density, a review of procedures. In J. Brozek & A. Henschel (Eds.), *Techniques for measuring body composition* (pp. 90-106). Washington, DC: National Academy of Sciences, National Research Council.

Buskirk, E.R., & Mendez, J. (1984). Sport science and body composition analysis: Emphasis on cell and muscle mass. *Medicine and Science in Sports and Exercise*, **16**, 584-593.

Cavagna, G.A. (1977). Storage and utilization of energy in skeletal muscle. *Exercise and Sport Sciences Reviews*, **5**, 89-129.

Christensen, C.S. (1972). Strength, the common variable in hamstring strain. *Medicine and Science in Sports*, **2**, 39-42.

Clarke, D.H. (1973). Adaptations in strength and muscular endurance resulting from exercise. *Exercise and Sports Sciences Reviews*, **1**, 73-102.

Corbin, C.B., & Noble, L. (1960). Flexibility: A major component of physical fitness. *Journal of Physical Education and Recreation*, **51**, 23-60.

Cornelius, W.L. (1985). Flexibility: The effective way. *National Strength and Conditioning Association Journal*, **7**(3), 62-64.

Darden, E. (1977). *Strength training principles: How to get the most out of your workouts*. Winter Park, FL: Anna.

DeLorme, T.L. (1945). Restoration of muscle power by heavy resistance exercises. *Journal of Bone and Joint Surgery*, **27**, 645-667.

DeLorme, T.L., & Watkins, A.L. (1948). Technics of progressive resistance exercise. *Archives of Physical Medicine*, **29**, 263-273.

Denny-Brown, D. (1949). Interpretation of the electromyogram. *Archives of Neurology and Psychiatry*, **61**, 99-128.

Eccles, J.C., Eccles, R.M., & Lundberg, A. (1958). The action potentials of the alpha motoneurones supplying fast and slow muscles. *Journal of Physiology*, **142**, 275-291.

Eyster, J.A.E. (1927). Cardiac dilation and hypertrophy. *Transactions of the Association of American Physicians*, **25**, 15-21.

Festa, S. (1988). Stretching: The truth. *Runner's World*, **23**(2), 39-42.

Fidanza, F., Keys, A., & Anderson, J.T. (1953). Density of body fat in man and other animals. *Journal of Applied Physiology*, **6**, 252-256.

Gandy, G. (1983). Overview of Coe's non-track training. In V. Gambetta (Ed.), *Track Technique Annual* (pp. 89-91). Los Altos, CA: Tafnews Press.

Garrett, W.E., Jr., Safran, M.R., Seaber, A.V., Glisson, R.R., & Ribbeck, B.M. (1987). Biomechanical comparison of stimulated and nonstimulated skeletal muscle pulled to failure. *The American Journal of Sports Medicine*, **15**, 448-454.

Hakkinen, K., & Komi, P. (1983). Electromyographic changes during strength training and detraining. *Medicine and Science in Sports and Exercise*, **15**, 455-460.

Hatfield, F.C. (1982). *Flexibility training for sports: PNF techniques*. Fitness Systems USA.

Henneman, E. (1957). Relation between size of neurons and their susceptibility to discharge. *Science*, **126**, 1345-1347.

Hettinger, T., & Muller, E.A. (1953). Muskelleistung und Muskeltraining [Muscle performance and muscle training]. *Arbeitsphysiologie*, **15**, 111-116.

Huxley, A.F., & Niedergerke, R. (1954). Structural changes in muscle during contraction. *Nature*, **173**, 971-973.

Huxley, H.E., & Hanson, J. (1954). Changes in the cross-striations of muscle during contraction and stretch and their structural interpretation. *Nature*, **173**, 973-976.

Jackson, A.S., & Pollock, M.L. (1978). Generalized equations for predicting body density of men. *British Journal of Nutrition*, **40**, 497-504.

Jackson, A.S., & Pollock, M.L. (1985). Practical assessment of body composition. *Physician and Sportsmedicine*, **13**(5), 76-90.

Jackson, A.S., Pollock, M.L., & Ward, A. (1980). Generalized equations for predicting body density of women. *Medicine and Science in Sports and Exercise*, **12**, 175-182.

Knapik, J.J., Mawdsley, R.H., & Ramos, M.V. (1983). Angular specificity and test mode specificity of isometric and isokinetic strength training. *Journal of Orthopaedic Sports Physical Therapy*, **5**, 58-65.

Komi, P., & Bosco, C. (1978). Utilization of stored elastic energy in leg extensor muscles by men and women. *Medicine and Science in Sports*, **10**, 261-265.

Kraemer, W.J., Deschenes, M.R., & Fleck, S.J. (1988). Physiological adaptations to resistance exercise: Implications for athletic conditioning. *Sports Medicine*, **6**, 246-256.

Laird, C.E., Jr., & Rozier, C.K. (1979). Toward understanding the terminology of exercise mechanics. *Physical Therapy*, **59**, 287-292.

Lesmes, G.R., Benhain, D.W., Costill, D.L., & Fink, W.J. (1983). Glycogen utilization in fast and slow twitch muscle fibers during maximal isokinetic exercise. *Annals of Sports Medicine*, **1**, 105-108.

Levin, A., & Wyman, J. (1927). The viscous elastic properties of muscle. *Proceedings of the Royal Society (London)*, **B101**, 218-243.

Lohman, T.G. (1981). Skinfolds and body density and their relation to body fitness: A review. *Human Biology*, **53**, 181-225.

Lohman, T.G., Roche, A.F., & Martorell, R. (1988). *Anthropometric standardization reference manual*. Champaign, IL: Human Kinetics.

MacDougall, J.D., Sale, D.G., Elder, G.C.B., & Sutton, J.R. (1982). Muscle ultrastructural characteristics of elite powerlifters and bodybuilders. *European Journal of Applied Physiology*, **48**, 117-126.

MacDougall, J.D., Wenger, H.A., & Green, H.J. (1982). *Physiological testing of the elite athlete*. Toronto: Canadian Association of Sports Sciences.

Malina, R.M. (1973). Biological substrata. In K.S. Miller & R.W. Dreger (Eds.), *Comparative studies of blacks and whites in the U.S.* (pp. 53-123). New York: Seminar Press.

Malone, T.R. (1988). Evaluation of isokinetic equipment. *Sports Injury Management*, **1**, 1-92.

Martin, D.E., Vroon, D.H., May, D.F., & Pilbeam, S.P. (1986). Physiological changes in elite male distance runners training for Olympic competition. *Physician and Sportsmedicine*, **14**(1), 152-171.

Matveyev, L. (1981). *Fundamentals of sports training*. Moscow: Progress.

McDonagh, M.J., & Davies, C.T. (1984). Adaptive response of mammalian skeletal muscles to exercise with high loads. *European Journal of Applied Physiology*, **52**, 139-155.

Moffroid, M.T., & Kusiak, E.T. (1975). The power struggle: Definition and evaluation of power of muscular performance. *Physical Therapy*, **55**, 1098-1104.

Moffroid, M.T., & Whipple, R.H. (1970). Specificity of speed and exercise. *Journal of the American Physical Therapy Association*, **50**, 1692-1699.

Moffroid, M.T., Whipple, R.H., Hofkosh, J., Lowman, E., & Thistle, H. (1969). A study of isokinetic exercise. *Physical Therapy*, **49**, 735-746.

Morgan, R.E., & Adamson, G.T. (1957). *Circuit training*. London: G. Bell and Sons.

Morpurgo, B. (1897). Uber aktivitats-hypertrophie der willkurlichen Muskeln [Concerning the hypertrophy of voluntary muscle]. *Virchow's Archiv fur Pathologie und Physiologie*, **150**, 522-554.

Morrow, J.R., Jackson, A.S., Bradley, P.W., & Hartung, G.H. (1986). Accuracy of measured and predicted residual lung volume on body density measurement. *Medicine and Science in Sports and Exercise*, **18**, 647-652.

Mueller, W.H., Shoup, R.F., & Malina, R.M. (1982). Fat patterning in athletes in relation to ethnic origin and sport. *Annals of Human Biology*, **9**, 371-376.

Nicholas, J.A. (1970). Injuries to knee ligaments: Relationship to looseness and tightness in football players. *Journal of the American Medical Association*, **212**, 2236-2239.

Olson, V.L., Schmidt, G.L., & Johnson, R.C. (1972). The maximum torque generated by eccentric, isometric, and concentric contractions of the hip abduction muscles. *Physical Therapy*, **52**, 148-149.

Perrine, J.J. (1968). Isokinetic exercise and the mechanical energy potentials of muscle. *Journal of Health, Physical Education, and Recreation*, **39**(5), 40-44.

Person, R.S., & Kudina, L.P. (1972). Discharge frequency and discharge pattern of human motor units during voluntary contraction of muscle. *Electroencephalography and Clinical Neurophysiology*, **32**, 471-483.

Pipes, T.V., & Wilmore, J.H. (1975). Isokinetic versus isotonic strength training in adult men. *Medicine and Science in Sports*, **7**, 262-274.

Rack, P.M.H., & Westbury, D.R. (1969). The effects of length and stimulus rate on tension in the isometric cat soleus muscle. *Journal of Physiology*, **204**, 443-460.

Robson, J.R.K., Bazin, M., & Soderstrom, R. (1971). Ethnic differences in skinfold thickness. *American Journal of Clinical Nutrition*, **29**, 864-868.

Schutte, J.E., Townsend, E.J., Hugg, J., Shoup, R.F., Malina, R.M., & Blomqvist, C.G. (1984). Density of lean body mass is greater in Blacks than in Whites. *Journal of Applied Physiology*, **56**, 1647-1649.

Siri, W.E. (1956). The gross composition of the body. *Advances in Biological and Medical Physics*, **4**, 239-280.

Sorani, R. (1966). *Circuit training*. Dubuque, IA: William C. Brown.

Thistle, H.G., Hislop, H.J., Moffroid, M., & Lohman, E.W. (1967). Isokinetic contraction: A new concept of resistive exercise. *Archives of Physical Medicine and Rehabilitation*, **48**, 279-282.

Thomas, D.W. (1988). Plyometrics—more than the stretch reflex. *National Strength and Conditioning Association Journal*, **10**(5), 49-51.

Verkhoshanskiy, Y. (1973). Depth jumping in the training of jumpers. *Track Technique*, **51**, 1618-1619.

Weltman, A., & Katch, V. (1981). Comparison of hydrostatic weighing at residual volume and total lung capacity. *Medicine and Science in Sports and Exercise*, **13**, 210-213.

Weltman, A., & Stamford, B. (1982). Strength training: Free weights versus machines. *Physician and Sportsmedicine*, **10**(11), 197.

Westcott, W.L. (1979). Female response to weight lifting. *Journal of Physical Education*, **77**, 31-33.

Wilmore, J.H., Buskirk, E.R., DiGirolamo, M., & Lohman, T.G. (1986). Body composition. *Physician and Sportsmedicine*, **14**(3), 144-162.

Wilmore, J.H., Parr, R.B., Girandola, R.N., Ward, P., Vodak, P.A., Barstow, T.J., Pipes, T.V., Romero, G.T., & Leslie, P. (1978). Physiological alterations consequent to circuit weight training. *Medicine and Science in Sports*, **10**, 79-84.

Young, D.C. (1984). *The Olympic myth of Greek amateur athletics*. Chicago: Aires.

Zinovieff, A.N. (1951). Heavy resistance exercises: The Oxford technique. *British Journal of Physical Medicine*, **14**, 129-132.

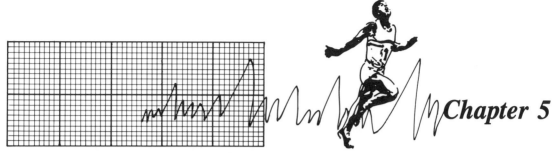

Successful Racing: Preparation and Achievement

Chapter 5

We direct this chapter primarily to the athletes who are reading this book. You (athletes) are the ones who will be executing race strategies as you compete, and thus you are the ones we desire to advise. In this chapter we discuss several of the Olympic distance events from the 800m through the marathon and present strategies for

- race assessment and preparation,
- getting a good start and establishing and maintaining good race position,
- running a race that best balances efficient use of energy resources with the sometimes energy-inefficient realities of racing, and
- considering tactics for varying race circumstances that will provide the best opportunity for a viable finish.

We must emphasize that this chapter is by no means a complete presentation of all the ''secrets'' of racing. Every race, along with the preparation leading up to it, is unique. For us to list all potential scenarios and suggested outcomes is both inappropriate and impossible. Even if we could do this, it would remove most of the enjoyment from racing—it is the element of the unknown that adds so much. We can, however, identify patterns of thought that might guide you into considering each event carefully and thereby give you some of the tools for creating your own best performance. You'll most likely find five underlying prin-

ciples in our discussion of each event. First, there is great value in being well prepared, realistic, and thoughtful before any race. But don't overdo it. Second, having an accurate sense of pace—estimating it, keeping it as even as possible for economy of effort, and knowing when and how to quicken it—is enormously important. Third, maintain physical and mental contact with your competitors. Fourth, know the definition of **tactics**: a structuring of the race pattern to suit you better than your opponents. In doing so, realize that employing tactics will be more demanding on you than not employing them. Thus, they should be used only if you can manage them and can do so with the idea that they are even more demanding on your opponents.

Finally, realize that it is not always necessary or appropriate to derive satisfaction only from winning. In the heats of a championship series, achieving a position high enough to move you up to the next race may be sufficient. In a race where you may find yourself in the company of some athletes with more skills than you have at that moment, running your best race is the key to placing well. It's also the surest way to score an upset victory! To glorify the adage that winning is everything makes defeat all the more devastating. Not winning is not losing if the quality of effort was excellent. An individual trains to race well; racing well is the single best indicator of being able to race better. Over a career, victories come most often from consistently good racing. Good racing requires knowledge and application of racing principles. That is what this chapter is all about.

THE 800-METER RUN

The 800m run is probably the most unforgiving of all track events. It requires a combination of strength, raw speed, anaerobic endurance, and split-second judgment to decide when tactics can be invoked to achieve a victory. The shorter events (100m through 400m) are run in lanes throughout, limiting many tactical options. The 100m is a straight, forward explosion of running, and starting technique is of utmost importance. The 200m demands good judgment of bend running. The 400m is now so fast that any attempt to float at 200 m to snatch a brief respite before the remainder of the race is no longer possible. The first bend of the 800m, however, is run in lanes. During the space of time between the break from lane assignments and when the bell announces the final lap, an athlete needs a very sharp tactical sense in addition to superb fitness to set up the best environment for the final lap. Victory goes to the runner with a combination of the greatest drive to win and the most accomplished ability to endure the remaining physiological race demands.

Not long ago the 800m distance was considered the shortest middle-distance event. But in 1981 Seb Coe lowered the men's 800m world record to 1:41.73. He achieved this by running laps of 49.7 and 52.1 sec. Two years later in 1983, Jarmila Kratochvilova lowered the women's 800m record to 1:53.28 by running laps of 56.1 and 57.2 sec. The thought of men coping with a sub-50-sec opening lap or women with a sub-56-sec opener makes it functionally more sensible to consider the 800m distance as an extended sprint. Such fast racing requirements place ever greater emphasis on the speed (anaerobic) aspect of speed endurance. Similar changes are occurring in the longer distances as athletes with greater inherent talent refine their performance abilities more successfully.

Running all-out for a large part of the distance, trying to remain afloat in a sea of hydrogen ions, is difficult enough without the added requirements of staying alert and thinking clearly. In a fast 800m race with a field of your peers, there is never time to recover from mistakes. Thus, mistakes can never be made. Yet to err is human. Therein lies the dilemma—minimizing your chance for error and coping where possible. Large variations in running pace are physically impossible, and one wrongly placed burst can be the undoing of a good race.

Anaerobic and Aerobic Expertise Are Essential

The requirement of both anaerobic and aerobic expertise for success at 800 m puts unique demands on your abilities. In effect, you must be expert at utilizing both energy systems. Think about what is required. An international-class male 800m runner needs the ability to run 400 m in roughly 45.5 to 47 sec, plus sufficient speed endurance to run a world-class mile. Similar effort output holds true for less accomplished runners performing to their limit, although the times will be appropriately slower.

Reconsideration of Table 3.4, which summarizes the relative balance between the aerobic and anaerobic energy contributions for various racing distances, not only adds some perspective to the logistics of running 800 m but also raises some interesting practical questions. The relative percentages of aerobic to anaerobic energy needs for 800 m are indicated as 57%:43%. For the 400m run, the ratio is 30%:70%. Let us create a race scenario and attempt to better understand its energy dynamics. We'll use in this example the split times for a top-level male and let the rest of you create split times that fit your own abilities. The concept is more important at this point than specific times.

Let's assume that you plan to run an 800m race in 1:43, with 400m split times of 50 and 53 sec. Your personal best for 400 m is 48 sec, and as you run your 800m race, you cover the first lap at 96% of your best 400m pace. What is the ratio of aerobic to anaerobic energy needs for this first 400 m? Certainly not 30%:70%, because it is not an all-out 400m race effort. Let us suggest that it is at 65%:35% or 60%:40%, and that a sizable O_2 debt has now accumulated as you begin the second lap. You run the second 400m lap (53 sec) at 90% of your maximum 400m velocity. Your effort is all-out, and you work very hard to maintain good form. Now, what is the aerobic percentage of your all-out second 400 m of this 800m race? We suspect the aerobic:anaerobic ratio is more on the order of 35%:65% or 40%:60%. Thus, the two laps are quite different in physiological terms. This kind of event analysis is useful, for it helps lay the basis for the methods by which you and your coach should be preparing for 800m competition. For each of these quite different metabolic loads, specialized intensive training must be included. This will give you an important edge over your competitors.

Your training for 800m racing must permit the development of both strength and endurance in your skeletal muscles, especially your legs. They must be able to tolerate an intense sustained work load. Only a truly total-body conditioning program (running plus weight-room and circuit training) will provide adequate preparation for 800m excellence. Your body must increase its ability to cope with acidosis so well that not only can you maintain pace, but you can also run steadily faster even when tissue discomfort is making your body plead with you to stop running altogether.

Be Alert at the Start

In contrast to the other middle- and long-distance events, in the 800m either of two different starting procedures may be used. In track jargon these are termed the *curved* and the *staggered* starts. With a large field of runners (more than 8 to 10), you will be arranged across the track, toeing a curved starting line. The start of such a race often creates a situation that, as with much of life itself, has no small amount of unfairness. The jostling that occurs can cause spiking and falls at worst, bumps and bruises at best. Some of the larger competitors frequently are not the most agile and often figure prominently in this initial melee, being least affected due to their size. Thus, it is not necessarily a disadvantage to be at the outside edge of the pack. This may provide the safest vantage point for choosing the proper moment to slip into the best position within the pack.

The curved start is relatively simple for several reasons. A quick glance allows a survey of most of the field of runners. It is easy to sense the pace. Fast starters will be in front, slower ones behind. The territory to be avoided if possible includes the inner two positions behind the leader. In these so-called "sled-dog" positions, there's just no option except to follow the pace of the runner in front. If the early leader slows and is passed, these two runners will soon find themselves in the rear of the field.

In major races and championships, a staggered start is used. With this method, you start in lanes and stay in them through the first turn. Then you may break away from this ordered sequence and use any lane suitable. This system delays the jockeying for optimum position until the back straightaway portion of the track.

Several strategic complications affect a staggered start. The outside runners are up front and cannot see those behind. (One coaching tip often given to the outside runners, however, is that if you can sense a runner on your left, you're behind.) The inside runners have a marked advantage in this regard as they can see most of their opposition. In a somewhat slow start, those who get out fast can opt to run hard from the gun. If inside runners do this, outside runners then have the double problem of closing the gap and also achieving their desired position early on in the race. In a fast start, however, the runners farthest back who start a bit slowly may not see the outside runners up front until the break from lanes is almost reached, and may not realize until then the deficit they need to remove. Bearing in mind the **rule of speed**—it's easier to ease up than it is to speed up—and realizing the psychological implications of finding yourself behind nearly from the beginning, it is clear that no matter which way the race begins, your strategies and attitudes should be geared toward a fast, safe start with the greatest odds of proper position as early as possible.

Run the Shortest Distance

We mentioned earlier the rule of speed. Now we remind you of the equally obvious **rule of distance:** The shortest distance between two points is a straight line. Failing to use this principle can get you into many difficulties in 800m races. If your starting position in the staggered start is in the outer lanes, when the breakpoint from lanes is reached, you should move to the outside of the inner lane gradually. Ideally you would reach it by the far back turn as illustrated in Figure 5.1, which shows the path you would take if you ran tangentially from lane 8 after the first 100 m to the outside edge of lane 1 by the start of the approaching bend. Remember your school geometry—a tangent to a circle is the straight line that just touches the circle but does not cut into it. We have drawn a tangent line from the edge of lane 1 on the far back turn in a manner such that it extends to lane 8 at the 100m mark. Following this path or a similar one should minimize participation in the associated collisions and elbowing that result from joining the immediate dash for the inside lane. If you overestimated the pace of your first 200 m it is easier to avoid taking the lead prematurely. Simply move over gradually and adjust your pace accordingly.

Even this tactic may have its problems, particularly if you are a runner caught in a middle lane, and being pushed by those outside bullying their way toward the inside. The 800m event is indeed a race with physical contact, and you must defend very firmly space fairly won. It is, however, entirely unacceptable to struggle with another competitor for space simply because it is desired. A fall or a blow in the wrong place could bring needless and premature loss of the race.

An enduring myth about track running holds that an enormous cost in distance results when running wide, that is, in the outer lanes. This is limited to bend running, and even then the added distance per bend

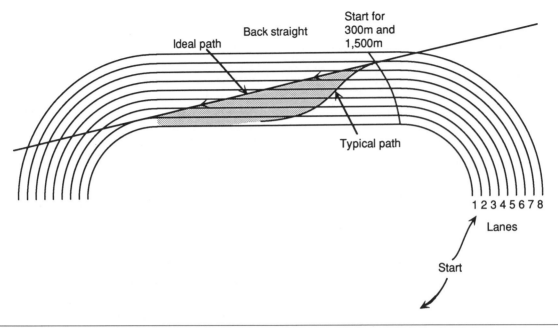

Figure 5.1   Diagram of an idealized (compared with the typically used) path for an 800m (or 1,500m) runner from the 100m breakpoint to reach the start of the back turn.

is not much—roughly 2.8 m in lane 2 compared to lane 1. But because it is very easy to run side by side in one lane, the added distance will be as little as 1.6 m. At a 52 sec/400m pace, this costs only 0.21 sec—a small price in time to pay for staying out of tactical trouble and also remaining free to take the lead. For top-level women running at a 58 sec pace, the time loss is still only 0.23 sec. Much more time— and perhaps victory in the race—could be lost by being trapped behind the front runner while the pack makes its move around.

Because of the extended-sprint nature of the 800m event, it is essential to distribute your effort as economically as possible. There are good reasons for this, whatever the specific race strategy. If you are aiming for a personal best, a more even pace instead of a fast/slow or slow/fast lap combination will minimize anaerobic energy production (although it still is high, as the intensity will be as high as 135% of your $\dot{V}O_2$max pace). If victory is your goal and if you fall a little behind early on, it may not be possible for you to muster the physical strength needed to catch up by increasing your stride length or stride frequency, even if you can endure the anaerobic stress. Thus, you must maintain contact with the leaders throughout.

However, strong front-runners typically avail themselves of a fast start. In part this is because they are still fresh during the first 14 to 16 sec, although an O_2 debt is developing rapidly as a result of blood perfusion to skeletal muscles initially falling short of metabolic demands. They hope that they will get far

enough in front that they can slow their pace slightly during mid-race, thereby having just enough recovery to permit a strong final-lap effort.

Use the First Lap to Establish Optimum Position

The best position for your first lap is probably in the wind shadow of the front-runners. You are conserving energy by drafting. You are applying psychological pressure to the leaders, who realize this and who are now the hunted, not the hunters. You have no catching up to do. Instead, as the hunter you are poised and ready, assessing the optimum moment to launch an assault that will overcome your prey and bring victory. An example using the real world of racing illustrates the point. In a 50-sec lap for the first 400 m, the average running velocity is 8 m/sec. As the bell lap begins, an athlete 6 m in back of the lead will need to race at a nearly 49-sec pace just to catch the leader. Any decision to wait until later brings a risk of the problem of accumulating acidosis, which tends to slow cadence as well as shorten stride length. Even if the leader is caught, victory isn't at hand, because now this potential winner must take the lead.

Sooner or later, every 800m racer gets into this dilemma. In one race, Seb found himself the better part of 2 sec behind in a world-class field, unable to achieve striking position until halfway up the finishing straight. It proved too late. His revenge over his conqueror came at their next meeting. Seb stuck to the fast early pace very closely so that his major assertive move drew him away from the rest of the field, and he directed virtually no energy at catching up.

Probably the best position to occupy as the race develops is the outside of the inside lane. This permits running wider if necessary and reduces the chances of being blocked by a runner in front. Picture the following scenario: You are running along the back straight, approaching the final bend just behind and slightly wide of the leader's shoulders. Someone from behind launches a sudden powerful surge to the front, darting past you and the leader and taking a position alongside the curb. This leaves the earlier leader trapped behind the new replacement, and to the inside of the smartest athlete in the race—you! Maintaining pace and position at the outer edge of the inside lane, you are still unimpeded, virtually at the front, ready to cope with other would-be front attackers, and poised to initiate your own assault at the proper moment.

Strategies for the Finish

If you are clearly the best athlete in the field, you may attempt the fastest possible time in addition to a victory. An all-out effort to leave the pack far behind always requires courage but is a dramatically powerful psychological tactic in its own right. So often, such an opportunity isn't provided. The presence of other talented athletes in the competition having a good race will put individual finish times much closer, making tactical decisions ever more important.

In these situations, the athlete must not only study both the field and the developing race while under increasing anaerobic stress, but must also determine the best kind of decisive maneuvering for the final stages. If the field has one or two well-known fast finishers, one of your options is to lead the entire field through the first lap at a rather fast pace, accepting the energy drain from breaking the wind but realizing that the edge must be removed from their fast finish abilities. If you do this carefully so as not to inhibit your finishing kick, the final lap then becomes a test of strength endurance more than speed endurance. Here is where the benefits of a long-term, total-body strength/endurance training program involving weight-room and circuit work has its delightful payoff.

After a good-quality first lap, a variant of this theme is for you to provide the pressure of a steadily increasing acceleration during the second lap. This application of gradually increasing speed calls for courage as much as gun-to-tape front-running, but it can shatter the will of your would-be pursuers, who must accelerate even more just to remain in contention with you. One of the more well-known proponents of this gradual acceleration tactic was Jurgen Straub of the German Democratic Republic, who in reality was a 1,500m specialist and steeplechaser. In the 1980 Moscow Olympic Games 1,500m final race, at the 800m point, he initiated a powerful dash for the finish at an 800m pace of 1:46. Beginning with the final 300 m, each succeeding 100 m was faster than the previous. After Straub had broken a fine field of runners, Seb Coe, who had stuck to him like glue, was able to beat him at the finish line using an even faster 12.1-sec final 100m effort. Again, such an achievement is your prerogative only if you have a profound background of complete conditioning.

In a race where many of the top competitors have similar abilities, your primary strategy becomes one of making the crucial attack first. This must be a shrewd blow, delivered as late as possible to avoid a counterattack but early enough that it is the first such strike. It needs to be a decisive breakaway in a few quick strides. Maintaining that gap or even only a part of it is much easier than trying to catch up, which all the rest must do.

In summary, then, total awareness of the ongoing race plus a willingness to commit completely and attack hard when the fleeting opportunity to strike presents itself are probably the two most crucial attributes for success in 800m racing. Sufficient talent, preparation, and authority to create opportunities is excellent, but the ability to assess and seize appropriate opportunities as well rounds out the creation of a grand master. Just as the race is multifaceted, so also must be the totality of your preparation. Superb fitness comes from a complete training plan—strength, quickness, stamina, and endurance—for all your major muscle groups. The gift of race confidence comes from practice in continuing to work when it hurts; that is, building the ability to tolerate anaerobic stress. This is not the fatigue of the long-distance runner. Rather, it's the raw pain of fast, prolonged speed. And it makes little difference whether you race among the fastest athletes in the world, or in your local club or school. Whether it is a 50 sec/400m lap (8 m/sec) or a 57.1 sec lap (7 m/sec), if it's a highly competitive 800m race, the principles are the same. Even the strategies of running wide remain the same—the time lost running wide will be longer for a slower race, but the distance covered by everyone each second is also less.

THE 1,500-METER RUN

A 1,500m race unfolds in roughly twice the time of an 800m event. This can be a double-edged sword. There is added time to recover from errors incurred but more time to encounter difficult circumstances.

Often, the field of starters may number as many as 12 to 15. Thus, positioning yourself early on and as the race proceeds takes on considerable importance.

Establish Good Position and Maintain Contact

An outside draw in the selection of track position in a 1,500m or mile race should not be a source of worry. It is a safe place; when you reach the start of the back straight, the same gradual angle toward the inside lane as described for the 800m staggered start (Figure 5.1) is the logical move. If your selection is on the inside, run the first 100 m briskly, regardless of the presence of a known pacemaker, to permit a gradual easing up with a position in the second lane at or near the front. If your initial pace was overestimated, it is safer to ease up in lane 2 than in lane 1, where you may be boxed in easily by surrounding athletes. If a pacemaker has been assigned to the race, this runner may not be the fastest of starters, and a place for that person needs to be "reserved" in lane 1, at the front, as he or she then takes direction of the initial stages of the race.

Gone are the days when fast-starting front-runners almost certainly came back to the pack. Now, once away, they are more likely to stay in front. Thus, to ensure being in contention, you must adequately maintain your contact with the leaders. Several circumstances can cause you to fall behind the lead pace. A slow start can bring some bumping and stumbling during the first lap and perhaps the second as well. A spike wound or a sharp elbow to your ribs can be so frightening that you tend to fall back simply from frustration or fear. Even if you are aggressive by nature, your rhythm can be disrupted, which can slow your pace. A tactical acceleration by the leaders has an effect on runners farther back in the pack similar to what occurs with a string of automobiles in highway traffic. Precious time is lost until space provided by the acceleration of the leaders permits those in the back of the pack to respond as well. By then, the leaders may have opened up a difference of 15 m or more.

One possible strategy for gaining lost distance, particularly when the deficit occurs early, is to steadily and economically reduce the gap by gradual acceleration. In theory this may appear logical, but theories must fit the exigencies of life, and life has a habit of adding unexpected complexities. If the front-runners begin another sudden acceleration, then the distance from front-runner to middle-pack runner will increase still more.

No, in today's races it is safest for any runner stuck early in the middle or back of the pack but still desirous of victory to insert a prompt submaximum short sprint to get up near the outside shoulder of the lead runner. Delivery of this kind of anaerobic burst is best developed by repeatable 400m sprint practice. This improves particularly well your nervous system's ability to recruit FT muscle cells. Distributing this anaerobic metabolism to larger numbers of muscle fibers optimizes energy production while minimizing excessive buildup of acidosis in each. Athletes often refer to this ability as "surging power" or the ability to quickly "shift gears."

A steady pace is, of course, most economical. The faster you attempt to run—for example, when a personal best is desired—the more sensible is an even pace. But many more races will be tactical battles, where victories often go to those who have imposed (and better managed) great demands of pace variation on their adversaries. Again, you must remain in good position close to the early leaders, ready to respond, whether it be to maintain pace or to initiate a tactical move.

Decide When to Strike

Three well-known racing tactics have been used with awesome effectiveness to win 1,500m and mile races. Each has been used distinctively by some of Britain's finest recent middle-distance runners. Steve Ovett was an accomplished fierce kicker during the later stages, especially in his sprints down the final straight. One racing response to this is the Steve Cram style of beginning a powerful acceleration from 300 m out, removing the sting from any accompanying sprinter experts. Two responses that Seb Coe perfected quite well were either to begin the final drive for home just before a long-surging competitor did, or to stay with that athlete's surge and then shift gears once again, increasing speed beyond an already very fast pace. The need for the comprehensive fitness required to permit such a fierce kick, long acceleration, or quick pace change has already been described for 800m racing, and in this regard the 1,500m run is similar.

Being up with the leader is crucial for each of these tactics to succeed. Not only do you gain the advantage of surprise, but virtually everyone else must accelerate more to remain abreast of you. An experienced athlete can sense when others around are laboring, which helps to determine the most opportune moment to strike. Also, if a competitor in the lead is attempting to maintain an optimum pace for his or her finish style, you may be well advised to insert a mid-race pace increase. This will help to neutralize, both psychologically and physiologically, that runner's notion of a race going according to an optimum plan. Front-running an entire 1,500m race is energy-costly and mentally stressful, but occasional front-running can have a useful purpose.

Some races are directed for a considerable period by prearrangement with an assigned pacemaker (often called a "rabbit"). Interestingly, not always do such paced races produce fast finish times. The psychological realization that much work is being done for these athletes by someone who intentionally takes them around at a preestablished pace can lessen their competitive resolve. Some runners will not break away from the field early on as they might in a less orchestrated race. These psychological negatives may not be negated completely by the physiological energy-saving benefit of drafting behind the pacemaker.

A real risk exists in such a race, especially if the pacemaker is also a gifted athlete, of the pacemaker stealing the show with an unexpected victory. Hardly a track fan during the early 1980s will forget the drama of the United States' gifted Tom Byers setting the pace for an excellent field in the Oslo Bislett Games 1,500m run in June 1981. Tom took the field through 400 m in 57.6 and 800 m in 1:54.9, developing an enormous 30 m lead. The trailing pack unknowingly was given Byers' split times instead of their own, thus clouding their usually unerring pace sense. Only too late did they realize the discrepancy. Tom was too far ahead for them to successfully close. They tried, but Tom earned his victory (over Ovett) by 0.52 sec with 3:39.01.

THE 5,000-METER RUN

We are now considering a race 6.25 times longer than the 800m; 3.3 times longer than the 1,500m. This event is contested at a pace approaching 100% of aerobic capacity. Thus, as with the 800m and 1,500m, we hope that your VO_2max has been raised as high as possible during training. Carbohydrates will by far be the predominant energy source for this race. Even with a steady pace, the energy requirement will be so great that anaerobic accumulation will begin to occur early, because the race pace in all probability will be faster than your lactate/ventilatory threshold pace. Your blood lactate level will soar during your final sprint to the finish, and the hope is that you time the start of that surge with sufficient precision that you'll be able to run all-out to the finish. The most economical strategy, therefore, is to run an evenly paced race to keep skeletal muscle and blood acidosis as low as possible until near the end. Elsewhere we have stressed the importance of learning good pace judgment in training. For the longer distance races, this facet of race savvy is crucial. A trait of particular value is accurate pace assessment during varying states of fatigue.

It is unwise, however, to expect a 5,000m race to be run in the most economical manner. It is more likely that the competitor lineup will have a mixture of runners who are famous for their fast strong finish, runners who may insert very fast mid-race laps, runners who insert shorter but even quicker and more sudden bursts of speed, and runners who prefer a strong pace throughout to remove the sting from any would-be final kickers. Among the top men in recent history, some well-known examples of each of these styles include, respectively, Marty Liquori (United States), Brendan Foster (Great Britain), Dave Bedford (Great Britain), and Antonio Leitao (Portugal). These racing styles are good examples of tactics—each style allows the athlete to take advantage of a particular talent, with the hope that use of it for that athlete will be less costly than for all the others. This points out the importance of knowing your competition in every event and devising your own individual strategy to utilize your strengths optimally.

Establish an Early Race-Pace Equilibrium

Running too fast too early has several consequences, all bad. The agonies of acidosis inhibit muscle operational efficiency prematurely. This brings discomforting thoughts ("I'm hurting this badly and it's so early in the race!?"), that reveal the importance of the mind–body interaction. A slower finish pace is the likely unfortunate result, with other runners passing you instead of being passed by you. Additional accessory muscles of the limbs and trunk are brought into play in a valiant but vain struggle to keep pace, but this decreases running economy and increases even further the O_2 consumption required. Even multi-tier training cannot rectify the mistakes of premature and unnecessarily excessive speed. However, it can provide the capability for enduring and initiating the sizable kinds of pace changes that may be required to either respond to or create conditions in which victory comes to the most prepared athlete.

The 5,000m race is run at too fast a velocity to be contested effectively with widely varying pace changes. After those first few laps done smartly because you feel fresh, you must resist the trend to begin pushing the pace or to take the lead because the pace seems slow unless you are in substantially better form than the rest and believe you can manage a faster pace. The reality is that after the first 2 laps, 10 laps and a little more yet remain. Reserve the fastest of these 10-plus laps for the end, not the beginning. Short bursts that are not sustained will quickly be closed by smarter runners not far behind who are keeping a more even pace. At this same time, those in the lead will have an increased energy requirement when compared to those behind because they are breaking the wind.

The easiest of all race options is simply to calculate a fixed per-lap pace that best estimates your potential performance given existing weather conditions and your level of physical fitness. If the early stages are run on the slow side of this pace, a feeling of freshness in the later stages permits a delightful increase in tempo. Feed off the positive psych that derives from passing those who were less accurate (or less sensible) in their pace judgment. Maintain good form throughout, and you'll have the best chance for your fastest possible race.

Such a strategy is wonderful in a race where you as an athlete face relatively little opposition. Take the lead and go for it. It can even work at the highest levels. Dave Moorcroft's world-record 13:00.42 at Oslo in 1982—where he found even 63-sec laps relatively easy—is an almost legendary example. We can only presume that on that day, Dave's lactate/ventilatory threshold pace was very close to an already high VO_2max pace, thereby keeping his tissue and blood acid accumulation minimal at his race pace.

How often have we heard spectators remark after witnessing a fine solo effort, ''What a splendid race! That runner was clear all the way; I wonder how much faster his finish time would have been had other runners been good enough to push him?'' The athlete clearly ran a smart race—optimally pace-efficient. But had the winner been challenged, would he or she necessarily have run faster? Not if that pace caused an excessive increase in blood acidity. The other challenging athletes wouldn't have been so gentle as to simply encourage the leader onward. We prefer to call these runners the ''spoilers'' because they delight in applying pressure in a most effective and unnerving way, using their own special tactics to spoil another runner's intended race plan. A well-known victim of such tactics was Dave Bedford, who had his very effective fast-pace running destroyed on several occasions by competitors who moved repeatedly to the front, then slowed ever so slightly and reduced the pace. He wasn't actually impeded, though he had the spike marks on his shins to show what had occurred. Such antics shattered his concentration.

The spoilers, of course, also run the risk of tiring, for it is physiological folly to insert short bursts to open gaps in a vain attempt to split the field. However, if several runners do this to slow the fast pace of a front-runner, they all can benefit, thereby neutralizing the would-be pacesetter and permitting the next phase of the battle to unfold. If you are a spoiler, be aware of the energy cost for such moves. If you are a front-runner in the process of being spoiled, you have an option, if it is in your repertoire. Use your repeatable 400m capability to make a serious and relatively long surge and hope it will drive you free of all attackers. This tactic is energy-costly as well, but if it brings home a victory, it is good use of proper training.

Viable Strategies for a Successful Finish

If a decisive push to set the stage for victory is to be attempted during the final five or six laps, it must indeed be a sustained drive—at the very least, one full lap; preferably two, and it may require a third to get clear. It should begin early enough to keep the would-be fast-finish sprinters from tagging along, remain modest enough to prevent you from slowing down toward the finish, and be sufficiently prolonged to let anyone in pursuit realize you are very serious. Once you have established your temporary supremacy, slow down to the overall pace that you believe you can manage and that you believe will win, because you most likely cannot maintain the accelerated pace throughout the race. For example, if you believe the race will be won in 13:20 or 13:45 (for men), or 15:00 or 15:25 (for women), resume running at the average pace per lap for each of those finish times—64, 66, 72, and 74 sec, respectively. Running any faster may require a pace faster than you can manage. If you run any slower you would not reap the benefit of that sudden injection of speed, because those behind will catch up too quickly. Ideally, they need to catch you only by about 5,001 m!

Not everyone can manage this strategy, however, and many have failed in the attempt. This tactic requires good anaerobic tolerance, an ability to cope with the pressure of knowing that you are ''the hunted,'' an excellent sense of pace judgment, and a feel for how others were handling the pace before you made your move. There is, however, the mental satisfaction of knowing that you have forced the others into running faster and (for them) less economically. If you have overestimated your competitors, you may be able to slow down slightly, thereby gaining a small measure of recovery as you prepare for your final acceleration to give your best effort. Of course, there is always the risk of one star in the field who is having a magnificent race and is still right beside you after your perfectly executed surge. Such is the nature of good competition, and of course the crowd loves it. What to do about it? The best you can, and hope that you can get more out of yourself than you believed possible.

Seb Coe remembers very well a two-lap, 5-mi road race in Italy in which a very good Italian distance runner simply was not intimidated by Seb's three long fast surges. It required a fourth, very close to the finish, before the race was decided. This points out an interesting similarity between successful racing in athletics and successful political negotiation: To win, you must be committed willingly, without any doubt, to endure at least one moment longer than your adversary.

If it is your preference to sit back throughout the race hoping to utilize a strong finish kick, realize that some of the aforementioned tactics may be used against you. Thus, you must cope accordingly, and this begins with your earlier training months before. Fast milers increasingly are showing forth as excellent 5,000m and 10,000m champions, so you would be well advised to keep your speed skills well honed. At the 1986 European Athletics Championships, Briton Jack Buckner, who took the 5,000m title, and Italy's Stefano Mei, 5,000m silver and 10,000m gold medalist, were both well-known middle-distance stars. Buckner had run a 3:57.29 mile that year, Mei 3:34.57 for 1,500 m.

Final-kick sprinting ability is not necessarily all genetic endowment. It can be developed in various ways to fit each athlete's natural tendencies, using multi-tier training. It is merely one facet of overall speed development. To race fast, you must have had fast training sessions, and that brings development of both speed strength and speed endurance. Today's 5,000m runners, both men and women, need to realize that both speed and strength must be incorporated into an extensive endurance base if they desire consistent success. Excellence in all areas provides the greatest number of options and thus the best chance for quality performances. Practice at racing distances on either side of 5,000m can provide such expertise by challenging your ability to manage speed with endurance (as in 3,000m track racing) as well as the reverse (as in 10km road racing).

The 8km road race (essentially 5 mi) is gaining popularity in both the United States and Britain. It is a race uniquely suited to both 5,000m and 10,000m runners, mixing the talents of those especially versed in speed and endurance. As might be suspected, it is most likely the expert in both who will have the best chance for victory. Keith Brantly scheduled an 8km road race early in July 1988 as a final tune-up to test his preparation for the U.S. Olympic Trials, in which he was prepared to run either the 5,000m or 10,000m events (or both). His 22:38 (in 71-degree F [22 degrees C] heat and 88% relative humidity) held up as the fastest time in the world that year over the 8km distance.

THE 10,000-METER RUN

From both physiological and tactical viewpoints, the 10,000m event has some similarity to the 5,000m.

The former is raced at roughly 92% of $\dot{V}O_2$max pace, the latter nearer to 100%. With optimal development, your lactate/ventilatory threshold will probably not exceed much beyond 88% to 90% of $\dot{V}O_2$max. Unless you can raise your $\dot{V}O_2$max or lactate/ventilatory threshold so high that a winning race pace would be within aerobic limits, a gradually accumulating metabolic acidosis is likely. This accumulation is less intense at 10,000m race pace than for the 5,000m run, however, which makes more viable the option of inserting occasional supra-race-pace surges as a tactic to increase the chances of victory. These observations give some clues as to those physiological systems that ought to be emphasized during training: good knowledge of pace, raising lactate/ventilatory threshold, raising $\dot{V}O_2$max, and honing an excellent speed capability for mid-race surging and a strong finish. As with the other events, periodic performance monitoring using treadmill testing as well as time trials in repeatable conditions can be useful to identify the extent to which training has in fact brought improvement over time. These principles were discussed earlier in chapters 2 and 3.

At first glance, the pace of a 10,000m race may not seem much slower than that of a 5,000m race, even at the world-record level. Compare the 65.1 sec/400m pace for Arturo Barrios' world-record 10,000m with the 62.3 sec/400m pace of Said Aouita's 5,000m world record (Table 5.1). Or on the women's side, compare the 72.6 sec/400m pace of Ingrid Kristiansen's world-record 10,000m race with the 70.2-sec pace for her own world-record 5,000m race. For the men, there's a 4.5% difference between the two events; for the women, 3.4%. However, as athletes, you are all fully aware of the accumulating stress of attempting to sustain (for 10 to 20 laps) a race pace that is even 1 sec/400 m beyond your manageable optimum. Effortwise, the few-second difference between the two race paces is enormous, and good pace sense thus becomes very important in these races. The pace difference also explains the greater requirement for stamina endurance training in 10,000m development, as compared to speed stamina for the 5,000m. Table 5.2 provides a detailed pace chart for use in determining the average 400m lap time for a wide range of 10,000m performances, as well as intermediate times at varying stages of such races. It can also calculate times for the various interval distances described in Chapter 3.

Abilities to sustain concentration during extended periods of track running—for pace identification and maintenance and for staying alert—are mandatory for 10,000m racers. This focus of attention can best be achieved by being mentally and physically rested before an important competition. Still, the length of

Table 5.1   Selected Noteworthy Running Paces—5,000m and 10,000m

Athlete	Time	Date	Venue	Pace (sec/400m)
5,000m				
Said Aouita—WR[a]	12:58.39	22 July 87	Rome	62.27
	13:00			62.4
	13:30			64.8
	14:00			67.2
	14:30			69.6
Ingrid Kristiansen—WR	14:37.33	05 Aug. 86	Stockholm	70.19
	15:00			72.0
	15:30			74.4
	16:00			76.8
	16:30			79.2
	17:00			81.6
	17:30			84.0
10,000m				
Arturo Barrios—WR[a]	27:08.23	18 Aug. 89	Berlin (West)	65.12
	27:30			66.0
	28:00			67.2
	28:30			68.4
	29:00			69.6
	29:30			70.8
	30:00			72.0
Ingrid Kristiansen—WR	30:13.74	05 July 86	Oslo	72.55
	30:30			73.2
	31:00			74.4
	31:30			75.6
	32:00			76.8
	32:30			78.0
	33:00			79.2
	33:30			80.4
	34:00			81.6
	34:30			82.8
	35:00			84.0

[a]WR = world record.

this event does provide considerably greater options for responding to changing conditions than do the shorter events just described. Unless the race is in the final stages, when a sudden pace change brings a competitor surging forth, you have adequate time to judge its significance—its potential effect on the race outcome and the extent to which you can fit it into the context of your own intended strategy for competitive effectiveness.

The elements of weather influence the outcome of 10,000m racing more profoundly than the shorter events, if for no other reason than the increased length of time that weather exerts its effects. Higher ambient temperatures mandate a shunting of blood flow to the skin for cooling, which reduces the amount of blood volume available for skeletal muscle perfusion. If the humidity is high as well, the evaporation rate decreases, even though perspiration may continue at a high rate. Reduced body cooling in the face of an elevated metabolism along with continued sweat loss can drastically slow the maintainable pace. A race of this kind tends to become a 24-lap exercise in running economy, with a final one-lap test of who has the greatest sprinting ability. It was under such conditions at the 1985 University Games in Kobe, Japan that Keith Brantly achieved thus far the United States' only

Table 5.2 200m and 400m Intermediate Split Times for Selected Metric-Measurement Race Distances Between 600m and 10,000m

Average per 200/400m (sec)	600	800	1,000	1,500	2,000	3,000	4,000	5,000	6,000	8,000	10,000
25.0/50.0	1:15.0	1:40.0	—	—	—	—	—	—	—	—	—
25.5/51.0	1:16.5	1:42.0	—	—	—	—	—	—	—	—	—
26.0/52.0	1:18.0	1:44.0	2:10.0	—	—	—	—	—	—	—	—
26.5/53.0	1:19.5	1:46.0	2:12.5	—	—	—	—	—	—	—	—
27.0/54.0	1:21.0	1:48.0	2:15.0	—	—	—	—	—	—	—	—
27.5/55.0	1:22.5	1:50.0	2:17.5	—	—	—	—	—	—	—	—
28.0/56.0	1:24.0	1:52.0	2:20.0	3:30.0	—	—	—	—	—	—	—
28.5/57.0	1:25.5	1:54.0	2:22.5	3:33.8	—	—	—	—	—	—	—
29.0/58.0	1:27.0	1:56.0	2:25.0	3:37.5	4:50.0	—	—	—	—	—	—
29.5/59.0	1:28.5	1:58.0	2:27.5	3:41.3	4:55.0	—	—	—	—	—	—
30.0/60.0	1:30.0	2:00.0	2:30.0	3:45.0	5:00.0	7:30.0	—	—	—	—	—
30.5/61.0	1:31.5	2:02.0	2:32.5	3:48.8	5:05.0	7:37.5	10:10.0	—	—	—	—
31.0/62.0	1:33.0	2:04.0	2:35.0	3:52.5	5:10.0	7:45.0	10:20.0	12:55.0	—	—	—
31.5/63.0	1:34.5	2:06.0	2:37.5	3:56.3	5:15.0	7:52.5	10:30.0	13:07.5	15:45.0	—	—
32.0/64.0	1:36.0	2:08.0	2:40.0	4:00.0	5:20.0	8.00.0	10:40.0	13:20.0	16:00.0	21:20.0	—
32.5/65.0	1:37.5	2:10.0	2:42.5	4:03.8	5:25.0	8:07.5	10:50.0	13:32.5	16:15.0	21:40.0	27:05.0
33.0/66.0	1:39.0	2:12.0	2:45.0	4:07.5	5:30.0	8:15.0	11:00.0	13:45.0	16:30.0	22:00.0	27:30.0
33.5/67.0	1:40.5	2:14.0	2:47.5	4:11.3	5:35.0	8:22.5	11:10.0	13:57.5	16:45.0	22:20.0	27:55.0
34.0/68.0	1:42.0	2:16.0	2:50.0	4:15.0	5:40.0	8:30.0	11:20.0	14:10.0	17:00.0	22:40.0	28:20.0
34.5/69.0	1:43.5	2:18.0	2:52.5	4:18.8	5:45.0	8:37.5	11:30.0	14:22.5	17:15.0	23:00.0	28:45.0
35.0/70.0	1:45.0	2:20.0	2:55.0	4:22.5	5:50.0	8:45.0	11:40.0	14:35.0	17:30.0	23:20.0	29:10.0
35.5/71.0	1:46.5	2:22.0	2:57.5	4:26.3	5:55.0	8:52.5	11:50.0	14:47.5	17:45.0	23:40.0	29:35.0
36.0/72.0	1:48.0	2:24.0	3:00.0	4:30.0	6:00.0	9:00.0	12:00.0	15:00.0	18:00.0	24:00.0	30:00.0
36.5/73.0	1:49.5	2:26.0	3:02.5	4:33.8	6:05.0	9:07.5	12:10.0	15:12.5	18:15.0	24:20.0	30:25.0
37.0/74.0	1:51.0	2:28.0	3:05.0	4:37.5	6:10.0	9:15.0	12:20.0	15:25.0	18:30.0	24:40.0	30:50.0
37.5/75.0	1:52.5	2:30.0	3:07.5	4:41.3	6:15.0	9:22.5	12:30.0	15:37.5	18:45.0	25:00.0	31:15.0
38.0/76.0	1:54.0	2:32.0	3:10.0	4:45.0	6:20.0	9:30.0	12:40.0	15:50.0	19:00.0	25:20.0	31:40.0
38.5/77.0	1:55.5	2:34.0	3:12.5	4:48.8	6:25.0	9:37.5	12:50.0	16:02.5	19:15.0	25:40.0	32:05.0
39.0/78.0	1:57.0	2:36.0	3:15.0	4:52.5	6:30.0	9:45.0	13:00.0	16:15.0	19:30.0	26:00.0	32:30.0
39.5/79.0	1:58.5	2:38.0	3:17.5	4:56.3	6:35.0	9:52.5	13:10.0	16:27.5	19:45.0	26:20.0	32:55.0
40.0/80.0	2:00.0	2:40.0	3:20.0	5:00.0	6:40.0	10:00.0	13:20.0	16:40.0	20:00.0	26:40.0	33:20.0
40.5/81.0	2:01.5	2:42.0	3:22.5	5:03.8	6:45.0	10:07.5	13:30.0	16:52.5	20:15.0	27:00.0	33:45.0
41.0/82.0	2:03.0	2:44.0	3:25.0	5:07.5	6:50.0	10:15.0	13:40.0	17:05.0	20:30.0	27:20.0	34:10.0
41.5/83.0	2:04.5	2:46.0	3:27.5	5:11.3	6:55.0	10:22.5	13:50.0	17:17.5	20:45.0	27:40.0	34:35.0
42.0/84.0	2:06.0	2:48.0	3:30.0	5:15.0	7:00.0	10:30.0	14:00.0	17:30.0	21:00.0	28:00.0	35:00.0
42.5/85.0	2:07.5	2:50.0	3:32.5	5:18.8	7:05.0	10:37.5	14:10.0	17:42.5	21:15.0	28:20.0	35:25.0
43.0/86.0	2:09.0	2:52.0	3:35.0	5:22.5	7:10.0	10:45.0	14:20.0	17:55.0	21:30.0	28:40.0	35:50.0
43.5/87.0	2:10.5	2:54.0	3:37.5	5:26.3	7:15.0	10:52.5	14:30.0	18:07.5	21:45.0	29:00.0	36:15.0
44.0/88.0	2:12.0	2:56.0	3:40.0	5:30.0	7:20.0	11:00.0	14:40.0	18:20.0	22:00.0	29:20.0	36:40.0
44.5/89.0	2:13.5	2:58.0	3:42.5	5:33.8	7:25.0	11:07.5	14:50.0	18:32.5	22:15.0	29:40.0	37:05.0
45.0/90.0	2:15.0	3:00.0	3:45.0	5:37.5	7:30.0	11:15.0	15:00.0	18:45.0	22:30.0	30:00.0	37:30.0

10,000m University Games gold medal; he combined carefully managed excellence in pace control with a slightly quicker last lap that involved an all-out sprint down the final straightaway. On an early-evening track still warm from the day's sun (temperature 29.5 degrees C [85 degrees F]; relative humidity 68%) his 29:11.24 victory was 0.47 sec ahead of Mexico's Jesus Herrera and 0.49 sec in front of Japan's Shuiji Yoneshige.

Wind can also affect performance. A headwind along one straightaway and a tailwind along the other typically produce an accordion-like effect as the space occupied by a pack of runners alternately shortens (into the wind) and lengthens (with the wind). For the leaders, the increased energy cost when running into the headwind is not regained as they proceed downwind. For those mid-pack during the upwind portion, the increased chances of being spiked by a runner in front and the need to shorten stride as the pack comes together can be unnerving and debilitating even to the freshest and most seasoned competitors. Both mental and physical toughness are crucial in combating the negative effects of these race conditions on performance.

When weather conditions are more favorable, the fantastic abilities of today's top-level racers to deliver fast final laps, even after fast racing for 23 or 24 laps, not only attest to the runners' well-rounded athletic abilities but also to the dependence on such developed speed to ensure a victory or good finish position. An excellent example of this occurred during the men's 10,000m final in the 1983 Helsinki World Championships in Athletics. At 9,400 m, 13 runners remained in a tight pack. As they passed the ringing bell, announcing the last lap, Werner Schildhauer (German Democratic Republic) launched a ferocious change of pace, eventually delivering a 54.8-sec final 400 m! But Hans-Jorg Kunze (German Democratic Republic) ran exactly as fast. Martti Vainio (Finland) ran even faster (54.5 sec), and Gidamis Shahanga (Tanzania) very nearly as fast (54.9 sec). Yet none of these athletes won the race. Alberto Cova (Italy) delivered a 53.9-sec 400 m to beat Schildhauer by 0.14 sec, in 28:01.04. The other three were so close that only 0.89 sec separated first place from fifth!

A quality finishing surge may also be mandated to ensure a very fast time, simply because of the physiological necessity to maintain the fastest sustainable pace for the longest possible time (to optimize economy), and then quicken the pace during the final moments to the fastest attainable before metabolic acidosis begins to slow performance. A notable example involves Mark Nenow's American record at the Van Damme Memorial meeting in Brussels in September 1986. The assistance of an effective pacer (Mauricio Gonzalez) brought Mark through 5,000 m in 13:47.1. Mauricio's 5,000m split was 13:46.79, and this 0.34-sec differential still allowed Mark to remain in his wind shadow without fear of tangling legs. Mark's second 5,000 m was essentially a lonely solo effort (he won the race by nearly 44 sec), that required enormous concentration to sustain evenly a pace of 65.5 sec per lap. He delivered a 60.2-sec final 400 m to achieve his record of 27:20.56, lowering Alberto Salazar's mark by 5.05 sec.

THE MARATHON

The marathon is quite a different event from the races just described in several respects. Racing for a much longer time is only one of the challenges; there are several more. Try to consider first the pace dynamics of this race; Table 5.3 will help in this regard. Had Ethiopia's Belayneh Dinsamo run his world-best marathon performance on a track, he would have averaged the equivalent of nearly 105 continuous laps of 400 m at a pace of 72.1 sec per lap. Similarly, Ingrid Kristiansen's world record represents an average pace of 80.3 sec per lap. There is thus the demand for well more than 2 hr of concentrated pace running while managing dehydration and fuel exhaustion and not encountering physical debilitation. The athlete may also need the reserve to insert a decisive increase in pace at a moment precisely timed to break a competitive field both mentally and physically. Anyone who believes that a marathon is a simple event to prepare for is terribly misinformed!

Unique Aspects of Marathon Preparation

These long, grueling races often give the impression that success is as much genetically determined as in the 100m dash. Thus, instead of possessing the reflexes of a squirrel with a genetic predominance of FT skeletal muscle fibers, you had better instead be primarily ST-endowed, with enormous running efficiency and low lactate production even at high work loads. But performance is determined by the interaction of genetic gifts with proper training. Just as training to build strength and improve technique is of great value for sprinters, so it is also with marathoners; training to increase stored energy supplies and aerobic power is essential. Of equal and perhaps even greater importance than a large VO_2max, however, is the ability to race at a high percentage of VO_2max pace without measurable anaerobic accumulation. Training brings lactate/ventilatory threshold pace closer to VO_2max pace.

Achieving fast performances when racing in marathons requires even more than genetics and training. Environmental conditions assume greater importance—a flat course that is correctly measured (to minimize the added stress of hills), cloudy skies (to minimize radiant heat gain), cool weather (to minimize sweat losses), and minimum wind (to reduce energy cost) are all key factors, along with a good competitive field to bring out the best in everyone. Admittedly, these may seem almost like laboratory conditions, but statistical records show that the vast majority of the world's best performances for both men and women have been achieved under such conditions. The most dependable circumstances for achieving these performances occur in Japan during the Japanese marathon season (December to March), and in Europe. Cities such as Rotterdam, London, Fukoka, Tokyo, Nagoya, and Osaka are meccas for those athletes who race the clock in an attempt for

Table 5.3 Approximate Pace Equivalents for Selected Marathon Performance Times

Athlete	Time	Venue	Date	Min/mile	Min/km
Belayneh Dinsamo—WR[a]	2:06:50	Rotterdam	17 April 88	4:50	3:00
	2:07:00			4:51	3:01
	2:08:00			4:53	3:02
	2:09:00			4:55	3:03
	2:10:00			4:57	3:05
	2:11:00			5:00	3:06
	2:12:00			5:02	3:08
	2:13:00			5:04	3:09
	2:14:00			5:07	3:11
	2:15:00			5:09	3:12
	2:20:00			5:20	3:19
Ingrid Kristiansen—WR	2:21:06	London	21 April 85	5:23	3:21
	2:25:00			5:32	3:26
	2:26:00			5:34	3:28
	2:27:00			5:36	3:29
	2:28:00			5:39	3:30
	2:29:00			5:41	3:32
	2:30:00			5:43	3:33
	2:31:00			5:45	3:35
	2:32:00			5:48	3:36
	2:33:00			5:50	3:38
	2:34:00			5:52	3:39
	2:35:00			5:55	3:40
	2:40:00			6:06	3:48

[a]WR = world record.

a personal record. Such performances are rarely achieved in the United States, where athletes all too commonly have the fruits of several months of hard training sadly spoiled by a hot day, subfreezing temperatures, or gusty headwinds—conditions that may leave a marathoner mentally destroyed and physically debilitated.

In addition to course conditions, a second challenge not encountered in racing shorter distances is the real risk of exhausting available energy supplies for maintaining a competitive race pace. Thus, tapering prior to a marathon race must involve nutritional considerations as well as physical rest. Fuel and water intake during the race are both appropriate and necessary, in contrast to the shorter races. Additional factors, often considered trivial, such as clothing and shoes that do not cause problems with chafing or blisters also acquire greater importance during marathon racing, with its greater-than-fourfold increase in competitive distance over the 10,000m run.

A third dilemma that you'll face in moving up to the marathon from shorter events comes in designing training plans. An important loss is the ability to include training runs considerably longer than your race distance. Top-level 800m and 1,500m men may run distances as long as 10 to 15 mi in training; the women typically a little less. Enormous confidence can come from training at distances from 15 to 30 times longer than your primary racing event. If you have decided to become a marathoner, you've just lost this option. Middle-distance runners have a much more favorable ratio of weekly training/racing distance than do marathon runners. For a male 1,500m runner, this may be 112,500 m/1,500 m = 69.9 mi/0.93 mi = 75/1. For a female 1,500m runner, it is less—perhaps 50/1. A marathoner's weekly training/racing ratio is from 3.5/1 to 5.5/1 at best. This may explain why the more consistently successful marathon runners can race effectively in no more than two to three marathons per year.

A fourth difference between marathon runners and shorter distance specialists is the marathoner's necessity for what we will term very long runs, ranging between 30 km (18.6 mi) and 35 km (21.7 mi) and done about once every 8 to 12 days during the 2- to three-month period before a marathon race. These are aerobic runs, typically at between 55% to 70% of $\dot{V}O_2$max pace or with a heart rate of 145 to 160 for women and 140 to 150 for men. The wearing effect of these very long runs is of such magnitude that they need to be considered almost as race equivalents. They will condition you mentally to tolerate sustained periods of running at a constant pace and introduce you to the sensation of profound fatigue that begins as muscle carbohydrate supplies begin to deplete.

When added to the remainder of a training week, the stress of these very long runs means that for marathon runners, a much greater chance exists than for runners in the other distance events for the results of training to initiate the sequence whereby fatigue → exhaustion → breakdown. In chapter 6 we will outline the various kinds of injury that occur—primarily tendon injuries as muscles fatigue and fail to do their share of bearing the load during training. If one warning can be issued for the prevention of injury, it is the **rule of specific quantity:** Do the least amount of the most sensible training to bring about improvement in performance. Do very long runs but not too frequently, and ensure proper recovery. Do shorter runs and longer distance interval runs, but again, ensure recovery. If the choice is yours, it is better to err on the side of undertraining rather than overtraining.

Another warning invokes the **rule of individuality:** Each athlete has a slightly different genetic endowment of FT and ST skeletal muscle fibers as well as a different training base and fitness level. The previous training load on the day before your very long runs and the ideal pace for these runs will be quite different for every athlete, depending on period in the training cycle, recovery, and genetics. For some in the group the pace will be too quick, producing excessive fatigue; for others it will be a perfect training stimulus. If your optimum training pace is 6:00/mi (3:44/km) for 20 mi, then running at a 5:50/mi (3:38/km) pace is needlessly fast. It isn't worth the risk of excessive fatigue or injury simply to have companionship on a long run. A winner crossing the finish line is all alone; here's your chance to practice just that (unless your training partners are your clones!).

Excellent marathoners quite often possess admirable shorter distance (i.e., 10,000m) racing abilities. This demonstrates once again the importance of strength, speed, and stamina in improving the ability of working muscles to endure a given submaximum work load for a long period. Within limits, the faster you can run, the easier any particular submaximum pace becomes. Dinsamo's 2:06:50 represents a 15:04/5,000m pace, while Kristiansen's 2:21:06 is at a 16:43/5,000m pace. The ability to race back-to-back 5,000m repeats at 15:50 for men (running at a 2:13:35 pace) or 18:00 for women (running at a 2:31:54 pace) can be developed nicely by training designed to raise as much as possible both your $\dot{V}O_2$max and your anaerobic threshold. We aren't necessarily suggesting here that men who are sub-4-min milers make fast sub-2:20:00

marathoners (scarcely 50 runners have achieved this double in the history of running). We are indeed suggesting, however, that good shorter distance racing ability, in both men and women, can contribute to competent marathon racing provided that the required marathon-training component of periodic very long runs is included to create connective tissue adaptation; increased skeletal muscle fuel reserves, mitochondria, and capillarization; and mental readiness for extended pace maintenance.

Marathons are raced by elite runners at a small fraction slower than lactate/ventilatory threshold pace. This means between about 78% and 88% of $\dot{V}O_2$max pace. For that portion of the race where carbohydrates are readily available (and hopefully this will extend to the end of the race), the respiratory exchange ratio is in the neighborhood of 0.93 to 0.95. This suggests a fat:carbohydrate ratio of between 24%:76% to 17%:83% for fuel consumption. If you possess a generous ST muscle fiber endowment, have a $\dot{V}O_2$max on the high side of that found among elite endurance athletes (e.g., > 75 ml/kg/min or higher for men, > 65 ml/kg/min for women), and are economical (i.e., consume less O_2 at submaximal paces than most other runners of similar expertise), then you have the best tools for fast performances. The key to achieving these fast performances is initiating a pace slow enough in the beginning to ensure an optimum ratio of fuel utilization, thereby maintaining adequate carbohydrate stores to carry you through the entire race. This topic of energy provision needs further discussion.

Fuel Replenishment for Marathon Training and Racing

In chapter 1 we identified the kinds of quantities of the various fuels used in metabolism and indicated that whereas fatty acids are plentiful, carbohydrates (muscle, blood, and liver glucose and glycogen) are not. The marathon distance is so long that carbohydrate exhaustion in working muscles with subsequent slowing of race pace is almost certain if this fuel is utilized excessively. Thus, successful marathon racing requires an optimum balance between fatty acid and carbohydrate utilization to prevent this slowing of performance. Though in chapter 1 we discussed how metabolites of these fuels control their relative rates of utilization during resting conditions, elevated activity levels such as during racing cause an additional challenge.

Consider the metabolic dilemma that you are up against. Fats are the logical energy source for such a long race because they are available in large quantity. But recall that fatty acid molecules contain very little O_2 and thus must rely on a plentiful circulating O_2 supply through the bloodstream. By comparison, glucose contains much more O_2 in its molecular structure and thus needs less additional O_2 for its metabolism. Thus, for every mole of O_2 provided by the blood, you will derive 5.05 kcal (21.1 kJ) of energy from glucose, but only 4.69 kcal (19.6 kJ) from fatty acids (Dwyer & Dyer, 1984). How is this important?

If you begin your marathon race at a sensible pace (slightly less than lactate/ventilatory threshold pace), your fuel consumption ratio will be at about 25%:75% fatty acids: carbohydrates. During the race, if your muscle carbohydrate supplies begin to dwindle, this ratio will change eventually to something like 40%:60% fatty acids:carbohydrates. This shift in fuel preference mandates an increased blood flow to your working muscles to provide the increased O_2 for fatty acid metabolism. However, developing dehydration as the race develops may not permit this unless the pace is quickened. If you are already racing at very near your lactate/ventilatory threshold pace, this option may not be feasible either. Such an increase in pace will not be sustainable due to accumulating acidosis. If carbohydrate depletion increases, shifting the fuel consumption to an even greater reliance on fatty acid metabolism, you may be forced to slow your race pace dramatically and may experience the profound sense of fatigue that accompanies such depletion. In runner's jargon, you have "hit the wall" due to carbohydrate exhaustion.

What can you do to ensure an acceptable ratio of fatty acids:carbohydrates throughout your marathon race? Clearly the answer is to have as much glycogen in your skeletal muscles as possible and in addition to have a supplemental source of glucose in the bloodstream that can enter your working muscles and provide a carbohydrate reserve as muscle glycogen stores diminish. The best way to increase this reserve is through the glycogen storage stimulus provided to working skeletal muscles by periodic very long runs during the months before your race, followed by a supplemental nutritional loading of the working tissues during the few days before your race. Then, during the race, the best way to ensure an additional incoming supplemental source of carbohydrate is to ingest fluids along the way which contain no more than 7% to 8% carbohydrate dissolved in water. Some background information and practical hints about these strategies may be useful.

The relationship of high-volume training and carbohydrate repletion dates back to the studies of Hultman and Bergstrom (1967). These workers (and others since) have shown that if skeletal muscle glycogen stores are largely depleted by prolonged exercise (e.g., a 20-mi [32.2-km] run), the depleted muscles would

respond during postexercise nutritional replenishment by storing even more glycogen than had been present before the depletion. This phenomenon was called *muscle glycogen supercompensation*. If your muscle cells had a personality, we could picture them not at all enjoying the loss of so much of their stored energy sources, and stuffing some extra fuel into their cytoplasm after such a depletion under the assumption that the owner of those muscles might attempt such a crazy antic again sometime in the future! Supercompensation will occur during the day or so following the long run if adequate nutritional replacement is provided. This increased glycogen-storing stimulus in your working muscles—which can best be triggered by the very long distance runs—is thus an essential part of your competitive marathon preparation.

During aerobic running you will consume about 1.04 kcal/kg body weight/km of distance (or 4.35 kJ/kg/km). Thus, a 20-mi (32.2km) run for a 60-kg man, or a 50-kg woman, has an energy requirement of 2,009 and 1,674 kcal (8,739 and 7,281 kJ) respectively (Anonymous, 1989; Margaria, Cerretelli, Aghemo, & Sassi, 1963). This requirement is related more to distance than to velocity (the faster the aerobic velocity, the greater the rate of energy production, but the training distance will be covered in less time). This puts you as much as two meals behind. Following this long run, energy intake should be greater than that lost to provide appropriate liver and muscle cell energy storage. Muscle glycogen will deplete quickly with daily high-volume distance running unless it is replenished adequately (Costill & Miller, 1980).

It is recommended that athletes doing high-volume aerobic training maintain a diet comprised of a 60%-25%-15% carbohydrate-fat-protein mixture to ensure adequate energy replacement (Hecker, 1987). One problem that occurs with athletes doing such high-volume training—even those who do two training sessions a day instead of one long run, which still may total 18 or more mi/day (29 km/day)—is that they find it difficult to schedule several feedings of such items as baked potatoes, rice, sweet potatoes, and pasta. It thus becomes easy to enter a state of negative energy balance in which outgo exceeds intake. Athletes in hard training need at least 5 (though optimally 6 to 7) grams of carbohydrate per kilogram body weight per day. This problem underscores the importance of periodic recovery days.

An interesting recent finding is that carbohydrate replacement immediately following training—within the first 30 min—will permit as much as 300% more carbohydrate assimilation (glycogen synthesis) than if it is delayed until a few hours postexercise (Ivy, Katz, Cutler, Sherman, & Coyle, 1988). Athletes typically do not eat much during this period, as they are either traveling to or from training or ending their training session with a shower or massage. It would thus be advantageous for runners to have liquid carbohydrate sources readily available for immediate ingestion at the site where they terminate their exercise. Such sources are now available in liquid polymer form as well as in the form of simple sugars, and there isn't any real advantage of one over the other except individual taste preference or ease of purchase. They are easily digested and absorbed, refreshing, and acceptable in flavor. Such rapid posttraining intake of high-energy fluids provides a beneficial alternative to the solid forms of complex carbohydrates mentioned previously and ensures a high-energy intake when the body is most receptive to it. Most of the research studies have involved cyclists rather than runners, in part because of the interest in the nutritional needs of athletes engaged in multi-day cycling competitions. There is no reason to believe that runners would have different metabolic dynamics than cyclists in terms of their daily energy needs because they often have similar energy requirements during heavy training and competition. However, running is very different from cycling in terms of jostling of the viscera. If this adversely affects the absorptive characteristics of the intestinal tract then runners as a group may be more variant in their responses to fluid ingestion during competition.

Most marathoners have experimented with various regimens suggested in the literature for topping up fuel reserves (especially carbohydrates) in the final few days preceding a marathon. This is popularly known as *carbohydrate loading*, and the strategies runners use have been based on the concept of glycogen supercompensation described earlier. An earlier preference was to do a long "depletion run" several days before, then have a day of noncarbohydrate dieting following by a reduction of training and dietary emphasis on complex carbohydrates, hoping to optimize glycogen supercompensation. The more recent preference is to eliminate the noncarbohydrate day. It's always difficult to presuppose what works best for you, because unlike in the world of laboratory science, you can't rerun the race the next week using a different loading regimen and still have exactly the same overall fitness and mental attitude, thus the difference cannot be assessed. Our experience with elite-level marathon runners suggests that most runners prefer not to tamper very much with their established dietary habits. Instead, they simply emphasize a slightly higher intake of complex carbohydrates in their diet during the several days preceding the race, skip the noncarbohydrate day and realize that increased fuel storage will occur automatically because

they are tapering their daily training distance. Thus, their energy intake exceeds their energy outgo, and if the intake has a substantial carbohydrate emphasis (60% or more), the excess will be stored.

Another important strategy occurs during the several hours before the race. The idea is to "top up" fuel stores from the preceding night's fast and also ensure optimum fluid on board for the race. It does no good to drink excessive amounts of water hours before a race, as it will simply be excreted as urine. However, fluids ingested during the final hour prerace will still be in the process of being absorbed when the race begins. Then, as kidney blood flow diminishes due to the shunting of blood from the viscera to the skeletal muscles, this absorbed fluid will remain available for use by the body. Four or five hours prerace, a light carbohydrate meal including such items as oatmeal, low-fat milk, unbuttered toast, and orange juice is easily absorbed and can top off fuel reserves quite nicely.

Oxford University biochemist Eric Newsholme (1986) suggests that carbohydrate-containing drinks and snacks be omitted from the near-race period (with just water being ingested). Costill et al. (1977) pointed out some of the rationale for refraining from carbohydrate ingestion between 2 hours and 30 minutes prerace. Such an ingestion typically increases insulin release into the blood, promoting glucose absorption throughout the body. The combination of insulin and an elevated blood sugar reduces the liver's usual glucose output into the bloodstream. Then, as the race begins, a gradually lowering blood sugar level deprives the working muscles of a steady glucose infusion until such time as insulin levels fall and liver output of glucose is restored. It would be preferable for you to maintain that steady infusion throughout the race. Thus, to eliminate this potential reduction in blood glucose, plain water would appear to be the best fluid to drink during the 3-hour period before starting the race.

During the race, many runners prefer to ingest only water, as it leaves no stickiness if spilled, has minimum chance for spoilage, and will be absorbed as quickly as (possibly more so than) most nutrient solutions. Because fluid losses from perspiration can exceed the maximum rate of fluid absorption, it is crucial not to compromise fluid absorption. However, we have already emphasized the need for supplemental and continual glucose diffusion into the working muscles to provide a carbohydrate source to supplement falling muscle glycogen supplies. Current research suggests that you can ingest carbohydrate solutions of up to 7% to 8% with acceptable absorption and no reduction in total water intake. This provides a ready source of blood glucose for working muscles (Coyle, Coggan, Hemmert, & Ivy, 1986). Thus, the threefold combination of

1. energy replacement during the race with energy-rich drinks,
2. training-related fuel increases as a result of very long runs followed by adequate energy replenishment, and
3. prerace carbohydrate loading

are all important strategies to help optimize marathon race performance.

Variation in athletes makes none of these regimens uniformly tolerable by your gastrointestinal system. Your own experimentation done as a part of very long training runs will provide the kind of information you need for developing a workable strategy. The gastrointestinal system works best by habitual periodic activity as typified by eating three meals a day. Altering the system's functional pattern by making sizable changes in mealtimes and type of food ingested often tends to increase the likelihood of dysfunction. Even mild diarrhea or constipation can be unpleasant and debilitating, particularly during a race. During a race, it would be sad to lose the rewards of months of preparation by experiencing stomach distress caused by inadequate ability to manage nutrient intake.

Strategies for Racing Marathons

More than for the shorter distance events, small elements of preparation, often seemingly insignificant, can affect the outcome of a marathon. Shoes must fit perfectly to prevent blisters and allow for foot swelling during the later stages. Clothing should not chafe or bind. Shoes and clothing that will be used in a race should all have been worn prior to the race to verify their suitability. For marathoners selected as part of traveling teams, early issue of team clothing should be a high priority. If on-course feeding stations are provided for runners to place bottles containing special fluids, care must be given to labeling (good visibility), shape (for easy capture), and content.

For athletes competing in their first marathon who have never (or very seldom) traversed the actual race distance, the experience is unique. Indeed, the varying terrain, weather, and past training history makes very nearly every marathon race quite different from any other. To gain a beneficial psychological perspective, many successful marathoners (especially those well versed in both the metric and Imperial measurement systems) divide the race into two parts: first, a 20-mi hard run, then a 10km race. This may be sensible from two perspectives: First, long runs typically

are in the neighborhood of 20 mi, so this distance is familiar. The 10km distance is also familiar as a racing distance. Many major world marathoners use both miles and kilometers. In a marathon, the "running" usually occurs during the first 20 mi, and the "racing" during the final 10 km. Thus, athletes generally wait until sometime after 30 km before inserting aggressive challenging surges. The 20-mi point is at about 32 km. If you can imagine a hard 20-mi run and then imagine a 10km race, psychologically you are always in familiar territory. Race pace for 10 km is faster than race pace for a 20-mi run, and although your marathon race pace may start to slow in the final kilometers you'll be better prepared psychologically for the more difficult effort sense. Second, for Imperially oriented runners a psychological advantage of imagining a 10km race is that the first digit of the mile markers beyond 20 (which are unfamiliar because they aren't encountered in training) can be ignored. Thus, the 21-mile mark becomes the 1-mile mark of the 6-plus-miles remaining.

Tables 5.4 and 5.5 provide a ready reference for split times, using both the metric and Imperial systems, for athletes attempting to chart even splits during marathon racing. Ideally, you should run the first portion of the race a little slower than your expected mean pace, thereby conserving carbohydrate supplies. Later on, as conditions become more tactical as you initiate or respond to pace increases intended by someone (you or your rivals) to break apart the lead pack, adequate carbohydrate supplies will be available to provide energy for these pace increases as well as for a strong finish. This is the concept of *negative-splitting* a marathon—running the second half in a shorter time than the first half. It seldom occurs, for three reasons: One is that very few marathon competitions are conducted over what we have termed "laboratory conditions;" that is, on a flat course, out and back, with minimum wind and unchanging temperature, and where accurate split times are recorded every 5 km to permit ongoing (and postrace) analysis. The second reason is that it is very difficult for runners to be patient enough initially to maintain a pace that seems well within their comfort zone; the temptation is to race faster. The agony of the second half of your last marathon raced has been all but forgotten, and you are about to make the same mistake twice! The third reason is that your lactate/ventilatory threshold pace most likely slows during the final stages of the race. The trend toward dehydration reduces blood volume, which reduces the extent of skeletal muscle perfusion. This decreases $\dot{V}O_2$ max and also causes hemoconcentration, effectively increasing the blood acidity. To keep this acidity from increasing further, running pace

Table 5.4　Metric Marathon Pace Chart With Selected Intermediate-Distance (Split) Times

1 km	5 km	10 km	15 km	20 km	Half	25 km	30 km	35 km	40 km	Marathon
3:00	15:00	30:00	45:00	1:00:00	1:03:18	1:15:00	1:30:00	1:45:00	2:00:00	2:06:35
3:05	15:25	30:50	46:15	1:01:40	1:05:03	1:17:05	1:32:30	1:47:55	2:03:20	2:10:06
3:10	15:50	31:40	47:30	1:03:20	1:06:49	1:19:10	1:35:00	1:50:50	2:06:40	2:13:37
3:15	16:15	32:30	48:45	1:05:00	1:08:34	1:21:15	1:37:30	1:53:45	2:10:00	2:17:08
3:20	16:40	33:20	50:00	1:06:40	1:10:20	1:23:20	1:40:00	1:56:40	2:13:20	2:20:39
3:25	17:05	34:10	51:15	1:08:20	1:12:05	1:25:25	1:42:30	1:59:35	2:16:40	2:24:09
3:30	17:30	35:00	52:30	1:10:00	1:13:50	1:27:30	1:45:00	2:02:30	2:20:00	2:27:40
3:35	17:55	35:50	53:45	1:11:40	1:15:35	1:29:35	1:47:30	2:05:25	2:23:20	2:31:11
3:40	18:20	36:40	55:00	1:13:20	1:17:21	1:31:40	1:50:00	2:08:20	2:26:40	2:34:42
3:45	18:45	37:30	56:15	1:15:00	1:19:07	1:33:45	1:52:30	2:11:15	2:30:00	2:38:13
3:50	19:10	38:20	57:30	1:16:40	1:20:52	1:35:50	1:55:00	2:14:10	2:33:20	2:41:44
3:55	19:35	39:10	58:45	1:18:20	1:22:38	1:37:55	1:57:30	2:17:05	2:36:40	2:45:16
4:00	20:00	40:00	60:00	1:20:00	1:24:24	1:40:00	2:00:00	2:20:00	2:40:00	2:48:48
4:05	20:25	40:50	61:15	1:21:40	1:26:09	1:42:05	2:02:30	2:22:55	2:43:20	2:52:18
4:10	20:50	41:40	62:30	1:23:20	1:27:54	1:44:10	2:05:00	2:25:50	2:46:40	2:55:49
4:15	21:15	42:30	63:45	1:25:00	1:29:40	1:46:15	2:07:30	2:28:45	2:50:00	2:59:20
4:20	21:40	43:20	65:00	1:26:40	1:31:25	1:48:20	2:10:00	2:31:40	2:53:20	3:02:51
4:25	22:05	44:10	66:15	1:28:20	1:33:11	1:50:25	2:12:30	2:34:35	2:56:40	3:06:21
4:30	22:30	45:00	67:30	1:30:00	1:34:56	1:52:30	2:15:00	2:37:30	3:00:00	3:10:57
4:35	22:55	45:50	68:45	1:31:40	1:36:42	1:54:35	2:17:30	2:40:25	3:03:20	3:13:14
4:40	23:20	46:40	70:00	1:33:20	1:38:47	1:56:40	2:20:00	2:43:20	3:06:40	3:16:55
4:45	23:45	47:30	71:15	1:35:00	1:40:13	1:58:45	2:22:30	2:46:15	3:10:00	3:20:26
4:50	24:10	48:20	72:30	1:36:40	1:41:58	2:00:50	2:25:00	2:49:10	3:13:20	3:23:57
4:55	24:35	49:10	73:45	1:38:20	1:43:44	2:02:55	2:27:30	2:52:05	3:16:40	3:27:28
5:00	25:00	50:00	75:00	1:40:00	1:45:30	2:05:00	2:30:00	2:55:00	3:20:00	3:31:00

may have to be slowed. Thus, run the first portion of the race only minimally faster than your expected mean pace to allow for late-race slowing.

Minimizing Fatigue and Coping With Altered Perceived Exertion

Two important psychophysiological considerations need to be clearly understood for appreciating what occurs during a marathon race. One is the problem of developing fatigue, which tends to slow the pace. This is in contrast to the other distance races we have thus far discussed, characterized often by a sizable pace increase near the end. To minimize this pace decrease, the marathoner must optimize mean race pace, which means deviating as little as possible from the mean pace of the intended finish time. We have been analyzing 5km split times for dozens of top-level marathon performances from the Japanese races, conducted often over virtually ideal conditions, and which provide such detail in their official results. These studies indicate that deviating from the mean race pace

by more than ±2% must be metabolically much more costly than remaining within this pace window, because early-race fast splits all too often result in proportionately even slower late-race splits. The crucial dilemma here, of course, is that you do not know how fast you'll run until the race is finished, making it difficult to decide on an acceptable mean 5km split pace. Given the strong probability that an early fast pace is more debilitating than an early slow pace, the odds of finishing faster are improved by beginning more slowly.

To examine this problem more specifically, in Figure 5.2 we show the 5km splits of Japan's Takeyuki Nakayama for three of his recent marathon races. This extraordinary athlete made a breakthrough in 1984 with a 2:10:00 victory at Fukuoka. In Figure 5.2a we see how sensibly he started that race, well within the ±2% window. He increased his pace between 25 and 30 km to break free of accompanying athletes, and only Michael Heilmann (German Democratic Republic) stayed with him. Although Nakayama moved outside the ±2% window during this surge, this

Table 5.5 Marathon Pace Chart With Selected Metric and Imperial Intermediate-Distance (Split) Times

Mile pace	5 km (3.1mi)	5 miles	10 km (6.2mi)	15 km (9.3mi)	10 miles	20 km (12.4mi)	Half marathon	15 miles	25 km (15.5mi)	30 km (18.6mi)	20 miles	35 km (21.7mi)	40 km (24.8mi)	Marathon
4:40	14:30	23:20	29:00	43:30	46:40	58:00	1:01:11	1:10:00	1:12:30	1:27:00	1:33:20	1:41:30	1:56:00	2:02:22
4:45	14:46	23:45	29:31	44:17	47:30	59:02	1:02:17	1:11:15	1:13:48	1:28:33	1:35:00	1:43:19	1:58:04	2:04:33
4:50	15:01	24:10	30:02	45:03	48:20	1:00:04	1:03:22	1:12:30	1:15:05	1:30:06	1:36:40	1:45:07	2:00:08	2:06:44
4:55	15:17	24:35	30:33	45:50	49:10	1:01:06	1:04:28	1:13:45	1:16:23	1:31:39	1:38:20	1:46:56	2:02:12	2:08:55
5:00	15:32	25:00	31:04	46:36	50:00	1:02:08	1:05:33	1:15:00	1:17:40	1:33:12	1:40:00	1:48:44	2:04:16	2:11:06
5:05	15:48	25:25	31:35	47:23	50:50	1:03:10	1:06:39	1:16:15	1:18:58	1:34:45	1:41:40	1:50:33	2:06:20	2:13:17
5:10	16:03	25:50	32:06	48:09	51:40	1:04:12	1:07:44	1:17:30	1:20:15	1:36:18	1:43:20	1:52:21	2:08:24	2:15:28
5:15	16:19	26:15	32:37	48:56	52:30	1:05:14	1:08:50	1:18:45	1:21:33	1:37:51	1:45:00	1:54:10	2:10:28	2:17:39
5:20	16:34	26:40	33:08	49:42	53:20	1:06:16	1:09:55	1:20:00	1:22:50	1:39:24	1:46:40	1:55:58	2:12:32	2:19:50
5:25	16:50	27:05	33:39	50:29	54:10	1:07:18	1:11:01	1:21:15	1:24:08	1:40:57	1:48:20	1:57:47	2:14:36	2:22:01
5:30	17:05	27:30	34:10	51:15	55:00	1:08:20	1:12:06	1:22:30	1:25:25	1:42:30	1:50:00	1:59:35	2:16:40	2:24:12
5:35	17:21	27:55	34:41	52:02	55:50	1:09:22	1:13:12	1:23:45	1:26:43	1:44:03	1:51:40	2:01:24	2:18:44	2:26:23
5:40	17:36	28:20	35:12	52:48	56:40	1:10:24	1:14:17	1:25:00	1:28:00	1:45:36	1:53:20	2:03:12	2:20:48	2:28:34
5:45	17:52	28:45	35:43	53:35	57:30	1:11:26	1:15:23	1:26:15	1:29:18	1:47:09	1:55:00	2:05:01	2:22:52	2:30:45
5:50	18:07	29:10	36:14	54:21	58:20	1:12:28	1:16:28	1:27:30	1:30:35	1:48:42	1:56:40	2:06:49	2:24:56	2:32:56
5:55	18:23	29:35	36:45	55:08	59:10	1:13:30	1:17:34	1:28:45	1:31:53	1:50:15	1:58:20	2:08:38	2:27:00	2:35:07
6:00	18:38	30:00	37:16	55:54	1:00:00	1:14:32	1:18:39	1:30:00	1:33:10	1:51:48	2:00:00	2:10:26	2:29:04	2:37:18
6:05	18:54	30:25	37:47	56:41	1:00:50	1:15:34	1:19:45	1:31:15	1:34:28	1:53:21	2:01:40	2:12:15	2:31:08	2:39:29
6:10	19:09	30:50	38:18	57:27	1:01:40	1:16:36	1:20:50	1:32:30	1:35:45	1:54:54	2:03:20	2:14:03	2:33:12	2:41:40
6:15	19:25	31:15	38:49	58:14	1:02:30	1:17:38	1:21:56	1:33:45	1:37:03	1:56:27	2:05:00	2:15:52	2:35:16	2:43:51
6:20	19:40	31:40	39:20	59:00	1:03:20	1:18:40	1:23:01	1:35:00	1:38:20	1:58:00	2:06:40	2:17:40	2:37:20	2:46:02
6:25	19:56	32:05	39:51	59:47	1:04:10	1:19:42	1:24:07	1:36:15	1:39:38	1:59:33	2:08:20	2:19:29	2:39:24	2:48:13
6:30	20:11	32:30	40:22	1:00:33	1:05:00	1:20:44	1:25:12	1:37:30	1:40:55	2:01:06	2:10:00	2:21:17	2:41:28	2:50:24
6:35	20:27	32:55	40:53	1:01:20	1:05:50	1:21:46	1:26:18	1:38:45	1:42:13	2:02:39	2:11:40	2:23:06	2:43:32	2:52:35
6:40	20:42	33:20	41:24	1:02:06	1:06:40	1:22:48	1:27:23	1:40:00	1:43:30	2:04:12	2:13:20	2:24:54	2:45:36	2:54:46
6:45	20:58	33:45	41:55	1:02:53	1:07:30	1:23:50	1:28:29	1:41:15	1:44:48	2:05:45	2:15:00	2:26:43	2:47:40	2:56:57
6:50	21:13	34:10	42:26	1:03:39	1:08:20	1:24:52	1:29:34	1:42:30	1:46:05	2:07:18	2:16:40	2:28:31	2:49:44	2:59:08
6:55	21:29	34:35	42:57	1:04:26	1:09:10	1:25:54	1:30:40	1:43:45	1:47:23	2:08:51	2:18:20	2:30:20	2:51:48	3:01:19
7:00	21:44	35:00	43:28	1:05:12	1:10:00	1:26:56	1:31:45	1:45:00	1:48:40	2:10:24	2:20:00	2:32:08	2:53:52	3:03:30
7:05	22:00	35:25	43:59	1:05:59	1:10:50	1:27:58	1:32:51	1:46:15	1:49:58	2:11:57	2:21:40	2:33:57	2:55:56	3:05:41
7:10	22:15	35:50	44:30	1:06:45	1:11:40	1:29:00	1:33:56	1:47:30	1:51:15	2:13:30	2:23:20	2:35:45	2:58:00	3:07:52
7:15	22:31	36:15	45:01	1:07:32	1:12:30	1:30:02	1:35:02	1:48:45	1:52:33	2:15:03	2:25:00	2:37:34	3:00:04	3:10:03
7:20	22:46	36:40	45:32	1:08:18	1:13:20	1:31:04	1:36:07	1:50:00	1:53:50	2:16:36	2:26:40	2:39:22	3:02:08	3:12:14
7:25	23:02	37:05	46:03	1:09:05	1:14:10	1:32:06	1:37:13	1:51:15	1:55:08	2:18:09	2:28:20	2:41:11	3:04:12	3:14:25
7:30	23:17	37:30	46:34	1:09:51	1:15:00	1:33:08	1:38:18	1:52:30	1:56:25	2:19:42	2:30:00	2:42:59	3:06:16	3:16:36
7:35	23:33	37:55	47:05	1:10:38	1:15:50	1:34:10	1:39:24	1:53:45	1:57:43	2:21:15	2:31:40	2:44:48	3:08:20	3:18:47
7:40	23:48	38:20	47:36	1:11:24	1:16:40	1:35:12	1:40:29	1:55:00	1:59:00	2:22:48	2:33:20	2:46:36	3:10:24	3:20:58
7:45	24:04	38:45	48:07	1:12:11	1:17:30	1:36:14	1:41:35	1:56:15	2:00:18	2:24:21	2:35:00	2:48:25	3:12:28	3:23:09
7:50	24:19	39:10	48:38	1:12:57	1:18:20	1:37:16	1:42:40	1:57:30	2:01:35	2:25:54	2:36:40	2:50:13	3:14:32	3:25:20
7:55	24:35	39:35	49:09	1:13:44	1:19:10	1:38:18	1:43:46	1:58:45	2:02:53	2:27:27	2:38:20	2:52:02	3:16:36	3:27:31

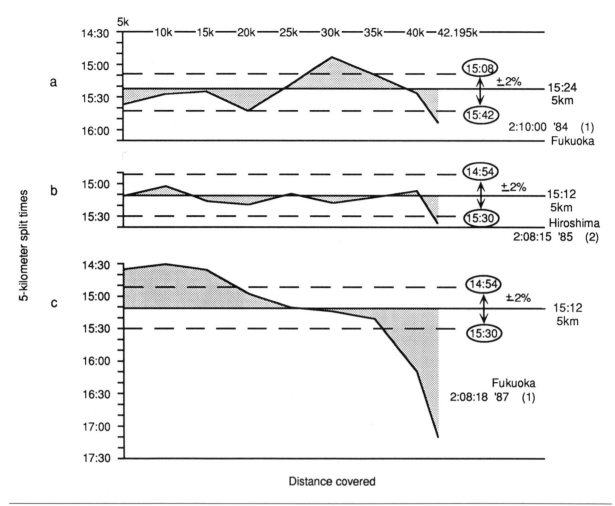

Figure 5.2 Racing the marathon: Examples, using 5km split times for three marathons of Takeyuki Nakayama, to illustrate how even-paced running throughout can reduce pace slowing at the end. Numbers in parentheses represent finish places.

increased pace was more within his limitations than it was for Heilmann, who slowed after 35 km, giving Nakayama a 36-sec margin of victory.

Figure 5.2b shows Nakayama's next marathon, a brilliant personal best (by 1:45) at Hiroshima (April 1985). It was also a new national record. He delivered virtually identical 5km splits throughout, head to head with Djibouti's Ahmed Salah through 40 km. Only then, as Ahmed gradually moved ahead and broke contact, did the cumulative physiological (and now psychological) effects of the competition begin to slow Nakayama's average pace. Finally, Figure 5.2c shows the debilitating effects of an excessively fast early pace. At the Japanese Olympic Trials in Fukuoka (December 1987), Nakayama felt obliged to deliver a performance of sufficient quality to ensure team selection. He led the pack through incredulous 5km splits of 14:30, 14:35, and 14:30 (on target for a sub-2:03:00 performance!), before slowing to paces (between 20 and 35 km) that would represent his mean

race pace. The effects of depleting carbohydrate availability then took their toll, and he began to slow. His decreased heat production from the slower pace coupled with the added hypothermic effects of a chilling rain gave him a finish time of 2:08:18, a scant 3 sec short of a personal best. We wonder just how much faster he would have run had his pace been as sensibly controlled as at Hiroshima, particularly because he had successfully improved his 10,000m racing speed from 28:07:0 to 27:35:33 during the preceding summer.

The second psychological consideration relates to the increased effort sense and elongated perception of time that occurs with developing fatigue. Thus, a given time-distance relationship—for example, running 1 mi in 6 min (or 1 km in 3:44)—is distorted so that more time seems to be required. We can imagine little worse than not only realizing that a slowing of pace is occurring from real fatigue, but also perceiving that slowing as even greater! The psychological explanation for the lengthened time perception is still being studied. Is it a reduction in neurotransmitter chemicals that link nerve cells with muscle cells, or a decreased sensory input, or neurological manifestations of the metabolic effects of prolonged fatigue? Perhaps the best way to deal with it is to prevent its occurrence by maintaining an early pace commensurate with the eventual mean pace for the race.

Breaking Records in the Marathon

One question we are asked frequently is "When will a woman break the 2:20:00 barrier in a marathon race?" Just as quickly, we respond, "As soon as a man runs 2:05:51." We certainly wouldn't suggest that it is impossible; we are well aware of the manner by which athletes respond when challenged. The barrier may indeed be broken. Our specific answer is based on the existing difference between the present women's (2:21:06) and men's (2:06:50) marathon record—10.1%. This is close to the mean 10.9% difference between the more frequently contested running events from the 800m through the marathon. Table 5.6 shows this more clearly. Thus, if a woman is to improve to 2:19:59, to maintain the 10.1% time differential an appropriate men's record would be 2:05:51. Or, using the mean of 10.9%, the men's time would lower to 2:04:44. It is remarkable that over such a wide range of distances, contested with such varied combinations of aerobic and anaerobic energy dynamics, this male/female differential seems to be similar. At the shorter distances, it is primarily due to the greater strength of male distance runners. At the longer distances where strength is less important, males still have an advantage in their greater blood O_2 content. We do not have the explanation. It is anyone's guess as to exactly when women will actually break the 2:20:00 barrier. We leave it to you athletes to tell us where and when!

PREPARING FOR AND DELIVERING SUCCESSFUL COMPETITIONS

It was probably John Landy who first went on record as stating that he would rather lose in a very fast race than win in a very slow one. That's the mentality of a pacer—a runner who is essentially challenging the clock. By contrast, Seb Coe stated in a televised interview, "I have to give up so many things, make so many personal sacrifices to perform at my level, that I cannot even contemplate losing." If Landy was the classic pacer, then Coe is the consummate racer. You as athletes will probably find yourselves in both sets of shoes on one occasion or another—perhaps during the same race! You may even use pace as a tactic in its own right, although your inner predilection may be solely striving to win. Seb Coe's medals in two consecutive Olympic Games and then the European Championships at Stuttgart were won in come-from-behind tactical battles. Many of his other top-level victories have come from shrewdly assessing what pace the race of the field could not manage and then proceeding to run away from them. Ideally, the best prepared athlete may be both racer and pacer—the complete athlete, developed optimally

Table 5.6   Performance Differences Between Male and Female Sea-Level World Records in Running (as of January 1, 1990)

Distance	Record	Velocity m/sec	mph	(male) Athlete	Year	Record	Velocity m/sec	mph	(female) Athlete	Year	% difference
100m	9.92	10.1	22.2	Lewis	1988	10.49	9.5	21.3	Griffith-Joyner	1988	5.4
200m	19.75	10.1	22.7	Lewis	1983	21.34	9.4	21.0	Griffith-Joyner	1988	7.5
400m	43.29	9.2	20.5	Reynolds	1988	47.60	8.4	18.8	Koch	1985	9.1
800m	1:41.73	7.9	17.6	Coe	1981	1:53.28	7.1	15.8	Kratochvilova	1983	10.2
1,000m	2:12.18	7.6	16.9	Coe	1981	2:30.6	6.6	14.9	Providokhina	1978	12.2
1,500m	3:29.46	7.2	16.0	Aouita	1985	3:52.47	6.5	14.4	Kazankina	1980	9.9
1 mile	3:46.32	7.1	15.9	Cram	1985	4:15.61	6.3	14.1	Ivan	1989	11.4
2,000m	4:50.81	6.9	15.4	Aouita	1987	5:28.69	6.1	13.6	Puica	1986	11.5
3,000m	7:29.45	6.7	14.9	Aouita	1989	8:22.62	6.0	13.4	Kazankina	1984	10.6
5,000m	12:58.39	6.4	14.4	Aouita	1987	14:37.33	5.7	12.7	Kristiansen	1986	11.3
10,000m	27:08.23	6.1	13.7	Barrios	1989	30:13.74	5.5	12.3	Kristiansen	1986	10.2
Marathon	2:06:50	5.5	12.4	Dinsamo	1988	2:21:06	5.0	11.1	Kristiansen	1985	10.1

through multi-tier training, who needs only to select the correct ploy for the race at hand. How utterly simple to desire, but so difficult to achieve!

Philosophical Considerations: Racer Versus Pacer

Each of you has your own basic philosophy about winning and losing, about racing and pacing, determined partly by your genes and partly by your training. A very few athletes are so gifted that their training eventually brings them to a level at which they have only themselves for competition. For them, the clock is the challenge. This can occur in younger athletes who are progressing faster than their peers. And at the highest levels, there are athletes like Said Aouita, Ingrid Kristiansen, or Seb Coe, who at various moments of their careers have been out in front of everyone else in performance capability. Typically, this is short-lived, however, and then they all find themselves becoming dictated to by the competition as to whether they will be racers or pacers.

The racer and the pacer form two ends of a spectrum of competitive possibilities. The pacer end is synonymous with the classic Olympic ideal, where participation and doing one's best (running fastest) is what matters, not simply winning. The racer end takes the view that failing to win, regardless of the pace, is unacceptable. Every nation's sport journalism probably has its notable quote that drives home this desire to win. In Britain, the 1,500/5,000m star Ian Stewart remarked, "First is first and second is nowhere." In the United States, the late Green Bay Packer football coach Vince Lombardi echoed this thinking with a phrase that goes something like, "Winning isn't everything, it's the only thing."

The desire to win is laudable for any athlete—it's the ultimate happiness in training to compete. But an athlete can run very well and not win. In the summer of 1987 at Oslo's Bislett Games, personal bests were set in the men's 5,000m race by the first six runners; five of these were national records. The race had only one winner (Jose Gonzalez of Spain in 13:12.34). Should the others have suffered disappointment at not winning? It depends on the extent to which they are more racer or pacer in their approach to sport. For the real racer, defeat is a very bitter pill to swallow, and rationalizing isn't easy.

In today's highly competitive world the choice of which camp to be in is not so simple. Very often three or four runners close in ability will find themselves racing each other, and all are very fit. Whatever the strategy, there is little room for error in planning exactly how best to utilize experience and aptitudes. If everyone holds back, it's a race of who has the fastest kick. If the pace is very fast from the start, then it's a race between those who have a combination of the greatest depth of fitness and natural talent. With both track and road races, it is becoming ever more difficult to win with slower times unless conditions of heat or humidity are influential, but still the work load is enormous. Thus, though an athlete may be interested primarily in winning (racing), the need to run the fastest possible time (pacing) to win may also be required. Here is where the confidence of knowing that you're fit as a result of having trained properly and optimally is of greatest ultimate benefit.

The decision of whether to be racer or pacer typically becomes blurred during actual competition, because in addition to those you are trying to defeat, you are also competing against yourself by attempting to do the best possible job. On occasion you may find it appropriate to select specific races or set up special race conditions in which racing or pacing can be emphasized. In his initial athletic years Seb Coe had a burning desire to win every race. But as time passed and he approached the world's best in capabilities, he became desirous of challenging a standing record with a definitive performance, hoping to get the most out of himself and to push the record just a little farther from the hands of anyone else. This attitude inevitably led him to several of his world records in races that he selected as fitting optimally with his preparation and that had some form of prearrangement in terms of competent pacesetters for the early stages.

Coaches have similar dilemmas in working with athletes: Do they desire racers or pacers? They would prefer to develop the optimally well-rounded athlete— the so-called Renaissance man (or woman)—and thus they are probably directed more toward producing winners. Athletes who are winners see themselves as successful athletes and successful people as well. They project a high personal image. The pursuit of excellence carries with it the idea of being numero uno— the very best. To challenge the best and win leaves no doubt. Coaches want their athletes to challenge the top spot, whether at the club, school, or world level. No one can win all the time, but a person's real character can develop and shine forth while he or she learns how to cope with both victory and defeat. That's also what keeps coaches interested in working with athletes—their interest in helping them be the very best athletes (and yes, people as well!) that they can be.

Mental Attitudes and Preparation

It is unlikely that a maximum training effect is ever achieved if it is not carried out with a strict mental discipline, with full concentration on the task at hand. An important part of your training, therefore, ought to be devoted to developing the willpower and mental discipline required to endure arduous physical training and competitive preparation. We can define at least five especially important mental characteristics that you can develop in this regard. These are confidence, motivation, controlled aggression, anxiety management, and relaxation. Let's describe each of these briefly.

Confidence.   Regardless of the level of competition, success is most likely to come consistently to physically prepared athletes who also have no doubts about their fitness. There are two facets to this mental confidence. One relates to training. Successful athletes feel certain that all possible aspects of training were adequately managed. They firmly believe that their training was not only correct for them but also ideal. The best way to ensure such confidence is by frequent communication between athlete and coach, discussing each phase of training and ensuring that no stone is left unturned along the way. If deviations in a training plan occur due to injury or extraneous difficulties, ensure that an alternate plan meets your approval as it is being created. Contribute actively to the creation of that plan and see to it that it is carried out. Then your confidence will remain high.

The other facet relates to competing. Wanting to win and even needing to win can be motivational in themselves, but at the starting line you must be all together mentally and physically as well. To genuinely have made the decision in your own mind that "This is *my* title" can be a very settling thought and a frame of reference geared toward control—control of yourself and your racing.

When you travel to competitions, small interferences can create large difficulties in maintaining a winning confidence. Changes that you had not predicted can add uncertainty or frustration. A roommate who snores, cafeteria food that is cold or greasy, transportation delays, a practice stadium that's locked instead of open—those and more can sap your energy and drain your confidence. Such occurrences can be minimized if you plan ahead, think clearly, and communicate well with the coaching staff or other appropriate authorities. It is better to expend energy in a positive way to create viable options than to expend the same amount complaintively, achieving no solution to the problem. Develop a checklist for trips and add to it each subsequent trip; this way you'll have contingency plans ready should deviations from the expected occur. This gives you better control over your own destiny, which in turn enhances your confidence. It reduces the effects of negative influences that are counterproductive to proper preparation.

An example of how mental attitudes are important in providing the environment for physical success, even over many months, can be found by briefly examining Seb Coe's preparation prior to the 1984 Los Angeles Olympic Games. During the first several months of 1984, Seb's physical preparation had progressed well, although it was delayed by illness. However, Seb was unsettled and unresolved in his attitudes about being prepared adequately. Two years of setbacks had left him unsure of himself. He needed to get back into the proper mental state that befitted his level of training. Both Seb and his coach decided that this was best done by Seb himself. The logic for that decision was quite simple: Even in a crowded competition, a track can be a lonely place. The larger the meeting, the lonelier it can become. When the big test comes, the athlete is out there on his own, and he had better have his mind and body together. It is something he would have to do by himself then, and in Seb's case, it was crucial that he begin to do it well in advance of the Games. Thus, it was decided that his coach would not go with him for his several-week pre-Olympic training camp (summarized in Table 5.7).

Shortly before making this decision, Seb had been defeated in a selection meeting, giving a poor performance in a slow time. His next race was in Oslo, where he won a top-class 800m race in a very fast time. The change for the better had already commenced. Knowing when and how to intervene is the key to coaching, but the athlete must also have the self-discipline to accept that there are times when the coach can do little more. This is not coaching defeatism; it is simply being wise enough to know when a rich and heady brew is best left to its own fermentation. Looking back, it seems that this is what Seb himself had desired, and his coach's decision to stay home served temporarily to better crystallize Seb's own thinking. Seb traveled to the Chicago area and proceeded through his pre-Olympic preparation at his own pace. When coach and athlete next met for a visit at the Olympic Village, Seb was radiantly confident as never before, permitting his coach the almost unnecessary observation that all was well.

If nothing else, what is important here is that the athlete was left to himself, to get himself together. The stresses of travel, training, and acclimatizing to village life were all very real, but they were Seb's to deal with. He knew it, and he set himself about doing it. This aggressive decision making more than anything else gave him the impetus he needed to begin the next phase—competition. Even after winning his silver medal in the 800m, Seb was happy and confident that a gold in the 1,500m could be his. He was buoyant throughout the qualifying rounds—so much so after the semifinal that his coach was rash enough

**Table 5.7   Training and Tapering for Competitive Excellence:
Sebastian Coe's 5 Weeks Before His 1984 Los Angeles 1,500m Gold Medal**

Week 1

—Tue. 10 JUL: Fly 18 hours from England to Chicago; easy, yet steady P.M. run @ a 6:00 to 6:30 per mile pace to get refreshed.

—Wed. 11 JUL: A.M. tempo session to ease into a faster pace and couple this with some speed endurance—3 × 1,600m @ a 4:40 per mile pace, 3 min recovery; cool-down of two laps @ a 90-sec pace followed by easy jogging.

—Thu. 12 JUL: A.M. easy recovery run of 6 miles; P.M. a tempo session to turn Wednesday's A.M. tempo session into a continuous run—3 miles in 14:30.

—Fri. 13 JUL: Introduction to race pace, but not deeply anaerobic—after warm-up, 30 × 200m @ 27/28 sec; cool-down of 2 laps @ a 90-sec pace followed by easy jogging.

—Sat. 14 JUL: Lengthening the short-distance intervals and speed, but keeping good recovery—after warm-up, 2 × (3 × 300m) @ 39 sec, with 3 min recovery, 9 min between sets; cool-down of 2 laps @ a 90-sec pace followed by easy jogging.

—Sun. 15 JUL: Easy run of 6 miles for recovery, rest, rehabilitation, and "charging the battery."

Week 2

Mon. 16 JUL: The first of the harder tempo runs—A.M. after warm-up, 6 × 800m @ 2:00 with 3 min recovery; cool-down of 2 laps @ a 90-sec pace followed by easy jogging; P.M. 4 miles easy.

—Tue. 17 JUL: The first cadence session—A.M. 5 miles easy; P.M. after warm-up, 10 × 100m steady acceleration to 60m, maximum speed to 80m, then float to 100m, walk back to start position and repeat.

—Wed. 18 JUL: Progressing from the Saturday 300m session but run 2 sec slower and as a single set—A.M. after warm-up, 6 × 300m @ 41 sec, with 3 min recovery; cool-down of 2 laps @ a 90-sec pace followed by easy jogging; P.M. 4 miles easy.

—Thu. 19 JUL: Short intervals to sharpen speed and still maintain a good heart/lung stimulus but keeping mileage low—A.M., after warm-up, 20 × 200m @ 27/28 sec; cool-down of 2 laps @ a 90-sec pace followed by easy jogging; P.M. 5 miles easy.

—Fri. 20 JUL: Adjusting to increasing speed with increasing distance—11 sprints, progressing in distance from 100m to 200m in 10m increments, @ 14, 15, 16, 17, 18, 19, 20, 21, 22, 23, 24, 25 sec, with jog-back recovery to the start position.

—Sat. 21 JUL: Maintained endurance run, but without locking into a set pace—6-7 miles including mixed accelerations (mini-fartlek).

—Sun. 22 JUL: Complete rest from running—traveled to Los Angeles and processed into Olympic Village.

Week 3

—Mon. 23 JUL: Start of alternating hard and easy sessions, taking particular care not to carry over fatigue from the previous day; A.M., after warm-up, 6 × 800m hard (@ 2:00 pace) with 2 min recovery; cool-down of 2 laps @ a 90-sec pace followed by easy jogging; P.M. 4 miles easy.

—Tue. 24 JUL: 30 min easy running over grassy slopes.

—Wed. 25 JUL: A 400m session as part of progression from 200m and 300m; A.M., after warm-up, 6 × 400m @ 51/52 sec with 5 min recovery; cool-down of 2 laps @ a 90-sec pace followed by easy jogging; P.M. 5 miles easy.

—Thu. 26 JUL: 30 min easy running over grassy slopes.

—Fri. 27 JUL: Similar to 300m intervals of 18 July but 2 sec faster; A.M., after warm-up, 6 × 300m @ 38/39 sec with 3 min recovery; cool-down of 2 laps @ a 90-sec pace followed by easy jogging; P.M. 5 miles easy.

—Sat. 28 JUL: Complete rest from running.

—Sun. 29 JUL: Not as fast as Wednesday, but shorter recoveries—after warm-up, 400m/600m/400m/300m/200m in 55/82/53/36/25 sec; cool-down of 2 laps @ a 90-sec pace followed by easy jogging.

Week 4

—Mon. 30 JUL: Interval pace maintained, but recovery reduced; A.M., 4 miles easy; P.M., after warm-up, 6 × 300m @ 38/39 sec with 2 min recovery; cool-down of 2 laps @ a 90-sec pace followed by easy jogging.

—Tue 01 AUG: A.M. 4 miles easy; P.M. a first session to maintain the feeling of 800m race pace—after warm-up, 10 × 200m @ 27 sec with 2 min recovery; cool-down of 2 laps @ a 90-sec pace followed by easy jogging.

—Wed. 02 AUG: A second session to maintain the feeling of 800m race pace—after warm-up, 3 × 400m @ 52/51/51 sec; cooldown of 2 laps @ a 90-sec pace followed by easy jogging.

—Thu. 03 AUG: Rest, but some easy jogging to stay loose.

—Fri. 04 AUG: A.M. easy 3 miles, including some strides during the run; P.M. race 800m heat #1; late evening easy jogging to stretch the legs.

—Sat. 05 AUG: Exactly identical to Friday; race 800m heat #2.

—Sun. 06 AUG: A.M. easy jogging to stretch the legs and stay loose; P.M. race 800m semifinal; late evening easy jogging to stretch the legs.

Week 5

—Mon. 07 AUG: A.M. easy jogging if desired; P.M. 800m final.

—Tue. 08 AUG: 8 miles easy running; no fast-paced racing-style efforts.

—Wed. 09 AUG: No fast-paced racing-style efforts; 10 × 100m easy strides and accelerations.

—Thu. 10 AUG: A.M. 3 miles easy plus a few faster paced strides than those of Wednesday; P.M. race 1,500m heat #1; late evening easy jogging to stretch the legs.

—Fri. 11 AUG: A.M. easy jogging as desired; P.M. race 1,500m semifinal; late evening easy jogging to stretch the legs.

—Sat. 12 AUG: A.M. easy jogging as desired; race 1,500m final.

Summary of approximate weekly training distance over the 5 weeks

Week 1	38 miles
Week 2	36 miles
Week 3	31 miles
Week 4	24 miles
Week 5	17 miles

Note. In the preceding summary, note carefully the pattern of progression of interval running. The principle is simple: First, establish the speed; then begin decreasing the recovery time to bring speed endurance into focus. This is done by eliminating the added rest time between sets. The intermediate step is a slight reduction of speed in going from sets to a continuous series of runs, with gradual return to the faster speed. This can best be done by simultaneous reduction in quantity of training. Speed and freshness become foremost in the athlete's mind, both of which are crucial for racing.

to tempt the gods by saying publicly that his athlete would win. Once again, coach and athlete were together, the coach's confidence now adding to Seb's increasing knowledge that indeed everything was coming together. At the final race, Seb went to the line with that "This medal is mine" attitude, and it was going to be very difficult to defeat him. No one did.

Motivation. Figure 5.3 identifies two basic types of motivation. One is an urge to succeed that originates from outside your own psyche. Recognition and praise from others, monetary rewards, a love of trophies—all have little to do with any inner desire to succeed but can strongly influence your desire to perform well. We believe it is preferable to be motivated intrinsically, to have the urge to do well because it gives you great personal pleasure and a sense of inner achievement. Malcolm Firth, a national coach to the British Cycling Federation, once remarked, "In the last analysis the athlete who aspires to the very top must

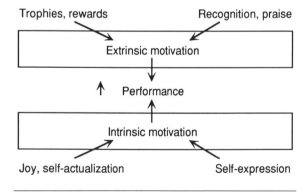

Figure 5.3 Intrinsic and extrinsic motivation.

have a high degree of self-motivation [that's intrinsic] and enthusiasm for the task. Athletes who get to the top and *remain there* [our emphasis] are capable of pulling themselves out of the depths of despair that overtake all athletes at some stage of their career."

No one enjoys fighting back after an illness, injury, or other serious setback. But once such problems occur, athletes who are motivated intrinsically have a better chance of returning to their former greatness. What attributes characterize intrinsically motivated athletes, and can these be developed? Figure 5.4 identifies two aspects that seem innate within us all, but to varying degrees: our perception of competence and our perception of control over our situation.

---

1. Perceived competence and ability to achieve

2. Perceived control and influence over circumstances

3. Opportunity for involvement in decision-making processes related to training

4. Pride in performance

5. Personal setting of attainable, high-quality long- and short-term goals that can be measurably assessed

6. Ongoing evaluation of progress

7. Emphasis on enjoyment as well as achievement

Figure 5.4 Intrinsic motivational factors important for performance in trained athletes.

It's anyone's guess as to whether these traits can be developed by coaching, but in Figure 5.4 we list five other factors that we believe can be incorporated into a training lifestyle to benefit the athlete. Be involved in the design of your own training plan. Take pride in your performance. Work toward attainable goals. Evaluate your progress periodically. Take the time to review these factors as a form of conscious self-assessment with a view toward self-improvement. But above all, enjoy what you are doing. Take a genuine self-interest in training and competing. This is what motivation is all about. It was such contemplation and such attitudes that kept Seb Coe in the proper frame of mind after his withdrawal (due to illness) from the 800m final in the 1986 Commonwealth Games. He needed to recover, regroup, take positive action, and continue on his course toward good performances at the European Championships just over a month later (where he earned his coveted first and only major championship 800m gold medal).

Controlled Aggressiveness. In running, aggressiveness is best identified as a single-minded determination to prevail over the opposition at all costs,

within the rules. In a race it can be achieved by unleashing an irresistible tactical maneuver at precisely the proper moment. Concentration and aggressiveness are interwoven inextricably in a successful athlete. Single-minded pursuit of any goal requires concentration to shut out the trivial. Then, aggressive behavior added to this competitive scene can make the athlete flourish. There is a high content of possessiveness—almost a greediness—in this behavior. Those who heard Keith Brantly's prerace assertion "When I'm gone, I'm gone" about his determined strategy to break away from the pack at 5 miles into the 1989 Gasparilla 15km Distance Classic in Tampa have a perfect example. His 2 months of prerace preparation had been flawless, and his confidence and motivation were both very high. The competitive field, however, was so good that only a powerfully decisive burst of aggresstive action—in the form of a sudden, maintained, and large surge in race pace—could be effective. It was, and his 42:50 victory was the third-fastest time in the race's 12-year history.

It should be clear, then, that aggressiveness in sport is beneficial only if it is controlled; that is, used at the proper moment and directed within reason toward a successful performance. All too often stories surface about athletes completing an absolutely awesome track session several nights before a weekend competition, ostensibly as a confidence-builder, only to be metabolically flat as a pancake on race day, delivering a dismal performance. Their aggressiveness was prematurely directed; their previous overall development should have given them the required confidence, with no need for a race effort before the actual race to provide some kind of last-minute assurance. That final track session should serve more to keep the engine fine-tuned rather than to damage the cylinders. You need to focus your aggressiveness toward the competition rather than toward your own self-destruction!

Anxiety. Anxiety is a form of nervous tension that usually stems from some sort of fear (of losing, of not performing up to a standard, of injury, or of competitors). Figure 5.5 (points 1 to 4) summarizes these aspects of fear and also identifies two more situations that can contribute to excessive arousal for competition. No one can predict who will win a race, so the outcome is uncertain. And you assign some level of importance to every race you run. You may always desire to perform well, but a club or national championship or the Olympic Games are very much different from a small local sports meeting.

As athletes, you are well aware of the concept of being "psyched"—either too much or not enough—for a competition or for training. The term relates to the interaction between arousal and attentiveness.

1. Fear of failing or looking bad
2. Fear of letting down those you hold in esteem
3. Fear of danger
4. Intimidation by opponents
5. Outcome uncertainty
6. Meaningfulness of the event

Figure 5.5 Causes of excessive arousal that affect optimum competitive performance.

In Figure 5.6, performance quality is plotted as a function of the extent of arousal. An inverted-U relationship results. Simply stated, best performances come from being aroused optimally (at the top of the curve) in terms of mobilizing nervous energy. Under- or overarousal results in poor performance. Attentional focus is also important: too broad, too focused, or too negatively focused attention detracts from performance.

With proper handling, the fear of losing can be lessened in a way that reduces total anxiety. This may improve the outcome of an upcoming performance. Again, think positively. Don't fear the worst or consider how disappointed you will be with a poor effort. Instead, use this attitude: "I'm going to see just how fit I am, and if I don't win I'm going to assess what still needs to be done for improvement; then I'll have the means for a better race next time." An understanding coach can suggest these subtle differences in attitudes about appraising performance and in so doing can reduce considerably an athlete's level of anxiety. Fear of the opposition is, of course, normal to some extent, unless everyone else in the competition is indeed considerably inferior to you in abilities. Then perhaps you shouldn't be in that race. Fear, along with other emotions, contributes to the required elevated state of arousal. It merely needs to be moderated.

Relaxation. The purpose of relaxation when an athlete is already motivated for competition may already be obvious. Relaxation is a governor for excessive anxiety, reducing nervous tension that can detract from optimum performance. How can you prepare to stay on top of the inverted U when it's time for competition? Balance anxiety with relaxation. Figure 5.7 illustrates a wide variety of identifiable tasks and activities that you may find useful to incorporate as part of your precompetition game plan. Note that the emphasis is on objective and positive goal-oriented tasks that when completed contribute to the confidence that you are doing the best possible for preparation.

Each successive level of activity (indicated by the Roman numerals) is more specific and occurs closer to the time of competition. Thus, well before any important race you will have evaluated your training success, included adequate racing simulations, and considered possible applicable racing strategies. You will have done this days or weeks before the competition. Such objective assessment reduces the anxiety that comes with panicked judgment of fitness equivalency that might arise when stories circulate about almost unbelievable training accomplishments of competitors.

Consistency of readying procedures should also reduce the incidence of anxiety. A master checklist of what's required when you travel to a competition will minimize the need for sudden frenzies of activity

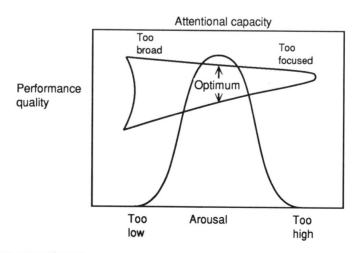

Figure 5.6 The inverted-U relationship between performance quality and arousal level and its relationship to attentional capacity.

I. Expectations in performance
   A. Know what you can do: assess your training.
   B. Practice possible racing scenarios using simulation.

II. Consistency in readying procedures
   A. Morning of a competition get a good night's sleep.
   B. Ensure suitable meals and adequate fluid replacement evening before a competition.
   C. During training practice any new racing innovations to be tried.
   D. Maintain previously familiar/effective routines.

III. Optimum competitive readiness
   A. Prepare as you did before previous best performances.
   B. Arrive early enough to ensure a proper warmup.
   C. Strive for an optimal attentional (mental, emotional) state.

IV. Use autogenic relaxation, imaging, and focusing
   A. Relax
      1. Develop mental images (words, experiences, colors, etc.) that evoke a relaxation response when brought to mind.
      2. Reduce excessive muscular tension to levels similar to those at the top of the inverted U.
   B. Image
      1. Imagine performing the event as desired for best results.
      2. If you imagine that you can do well, then the psychological environment for doing well is optimal.
   C. Focus
      1. Concentrate on one or two relevant elements of the competition.
      2. Do not be overattentive to irrelevant cues.

Figure 5.7 Task/activity sequence, with minimal anxiety risk, to permit an orderly approach to competition.

during last-minute packing. Do not try dramatically new preparation techniques without having practiced them at home. Identify with what has worked best previously, and at the same time keep an open mind toward including improvements.

The finishing touches to optimum competitive readiness are often found in the prerace warm-up. Ensure that this is not so ritualized and specialized that it is likely to cause you irritability due to inappropriate requirements for specific facilities or time. At this moment you as well as your competitors will be reaching your highest level of pre-event focusing. You are now different people than you are during periods of noncompetitive social interaction. Statements made to you by friends or coaches may be interpreted differently or ignored. These changes from the norm can be sources of frustration and misunderstanding to both parties. It is here that being alone can be an advantage. Coaches must also realize that you are a different person; they should minimize the detailed instructions or last-minute advice. Only relevant cues for that race are needed or appropriate.

The use of autogenic (self-induced) relaxation can be effective in reducing excessive muscular tension. Powerful emotions are often accompanied by muscular tension in various parts of the body. Such tension is needlessly energy-wasteful, much like when an automobile engine idles too fast. Thought processes directed toward return of more manageable levels of neuromuscular tone will thus reduce the overall level of arousal. For some, a single word, or for others, a phrase or recalling a particular experience elicits memories of activity sufficiently low-key to bring about relaxation of excessively tense musculature.

Two other techniques, imaging and focusing, can assist in this regard. Mentally picturing the race as you would ideally like to have it proceed, or imagining yourself delivering the correct racing response to specific attacks by competitors are both effective in removing anxieties about fear of failure. You are taking positive action and acting with control, which has a relatively low fear component. This kind of behavior serves as a prelude for the final prerace (and even during-race) task of focusing. Identify and prioritize the primary focal points on which you will base your race assessment as it develops. Is it not losing contact with the leaders? Is it remembering to use strong arm action and lift with hip flexors to better attack hills in cross-country or road races? Is it not being boxed in behind the leader in a track race, unable to change position? Focusing squarely on key items permits quicker response to their presence when they appear.

A number of quite good books have emerged in recent years on sport psychology. Though some of these deal with sport in general (Bell, 1983; Elliott, 1984; Loehr, 1982; Orlick, 1980), some include considerable useful emphasis on the running events (Lynch, 1987; Nideffer, 1976). As athletes, you would do well to read as many of these as possible; the psychological aspect of sport preparation is as integral a part of total development as the physiological aspect. When the two work as one, the synergism is incredibly powerful.

Tactics

It has often been said that tactics are only the icing on the cake, and the basis of it all is fitness and preparation. Back in the 1960s when a few New Zealand runners were seemingly on top of the distance-running world, their coach, Arthur Lydiard, suggested that the days of utilizing tactics were numbered. When well-trained athletes were running at their limit, tactics wouldn't be used because everyone would be maintaining a fairly similar pace to optimize efficiency, each hoping he or she had more left at the end than anyone else. Indeed, in many close, fast races, this often is true. But just as often, tactics can add a sparkle of decisiveness that clearly sets the stage for the supremely fit athlete to run away with a victory.

The use of tactics, however, need not be left until the race itself. In training, tactics can be practiced as you prepare for specific race requirements. Identify any aspect about the manner in which a race may need to be run to achieve victory, and then plan for it during the days of training. An example from Seb Coe's experience occurred when Steve Ovett's enormous and precocious talent for kicking into a very fast final few hundred meters became well known to all the world's 1,500m men. In Seb's training some very specific sessions were directed at teaching him to kick off a variety of paces and maintain the fastest speed possible for as long as possible. This gradually improved Seb's mental and physical ability to cope with such race problems. Then, fitting the definition of tactics, when Steve Ovett unleashed a furious sprint, it may have been debilitating to most competitors but it wasn't for Seb, who confidently countered with equal fury.

Remember that the tactics available to any one of you will depend in part on your genes and in part on your race preparation. If your genes don't allow you to perform as a sprinter, then don't plan to rely on a fast finish as the key to success. Perhaps you are a better front-runner, more able to maintain a steady fast pace throughout that is just a little too fast for all the rest. Select your best option and go with it.

An excellent example of this was seen when Ingrid Kristiansen established a lead of as much as 15 sec, beginning with lap 2 in her 10,000m final at the 1987 Rome World Athletics Championships. Coming off a period of injury without having had opportunities to hone her speed, she was concerned that a sprint down the final straightaway would more likely play into the hands of runners who had excellent speed training, such as the Soviet Union's Elena Zhupieva. Ingrid opted valiantly to maintain a very lonely position well in front of the greatest field of women's 10,000m runners that had ever been assembled. She eked out a victory by a scant 3.55 sec as Elena's brilliant 61.1-sec final 400 m came not quite close enough to matching Ingrid's sense of independently sustainable pace in front.

Being Prepared for Important Races

Whatever the kind of basic tactic that is to be employed, you simply must be on par with your finest competitive abilities at your top-level meetings, wherever they might be. Thus, a mix of intelligent training, tapering, and handling of prerace details all become very important considerations for both athlete and coach. After every race a debriefing of sorts should be done, with written notes made of what could have been improved—from all viewpoints. Later, as these notes are reread, the added experience of further consideration will add more accuracy. Eventually a pattern will emerge as to the overall strategy that is most effective for you when racing season arrives.

At major competitions, it is sometimes incredible how penalizing even the slightest deviation from peak form can be; and it hurts here the most, particularly if it prevents you from advancing through heats or semifinal rounds. A few illustrations will make the situation painfully clear. As a theoretical example, let's consider a 1,500m final race that will be won in 3:35, a time that is also your personal record. To be only half of 1% below this ability is to concede 7 m, roughly 1.08 sec—enough to leave you unplaced in a tight finish. As a specific example, let's use a longer distance race, the Helsinki World Championships men's 10,000m final. It was won in 28:01.04, a time slower than the personal best times of most of the finalists. If you ran half of 1% slower than Alberto Cova's winning time, you would have been 8.4 sec back, relegated to 9th place. In each of the two heats, the same closeness prevailed: Half of 1% back of the winning time would have been 9th for the faster heat (won in 27:45.54), 11th place for the slower (won in 28:04.69).

Top-level finals in the longer distances usually tend

not to be quite so close and so deep at the same time. But great care must be reserved for the qualifying rounds. Very close races may occur when a large group of runners who have not run a completely exhausting race because they are keeping as much in reserve as possible for the upcoming final make an ending dash to the finish tape. As a specific example, consider the two semifinal races of the 1988 Seoul Olympic Games 5,000m. The first race was won in 13:22.44, the second in 13:24.20. In either race, if you had finished 1 sec behind the winner, you would have been in eighth place. In each race the top six finishers qualified for the final on place, and the seventh qualified on time. In the second semifinal, only 0.61 sec separated first place from seventh! The lessons to be learned are (a) be sure your sense of pace is excellent for proper acceleration during the final stages, (b) have a readily mobilizable speed component developed during training to permit such acceleration, and (c) aim always for qualification on the basis of place rather than time.

The tapering period for a major race is as important as the training and actual competition. When we recall that the preparation process consists of the tearing-down phase (the training) and the building-back phase (recovery), tapering becomes the final aspect of the recovery process. Several guiding principles might assist in final preparation. First, once a racing phase is about to begin, particularly for middle-distance runners, the more endurance-oriented aspects (such as long runs) are replaced by rest, recovery runs, or some form of interval training (recall our discussion of periodization in chapter 3). Marathoners fit into a special category here, as their racing phase may be only one event, requiring little final preparation in the way of high-velocity, short-distance intervals. For all events, the mental state of an athlete prepared for racing is not conducive to coping with continued serious training. Second, to permit the supercompensation phase of recovery to have full effect, rest during the period of tapering should be considerable. Give the body time to heal itself. Third,

the quickness aspect of the training process, rather than the endurance aspect, begins to deteriorate first when training ceases or dramatically decreases. Thus, faster sessions ought to be the mainstay of maintenance training during a tapering phase. The athlete begins to ''think speed'' in the context of feeling fresh and desirous of racing; both feelings are essential in producing a mentality geared toward racing to win. Shorter, faster training sessions can maintain cardiovascular and neuromuscular systems in a high state of readiness between races scheduled over a period of a few weeks.

More careful analysis of Table 5.7, which summarizes Seb Coe's pre-Los Angeles Olympic Games pattern of final preparation, shows how these concepts were utilized effectively. Our old friends volume, intensity, density, and frequency were adjusted to permit reduction in total work but maintenance of quickness. Seb commenced with 200m-interval runs, initially with full recoveries; then these were gradually reduced in number, with recovery maintained and then discontinued as faster work was introduced. Similarly the 300m repetitions began during week 1 as two separate sets of three, run fairly quickly but with adequate recovery between repetitions and added recovery between sets. The running time was steadily decreased (the pace was increased) and the recovery time shortened (but each week only one variable was altered). This same logic was continued with the 800m runs. Always, the emphasis was on staying sharp (fresh and quick), ensuring good form, not getting tired, and feeling good about the results. Although some might term these ''build up'' weeks to the Olympic Games, the difficult, exhausting work was done many weeks before. By use of short-distance, faster paced work (200m, 300m, 400m) as well as longer distance, slower paced work (1,600m runs and a pyramid-style combination of 200m, 300m, 400m, and 600m runs), the multi-tier training philosophy was maintained in a context of work reduction to ensure freshness when required.

SUMMARY

1. Running quickly and intelligently during races provides the best opportunity for victory. To run quickly, an athlete must develop fatigue resistance, strength, and speed. Running intelligently demands proper management of pace and tactics. The longer the race distance, the greater the influence on racing effectiveness by such factors as heat, humidity, wind, and the dynamics of energy replacement.

2. In any race, it is crucial to (a) be prepared physically and mentally, (b) run efficiently but effectively, (c) be poised to act and react as necessary to remain in the best possible

position to win, and (d) use tactics as appropriate to gain additional advantage. As athletes, you are not robots; and as coaches, we are not dictators. We both must adapt. Every race will be unique but will have striking similarities to other races. Learning from every race you run should be an important goal.

3. A successful athlete has geared his or her preparation to match all possible needs of the distance being raced. This includes (a) scheduling appropriate proportions of aerobic and anaerobic work, (b) completing race-scenario simulations, (c) assessing personal strengths and weaknesses as well as those of competitors, and (d) improving the intuitive sense of pace.

4. The best competitor is one who is completely fresh—physically tapered and mentally confident. When training load is reduced, speed is lost more quickly than endurance. Thus, during tapering, reduce the volume of endurance training and maintain speed. The accompanying volume reduction permits physical recovery and builds increasing hunger for competition. With motivation and confidence high and aggressiveness and anxiety under control, good racing is the logical sequel.

5. Although a mind-set focused on an excellent race effort is essential, winning is not always of sole importance. A personal best may be satisfaction enough. In heats or semifinals, however, the primary goal is to advance to the next round of competition; racing for place thus is the foremost priority.

6. When you race against peers, there are no guaranteed formulas for winning any race, let alone every race, because the possible strategies are limitless. Being fit and well trained are essential. But being alert, sharp-witted, and ready to respond are all virtues that increase the chances for achieving your best performance. Excessive mental rehearsal can leave you perplexed and beaten before the race, particularly if it has produced a plan that cannot be amended or dropped in an instant to fit a better alternative caused by changing circumstances.

7. Remember to put competitive sport into the perspective of your overall living environment. Success in sport is not final, and failure is not fatal. What is important is to work hard to be better than yourself in the past, and better than someone else in your race today. Competitive sport is and must be only a wonderful game whose rules set an exciting stage for helping you achieve the best years of your life yet to come. So do the very best you can, and put the results into a healthy perspective.

REFERENCES

Anonymous. (1989). *Walking and running*. Alexandria, VA: Time-Life Books.

Bell, K.F. (1983). *Championship thinking*. Englewood Cliffs, NJ: Prentice-Hall.

Costill, D.L., Coyle, E., Dalsky, G., Evans, E., Fink, W., & Hoopes, D. (1977). Effects of elevated plasma FFA and insulin on muscle glycogen usage during exercise. *Journal of Applied Physiology*, **43**, 695-699.

Costill, D.L., & Miller, J.M. (1980). Nutrition for endurance sport: Carbohydrate and fluid balance. *International Journal of Sports Medicine*, **1**, 2-14.

Coyle, E.F., Coggan, A.R., Hemmert, M.K., & Ivy, J.L. (1986). Muscle glycogen utilization during prolonged strenuous exercise when fed carbohydrate. *Journal of Applied Physiology*, **61**, 165-172.

Dwyer, T., & Dyer, K.F. (1984). *Running out of time*. Kensington, New South Wales: New South Wales University Press.

Elliott, R. (1984). *The competitive edge*. Englewood Cliffs, NJ: Prentice-Hall.

Hecker, A.L. (1987). Nutrition and physical performance. In R.H. Strauss (Ed.), *Drugs and performance in sports* (pp. 82-151). Philadelphia: W.B. Saunders.

Hultman, E., & Bergstrom, J. (1967). Muscle glycogen synthesis in relation to diet studied in normal subjects. *Acta Medica Scandinavica*, **182**, 109-117.

Ivy, J.L., Katz, A.L., Cutler, C.L., Sherman, W.M., & Coyle, E.F. (1988). Muscle glycogen synthesis after exercise: Effect of time of carbohydrate ingestion. *Journal of Applied Physiology*, **64**, 1480-1485.

Loehr, J.E. (1982). *Mental toughness training for sports*. Lexington, MA: Stephen Greene.

Lynch, J. (1987). *The total runner*. Englewood Cliffs, NJ: Prentice-Hall.

Margaria, R., Cerretelli, P., Aghemo, P., & Sassi, J. (1963). Energy cost of running. *Journal of Physiology*, **18**, 367-370.

Newsholme, E.A. (1986). Application of principles of metabolic control to the problem of metabolic limitations in sprinting, middle-distance, and marathon running. *International Journal of Sports Medicine*, **7**(Suppl. 1), 66-70.

Nideffer, R.M. (1976). *The inner athlete*. New York: T.Y. Crowell.

Orlick, T. (1980). *In pursuit of excellence*. Champaign, IL: Human Kinetics.

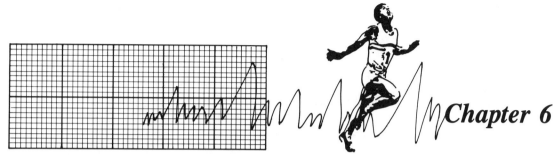

Stress Management in Training

Chapter 6

The training process causes alterations in physiological and psychological functions. We respond to these alterations in a reasonably predictable manner over time. When the stimulus is removed, performance ability is restored or improved. This stimulus removal can be short-lived, as during the interim between one day's training and the next. It can be longer lasting, as with a day off during a microcycle or a few days' break following a competition or the completion of a microcycle. Many of these adaptive processes were described in chapters 1 and 2. Harvard University physiologist Walter Cannon described the physiological alterations in the 1920s, coining the term **homeostasis** to refer to those dynamic, self-regulating processes by which the body's internal cellular environment is maintained at a constant level of function.

For example, during a long run on a warm day, evaporative cooling will cause a sizable depletion of body fluids. Partial depletion of energy reserves will also occur. Mild accumulation of metabolites such as lactic acid in working muscles may cause muscle cell swelling as water moves in to restore the osmotic balance. During the body's recovery process in the hours after the run, increased thirst and hunger will promote ingestion of sufficient fluids and fuels to promote restoration of nutrient, electrolyte, fluid, and fuel supplies. Massage, a relaxing bath, and a good night's sleep will also promote restoration of normal cell function. The next day finds the athlete feeling fresh, rested, and able to train effectively.

During training, the stimulus of hard work causes a partial breakdown (catabolism) of tissue integrity in both skeletal muscle cells and their associated connective tissues. Sensations of fatigue and soreness as well as energy and electrolyte imbalances in the working muscles are common. Psychological changes also occur that parallel these physiological changes—tiredness and decreased motivation are commonly seen. Then, during the subsequent recovery phase, intracellular metabolic function is restored (anabolism) back to the prestimulated state or even beyond, thereby providing recovery and (it is hoped) enhancement of performance ability. Psychologically, increased vigor and the urge to compete return as well. This again is homeostasis in action.

Thus, the rewards from the physical aspects of training come after recovery, when a sense of freshness replaces the dullness of fatigue, and performance abilities are improved. A key ingredient to achieving a successful race effort, therefore, is performing under the influence of an optimal combination of physical training and recovery. Ideally, when it is time for an athlete's major competitions, the beneficial adaptive effects of training should by far dominate over any residual detrimental debilitating effects of fatigue. The art of achieving optimum athlete preparation, therefore, is in designing a training stimulus as challenging as can be managed, followed by an appropriate recovery period, that is timed to put the athlete at the site of competition in perfect harmony for an excellent performance. Unfortunately, a very small difference exists between training just enough for optimum preparation and good health, and training too much, which can bring injury, illness, staleness, or a combination of these. Both science and artistry are involved on the part of athletes, coaches, and their technical support people to ensure that this threshold of excessive total stress load is not reached.

THE CONCEPT OF FATIGUE IN METABOLIC SYSTEMS

What are the characteristics of fatigue, overtraining, and staleness? Are they different, and if so, how? What causes limb soreness? Is it a problem with the muscles, with their associated connective tissues, or with both? Does excessive fatigue or soreness in muscle tissues represent injury? If so, what is the causal mechanism of such injury? Is there truth to the oft-heard comment that the incidence of illness and injury increases when an athlete is in an overtrained or stale state? If so, what causes this susceptibility? When athletes get so overtrained that staleness results, what explains the very long time required for recovery? How can overtraining be avoided? How does an athlete strike a balance between quantity of training and adequate recovery to permit optimum adaptive benefits for beginning the ensuing training or competitive phase?

It is far easier to ask these questions than to provide answers. Knowing both the correct questions to ask regarding assignment of appropriate training and the correct answers to give, either when explaining fatigue, overtraining, and staleness or when providing hints for coping with preventing such conditions, are essential for the long-term health maintenance of athletes. A winning athlete (temporarily, at least) is a model of optimally managed response to training, recovery, and other aspects of lifestyle. Fatigue and pain are no longer present; freshness prevails. Staleness and injuries are absent; fine-tuned athletic excellence predominates.

The Training Process: When Does Enough Become Too Much?

It is appropriate to view overuse injuries, overtraining, and staleness as pathological elements of the training process. Ideally, none of these should occur, but if they do occur, careful athlete management is required to bring prompt recovery. Fatigue and muscle soreness are quite different from overtraining or staleness, although they may exist during such states. They are normal physiological elements of what may be termed the **training process**, which is defined as a set of interactions between a stimulus and a response intended to initiate adaptive (beneficial) physiological changes. This process has both somatic and psychological aspects (body and mind) that are linked inseparably. When the training process is overdone, then overtraining, staleness, and overuse injuries are very likely to occur. Their pathological effects can severely limit or inhibit performance and can be bad enough to shorten career longevity. In this chapter we will attempt to identify how the transition from acceptable, challenging training, to which physiological adaptation can occur, can progress to unacceptable training, in which excessively difficult work loads maintained for too long, especially in the face of other lifestyle constraints, bring pathological debilitation. Once these concepts are understood, guidelines for preventing this transition from occurring may be more logically identifiable.

Figure 6.1 depicts the relationship between training, recovery, and performance over time for three different training loads. In the context of a training athlete, these loads could quite nicely represent the 2- to 3-week requirement to complete a particular microcycle of training. In Figure 6.1a we see that while applied, a given training stimulus (notice the T for training in the hatched area) decreases immediate performance abilities. Following adequate recovery, shown by the hatched area labeled R, the original performance level is restored or perhaps even enhanced to a small extent. A highly talented athlete interested in ever-greater performance excellence would not enjoy the adaptive effects of this training stimulus—they weren't adequate to improve performance significantly. For thousands of serious fitness devotees, however, this is exactly what they seek: excellent health through vigorous activity, a minimum injury risk, and maintenance of good-quality performance characteristics. Fatigue and some mild soreness may likely occur, but this is transient, expected, and easily manageable.

In Figure 6.1b, the training stimulus is quantitatively more profound, intended for the competitive athlete. The stimulus either is applied longer or is more intense. Thus, the energy cost is higher, the adaptive challenge is larger, and muscle fatigue and soreness will be greater. The initial performance decrements are more sizable than those in Figure 6.1a, and additional recovery time is required after removal of the training stimulus. But the performance ability following full recovery is now increased considerably. The greater training load has initiated homeostatic changes designed to permit greater tolerance to such a challenge. The athlete has improved, that is, performance abilities are now greater than they were pre-

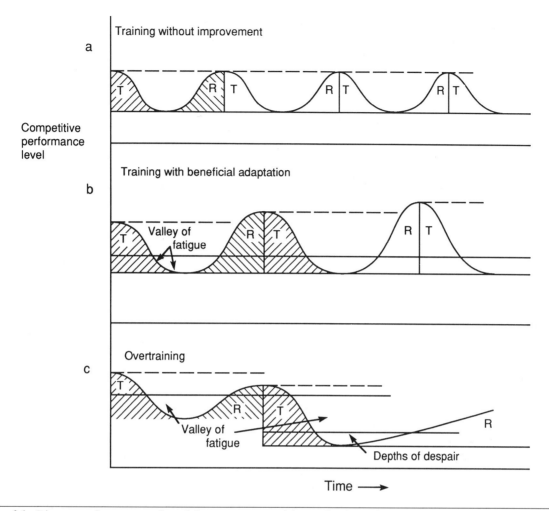

a Training without improvement

Competitive
performance
level

b Training with beneficial adaptation

Valley of
fatigue

c Overtraining

Valley of
fatigue

Depths of despair

Time ——→

Figure 6.1 Diagrammatic representation of the response to training under three different conditions. In Figure 6.1a, insufficient training occurred to elicit performance improvement upon recovery. In Figure 6.1b, such a performance improvement did occur, caused by a beneficial training effect. In Figure 6.1c, a performance decrement occurred as a result of not only an excessive training stimulus but also its beginning before recovery had fully occurred; overtraining was the result.

viously. Optimum management of the volume of training and the extent of recovery should minimize the injury risk.

One of the coaching "grand masters" in the art of varying the quantity and quality of such work loads to provide an adequate stimulus just long enough to yield excellent results without putting athletes over the edge was Indiana University swimming coach James Counsilman. His excellent book, published in 1968, served as a stimulus for others to consider carefully the strategies for training and peaking for top-level performance when it was most important. Since then, although much jargon has sometimes confused the picture, some general concepts that refer to applying and withdrawing training stimuli have become reasonably clear.

In Figure 6.1a our athlete has been within what we

could term a *zone of normalized homeostatic adaptation*. By this we mean that when recovery was permitted (note the *R* in the hatched area) through reduction in the training load (indicated by *T*), there was not necessarily an actual improvement in performance ability. In Figure 6.1b, however, our training athlete progressed into a *zone of improved homeostatic adaptation*. The extra training load, characterized by a psychological appreciation in athletes that they are working very hard, puts them into a so-called *valley of fatigue*. Physiologically, this manifests itself in terms of extensive skeletal muscle fuel depletion and possibly also muscle protein breakdown. The enlarged training load (T) must then be followed by an increased recovery period (R). The reward is an improved performance level due to the various physiological adaptive changes which should have taken place—increased $\dot{V}O_2$max, restored (perhaps expanded) fuel supplies to the working muscles, increased size and numbers of mitochondria, etc. Slower training paces will initiate this adaptive response primarily in the ST fibers, providing little, if any, stimulus to the FT fibers. Faster paced work would provide a continuing adaptive stimulus to both ST and FT muscle fibers. This explains the need for never venturing very far away from speed all through the training year. To climb out of this valley and reap the training benefits in the form of improved work tolerance, proportionately more recovery time to regain optimum organ function is required than for the earlier example given in Figure 6.1a.

Thus, improved athletic performance has a psychological component (the athlete knows that hard training has been managed well and has a proper attitude geared toward the use of the performance improvements) and a physiological component, which in turn has two aspects. There is a neuromuscular improvement (better fiber recruitment; more tension generation with less fatigue) and a metabolic component (improved fuel storage and utilization). Few scientists studying human performance have emphasized enough the intricate interaction of these two components—physiological and psychological (Morgan, 1985)—in raising performance potential. Even fewer physiologists have emphasized the interaction of the two physiological aspects involved (Noakes, 1988). Appreciation of this latter interaction, for example, helps to explain observations from both animal experiments and human training experience. Sprint training in rats (Davies, Packer, & Brooks, 1982) as well as strength training in young men (Weltman et al., 1986) can increase $\dot{V}O_2$max without increasing mitochondrial numbers or mitochondrial enzyme content in individual muscle cells, suggesting that it is tension-generating ability that is improved (through recruitment of more muscle cells and therefore more muscle protein) rather than increasing O_2 usage in individual muscle cells. When performance capacity falls, we ought to look at any or all of these three components as possible causes.

Fatigue as a Manifestation of the Response to Training

When we defined fatigue in chapter 3 as a sensation of increased difficulty to maintain a previous level of working effectiveness, we were implying that specific physiological processes such as muscle tension generation were being limited, giving us a diminished ability to sustain submaximum or maximum work. Appreciation for how such physiological changes bring about such limitation in function is quite important for athletes and coaches alike. Fatigue can be a friend or foe depending on how it is used or abused in the training process. Recall that skeletal muscle cells exist in several varieties. Some emphasize glycolytic (anaerobic) work (FT Type IIb), others oxidative (aerobic) work (ST), and some do both quite well (FT Type IIa). Whereas ST fibers are used predominantly to maintain posture and allow walking, jogging, and lesser-intensity running, FT fibers are not recruited in appreciable numbers except during higher-intensity running (faster speeds or uphill).

Fatigue decreases the maximum tension-generating velocity attainable by skeletal muscle fibers. Increasing numbers of H^+ ions from anaerobic metabolism at higher work rates decrease the effectiveness of myosin ATPase as an enzyme in permitting interaction with adjacent actin myofilaments. The slower the rate of cross-bridge linking between actin and myosin myofilaments (see Figures 1.18, 1.19), the slower these myofilaments can slide past each other, and the slower the rate of tension generation in the muscle. Because power is the time rate of performing work, this decreased power output manifests itself as a slowing of performance. Free H^+ ions also decrease the rapidity with which actin-myosin complexes are broken. In turn, relaxation of skeletal muscle tension is slowed; this is noticeable as a shortened running stride.

Runners are keenly aware of the limitations brought about by fatigue. An athlete running a competitive middle-distance race typically finds it difficult to maintain pace due to the effects of increasing acidosis. However, athletes reaching the end of an exhausting and intensive weight-room session, attempting eight repetitions of the bench press or quarter-squat with a sizable amount of resistance, particularly if they have already completed three or four sets in addition to other exercises, may find fatigue occurring not only because of acidosis but also because their muscle cells are depleting their stores of carbohydrate. The desire to work was there but the fuel delivery would not occur.

But fatigue can be an even more complex phenomenon. For a first-time marathon runner who is marginally trained to complete the distance and trying as hard as possible to do so, or for an experienced marathoner who has attempted (and failed) to maintain an excessively fast pace relative to performance abilities, fatigue has a different feeling. For them, there is simply an utterly overwhelming urge late in the race to sit down at the edge of the road, quit the race altogether, and have a cold drink. Clearly the desire to endure has been lost almost completely.

Endurance—the ability to continue at a given work intensity over increasingly long periods—might thus be considered as the opposite of fatigue.

Why did our marathon runners experience the overwhelming urge to stop? Unlike the two examples of the track runner and weight lifters who had continuing motivation but still had to slow their work rate (the mind said "go" but the body said "no"), with our marathon runners it was an eventual central nervous system decision to stop (the mind said "stop" and the body said, "I'm glad you agree; I've been suggesting this for some time!"). Fatigue is thus a psychophysiological phenomenon, explainable completely only by the interactive result of many cellular functions that are no longer in a stable equilibrium. Depleted fuel supplies and accumulating acidosis in the working muscles as well as other less-understood central nervous system signals from these overworked tissues all contribute to a reduction in work intensity. An increase in these central nervous system signals, for example, by cheering from friends to continue working hard, can recruit additional less-fatigued motor units. The result of such stimulation, of course, will eventually bring even greater fatigue. This same cheering, however, from a full stadium can provide the additional stimulation for an athlete to achieve a superlative performance.

No single physiological or psychological measurement can quantitate fatigue, and its complete explanation remains a dilemma. In 1905, an Italian worker, Mosso, described its most important features. Research since then has not added much more to our understanding. As outlined in a 1915 translation of Mosso's work, with fatigue "two sets of phenomena demand attention. The first is diminution of the muscular force. The second is fatigue as a sensation." Thus, muscle cells seem to weaken, and the central drive to work is reduced. The sensation can occur long into the resting state after the physical activity has ceased.

Over the years, various alterations in cellular physiology have been proposed as contributing to fatigue in working muscles. Some workers have suggested that ATP supplies become exhausted. Studies of biopsied muscle tissue, however, as well as newer reports using magnetic resonance imaging, show that ATP levels aren't changed very much during intense or prolonged work. ATP is never in very large supply, and it is quickly regenerated from ADP (using the CP reservoir) as it is broken down (recall chapter 1).

Other workers have suggested reduced intracellular O_2 availability, and thus the increasing inhibitory effects of acidosis from anaerobic metabolism, as a causal agent in fatigue. Though this may play a role in high-intensity exercise, it doesn't explain the reason why marathon runners working within their aerobic limits achieve such a state of fatigue that they simply run out of reasons for running. Inhibition of performance by the accumulation of acidosis should be minimal in less competitive runners, including those thousands of serious fitness athletes who run primarily at an aerobic pace as they enjoy participating in popular marathons and other long-distance road races. But they fatigue as well.

Probably the best single physiological indicator that correlates well with the sensation of fatigue is a fall in muscle glycogen levels. Major credit goes to David Costill and his co-workers for their pioneering nutritional and fuel metabolism studies in working muscles of athletes, recently summarized (Costill, 1988). (This glycogen depletion probably accounts for a large part of the eventual decision of the two marathon runners described earlier to quit their race efforts.) The practical results of Costill's work have emphasized the importance of including adequate recovery time following intense training periods to permit proper nutrient, electrolyte, and fuel replenishment. Other suggestions include

- using multiple muscle groups during exercise (for example, in running up hills, use an efficient arm swing to accompany leg motion), thereby diminishing the fall in muscle cell glycogen for any particular muscle group;
- enhancing fuel supplies in the working muscles before a major competition (such as through techniques of carbohydrate loading for marathon racing); and
- matching energy losses from training and competition by appropriate increases in dietary intake. (Strategies for marathoners to achieve this were outlined in chapter 5.)

Returning to Mosso's conceptualization of fatigue, we see that characterization of this phenomenon derives only in part from actual weakness, but it also involves several other variables that we know very little about. There is a decrease in the central nervous system drive to motor units—a fatigued runner has less desire to compete than one who is fresh. There are the decreased intracellular energy reserves we referred to earlier. Fatigued endurance runners may have decreased plasma volume from prolonged perspiration, which in turn decreases optimum perfusion of their working muscles. There are most likely several other aspects contributing to fatigue, which can occur well after the termination of exercise. Fatigued muscles can be sensed by their owners even when they are not in use. Unfortunately, this suggests that it may be unlikely that we will find any single blood chemistry variable or other criterion, other than our own sensual perception, more reliable as an indicator of either the onset or the cessation of fatigue.

Muscle Soreness From Unusually Challenging Exercise

Athletes in hard training often report considerable soreness in their lower limbs, usually a day after intense fast-paced running sessions, or following back-to-back, very hard–training days, or after a hard race. The longer and more intense the effort, the greater the chance for such discomfort. This **delayed-onset muscular soreness** was defined by Robert Armstrong (1984) as a sensation of discomfort or pain in the skeletal muscles that occurs following unaccustomed muscular exertion. The key word here is "unaccustomed," because such soreness does not typically occur following routine submaximal-intensity training. Athletes do not adapt completely to large volumes of maximum or near-maximum effort—it's simply too stressful. Some adaptation occurs, of course, and the amount of adaptation determines how well such sessions will be tolerated the next time they are scheduled.

Lower-limb muscle soreness develops after a marathon. Athletes discover about a day following their race that their quadriceps and gluteal muscles are especially tender to palpation and sore as they descend stairs. The soreness peaks between 2 and 4 days postexercise, varies in intensity depending on the athlete's fitness and the stress of the race, and disappears completely within a week. It seems to represent a combination of tenderness and stiffness. Is this pain indicative of actual tissue injury? If so, are the muscles or the connective tissues (or both) affected? Is inflammation present? Because such soreness may be nearly unavoidable after racing efforts, should training that produces such soreness be avoided at all costs? These and other questions have characterized a quite active recent investigation of the problem, although scientists have studied the phenomenon for a long time.

More than 80 years ago, the notion was advanced (Hough, 1902) that hard work in muscle unadapted to such loads caused a microscopic tearing or rupturing of the cells. This could, of course, involve damage to the muscle cells, to their associated connective tissue, or to both. The soreness may occur all along the involved muscles and is often greatest near the muscle-tendon junctions. Newham, Mills, Quigley, and Edwards (1982) have suggested that here the long axes of muscle fibers are least parallel to the long axis of the entire muscle. Also, pain receptors are very common in the tendons and connective tissue. In several of the long lower-limb muscles, the tendons, instead of being restricted to the ends of the muscle (e.g., near the hip, knee, or ankle), extend a considerable distance along the muscle to which they connect (recall the diagram of penniform hamstring muscles in Figure 1.15). During soreness, the tension-generating abilities of the muscle cells are reduced (Francis & Hoobler, 1988). Or, again according to Newham et al. (1983), more muscle cells than previously (i.e., before the onset of the soreness) will need recruiting to achieve a given level of force output. This may explain why racing effectiveness (or continued fast-paced work) is so difficult during such a period.

Armstrong (1984) has surmised that this debilitation of muscular force occurs because of an increased Ca^{++} ion level in the muscle cells. Cell membrane damage from intense activity permits more Ca^{++} ions to diffuse inward (because their concentration outside these cells is greater than inside). An elevated cell Ca^{++} level inhibits the rate at which Krebs cycle enzymes permit fuel breakdown. The ionic disruption is entirely transitory, thanks to homeostatic processes that permit complete regeneration of membrane integrity during the recovery period. Calcium entry is reduced back to an acceptable rate, and fuel metabolism proceeds normally.

During the days when delayed-onset muscular soreness is manifested, the best way to remove its symptoms is to engage in very mild exercise. There may be several reasons for this. Breaking up the connective tissue adhesions between muscle cells may decrease the stretch that stimulates pain-mediating neurons in the region. The brain and spinal cord produce opium-like substances called endorphins that, when released into the bloodstream and allowed to circulate, have potent analgesic properties; they are released with even mild exercise. A third possibility involves the elevated activity of sensory neurons from working muscles and tendons, which in turn inhibit the activity of smaller pain-mediating neurons. Whatever the mechanism, it doesn't appear that such mild exercise necessarily enhances the recovery process (it doesn't appear to inhibit it either). Shortly after the mild exercise period, the muscular soreness returns and continues until recovery processes restore the cells to normal health.

Recent studies of athletes following completion of marathon races (Evans, 1987; Hagerman, Hikida, Staron, Sherman, & Costill, 1984; Siegel, Silverman, & Lopez, 1980; Warhol, Siegel, Evans, & Silverman, 1985) and multi-day ultra-endurance races (Dressendorfer & Wade, 1983) have documented clearly the extensive pathological disruption that can occur in skeletal muscle cells from such prolonged physical work. Cellular destruction is sufficient to cause the dissolution of tension-generating proteins and the complete destruction of sizable numbers of sarcomeres. Intracellular enzymes leak into the bloodstream as a result of increased muscle membrane permeability, the most well-known of these enzymes being creatine kinase (CK). This is also observed in the milder forms of delayed-onset muscular soreness caused by intense short-term training. Studies often report peak serum CK levels correlating positively with the subjective sensation of muscle soreness (Dressendorfer & Wade, 1983; Schwane, Johnson, Vandenakker, & Armstrong, 1983). White blood cells eventually move into these damaged muscle cells and metabolize the intracellular debris, permitting recovery so that renewed protein synthesis will restore cellular integrity (tension-generating abilities and membrane stability). In marathon runners, muscular soreness may subside within a week, but as long as a month may be required for reasonable repair of the muscle cell destruction (Warhol et al., 1985). This is one good reason why training and racing should be minimal for several weeks after a marathon race. For the shorter races and training sessions, damage is minimal and repaired within a few days.

Lengthening (eccentric) tension generation seems more prone to cause soreness than shortening (concentric) tension generation, although both can do it (Ebbeling & Clarkson, 1989; Schwane et al., 1983). Examples of lengthening tension include running downhill, stepping down, or reverse bicycle pedaling. Eccentric tension is an integral part of running even on level ground, occurring with every stride as the gastrosoleus, anterior and posterior tibialis, and quadriceps absorb much of the impact forces placed on the knee joint and foot at footstrike. This explains the soreness an athlete often experiences in these muscle groups after a marathon race. Perhaps this provides a partial explanation for the general consensus among marathoners that considerably more recovery time is required before resuming normal training patterns following a downhill marathon (such as at Boston) than following other marathons. The marathoners are less adapted to its specific challenge.

At least three mechanisms may explain this debilitation. First, electromyographic evidence suggests that fewer muscle fibers are recruited during lengthening tension generation. Thus, fewer involved muscle fibers must generate relatively more force at any given work rate than if they were active during shortening tension. Second, the force production requirements are greater during downhill running because the body's center of mass is lowered (Margaria, 1972).

Braking against gravity is required when running downhill. Additional momentum of limb movements must be counteracted by antagonistic muscles, requiring a greater involvement of connective tissue elements such as tendons. It is not surprising, therefore, that delayed muscle soreness and elevated CK levels are both greater when running is predominantly downhill rather than uphill or on level terrain (Schwane et al., 1983). Third, during prolonged exercise FT muscle cells that may have been used and subsequently fatigued enter a state of rigor. Passive lengthening from eccentric exercise can mechanically damage or destroy them (Lieber & Friden, 1988).

The venerable British exercise physiologist Archibald Hill suggested as far back as 1951 the novel theoretical viewpoint that the best way to prevent delayed-onset muscular soreness may in fact be to train harder. Assuming that adaptation occurred, this would make the routine tolerable work load more similar to the work load producing the soreness (remember that it is the *unaccustomed* load that causes the soreness). As one might expect, the training stimulus must be very specific. That is, hard eccentric training will protect against muscular soreness from a very difficult eccentric session much better than it will from a sudden concentric session, and vice versa. More recent work (Schwane, Williams, & Sloan, 1987) has confirmed this notion. Thus, an appropriate consideration for a marathoner training to race the Boston course, which drops 120 m along its length, might be to include long downhill training runs. Level or uphill runs would not provide protection from muscle soreness nearly as well. It is usually difficult for athletes to find such long downhill terrain in their training environments. And even if they could, such training chances injury, which would require additional recovery/rest time. This injury risk very quickly makes the theoretically sound solution to the problem of adaptation less practical or sensible than athletes would desire.

Overuse Injuries in Connective Tissue

We have just offered the notion that training so intensely as to bring delayed-onset muscular soreness may be required to stimulate sufficient adaptation that such work loads no longer elicit soreness. Such a challenge followed by beneficial adaptation ought to provide noteworthy tolerance to intense work and improve performance potential. Athletes and coaches are always aspiring toward better performance, and thus all too often they are willing to assign or to endure the most difficult of sessions. But is such intense training a wise idea? What occurs when insufficient recovery/rest time is provided, when too many back-to-back sessions are assigned, or when the athlete does this increased training in the face of notable biomechanical imperfections (such as excessive genu valgum [knock-knees], or ligamentous laxity, or wearing overworn shoes)? Aren't we suggesting that athletes push themselves very close to the point of doing too much (overuse) and developing injury? Yes, we are. And as long as training is not overdone, then forward progress should be optimal. But the dilemma for coach and athlete should be strikingly obvious.

To become the best, an athlete must challenge the body to its reasonable limits, allowing the resulting adaptation to improve performance potential. As long as the training stimulus is not overdone, improvement will continue, with racing effectiveness the benefactor. A crucial aspect of the art of good coaching, therefore, is always to stop short of requiring excessively intense or prolonged hard training. This is the sure way to prevent the overuse that produces injury. First realizing that there must be a limit to hard training and then not only identifying but working within this limit become paramount to injury-free success. Knowing this limit comes from

- keeping good records,
- understanding from experience the kinds of loads that can be tolerated,
- emphasizing a feeling of freshness rather than excessive fatigue and remaining within that working condition, and
- assigning difficult work loads for relatively brief periods.

The key to comprehending the concept of an overuse injury risk is to realize that this implies excessive working tissue use (i.e., training) over time. Although a single training session may provoke the clinical symptoms of an overuse injury, the *totality* of a long period of very challenging training, rather than the single session, causes the problem.

Remembering that our limbs are interconnected bone-tendon-muscle links in a kinetic chain responsible for absorbing impact stress and providing pushoff forces, we know that the weakest link in this chain will deteriorate first. Bones and ligaments are structurally very stable, and muscle-tendon and tendon-bone insertions are also very sturdy. Ligaments are very strong too, connecting bone to bone, whereas tendons connect bone to muscle. Muscles have excellent circulation and energy provisions, although their energy stores are, of course, limited. The tendons and ligaments, however, are the most poorly equipped of these tissues to adapt to long-term repeated stimula-

tion. There is a fine line indeed between a healthy challenge (with physiological adaptation) and the onset of chronic overuse (with pathological consequences). The trick is to realize how much will be excessive, and then provide periodic rest to ensure that training serves as a temporary rather than continual overload. The rest period must be long enough to permit recovery. Some understanding of the physiology of connective tissue is helpful in providing an understanding of its recovery dynamics.

Whereas ligaments are composed largely of a connective tissue molecule called elastin, a stretchable fibrous protein, tendons are essentially nonstretchable and comprised of collagen molecules. Collagen is the most common protein in the body. In tendons, collagen fibrils are arranged in parallel bundles and have a greater tensile strength than steel wire. Unfortunately, tendons have a poor blood circulation. The repetitive mechanical stresses of running increase collagen metabolism. There is a limit to the dynamics of this tissue maintenance (breakdown and buildup) in its healthy state. When tendons are stressed beyond this limit, tendon disruption occurs in the form of microtears. These tears heal, either by the formation of good-quality new collagen or lesser quality fibrotic scar tissue. The poorer a tendon's vascularity, the greater the incidence of inadequate recovery from excessive use. The more incomplete the healing process, caused most frequently by depriving the tissue of adequate rest, the greater the risk of chronic inflammatory processes forming additional scar tissue.

All overuse injuries to muscle and connective tissues are caused by repetitive microtrauma, which results in inflammation as the pathological response. The action of prostaglandins within circulating blood brings vasodilation, increasing capillary permeability and thereby causing transudation of fluid, with accompanying swelling and pain. Anti-inflammatory agents such as aspirin work by blocking prostaglandin synthesis. Incoming white blood cells, especially lymphocytes, neutrophils, and macrophages (specialized monocytes) digest cellular debris and clear the area for repair to begin. Recapillarization and growth of new collagen then begin, but this takes time. Only limited motion can occur during this period, which varies depending upon tissue and extent of injury. Since inflammation is a mandatory component of the post-injury healing process, and since chronic inflammation should be avoided because that indicates no progress in repair, athletes must be advised strongly that the rest period is long enough to permit recovery.

Collagen and elastin contain sizable quantities of a unique amino acid called 4-hydroxyproline. When the connective tissues break down, their metabolites appear in the blood and are eventually excreted in the urine. Thus, urinary excretion of 4-hydroxyproline can serve as a marker for increased tendon and ligament metabolism (Abraham, 1977). It is not surprising, therefore, that studies of delayed muscle soreness that have included urinary measurements of 4-hydroxyproline in the days following very hard muscular exercise have shown increases in this metabolite. Increased plasma hydroxyproline levels will also be seen (Hodgdon et al., 1988). To ensure that what is being measured actually reflects extracellular structural collagen breakdown from tissue such as tendons, it might be preferable to measure plasma levels of metabolites (such as hydroxypyridinoline) that are restricted to this type of collagen (Riedy et al., 1988).

Depending on the intensity of exercise or the challenge to the metabolic integrity of the tendons involved, these connective tissue metabolites and skeletal muscle enzyme elevations in the blood may parallel nicely the occurrence of delayed muscle soreness. Such elevations are not always observed, however (Dressendorfer & Wade, 1983), showing that a particular threshold of volume and intensity overload is required. In turn, this will be determined individually by the athlete's fitness, the environmental conditions, and the athlete's genetic constitution (muscle fiber type and biomechanical efficiency). Another variable that may require consideration in such studies is dietary vitamin C intake. Vitamin C is ascorbic acid, which is required for the enzymatic hydroxylation of proline to form 4-hydroxyproline for collagen biosynthesis. Distance runners frequently include oral vitamin C supplementation of as much as 500 mg to 1 gm/day as part of their diets. The interrelationships between high weekly training volumes, measured connective tissue turnover, and possible benefits of increased vitamin C intake have not yet been determined precisely.

The calcaneal tendon (or tendon of Achilles) is often a victim of the strain of such overuse. This tendon originates about halfway down the lower leg and is formed when the superficial and deep fascia of the triceps surae (the soleus plus the two heads of the gastrocnemius) merge. It inserts on the posterior portion of the calcaneus (or heelbone). Overpronation is a common cause of Achilles tendinitis. Excessive internal tibial rotation causes pronation (as outlined in chapter 1) and draws the Achilles tendon medially, producing a whipping action of the tendon that can cause microtears.

Chronic stress can also bring inflammation, thickening, and fibrosis to the tendon sheath (called the mesotenon). When such changes occur in the calcaneal tendon, for example, the resulting condition is termed *Achilles tenosynovitis*. The blood supply to tendons is usually via their surrounding mesotenon. Thus, reduction in mesotenon vascularity can even further deprive the tendon's ability to cope with chronic loading. If the accompanying pain from tenosynovitis does not cripple the runner, partial tendon rupture may. Excessive strain on an inflamed tendon (particularly sudden overload) can initiate partial rupture.

Interval training and hill sessions are particularly stressful on lower limb muscles and tendons. Thus, as such sessions are increased in progressing through a training plan, special care must be given to providing plenty of adaptive rest. Adaptation may never be sufficient to permit strong daily challenges to the lower-limb tendons with such training. This explains why repeat speed or hill sessions are often the triggering cause of a painful flare-up of Achilles tenosynovitis. There is no substitute for rest in permitting micro-healing to replace micro-tearing in tendon repair. Once such injurious processes have begun, considerable rest and tissue freedom from further insult are required to ensure timely recovery. This is why even easy running on an inflamed Achilles tendon is ill advised. The tendon itself is compromised in its ability to tolerate impact stress. Alternative activities (such as deep-water pool swimming using a flotation vest) should be considered to maintain cardiorespiratory fitness.

Another related problem of overuse involves inflammation in the bursa that is often associated with tendons or muscles that must glide over bony prominences. A bursa is a closed sac lined with a synovial membrane that produces a thick, viscous fluid with a texture similar to that of the white of an egg. One example is the retrocalcaneal bursa, which lies between the calcaneus and the Achilles tendon. Only a small amount of fluid, sufficient to serve as a marvelously effective lubricant, is produced. Repetitive trauma caused by excessive pressure of the tendon on this bursa can lead to inflammation, increasing synovial fluid production and causing even greater tissue pressure in this region. Eventually, debilitating pain and decreased mobility result. A typical diagnostic feature in retrocalcaneal bursitis is a decreased passive dorsiflexion of the foot. An effective ongoing health maintenance program designed to stretch and strengthen the gastrocnemius-soleus muscle complex and Achilles tendon is ideal for minimizing not only the pressure of the Achilles tendon on its bursa but also the developmental risk of bursitis (and tendinitis) from high-volume training.

It is not solely the effects of overload training that can predispose an athlete to overuse pathology. Biomechanical imbalances, particularly when coupled with improper footwear, can hasten the development of overuse problems. In chapter 1 we mentioned the need for a certain amount of pronation to occur as each foot lands on its running surface. Wearing shoes that unduly limit subtalar joint pronation reduces the foot's ability to absorb landing shock. Running on crowned roads also tends to limit pronation in the downhill foot. Frequently the iliotibial band (see Figure 1.14) is affected, with pain manifested on the lateral surface of the knee as this band of connective tissue moves over a bony protuberance on the femur called the lateral femoral epicondyle (Jones & James, 1987). The pain arises predictably after a certain distance is covered, is especially noticeable with downhill running, and subsides when the athlete stops running and switches to walking (because the band no longer moves over the epicondyle).

Ironically, this iliotibial band friction syndrome may occur after a runner has been told to wear shoes and special inserts (orthoses) intended to limit the excessive pronation that had produced a pain syndrome called *runner's knee*. The twisting of the lower limb resulting from excess pronation causes excessive asymmetric tension on the ligaments supporting the patella (or kneecap). The stress process occurring at the ligament-bone junction produces an inflammation response. Pain around the patella has an onset after a predictable running distance, is noticeable when ascending or descending stairs, and increases while sitting for prolonged periods with the knees bent. The proper amount of correction will alleviate the symptoms of runner's knee. But it must not be overcorrected.

There is perhaps only one thing worse than when an athlete corrects one overuse problem by creating another. And that is when the athlete displays some symptoms of both situations, not knowing in which direction (resolution or exacerbation) the injured tissues are responding in view of the treatment being applied. This explains a situation that occurs frequently in runners who, because of travel to different locales or frustration over being told that they should briefly curtail their running, visit several physicians and are given different diagnoses or suggested therapeutic regimens. The presenting problem is indeed different at various times due to the changing nature of the injury. For good reason, both athletes and physicians are dismayed. The athletes do not enjoy hearing different diagnoses or requests for rest, and the physicians are often insufficiently aware of the athletes' preceding medical history to integrate it with the presenting problems. Clearly, then, we see that prevention is by far the best way to manage this situation. Given that this ideal may not always be achieved, it is probably most useful for athletes to

maintain close contact with the same group of competent, medically knowledgeable experts as a support team. This ensures consistency in health care.

What is the best way to achieve the ideal of preventing assigned training loads from being so excessive that pathology replaces physiology, that is, maladaptation replaces adaptation? Probably the best advice is to ensure that periodic rest is programmed into all training regimens. This implies keeping careful records to document assigned (and accomplished) training loads and developing an attitude in both athlete and coach that because rest is part of training, it must be assigned. Some of the principles of psychological counseling are useful here in providing guidance. Any type of lasting behavioral change must be coupled with an attitude change, which in turn requires a change in thought patterns. Here, athletes and coaches must not think of the need for rest as a sign of an inability to tolerate arduous training, but rather as a mechanism for ultimately being able to tolerate more. If there is ever a doubt as to whether an athlete should insert additional rest or press onward relentlessly, by all means rest is the preferred choice. The physiological recovery will certainly be beneficial because the risk for injury will have been reduced. Also, the mental respite will bring renewed enthusiasm for the ensuing training session. Again, freshness is far more functional than fatigue in achieving overall quality in training.

OVERTRAINING AND STALENESS: BEYOND FATIGUE

Let us now return to Figure 6.1c and examine a third possible scenario of training and recovery. In Figure 6.1c our athlete did not allow adequate homeostatic recovery from the first sizable work load before resuming intense training. And this next training load is even more intense than the previous one. Often such an increased load/decreased recovery sequence results when the previous training mesocycle went very successfully. Both athlete and coach decide (in this instance, erroneously), "We're ahead of schedule, so let's pick up the pace." In this enthusiasm, a training excess occurs. Now, during the second training period, the athlete not only reaches the bottom of the valley of fatigue, but enters the depths of despair, or fatigue-plus. This athlete is experiencing **short-term overtraining**, which we will refer to as **overtraining** and define as a condition characterized by a temporary imbalance between training and recovery most easily noticed as fatigue that doesn't disappear with normal rest and which is accompanied by a wide variety of additional signs and symptoms. Just as with the previous two training intensities, the metabolic tearing down of tissues, occurring as a normal part of the training process, is greater than the rate of metabolic recovery, but the challenge has affected the body much more profoundly. Figure 6.2 outlines some of the adaptive mechanisms that occur with high-volume training and gives an idea of some of the events that can bring on fatigue if recovery is inadequate (either because the stimulus was excessive or because the time provided for recovery was insufficient).

When athletes enter this state, they quite often wisely opt to take a few days off and then resume training. Unfortunately, because they virtually never take days off due to their devotion to training, the notion that three or four days off is preferable to two or three never enters their minds. Thus, the likelihood that athletes will resume training prematurely is very high, and their rapid increase of training loads to make up for lost time worsens the problem.

If our athlete in Figure 6.1c continues to push onward with training despite these symptoms of overtraining—which we shall describe shortly—eventually (in anywhere from a few weeks to many weeks) a kind of physiological and psychological breakdown can occur. This marks the onset of what is called **long-term overtraining**, or simply **staleness**. It can be defined as a complex combination of psychophysiological signs and symptoms of a more far-reaching nature than simple fatigue, suggesting a trend toward actual cellular injury, profound fuel exhaustion, breakdown of the body's defense mechanisms, neurological and endocrine disturbances, or perhaps all of these together! Detriments in performance that before were occasional are now chronic and large. Along with increased risk of injury, illness occurs with increasing frequency. Altered mood states, altered hormonal patterns, and other metabolic changes can occur, and these can vary enormously among individuals. A very long time will be required for recovery to restore performance abilities—weeks, months, maybe even a year!

Using the psychological approach of Morgan, Brown, Raglin, O'Connor, and Ellickson (1987), it is convenient to view excessive training and overtraining as stimuli in the context of the classic stimulus-response paradigm. If excessive training is the stimulus, then overtraining is the response. Similarly, if overtraining is the stimulus, then staleness, however it is manifested, is the response. Long-term overtraining in athletes should be avoided like the

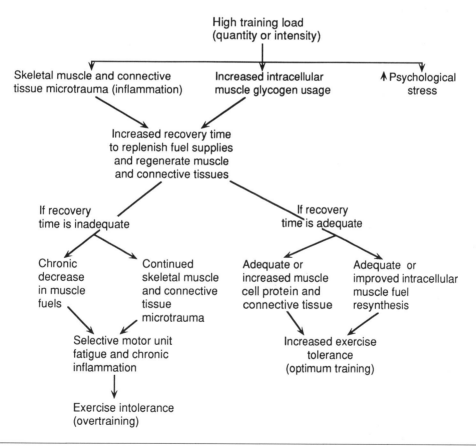

Figure 6.2 Variable responsiveness to a high load training.

plague, because it could spell the end of a competitive season or a career, particularly if it merges into staleness. Optimal training ought to be the goal of all athletes, but overdoing it becomes almost a fact of life in those who are highly motivated. Being sensitive to the early identification of overtraining and having the good sense and strategy to take the proper corrective steps to return to optimum training is of crucial importance for proper development.

Characterizing Overtraining and Staleness

Considerable difference exists between hard training and overtraining. In Figure 6.3 we attempt to depict the interrelationships and differences between hard training and overtraining as they can potentially contribute to or affect adaptation, fatigue, muscular soreness, overuse injury, and staleness. Hard training is required for eventual improvement in performance. Although it causes a temporary worsening of performance abilities through catabolic changes in the working muscles and other energy storage tissues, it is done for relatively short periods. Thus, the typical recovery phase can also be somewhat short, but it must be adequate and will be followed by increased work capacity.

Overtraining, however, is the result of overdoing hard training, which produces a comprehensive breakdown in the body's adaptive responsiveness to hard training. The ongoing very high level of activity can no longer be managed effectively. There is a fine line between hard training, to which the body can adapt if the stimulus is not too great and if the recovery is adequate, and excessive hard training, which is simply too much to manage. As soon as that line is crossed, a major reduction in work load must be initiated until regenerative processes restore homeostatic equilibrium. Athletes need to be sensitive to the identification of early warning signs that might suggest the transition from hard training to overtraining and then to focus clearly on the need for rest to turn the situation around in their favor quickly. Admittedly, this is tantamount to being able to predict the future and goes counter to athletes' innate desires to keep on training (or competing) as long as they see improvement. But it is simply too risky and not useful over the long term to push too far, reach the overtraining or staleness states, and then require considerable downtime.

An analogy we have found comprehensible by some of our runners, particularly those with academic business backgrounds, is to think of fatigue as a process similar to going into debt, and overtraining and stale-

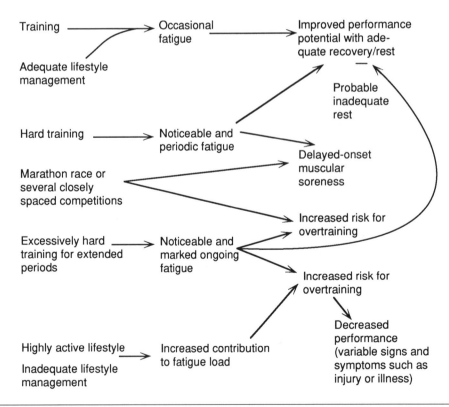

Figure 6.3 Interrelationships between training, fatigue, overtraining, lifestyle, overuse injury, staleness, and athletic performance.

ness as entering into bankruptcy with subsequent corporate reorganization. Fatigue can be dealt with and removed, just as with debt, by a reduction in the expenditure of resources and more careful resource (energy) management. Bankruptcy and overtraining, however, are situations in which a marked, identifiable failure of the system prevents adequate coping with environmental conditions. More than the usual homeostatic restructuring will be required—with activity temporarily halted in the interim—to permit recovery and a return to some semblance of normal operational efficiency. Without this time and effort directed toward recovery, there is a reasonable risk of never turning the situation around.

Lifestyle Overload and Overtraining

From a holistic or total-body viewpoint, the performance abilities of athletes for training and competition become a function of coping adequately with their lifestyles. If the athlete's adaptation to training is excellent, performance will likely improve, showing that other lifestyle activities are not excessive. If adaptation is inadequate, then substandard or diminishing performance may occur, suggesting the onset of overtraining unless the athlete redesigns lifestyle. Mechanical engineers define stress as load per unit area. We might analogize here and write the following relationship:

$$\text{stress} = \text{lifestyle load/athlete performance} \quad (6.1)$$

Lifestyle load refers to enhancing factors (adequate nutrition, rest, and relaxation; emotional stability; and proper training) as well as inhibitory factors (imbalances in any of the aforementioned enhancers as well as other competing pressures caused by ongoing problems of life in the real world).

Athletes differ in important ways regarding their likelihood to develop overtraining or staleness when presented with a given high-volume training work load. An excessive load for one athlete may not necessarily be excessive for another, even if the athletes are of similar age, weight, and $\dot{V}O_2\text{max}$ and have similar previous personal bests. The many aspects of total lifestyle, including the other activities that compete for the athlete's available energy supplies—a full-time job, frequent promotional or other travel related to sport, demands imposed by media, a newborn child, responsibilities of maintaining a complete household, and so on—must also be considered, along with differing states of fitness at the time the work load is assigned.

One of the difficulties that coaches attempting to work effectively with elite athletes often experience is that they do not understand some of the unique personality traits of these gifted performers. The work of psychologist Frank Farley (1986) has been quite illuminating in this regard. These talented people exhibit what Farley classifies as a "type T" personality—T for "thrill-seeker" and implying a high predilection for taking risks. These individuals become bored quickly, have a large need for ongoing stimulating activities, are very adventuresome, have an enormous capacity for energy-consuming activity, and have no difficulty rationalizing putting all their abilities on the line in risky (competitive) environments. They may lose everything, but they have the resiliency (and the temperament) to recover, regroup, and do it all over again.

It may now be easier to comprehend why the most motivated athletes may have the greatest risk for overtraining and staleness. The type of personality just described is a prerequisite for the mind-set with which the athlete is able to achieve goals that have a relatively small chance of success. To optimize the chance for success, no amount of energy output in preparation is considered excessive. This high-level enthusiasm carries over into the athlete's daily affairs, which can also be energy-draining. If an active lifestyle coupled with intense training eventually becomes too demanding, manifestations can be evident in the form of poor competitive performance, overuse injury, or profound fatigue. Figure 6.4 illustrates this cycle of events that sets the scene for the development of staleness from too much training. This is a sad irony that needs attentive intervention for its prevention. Very often, the best coach is not necessarily one who emphasizes solely the motivation to work harder. The best coach instead may be someone who realizes when motivation is indeed appropriate

Figure 6.4 Psychophysiological event sequence causing overtraining.

but who also is ever alert to the need for moderation, reassessment, and redirection of the total work output. This is in keeping with our previously stated view that the least amount of specific work required to achieve the best results is a powerfully effective training strategy.

It should be obvious from the preceding that it is not just excessive training loads that can culminate in overtraining. Training itself may be within reasonable limits, but the sum of all the other facets of the athlete's lifestyle may compete inappropriately with the total energy available. An athlete's so-called "energy pie" (the total energy level at which the athlete can maintain daily activities over extended periods) can have many or few pieces. Increasing the size of those pieces unrelated to running, or increasing the number of pieces (the number of lifestyle activities) mandates that the training, racing, and recovery pieces must be appropriately reduced. Athletic performance diminishes accordingly. The intelligent athlete with a passion for excellence must choose wisely in lifestyle management.

A short practical anecdote can exemplify this interrelationship of training and lifestyle as well as the need to monitor total lifestyle demands. It concerns the buildup to Seb Coe's first world record in the 800m, run in Oslo on July 5, 1979. During the previous winter and on into the early spring of 1979 Seb had been studying diligently for his honors degree in economics and social history. At the same time, of course, he was training very hard for the coming Olympic season. As a means of deriving a sense of whether he was on target for good development in preparation for the Moscow Olympic Games, on May 31 he ran an 800m race for his University against a representative team from the British Amateur Athletic Association. His time was 1:47.8, and he was feeling slightly ill at the time. In the eyes of his coach, Seb looked a bit drawn from the effort. Nothing at all would have suggested that Seb had anything in him to permit running much faster. He ended up with subsequent sniffles and the aches and pains all over that characterize a typical viral cold.

The obvious realization was to accept the fact that an overload was occurring and to back off training, because it was impossible to dismiss the difficult academic regimen that was coming to a peak. In addition to his head cold, a few psychological symptoms of overtraining were also noticeable. With the training stimulus greatly reduced, Seb finished his final exams in fine style, with excellent results. Then it was as if a huge element of strain that had been consuming his energy reserves was lifted. His academic load was removed, and his volume of physical training had already been reduced. In the transition back to high-level athletic work, his spirits brightened, and his physical freshness returned just as quickly. His subsequent achievement was extraordinary. Two races later and a Bislett Games 1:42.33 world record was his. The decision not to push on in view of the warning signals, and thus interpreting them properly, was by far more proper than to have pushed on *despite* the warning signs. Good grades were crucial, as was good athletic performance. Both simultaneously were too much. The writing was on the wall, and the message, fortunately, was both read and heeded. Seb had rearranged his priorities correctly. Doing less ultimately meant gaining more.

Physiological Dimensions of Overtraining and Staleness

The noted Canadian biochemist Hans Selye identified in somewhat general terms (1976) what might be occurring as the temporary challenge of overtraining merges with the more prolonged response of staleness. Hans Selye and Walter Cannon were contemporaries, both attempting to quantify a concept introduced by W.A. Engelhardt (1932) which defined the **training process** as a physiological breakdown that serves as a specific stimulus for subsequent synthetic recovery processes. Selye became particularly interested in the difference between short-term physiological breakdown (i.e., hard training, from which normal recovery occurs without problems) and pathological breakdown (i.e., overtraining and then staleness, where recovery requires much additional time, and it is likely that complete functional restoration of homeostatic processes may not occur). His most well-known experiments did not involve athletes in physical training but rather laboratory animals injected with noxious agents. He found in his animals a predictable series of events, initiated through increases in pituitary and adrenal gland hormonal activity, in essence directed at mobilizing increased amounts of circulating fuels—carbohydrates, fats, and proteins—to provide energy for the body to fight off the effects of the injected agents.

Initially, there is an alarm reaction, as shown in Figure 6.5, as the body fails to keep up with the sudden increased metabolic demands and characterized also by a lowered resistance, perhaps due to a depletion in lymphatic tissue. Following this is a period of varying duration, depending on the assault, whereby the animals maintain a heightened state of resistance and tolerance to the noxious agents. Presumably, during this period adequate energy reserves are available to cope with the body's needs to combat the effects of the injected agents. Eventually, however, unless recovery occurs as a result of the elevated

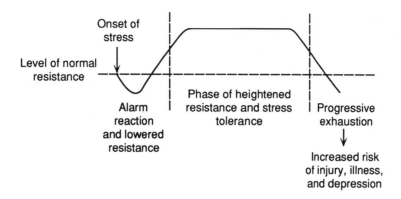

Figure 6.5 The three phases of Hans Selye's general adaptation syndrome. *Note.* From *The Lore of Running* by T. D. Noakes, in press, Champaign, IL: Leisure Press. Copyright by Timothy D. Noakes. Adapted by permission.

metabolism being sufficient to combat the tissue assault, a state of progressive exhaustion will develop, with death or illness resulting shortly thereafter. The staleness seen with prolonged overtraining in athletes may be analogous to Selye's stage of exhaustion.

Galbo (1983) and Berdanier (1987) have reviewed the major aspects of the hormonal and metabolic responses that are mobilized to help the body combat the kind of intense chronic severe work loads that mimic the stress placed upon Selye's laboratory animals, and that very likely athletes place upon themselves during excessive prolonged training periods, resulting in staleness. The response is multidimensional, involving a teamwork operation by several organ systems. The adrenal glands increase their output of adrenaline and noradrenaline, the former more than the latter. Both increase liver blood flow and increase the metabolism of glycogen, fats, and proteins in an attempt to provide the additional fuel required. The pituitary gland is also stimulated, increasing its output of adrenocorticotropic hormone. This substance in turn stimulates the adrenal cortex to increase its release of steroid hormones, notably aldosterone and a group of hormones best known as glucocorticoids (a good example is cortisone). Aldosterone assists with maintaining electrolyte balance; glucocorticoids have anti-inflammatory properties and also help mobilize fats and proteins for energy purposes. Pituitary growth hormone levels are also elevated, increasing the potential for protein synthesis. Because many of the immune system substances (such as immunoglobulins) are proteins, this may be of benefit for improving the body's immunocompetence. And intense physical exercise stimulates protein breakdown in the working muscles.

All of the previously mentioned hormones inhibit both the release and the action of insulin on glucose uptake by muscle and fat cells. In turn, the liver responds by increasing its own glucose production. Along with an increased fatty acid secretion into the

bloodstream, this provides an additional fuel source. An increased level of heat production with this fuel metabolism decreases the amount of chemical energy that can be harvested (as ATP) for any given quantity of fuel consumed. During severe stress, this energy inefficiency can be increased as much as 10-fold, which mandates a considerably increased nutritional requirement.

A nonscientific analogy to the body's reaction to stress could bring to mind a "reservoir of anti-stress" in the body that can be used to counteract the effects of applied stress. This reservoir could represent stored energy fuels, the immune system, and all the hormones and enzymes related to fuel metabolism and maintenance of immunological integrity. Overtaxing the performance limits of these systems may disrupt their synergistic interactions and deplete energy supplies, thereby decreasing the effectiveness of homeostatic mechanisms that previously were effective in handling the body's response to hard work. When this reservoir is depleted, continued resistance to the stress is not possible, and breakdown occurs.

Selye's work did not include the psychological and illness manifestations of stress because he worked with laboratory animals, but these aspects are no less important. In particular, the studies of Rahe (1972) provide useful insight. It was Rahe's contention that life experiences relate to disease prevalence. He developed a life stress and illness model whereby the ability of an individual's psychological defenses to cope with life problems determines the likelihood of acquiring illness. Excessive and prolonged anxiety, depression, and emotional distress, representing the inability to manage life problems effectively, carry with them a sizable increased risk for physical symptoms of illness. In part this is developmental. The studies of Weiner (1972) suggest that early behavioral experiences in growing up influence the nature of our responses to changing environmental situations. We'll describe additional psychological aspects of overtraining and staleness shortly.

The possibility of immunological suppression and thus an increased risk of infection accompanying hard training and excessively hard training (which can produce overtraining or staleness) has been difficult for epidemiologists to quantify. Three major difficulties have hindered forward progress:

1. The great variability among individuals in response to exercise
2. The difficulty in assigning equivalent long-term work loads in study subjects for experimental studies
3. The still not completely understood nature of the immune system.

There is both anecdotal (Jokl, 1974) and epidemiological (Peters & Bateman, 1983) evidence that athletes seem to exhibit less resistance to minor infections than untrained people, suggesting a decreased effectiveness of the acquired (or specific) immune system. Through the abilities of specialized cells to recognize foreign macromolecules of infectious agents, this system results in the production of antigen-specific antibodies and certain other chemicals (called interleukins) that can increase the potency of the overall immunological response. The cells involved are lymphocytes, which become very specialized and metabolically highly active to carry out their task.

Work by Ardawi and Newsholme (1985) has suggested an almost certain interdependence between skeletal muscle cells and lymphocytes. Lymphocytes derive their energy from two fuel sources: glucose and glutamine. A major site for glutamine biosynthesis in the body is skeletal muscle, and its ability to produce adequate glutamine seems to be compromised when it is in a state of extensive repair following long-term intense exercise. If a glutamine debt should occur, the extent to which lymphocyte function is compromised may determine the prevalence of viral invasions or the rate of recovery from the effects of viral illnesses or fever.

A variety of recent studies have described the extent to which specific subtypes of lymphocytes are either increased or decreased in numbers as a result of long-term intense exercise. Current evidence points toward ratios of these subtypes that are altered in such a manner as to produce temporary immunological suppression (MacKinnon & Tomasi, 1986; Nieman et al., 1989). Whether this is hormonally induced has not yet been clearly established. Corticosteroid hormones, elevated during exercise, are typically immunosuppressive, but hormones such as adrenaline and noradrenaline can increase lymphocyte populations

(Galbo, 1983). It also isn't clear yet how specific cell subtype ratios are changed in favor of immunosuppression or activation during chronic hard training.

Decreased resistance to infection is not limited to human athletes. Veterinarians working with racehorses have also characterized a poor performance syndrome (Mumford & Rossdale, 1980) that involves a positive relationship between upper respiratory tract infections and lackluster race efforts.

The interaction of psychological aspects of stress with immunological competency is also only beginning to be explored. The discovery of decreased immunoglobulin A levels in the saliva of students under the duress of major university examinations (Jemmott et al., 1983) suggests that immunosuppression to some extent can occur. In this instance, it is probably related to elevated adrenaline levels. The interaction of psychological with physiological mechanisms in permitting proper adaptation to a training load is well known. It appears as though physiological maladaptation can also be affected by the negative interaction of psychological factors.

Psychological Dimensions of Overtraining and Staleness

What are the psychological dimensions of overtraining and staleness that interact with physiological changes? A common subjective report of an athlete who has entered an overtrained state is, "I'm training as hard as I ever have, but my gains are getting smaller and smaller. I just feel like giving up, but I know I shouldn't." The increased frustration, accompanied by decreased enthusiasm and dedication, can be so profound as to bring clinical signs of depression. Table 6.1 lists the wide variety of symptoms that may be observable to a limited extent with overtraining but which will become more prevalent in both number and severity during staleness. A perusal of this list suggests that we are seeing a psychophysiological deterioration of stability—both mind and body are affected. Eventually, this deterioration can have pathological consequences as well. This is to be expected because of the complex neuroendocrine interactions that direct the subtleties of human performance. A review of recent studies in this area (Kuipers & Keizer, 1988) suggests that two types of staleness may be identifiable, depending on whether the sympathetic or parasympathetic portions of the autonomic nervous system are increased in their activity.

Staleness thus may be an athlete's manifestation of a combination of the pathophysiological exhaustion identified by Selye coupled with additional psychological components. In athletes, the kinds of detailed

Table 6.1   The Major Warning Signs of Overtraining and Staleness

Training-related

Unusual muscle soreness the day after a training session
Progressive increases in soreness with continued training
Performance plateau or decrement despite increased training
Inability to complete previously manageable training load
Elevated effort sense; delay in recovery from training
Thoughts of quitting training, skipping training

Lifestyle-related

Increased tension, depression, anger, fatigue, confusion; inability to relax
Decreased vigor in completing daily activities; things once pleasurable now are not
Poor-quality sleep

Health-related

Swelling of lymph nodes
Constipation, diarrhea
Increased incidence of illness (fever, head colds, etc.)
Increased blood pressure; increased morning pulse
Loss of weight; loss of appetite

metabolic investigations that might identify the extent to which Selye's stress syndrome is similar to staleness are just beginning to be carried out. There are indeed some similarities (Kuipers & Keizer, 1988), but the picture is far from clear. Medical diagnosticians have reported a condition seen in the general population known variously as postviral fatigue syndrome (David, Wessly, & Petosi, 1988) or chronic fatigue syndrome (Eichner, 1989a) and characterized by a similarly wide variety of psychological and physiological symptoms, persistent malaise, and frequently a positive titer to Epstein-Barr virus. Distance runners who have entered what we would term staleness, characterized by their exhibiting a sizable number of the characteristics listed in Table 6.1, frequently also give a positive response when tested for Epstein-Barr virus. The multifaceted nature of staleness frustrates those who would like to more precisely define it. Perhaps staleness and chronic fatigue syndrome are the same thing; we do not know at present. Eichner (1989b) brushes the syndrome aside, as far as distance runners are concerned, as psychosomatic, suggesting that positive thinking is the solution for affected runners who desire to restore their presyndrome excellence. We would suggest the alternative view, that the head does indeed have a body and that the two work together.

Given the enormous mental drive that powers a runner to train and compete at a high level, an overtrained runner who continues to overwork may likely find it necessary to recruit more than the usual additional muscle fibers from accessory muscles to complete a workout at a prescribed pace. These muscle fibers may not be as fatigued as those from the muscles that ordinarily serve as the prime movers. Their tension-generation velocities may be relatively normal, and their recruitment may permit attainment of the desired running paces. However, these muscles are not designed for the task at hand as specifically as the (now fatiguing) prime movers. We could hypothesize that there is a greater O_2 cost for this submaximum work output and that this runner's economy or movement efficiency has decreased. If true, and if the decrease is large enough, this could be detected by comparing $\dot{V}O_2$ consumption at various submaximum paces with previous values. Subjectively it can be detected as an increased effort sense, but thus far no evidence exists to show that a runner who feels fatigued in fact runs less economically.

Athletes experiencing overtraining have a greater chance of performing worse in competition than if they were undertrained or optimally trained. This may not be related as much to physiological performance decrements as to the interaction of these with psychological attitudinal deficits, as indicated in Table 6.1. The two summate, and during a competitive phase, when an optimum mental attitude directed toward successful performance assumes enormous importance, the interaction is seen clearly. A useful testing instrument for profiling psychological tension (McNair, Lorr, & Droppelman, 1971) known as the Profile of Mood States (POMS) describes these attitudinal changes predictably. The pioneering studies of University of Wisconsin sport psychologist William Morgan characterized the onset of performance decrements in elite runners using this evaluation instrument. He found similar attitudinal changes in both men (Morgan & Pollock, 1977) and women (Morgan, O'Connor, Sparling, & Pate, 1987) as manageable training transitioned into overtraining and, just as importantly, as marginal overtraining transitioned back to recovery when tapering preceded a competitive period. Figure 6.6 illustrates two profiles, one from an athlete training normally in a properly prepared state for top-level competition and one from the same athlete showing symptoms of overtraining. During optimal preparation, attitudes such as depression, fatigue, confusion, anger, and tension are minimal in comparison to vigor. The overtrained athlete has essentially an inversion of these measures of affective behavior.

In the jargon of sport psychologists, if the profile of the optimally prepared athlete is likened to a floating

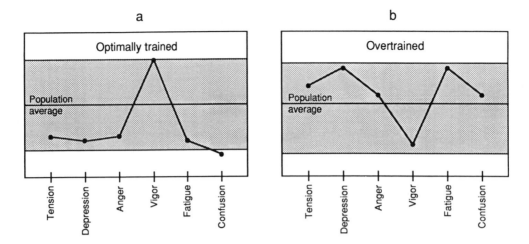

Figure 6.6 Use of the Profile of Mood States (POMS) test to illustrate predictably different mood states in overtrained and optimally prepared athletes. During optimal preparation, athletes score quite low in such measures of affective behavior as tension, depression, anger, fatigue, and confusion but very high in vigor, giving the so-called "iceberg profile" as shown in Figure 6.6a. The overtrained state is characterized by a reversal of these mood states, causing a so-called "flipped iceberg profile," indicated in Figure 6.6b. *Note.* From "The Facts and Fallacies of Overtraining and Staleness" by J. Kimiecik, 1988, *American Coach*, March/April, p. 12. Copyright 1988 by Human Kinetics. Reprinted by permission.

iceberg (Figure 6.6a), giving an iceberg profile, then the overtrained athlete (Figure 6.6b) will likely exhibit a flipped iceberg profile (Morgan, 1985). This is where long-term monitoring of athlete performance and behavior can be useful for optimizing preparation. As training intensities are manipulated, appropriate changes in mood states may likely occur. Though fatigue and vigor may, respectively, increase and decrease during a period of intense training, these mood states should reverse during recovery or tapering. The continuum of performance abilities with training thus has undertraining at one end and staleness at the other, with optimum training and overtraining fitting somewhere in between. Both physiological and psychological variables can be monitored to assess the possible shift from an optimally productive state to one suggestive of overtraining or staleness.

Identifying the Onset of Overtraining and Minimizing its Effects

The earlier the symptoms of overtraining can be identified and managed, the more rapid and successful will be a return to effective progress and the less likely will be the development of staleness. This often is not easy to do. It is unfortunate but evident that a peculiar tunnel vision frequently clouds the perception of outstanding athletes and their coaches (perhaps due to their T personalities) regarding total work load management. They do not want to anticipate the problem before it occurs. Too often an individualized training plan has not been provided with periodic rest as well as frequent assessment of progress.

An athlete's body cannot become a bottomless sinkhole for physical training and mental accumulation of the fear of failing. Such a preparation regimen is a near-guaranteed prescription to initiate overtraining, overuse injury, or eventual staleness. In fact, it is useful to think of exercise as a drug in this instance. A small dose of exercise, just as with a medication, brings a hardly measurable effect. An optimum dose brings just the proper effect. Excessively high doses carry with them the risk of toxic side effects in addition to no greater improvement of the condition for which the optimum dose was prescribed. Any licensed physician found guilty of prescribing such improper doses would be liable for malpractice suits or penalties. They are therefore careful to identify the rational need for the dose prescribed by documenting its effects. Coaches and athletes who are prescribing exercise by designing training plans need to use the same logic and restraint. And frequently they do. Athletes who are products of such an environment have long and productive careers, with few setbacks. But often such logic and restraint are not employed. Training is pushed into the realm of excess, either unknowingly (because coach and athlete do not jointly assess the results of work assigned) or simply because of a work ethic that continually promotes the attitude that more is better, that there is no gain without pain, and that the need for rest is a sign of weakness.

Imagine the scenarios resulting with an enthusiastic

coach, particularly one who in unbending fashion dictates to his athletes that they tolerate his assigned training loads and do them without discussion or debate (Newton & Durkin, 1988), or with a coach who writes generic training assignments for a group of athletes of varying abilities and event specialties. The athletes in the former category must follow the orders of the coach (*do it my way or else*), who has no intention of even considering the reality of the athletes' comments that the training assignments are provoking excessive fatigue and causing the beginnings of muscle or tendon irritation that signal the onset of overtraining or overuse injury.

If the athletes do accept the fact that, as their coach demands, thinking is out of the question and obeying is the only alternative, they will simply push on and not admit that they are unduly fatigued, depressed, or even marginally injured. If the coach's past record in previous years has been successful, the athletes may even convince themselves that this state of profound fatigue, depression, or injury is necessary or appropriate for victory. Even if conversations between coach and athletes now occur, the athletes may be afraid to admit any deficiencies that could be construed as signs of weakness. The coach may rationalize any orneriness from the athletes as simply a little irritability from a certain amount of expected fatigue caused by hard training. An emotional environment simply does not exist where athletes and coach can appreciate that by continuing high-level work output without compensatory rest, a high risk of developing overtraining or overuse injury is inevitable.

Attempting to resolve such a situation reminds us of trying to pick up an irritated porcupine. There is no good direction from which to begin making progress. Individual athletes eventually become incapable of good performance, or get injured and are eliminated from further competition. The coach doesn't learn the reasons for the various causes of athlete overstress partly because the environment for two-way exchange hasn't developed. And if the team does well, thanks to a sufficiently large group of athletes still running well who can amass scoring points in the championship meet, the injured athletes are simply viewed as people who didn't respond properly to the training program. Are there any solutions? Yes. One, of course, is that the kind of coaching mentality portrayed here seems to be on its way out of the profession, thanks to the improving tenets of acceptable coaching strategies. Another is that we would plead for coaches and athletes to develop an effective two-way relationship based on a mutual desire for forward progress rather than a one-sided game of imposition of forced dominance and control by one over the other. We would also suggest keeping good records

of progress, thereby permitting easy identification of steady rise, plateau, or decline in performance.

Preventing Overtraining as Part of the Art of Good Coaching

Three primary circumstances in the training environment most frequently set the stage for the kind of fatigue that elicits either overtraining or overuse injury. One occurs because of the conclusion that performance in either training or racing has started to deteriorate because the athlete simply has not been training enough in quantity, in quality, or in both. The rationale is simple. Because training should bring improvement of performance, and no training should result in no improvement, then a falling-off in performance can be caused only by inadequate training. This logic is incorrect because at the point of performance deterioration, we have an athlete who is no longer capable of responding in the usual manner to a training stress. No longer does more beget more; here, more will beget less and less will beget more. The third side of the developmental coin—recovery/rest in addition to quantity and quality—needs to be larger.

The second circumstance occurs following a successful series of races or a few successful mesocycles of training. A feeling of invincibility or that better results would accrue through more training, particularly because the athlete achieved good results without feeling overtaxed from a previous difficult training load, helps ingrain the rationale that more work can be tolerated. In fact, the situation may be quite the opposite. The good results probably resulted from just the correct balance of quantity, quality, and recovery. Very slight increases in work load may continue to raise the athlete to a new plateau. Substantial increases may very likely be excessive.

The third circumstance occurs when an athlete has recovered from a setback such as an injury or illness, particularly when relatively little time remains for proper preparation for an upcoming important competitive period. Instead of not competing and adjusting goals for a later competitive period, the athlete rapidly increases the quantity and quality of training without incorporating adequate rest. Initially, the athlete is fresh, both physically and mentally, from the layoff. But the body is inadequately prepared to manage the training load. Enormous improvements occur initially, but benefits do not accrue because of either inadequate rest or excessive loads.

Athletes and coaches thus find themselves in a dilemma when they devise a training plan. Three crucial questions need answers. First, how much training can be done so that improved performance will occur but overtraining will not? Second, what kinds of training or other lifestyle patterns pose increased risks of overtraining? And finally, are there any telltale early warning signs that may mark the onset of overtraining and staleness?

The first question is the most difficult to answer, because for each athlete it is different. The three major groups of variables that contribute to stress as training volume begins to increase are

1. lifestyle,
2. genetic factors, and
3. initial fitness level.

One suggestion for identifying optimum manageable training loads resides in careful examination of training logs from similar training periods to identify the combination of lifestyle and training loads previously manageable for favorable progress. A rule of thumb (with only the evidence of experience to back it up) suggests that no more than a 5% increase in training load each week can be managed effectively over a period such as a microcycle with healthy and progressive homeostatic adaptation. Also, volume and intensity of training should not be increased simultaneously.

Such deliberations, however, demand well-documented training records and a healthy athlete at the start of the training period. Tabulations should include data such as the weekly and monthly distance run, the total weekly distance that represents aerobic, long-interval (marginally anaerobic), and short-interval (considerably anaerobic) work, the number of rest days per week or month, quantitation of running paces and interval rests for faster sessions, and a summary of interruptions in the continuity of routine (family or job difficulties, long-distance travel, illness, small injuries, etc.). Often, when such data are viewed in tabular fashion and are not hidden among pages of daily training details, trends regarding shifts away from an optimum pattern of work and rest can be discerned clearly.

An important unsolved problem for coaches that scientists ought to help them resolve is developing a method for assigning a numerical indicator of intensity to all training sessions, permitting a more specific comparison of various sessions and a cumulative indicator of training load. The body does this very nicely as it accommodates to each day's training assignment. Weather, terrain, psychological factors, muscle cell O_2 and fuel availability, range of motion, and many other factors all contribute to the totality of the body's response to a training session. As soon as we can quantitate this net effect as well as the body itself does, we can then be in a better position to distinguish between training load and overload. With the computer age upon us, this should be simple. The data manipulation is simple; what is difficult is developing a system for numerically recording the effects of training on all the various aspects of bodily function. A major breakthrough in quantifying training will occur when such analyses are possible.

The second question is a little easier to answer, again provided that adequate documentation of training records and responses is available for perusal. Several kinds of activity patterns should be red-flagged (and treated as such) because of their high risk of causing the kind of overwork that brings on overtraining. These include the following:

- Too many competitions closely spaced without adequate recovery between them or without a well-defined rest break after the series
- A sudden rather than gradual increase in quantity or intensity of training
- Increased emphasis on one training format, so that certain muscle groups are challenged excessively
- Increased non-training-related extraneous stress (travel, irregular daily schedule, inadequate sleep, emotional confrontations, negative energy or water balance, etc.)

Although we mentioned this earlier, the inhibitory and summating nature of these extraneous factors on optimum recovery from hard training should be reiterated. Their effects cannot be psychologically repressed or brushed aside as noncontributory to total lifestyle load. In contrast, the wise athlete accepts objectively their influencing role and attempts to reduce their total input.

Conversely, the enhancement of recovery and thereby a possibility for absorbing even more difficult training as a result of having these extraneous stressors removed points to the desire of many athletes to adjourn periodically to "training-camp" environments. Some nations maintain such camps on a year-round basis for their developing athletes. Good food at regular hours, excellent training facilities, massage and other recuperative therapeutic modalities, recreational diversions, and minimal outside influences form an ideal environment for a motivated athlete. However, the risk of excessive training in such a sports haven is very great. Therefore, these training camp sessions are usually restricted to no more than two weeks, following which recovery, tapering, and some form of small competition or time trial is typically scheduled in the following week.

Four Signs of Overtraining. We have some empirically based suggestions for identifying the early warning signs of overtraining. Any of the warning signs summarized in Table 6.1 may occur on occasion in isolated fashion and simply suggest a temporary setback in training continuity. But when hard training crosses the threshold into overtraining, these symptoms begin to summate. Performance shows consistent deterioration. Our collective experience in the close management of several dozen elite-level distance runners suggests that four primary indicators—when they begin to occur in combination—are signs of developing overtraining and possibly staleness unless prompt and aggressive recovery measures are begun.

Indicator 1: A clearly greater effort sense required to finish a speed session, time trial, or race effort at a pace that previously was entirely manageable under similar environmental conditions. Running intervals cannot be done at previously manageable paces unless considerably longer recovery is provided.

Indicator 2: A clearly recognizable inadequacy of the usual day-to-day recovery time for completion of a training assignment, often seen as an increased morning heart rate or poor-quality sleep and an ongoing feeling of dehydration.

Indicator 3: A noticeable increase in general irritability in dealing with the routine, normally unstressful problems of life (moodiness, being argument-prone and complaining, etc.). This might be likened to the "burnout" that workers in high-stress, executive-type workaday world jobs experience.

Indicator 4: A decreased drive to train. Athletes no longer look forward to the challenge of a hard training session and have almost a dread of achieving expected poor results.

Heeding the signs immediately and taking aggressive recovery measures such as reducing the training load by 50% to 60%, foregoing an upcoming competition, improving regularity and quality of sleep and nutritional intake, and removing the effects of other extraneous stressors by rearranging priorities may restore optimum function within a week or two. But the previously intense training regimen should be resumed only slowly, with appropriate changes to prevent a return to the earlier total stress load. The signal to resume full training is evidenced by a renewed interest in and ability to train hard in a normal adaptive fashion. Overtraining and staleness are best considered as very real and important setbacks in forward development. Their effects must be removed by decreasing the stress load. There is absolutely no other choice.

In our discussions over the years with elite-level runners who have sustained overuse injuries or suffered staleness, it has become evident that they indeed did experience the previously described early warning signs. But they ignored them. Their training goals had been identified in terms of an upcoming competitive phase, and the thought that overtraining or overuse injury could ever occur was simply not in those plans. When these symptoms occurred, it was simply assumed that somehow they would go away, with the athlete's tolerance to their developing effects seen as another indicator of overall toughness. Just as often, these athletes were under the direction of coaches who would not tolerate injury or the suggestion of recovery time inserted to permit restoration of normal adaptive mechanisms. Only when it was too late, when injury, illness, or profound staleness developed, did the athletes realize that their training plan design was inappropriate to their adaptive abilities. They felt inferior and tended to blame themselves for their demise rather than even considering as a contributory element the unbending coach who permitted no deviation or discussion and who concluded that the reason the athletes failed was that they simply didn't respond adequately to the training regimen.

Using Objective Criteria to Identify Overtraining

Just as a physician makes use of the clinical laboratory to monitor the patient's health status, so also it is appropriate and useful for athletes coaching themselves (and coaches as well) to develop collaborative relationships with knowledgeable sports science or sports medicine personnel who have a sincere interest in the performance success of the athletes being monitored. Increasing study of overtraining and staleness has provided a better diagnostic awareness for early detection through the use of psychological evaluation (such as the POMS test for mood changes described earlier) and blood chemistry profiling (quantifying variations in blood chemistry variables that suggest metabolic imbalance).

The serious setback resulting from staleness has stimulated great interest in a search for either one or a small number of easily measurable physiological variables that would be highly suggestive of overtraining and its sequelae. Because the overstress phenomenon is multifaceted, the likelihood of such a simple solution seems illogical. But the search goes on. Ideally, to identify overtraining before it occurs is best. But this in itself may be difficult. If specific variables unique to overtraining are identifiable, these wouldn't occur until after overtraining had begun. A primary difficulty in identifying such variables is that arduous training by itself causes measurable changes in cellular physiology that can be seen by profiling various blood chemistry and physiological values. The difference between serious but manageable training and the onset of overtraining is essentially one of degree. There is a gray area where adaptive physiological responses are not quite keeping up with demand. There is also a problem with inter- and intra-individual variability in blood chemistry variables, making it difficult to suggest specific overtraining threshold values applicable to everyone. However, deviations from normal limits in a group of selected variables measured somewhat frequently (e.g., monthly or quarterly) and compared to the particular athlete's baseline blood chemistry profile may be enough to suggest that the body is not maintaining homeostatic equilibrium, with overtraining a likely result. Some of the more commonly measured blood chemistry variables, which we have already discussed in this chapter or in chapter 2, include hemoglobin (as an indicator of anemia), ferritin (as an indicator of prelatent anemia), creatine kinase (as an indicator of muscle cell membrane permeability increases), hydroxyproline (as a marker for tendon breakdown), reticulocytes (as an indicator of adequate red blood cell production), and haptoglobin (as an indicator of increased hemolysis).

Our policy in working with elite distance runners for whom we have developed blood chemistry profiles is to suggest a substantial reduction in training together with reevaluation of training loads and nutritional status when four of the markers described on page 273 are substantially altered and some of the other physiological changes, to be mentioned shortly, occur. These athletes typically have not developed symptoms of overtraining, so it's tempting to suggest that this is one acceptable regimen for preventing overtraining. Scientifically, of course, such a statement isn't valid. We would need to repeat the study with these same athletes, now allowing these altered variables to continue with no suggestion of training plan alteration. If overtraining symptoms and eventual staleness resulted, then we would be on firmer ground. Unfortunately, we cannot go back in time and recreate such conditions to determine the new outcome.

Some have suggested the value of monitoring more generalized human performance data, such as hours of sleep each night or morning heart rate (Ryan, Brown, Frederick, Falsetti, & Burke, 1983; Dressendorfer, Wade, & Scaff, 1985). Similar difficulties occur in acquiring and interpreting these data as well. As an example, recording hours of sleep each night may provide a useful estimate of needed rest. But going to bed late and sleeping late the next morning does not typically provide as restful a night's sleep as the usual habit pattern. Thus, quality of sleep and also sleep patterns should be documented. The measurement of morning pulse may be useful as an index of generalized recovery. But different conditions of measurement can increase variability considerably: awaking naturally versus with an alarm, measuring before or after arising from bed, and so on.

A third potentially useful variable is body weight. Again, when and how to measure is critical. The same weighing device ought to be used for each measurement. Following a training session might be the best time to measure this so-called training weight. But not all sessions are similar, because of weather conditions and the nature of the training load. And depending on circumstances, athletes may or may not drink fluids during the session, further modifying the weight loss picture. Morning weight is also sometimes used, following bladder and bowel activities and before breakfast. Notable elevations in heart rate, decreases in body weight, or either decreased sleep or insomnia, particularly when they occur together, should raise suspicion that an overtrained state is imminent. The lesson to be learned from this is that poorly collected data can be an excellent source of noninformation. Useful conclusions can be derived only from well-collected data obtained through meaningful preplanning.

SUMMARY

1. Optimum training loads should bring optimum improvement in performance capability. A crucial question is how to ensure an optimum training load. The nature of competitive sport, that is, a contest requiring athletes to perform at their very best, mandates a high level of motivation for doing all the work required to achieve the greatest possible fitness. This intense motivation, a personality trait in gifted athletes, often clouds athletes' ability to discern the difference between optimum and excessive work.

2. Fatigue and delayed-onset muscle soreness are accompanying components of the training process for athletes desirous of substantial improvements in their performance capabili-

ties. This is because they are manifestations of the metabolic effects of hard training on organ systems. Unusually challenging exercise of a temporary nature typically induces delayed-onset muscular soreness, recovery from which occurs in a few days. Overuse injuries are more likely to result from extended periods of inappropriately high training volume or intensity (overtraining). Rapid turnover rates for tissues such as muscles and tendons occur as a result of sizable periods of anaerobic metabolism, and thus near-maximum or maximum work rates. If optimum physiological adaptation occurs, recovery should find the trained individual more capable of enduring similar work loads.

3. Short-term overtraining (or simply overtraining) results when inadequate recovery is permitted from a challenging training load. Both psychological and physiological signs and symptoms announce its presence, and a considerably greater period of recovery is required than usually is provided for homeostatic restitution to occur. Performance in races is typically poor.

4. Long-term overtraining (or staleness) results when overtraining continues unabated. Again, psychological and physiological indicators indicate its existence, but these now are more numerous and obvious, accompanied by increased incidence of illness and a predilection to overuse injuries. Recovery may require anywhere from weeks to a month or more.

5. The risks of inhibiting good performance because of fatigue or preventing continued progress because of overuse injury or staleness are so great that all athletes and coaches desirous of achieving sport excellence must make it a top priority to take appropriate steps to minimize their occurrence. Hard training does not become overtraining at any precise moment because the latter occurs as a result of the sum of hard training occurring too long without adequate compensatory recovery/rest. Although it is difficult to back away, even temporarily, from continued hard training when one feels confident that development is proceeding well, somehow the mind-set of an athlete must be geared toward the reality that planned adequate rest is a part of training and essential for continuing this excellent development. When rest is indeed adequate, athletes consistently feel good about themselves and their training and have a positive attitude and sense of confidence.

6. The single best method for minimizing the risk of overtraining includes careful monitoring of the past and present training history and present lifestyle status, and using this knowledge in the training plan design with appropriate reassessment. Combinations of unusual increases in training volume or quality, adverse changes in training environment (warmer weather or the addition of hilly terrain), or the addition of other lifestyle stress factors when unaccompanied by a corresponding increase in rest, nutrition, or use of recuperative and restorative therapeutic modalities are unwise, and can best be identified by careful consideration of written training records. Good record keeping with periodic objective review and analysis should form the first line of defense against overtraining. The conclusions from such analyses can also be prospective (i.e., they can project the possibility of risk).

7. Subjective indicators of the accumulating effects of very hard training can be effective early warning signs that overtraining is occurring. The best subjective indicators include (a) increased effort sense for a given pace, (b) decreased performance abilities despite the typically allocated rest, (c) increased irritability and moodiness, and (d) decreased drive to train.

8. Individualized training plans, updated continually to reflect an athlete's ongoing adaptations to training, have far less risk of inducing overtraining than generic training plans intended for a group. Too often such group plans stimulate overtraining in the less fit or less talented athletes and understimulate the more gifted ones, causing the latter to include additional work that may also bring overtraining if not controlled appropriately.

9. Metabolic indicators, as measured by changes in the values reported for blood chemistry variables, are at present imprecise indicators for the actual onset of overtraining, because no consistently identifiable threshold level exists for this condition. Individual differences are sizable. Periodic blood chemistry profiling as part of routine health evaluation of athletes in training will be valuable in providing an ongoing accurate picture of what is typical

for each one. Those athletes with the luxury of periodic long-term (i.e., several years) health care monitoring are in the best position to have such changes be useful indicators that overtraining may be likely. When alterations from this normally stable blood chemistry picture occur in a direction that logically suggests possible metabolic imbalance, prompt consideration of these changes in the context of that athlete's training and lifestyle can be useful for restoring equilibrium. A few such blood chemistry variables have been described. Important other physiological alterations that can accompany this monitoring include an increase in morning heart rate, progressive weight loss, decreased sleep effectiveness, and a loss of appetite. Caution must be taken, however, to obtain information that has consistency and validity for useful interpretation.

REFERENCES

Abraham, W.M. (1977). Factors in delayed muscle soreness. *Medicine and Science in Sports*, **9**, 11-20.

Ardawi, M.S., & Newsholme, E.A. (1985). Metabolism in lymphocytes and its importance in the immune response. *Essays in Biochemistry*, **21**, 1-43.

Armstrong, R.B. (1984). Mechanisms of exercise-induced delayed onset muscular soreness: A brief review. *Medicine and Science in Sports and Exercise*, **16**, 529-538.

Berdanier, C.D. (1987). The many faces of stress. *Nutrition Today*, **22**(2), 12-17.

Cannon, W.B. (1929). Organization for physiological homeostasis. *Physiological Reviews*, **9**, 399-431.

Costill, D.L. (1988). Carbohydrates for exercise: Dietary demands for optimum performance. *International Journal of Sports Medicine*, **9**, 1-18.

Counsilman, J.E. (1968). *The science of swimming*. London: Pelham.

David, A.S., Wessly, S., & Pelosi, A.J. (1988). Post-viral fatigue syndrome: Time for a new approach. *British Medical Journal*, **296**, 696-699.

Davies, K.J.A., Packer, A., & Brooks, G.A. (1982). Exercise bioenergetics following sprint training. *Archives of Biochemistry and Biophysics*, **215**, 260-265.

Dressendorfer, R.H., & Wade, C.E. (1983). The muscular overuse syndrome in long-distance runners. *Physician and Sportsmedicine*, **11**(11), 116-130.

Dressendorfer, R.H., Wade, C.E., & Scaff, J.H. (1985). Increased morning heart rate in runners: A valid sign of overtraining? *Physician and Sportsmedicine*, **13**(8), 77-86.

Ebbeling, C.B., & Clarkson, P.M. (1989). Exercise-induced muscle damage and adaptation. *Sports Medicine*, **7**, 207-234.

Eichner, E. (1989a). Chronic fatigue syndrome: Searching for the cause and treatment. *Physician and Sportsmedicine*, **17**(6), 142-152.

Eichner, E. (1989b). Chronic fatigue syndrome: How vulnerable are athletes? *Physician and Sportsmedicine*, **17**(6), 157-160.

Engelhardt, W.A. (1932). Die Beziehungen zwischen Atmung und Pyrophatumsatz in Vogelerythrocyten (The relationships between respiration and phosphate turnover in bird erythrocytes). *Biochemische Zeitschrift*, **251**, 343-368.

Evans, W.J. (1987). Exercise-induced skeletal muscle damage. *Physician and Sportsmedicine*, **15**(1), 89-100.

Farley, F. (1986). The Big T in personality. *Anthropology and Education Quarterly*, **20**(5), 44-52.

Francis, K., & Hoobler, T. (1988). Delayed onset muscle soreness and decreased isokinetic strength. *Journal of Applied Sports Science Research*, **2**, 20-23.

Galbo, H. (1983). *Hormonal and metabolic adaptation to exercise*. Stuttgart: Georg Thieme Verlag.

Hagerman, F.C., Hikida, R.S., Staron, R.S., Sherman, W.M., & Costill, D.L. (1984). Muscle damage in marathon runners. *Physician and Sportsmedicine*, **12**(11), 39-46.

Hill, A.V. (1951). The mechanics of voluntary muscle. *Lancet*, 261:947-954.

Hodgdon, J., Riedy, M., Goforth, H., Norton, J., Murguia, M., Mandelbaum, B., & Vailas, A.C. (1988). Plasma hydroxyproline and its association to overuse training. *Medicine and Science in Sports and Exercise*, **20**, S10.

Hough, T. (1902). Ergographic studies in muscle soreness. *American Journal of Physiology*, **7**, 76-92.

Jemmott, J.B., Borysenko, J.Z., Borysenko, M., McClelland, D.C., Chapman, R., Meyer, D., & Benson, H. (1983). Academic stress, power motivation, and decrease in secretion rate of salivary secretory immunoglobin A. *Lancet*, 1:1400-1402.

Jokl, E. (1974). The immunological status of athletes. *Journal of Sports Medicine*, **14**, 165-167.

Jones, D.C., & James, S.L. (1987). Overuse injuries of the lower extremity. *Clinics in Sports Medicine*, **6**, 273-290.

Kuipers, H., & Keizer, H.A. (1988). Overtraining in elite athletes. *Sports Medicine*, **6**, 79-92.

Lieber, R.L., & Friden, J. (1988). Selective damage of fast glycolytic muscle fibers with eccentric contraction of the rabbit tibialis anterior. *Acta Physiologica Scandinavica*, **133**, 587-588.

MacKinnon, L.T., & Tomasi, T.B. (1983). Immunology of exercise. *Annals of Sports Medicine*, **3**, 1-4.

Margaria, R. (1972). Positive and negative work performances and their efficiencies in human locomotion. In G.R. Cummings, D. Snidal, & A.W. Taylor (Eds.), *Environmental effects on work performance* (pp. 215-228). Toronto: Canadian Association of Sports Sciences.

McNair, D.M., Lorr, M., & Droppelman, L.F. (1971). *Profile of mood states manual*. San Diego: Educational and Industrial Testing Service.

Morgan, W.P. (1985). Selected psychological factors limiting performance: A mental health model. In D.H. Clarke & H.M. Eckert (Eds.), *Limits of human performance* (pp. 70-80). Champaign, IL: Human Kinetics.

Morgan, W.P., Brown, D.R., Raglin, J.S., O'Connor, P.J., & Ellickson, K.A. (1987). Psychological monitoring of overtraining and staleness. *British Journal of Sports Medicine*, **21**, 107-114.

Morgan, W.P., O'Connor, P.J., Sparling, P.B., & Pate, R.R. (1987). Psychological characterization of the elite female distance runner. *International Journal of Sports Medicine*, **8**, S124-S131.

Morgan, W.P., & Pollock, M.L. (1977). Psychologic characterization of the elite distance runner. *Annals of the New York Academy of Sciences*, **301**, 383-403.

Mosso, A. (1915). *Fatigue*. (M. Drummond & W.G. Drummond, Trans.) (3rd ed.). London: Allen & Unwin. (Original work published 1905)

Mumford, J.A., & Rossdale, P.D. (1980). Virus and its relationship to the "poor performance syndrome." *Equine Veterinary Journal*, **12**, 3-9.

Newham, D.J., Mills, K.R., Quigley, R., & Edwards, R.H.T. (1982). Muscle pain and tenderness after exercise. *Australian Journal of Sports Medicine and Exercise Science*, **14**, 129-131.

Newham, D.J., Mills, K.R., Quigley, B.M., & Edwards, R.H.T. (1983). Pain and fatigue after concentric and eccentric muscle contractions. *Clinical Science*, **64**, 55-62.

Newton, J., & Durkin, J.D. (1988). *Running to the top of the mountain*. Roselle, IL: J & J Winning Edge.

Nieman, D.C., Berk, L.S., Simpson-Westerberg, M., Arabatzis, K., Youngberg, S., Tan, S.A., Lee, J.W., & Eby, W.C. (1989). Effects of long-endurance running on immune system parameters and lymphocyte function in experienced marathoners. *International Journal of Sports Medicine*, **5**, 317-323.

Noakes, T.D. (1988). Implications of exercise testing for prediction of athletic performance: A contemporary perspective. *Medicine and Science in Sports and Exercise*, **20**, 319-330.

Peters, E.M., & Bateman, E.P. (1983). Ultramarathon running and upper respiratory tract infections: An epidemiological survey. *South African Medical Journal*, **64**, 582-584.

Rahe, R.H. (1972). Subjects' recent life changes and their near-future illness susceptibility. *Advances in Psychosomatic Medicine*, **8**, 2-19.

Riedy, M., Hodgdon, J., Goforth, H., Norton, J., Murguia, M., Mandelbaum, B., & Vailas, A.C. (1988). A serum marker for monitoring the exercise-induced degradation of connective tissues. *Medicine and Science in Sports and Exercise*, **20**, S10.

Roberts, J.A. (1986). Virus illness and sports performance. *Sports Medicine*, **3**, 298-303.

Ryan, A.J., Brown, R.L., Frederick, E.C., Falsetti, H.L., & Burke, E.L. (1983). Overtraining of athletes: Round table. *Physician and Sportsmedicine*, **11**(6), 93-110.

Schwane, J.A., Johnson, S.R., Vandenakker, C.B., & Armstrong, R.B. (1983). Delayed-onset muscular soreness and plasma CPK and LDH activities after downhill running. *Medicine and Science in Sports and Exercise*, **15**, 51-56.

Schwane, J.A., Williams, J.S., & Sloan, J.H. (1987). Effects of training on delayed muscle soreness and serum creatine kinase activity after running. *Medicine and Science in Sports and Exercise*, **19**, 584-590.

Selye, H. (1976). *The stress of life*. New York: McGraw-Hill.

Siegel, A.J., Silverman, L.M., & Lopez, R.E. (1980). Creatine kinase elevations in marathon runners: Relationship to training and competition. *Yale Journal of Biology and Medicine*, **53**, 275-279.

Warhol, M.J., Siegel, A.J., Evans, W.J., & Silverman, L.M. (1985). Skeletal muscle injury and repair in marathon runners after competition. *American Journal of Pathology*, **118**, 331-339.

Weiner, H. (1972). The transduction of experience by the brain. *Psychosomatic Medicine*, **34**, 355-380.

Weltman, A., Janney, C., Rians, C.B., Strand, K., Berg, B., Tippitt, S., Wise, J., Cahill, B.R., & Katch, F.I. (1986). The effects of hydraulic resistance strength training in pre-pubertal males. *Medicine and Science in Sports and Exercise*, **18**, 629-638.

Name Index

Subject Index

A

Abduction (external rotation), 10
Ability, athletic, 2-3
Acceleration, 161-162
Accommodating (isokinetic) resistance equipment, 188-189
Acetylcholine, 75
Acetyl Coenzyme A, *35*, 49-51, 52
Acetyl group, 49
Achilles tendinitis, 261
Achilles tenosynovitis, 261
Acidosis, 41, 49, 53, 69, 73, 90, 93, 107. *See also*
    Lactate threshold
Actin, *23*, 24-25
Action, and reaction, 7-8
Adduction (internal rotation), 10
Adductor muscles stretch (exercise), 206, *208*
Adenosine diphosphate (ADP), 33, 34, *35*, 37
Adenosine monophosphate (AMP), 33, *35*
Adenosine triphosphate (ATP), 24, 30, 33-38, *35*, 48, 52
Adenyl cyclase, 45
Adipose tissue, 41
Adrenaline, 44-45
Aerobic capacity training, 141-142
Aerobic conditioning, 136-139
Aerobic endurance, 122. *See also* Stamina
Aerobic energy contribution, 60-63, *62*
Aerobic exercise programs, 64
Aerobic glucose metabolism, 49-51
Aerobic metabolism
  definition of, 39
  generalized equations for, 40
  muscle capacity for, 26, 30
Aerobic threshold (2 mM). *See* Anaerobic threshold
Age. *See also* Aging
  and body fat, 212
  and flexibility, 204

Aggressiveness, controlled, 246
Aging, and decline in $\dot{V}O_2$max, 64-65
Agonist muscles, 3, 21
Air resistance, 97
Alveoli, 81
Alveolocapillary membrane, *81*, 81, 82, *84*
Amateur Athletic Association (AAA)
  British, 116-117, *118*
  Five-Star Award Scheme, 149, *150*
American College of Sports Medicine (ACSM), 64, 65,
    104
American Thoracic Society, 86
Anabolism, 33
Anaerobic capacity training, 142-143
  and running economy, 105
Anaerobic conditioning, 139-141
Anaerobic endurance (speed endurance), 123
Anaerobic energy contribution, 60-63, *62*
Anaerobic glycolysis, 46-49, *47*, 52
Anaerobic metabolism
  definition of, 39
  muscle capacity for, 26, 28, 30
  threshold of, 66-67, 68
Anaerobic threshold (4mM), 66-67, 68
Anemia, incidence of, 89. *See also* Iron
Ankle joint, 10, 16
Antagonist muscles, 3
Anthropometry, 211-212
Anxiety, 166-167, 246-247
Appetite, decreased during training, 92, 93. *See also* Diet
Archimedes' principle, 209
Arms
  analysis of style of, 17-18
  energy-efficient movement of, 7
  rapid swing of, 8
Arterial hypoxemia, 83

Sebastian Coe   **Peter Coe**   **David Martin**

No two authors are better qualified than **David Martin** and **Peter Coe** to address the subject of distance running from the combined perspective of physiology and coaching.

Martin has served as marathon chairman of The Athletics Congress's Men's Development Committee since 1979 and long distance running physiology coordinator for the USOC/TAC Elite Athlete Special Project since 1981. He also chairs the Sports Science Subcommittee of TAC, a position he has held since 1984. A Fellow of the American College of Sports Medicine, Dr. Martin is the author of more than 50 scientific articles as well as 3 books: *Respiratory Anatomy and Physiology, The High Jump Book,* and *The Marathon Footrace.*

Peter Coe has devoted more than 20 years to coaching his son Sebastian, an effort that has paid off in 4 Olympic medals (two gold, two silver); a bronze, a silver, and a gold medal in three successive European championships; and 12 world records. A retired professional engineer, Coe coaches a small elite squad of runners in Great Britain that includes an Olympic medalist and several national title holders.

Coe is past chairman of the British Milers Club and recipient of the club's Coach of the Year trophy in 1984. He is a frequent lecturer on middle-distance running throughout the world and is the author of *Running for Fitness.*